The HOVE
BLUE BOOK
Millennium Edition

The HOVE International
BLUE BOOK
Millennium Edition

HOVE
COLLECTORS
BOOKS

The Blue Book

Millennium Edition

Published September 1999

Hove Collectors Books

30, The Industrial Estate

Small Dole

West Sussex, BN5 9XR, UK

Fax: +44(0)1273-494992

British Library Cataloguing-in-Publication Data

A catalogue record for this book is available from the British Library

ISBN 1-874707-32-4

Millennium Edition edited by *John Wade*

Design and layout by ʻFacing ʻPages, Southwick.

Front cover picture by courtesy Nikon UK.

Printed by Biddles Ltd, Guildford and Kings Lynn.

Additional photographs courtesy of Canon Camera Company, Inc., Tokyo, Christie's, South Kensington, Philip Condax, KEH Camera Brokers, Mamiya Camera Company, Jack Naylor, Auction House, Germany, Geoff Wilkinson, John Wade and many users who have contributed photographs

Contents

Publisher's Note

The Millennium Edition of the *Blue Book* is now with us, but photography has been with us for 170 years or so and cameras manufactured 100 years ago are now of historic interest. 100 years ago 35mm cameras did not exist but they have now been in continuous production by Leica and others since 1925. It's the same for many other styles from roll film SLRs and TLRs, to auto-exposure cameras.

This new edition is again different from its predecessors, in particular the pricing, which is explained in the introduction. I am sure this will go a long way to solving the problem of fluctuation in rates of exchange.

Many more cameras have been inserted in the new *Blue Book,* in particular the more interesting era post-WWII, which is the market that is fast drawing collectors' attention.

You may consider the price of a camera listed too high or too low. At the end of the day only a willing seller and a willing buyer can determine the price at which a particular camera changes hands. Condition is always the most important factor in determining whether the price may be higher or lower. An almost pristine camera, perhaps in its original packaging, may well tempt you to a much higher price than the *Blue Book* or indeed any price guide indicates.

John Wade, as the Editor, has introduced several new sections, including restoration, tomorrow's collectables and a new look at dating and advice for new collectors.

As in every previous edition, the comment must be made that the *Blue Book,* in common with all price guides, just gives you an indication of the possible price you may have to pay for an item.

R.W.F.C.

Introduction

More data, more pictures, more information for the collector... that's the promise for this latest, Millennium Edition of the Hove International Blue Book.

The Blue Book has, for the past quarter of a century, been recognised as a major player in the field of camera collecting, not only as a guide to the prices of collectable cameras, but also in the information it supplies with each entry and its general advice to the collector. The latest edition brings you all this and more.

The data and price directory still plays the largest role in the book, but with this edition, we have opened up the general information sections more. For the first time, we have advice on repair and restoration of collectable cameras. We have much more informed advice for new collectors on how, where, when and why to buy. And we have significantly expanded the section on identifying and dating classic and collectable equipment.

All this adds up to a book that is designed to be a companion to collectors, still just about pocketable despite its wealth of information, and ideal for anyone visiting a camera fair or auction and who needs a fast way of checking, not only the right sort of price to pay, but also the relevance of a particular item in the history of photography.

Blue Book ancestry

It's something that few other camera collector guides have attempted, but there again, few other guides have the ancestry that the Blue Book boasts. Unlike other guides, which are most often the work of one person, the Blue Book has been put together, added to and amended over the years by a series of editors, each of whom is an expert in his own field.

The first Blue Book was edited by Myron Wolfe, an American author who had been publishing directories of collectable cameras back in the 1970s when camera collecting first began to take a hold and before many others had thought about producing books or guides on the subject.

In 1989, the rights to the book were acquired by another American, Douglas St Denny, an author and photo historian who, in turn, sold the rights to the English photographic dealership Jessop of Leicester. It was at a time when Jessop was beginning to open up branches around the UK and one, opened in London, was dedicated to the sale of antique and collectable cameras. Two editions of the Blue Book were then produced under the imprint of Jessop Specialist Publishing, before the rights were sold again, this time to Hove Photo Books, Britain's foremost publisher of books for the photographic collector. This is the fourth Blue Book published by Hove and, for this edition, the Editor's chair has been taken by John Wade, a collector himself who has been writing books and articles on collectable cameras in the British photo press for more than twenty years.

A new look at valuations

One new feature of this latest edition is the way we have taken a new look at the pricing of collectable cameras. In the past, we have put precise values on every piece of equipment listed, but now we have come to accept that this is not always the most practical approach. The fact is that values fluctuate. They go up and down slightly with the state of the market in general. They vary according to the condition of the equipment on offer. They can also vary according to who is selling the item in question, with the price charged by a prestigious dealer sometimes considerably higher than you might expect to pay for a similar camera from a fellow collector. Likewise, prices can vary at auctions, dependent on how many collectors present are desperate to buy a particular lot. Two collectors determined to outbid each other for an item will force up its price unnecessarily, whilst the absence of rival bidders might allow the item to go for a song.

The Blue Book is, of course, a guide, and the values put on the equipment in its directory have, in the past, been only guide prices, rather than the absolute, precise amount for which you should buy or sell. For this reason, we have now replaced specific prices with a price code from 'A' to 'L'. These codes can then be interpreted by the collector as a working guide to the value in Pounds Sterling, US dollars or Euros. You will find a key to these price codes printed in different denominations of money on cards throughout the book, and you can remove these to use as bookmarks.

This is how the codes line up:-

		UK	US	
A:	Cameras valued to	£10	$15	€30
B:	Valued between	£12-20	$17-40	€16-30
C:	Valued between	£25-45	$50-75	€35-60
D:	Valued between	£50-90	$80-150	€60-125
E:	Valued between	£100-125	$160-350	€140-315
F:	Valued between	£250-450	$375-750	€350-630
G:	Valued between	£500-900	$800-1,400	€700-1,330
H:	Valued between	£1,000-2,250	$1,500-3,500	€1,400-3,150
I:	Valued between	£2,500-4,500	$4,000-7,500	€3,500-6,300
J:	Valued between	£5,000-9,000	$8,000-15,000	€7,000-12,600
K:	Valued between	£10,000-24,000	$17,000-35,000	€ 14,000-34,000
L:	Above	£25,000	$45,000	€35,000

At the top end of this scale, where the range of values vary by greater increments, we have also added '+' or '—' signs to give a more accurate valuation.

Another innovation with this Millennium Edition of the Blue Book is the way we have converted values into different currencies. Although the Blue Book is an English publication, past editions have given valuations only in US dollars — what is usually accepted as the international currency for collecting. But whilst it is easy enough to apply current conversion rates to US dollars to obtain an equivalent price in any other currency, we have come to accept that this is not always the most accurate of indications to actual value. A camera which is fairly common in America might be rare in Europe, and vice versa — and the value of said camera reflects that fact in different countries. So, for this edition, the price code valuations have been checked over by independent experts in each country.

New directions in collecting

So what changes have we seen in the world of camera collecting in the three years since the last Blue Book was published?

One of the most significant changes must be the shift in emphasis for many collectors to later models. When camera collecting first began to be taken seriously as a hobby, back in the 1970s, most collectors concentrated on cameras produced before the Second World War, which meant a cut-off date of 1939. This led on to an interest in the 1950s and into the 1960s. Today, the most cursory glance around a camera fair, will show more and more tables selling cameras from the 1970s and even into the 1980s, right up to the advent of autofocus. Once thought of as usable classics, these cameras are now becoming the latest collectors' items.

Several reasons for this shift in interest can be put forward. Firstly, there is only a finite number of collectable cameras actually in existence, and as the hobby becomes more and more popular, more and more of these find their way into private collections, so that to some extent, the source for older models is beginning to dry up.

Then there's the fact that the hobby is still attracting newcomers, who are somewhat younger than the original, established collectors. To a great extent, collecting is all about reliving our youth — and the cameras from the youth of this new generation are correspondingly newer than those from the first generation of collectors.

Another point is that these post-Second World War cameras are less expensive than their pre-war counterparts, making them more accessible to the collector on a budget.

Cameras like this Olympus OM-1 from the 1970s are beginning to be sort after almost as much as more traditional collectable models such as those made by Leica, Contax or Sanderson.

It is also a fact that many established collectors have actually bought all they want of the older models and so are looking in new directions for cameras to collect, so turning their attention to cameras of the past three decades.

Another aspect of this need to find a new direction to take has manifested itself in the past year or so in the collection of cine cameras. Especially early models from before 1920 have always been collectable, but today, the later models that began with the advent of true amateur cinematography in 1923, are beginning to appeal to collectors. Where once these cameras were to be found in the junk boxes below tables at camera fairs, they are now beginning to be elevated to the top of the table. Prices are still very modest compared to those for still cameras, but they are beginning to creep up. So the message is clear. If you want to hedge your bets against the future, cine is a good place to look.

We do not include cine cameras in the Blue Book yet, but in acknowledgement of the general shift towards later cameras, most of the 500 or so extra items included in this edition are from the post-1945 period, up until the early 1980s.

Price changes

What about prices? How have they changed since our last edition, and what seems to be the trend for the future?

Up until early 1998, prices of what we might call the traditional collectable cameras continued to rise at a small but steady rate, although Russian cameras have continued to fall in prices as more and more equipment finds its way into the West, following the opening up of the country. Some of the older wood and brass cameras still do not command the prices they once did, compared to later and more mechanically sophisticated cameras such as those from Zeiss or Leitz. At the same time, some of the newer items of interest (such as the post-war models and cine cameras mentioned above) came onto the market at low prices, then began to escalate at a faster rate than the traditional equipment as more interest was shown.

Then, early in 1998, the Japanese Stock Market collapsed. It might, at first, seem that this would have little effect on the prices of cameras in other parts of the world, but to assume this is to deny the impact that Japanese collectors had, until then, on the global market.

The Japanese were prolific collectors, and seemed to have more money to spend than their western counterparts. Without even leaving their own country, many of them bought by mail order from dealers elsewhere in the world, and they bought by postal bids at auctions, also from places outside Japan. For dealers, the prices that Japanese collectors were prepared to pay became the official prices for certain cameras, however inflated they might have seemed. And, as those Japanese collectors fought to outbid each other, buying from dealers who were quick to see a way of making more profit, so the prices went up and up.

The same was true of auctions, both in international sales, such as those at Christie's, and in smaller postal auctions such as those organised by the Photographic Collectors Club of Great Britain. Once again, the price that the Japanese were prepared to pay forced up the prices for other collectors.

When the Japanese Stock Market collapsed, Japanese collectors stopped buying, almost overnight. Such was the impact of their sudden absence from the collectors' market, that one major London dealer who had relied on Japanese custom for a major area of sales, went into voluntary liquidation in April 1998, citing the collapse of the Japanese economy as a major reason for the failure of his business.

Introduction

Logically, the result should have been a fall back to the prices of a year or so ago. In fact, what happened was that prices dropped back a little, held steady for a while, then began to show small increases again.

The Japanese have not, as yet, come back with the force they once represented, but there has been no significant drop in interest among collectors in Europe, America and other parts of the world, and so the prices which in many cases were originally dictated by Japanese collectors, have remained stable.

The overall effect of all this is that although many dealers might have a little more stock left on their shelves than they once had, and although auction houses might be left with a few more unsold lots than they have previously been accustomed to, prices are still buoyant. As for the future, most dealers, professional and amateur, see the next year as one in which prices should not escalate out of proportion, but in which they should see small but significant increases.

Condition

Guide prices are for cameras in generally excellent condition. That means 80% to 100% original finish and no evidence of restoration. There are a number of instruments that rarely ever will be found in good working condition. For example, the Contaflex TLR and a number of Zeiss 35mm cameras made in the 1930's fitted with focal plane shutters will rarely be functional. Furthermore they are extremely difficult to have serviced and the older they get the problem only gets worse as the service people, who once did the work, and the parts become increasingly scarce. The same is true of the Super Kodak 620, a very rare camera with an equally delicate shutter and automatic exposure control system. In this instance, the cosmetic condition of the camera will be the most important consideration.

The presence of the original packaging is particularly important if it is very old and or a special type such as the first Brownies, or the *art-deco* cameras of Eastman Kodak in the 1930's.

For cameras in other states of condition, add or subtract from the Guide price as follows:

Mint Condition

100% original finish,everything perfect, in new condition in every respect, add 50% to the list prices. If the camera is over 50 years old, this number may go higher. Very rare cameras R4 to R5, this figure raises to 100% or more.

Very Good Condition

60% original finish, item complete but wood, or leather slightly scratched; scuffed or marred metal work, but no corrosion or pitmarks. Lens and viewfinder clean, shutter and other mechanical parts in working order (with exceptions noted above), restorable with minimum effort and expense. Deduct 15-25% from listed prices.

Good Condition

50% original finish, minor wear on exposed surfaces, no major parts broken or missing but may need some minor replacements, metal rusted or pitted in places but can be cleaned, leather scuffed and/or aged, wood scratched, marred and may have minor cracks, but restorable. The lens will show use and the shutter may be in questionable mechanical condition, but repairable. Collectors are less and less interested in these cameras, and you might find you have a difficult time trading them off or selling them.

The other side of this coin is that they are easier to find and if you are skilled in restoration techniques and prepared to invest the time they can be a bargain. Deduct about 40% to 60% from listed price.

Fair Condition

25% original condition, well used and worn, in need of parts replacement and refinishing, leather cracked or missing, lens clouded or damaged, metal parts pitted and gears rounded, shutter inoperable, wood finish almost gone and in need of complete restoration. These cameras are usually sold for parts, to someone who has the same camera in better condition, but maybe needs a screw or spring which can be salvaged from the fair camera. Even worse than the "fair" camera is a strictly parts-only camera. Deduct 60% to 90% from listed price.

Exceptions

Very rare cameras, those with a four to five star or considered unavailable are frequently exceptions to the preceding rules. The older and rarer a camera becomes the more difficult it is to find in truly mint condition. If one does turn up, it may be worth triple the listed price. At the same time a camera that is considered in good condition, but very rare, may still command a very high price. Collectors are cautioned to be very careful of evidence of extensive restoration with valuable instruments. Restored cameras are usually less interesting to collectors than cameras in original condition; it can depend very much on the country and particular collecting speciality. They are usually an attempt by a shrewd dealer to make a poor camera into something it is not. Few serious collectors will be willing to pay the money asked for such mutilations.

For usable cameras, such as the Leica M3 (EL134), or the Bessa II (V0105), needing repair, deduct the cost of repair from the listed price. Be warned, though, that the repair of complex rangefinder or SLR cameras can prove expensive. Competent repair people are becoming increasingly harder to find (and more costly), a trend that can easily depress the prices of cameras needing work, that you may wish to use.

Rarity

Rarity indicates a camera's accessability for purchase to the collector. The harder it is to find, the higher the rarity factor. Rarity factors are indicated by a star rating system, ranging from 1* to 5*, as in previous editions. We have added an additional category in this issue: UNAVAILABLE. A camera in this category exists in such limited quantities that they are either all in museums or a very few private collections.

When they do come on the market, the price can be staggering. Very few cameras in this category are in the Guide, however several are listed mainly for reasons of historical interest.

Rare cameras are usually in that category regardless of the country they are found in. They are recognized as being in limited supply by collectors internationally. At the lower end of the scale in categories 1, 2 or even 3, there is a strong geographic factor working. For example, a Kodak collector will find their task considerably easier for US products at home, likewise, a collector in Europe or Japan will find it easier to locate the more common domestically made cameras in their own countries. As is the case with prices, it is important to think of Rarity ratings as **guides**, adjusting them for location. The ratings are defined as follows:

1*Cameras with a **one-star** rating can be found easily. They are frequently found in box lots at lower level auctions or market stalls. Since they are so easily obtained, a collector has large choice. They were mass-produced and widely distributed for a number of years. Most simple box and folding cameras fall into this category. A good example is a 3A Folding Kodak made for nearly a quarter-of-a-century with minor changes.

2*Cameras with a **two-star** rarity are slightly more difficult to find. They were usually more costly to purchase new. Rather than finding them at virtually all jumble sales, a collector will need to work a bit harder to find a good sample. Folding plate cameras such as the Zeiss Contina II are in this grouping.

Before World War II folding plate cameras and the better grade folding roll film instruments were offered with a large variety of lens and shutter combinations, sometimes the available choice being determined by the country it was sold in. At the lowest end of the scale it may be fitted with a simple achromat in a three speed shutter. The same basic camera was also being sold with a Zeiss Tessar lens in a Compur shutter. Although the first cost was much higher for the expensive models, this difference is not necessarily reflected in the collectors' market.

3*Three-star cameras will take more searching out. Camera fairs with itinerant dealers, many with excellent inventory, will generally be a good source of three-star cameras, but they do turn up in flea markets from time-to-time. The Kodak Chevron and the Foth-Flex are examples of three-star cameras.

4*A camera may be of **four-star** rarity for a number of reasons. If it is very old, say early Victorian, time and the changing needs of evolving technology may have combined to destroy most of them. The surviving instruments are in very short supply, or the original production run may have been very small.

5*Five-star level of rarity instruments exist mostly in museums or very large private collections. As recently as a decade ago instruments at this level still turned up occasionally in antique shops etc., but an increasing number of collectors and a greater amount of knowledge about cameras makes such "lightning strikes" increasingly unlikely. The Ben Akiba Cane Camera, and a number of daguerrotype cameras fall into this area.

U – Unavailable. Instruments in this category are sometimes difficult to define. To a large extent you can use the definition of five-star cameras with an important difference. The original production run was very low and the surviving instruments have all been accounted for. The O-Series Leica is a good example of such a camera.

Leica Cameras and Accessories

Leica collecting is the most highly developed and specialised field of camera collecting. There are three main reasons for this. The Leica, although not the first to use 35mm cine film, was the first serious 35mm camera and it revolutionised photography. Leica users pioneered the real-life style of photography we are familiar with today. So it has immense historic significance. Secondly, its makers, Ernst Leitz, from the beginning saw it as a system camera. They developed interchangeable lenses and a myriad of accessories to expand its use into all types of photographic applications, so there are literally thousands of individual items, all beautifully engineered. Thirdly, and most significantly, there is more information available about the Leica than any other camera. This is because the archives of Ernst Leitz at Wetzlar survived the war, being neither destroyed nor looted.

A tremendous amount of research on the Leica has been carried out and published. Complete serial number lists are available, pinpointing the year of manufacture of each individual camera and lens. The history of many individual cameras is known, giving them a special value.

For the camera collector wanting to add some Leica examples to a general collection the *Blue Book* will provide adequate guidance, and furthermore place the Leica cameras in the context of cameras generally. The Leica specialist collector, however, needs much more detailed information and should turn to the Hove specialist Leica publications listed in the advertisement section of the book. In particular, the *Hove Leica International Price Guide* gives a finer division of rarity on a scale of 1 to 10 for cameras, lenses and accessories, necessary because of the many variations within individual models and the very limited production of some.

Abbreviations

Certain abbreviations are used throughout the listings in the *Blue Book*. Here's how to read them...

(?):	approximate.
*:	one lens and shutter combination of several variations.
+:	the "+" sign after a price indicates that the camera would probably sell for considerably more on today's market than it sold for when the price was originally figured.
BIM:	built-in light meter.
C:	Year of manufacture. The dates in the Zeiss section are precise; elsewhere the dates are approximate. A single date usually indicates the year the camera model first appeared.
CFPS:	cloth focal-plane shutter.
Counterfeit:	a camera, represented by the seller to the buyer as being historically accurate, but appearing to be of a make or model different from that which it really is. Counterfeit Leica cameras are usually Russian.
CRF:	coupled rangefinder.
exp:	exposure.
Fake:	a camera which has been made to seem that which it is not, and which is represented by the seller to the buyer as original. A Leica "Luxus"which is really a re-worked Leica I(A) but found on a dealer's table at a show as a true "Luxus"would be called a fake. Beware of fakes, before making an expensive purchase, know all the facts about the camera and the seller. More and more"Fakes" are being made in Eastern Europe, and shipped into the West for the chance to turn a fast mark or pound.

FPS: focal plane shutter.
mfg: manufactured.
MFPS: metal focal-plane shutter.
NSR: no sales recorded.
Qty: quantity.
Replica: a camera, represented to the buyer by the seller as being not historically accurate. Replica cameras are not sold to fool anybody. Leica "Luxus" cameras are sometimes made from Leica I(A) cameras, "Ur" Leica cameras are indeed made by Leitz, and are faithful to the original, but alas......
RFR: rangefinder.
s: seconds.
Slr: single lens reflex.
Snr: serial number range.
VFR: viewfinder.

On cameras where more than one price is quoted for variations of the same type (e.g. chrome/black/military markings, etc) the value and rarity ratings apply to that of the basic camera in the section.

New Collectors Start Here

Camera collecting began to take off as a major hobby during the early to middle 1970s. Until then, there were camera collectors, but they were few and far between, rarely meeting with one another or even knowing of each other's existence.

These people were often amateur photographers who had originally bought an older camera to use, only to become fascinated by its operation and craftsmanship, and one thing inevitably to another. Independent of each other, they began looking for old cameras. Photographic dealers, where customers traded in old equipment for new, were prime targets and collectors would leave their names and phone numbers with dealers in the hope of a call. Junk shops were a source of collectable equipment, although very few cameras had yet to attain the respect of real antique dealers.

Gradually, over the course of a few brief years, the hobby took off. Collectors' clubs were formed. Fairs began to be organised. Big auction houses like Christie's started to feature camera auctions. Photographic dealers gave over some of their shelf space to older, more collectable equipment. And eventually, specialised dealers, selling nothing but collectable cameras, opened their doors.

If you are new to camera collecting, you probably find yourself regretting not having started years before when prices were cheaper. If so, you have just stumbled on the first rule of collecting: "The best time to start was ten years before you did."

Yes, prices were cheaper in those days, mainly because there wasn't the demand. But the demand has, in itself, opened up the market, so that today it is far easier to buy collectable cameras — a fact that actually keeps prices stable. Also, if you compare the price of an average (as opposed to a super-rare) collectable camera of today with what it cost ten or twenty years ago, taking its value against national wage averages, you might be surprised to learn that a great many collectable cameras haven't soared in price in real terms, only kept pace with inflation.

Where to buy

The first thing a new collector should do — if you haven't done so already — is join a club. The Photographic Collectors Club of Great Britain (PCCGB) is one of the best world-wide, holding not only an annual national meeting and fair, but any number of regional meetings at regular intervals throughout the year. Here collectors meet, listen to talks, gather new information and sell or swap cameras between themselves. The club also has many sub-divisions for members interested in specific camera manufacturers.

Many other clubs for camera collectors exist elsewhere around the world. Check the lists on pages 63-68 to find the one nearest to you.

Where else can the newcomer find cameras to collect and what is the best way of buying?

Camera fairs make an ideal starting point. Members of the PCCGB get a listing of fairs all over the country, published on a regular basis, otherwise watch out for them advertised in the classified sections of photographic magazines. Camera fairs attract recognised dealers, but also private collectors. These are the best people to buy from, because they are not there to make huge profits, only to charge a fair price, and because they have been collecting for so many years, they often have some fascinating cameras to sell on.

Prices at specialised dealers are usually higher than at camera fairs, but on the other hand, the equipment might be in better condition, and if there is anything wrong with it, they'll tell you, reducing the price accordingly. That's

Classic camera dealers can be expensive, but the equipment on offer will be of top quality

something you won't always get at a camera fair! It's also worth remembering the sheer range of equipment that they have available. Dealers can get their hands on equipment that ordinary collectors can only dream about finding elsewhere. Also because they have contacts among a great many collectors, they know who wants what and are consequently in a good position to offer you a decent price if you are selling or part exchanging.

Auctions come in two types: national and local. Nationally, auction houses like Christie's have regular sales entirely of collectable camera gear every few months. Locally, look out for auctions of house clearance items. These are the places to pick up bargains. If you are a newcomer to collecting, you might not fully understand how an auction works, so let's pause for a moment to look at how you buy at one.

It starts with the viewing, which is usually held the day before or sometimes right up to just before the sale starts. This is where you go to look at what's on offer. Before the start of the sale, go to the registration desk, where someone will take your name, address, possibly your telephone number and maybe proof of identity. Then they will give you a number. In the sale room, the auctioneer calls up each lot, and he (not you) starts the bidding by suggesting a price. If you are interested, raise your hand. The auctioneer will then increase the price and someone else will bid, and he raises the price again. You keep bidding until you are the last one in, at which point the item is knocked down to you. You then hold up your number. Afterwards, you go to the collection point, quote your number, pay your money and collect your goods. But beware, because the price you bid might be less than the price you are asked to pay. That's because a buyer's premium — usually around ten per cent — is added to the price and, at the larger auction houses, if the camera you are buying is subject to VAT or other sales taxes, that too could be added.

Antique markets rarely include specialist camera dealers, but you might find cameras on more general stalls, among the china and glassware. Although not a major source for collectable cameras, they can be fruitful at times and are often good places to look for accessories like exposure meters as opposed to actual cameras.

Flea markets and junk fairs are much the same as antique markets, except that the items on sale are a lot less prestigious. Although you do hear stories of unbelievable bargains, it is actually quite rare to find anything really valuable at a junk fair or flea market. For the camera collector, they make better places for building up a collection of simple snapshot cameras.

What to buy

So if you know *where* to buy, the next question is *what* to buy.

When you start out, you'll probably buy everything and anything. But as you get more into the hobby, you might decide you would prefer to specialise.

Some collectors specialise in cameras made by a specific manufacturer, and perhaps the most popular of all is Leitz, the makers of Leica equipment. There are collectors who buy nothing but Leica cameras, lenses and accessories, and there are whole books devoted to nothing but the many different variations of this marque. Leica cameras are perhaps the most expensive of collectable cameras, but other manufacturers are of interest to other collectors, who might specialise in Zeiss Ikon, Voigtlander, Kodak, Nikon, Canon, etc. If you want to know more about that approach it's a good idea to join one of the specialist groups of enthusiasts. (See the club listings starting on page 63).

Another alternative is to collect certain types of camera: single lens reflexes, twin lens reflexes, small format plate cameras, larger wood and brass types, box cameras, stereo, 35mm models. One especially popular category is subminiatures. Here you can find just about all the other types, each reduced in size to take small format film. Subminiatures are attractive and also have the advantage of taking up less display space than others.

Actual styles can also form a collection, with the art deco period perhaps being the most popular. Art Deco was a decorative arts style that was popular

Subminiatures can make an interesting collecting category

between 1910 and 1940. Its themes were based on classical motifs, reduced to simple, geometric shapes, often seen in architecture and sculpture, but equally seen in cameras, notably those produced in and around the 1930s.

Landmarks provide another interesting route to take, looking at specific models which introduced the earliest model of a popular camera style: the first 35mm single lens reflex, the first rollfilm twin lens reflex, the first camera to take 127 or 120 film, the first camera with auto exposure, the first with a coupled rangefinder, or perhaps the first model made by each of several different well-known manufacturers.

The Sport appeals to collectors of Russian cameras and is also interesting for being a very early 35mm single lens reflex.

Or how about looking for cameras from certain countries? Japan is an obvious one and perhaps just a little too prolific to form the basis for a single collection. But English camera makers provide an interesting focal point, covering a wide span in both time and styles. The same goes for French manufacturers. Russian cameras are particularly interesting because many of them are copies of well-known makes from the West, whilst others show real innovation in design not seen before or since. At one time, Russian cameras, with the exception of makes like Zenit, Zorki and Fed, were difficult to buy in the West. But since the opening up of the country, many more Russian cameras have come on to the market and prices of what were once considered exceptionally rare models have consequently fallen.

Even Chinese cameras have their devotees, and for much the same reason as Russian cameras.

Dates are worth keeping in mind, and it's not a bad idea to draw certain boundaries in your collecting. Camera manufacture really began in 1839 with the launch of the daguerreotype process, and cameras from this early era are both rare and expensive. For these reasons, most general collectors will have few cameras made before 1900.

Some collectors draw the line at 1939, the year the Second World War broke out. It makes a convenient stopping point, since the post-war years saw so many changes in camera styles. By the same token 1945, the year the war ended, makes an interesting starting point, and one that is currently growing in popularity among collectors. In fact, if you are new to collecting, the period between mid-1940s, into the 1970s and even into the early 1980s is one that is certainly worth considering. It was a time when many new designs came on to the market and many of the older ones died. The 1960s saw the real start of the SLR revolution, the 1970s refined the SLR and the 1980s started the autofocus boom.

Cameras from this era are certainly easier to find than the much earlier models, and for the newcomer, the prices are more attractive than what might be paid for a super-rare camera from the really early days of photography.

Collecting tips

However you organise your collection, there are a few general points that the beginner should keep in mind. Perhaps the most important aspect is cosmetic appearance. For a camera to be truly collectable, it needs to be in the best possible condition. Some minor examples of use do no harm, but whenever possible, avoid really tatty examples with torn leatherwork, brass showing through enamelling, fungused or misty lenses, jammed aperture blades and sticky shutters. They look ugly when displayed and they invariably fail to sell on when you want to replace them.

That said, there is no harm in buying a camera in bad condition, if the price is right and if you are sufficiently skilled to renovate it (see pages 46-50 for hints and tips on renovation). It is also permissible to buy a rough version of a model that you really want, providing you have the strength of will to replace it with a better version when the opportunity arises. The big mistake is to ignore the opportunity of upgrading your collection and to use any spare cash to buy further tatty cameras.

Remember that camera collecting is an investment as much as a hobby and it's the camera in the best condition that increases in value.

Finally, watch out for fakes, and don't confuse them with replicas.

A replica is a modern-day version of a truly historic camera, made and genuinely sold as a replica rather than the real thing. The two main examples that come to mind are the Ur Leica and the first Kodak. There's not much chance that you might be fooled by the Ur Leica, because although there are a fair number of replicas on sale, only two (or some claim, three) of the real thing were ever made. So it's a certainty that the one you see at a camera fair will be identified as, and sold as, a replica. The Kodak might be a little more difficult to identify. This was made in a limited edition in 1988 to celebrate the centenary of the first model. When it is sold, it is still usually identified as a replica, but would be a little easier to pass off as one of the originals if some clever faker managed to age it convincingly.

Which brings us to true fakes. At one time, fakery was confined to the Victorian era of cameras, where it was relatively easy to make what was essentially little more than a wooden box with a contemporary lens on it. But today, fakers are getting more ambitious and there are rumours of factories in places like Poland set up for the sole purpose of faking collectable cameras. You should be particularly wary of what appears to be a super-rare camera such as the Leica Luxus — a gold-plated Leica I with lizard skin covering — turning up at a camera fair.

Even certain collectors are guilty of faking, albeit in a perfectly innocent way. Those who are especially good at repairs and restoration will often make one good camera out of the parts of several others, ending up with a camera that is different in its specification from any true model, and which could get mistaken for a one-off rarity. There is one English collector who has developed the knack of making stereo cameras out of Prakticas. He has no intention of passing them off as fakes, but imagine the scene some

Not a rare prototype, but a stereo Praktica, purpose made by a keen collector.

50 years hence when one of his cameras turns up at some future camera fair on in an auction and gets mistaken for a rare prototype from the Praktica factory.

The problem is that the better the fake, the more difficult it is for the lay person to identify it as such and the truth of the matter is that you could easily buy a faked version of one of the more common collectables without ever knowing it. But if you see, or are offered, what you know to be a very rare camera at a surprisingly good price, then beware, and if in any doubt walk away from it. You owe it, not only to yourself, but also to future collectors, to do everything you can to prevent fakes getting into the open market.

Dating Collectable Cameras

Dating a collectable camera is, at best, an imprecise science. Some camera manufacturers, throughout their history, have been very good at keeping detailed records of serial numbers and the dates they apply to, and this of course will give you information that is about as accurate as it's possible to get. Perhaps the very best of these companies is Leica, who freely publish their lists from day one to fairly recent years, and the latest of these lists is printed starting on page 37. So for Leica enthusiasts, camera dating is easy and straight forward.

Some other companies have made efforts to keep records and, where such lists are available, we have also included these at the end of this chapter. But, with the notable exception of Leica, most lists are incomplete. Mergers, take-overs, company name changes, lost records particularly during the years of World War Two, have all contributed to confusion and omissions.

That said, it is possible, with a little detective work, to compare names, features, body types, lenses, shutters, patent dates and other sundry information, and between them to get as close as possible, even to often hit the date spot on.

Here are some clues to watch out for.

Books and magazines

The Blue Book that you are reading gives dates for as many of its entries as possible, and these are as accurate as it has been possible to get them. But if you think we are wrong and can prove it, we want to hear from you, so that we can correct later editions.

Other modern books also date cameras as accurately as possible, but you should never accept what the author says as gospel truth. Where possible, check other sources and try to get at least two that agree. Don't forget also that authors often take information from each other, and mistakes can get passed on from book to book.

A better bet is to go back to source. Whenever possible, buy old photographic magazines, in particular Amateur Photographer, which was first published in 1894 and the British Journal of Photography, which was first published in 1854. If they talk about a new piece of equipment that they say has just been launched, then the date of the magazine is a pretty safe bet. But do bear in mind that the date the news of the item arrived in the UK (or any other country whose magazines you are using) might be a year or so after the camera was officially launched in its home country.

Another good source is the British Journal Photographic Almanac, which was first published in its original form in 1860 and thereafter at yearly intervals. By comparing issues year by year and checking the first appearance of a particular camera in the advertisements, you can get a pretty good idea of its launch date. In early issues, the BJ, as it is known among collectors, listed equipment in a regular section called *Epitome of Progress,* but in 1924, the equipment news was separated out in a section called *Recent Introductions in Apparatus and Materials,* which speaks for itself. From 1925 on, this became a section simply called *New Goods.* One point to be aware of, though. Being an annual publication, the BJ was up to a year in production, so publication dates of issues in which equipment appears for the first time, are very often one year later than the date of the actual launch or the appearance of the camera in the UK.

Patent dates

You'll sometimes find patent dates stamped inside camera backs, particularly on Kodak cameras, but don't be fooled by these. If a camera carries a patent date or series of dates, that doesn't guarantee when it was made, since a camera might be actually built several years after its design was patented. What the patent date will give you is a time before which the camera could *not* have been built.

Film sizes

Older cameras used a wide variety of different film sizes and, if the required film is printed or stamped somewhere inside the body, then once again you have a date before which the camera couldn't have existed. On the next page you will find some examples of film size numbers and the approximate dates of their launch.

Company and camera names

Here in the Blue Book, we have tried to give you potted histories of many of the companies — when they first started, when their names changed, etc —and this of course can also tell you the earliest date that a particular manufacturer might have built a camera. For example...

During a period of a little over 30 years, Eastman Kodak absorbed a number of American camera manufacturers: the Blair Camera Company in 1899, the Boston Camera Manufacturing Company in 1895, the American

American Film Numbers by date of introduction

101:	1895	110:	1898	119:	1900	129:	1912
102:	1895	111:	1898	120:	1901	130:	1912
103:	1896	112:	1898	121:	1902	616:	1932
104:	1897	113:	1898	122:	1903	620:	1932
105:	1898	114:	1898	123:	1904	135:	1935
106:	1898	115:	1898	124:	1905	828:	1935*
107:	1898	116:	1899	126:	1906	126:	1963**
108:	1898	117:	1900	127:	1912	110:	1972***
109:	1898	118:	1900	128:	1912	Disc:	1981
						APS:	1996

*also known as Bantam

**also known as Instamatic, not the same as 126 of 1906

***also known as Pocket Instamatic, not the same as 110 of 1898

Camera Company in 1898, the Rochester Optical Company in 1903, Folmer and Schwing in 1907 and Nagel in 1932.

G. Houghton and Son became Houghtons Ltd in 1904. The company merged with Butchers to form Houghton-Butcher in 1925. They sold cameras under the name of Ensign from 1930.

Amalgamated Photographic Manufacturers Ltd, otherwise known as APM, was formed in 1921, from the amalgamation of a number of well-known British manufacturers that included Marion, Paget and Rajar. In 1929, the company split, and camera making continued under the name of Soho Ltd.

Zeiss Ikon was formed from the amalgamation of Goerz, Ica, Ernemann and Contessa-Nettel in 1926.

The Miroflex was made by Contessa-Nettel before 1926 and continued to be made by Zeiss Ikon after the merger.

Shutters and lenses

Camera manufacturers of the past didn't always make their own shutters or lenses, but preferred to add other well-known names to their bodies. So knowing when certain shutters or lenses first appeared also gives you an earliest date from which to work...

Shutters

Unicum	1897
Automat	1901
Goerz Sector	1904
Compound,	1904
Compur dial set	1912
Compur rim set	1928.

The shutter on a camera can help you date it. Left to right are a Compur dial set (1912), Compur rim set (1928) and Unicum (1897).

Lenses

Aldis Anastigmat	1901
Aviar	1918
Cooke	1893
Dagor	1904
Helia	1902
Protar	1895
Tessar	1902
Xpres	1914.

Lens coating appeared mostly after 1945, although beware of earlier lenses that were coated several years after their original manufacture.

Zeiss lenses (often coupled with Compur shutters) were used on a great many different camera bodies, even in Japan before the Japanese began their

The Tessar lens was introduced in 1902 and remained popular for many years thereafter.

own lens production, so knowing the dates and serial numbers of lenses from this particular company can be a strong clue to the date of the camera. Here's a list of Zeiss serial numbers with their appropriate dates.

Zeiss Lens Serial Numbers:

Year	Serial Numbers	Year	Serial Numbers	Year	Serial Numbers
1912	173400-200500	1923	561250-578300	1933	1436650-1456000
1913	208500-249350	1924	631850-648500	1934	1500450-1590000
1914	249900-252700	1925	652200-681751	1935	1615750-1752300
1915	282800-284500	1926	686800-703200	1936	1774800-1942800
1916	285200-288100	1927	722200-798250	1937	1950100-2220000
1917	289000-298150	1928	903100-908150	1938	2268000-2528000
1918	298200-322750	1929	919800-1016900	1939	2528001-2651200
1919	322800-351600	1930	1020500-1239700	1940	2652000-2678000
1920	375200-419800	1931	1239701-1365600	1941	2678001-2790350
1921	433250-438350	1932	1365601-1389300	1942	2799600- ?
1922	438900-498000				

It is worth noting that many cameras originally sold with one lens and shutter combination, might have been changed later as owners updated their equipment. Also remember that many camera models were originally sold with a choice of shutter and lens combinations, according to the price and the taste of the customer. These combinations might also be affected by the country in which a camera was sold, as importers and distributors often changed the specifications. A French lens on a German camera, for example, could indicate that a particular item, though maufactured in Germany, was originally sold in France.

Camera features

Certain features that are common to different manufacturers can also help identify a date.

Red windows for film winding first appeared in 1892 and fairly regularly from 1895.

The Autographic Back, identified as a small flap on the back of mostly Kodak cameras, lasted from 1914 until 1933.

Metal plating changed through the years. Nickel (shiny and looking a little yellow) dates from the 1890s, chrome from the mid 1930s.

Bellows were mostly red until about 1910, then black. They were designed with square corners until around 1900, before changing to chamfered corners.

The very first coupled rangefinder was on a Kodak camera in 1916, but mostly they date from around 1930.

Folding cameras with a bed that drops down for the lens to pull out along it on rails date from 1900. Self-erecting folders were rare before 1920.

The No.3A Folding Pocket Kodak, made in 1900, was the first of this style of folding camera.

The first really viable 35mm camera, taking the now traditional 24x36mm format dates from 1925.

The first twin-lens camera appeared in 1881, but the first true rollfilm twin lens reflex dates from 1928.

Bakelite was used in camera making from 1929.

Two red windows for 16-on first appeared in 1922 for 120 film, but didn't take off properly until the idea was introduced for 127 film in 1930, after which the feature was applied to both 127 and 120.

The first truly compact single lens reflex came in 1933, but was made for 127 film. The first 35mm single lens reflex was in 1935 or 1936, depending on whether or not you accept that the Russians produced the Sport before Ihagee produced the Kine Exakta. There are schools of though for both, but the Exakta, dated for 1936, is the best guide.

The first camera with a built-in exposure meter arrived in 1938. The same year saw the first camera with automatic exposure control.

The instant return mirror first appeared in 1947, but only really became popular after 1954.

The first instant picture camera appeared in 1948.

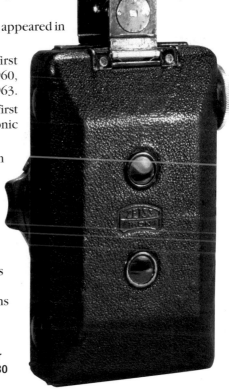

Through-the-lens metering first appeared in a subminiature in 1960, then in a single lens reflex in 1963.

The same year also saw the first camera with an automatic electronic shutter.

Instamatic cameras for 126 film date from 1963, for 110 film from 1972.

The first automatic single lens reflex appeared in 1968.

The first autofocus compact cameras came in 1978, with autofocus lenses for manual focus cameras in 1980 and the first purpose-built autofocus single lens reflex in 1985.

Twin red windows became popular after the they were used in the 1930 Kolibri.

Disc cameras were launched in 1981.

The first of the modern-style disposable cameras appeared in 1988.

Electronic imaging in a commercially available camera first appeared in 1989.

Camera names

The first appearance of a well-known name gives a cut-off point before which those names would not have been seen. Here's a list of when certain household names first appeared on a camera (as opposed to the dates the various companies were actually founded).

Agfa	1928
Canon	1935
Ensign	1930
Ernemann	1900
Exakta	1933
Fed	1934
Graflex	1902
Hasselblad (SLRs)	1948
Ilford	1951
Kodak	1888
Kodak Brownie	1900
Leica	1925
Minolta	1931
Minox	1937
Nikon	1948
Olympus	1936
Pentax	1957
Polaroid	1948
Rolleiflex	1928
Sanderson	1896
Voigtlander	1840
Zeiss Ikon	1926
Zorki	1948

Hidden codes

In the 1940s and 1950s, Kodak used a hidden code in the serial numbers of some of their lenses to indicate when they were built. The code consists of a series of letters that translate into numbers, like this:-

C A M E R O S I T Y

1 2 3 4 5 6 7 8 9 0

To date the lens, look for the letters and compare them to the appropriate numbers below them in the table. For example, a serial number beginning with the letters 'ER' denotes the lens was made in 1945.

At one time, Hasselblad used a similar system on bodies and film magazines that ran like this:-

V H P I C T U R E S

1 2 3 4 5 6 7 8 9 0

You will also find a hidden code on some Chinese cameras, that uses the first two figures of the serial number to denote the number of years after liberation that the camera was made. Liberation was in 1949, so a camera whose serial number begins, for example, with the figures '21', was made in 1970 (1949 + 21 = 1970).

Many Russian cameras and lenses made between 1950 and 1980, show the year of manufacture in the first two digits of the serial number. So if, for example, the serial number is quoted as 56083307, the camera was most likely made in 1956. This offers an ideal way of comparing bodies and lenses to see if a later lens has been added to an earlier body.

Serial numbers

The following serial number lists with their dates will help to identify years of manufacture for certain camera makers

FED Serial Numbers

Year	Serial	Year	Serial
1934	31 - 4000	1947	176000 - 186000
1935	4000 - 16000	1948	186000 - 203000
1936	16000 - 31000	1949	203000 - 221000
1937	31000 - 53000	1950	221000 - 248000
1938	53000 - 82000	1951	248000 - 289000
1939	82000 - 116000	1952	289000 - 341000
1940	116000 - 148000	1953	341000 - 424000
1941	148000 - 175000	1954	424000 - 560000
1942-45	No Camera Production	1955	560000 - 700000
1946	175000 - 176000		

Foca models and dates

Foca "PF1", one star

1946	16,001-20,300
1947	20,301-21,200
1948	60,001-61,300
1949	61,301-65,200
1950	65,201-67,700
	68,201-68,700
1951	67,701-68,200
	68,701-69,200
	69,701-69,999
	100,001-101,150
1952	69-201-69,700
	101,151-101,550
	160,001-161,000
1953	101,551-101,999

Foca "Standard" one star

1953	500,001-502,050
1954	502,051-503,150
1955	503,151-504,100
1956	504,101-505,300
1957	505,301- ?

Foca "PF2" two stars

1946	10,001-15,999

Foca "PF2b" two stars

1947	25,001-37,000
1948	37,001-46,600
1949	56,601-53,000
	54,401-55,350
1950	53,001-54,401
	55,351-56,000
1951	56,001-59,500
	125,000-150,000
1952	59,501-60,000
	90,001-92,700

1953	300,000-300,550
	92,701-94,999
1954	300,551-302,100
1955	302,101-303,700
1956	303,701-306,000
1957	306,001- ?

Foca "PF3" three stars

1952	90,001-92,700

(taken from the PF2b list from the same year)

1953	92,701-89,999

(taken from the PF2b list from the same year)

	400,001-400,650
1954	400,651-402,400
1955	402,401-404,100
1956	404,101-406,400
1957	406,401- ?

Foca Universal no stars

1949	70,001-74,800
1950	74,801-80,400
1951	80,401-84,650
1952	170,000-174,000
1953	84,651-86,900
1954	86,901-87,999
1955	200,501-201,250

Foca Universal "R" no stars

1955	200,001R-
1956	200,900R-
1957	203,300R ?
	-

FOCASPORT

1955	10,001S-23,600S
1956	23,601S-48,500S
1957	48,501S- ?

*From 1947 until 1951, about 1200 PF3 cameras were made. These cameras used serial numbers taken from the "PF2b" list. They fall between two ranges. 25,000-59,999, and 125,000-150,000.

Zeiss United States Patent numbers

United States Patent numbers by year of issue

Year	Number	Year	Number	Year	Number
1850	6891	1882	251,685	1914	1,083,267
1851	7865	1883	269,820	1915	1,123,212
1852	8622	1884	291,016	1916	1,166,419
1853	9512	1885	310,163	1917	1,210,389
1854	10,358	1886	333,494	1918	1,251,458
1855	12,117	1887	355,291	1919	1,290,027
1856	14,009	1888	375,720	1920	1,326,899
1857	16,324	1889	395,305	1921	1,364,063
1858	19,010	1890	418,665	1922	1,401,948
1859	22,477	1891	443,987	1923	1,440,362
1860	26,642	1892	466,315	1924	1,478,996
1861	31,005	1893	488,976	1925	1,521,590
1862	34,045	1894	511,744	1926	1,568,040
1863	37,266	1895	531,619	1927	1,612,790
1864	41,047	1896	552,501	1928	1,654,521
1865	45,085	1897	574,369	1929	1,696,897
1866	51,784	1898	596,467	1930	1,742,818
1867	60,658	1899	616,871	1931	1,787,424
1868	72,959	1900	640,167	1932	1,839,190
1869	85,503	1901	664,827	1933	1,892,66
1870	98,460	1902	690,385	1934	1,941,449
1871	110,617	1903	717,521	1935	1,985,878
1872	122,304	1904	748,567	1936	2,026,516
1873	134,504	1905	778,834	1937	2,066,319
1874	146,010	1906	808,618	1938	2,014,004
1875	158,350	1907	839,799	1940	2,185,170
1876	171,641	1908	875,679	1941	2,227,418
1877	158,813	1909	908,436	1942	2,268,540
1878	198,733	1910	945,010	1943	2,307,007
1879	211,078	1911	980,178	1944	2,338,081
1880	223,211	1912	1,013,095	1945	2,366,154
1881	236,137	1913	1,049,326	1946	2,391,856

Identifying Leica Cameras

The list of Leica camera and lens serial numbers are reproduced here by kind permission of Leica Camera G.m.b.H. This listing is essentially for use as a quick reference guide for the dating of a Leica camera or lens. The lists are in manufacturing batches. In a number of cases, particularly in the more recent post-war period, not all allocated numbers were used.

In the Leica screw period the individual batches were often much smaller than would be indicated by this quick reference list. You will often find individual cameras that are of a different model than that indicated in the list. For example, you might come across a Leica Standard with a serial number that indicates it should be one of a batch of 1000 Leica IIIa cameras. This is because, before the war, the Leitz company were willing to supply a special order camera to an individual customer: it would then be allotted a number from the current production batch. Leica Historica, the German Leica historical society, once published a screw camera listing that analysed production almost down to individual cameras by model and date and ran to 190 A4 pages of detail. This listing was compiled from the hand-written ledgers, which still exist in the factory, where every single camera produced was recorded, with its model type, date and destination.

Another anomaly that can arise with screw, and some M cameras, is caused by the Leitz policy, up to at least the end of the 1960s, of offering an upgrading service. Examples might be from Leica I to Leica II, or Leica II to Leica III or IIIa. After the war, flash synchronisation was also offered for earlier models. For these reasons you can see that an original Leica I could have been converted several times during its life, but it always retained its original serial number. This can be disappointing for the collector who comes into possession of a camera with the serial number of what should have been a valuable collector's item, but which has been converted into something much more up-to-date but far less valuable now!

Leitz also upgraded lenses for customers by changing the front ring on, say, an Elmax to a standard Elmar ring. Later they offered to change the aperture scale to the later type. They also coated earlier lenses. So it is quite possible to find an early unnumbered lens, that was not originally rangefinder coupled, that has been converted to a later, coated specification.For all the above reasons, use these serial number lists with caution. They are only a quick reference guide. The more detailed Leica publications from HOVE BOOKS will give further help in identifying Leica cameras, lenses and accessories and act as guides into the fascinating Leica world.

Leica Serial Numbers up to 1992

This information reproduced by kind permission of Leica Camera GmbH

Leica No	Model	Year	Leica No	Model	Year	Leica No	Model	Year
100 - 130	I	1923	144201 - 144400	II	1934	161601 - 161800	IIIa	1935
131 - 1000	I	1925	144401 - 144500	Standard	1934	161801 - 161950	III Chrom	1935
1001 - 2445	I	1926	144501 - 145600	III	1934	161951 - 162100	IIIa	1935
2446 - 5433	I	1926/27	145601 - 145800	Standard	1934	162101 - 162175	III	1935
5434 - 5700	I	1928	145801 - 146200	III	1934	162176 - 162350	IIIa	1935
5700 - 6300	Compur	1926-29	146201 - 146375	II	1934	162351 - 162400	III	1935
6301 - 13100	I	1928	146376 - 146675	III	1934	162401 - 162500	IIIa	1935
13101 - 13300	Compur	1929	146676 - 146775	II	1934	162501 - 162625	III	1935
13301 - 21478	I	1929	146776 - 147000	III	1934	162626 - 162675	IIIa	1935
21479 - 21810	Compur	1930	147001 - 147075	Standard	1934	162676 - 162750	III	1935
21811 - 34450	I	1930	147076 - 147175	II	1934	162751 - 162800	IIIa	1935
34451 - 34802	Compur	1930	147176 - 147875	St Chrom	1934	162801 - 162825	IIIa	1935
34803 - 34817	I(Luxus)	1930	147876 - 148025	II Chrom	1934	162826 - 162925	III	1935
34818 - 60000	I	1930	148026 - 148850	III Chrom	1934	162926 - 163050	IIIa	1935
60001 - 71199	I	1931	148851 - 148950	II Chrom	1934	163051 - 163100	III	1935
71200 - 101000	II	1.2.32	148951 - 149350	III Chrom	1935	163101 - 163225	IIIa	1935
101001 - 106000	Standard	21.10.32	149351 - 149450	St Chrom	1934/35	163226 - 163250	III	1935
106001 - 107600	II	1933	149451 - 149550	II Chrom	1934/35	163251 - 163400	IIIa	1935
107601 - 107757	III	1934	149551 - 150000	III Chrom	1935	163401 - 163450	Standard	1935
107758 - 108650	II	1934	150001 - 150200	Reporter	1934-36	163451 - 163550	IIIa	1935
108651 - 108700	III	1933	from 150125 with ^{1}/1000 from 14.7.36			163551 - 163775	III	1935
108701 - 109000	II	1933	150201 - 150850	III Chrom	1934/35	163776 - 163950	IIIa	1935
109001 - 111550	III	1933	150851 - 151100	Standard	1935	163951 - 164150	Standard	1935
111551 - 111580	II Chrom	1933	151101 - 151225	III	1935	164151 - 164275	IIIa	1935
111581 - 112000	III	1933	151226 - 151300	II	1935	164276 - 164675	III	1935
112001 - 112500	II Chrom	1933	151301 - 152500	III	1935	164676 - 164900	IIIa	1935
112501 - 114400	III	1934	152501 - 152600	St Chrom	1935	164901 - 165000	II	1935
114401 - 114050	St Chrom	1933	152601 - 153175	III Chrom	1935	165001 - 165100	III	1935
114051 - 114052	Reporter	1933	153176 - 153225	II	1935	165101 - 165300	II	1935
114053 - 114400	III	1934	153226 - 153550	III	1935	165301 - 165500	Standard	1935
114401 - 115300	II Chrom	1933	153551 - 153700	II	1935	165501 - 165975	II	1935
115301 - 115650	III	1934	153701 - 154150	III	1935	165976 - 166075	IIIa	1935
115651 - 115900	II Chrom	1934	154151 - 154200	II	1935	166076 - 166600	III	1935
115901 - 116000	St Chrom	1934	154201 - 154800	III	1935	166601 - 166750	IIIa	1935
116001 - 123000	III Chrom	1933	154801 - 154900	St Chrom	1935	166751 - 166900	III	1935
123001 - 123580	Standard	1934	154901 - 156200	III	1935	166901 - 167050	IIIa	1935
123581 - 124800	III Chrom	1933	156201 - 156850	IIIa ^{1}/1000	1935	167051 - 167175	III	1935
124801 - 126200	III Chrom	24.11.33	156851 - 157250	III	1935	167176 - 167200	IIIa	1935
126201 - 126800	III	1934	157251 - 157400	II	1935	167201 - 167225	III	1935
126801 - 137400	III	1934	157401 - 158300	IIIa	1935	167226 - 167700	IIIa	1935
137401 - 137625	Standard	1934	158301 - 158350	Standard	1935	167701 - 167750	III	1935
137626 - 138700	III Chrom	1934	158351 - 158400	II	1935	167751 - 168000	Standard	1935
138701 - 138950	St Chrom	1934	158401 - 158650	IIIa	1935	168001 - 168200	II	1935
138951 - 139900	III Chrome	1934	158651 - 159000	III	1935	168201 - 168250	III	1935
139901 - 139950	Standard	1934	159001 - 159200	II	1935	168251 - 168325	IIIa	1935
139951 - 140000	II	1934	159201 - 159350	Standard	1935	168326 - 168400	III	1935
140001 - 141500	III Chrom	1934	159351 - 159950	III	1935	168401 - 168500	IIIa	1935
141501 - 141850	Standard	1934	159951 - 159625	IIIa	1935	168501 - 168600	III	1935
141851 - 141900	II	1934	159626 - 159675	II	1935	168601 - 168725	IIIa	1935
141901 - 142250	III Chrom	1934	159676 - 160325	IIIa	1935	168726 - 168750	III	1935
142251 - 142350	II	1934	160326 - 160375	III	1935	168751 - 168850	IIIa	1935
142351 - 142500	III	1934	160376 - 160450	I	1935	168851 - 169000	Standard	1935
142501 - 142700	I Standard	1934	160451 - 160700	II	1935	169001 - 169200	III	1935
142701 - 143425	III	1934	160701 - 161150	I Standard	1935	169201 - 169350	Standard	1935
143426 - 143750	III Chrom	1934	161151 - 161450	II	1935	169351 - 169450	II	1935
143751 - 143900	Standard	1934	161451 - 161550	IIIa	1935	169451 - 169550	III	1935
143901 - 144200	III	1934	161551 - 161600	III	1935	169551 - 169650	II	1935

Leica No	Model	Year	Leica No	Model	Year	Leica No	Model	Year
169651 - 170150	IIIa	1935	180701 - 180800	Standard	1935	192501 _ 192800	III	1936
170151 - 170500	III	1935	180801 - 181000	II	1935	192801 - 192950	II	1936
170501 - 171300	IIIa	1935	181001 - 181450	IIIa	1935	192951 - 193200	IIIa	1936
171301 - 171550	II	1935	181451 - 181550	III	1935	193201 - 193450	Standard	1936
171551 - 171900	Standard	1935	181551 - 181600	IIIa	1935	193451 - 193500	IIIa	1936
171901 - 172250	IIIa	1935	181601 - 181700	III	1935	193501 - 193600	III	1936
172251 - 172300	III	1935	181701 - 182000	IIIa	1935	193601 - 194300	IIIa	1936
172301 - 172350	IIIa	1935	182001 - 182050	III	1935	194301 - 194650	III	1936
172351 - 172600	III	1935	182051 - 182300	IIIa	1935	194651 - 194850	II	1936
172601 - 172800	II	1935	182301 - 182350	III	1935	194851 - 194950	Standard	1936
172801 - 173000	Standard	1935	182351 - 182500	IIIa	1935	194951 - 196200	IIIa	1936
173001 - 173125	IIIa	1935	182501 - 182700	Standard	1935	196201 - 196300	III	1936
173126 - 173176	III	1935	182701 - 182850	II	1935	196301 - 196400	IIIa	1936
173177 - 173425	IIIa	1935	182851 - 183500	IIIa	1935	196401 - 196550	II	1936
173426 - 173475	III	1935	183501 - 183600	II	1935	196551 - 196750	Standard	1936
173476 - 173500	IIIa	1935	183601 - 183750	Standard	1935/36	196751 - 197400	IIIa	1936
173501 - 173650	Standard	1935	183751 - 184400	IIIa	1936	197401 - 197500	Standard	1936
173651 - 173675	IIIa	1935	184401 - 184450	III	1936	197501 - 197550	IIIa	1936
173676 - 173725	III	1935	184451 - 184700	IIIa	1936	197551 - 197800	III	1936
173726 - 173825	IIIa	1935	184701 - 184750	III	1936	197801 - 198200	IIIa	1936
173826 - 173900	III	1935	184751 - 184800	IIIa	1936	198201 - 198400	III	1936
173901 - 174025	IIIa	1935	184801 - 184950	III	1936	198401 - 198800	IIIa	1936
174026 - 174075	III	1935	184951 - 185200	IIIa	1936	198801 - 198900	III	1936
174076 - 174100	IIIa	1935	185201 - 185350	III	1936	198901 - 199200	IIIa	1936
174101 - 174125	III	1935	185351 - 185500	II	1936	199201 - 199300	III	1936
174126 - 174150	IIIa	1935	185501 - 185650	Standard	1936	199301 - 199500	IIIa	1936
174151 - 174400	III	1935	185651 - 185700	III	1936	199501 - 199600	III	1936
174401 - 174650	II	1935	185701 - 185800	Standard	1936	199601 - 199800	II	1936
174651 - 174675	IIIa	1935	185801 - 186100	IIIa	1936	199801 - 200100	IIIa	1936
174676 - 174750	III	1935	186101 - 186200	III	1936	200101 - 200200	III	1936
174751 - 174950	IIIa	1935	186201 - 186500	IIIa	1936	200201 - 200500	IIIa	1936
174951 - 175125	III	1935	186501 - 186550	III	1936	200501 - 200650	II	1936
175126 - 175200	IIIa	1935	186551 - 186800	IIIa	1936	200651 - 200750	Standard	1936
175201 - 175350	III	1935	186801 - 186900	III	1936	200751 - 201100	III	1936
175351 - 175450	IIIa	1935	186901 - 186950	IIIa	1936	201101 - 201200	III	1936
175451 - 175500	III	1935	186951 - 187000	III	1936	201201 - 201300	IIIa	1936
175501 - 175700	Standard	1935	187001 - 187100	IIIa	1936	201301 - 201400	III	1936
175701 - 175750	III	1935	187101 - 187200	III	1936	201401 - 201600	IIIa	1936
175751 - 175850	IIIa	1935	187201 - 187400	IIIa	1936	201601 - 201700	Standard	1936
175851 - 175900	III	1935	187401 - 187500	III	1936	201701 - 202300	IIIa	1936
175901 - 176100	IIIa	1935	187501 - 187650	II	1936	202301 - 202450	II	1936
176101 - 176150	III	1935	187651 - 187775	III	1936	202451 - 202600	IIIa	1936
176151 - 176250	IIIa	1935	187776 - 187785	IIIa	1936	202601 - 202700	III	1936
176251 - 176300	III	1935	187786 - 187850	III	1936	202701 - 202800	IIIa	1936
176301 - 176600	IIIa	1935	187851 - 188100	IIIa	1936	202801 - 202900	II	1936
176601 - 177000	III	1935	188101 - 188300	III	1936	202901 - 203100	III	1936
177001 - 177400	IIIa	1935	188301 - 188600	Standard	1936	203101 - 203300	III	1936
177401 - 177550	III	1935	188601 - 188750	II	1936	203301 - 203400	Standard	1936
177551 - 177600	IIIa	1935	188751 - 189300	IIIa	1936	203401 - 204100	IIIa	1936
177601 - 177700	III	1935	189301 - 189475	III	1936	204101 - 204200	III	1936
177701 - 177800	Standard	1935	189476 - 189800	IIIa	1936	204201 - 204300	IIIa	1936
177801 - 177900	IIIa	1935	189801 - 189900	III	1936	204301 - 204500	II	1936
177901 - 178000	III	1935	189901 - 190200	IIIa	1936	204501 - 204600	III	1936
178001 - 178100	IIIa	1935	190201 - 190500	III	1936	204601 - 204800	IIIa	1936
178101 - 178250	III	1935	190501 - 190700	IIIa	1936	204801 - 205000	III	1936
178251 - 178550	IIIa	1935	190701 - 190900	III	1936	205001 - 205100	IIIa	1936
178551 - 178600	III	1935	190901 - 191100	IIIa	1936	205101 - 205300	III	1936
178601 - 179200	IIIa	1935	191101 - 191200	III	1936	205301 - 205400	IIIa	1936
179201 - 179250	III	1935	191201 - 191300	II	1936	205401 - 205500	II	1936
179251 - 179500	IIIa	1935	191301 - 191350	IIIa	1936	205501 - 205700	Standard	1936
179501 - 179575	II	1935	191351 - 191500	III	1936	205701 - 207300	IIIa	1936
179576 - 179800	Standard	1935	191501 - 191650	II	1936	207301 - 207400	II	1936
179801 - 179900	II	1935	191651 - 191750	Standard	1936	207401 - 207600	Standard	1936
179901 - 180100	IIIa	1935	191751 - 191850	III	1936	207601 - 207800	III	1936
180101 - 180400	III	1935	191851 - 192100	IIIa	1936	207801 - 208000	III	1936
180401 - 180475	IIIa	1935	192101 - 192400	III	1936	208001 - 208300	III	1936
180476 - 180700	III	1935	192401 - 192500	IIIa	1936	208301 - 208600	IIIa	1936

Leica No	Model	Year	Leica No	Model	Year	Leica No	Model	Year
208601 - 208800	III	1936	227001 - 227050	III	1936/37	245101 - 245300	III	1937/38
208801 - 209000	IIIa	1936	227051 - 227600	IIIa	1936/37	245301 - 246200	IIIa	1937/38
209001 - 209600	III	1936	227601 - 227650	III	1936/37	246201 - 246300	III	1937/38
209601 - 209900	II	1936	227651 - 231500	IIIa	1936/37	246301 - 246400	IIIa	1937/38
209901 - 210100	IIIa	1936	231501 - 231600	III	1936/37	246401 - 246500	III	1937/38
210101 - 210200	III	1936	231601 - 231800	IIIa	1936/37	246501 - 246700	II	1937/38
210201 - 210400	IIIa	1936	231801 - 231900	III	1936/37	246701 - 247500	IIIa	1937/38
210401 - 210900	Standard	1936	231901 - 232200	IIIa	1936/37	247501 - 247600	II	1937/38
210901 - 211000	III	1936	232201 - 232500	III	1936/37	247601 - 248300	IIIa	1937/38
211001 - 211600	IIIa	1936	232501 - 232800	IIIa	1936/37	248301 - 248400	II	1937/38
211601 - 211700	III	1936	232801 - 232900	III	1936/37	248401 - 248600	Standard	1937/38
211701 - 211800	IIIa	1936	232901 - 233400	IIIa	1936/37	248601 - 248900	IIIa	1937
211801 - 211900	II	1936	233401 - 233500	III	1936/37	248901 - 249000	III	1937
211901 - 212400	IIIa	1936	233501 - 233700	Standard	1936/37	249001 - 249200	IIIa	1937
212401 - 212700	Standard	1936	233701 - 233800	III	1936/37	249201 - 249400	II	1937
212701 - 212800	IIIa	1936	233801 - 234000	IIIa	1936/37	249401 - 249500	III	1937
212801 - 213200	III	1936	234001 - 234100	II	1936/37	249501 - 249700	Standard	1937
213201 - 213300	IIIa	1936	234101 - 234200	III	1936/37	249701 - 249800	IIIa	1937
213301 - 213600	Standard	1936	234201 - 234500	IIIa	1936/37	249801 - 249900	III	1937
213601 - 213700	II	1936	234501 - 234600	III	1936/37	249901 - 250300	IIIa	1937
213701 - 214400	IIIa	1936	234601 - 235100	IIIa	1937	250301 - 250400	III	1937
214401 - 214800	Standard	1936	235101 - 235200	III	1937	250401 - 251200	IIIa	1937
214801 - 215300	IIIa	1936	235201 - 235800	IIIa	1937	251201 - 251300	II	1937
215301 - 216000	III	1936	235801 - 235875	III	1937	251301 - 251500	Standard	1937
216001 - 216300	IIIa	1936	235876 - 236200	IIIa	1937	251501 - 251600	IIIa	1937
216301 - 216500	II	1936	236201 - 236300	III	1937	251601 - 251800	II	1937
216501 - 216800	IIIa	1936	236301 - 236500	IIIa	1937	251801 - 252000	III	1937
216801 - 217000	III	1936	236501 - 236700	II	1937	252001 - 252200	II	1937
217001 - 217200	IIIa	1936	236701 - 236800	IIIa	1937	252201 - 252900	IIIa	1937
217201 - 217300	III	1936	236801 - 236900	III	1937	252901 - 253000	III	1937
217301 - 217500	Standard	1936	236901 - 237000	IIIa	1937	253001 - 253200	IIIa	1937
217501 - 217700	III	1937	237001 - 237200	III	1937	253201 - 253400	III	1937
217701 - 217900	II	1936/37	237201 - 237500	IIIa	1937	253401 - 253500	IIIa	1937
217901 - 218300	IIIa	1936/37	237501 - 237600	III	1937	253501 - 253600	III	1937
218301 - 218700	II	1936	237601 - 238000	IIIa	1937	253601 - 253800	Standard	1937
218701 - 218800	III	1936	238001 - 238100	III	1937	253801 - 254000	IIIa	1937
218801 - 219600	IIIa	1936	238101 - 238500	IIIa	1937	254001 - 254200	III	1937
219601 - 219800	II	1936	238501 - 238600	III	1937	254201 - 254600	IIIa	1937
219801 - 219900	IIIa	1936	238601 - 238800	IIIa	1937	254601 - 254800	II	1937
219101 - 220000	III	1936	238801 - 238825	III	1937	254801 - 254900	III	1937
220001 - 220300	IIIa	1936	238826 - 238900	IIIa	1937	254901 - 256400	IIIa	1937
220301 - 220500	II	1937	238901 - 239000	III	1937	256401 - 256600	Standard	1937
220501 - 220600	IIIa	1936	239001 - 239100	IIIa	1937	256601 - 256800	IIIa	1937
220601 - 220700	III	1936	239101 - 239300	III	1937	256801 - 256900	III	1937
220701 - 220900	IIIa	1936	239301 - 239400	IIIa	1937	256901 - 257400	IIIa	1937
220901 - 22100	III	1936	239401 - 239600	III	1937	257401 - 257525	III	1937
221001 - 221300	IIIa	1936	239601 - 239700	IIIa	1937	257526 - 257600	IIIa	1937
221301 - 221400	III	1936	239701 - 239800	III	1937	257601 - 257800	Standard	1937
221401 - 222150	IIIa	1936	239801 - 240000	Standard	1937	257801 - 258200	III	1937
222151 - 222200	III	1936	240001 - 241000	IIIb	1937/38	258201 - 259500	IIIa	1937
222201 - 222300	IIIa	1936	241001 - 241100	IIIa	1937/38	259501 - 259800	II	1937
222301 - 222700	Standard	1937	241101 - 241300	III	1937/38	259801 - 259900	Standard	1937
222701 - 223000	II	1937	241301 - 241500	IIIa	1937/38	259901 - 260000	IIIa	1937
223001 - 223300	III	1937	241501 - 241700	II	1937/38	260001 - 260100	Reporter	1937
223301 - 223600	IIIa	1936	241701 - 241900	Standard	1937/38	260101 - 260200	IIIa	1937
223601 - 223700	III	1936	241901 - 242000	II	1937/38	260201 - 260600	III	1937
223701 - 224600	IIIa	1936/37	242001 - 243000	IIIb	1937/38	260601 - 260800	IIIa	1937
224601 - 224800	Standard	1936/37	243001 - 243400	IIIa	1937/38	260801 - 260900	III	1937
224801 - 224900	IIIa	1936/37	243401 - 243500	III	1937/38	260901 - 261200	IIIa	1937
224901 - 225000	III	1936/37	243501 - 243800	II	1937/38	261201 - 261300	III	1937
225001 - 225200	IIIa	1936/37	243801 - 244100	IIIa	1937/38	261301 - 261500	IIIa	1937
225201 - 225300	III	1936/37	244101 - 244200	III	1937/38	261501 - 261600	III	1937
225301 - 225400	IIIa	1936/37	244201 - 244400	Standard	1937/38	261601 - 261800	IIIa	1937
225401 - 225600	III	1936/37	244401 - 244600	III	1937/38	261801 - 262000	Standard	1937
225601 - 226300	IIIa	1936/37	244601 - 244800	IIIa	1937/38	262001 - 262800	IIIa	1937
226301 - 226400	III	1936/37	244801 - 245000	Standard	1937/38	262801 - 263000	III	1937
226401 - 227000	IIIa	1936/37	245001 - 245100	IIIa	1937/38	263001 - 263600	IIIa	1937

Leica No	Model	Year	Leica No	Model	Year	Leica No	Model	Year
263601 - 263900	II	1937	287601 - 288000	IIIa	1938	303701 - 303800	II	1938
263901 - 264000	III	1937	288001 - 290200	IIIb	1938/39	303801 - 303900	Standard	1938
264001 - 264800	IIIa	1937	290201 - 290500	IIIa	1938	303901 - 304400	IIIa	1938
264801 - 265000	Standard	1937	290501 - 290800	III	1938	304401 - 304500	III	1938
265001 - 266000	IIIb	1937	290801 - 291000	IIIa	1938	304501 - 304700	IIIa	1938
266001 - 266100	IIIa	1937	291001 - 291200	Standard	1938	304701 - 304800	III	1938
266101 - 266200	III	1937	219201 - 291500	IIIa	1938	304801 - 304900	IIIa	1938
266201 - 266400	IIIa	1937	291501 - 291600	III	1938	304901 - 305000	III	1938
266401 - 266500	III	1937	291601 - 291800	IIIa	1938	305001 - 305600	IIIa	1938
266501 - 266800	II	1937	291801 - 292000	Standard	1938	305601 - 305700	III	1938
266801 - 266900	IIIa	1937	292001 - 292200	II	1938	305701 - 305800	Standard	1938
266901 - 267000	III	1937	291201 - 292400	Standard	1938	305801 - 306200	IIIa	1938
267001 - 267700	IIIa	1937	292401 - 292600	IIIa	1938	306201 - 306300	III	1938
267701 - 267800	III	1937	292601 - 292700	III	1938	306301 - 306500	II	1938
267801 - 267900	IIIa	1937	292701 - 293000	IIIa	1938	306501 - 306600	III	1938
267901 - 268000	Standard	1937	293001 - 293100	III	1938	306601 - 306800	IIIa	1938
268001 - 268100	IIIa	1937/38	293101 - 293200	IIIa	1938	306801 - 307000	III	1938
268101 - 268200	III	1938	293201 - 293400	III	1938	307001 - 307500	IIIa	1938
268201 - 268400	IIIa	1937	293401 - 293500	II	1938	307501 - 308000	Standard	1938
268401 - 268500	III	1938	293501 - 293900	IIIa	1938	308001 - 308100	IIIa	1938
268501 - 268700	IIIa	1938	293901 - 294000	Standard	1938	308101 - 308200	III	1938
268701 - 268800	III	1938	294001 - 294600	IIIb	1938	308201 - 308300	II	1938
268801 - 269300	IIIa	1938	294601 - 294800	II	1938	308301 - 308500	Standard	1938
269301 - 269400	III	1938	294801 - 294900	III	1938	308501 - 308600	III	1938
269401 - 269600	IIIa	1938	294901 - 295100	IIIa	1938	308601 - 308700	IIIa	1938
269601 - 269700	III	1938	295101 - 295200	III	1938	308701 - 308800	III	1938
269701 - 270100	IIIa	1938	295201 - 205300	IIIa	1938	308801 - 309000	IIIa	1938
270101 - 270200	III	1938	295301 - 295400	Standard	1938	309001 - 309200	Standard	1938
270201 - 270300	IIIa	1938	295401 - 295500	III	1938	309201 - 309300	IIIa	1938
270301 - 270400	III	1938	295501 - 296000	IIIa	1938	309301 - 309400	III	1938
270401 - 271000	IIIa	1938	296001 - 296200	II	1938	309401 - 309500	IIIa	1938
271001 - 271100	II	1938	296201 - 296500	IIIa	1938	309501 - 309700	II	1938
271101 - 271600	Standard	1938	296501 - 296600	III	1938	309701 - 310000	IIIa	1938/39
271601 - 271700	II	1938	296691 - 296900	Standard	1938	310001 - 310200	III	1938/39
271701 - 271800	III	1938	296901 - 297100	II	1938	310201 - 310400	IIIa	1938/39
271801 - 272300	IIIa	1938	297101 - 297200	IIIa	1938	310401 - 310500	III	1938/39
272301 - 272400	II	1938	297201 - 297400	III	1938	310501 - 310600	IIIa	1939
272401 - 274800	IIIa	1938	297401 - 297900	IIIa	1938	310601 - 311000	III	1938/39
274801 - 275200	III	1938	297901 - 298000	III	1938	311001 - 311200	II	1938
275201 - 275350	IIIa	1938	298001 - 299000	IIIa	1938	311201 - 311400	IIIa	1939
275351 - 275650	II	1938	299001 - 299200	III	1938	311401 - 311700	III	1939
275651 - 275675	IIIa	1938	299201 - 299500	IIIa	1938	311701 - 311800	IIIa	1939
275676 - 275700	III	1938	299501 - 299600	III	1938	311801 - 311900	III	1939
275701 - 275800	IIIa	1938	299601 - 299800	IIIa	1938	311901 - 312000	IIIa	1939
275801 - 276400	III	1938	299801 - 299900	III	1938	312001 - 312200	Standard	1939
276401 - 277000	IIIa	1938	299901 - 300000	Standard	1938	312201 - 312400	IIIa	1939
277001 - 277100	III	1938	300001 - 300100	Reporter	1938	312401 - 312500	III	1939
277101 - 277500	IIIa	1938	300101 - 300200	Standard	1938	312501 - 312800	Standard	1939
277505 - 277900	Standard	1938	300201 - 300300	II	1938	312801 - 313000	IIIa	1939
277901 - 278100	II	1938	300301 - 300400	Standard	1938	313001 - 313100	III	1939
278101 - 278200	III	1938	300401 - 300700	IIIa	1938	313101 - 313200	IIIa	1939
278201 - 278500	IIIa	1938	300701 - 300800	III	1938	313201 - 313300	III	1939
278501 - 278525	III	1938	300801 - 301000	III	1938	313301 - 313400	IIIa	1939
278526 - 278550	IIIa	1938	301001 - 301100	III	1938	313401 - 313500	Standard	1939
278551 - 278600	III	1938	301101 - 301400	IIIa	1938	313501 - 313600	III	1939
278601 - 278800	Standard	1938	301401 - 301500	III	1938	313601 - 314000	III	1939
278801 - 279000	IIIa	1938	301501 - 301600	III	1938	314001 - 314100	III	1939
279001 - 279200	III	1938	301601 - 201700	Standard	1938	314101 - 314300	II	1939
279201 - 279400	II	1938	301701 - 301800	III	1938	314301 - 314500	Standard	1939
279401 - 280000	IIIa	1938	301801 - 310900	IIIa	1938	314501 - 314600	II	1939
280001 - 286500	IIIb	1938	310901 - 302000	III	1938	314601 - 314700	III	1939
286501 - 256600	Standard	1938	302001 - 302500	IIIa	1938	314701 - 314800	IIIa	1939
286801 - 287000	III	1938	302501 - 302800	II	1938	314801 - 314900	III	1939
287001 - 287200	IIIa	1938	302801 - 302900	III	1938	314901 - 315000	IIIa	1939
287201 - 287300	III	1938	302901 - 303200	IIIa	1938	315001 - 315100	II	1939
287307 - 287400	IIIa	1938	303201 - 303300	III	1938	315101 - 315400	IIIa	1939
287401 - 287600	II	1938	303301 - 303700	IIIa	1938	315401 - 315500	II	1939

Leica No	Model	Year	Leica No	Model	Year	Leica No	Model	Year
315501 - 315700	IIIa	1939	334401 - 334600	III	1939	369451 - 390000	IIIc	1941/42
315701 - 315800	III	1939	334601 - 335000	IIIa	1939	390001 - 397650	IIIc	1943/46
315801 - 316100	IIIa	1939	335001 - 337000	IIIb	1939/40	397651 - 399999		
316101 - 316400	III	1939	337001 - 337200	II	1939	400000 - 440000	IIIc	1946/47
316401 - 316700	IIIa	1939	337201 - 337400	IIIa	1939	440001 - 449999	IIc	1948/51
316701 - 316900	Standard	1939	337401 - 337500	III	1939	450000		IIIc	1949
316901 - 317000	II	1939	337501 - 337900	IIIa	1939	450001 - 451000	IIc	1951
317001 - 318000	IIIb	1939	337901 - 338100	II	1939	451001 - 455000	IIf	1951
318001 - 318200	IIIa	1939	338101 - 338200	IIIa	1939	455001 - 460000	Ic	1949/50
318201 - 318300	II	1939	338201 - 338600	III	1939	460001 - 465000	IIIc	1948/49
318301 - 318500	Standard	1939	338601 - 338900	IIIa	1939	465001 - 480000	IIIc	1949
318501 - 318800	II	1939	338901 - 339000	III	1939	480001 - 495000	IIIc	1949/50
318801 - 318900	IIIa	1939	339001 - 340000	IIIb	1939/40	495001 - 520000	IIIc	1950
318901 - 319901	III	1939	340001 - 340200	IIIa	1939	520001 - 524000	Ic	1950/51
319001 - 320000	IIIb	1939	340201 - 340400	III	1939	524001 - 525000	IIIc	1950/51
320001 - 320200	II	1939	340401 - 340600	IIIa	1939	525001 - 540000	IIIf	1950/51
320201 - 320400	III	1939	340601 - 340700	III	1939	540001 - 560000	IIIf	1951
320401 - 320600	IIIa	1939	340701 - 341000	IIIa	1939	560001 - 562800	Ic	1951
320601 - 320700	II	1939	341001 - 341300	II	1939/40	562801 - 565000	If	1951
320701 - 321000	Standard	1939	341301 - 341500	Standard	1939	565001 - 570000	IIIf	1951
321001 - 322000	IIIb	1939	341501 - 341700	III	1939	570001 - 575000	IIf	1951/52
322001 - 322200	II	1939	341701 - 341900	IIIa	1939	575001 - 580000	IIf°	1952/53
322201 - 322700	Standard	1939	341901 - 342000	III	1939	580001 - 610000	IIIf	1951/52
322701 - 322800	IIIa	1939	342001 - 342200	Standard	1939	610001 - 611000	IIIf/ELC	1952
322801 - 323000	III	1939	342201 - 342300	III	1939	611001 - 615000	IIf°	1952/53
323001 - 324000	IIIb	1939	342301 - 342900	IIIa	1939	Leica with light weight shutter		
324001 - 324100	Reporter	1939	342901 - 343100	III	1939	615001 - 650000	IIIf	1952/53
324101 - 324700	IIIa	1939	343101 - 344000	IIIa	1939	650001 - 655000	IIf	1953
324701 - 324800	III	1939	344001 - 348500	IIIb	1939/40	655001 - 673000	IIIf	1953
324801 - 325000	II	1939	348501 - 348600	Standard	1939/40	673001 - 674999	If	1953/54
325001 - 325200	IIIa	1939	348601 - 349000	IIIb	1940	675000		IIIf	1953
325201 - 325275	III	1939	349001 - 349050	Reporter	1940	675001 - 680000	IIf	1953/54
325276 - 325300	IIIa	1939	349051 - 349300	Standard	1940	680001 - 682000	IIf	1954
325301 - 325400	I	1939	349301 - 351100	IIIb	1940	682001 - 684000	If	1955
325401 - 325600	IIIa	1939	351101 - 351150	II	1940	684001 - 685000	IIIf/ELC	1953
325601 - 325800	III	1939	351151 - 352000	IIIb	1940	685001 - 699999	IIIf Vorl.	1954
325801 - 325900	IIIa	1939	352001 - 352100	II	1940	700000		M3	1954
325901 - 326000	II	1939	352101 - 352150	Standard	1940	700001 - 710000	M3	1954
326001 - 327000	IIIb	1939	352151 - 352300	II	1940	710001 - 711000	IIIf Vorl. ELC	1954
327001 - 327200	II	1939	352301 - 352500	Reporter	1940/41/42	711001 - 713000	IIf	1954
327201 - 327400	III	1939	352501 - 352900	II	1940/41/42	713001 - 729000	IIIf Vorl.	1954
327401 - 327500	IIIa	1939	352901 - 353600	Standard	1940/41/42	729001 - 730000	IIIf Vorl. ELC	1954
327501 - 327600	III	1939	353601 - 353800	Reporter	1942/43	730001 - 746450	M3	1955
327601 - 327800	IIIa	1939	353801 - 354000	Standard	1942/47	746451 - 746500	M3 ELC	1955
327801 - 328000	Standard	1939	354001 - 354050	IIIa	1941/47	746501 - 750000	M3	1955
328001 - 329000	IIIb	1939	354051 - 354075	IIIa	1941/46	750001 - 759700	M3	1955
329001 - 329400	Standard	1939	354076 - 354100	II	1947	759701 - 760000	M3 ELC	1955
329401 - 329600	II	1939	354101 - 354200	IIIa	1947	760001 - 762000	If	1955
329601 - 329800	IIIa	1939	354201 - 354400	II	1942/44	762001 - 765000	IIf	1955
329801 - 329900	III	1939	354401 - 355000	IIIb	1946	765001 - 773000	IIIf Vorl.	1955
329901 - 330000	IIIa	1939	355001 - 355650	Standard	1947/48	773001 - 774000	IIIf ELC	1955
330001 - 330200	III	1939	355651 - 356500			774001 - 775000	IIIf	1955
330201 - 330300	II	1939	356501 - 356550	IIIa	1947/48	775001 - 780000	M3	1955
330301 - 330500	Standard	1939	356651 - 356700	II	1947/48	780001 - 780090	M3 ELC	1955
330501 - 330700	III	1939	356701 - 357200	IIIa	1948/50	780091 - 780100	If	1957
330701 - 330800	IIIa	1939	357201 - 358500			780101 - 787000	M3	1955
330801 - 331000	Standard	1939	358501 - 358650	II	1948	787001 - 789000	IIf	1955
331001 - 332000	IIIb	1939	358651 - 360000			789001 - 790000	If	1955
332001 - 332500	IIIa	1939	360001 - 360100	IIIa	1940/42	790001 - 799000	IIIf	1955
332501 - 332600	III	1939	360101 - 367000	IIIc	1940	799001 - 799999	IIf	1956
332601 - 333000	IIIa	1939	367001 - 367325	IIIc	1941/44	800000 - 805000	M3	1955
333001 - 333100	III	1939	367326 - 367500	IIIc	1945	805001 - 805100	M3 ELC	1955
333101 - 333300	IIIa	1939	367501 - 368800	IIIc	1940/41	805101 - 807500	M3	1955
333301 - 333600	Standard	1939	368801 - 368950	IIIc	1941	807501 - 808500	If	1956
333601 - 334000	IIIb	1939	368951 - 369000	IIIc	1941	808501 - 810000	IIf	1956
334001 - 334200	III	1939	369001 - 369050	IIIc	1941	810001 - 815000	IIIf	1956
334201 - 334400	IIIa	1939	369051 - 369450	IIIc	1941	815001 - 816000	If	1956

Identifying Leica Cameras

Leica No	Model	Year	Leica No	Model	Year	Leica No	Model	Year
816001 - 816900	M3	1956	929001 - 931000	M2	1958	988026 - 988350	IIIg	1960
816901 - 817000	M3 ELC	1956	931001 - 933000	M2	1958	988351 - 988650	M2	1960
817001 - 820500	M3	1956	933001 - 934000	IIIg	1958	988651 - 989250	M2 Vorl.	1960
820501 - 821500	IIf	1956	934001 - 934200	IIIg ELC	1958	989251 - 989650	M2 Vorl.	1960
821501 - 822000	IIf	1956	934201 - 935000	IIIg	1958	989651 - 989800	M2	1960
822001 - 822900	If	1956	935001 - 935512	MP2	1958	989801 - 990500	M2 Vorl.	1960
822901 - 823000	IIIf kältef.	1956	935513 - 937500	M2	1958	990501 - 990750	M2 schw. l.	1960
823001 - 823500	IIIf	1956	937501 - 937620	M2	1958	990751 - 993500	M3	1960
823501 - 823867	IIIf ELC	1956	937621 - 937650	M2 ELC	1958	993501 - 993750	M3 schw. l.	1960
823868 - 825000	IIIf	1956	937651 - 940000	M2	1958	993751 - 995000	M2	1960
825001 - 826000	IIIg	1956	940001 - 942900	M2	1958	995001 - 995100	M2 ELC	1960
826001 - 829750	IIIg	1956	942901 - 943000	M2 ELC	1958	995101 - 995400	M2 Vorl.	1960
829751 - 829850	IIIf ELC	1956	943001 - 944000	IIIg	1958	995401 - 996000	M2	1960
829851 - 830000	M3 ELC	1956	944001 - 946000	M2	1958	996001 - 998000	M3	1960
830001 - 837500	M3	1956	946001 - 946300	M2	1958	998001 - 998300	M3 ELC	1960
837501 - 837620	M3 ELC	1956	946301 - 946400	M2 ELC	1958	998301 -1000000	M3	1960
837621 - 637720	IIIf ELC	1956	946401 - 946900	M2	1958	100001 -1003700	M3	1960
837721 - 839620	M3	1956	946901 - 947000	M2 ELC	1958	1003701 -1004000	M3 ELC	1960
839621 - 839700	M3 ELC	1956	947001 - 948000	M2	1958	1004001 -1005100	M2 VW	1960
839701 - 840500	M3	1956	948001 - 948500	IIIg	1958	1005101 -1005350	M2 VW	1960
840501 - 840820	M3 ELC	1956	948501 - 948600	M2 ELC	1958	1005351 -1005450	M2 ELC	1960
840821 - 844780	M3	1956	948601 - 949100	M2 schw. l.	1958	1005451 -1005750	M2	1960
844781 - 845000	M3 ELC	1956	949101 - 949400	M2 Vorl.	1958	1005771 -1007000	M2	1960
845001 - 845380	IIIg ELC	1956	949401 - 950000	M2	1959	1007001 -1011000	M3	1960
845381 - 850900	IIIg	1956	950001 - 950300	M1	1959	1011001 -1014000	M2	1960
850901 - 851000	If	1956	950301 - 951900	M3	1959	1014001 -1014300	M3 ELC	1960
851001 - 854000	M3	1956	951901 - 952000	M3 ELC	1959	1014301 -1017000	M3	1960
854001 - 858000	M3	1957	952001 - 952015	MP2	1959	1017001 -1017500	M1	1961
858001 - 861600	IIIg	1957	952016 - 952500	M1	1959	1017501 -1017900	M2	1961
861601 - 862000	IIIg ELC	1957	952501 - 954800	M3	1959	1017901 -1018000	M2 ELC	1961
MP. 1 - 11	MP	1956	954801 - 954900	M3 ELC	1959	1018001 -1020100	M2	1961
862001 - 866620	M3	1957	954901 - 955000	M3 ELC	1959	1020101 -1020200	M2 ELC	1961
866621 - 867000	M3 ELC	1957	955001 - 956500	IIIg	1959	1020201 -1022000	M2	1961
867001 - 871200	IIIg	1957	956501 - 957000	M1	1959	1022001 -1022700	M3	1961
871201 - 872000	IIIg ELC	1957	957001 - 959400	M3	1959	1022701 -1023000	M3 ELC	1961
872001 - 877000	M3	1957	959401 - 959500	M3 schw. l.	1959	1023001 -1027800	M3	1961
877001 - 882000	IIIg	1957	959501 - 960200	M2 Vorl.	1959	1027801 -1028000	M3 ELC	1961
882001 - 886700	M3	1957	960201 - 960500	M2	1960	1028001 -1028600	M1	1961
MP. 13 - 150	MP schw. l.	1957	960501 - 961500	M2	1959	1028601 -1031800	M2	1961
MP-151 - 450	MP chrom.	1957	961501 - 961700	M3 ELC	1959	1031801 -1032000	M2 schw. l.	1961
886701 - 887000	M3 ELC	1957	961701 - 966500	M3	1959	1032001 -1035400	M3	1961
887001 - 888000	Ig	1957	966501 - 967500	M1	1959	1035401 -1035925	M1	1961
888001 - 893000	IIIg	1957	967501 - 968350	M2	1959	1035926 -1036000	M1 oliv. l.	1961
893001 - 894000	M3	1957	968351 - 968500	M3 ELC	1959	1036001 -1026050	M2 ELC	1961
894001 - 894570	M3 ELC	1957	968501 - 970000	IIIg	1959	1036051 -1036350	M3 ELC	1961
894571 - 898000	M3	1957	970001 - 971500	M2	1959	1036351 -1037950	M2	1961
898001 - 903000	M3	1957	971501 - 972000	IIIg	1959	1037951 -1038000	M2 ELC	1962
903001 - 903300	M3 ELC	1957	972001 - 974700	M3	1959	1038001 -1038800	M3	1961
903301 - 907000	IIIg	1957	974701 - 975000	M3 ELC	1959	1038801 -1039000	M3 schw. l.	1961
907001 - 910000	Ig	1957	975001 - 975800	M2	1959	1039001 -1040000	M3	1961
910001 - 910500	M3	1957	975801 - 976100	M2 Vorl.	1960	1040001 -1040066	M1	1962
910501 - 910600	M3 oliv. l.	1957	976101 - 976500	M2	1959	1040067 -1040068	M3	1962
910601 - 915000	M3	1957	976501 - 979500	M3	1959	1040069 -1040070	M1	1961
915001 - 915200	M3	1957	979501 - 980450	M1	1959	1040071 -	M3	1961
915201 - 916000	M3	1957	980451 - 980500	M1 oliv. l.	1960	1040072 -1040094	M1	1961
916001 - 919250	M3	1958	980501 - 982000	IIIg	1959	1040095 -1040096	M3	1962
919251 - 920500	M3	1958	982001 - 982150	M2 Vorl.	1960	1040097 -1040600	M1	1961
920501 - 920520	M3	1958	982151 - 982900	M2	1959	1040601 -1043000	M3	1961
920521 - 924400	M3	1958	982901 - 983500	M2 Vorl.	1959	1043001 -1043800	M2	1962
924401 - 924500	M3 ELC	1958	983501 - 984000	M2	1959	1043801 -1044000	M2 schw. l.	1962
924501 - 924568	Ig	1958	984001 - 984200	M3 ELC	1959	1044001 -1046000	M2 schw. l.	1962
924569 - 924588	Ig	1958	984201 - 987000	M3	1959	1046001 -1046500	M1	1962
924589 - 926000	Ig	1958	987001 - 987200	M3 ELC	1959	1046501 -1048000	M3	1962
926001 - 926200	M2	1957	987201 - 987300	M2 ELC	1960	1048001 -1050000	M3 ELC	1962
926201 - 926700	Ig	1958	987301 - 987600	Ig	1960	1050001 -1050500	M1	1962
926701 - 928922	M3	1959	987601 - 987900	IIIg	1960	1050501 -1053100	M2	1962
928923 - 929000	Postk.	1958	987901 - 988025	IIIg schw. l.	1960			

Leica No	Model	Year	Leica No	Model	Year	Leica No	Model	Year
1053101 - 1053250	M2 lack.	1962	1139001 - 1140900	M3	1966	1287251 - 1288000	M5 schwarz	1971
1053251 - 1054900	M2	1962	1140901 - 1141000	M3 ELC	1966	1288001 - 1289000	M5 hell	1971
1054901 - 1055000	M2 ELC	1962	1141001 - 1141896	MD	1966	1289001 - 1291400	M5 schwarz	1971/72
1055001 - 1059849	M3	1962	1141897 - 1141968	Postk.	1966	1291401 - 1293000	M5 hell	1971/72
1059850 - 1059999	M3 lack.	1962	1141969 - 1142000	Postk. 24x27	1966	1293001 - 1293672	MDa	1971/72
1060000 -	M3	1962	1142001 - 1145000	M2	1966	1293673 - 1293700	MDa Blitzsp.	1972
1060001 - 1060500	M1	1962	1145001 - 1155000	Leicaflex	1966	1293771 - 1293775	M4-KE 7	1972
1060501 - 1061700	M2	1962	1155001 - 1157590	M3	1966	1293776 - 1293877	MDa Blitzsp.	1972
1061701 - 1061800	M2 ELC	1962	1157591 - 1157600	M3 lack.	1966	1293878 - 1294000	Postk. 24x27	1972
1061801 - 1063000	M2	1962	1157601 - 1158995	M3	1966	1294001 - 1294500	M5 hell	1972
1063001 - 1065000	M3	1962	1158996 - 1159000	M3 oliv. l.	1966	1294501 - 1295000	M4-KE 7	1972
1065001 - 1065200	M3 ELC	1962	1159001 - 1160200	MDa	1966	1295001 - 1296500	Leicaflex SL	1972
1065201 - 1067500	M3	1962	1160201 - 1160820	MD	1966	1296501 - 1300000	M5 schwarz	1972
1067501 - 1067870	M1	1963	1160821 - 1161420	MDa	1966	1300001 - 1335000	CL	1973/74
1067871 - 1068000	Postk.	1963	1161421 - 1163770	M2	1966	1335001 - 1336990	Leicaflex SL	1972
1068001 - 1070000	M2	1963	1163771 - 1164046	M2 Motor	1966	1336991 - 1337110	LeicaflexSLmot	1972
1070001 - 1074000	M3	1963	1164047 - 1164845	M2	1966	1337111 - 1338220	LeicaflexSL	1972
1074001 - 1074500	M1	1963	1164846 - 1164865	M3	1966	1338221 - 1338300	LeicaflexSLmot	1972
1074501 - 1077000	M2	1963	1164866 - 1164940	Postk. 24x36	1967	1338301 - 1339870	LeicaflexSL	1972
1077001 - 1080000	M3	1963	1164941 - 1165000	M2	1967	1339871 - 1339900	LeicaflexSLmot	1972
1080001 - 1085000	Leicaflex	1964/65	1165001 - 1173000	Leicaflex	1967	1339901 - 1341450	LeicaflexSL	1972
1085001 - 1085450	M1	1963	1173001 - 1173250	Leicaflex SL	1968	1341451 - 1341470	LeicaflexSLmot	1972
1085451 - 1085500	M1	1963	1173251 - 1174700	Leicaflex	1968	1341471 - 1342020	LeicaflexSL	1973
1085501 - 1088000	M2	1963	1174701 - 1175000	Leicaflex SL	1968	1342021 - 1342050	LeicaflexSLmot	1973
1088001 - 1091000	M3	1963	1175001 - 1178000	M4	1967	1342051 - 1342900	LeicaflexSL	1973
1091001 - 1091300	M1	1964	1178001 - 1178100	M4 ELC	1967	1342901 - 1343000	LeicaflexSLmot	1973
1091301 - 1093500	M2	1964	1178101 - 1185000	M4	1967	1343001 - 1344400	LeicaflexSL	
1093501 - 1093750	M2 lack.	1964	1185001 - 1185150	M4 Motor	1968	1344401 - 1344500	LeicaflexSLmot	1973
1093751 - 1093800	M2 ELC	1964	1185151 - 1185290	M4 lack.	1968	1344501 - 1345000	LeicaflexSL	1973
1093801 - 1097700	M3	1964	1185291 - 1185300	Postk. 24x27	1968	1345001 - 1347000	M5 hell	1972
1097701 - 1097850	M3 lack.	1964	1185301 - 1195000	M4	1968/69	1347001 - 1354000	M5 schwarz	1972
1097851 - 1098000	M3 ELC	1964	1195001 - 1205000	Leicaflex SL	1968	1354001 - 1355000	M5 hell	1972
1098001 - 1098100	M1	1964	1205001 - 1206736	MDa	1968/69	1355001 - 1356500	M5 hell	1973
1098101 - 1098183	M1 oliv. l.	1964	1206737 - 1206891	M4 Motor	1969	1356501 - 1360000	M5 schwarz	1973
1098184 - 1098300	M1	1964	1206892 - 1206941	Postk. 24x36	1969	1360001 - 1361500	MDa	1973/74
1098301 - 1199800	M2	1964	1206942 - 1206961	Postk. 24x27	1969	1361501 - 1363000	M5 hell	1973/74
1099801 - 1099900	M2 ELC	1964	1207000	M2 lack.	1968	1363001 - 1365000	M5 schwarz	1973
1099901 - 1100000	M2	1964	1207001 - 1207480	M4 lack.	1968/69	1365001 - 1365380	LeicaflexSL	1973
1100001 - 1102000	M3	1964	1207481 - 1215000	M4	1968/69	1365381 - 1365470	Leicaflex SLmot	1973
1102001 - 1102500	M1	1964	1215001 - 1225000	Leicaflex SL	1969	1365471 - 1366990	LeicaflexSL	1973
1102501 - 1102800	MD	1964	1225001 - 1225800	M4 lack.	1969	1366991 - 1367090	LeicaflexSLmot	1973
1102801 - 1102900	M1	1964	1225801 - 1235000	M4	1969	1367091 - 1367950	LeicaflexSL	1973
1102901 - 1103000	M3	1965	1235001 - 1245000	Leicaflex SL	1969/70	1367951 - 1368020	LeicaflexSLmot	1973
1103001 - 1104900	M2	1965	1245001 - 1246200	MDa	1969	1368021 - 1368850	LeicaflexSL	1973
1104901 - 1105000	M2 ELC	1965	1246201 - 1248100	M4 lack.	1969/70	1368851 - 1368900	LeicaflexSLmot	1973
1105001 - 1106900	M3	1965	1248101 - 1248200	M4 Motor	1969	1368901 - 1369800	LeicaflexSL	1973
1106901 - 1107000	M3 ELC	1965	1248201 - 1250200	M2R	1969/70	1369801 - 1369875	Leicaflex SL2	1974
1107001 - 1109000	M2	1965	1250201 - 1254650	M4	1970		(Nullserie)	
1109001 - 1110500	M3	1965	1254651 - 1255000	MDa	1970	1369876 - 1370700	LeicaflexSL	1973
1110501 - 1112000	M3	1965	1255001 - 1265000	Leicaflex SL	1970	1370701 - 1372440	LeicaflexSL	1974
1112001 - 1114975	M2	1965	1265001 - 1266000	MDa	1970	1372441 - 1372630	LeicaflexSLmot	1974
1114976 - 1115000	Postk.	1965	1266001 - 1266100	M4 lack.	1970/71	1372631 - 1374000	LeicaflexSL	1974
1115001 - 1128000	Leicaflex	1965	1266101 - 1266131	M4 olivegr.	1970	1374001 - 1375000	LeicaflexSL	1974
1128001 - 1128400	MD	1965	1266132 - 1267100	M4 lack.	1970	1375001 - 1378000	M5	
1128401 - 113000	M3	1965	1267101 - 1267500	M4 Motor	1970		schwarz	1973/74
1130001 - 1130300	M2 lack.	1965	1267501 - 1273921	M4	1970/71	1378001 - 1379000	M5 hell	1973/74
1130301 - 1132900	M2	1965	1273922 - 1273925	Postk. 24x27	1971	1379001 - 1380000	MDa	1974
1132901 - 1133000	M2 ELC	1965	1273926 - 1274000	Postk. 24x36	1971	1380001 - 1381650	M4 schwarz	1974
1133001 - 1134000	M3	1965	1274001 - 1274100	M4 Motor	1971	1381651 - 1382600	M4 schwarz	1974
1134001 - 1134150	M3 lack.	1965	1274101 - 1275000	MDa	1971		(Leitz Canada-Gravur)	
1134151 - 1135000	M3	1965	1275001 - 1285000	Leicaflex SL	1971	1382601 - 1383000	M5 hell	1974/75
1135001 - 1135100	M3 ELC	1965	1285001 - 1286200	MDa	1971	1383001 - 1384000	M5	
1135101 - 1136000	M3	1965	1286201 - 1286700	M4 lack.	1971		schwarz	1974/75
1136001 - 1136500	MD	1965	1286701 - 1286760	Postk. 24x27	1972	1384001 - 1384600	M4 schwarz	1974
1136501 - 1137000	MD	1966	1286761 - 1287000	unbelegt.		1384601 - 1385000	MDa	1974/75
1137001 - 1138900	M2	1966	1287001 - 1287050	M5 Nullserie	1971	1385001 - 1386000	Leicaflex	
1138901 - 1139000	M2 ELC	1966	1287051 - 1287250	M5 hell	1971		SL2	1974/75

Leica No	Model	Year	Leica No	Model	Year	Leica No	Model	Year
1386001-1386100	LeicaflexSL2	1975	1492251-1502000	R3 mot LP	1978	1782001-1783000	R5,R6,	
1386101-1386600	Leicaflex		1502001-1508000	M4-2	1978/79		R-E schw.	1990
	SL2	1974/75	1508001-1523750	R3 mot LP	1979	1783001-1786000	M6 schw.	1990
1386601-1386700	Leicaflex		1523751-1523850	R3 schw. LP	1979	1786001-1788000	R5, R-E schw.	1990
	SL2mot	1975	1523851-1524850	R3 gold LP	1979	1788001-1790000	R5, R-E schw.	1991
1387451-1387450	Leicaflex		1524851-1525350	R3 hell LP	1979	1790001-1790500	M6 hell	1991
	SL2	1974/75	1525351-1527200	M4-2	1979	1790501-1791000	M6 hell	1991
1387451-1387500	Leicaflex		1527201-1527700	M4-2 gold	1979/80	1791001-1793000	R5,	
	SL2mot	1975	1527701-1528150	M4-2	1980		R-E schw.	1991
1387501-1391760	Leicaflex		1528151-1528650	M4-2 gold	1980	1793001-1794500	M6 hell	1991
	SL2	1974/75	1528651-1533350	M4-2	1980	1794501-1797000	M6 schw.	1991
1391761-1392000	Leicaflex		1533351-1543350	R4 schw.	1980/81	1797001-1800000	R5,	
	SL2mot	1975	1543351-1545350	M4-P	1980/81		R-E schw.	1991
1392001-1393420	LeicaflexSL2	1975	1545351-1546350	MD-2	1980/81	1800001-1850000	Leica Mini	1991
1393421-1393510	Leicaflex		1546351-1552350	M4-P	1981	1850001-1900000	—	—
	SL2mot	1975	1674351-1678350	M6	1985	1900001-1903500	R-E,	
1393511-1394300	LeicaflexSL2	1975	1678351-1682350	M6	1985		R6.2 schw.	1991
1393511-1394300	LeicaflexSL2	1975	1682351-1682950	M6 hell	1986	1903501-1904500	M6 hell	1991
1394301-1394600	Leicaflex		1682951-1687950	R4s-2	1985-86	1904501-1906500	M6 schw.	1991
	SL2mot	1975	1687951-1691950	M6	1986	1906501-1907500	M6 hell	1991
1394601-1395000	Leicaflex SL2	1975	1691951-1692950	M4-P	1986	1907501-1908500	R-E,	
1395001-1410000	CL	1974/75	1692951-1694950	R4s	1986		R6.2 schw.	1991
1410001-1412550	MDa	1975/76	1694951-1696450	R4	1986	1908501-1912000	R7 schw.	1991
1412551-1413350	M4 schwarz	1975	1696451-1701450	R5	1986	1912001-1914000	R6.2 schw.	1991
	(Leitz Canada-Gravur)		1701451-1705450	M6	1986	1907101-1907300	M6	1992
1413351-1415000	M4 schwarz	1975	1704601-1704800	MD-2	1986		Columbus '92	
1415001-1415140	LeicaflexSL2	1975	1705451-1707450	M6 hell	1986	1914001-1915000	M6 hell	1992
1415141-1415230	Leicaflex		1707451-1711450	M6 schw.	1986	1915001-1918000	M6 schw.	1992
	SL2mot	1975	1711451-1714450	M6 hell	1987	1918001-1919020	M6 hell	1992
1415231-1421000	LeicaflexSL2	1975	1714451-1719450	R5 schw.	1987	1919021-1920000	R7 hell	1992
1421001-1421150	Leicaflex		1719451-1720450	R5 hell	1987	1920001-1923000	R6.2 hell	1992
	SL2mot	1975	1720451-1724450	R5	1987	1923001-1924000	R7 hell	1992
1421151-1425000	LeicaflexSL2	1975	1724451-1728450	M6 schw.	1987	1924001-1926000	R7 schw.	1992
1425001-1440000	CL	1975/76	1728451-1732450	R6 schw.	1987	1926001-1932000	M6 hell	1992
1440001-1443000	Leicaflex		1732451-1733450	R5 hell	1987	1920001-1923000	M6 schw.	1992
	SL2	1975/76	1733451-1738450	R5 schw.	1988	1923001-1924000	R6.2 chrome	1992
1443001-1443170	M4 schwarz	1975	1738451-1741450	M6 hell	1988	1924001-1926000	R7 chrome	1992
1443501-1446000	LeicaflexSL2	1976	1741451-1745450	M6 schw.	1988	1926001-1932000	M6 chrome	1992
1446001-1446100	R3 hell LW	1976	1745451-1755450	R6 schw.	1988	1932001-1933000	R6.2 chrome	1993
1446101-1447100	R3 hell LP	1976	1755451-1758450	M6 hell	1988	1933001-1935000	R7 black	1993
1447101-1449000	R3 schw.		1758451-1762450	M6 schw.	1988	1935001-1937000	M6 chrome	1993
	LP	1976/77	1762451-1765750	R5 schw.	1988	1937001-1937101	M6 black	1993
1449001-1450500	R3 schw. LW	1976	1757001-1758001	M6 platinum	1989	1937102-1937999	R6.2 black	1993
1450501-1450900	R3 hell LW	1977	1758002-1758251	M6 platinum	1989	1938000-1938150	M6 chrome	1993
1450901-1468000	R3 schw.		1765751-1768000	R6 hell	1989	1938151-1940000	R7 black	1993
	LP	1977/78	1768001-1770220	R5 schw.	1989	1940001-1941000	R7 black	1993
1468001-1470000	R3 oliv. LP	1977/78	1770221-1770485	R5 schw.	1989	1941001-1991000	Mini zoom	1993
1470001-1479000	R3 schw.		1770486-1772500	R5/R6 hell	1989	1991001-1993000	M6 chrome	1993
	LP	1977/78	1772501-1775000	M6 hell	1989	1993001-1995000	R6.2 black	1993
1479001-1480000	R3 hell LP	1978	1775001-1777000	R5/R6 hell	1990	1995001-1997000	M6 black	1993
1480001-1482000	M4-2	1978	1777001-1777500	M6 hell	1990	1997001-1998000	R6.2 chrome	1993
1482001-1485000	R3 oliv. LP	1978	1777501-1779000	R5/R6/		1998001-1999000	R7 black	1993
1485001-1491000	R3 schw. LP	1978		R-E schw.	1990			
1491001-1492250	R3 hell LP	1978	1779001-1782000	M6 schw.	1990			

List of Leica Lens Numbers

Year	From	To	Year	From	To
1933	156 001	195 000	1964	2 015 701	2 077 500
1934	195 001	236 000	1965	2 077 501	2 156 300
1935	236 001	284 600	1966	2 156 301	2 236 500
1936	284 601	345 000	1967	2 236 501	2 254 400
1937	345 001	416 500	1968	2 254 401	2 312 750
1938	416 501	490 000	1969	2 312 751	2 384 700
1939	490 001	538 500	1970	2 318 701	2 468 500
1940	538 501	565 000	1971	2 468 501	2 503 100
1941	565 001	582 290	1972	2 503 101	2 556 500
1942	582 295	593 000	1973	2 556 501	2 663 400
1943	593 001	594 880	1974	2 663 401	2 731 900
1944	594 881	595 000	1975	2 731 901	2 761 100
1945	595 001	601 000	1976	2 761 101	2 809 400
1946	601 001	633 000	1977	2 809 401	2 880 600
1947	633 001	647 000	1978	2 880 601	2 967 200
1948	647 001	682 000	1979	2 967 201	3 013 600
1949	682 001	765 000	1980	3 013 601	3 087 000
1950	765 001	840 000	1981	3 087 001	3 160 500
1951	840 001	950 000	1982	3 160 501	3 249 100
1952	950 001	1 051 000	1983	3 249 101	3 294 900
1953	1 051 001	1 124 000	1984	3 294 901	3 346 200
1954	1 124 001	1 236 000	1985	3 346 201	3 383 200
1955	1 236 001	1 333 000	1986	3 383 201	3 422 890
1956	1 333 001	1 459 000	1987	3 422 891	3 455 870
1957	1 459 001	1 548 000	1988	3 455 871	3 478 900
1958	1 548 001	1 645 300	1989	3 478 901	3 503 150
1959	1 645 301	1 717 000	1990	3 503 151	3 540 467
1960	1 717 001	1 827 000	1991	3 540 468	3 583 830
1961	1 827 001	1 913 000	1992	3 583 831	3 610 679
1962	1 913 001	1 967 100	1993	3 610 680	
1963	1 967 101	2 015 700			

NOTE: These numbers are allocated at the beginning of each year and this does not necessarily mean that they are all used in that year. Some may not be used until the next year, or even later.

Repair and Restoration

The first question you should ask yourself before you even consider restoring a collectable camera is this: Will my attempts to transform this camera improve it aesthetically or in terms of its value? The second questions should be: Do I have the skills to carry out the job?

The fact is that although it is worth attempting to restore a particularly tatty camera, there are times when restoration is best left alone. You can get to a point where you 'over restore', so that the camera looks too new for its age and so appears completely false. Sometimes, the appeal of an older camera lies in the fact that it has seen some use. This is especially true of older wood and brass cameras which, over the years, have developed a patina, in the way of old furniture, that is a major part of their appeal. Restore them to the way they were when new and they will no longer look authentic.

That aside, a sympathetically restored camera will always look better on display than a tatty one, and providing your restoration does no harm to the camera mechanically or aesthetically, it will undoubtedly increase its value.

Here, then, are a few tips on repair and restoration.

Restoring leather

Rather than using standard cleaning materials, you need one specially designed for old leatherwork, and although no such cleaner is made specifically for cameras, it is possible to use one designed for the restoration of old book bindings.

One such is a product called Fortificuir, which is ideal for reviving old leather. At the time of writing, it can be obtained from Alfred Maltby & Sons, 28-30 St. Michael's Street, Oxford OX1 2EB. Call them first on 01865 213113.

Failing that, shoe polish can be used, providing you use the right type and apply it correctly. The leather on old cameras very often loses its sheen, and if you apply standard shoe polish, it simply seeps into the pores of the leather, which will remain dull.

A better bet is to use the kind of shoe polish designed, not so much to clean shoes as to restore scuff marks, particularly on children's shoes. Ask your local shoe shop for a restoring or an anti-scuff polish. Then use it sparingly. Dab it on lightly a little at a time, and polish it off with a cloth or tissue almost immediately.

Removing old leather

Leather on older cameras was usually attached to the metal beneath with shellac. To remove it without damage, carefully lift an edge and run a small brush loaded with methylated spirits across the line where the leather is attached to the metal.

As the methylated spirit softens the shellac, gently peel the leather back and apply more methylated spirits as fresh shellac is revealed.

Continue until all the leather has been removed.

Replacing leather

The first task is to find a source for suitable leather, and you can often find that at flea markets and in secondhand shops. Look for old leather handbags, gloves, diaries and the like that are made of, or covered in, leather that has a similar grain to that on the camera you are restoring. Or, if you are starting from scratch, choose a grain that won't look out of place on the camera.

Start by cutting the leather to the required shape. If you have managed to take the old leather off in one piece, you can use this as a template. Otherwise, try making a template out of paper first, get that to fit correctly, then use it to cut out your pattern. Leather can be cut with a sharp scalpel, obtainable from a modelling shop. Use a steel ruler to cut straight edges and work on a cutting board, obtainable from good artists' supply shops. And take care — one slice of a sharp scalpel and you could loose a finger!

Sometimes the leatherwork on a camera body has an embossed line that matches a groove in the metal or wood beneath. To match that, start by cutting the leather a little oversize, then soak it in water. When it is completely limp, place it over the bare area of the camera body and run a tool over the leather, digging it gently into the groove beneath. When the line has been clearly marked, allow the leather to dry naturally at room temperature before gluing into position.

To attach the leather to the body, use a glue such as Evostick, coating it on the leather side only and applying whilst the glue is still wet. You will find this should hold firmly, but will still peel back if necessary.

Stiffening bellows

Old and sagging bellows can be given a new lease of life by first of all opening them and propping them up with pieces of cardboard to keep them in their correct position. Next, using a paintbrush, apply a five per cent solution of Unibond in water to the inside surface of the bellows and, when complete, use a hair dryer to dry it. Make sure that the folds do not touch each other while the bellows are still wet.

Cleaning shutters

With a little care, shutters such as those made by Compur and Prontor can be cleaned and slow speed mechanisms persuaded to work again if you go about things in the right way.

Most importantly, never be tempted to oil them with household lubricants. Instead, start by removing the shutter from the camera and carefully dismantling it to strip out all the glass elements. A set of jewellers screwdrivers will be found useful for the purpose.

With the glass removed, place the shutter in a de-greasing solvent, which you can buy in a motoring accessories shop. This will remove grease without leaving any residue. Remove it and allow to dry naturally.

When the mechanism is completely dry, place it in a capped jar containing a small amount of finely powdered graphite, which you can make yourself by shaving off the lead from a hard pencil. Shake the jar carefully then remove the shutter and blow off the loose graphite powder.

Then reassemble the shutter, putting back the glass elements and reattach it to the camera. Keep the jar of graphite powder for future use.

Cleaning old brass.

If old brasswork on a camera has developed a patina with age, then it should be left as it is. This is a good example of the way a camera can be 'over restored' to a point were it no longer looks natural.

Black marks on the brass can be lightly buffed with very fine emery paper, making sure to move it in one direction only, then the brass polished with metal or brass cleaner.

Removing the lacquer from brass is not particularly recommended, because it is not easy to replace. Some collectors have been known to use model maker's varnish for the purpose, but the final effect isn't to everyone's taste. If you want to try it, once again experimentation on an unimportant piece of brass first is advised.

If you do decide to take this route, old lacquer can be removed by soaking the fittings overnight in a solution of washing soda. Verdigris can be removed with vinegar.

Renovating wooden cameras

The body of wooden camera can be carefully sponged with water containing a few drops of liquid ammonia to remove dirt. Holes and cracks can be filled with plastic wood, which should be left for a few days to harden. Once dry and hard, any surplus can be removed with fine glasspaper, then stained with water-colour paints to match the rest of the body. Finish the job by polishing the repaired area with red shoe polish.

Making ground-glass

Valve grinding paste from motoring accessory shops or engineering companies is useful for grinding plain glass and turning it into ground-glass to replace missing or broken focusing screens. Apply it with fine wire wool, rubbing lightly to get the best effect, continually washing and checking until the opacity of the glass is right.

The problem of finding the right kind of glass to begin with is easily solved by using photographic plates, very often found in junk boxes at camera fairs. Not only is the glass used in photographic plates thin and perfectly flat, it is also cut to precisely the right size, depending on the format of the plate and the camera it is made for.

The emulsion can be removed from the plate by dissolving it in hypo or any standard black and white darkroom fixer, before washing and allowing it to dry naturally.

When you have finished, you will have a matt or slightly rough side to the glass where you have been grinding it, backed by the untouched glossy side. The screen goes into the camera with the rough side towards the lens.

Black enamelling

Where the black enamel wears away from the base metal of a camera body, it can be replaced with care, using enamel paint from a model shop. The overall effect, however, can sometimes look too glossy, so it's worth experimenting with mixing matt and glossy paints together in various ratios to get exactly the right look. Practising on an old piece of metal is important before committing yourself to the actual camera.

To apply the enamel to small areas, use a suitably-sized paintbrush and allow the enamel to flow from its tip onto the surface. It is possible to develop a technique in which the enamel is allowed to flow off the end of the brush without its hairs actually making physical contact

Before: A Debrie Sept in particularly poor cosmetic condition.

---

with the camera itself. The important thing is to apply the enamel in one direction only. Never return to the same area and paint over it as this will lead to brush marks.

If it's possible to remove a top plate, base plate or any other part of as body completely from the camera, then paint can be sprayed onto the surface, using a car paint spray can. Several coats are needed, allowing each to dry before the next is applied.

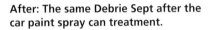

After: The same Debrie Sept after the car paint spray can treatment.

Tomorrow's Collectables

Which cameras around today will be the collectors' items of tomorrow? The fast and easy answer to that is quite simply all those models that are made new, specifically as collectors' items. This is an industry that has been around for some time, but has certainly escalated in the years since the last Blue Book was published, with Leica undoubtedly leading the way.

High budget collectables

In recent years, Leica has produced a number of special limited editions which have gone straight into the collectable category. They include the following.

A special edition of the Leica M6, commissioned by Jaguar to mark the 50th anniversary of the Jaguar XK120 sports car in 1948, and made in a limited run of 50 cameras, numbered XK1 to XK50.

The Ein Stück Leica, an M6 produced in a limited edition of 996 and covered in calf skin embossed with the Leica logo, to mark the listing of Leica AG on the stock exchange.

The Anton Bruckner Leica, an M6 covered in grey-blue embossed iguana leather to commemorate the 100th anniversary of the death of the famous Austrian composer, produced in a limited edition of 200, representing 20 cameras for each of his 10 symphonies.

The Leica M6 Royal Wedding, engraved with the Danish Royal Crest and the wedding date, 18th November 1995, produced in a limited edition of 200.

The Leica M6J, a camera that is basically an M6 with strong design influences from the original M3, made in a limited edition of 1,640, to mark 40 years of Leica M cameras.

The Royal Photographic Society M6, made in a limited edition of 100 to mark the centenary of the Royal Photographic Society in England, the top plate engraved with the RPS coat of arms.

Minox too has leapt on this particular bandwagon with cameras that have included the following over the past few years:

The Minox AX subminiature, produced in black in a limited edition of 222.

The Walter Zapp Minox AX, a 24-carat gold-plated subminiature, made in a limited edition of 250 to celebrate 50 years of Minox manufacture in

Germany and engraved with the signature of Walter Zapp, the camera's inventor.

The Minox MDC Gold, a 24-carat gold-plated version of the traditional MDC 35mm camera, made in a limited edition of 555, for no particular reason other than to appeal to the collector's market.

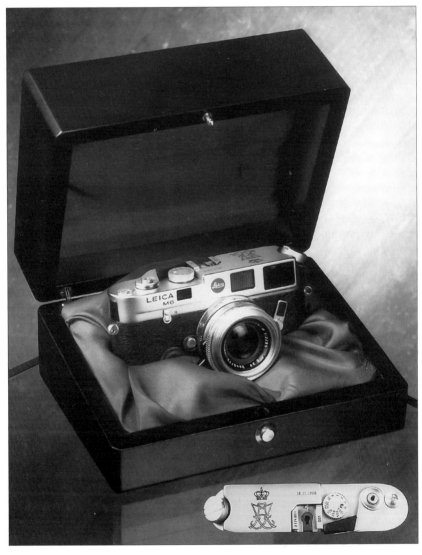

This Leica M6 with the Danish Royal Crest was made to celebrate the Royal Wedding in 1995.

Although Hasselblad isn't always considered to b[e] that, say, Leitz or Zeiss cameras are, the marque is att[ractive to a wide range] of enthusiasts, and it's a manufacturer that has produced [a] and limited editions in recent years. Since Hasselblad w[as] for the moon landings, they include a special EL/M, made i[n a limited run of] 1,500 in 1979 to celebrate ten years on the moon; and a chro[me version] w[ith] a light grey vinyl body, made in a limited run of 1,500 in 198[4 to] [ma]rk the 20th anniversary of Hasselblad's participation in the US space p[r]ogramme. The company has also produced a number of special editions to celebrate anniversaries of landmark models.

Some other manufacturers too have occasional excursions into the special, one-off camera, aimed at collectors: Olympus with its 'O' product, a few specials from Minolta, Rollei with special editions of its 35mm range and TLRs dedicated to famous users of the marque.

Cameras like these are made purely to entice rich collectors to add to their growing collection, something which Leica fanatics in particular can rarely resist — assuming they have the cash to afford them. Such cameras are nearly always sold in special commemorative boxes, usually made of quality wood with silk linings, and there are stories of collectors who buy them, keeping them sealed in their original packaging without even unwrapping them.

This, it must be said, is taking collecting to its most extreme, like wine collectors who buy and sell bottles of the stuff and never dream of drinking it.

Some modern cameras, whilst not specifically made as collectors' items, still command the attention of the collector, because of their unusual or unique design concepts. The Contax G1, now superseded by the G2, is a prime example. Although a modern camera in every sense of the word, with its electronic systems, automated exposure modes and autofocus options, it was, at the time of its launch, the first real interchangeable lens, non-reflex camera made in years. Unlike other cameras mentioned above, it was never intended to be produced as a special or limited edition, but is nevertheless becoming a collector's item.

All of these cameras were immediately collectable at the time of their launch and will undoubtedly remain collectable for years to come, their values steadily growing as long as the collector's market remains buoyant. The problem, for the average collector, is that their prices are prohibitively expensive, usually running into several thousands of pounds at the very least, especially when it comes to limited editions.

Medium budget collectables

Between the high budget collectables just mentioned and modern cameras for collectors on a lower budget that we will come to in a moment, lies that

... cameras which might not have been thought of as collectable until ... rly recently. These are the cameras that can still be bought on a fairly restrained budget, but which are destined to attract more collectors in the coming years.

Top of this list must be cameras from the 1970s. Since this is the era in which many established collectors began collecting, it's a decade that is still considered by many to be too modern for consideration. A new generation of collectors, however, is beginning to think differently, and as more interested develops, so prices will begin to climb.

We're talking here about cameras such as the Olympus OM-1, first of the compact 35mm single lens reflexes; the Nikon EM, that company's first real foray into cameras for the amateur; or perhaps the Konica FS-1, first 35mm single lens reflex with a built-in electric motor drive.

Russian cameras are today cheaper than they have been for years, simply because the opening up of the country has led to more cameras reaching the market. But as that supply begins to dry up, these too could begin to rise again.

So too could older brass and mahogany cameras. Today, they are not considered as collectable as they once were. But the trend could well change, so it's worth keeping an eye on prices to see when they start to rise again.

Some Polaroid cameras are worth keeping an eye on. Models like the Swinger are worth very little now and probably won't be for many years to come. But models like the first SX-70 and the SLR680 are starting to command serious prices, which appear to be on the rise.

Like Polaroid, some of the more unusual Kodak Instamatic cameras — such as the Instamatic 400 with its built-in clockwork motordrive — are also attracting interest, and it's probably only a matter of time before disc cameras go the same way.

Look out too for examples of early autofocus cameras. The Konica C35AF, which was the first automatically focusing 35mm compact, can still be bought for next to nothing. But as the 1970s become more acceptable to the collector, this is a 1978 collectable that could begin to grow in value. Likewise, early autofocus single lens reflexes like the Canon T80, or the special autofocus lenses made by Canon and Ricoh to convert manual focus cameras for automatic focusing.

Cine cameras are only now beginning to interest collectors, but evidence over the past year has shown that it's an interest that is on the increase, and as it grows, so too will the prices. The cameras to look for here are those from the early days of amateur cinematography from 1923 onwards, particularly cameras made for 16mm, 9.5mm and 8mm in its various forms: the double eight version that was actually 16mm run through the camera twice, and the version usually, but not always, found in its own cartridge to be run through just once.

These are all cameras from the recent past that can still be bought today on a medium budget, but which are currently showing signs of increasing in popularity.

Low budget collectables

So which modern cameras today can the collector on a budget look for as an investment for the future?

Consider for a start, cameras that epitomise an era and which have been innovations of their own. The obvious choice here is the vast range of disposable cameras on sale today. There are many different types and styles, including specials such as one produced by Harrods, the world-famous department store, or the one produced to celebrate the 1998 World Cup.

The fact that they are made to be disposable means that the vast majority of them won't survive and, as the different types are superseded, the old ones are already beginning to be sort after by specialist collectors.

Then there are cameras which the manufacturers obviously thought to be a good idea at the time, but which never really caught on. The Sirius Action Tracker is a prime example. A fairly basic, plastic snapshot camera, it has the unusual feature of taking four pictures, in sequence, on a single frame of

Collectors are already showing an interest in different types of disposable camera.

35mm film. It was aimed at snapshotters who wanted to record sporting action, but it never found its market and, within a short while of being launched, it was being discounted. Today, it is beginning to appear at camera fairs.

Polaroid is another manufacturer worth keeping an eye on. This company is fond of producing special editions of their cheaper models. Currently, they have one called the Spicecam, which relates to the Spice Girls, an all-girl singing sensation whose popularity will undoubtedly wane in the next few years, and who one day might only be remembered by their association with an instant picture camera.

Or how about cameras that are given away for promotional purposes? The inclusion of a trade name on a camera of the past, made for a specific company or exhibition, usually ups its value today. So watch out for the modern equivalents on 35mm compacts and other snapshot models.

Then there are the fun cameras and special one-offs that usually arrive in the shops around Christmas, produced principally as presents for children. They often take the same basic design, but add to it with special mouldings of subjects like animals, or children's fictional characters. The Wallace and Gromit characters, for example, have been immortalised on one such camera, which has been selling in a special pack that includes film in its own specially designed box, a photo album and instructions for getting the best pictures from the camera. Imagine the current value of an equivalent complete box set made, say, back in the 1930s and you can understand why it's no bad idea to buy this kind of equipment today and keep it for the future.

Cameras like these are, in their own way, limited editions, because once a current fad or phase has finished, then they cease to remain popular. The

Novelty cameras of today could well be the collectors' items of tomorrow.

manufacturers know that and produce only enough to satisfy current trends, before moving on to the next craze.

This is, in fact, something that some collectors and dealers are already seeing the value of. In the UK, novelty cameras of this type have been sold principally by the Boots chain of stores. One collectable camera dealer, in the past year, bought up the entire stock from a London branch of Boots, put them in his catalogue and immediately started making sales to customers in the USA.

A Gerry the Giraffe plastic snapshot camera might not have quite the appeal of a Leica M6 Royal Wedding camera, but in its own way it is an attractive special edition, easily found today and worth buying for the future.

These are all cameras that have only a short lifespan — and those are the very models that will become collectable in the years to come.

Museums for Collectors

AUSTRALIA

Michaels Classic and Antique Camera & Video Museum. Over seven thousand collectable photographic items displayed. Contact Curator John Tracey; Michaels Buildings, Cnr. Elizabeth & Lonsdale streets, Melbourne, Australia. PO.Box 2047S GPO Melbourne Phone; + 61 3 670 2259 FAX; + 61 3 670 0074

BELGIUM

Museum Voor Fotografie, Waalse Kaai 47 Antwerpen, Belgium, B-2000 A wide view on the world of photography, yesterday, today and tomorrow. Open 10:00-5:00pm, except Mondays. Contact Roger Coenen at (03) 2162211.

THE CZECH REPUBLIC

National Museum of Technology, Holesovice, Kostelni 42,Prague-7, The Czech Republic. Telephone (2) 373651. Excellent display of still and motion picture cameras, the finest in central Europe and ranks right up with the best.

FRANCE

Musée Français de la Photographie, 78 rue de Paris, PO Box 03-Bievres, France 91570. Cameras, photographs, accessories, and documentation. Open everyday from 10:00-12:00 and 2:00-6:00, holidays included. Contact Andrè Fage, Conservateur en Chef at (6941)1060

Musée National des Techniques, Conservatoire National des Arts et Mètiers, 270 Rue Saint-Martin, Paris, France, 75003. Cameras from 1850 to present day. Microphotography by Dagron for carrier pigeons, stereo cameras and spy cameras, motion study photography by Marey and Muybridge. Open 10:00-5:30 Tuesday- Saturday. Contact Mr. Jaques Foiret at (1) 402-72220 or 402-72371. The camera section has been closed for renovation for several years, but may be open by now. It is suggested you contact them before visiting.

GERMANY

Agfa-Gevaert Foto Historama, Bischofsgartenstrasse-1. D-50667 Köln, West Germany. Contact Dr. Bodo von Dewitz, Director, at (0221) 2212411.

Berlin Museum fur Verhehr und Technic. Trebbiner Strasse 9 DW-1000 Berlin 61. (030) 254-840.

Deutsches Museum, Museuminsel,D-80536 Munich, West Germany

Essen, Abring Foto Museum. Burg-Horst,Haus Horst 1, DW-4300, Essen14. (0201) 53 86 90. Large camera display plus private museum; by Appointment;

Leica Museum, Leica Camera GmbH, Oskar Barnack Strasse 11, Postfach 11 80, D-6336 Solms, Germany. Leica Cameras and accessories. Open 9:00-5:00pm by arrangement. Telephone (6442) 2080.

Münchner Stadt Museum, St Jakobsplatz,D-80334 Munich, West Germany.

Optisches Museum Oberkochen, Am ülweiher 15, D-73447. Oberkochen, Baden-Würtemberg, West Germany, Historical and modern eyeglasses, telescopes, binoculars, surveying instruments, cameras and microscopes. Open 10:00-1:00pm and 2:00-4:00pm Monday-Friday, 9:00-12:00 Sunday. Closed Saturdays and holidays. Telephone (07364) 202878.

ITALY

Museo Nationale del Cinema, Palazzo Chiablese, piazza San Giovanni, 2, Turin, Italy, 10122. Photograph and camera collections, Cinema Massimo magazine, vintage film and magic lantern shows. Contact for Camera collections, Ms. Donata Pesenti; Photograph collections, Ms. Marica Marcellino, at (011) 5661148 or 5661387.

JAPAN

JCII Museum, 23 Ichiban-cho, Chiyoda-ku, Tokyo, 102, Japan. Although small, this museum has a truly extraordinary collection with frequently changing exhibits. The only example of a Giroux Daguerrotype Camera in Asia is in the collection of this museum. A must-see for anybody visiting Japan with an interest in cameras.

City of Yokahama Camera Museum, Cultural Officer, Yokahama, Japan. Recently the city of Yokahama acquired the very large Naylor Collection and expects to build a museum to house it which will open next year. This is all the information we have at this time. A visitor to Japan later next year is advised to contact the above address for up-to-date information.

REPUBLIC OF SLOVAKIA

Petzval Museum, Spisska Bela, Republic of Slovakia. Located in the home which was his birthplace, the museum is dedicated to Josef Max Petzval, who designed the first high-speed lens. The museum contains an excellent exhibit of early Petzval lenses and the cameras that used them.

SOUTH AFRICA

Bensusan Musuem of Photography, 17 Empire Rd., Parktown, South Africa.

THAILAND

Department of Photographic Science, Faculty of Science, Chulalongkorn University, Phyathai Road, Bangkok, Thailand. The Photographic Science Department of this university administers a recently opened museum of photographic technology that occupies a new building on the campus. It is the first and only photographic museum in SE Asia. An excellent collection includes cameras used by more than a century of Thai royalty. Contact above address for opening times.

UK

Barnes Museum of Cinematography, 44 Fore Street, St. Ives, Cornwall, England.

Buckingham Movie Museum, Printers Mews, Market Hill, Buckingham, England.

Fenton Photography Museum, Port Erin, Isle of Wight, England.

Fox Talbot Museum of Photography, Lacock, Near Chippenham, Wiltshire, England, SN15 2LG. Fox Talbot collection, Open 11:00-6:00 pm everyday except Good Friday, March 1st to November 5th Telephone 0124 973459.

Medina Camera Museum, Golden Hill Fort, Freshwater, Isle of Man, England.

Museum of the History of Science, Broad Street, Oxford, England, OX1 3AZ. Cameras and photographic accessories, early and experimental photographs, Specimens of scientific interest, (early Colour). Open 10:30-1:00pm and 2:00-4:00pm, Monday-Friday, except bank holidays, and Easter and Christmas weeks. Telephone (01865) 277280.

National Museum of Photography, Film, and Television, Princes View, Bradford, West Yorkshire, England, BD5 0TR, Kodak Museum, Interactive and Theatrical reconstruction in museum displays on the past, present and future of photography and television. Changing special exhibitions. Open 11:00-6:00 Tuesday-Sunday, Contact Roger Taylor at (01274) 727488.

Science Museum, Exhibition Rd., South Kensington, London, England, SW7 2DD. Photographic and Cinematographic equipment and photographs from 1835 to present day. Open 10:00-6:00 Monday-Saturday, 11:00-6:00 Sundays.

The Royal Photographic Society, The Octagon, Milsom Street, Bath, England BA1 1DN. Comprehensive collection of cameras photographs from the very beginning of photography. Open 9:30-5:15 pm, Contact Mrs. P. Roberts, or Miss K. Rouse at (01225) 62841 ext. 212.

Woodspring Museum, Burlington Street, Weston-super-Mare, Avon, England BS23 1PR. A good cross section of the progress of photography since the 1890s. Of special interest is a Bertsh "Chambre Automatique" from about 1861. Photo accessories are also on display. Free admission. Open 10:00-5:00, Monday-Saturday, open Bank holidays except Good Friday, Christmas and New Year. Telephone (01934) 621028.

Woolstaplers Hall Museum, High Street, Chipping Campden, Gloucestershire, England, GL55 6HB. Projectors, plate cameras, Kodak cameras, Contax cameras and other photographic paraphenalia.Open 11:00-6:00 daily from April 1st to October 31st. Contact Mrs. J. Griffiths, Curator at (01386) 840289.

The British Photographic Museum, Bowden House, Totnes, South Devon, England, TQ9 7PW. Camera collection on display, gift shop and Tea Room available. Contact Christopher or Belinda Petersen at (01803) 863664.

Royal Museum of Scotland, Chambers Street, Edinburgh, Scotland.

USA

California Academy of Science, Golden Gate Park, San Francisco, California, USA, 94118. 400 items late 19th and 20th century cameras and equipment. Open 9:00-5:00 pm Monday-Friday Display partially up. Contact Dr. Robert Sayers, Anthrology Dept. at 415-750-7163.

Florida State Museum, Gainesville, FL, USA Gallery of Photographic History, 10010 Lanehart Road, Little Rock, Arkansas, USA, 72204. Major photographic library, prints, but very little equipment. Open by appointment only. Contact Greer H. Lile at (501) 666-7409 or 455-0179.

George Eastman House, The International Museum of Photography, 900 East Avenue, Rochester, New York 14622. Tel: 716/271-3361. Certainly the finest museum of photography in North America, possibly the world. A must for anyone interested in photographic technology. Open Tue.-Sunday 10-5. Archives may be visited by appointment. Contact Todd Gustavson, Technology Archivist.

Henry Ford Museum and Greenfield Village, PO Box 1970, 20900 Oakwood Blvd, Dearborn, MI, USA, 48121. Small collection of cameras from 1890-1980. Open 9:00-5:00pm daily except Christmas and Thanksgiving. Contact the Curator of Communications at (313) 271-1620

Jacksonville Museum, Courthouse Sq., Jacksonville, FL, USA. Housed in a large old Courthouse and maintained by the Southern Orega Historical Society. The Peter Britt Gallery is a display of the life and times of photographer Britt. Daguerrean images; studio artifacts but very limited camera diplay, makes this a fascinating display.

Los Angeles County Museum of Natural History, 900 Exposition Blvd., Los Angeles, California USA, 90007. Historical photographs concerning the growth and development of Los Angeles, and southern California. Includes Southwest Indians. Open 1:00-4:00 pm Monday-Friday at the Seaver Center. Telephone (213) 744-3359.

The Magic Lantern Castle Museum. The only purely Magic Lantern Museum in the World; Research and library facilities. Contact; Jack Judson,Jr. Castellen/Curator. 1419 Austin Highway, San Antonio, Texas 78209 at (210)-805-0011. FAX.210-822-1226.

National Museum of American History, Smithsonian Inst.,Washington, DC, USA, 20560 Part of the vast Smithsonian collection. Often called "America's attic". Camera and photography display in general has been taken down. No indication as to when it will be restored in any form. Open 10:00-5:30 pm, every day but Christmas Day. Contact Eugene Ostroff, Curator at 202-357-2059.

Stonefield Village, Nelson Dewey State Park, Cassville, Wisconsin,USA, 53806. Replica of 1890s Photographer's Shop. Open 9:00-5:00 pm. Telephone (608) 725-5210.

University of Texas, Harry Ransom Humanities Research Center, Box 7219, University of Texas at Austin, Austin, TX, USA, 78713-7219. Excellent collection based on the former Helmut Gernsheim Collection (which contained the world's earliest photograph by Niepce). It relates to the entire history of photography, its growth and impact on world culture. Open 9.00-5.00 p.m. Monday-Friday. Appointments and reservations requested. Contact Roy Flukinger, Curator, at 512-471-9124.

Clubs for Collectors

AUSTRALIA

Photographic Collectors Society, 14 Warne Street, Eaglemont, Victoria, 3084, Australia. Newsletter, published quarterly. Phone, (03) 457-1050.

Sydney Stereo Camera Club, PO Box 465, Pymble, NS, 2073, Australia, For Stereo photographists, Bi-monthly newsletter, monthly membership meetings. Contact Judy Archer, Secretary.

BELGIUM

Photographica, Chausee de la Hulpe 382, Brussels, 1170, Belgium, Telephone (2) 673-8490.

CANADA

Photographic Historical Society of Metropolitan Toronto, PO Box 115, Postal Station "S", Toronto, Ontario, M5M 4L6, Canada, Telephone (416) 483-4185.

Western Canada Photographic Historical Association, PO Box 33742, Vancouver, British Columbia, V6J 4L6, Canada, (614)-873-2128.

The Photographic Historical Society of Canada, 10 Northolt Court, Islington, Ont.,M9A 3B1, Canada.

FRANCE

Club Niepce Lumiere, 35 Rue de la Mare a l'Ane, Montreuil, 93100, France.

GERMANY

Club Daguerre, Mohlenstrasse 5, Leverkusen, Hitdorf, D-5090, West Germany. (02173)-40080. Two news letters published four times a year. Annual membership meeting, more frequent regional meetings. About 450 members. Membership fees 100 Dm/year. Contact Klaus Storsberg.

Ihagee Historiker Gesellschaft, Charlottenburger Strasse 22A, Leverkusen, D-5090, West Germany.

Leica Historica, C/O Klaus Grothe, Bahnhof Str.53, D3252, Bad Münder 1, Germany, Membership DM50/year, includes 3-4 newsletters (Vidom) published each year, two annual meetings per year, usually at a location near Wetzlar, about 470 members.

HOLLAND

Dutch Society of Photographica Collectors, PO Box 4262, Haarlem, 2003EG, Netherlands. Illustrated magazine published four times a year. International camera shows twice a year, with more than 200 dealers, and 2,300 visitors. Regional meetings two or three times a year with 60 dealers. Postal auction four times a year. Museum outings several times each year. More than 1,100 members including 1,000 Dutch members, and more than 100 world wide members. Hfl 40 for Dutch membership, Hfl 47 for foreign membership, US$ 25.00 foreign. Contact Harry van Kohl, secretary.

Ihagee Historiker Gesellschaft, Tesselschadelaan 20, Hilversum, 1217LH, Netherlands.

UK

Hasselblad Forum Magazine. The *'Hasselblad Forum'* magazine is published in Sweden by Victor Hasselblad AB and is normally only available on annual subscription. Four issues, containing many excellent contributions from expert photographers from all over the World, are printed each year and these will be sent to members free of charge. Hasselblad (UK), York House, Empire Way, Wembley, Middlesex, HA90 QQ. Tel: 0181 903 3435. Fax. 0181 902 2565.

Ihagee Historical Association, c/o Teamwork, 11 Shelton St., London, WC2H 9JN, England, FAX (1) 379-0981.

Leica Historical Society, Greystoke, 8 Driffold, Sutton Coldfield, West Midlands, B73 6HE, England.

MPP Club. The Club aims to foster the use and application of MPP cameras and products by the free exchange of information between members through the postal circulation of notebooks with members hints and tips and the issue of periodic Gazettes. By that means members can seek solutions to some of the problems they may encounter in using or collecting MPP cameras. Meetings will mostly be at the Photo-collectors fairs, such as Dartford or others in the London region. Locations which are idea opportunities to meet and discuss matters of mutual interest. The repair of members cameras may well depend upon sourcing of spare parts. The Club can already assist to some degree in this, and provide flat lens panels which can be supplied to order as well as bellows ex-stock for some models at modest prices. Membership is open to professional and amateur users and to collectors, and to those who may seriously be considering the purchase of an MPP camera to further their photographic interests. To all those who thereby qualify, the Club has a lot to offer and they should become members.

The annual subscription is only £6. Further information and additional application forms are available from: Mr Mike Meurisse, Hon. Secretary MPP Users' Club. Tel: 01932 863769.

Magic Lantern Society of Great Britain, "Prospect", High Street, Nutley, East Sussex TN22 3NH. UK subs, £15 for Journal and newsletter.

Pentax Club and Magazine. Tel: 01483 418473. Fax: 01483 419270. E-mail: Pentax.magazine@ski.co.uk. Please call for more information.

Photographic Collectors Club of Great Britain, Membership Secretary, 5 Station Industrial Estate, Low Prudhoe, Northumberland, NE42 6NP, England. Photographica World and Tailboard newsletter published quarterly. Meetings regularly, all over Great Britain. Annual fair in May. Telephone 01434 688129.

The Historical Group of the Royal Photographic Society, The Octagon, Milsom Street, Bath, Avon, BA1 1DN, England.

The Pen F Register, c/o 1 Sylvan Close, Hemel Hempstead, Hertfordshire, HP3 8DN, England.

The Stereoscopic Society, Hon. Secretary Sue Makinson, 36 Silverthorn Drive, Hemel Hempstead, Herts HP3 8BX, UK. Quarterly magazine, monthly meetings from September to May in London and Coventry. Also annual convention. Current membership fee £13/year. Web site http://www.stereoscopy.com/stereosociety. *Write or fax 01442 250266 for colour leaflet and application form.*

The Voigtländer Verein. Hon. Secretary, Chris Haupt, 33 Woodhayes Road, Frome, Somerset BA11 2DG. The group was formed in 1994 by a small group of enthusiasts. We now have around 100 members worldwide. The word 'Verein' in German means 'fellowship.' We are not dealers but amateur collectors and historians. Our quarterly magazine 'Voigtländer Matters' comprises of members' articles on, and the gathering of detailed information about, all Voigtländer products and history, but mainly about their cameras and lenses. We always encourage active participation from our members and their responses to questionnaires on various cameras and accessories has added considerably to our detailed knowledge of Voigtländer camera development. We are currently updating and revising Dr Neil Wright's definitive 'Checklist of Voigtländer Cameras', the copyright of which he has most generously given to us.

Third Dimension Society, 2, Davison Road, Darlington, Co. Durham, DL1 3DR, England. Telephone (0325) 59272, quarterly magazine. Membership fee £7/year, contact D.C. Wardle, Membership Secretary.

USA

American Photographical Historical Society, 520 West 44th Street, New York, NY, 10036, USA, Telephone (212)-594-5056. Photographica magazine published four times a year. Eight membership meetings a year, and two camera shows annually. Over 400 members worldwide. Annual dues in the

---

United States US$ 22.50. Foreign membership is available. Contact George Gilbert.

American Society of Camera Collectors, 4918 Alcove Avenue, North Hollywood, CA, 91670, USA, Telephone (213)-769-6160.

Atlanta Photographic Collectors Club, PO Box 98291, Atlanta, GA, 30345, USA.

Bay Area Photographic Association, 2538 34th Avenue, San Francisco, CA, 94116, USA, Telephone (415)-664-6498.

Chicago Photographic Collectors Society, PO Box 375, Winnetka, Ill, 60093, USA.

Club Daguerre-Darrah, 2562 Victoria, Witchita, KA, 67216, USA, Telephone (316)-265-0393.

Delaware Valley Photographic Association, PO Box 74, Delanco, NJ, 08075, USA.

International Kodak Historical Society, PO Box 21, Flourtown, PA, 19031, USA.

International Photographic Historical Organization, PO Box 16074, San Francisco, CA, 94116, USA, Telephone (415)-681-4356.

Leica Historical Society of America, 7611 Dornoch Lane, Dallas, TX, 75248, USA, (214) 387-5708. *Viewfinder* magazine and *Leica Catalogue* published four times a year. Annual membership meeting. More than 1,000 members. US$ 28.00 membership fee for the USA, Canada and Mexico,. All other countries, US$ 28.00 by surface mail, US$ 37.00 by airmail.

Michigan Photographic Historical Society, PO Box 202, Wayne, MI, 48184, USA, Telephone (313)-721-5126.

Midwest Photographic Historical Society, 19 Hazelnut Court, Florissant, MO, 63033, USA.

Miranda Club, PO Box 2001, Hammond, Indiana, 46323, USA, Contact Thomas Surovek.

The Magic Lantern Society; Contact the President Jack Judson,Jr. 445 Burr Road, San Antonio Texas 78209. Phone (210) 824-9995. FAX (210) 822-1226). The Magic Lantern Castle museum is associated with the club.

National Stereoscopic Association, PO Box 14801, Columbus, OH, 43214, USA. Magazine published six times a year. Regional meetings and annual convention held in the US. More than 2200 members, worldwide. US$ 22 in the United States, US$32 foreign surface mail, and US$ 46 by airmail., US$ 22/year, foreign US$32 by surface, US$ 46 by air.

Nikon Historical Society, PO Box 3213, Munster, IN, 46321, USA. Telephone(708)-895-5319. The Nikon Journal is published four times a year. The Nikon Historical Society held its second convention in March of 1990. More than 150 members worldwide. Annual dues is US$ 25/year for the United States and Canada, Foreign membership is US$ 35/year. Contact Robert Rotoloni.

Pennsylvania Photographic Historical Society, Inc., PO Box 862, Beaver Falls, PA, 15010, USA. Flash Pan newsletter five times a year. Five meetings are held annually. 40 regional members, US$10 annual dues, US$ 15 for family membership. No foreign membership is available at the present time. Membership fees are US$ 10/year, US$ 15 for family. Contact B.J. Tarr.

Photographic Collectors of Houston, 1201 McDuffie, #104, Houston, TX, 77019, USA.

Photographic Collectors of Tucson, PO Box 18646, Tucson, AR, 85731, USA. Telephone (602) 721-0478.

Photographic Historical Society of New England,Inc., PO Box 189, West Newton Branch, Boston, MA, 02165, USA. Telephone (617)-277-0207 Magazine, New England Journal of Photographic History, published four times a year. Monthly meetings held, except July and August. Over 450 members worldwide. Dues are US$ 18 for US and Canada, US$ 35 for foreign each year. Contact Jack Naylor.

Puget Sound Photographic Collectors Society, 10421 Delwood Dr. SW, Tacoma, WA, 98498, USA. Telephone (206)-582-4878, Membership fee US$ 10.00.

Rochester Photo Historical Society, PO Box 9563, Rochester, New York 14604. This was the first club for camera collectors in the United States.

The Movie Machine Society, 50 Old Country Road, Hudsen, MA, 01749, USA, Quarterly Bulletin Sixteen Frames.

The Ohio Camera Collectors, PO Box 282, Columbus, OH, 43216, USA, Annual show Memorial Day weekend. Membership meeting on the first Saturday of each month, more than 100 members. Contact John Durand (614) 885-3224.

The Photographic Historical Society, PO Box 9563, Rochester, NY, 14604, USA.

The Photographic Historical Society of the Western Reserve. PO Box 25663, Cleveland, OH, 44125, USA. Phone (216)-382-6727. Membership meetings on the third Wednesday of each month, except August. 100 members. Contact William S. Nehez.

Tri-State Photographic Collectors Society, 8910 Cherry, Blue Ash, OH, 45242, USA. Telephone (513)-891-5266.

Western Photographic Collectors Assoc., PO Box 4294, Whittier, CA, 90607, USA. (213) 693-8421. Quarterly, 24 page Journal on coated stock. Membership meetings held monthly, plus two trade shows a year. 450 Members. Regular membership fee (receiving meeting notices) US$ 25, Corresponding US$ 20, Foreign US$ 30. Contact William P. Carroll.

Zeiss Historical Society, PO Box 631, Clifton, NJ, 07012, USA. (201)-472-1318.

Camera Directory

A-Z

Collectible Cameras,
Specifications, Prices,
Values, Rarity Ratings
and Years of Manufacture

film changing systems and accurate, vibrationless shutters.

Acro Scientific Products Co.,
Chicago, USA.

ACRO R: c1938, Bakelite RFR camera for 3 x 4cm frames on 127 roll film, f3.5 lens, Alphax shutter, built-in extinction meter, un-coupled RFR.

R3*   **C+**

ACRO IV: Without extinction meter or RFR.

R3*   **B**

Adams & Co.,
London, England.

The firm of A.Adams was founded in 1886 by Arthur L. Adams in London. By the 1890's they were general photographic suppliers, offering studio furniture, painted backgrounds and all the other requirements of the photographers of the day. Eventually they began making cameras for sections of the market, at prices from £1 to £20. In the early 1900's Adams dropped their cheaper range of cameras to concentrate on high quality, exquisitely made cameras for the professional and advanced amateur. Two of these were the square bellows "Challenge" and the tapered bellows "Club", both in production until the late 1930's. Arthur Adams designed most of the cameras himself, concentrating on reliable plate and

ADAMS DELUXE HAND CAMERA: box magazine camera; pneumatic shutter to $\frac{1}{1000}$s; dark focusing red Russian leather bellows; could be used with Eastman-Walker roll holder; polished wood magazine holder. Same camera covered in red leather with 18 karat gold fittings, shutter and handle was made for Queen Victoria. C 1890's. 3 models made: No.1. Single ext; Quarter and Half-plate, 4"x 5" Dallmeyer Stigmatic Series 1 F6 lens.: No.2. Double ext. 4"x5" Quarter-plate;Zeiss Satz Convertable F6.3 lens: No.3. Triple ext.;4"x 5" Quarter-plate; Zeiss Satz Convertable F7 lens: No.4: C.1902; As no.3 with addition of Adams FP shutter $\frac{1}{150}$ – $\frac{1}{1000}$s.

R4*   **F**

NO. 1 YALE PHOTOGRAPHIC OUTFIT: C 1890's. Black paper covered cardboard box camera; 2" x 2" exp on plates.

R3*   **C+**

NO. 5 YALE STEREO DETECTIVE: c1890's. Leather covered camera; 7½" Zeiss lenses; rack focusing; concealed bellows. Leather changing bag back.

R4*   **G**

MINEX: c1939. 3¼" x 4¼" SLR camera. C.1910. Made in various sizes until 1939 and maybe later.

R4*   **E**

MINEX TROPICAL: c1930. 3¼" x 4¼" tropical SLR camera; CFPS ⅛-¹⁄₁₀₀₀s. Teak wood construction with polished brass fittings.
R4*   **I**

IDENTO: c1908 3¼" x 4¼" folding camera; Ross Homocentric 5" f5.3 lens.
R3*   **E**

VIDEX: c1904. 3¼" x 4¼" SLR camera; Tessar 21cm f4.5 lens.
R3*   **E**

Adox Kamerawerk,
Wiesbaden, Germany.

(Also Dr. C. Schleußner Fotowerk, Frankfort a/M, Germany)

ADOX ADRETTE: c1939, 35mm camera with telescoping front; Schneider Radionar 50mm f2.9 lens; Compur Rapid shutter, 1-¹⁄₅₀₀ s, 36 exp, 24 x 36mm. This camera is identical to the Wirgin Edinex, and may be made by Wirgin.
R2*   **C−**

ADOX SPORT: c1935-51, folding VFR camera for 6 x 9 or 6 x 4.5cm frames on 120 rollfilm, Anastigmat f6.3 or f4.5/105mm lens.
R2*   **B**

ADOX SPORT O: c1949, folding VFR camera for 6 x 9 or 6 x 4.5cm frames on 120 roll film, Radionar f4.5/10.5cm lens, Vario shutter, ¹⁄₂₅ − ¹⁄₁₀₀s, synch. Postwar version Sport.
R2*   **B**

ADOX SPORT I: c1950, Pronto shutter.
R2*   **B**

ADOX SPORT II: c1950, Prontor shutter.
R2*   **B**

ADOX SPORT IA: c1952, folding VFR camera for 6 x 9cm or 6 x 6cm frames on 120 roll film, Cassar f4.5/105mm lens, Pronto shutter, synch. Addition of new chromed top plate, double exposure prevention, and accessory shoe. Both formats visible in optical VFR.
R2*   **B**

ADOX SPORT IIA: c1952, Prontor S shutter.
R2*   **B**

ADOX SPORT IIIA: c1952, Prontor SV shutter.
R2*   **B**

ADOX SPORT ROUGE: c1952. With special red leatherette body covering, and red leather bellows.
R4*   **D**

ADOX TEMPO: c1935, folding vrf camera for 6 x 4.5cm frames on 120 roll film, many lens/shutter combinations including the top of the line Xenar f2.8/75mm lens in Compur Rapid shutter.
R3*   **C−**

ADOX TRUMPF: c1932, folding VFR camera for 6 x 9 or 6 x 4.5 frames on rollfilm, Anastigmat f4.5/105mm lens, Vario shutter.
R3*   **B**

ADOX TRUMPF II: c1934, folding VFR camera for 6 x 9 or 6 x 4.5 frames on roll-film, many lens/shutter combinations, typically Xenar f4.5/105mm lens, Compur Rapid shutter. Addition of body release, new film pressure plate, and better lens availability.

R3*   **B**

JUNKA: c1949, metal VFR camera for 3 x 4cm frames on special Schleussner/Junka film, f8/45mm lens, simple shutter.

R3*   **B**

ADOX 66: c1950, black Bakelite TLR type box camera for 6 x 6cm frames on rollfilm, f8 lens, simple shutter, choice of three lenses with focusing from 1m to inf.

R1*   **B**

ADOX BLITZ: c1950, black Bakelite TLR type box camera for 6 x 6cm frames on roll film, f8 lens, simple shutter, basically the 66 camera with provision for flash.

R2*   **A**

ADOX GOLF: c1952, folding VFR camera for 6 x 6 frames on roll film, Cassaren f4.5/75mm lens, Pronto shutter, accessory shoe, body release, knob wind.

R2*   **B**

ADOX GOLF II: c1952, folding VFR camera for 6 x 6 frames on roll film. Prontor S shutter.

R2*   **B**

ADOX GOLF IV: c1952, folding VFR camera for 6 x 6 frames on roll film, Cassar f3.5/75mm lens. No model III is known to exist.

R2*   **B**

ADOX GOLF 63: c1954, folding VFR camera for 6 x 6 frames on roll film, Adoxar f6.3/75mm lens, Vario shutter, accessory shoe, body release, knob wind. The cheapest version of the Adox Golf family.

R2*   **A**

ADOX GOLF 63 S: c1956, folding VFR camera for 6 x 6 frames on roll film. Addition of a selftimer.

R2*   **B**

ADOX ME-GOLF: c1955, folding RFR camera for 6 x 6cm frames on roll film, CRF, Cassar f3.45 or 4.5/75mm lens, Pronto or Prontor S shutter, self timer, synch. Advertised as the "cheapest 6 x 6 RFR of the day!".

R3*   **C**

ADOX 300: c1956, 35mm RFR camera with *interchangeable film magazine backs,* each back having its own film counter and film reminder system, built-in light meter, Cassar f2.8/45mm lens and Synchro Compur MXV shutter with EV scale, or Xenar f2.8/45mm lens and Compur Rapid XV shutter with EV scale. Original price included *one* magazine, not three as is sometimes mentioned. Additional magazines were available for 56DM each.

R4*   **E**

ADOX GOLF IA: c1963, 35mm VFR camera, (not to be confused with the folding roll film Golf series), Adoxon f2.8/45mm lens, Prontor 125 shutter.

R2*   **A**

ADOX GOLF IA: c1964, 35mm VFR camera, (not to be confused with the folding roll film Golf series), Adoxon f2.8/45mm lens, Prontor-matic shutter, built-in light meter, red green diode light metering.

R2*   **A**

ADOX GOLF IIIA: c1954. 35mm VFR camera, (not to be confused with the folding roll film Golf series), Radionar L f2.8/45mm lens, Prontor 500 shutter, built-in light meter. The most expensive of the 35mm Golf series, using a rare earth glass lens.

R3*   **B**

ADOX POLO: c1959. metal 35mm VFR camera, Adoxar f3.5/45mm lens, Pronto shutter.

R2*   **A**

ADOX POLO IS: c1959, metal and plastic 35mm VFR camera, Radionar L f2.8/45mm lens, Pronto shutter.

R2*   **A**

ADOX POLO IB: c1964, metal and plastic 35mm VFR camera, Adoxar f3.5/45mm lens, Prontor shutter.

R2*   **A**

ADOX POLOMAT: c1959, 35mm VFR camera with built-in coupled light meter, Radionar L f2.8/45mm lens, Prontor LK shutter.

R2*   **A**

ADOX POLOMAT 1: c1959, 35mm VFR camera with built-in coupled light meter, Radionar L f2.8/45mm lens, Prontor 500LK shutter, bright line parallax marking in the VFR.

R2*   **B**

ADOX POLOMAT 2: c1959, 35mm VFR camera with built-in coupled light meter visible in the VFR and on the top plate, Radionar L f2.8/45mm lens, Prontormat shutter.

R2*   **A**

ADOX POLOMATIC 2: c1961, 35mm VFR camera with built-in coupled light meter, Radionar L f2.8/45mm lens, Prontor Lux shutter.

R2*   **A**

ADOX POLOMATIC 3: c1961, 35mm VFR camera with built-in coupled light meter, Radionar L f2.8/45mm lens, Prontormat-S shutter.

R2*   **A**

ADOX POLOMATIC 3S: c1961, 35mm VFR camera with built-in coupled light

meter, Radionar L f2.8/45mm lens, Prontor-Matic shutter, lens opening visible in the VFR.

R2*   **A**

L'AIGLON: c1934. Meniscus lens; single speed shutter; 8 exp, 12 x 14mm on special roll film. Mfd in France.

R3*   **E–**

Agilux Ltd
Croydon, England.

AGIFLASH: c1954. Bakelite covered in leatherette. 8 exp. on 127. Built-in socket for flashbulbs. Detachable flash reflector.

R1*   **A+**

AGIFLEX: c1947. Rigid body SLR for 8 exp. on 120. Leather-covered metal body, based on the Reflex Korelle. Waist-level finder. 80mm f/3.5 Agilux with helical focusing. Shutter 1/25-1/500s. Slight redesign of bayonet to take extra lenses with the Model II in 1949, which also added shutter speeds to 2s. Restyled in 1854 for Model III.

R2*   **C+**

AGIFLEX II: 1949; 6 X 6cm SLR camera;FPS 1/25-1/500s. 12 exp on 120 roll film;

several versions; Models- I £50 II £100 III £150

R2*   **C+**

AGIFOLD: c1956. 12 on 120 folding camera. Built-in uncoupled rangefinder and extinction meter. 75m f/4.5 Agilux Anastigmat. Shutter 1-1/350s. Removable back for easier film loading.

R2*   **C–**

AGIMATIC: c1956. 35mm with uncoupled rangefinder. 45mm f/2.8 Agilux. Shutter 1-1/300s.

R2*   **C**

Aires Camera Industries Co.
Tokyo, Japan.

AIRES 35-IIIL: c1955, 35mm RFR camera, Coral f1.9/45mm coated lens, Seikosha MXL 1-1/500 s, CRF.

R2*   **C–**

AIRES 35 IIIA: c1957, 35mm RFR camera.

R2*   **C–**

AIRES 35-V: c1960, 35mm RFR camera, interchangeable Coral f1.5/4.5cm lens, Seikosha MX shutter 1 – 1/400s, built-in light meter, CRF, bright line fields of view for 50mm and 100mm in VFR.

R3*   **D–**

ACCESSORY LENSES FOR AIRES 35-V:

W/A Coral f3.2/35mm lens: **B+**

Tele Coral f3.5/100mm lens: **C**

A.F.I.O.M.,
Pordenone, Italy.

WEGA: 1950. Cfps, $\frac{1}{20}$ – $\frac{1}{1000}$ sec, Vfr only, no Rfr, flash synch. Screw mount Trixar F3.5/50mm lens. *Only about 1000 cameras are thought to have been made.*

R3*   **F–**

WEGA IIA: 1950-51. Cfps, 1/20 -1/1000 sec, seperate Rfr/Vfr windows, flash synch. Screw mount Trixar F3.5/50mm lens.

R3*   **F**

Air King Products Companies Inc,
New York.

AIR KING CAMERA RADIO: c1948. Combination tube-type radio and plastic 828 roll film camera; finished in brown "lizard-skin".

R3*   **E–**

Aivas and Chauvet,
France.

LE FIN DE SIECLE: c1892. Aplanat f8 lens; 9 x 12cm plates; magazine back.
R4*   **F+**

Charles Alibert,
Paris, France.

PHOTO-SAC A MAIN: c1895. Lady's handbag detective camera; Rapid Rectilinear 150mm f12 lens; non-capping rotary shutter; single exp. 9 x 12cm on dry plates.
R4*   **I**

Alpa –
refer to PIGNONS, S.A.

Alsaphot
(Société Alsacienne d'Optique et de la Photographie), France

DAUPHIN: c1950, simple TLR camera for 6 x 6cm frames on roll film.
R3*   **B**

AJAX: c1950, metal bodied VFR camera for 6 x 6cm frames on roll film, collapsible

Alsar f3.5/75mm lens, Alsaphot shutter, 1 - 1/300s, accessory shoe.
R3*   **B**

CADY: c1950, metal bodied VFR camera for 6 x 6cm frames on roll film, collapsible Alsaphot Anastigmat f6.3/75mm lens, simple shutter, accessory shoe.
R3*   **B**

D'ASSAS: c1950, metal bodied VFR camera for 6 x 6cm frames on roll film, collapsible Boyer Topaz f4.5/75mm lens in Alsaphot shutter, ½₅ – ½₀₀s, tubular VFR, accessory shoe.
R3*   **B**

MAINE: c1957, simple metal bodied 35mm VFR camera, knob advance, Berthiot f2.8/45mm lens in Alsaphot shutter, 1/25 – 1/200s, accessory shoe.
R2*   **A**

MAINE II: c1960, Lever advance instead of wind knob.
R2*   **B**

MAINE IIIA: c1962, with built-in light meter.
R2*   **B**

CYCLOPE: 1950-52, aluminium bodied VFR camera for 6 x 9cm frames on roll film, unique rigid construction using internal mirrors to lengthen the light path, eliminating the need for bellows, making a

solid, compact camera. coated Boyer Saphir f4.5/ 105mm lens, Prontor II shutter to ¼₅s, lens placement makes this camera hard to miss. Designed by Lucien Dodin, father of the split-image RFR, about 1800 made. Though very rare, one or two of these cameras show up at the annual camera fair at Bievre, France.

R3* **F**

CYCLOPE II: 1953. Boyer Saphir f3.5/105mm lens, Prontor II shutter to ½₀₀s, and "Deluxe" finish, *only 200 made*, and these were made against the advice of Mr. Dodin, whose calculations showed that there was too much light fall-off with the lens wide opened at f3.5 for the mirror system to work well.

R4* **G+**

Altissa Kamerwerk,
Dresden, former East Germany

(Post war continuation of Eho-Kamera-Fabrik GmbH, Emil Hofert, Dresden, Germany, see Eho listing for pre-war cameras)

ALTUCA: c1949, metal roll film camera for 6 x 6 frames, collapsible f3.5/75mm lens, simple three speed shutter.

R3* **B**

ALTIX II: c1947 35mm VFR camera for 24 x 24mm frames, f3.5 35mm lens in simple bti shutter. Name written on the camera front. Interesting as a continuation of the pre-war Altissa, pleasing body style, quite rare.

R4* **C–**

ALTIX III: 1950, 35mm VFR camera for 24 x 36mm frames, Meritar f2.9/50mm lens in simple bti shutter. The first full-frame Altix.

R3* **C–**

ALTIX IV: c1951, 35mm VFR camera, now with accessory shoe and flash synch outlet, Trioplan f2.9/50mm lens in Cludor 1 – ½₀₀s or Vebur 1 – ½₅₀ shutter, with and without film reminder dial.

R3* **C–**

ALTIX V: c1957, 35mm VFR camera with interchangeable Trioplan f2.9 or CZ Jena f2.8/50mm lens in Tempor shutter, 1 – 1/250. The first Altix with interchangeable lens, quite rare.

R4* **C–**

ALTIX N: c1958, 35mm VFR camera, interchangeable CZ Jena f2.8 or Trioplan f2.9/50mm lens in Tempor shutter 1 – ½₅₀, new body style, The first Altix to be identified on the camera itself, "Altix-n" on the front or top of the camera.

R2* **C–**

ALTIX-NB: c1958, 35mm VFR camera, interchangeable CZ Jena f2.8 or Trioplan f2.9/50mm lens in Tempor shutter, with the addition of uncoupled built-in light meter.

R2* **C–**

ALTISSA: c1957, all metal box camera for 6 x 6 frames on roll film, top mounted optical finder, simple shutter, Altissar Periscope f8 lens, not to be confused with the pre-war Altissa. This camera was copied by the Chinese and called the Xing Fu.

R2* **C+**

ACCESSORIES FOR ALTIX CAMERAS

Primagon f4.5/35mm lens: **B**

Telefogar f3.5/90mm lens: **B+**

American Advertising & Research Corp.
Chicago, Illinois.

CUB: c1950's. Plastic roll film box camera; meniscus lens and sector shutter; 828 roll film; side comes off to load. Later known as Scenex. Original cost was $15 – less than the cost of a roll of film; also given away as toothpaste premium.

R2*   **A**

American Camera Mfg. C0.
Northboro, Massachusetts.

Founded in 1895 by Thomas Blair, the American Camera Mfg. Co. marketed Buckeye Brand cameras, and also supplied them to E.& H.T. Anthony and Co. In 1896 the company was sold to George Eastman, who wanted control of a number of important patents.

NO. 2 BUCKEYE: c1899. Box roll film camera; 4" x 5" exp on plates. Method of shutter tensioning and arrow in lens opening similar to Blair box cameras.

R2*   **C+**

NO. 1 TOURIST BUCKEYE: c1895. Folding roll film camera; 3½" x 3½" exp on roll film.

R3*   **D+**

American Optical Co. –
refer to SCOVILL MFG. CO.

American Safety Razor Corp.,
Camera Division, New York.

ASR FOTODISC: c1960. Two part camera consisting of film disc and lens mount; 32mm Rapodis-ASR lens; single speed shutter. 8 exp, 22 x 24mm on circular film, 10cm in diameter in special holder.
R4*   **F**

Ansco Inc. (AGFA, G.A.F.),
Binghamton, New York.

In 1902, E. & H. T. Anthony and Company merged with the Scovill and Adams Company, forming the Anthony and Scovill Company; in 1907, the company name was shortened to Ansco. In 1928 the company was merged with Agfa Products Inc. and Agfa Rawfilm Corp. of New York under the name of Agfa Ansco Corp. In 1939 the company name was changed to General Aniline & Film Corp., commonly referred to by its initials, G.A.F. Corp. For simplicity , German Agfa cameras are included in the following listing.

ANTHONY & SCOVILL SOLOGRAPH PLATE CAMERA: c1901. 4" x 5" plate view camera; Scovill & Adams Co. lens and shutter; red bellows.
R3*   **E–**

Anthony & Scovill Roll Film Camera

ANTHONY & SCOVILL STEREO SOLO-GRAPH: c1901. 4" x 6" folding stereo camera; 4" x 6" exp on dry plates.

R3*   **F**

ANTHONY & SCOVILL ROLL FILM CAMERA: c1901. Wollensak lens; wood interior with detailed engraving. Separate roll film back. In 1907 this became the No. 8 Ansco.

R3*   **D+**

ANTHONY & SCOVILL 4" X 5" BOX CAMERA: c1902. No variable aperture control; red window; 6 or 12 exp, 4" x 5" on roll film. In 1907 this became the No. 3 Ansco.

R3*   **C–**

ANTHONY & SOVILL 3¼" X 4¼" BOX CAMERA: c1903; side variable aperture

setting; dual vf; side shutter release; dual pushbutton rear opening; wood interior; 6 or 12 exp, 3¼" x 4¼". In 1907 this became the No. 2 Ansco.

R2*   **C**

ANTHONY & SCOVILL 3¼" X 4¼" BOX CAMERA: c1900; key wind top shutter release; single top vf; rear slide back opening; wood interior; 6 or 12 exp on roll film. In 1902 this became the No. 1 Ansco.

R2*   **C**

NO. 4 ANSCO MODEL D: c1905; Wollensak lens; 3¼" x 4¼" exp on 118 roll film.

R3*   **C–**

DOLLAR BOX CAMERA: c1910; 3½" x 2½" box camera.

R2*   **A**

NO. O BUSTER BROWN CAMERA: c1921. The Buster Brown box camera was available in six basic models plus several special versions covered in coloured leather with polished brass fittings. The #0,2,2A,2C,3,3A are worth about the same.

R3*   **B**

NO. 3A FOLDING BUSTER BROWN CAMERA: c1915; Actuf shutter; 6 or 10 exp, 3¼" x 5½".

R2*   **C+**

NO. 5 ANSCO, MODEL C: roll film camera; horizontal format; red bellows.

R2*   **C–**

ANSCO JR. MODEL A: c1912, 6 or 12 exp, 2¼" x 4¼".

R2*   **C+**

ANSCO JR. MODEL B: c1912, 6 or 12 exp, 2¼" x 4¼"

R2*   **C**

**Vest Pocket
Ansco No. 2**

*Ansco Folding Buster Brown, Junior,
Model A and Model B*

NO. 4 ANSCO: c1912, 6 or 12 exp, 3¼""
x 3¼".

R2*   **C**

NO. 6 ANSCO MODEL D: c1912, 6 or 12
exp, 3¼" x 4¼"

R2*   **C**

NO. 0 ANSCO: c1914, vest pocket
camera; Ansco Anastigmat f6.3 or Modico
Anastigmat f7.5 lens; 1⅝ x 2½" exp; front
pulls straight out.

R2*   **C**

VEST POCKET ANSCO NO. 2: c1914, 6 x
9cm roll film camera; Ansco Anastigmat
lens; Bionic shutter; 8 exp, 6 x 9cm on 120
roll film.

R2*   **B+**

NO. 1A AUTOMATIC CAMERA: c1925,
clockwork motor drive roll film camera;
Ilex Anastigmat f6.3 lens; Ilex Semi-Automatic shutter ½₅-¹⁄₁₀₀ s; 2¾" x 4⅛" exp on D6
or D12 roll film. Spring wound motor automatically advances film after each exp at
rate of approx 1 exp per sec.

R3*   **E**

ANSCO READYSET CAMERA: c1926,
120 roll film folding camera; maroon
leather, brass hardware.

R2*   **C**

NO. 1A READYSET ROYAL: c1926, 116
roll film folding camera; 116 Antar lens;
Readyset shutter I, T; brown ostrich
covering, matching brown bellows.

R2*   **C+**

NO. 1A READYSET SPECIAL: c1926, 116
roll film folding camera; Antar lens;
Readyset shutter I, T and B; dark reddish
brown covering, brown bellows.

R2*   **C–**

NO. 1 READYSET ROYAL: c1926, 120 roll
film folding camera; 120 Antar lens and
shutter; dark tone coloured sealskin
covering, grey bellows.

R2*   **C+**

NO. 1A READYSET ROYAL: c1926, 116
roll film folding camera; Wollensak
Velostigmat f6.3 lens; shutter ¹⁄₁₀-¹⁄₁₀₀ s, I, T;
brown ostrich covering, brown bellows.

R3*   **C+**

PHOTO-VANITY: c1926, vanity-case type
detective camera; containers for rouge,
powder and lipstick; small Ansco box
camera fitted; operates through exterior of
case. 8 exp, 4 x 6.5cm on 127 roll film.

R4*   **G+**

MEMO (1927): c1927,
half-frame
35mm box
camera; Ilex-
Ansco Cinemat
40mm f6.3
lens; Ilex
shutter ¹⁄₂₅-¹⁄₁₀₀ s.
Rapid film shift
mechanism.
The Memo
used special
cassettes, origi-
nally wood and
later metal.

R2*   **D**

OFFICIAL BOY SCOUT MEMO CAMERA:
c1927, wooden bodied, olive drab finish,
with boy Scout insignia, miniature camera;
50 exp, 18 x 23mm on 35mm film.

R3*   **E+**

BILLY I: c1928, folding VFR camera for 6
x 9cm frames on roll film, Igestar 105mm
f8.8 lens; Agfa shutter ¹⁄₂₅-¹⁄₁₀₀s, squarish
body ends make this camera easy to identify.

R3*   **A**

BILLY II: c1930s, folding VFR camera for
6 x 9cm frames on roll film, Agfa Anastigmat f7.7 lens; Agfa shutter ¹⁄₂₅- ¹⁄₁₀₀s.

R2*   **A**

BILLETTE F4.5: c1930s, folding VFR
camera for 6 x 9cm frames on roll film,
either Oppar or Solinar Anastigmat f4.5
lens, Compur shutter, the top of the line
"Billy".

R3*   **A**

BILLY RECORD 8.8: c1930s, folding VFR camera for 6 x 9cm frames on roll film, Igestar f8.8/10cm lens, Automat shutter.

R2*   **A**

BILLY RECORD 7.7: c1930s, folding VFR camera for 6 x 9cm frames on roll film, Igestar f7.7/10cm lens, Automat or Automat S shutter.

R2*   **A**

BILLY RECORD 6.3: c1930s, folding VFR camera for 6 x 9cm frames on roll film, Igestar f6.3/10cm lens, Vario or Pronto S shutter.

R2*   **A**

BILLY RECORD 4.5: c1930s, folding VFR camera for 6 x 9cm frames on roll film, Apolar f4.5/10.5cm lens, Prontor II-S shutter.

R2*   **B**

BILLY COMPUR: c1935, folding VFR camera for 6 x 9cm frames on roll film, Apotar or Solinar f4.5/10.5cm lens, Compur or Compur Rapid shutter.

R2*   **B**

AGFA RECORD I: c1950s, folding VFR camera for 6 x 9cm frames on roll film, Agnar f6.3 or f4.5/105mm lens, Vario or Pronto shutter, with and without accessory shoe or body mounted shutter release.

R3*   **B**

AGFA RECORD III: c1950s folding RFR camera for 6 x 9cm frames on roll film, Solinar f4.5/105mm lens, Synchro Compur shutter, accessory shoe, built-in un-coupled RFR, body mounted shutter release

R3*   **D**

TROLITA: c1938, plastic folding VFR camera for 6 x 9cm or 6 x 4.5fcm frames on roll film, Apotar f4.5/10.5cm lens, Compur or Prontor II shutter. Produced at the same time as the Trolix box camera (AS156) from "Trolit", a kind of thermo plastic.

R3*   **C–**

STANDARD 6 X 9: c1930s, metal folding VFR camera for 6 x 9cm frames on roll film, marked "Standard" on the lens stand, Anastigmat f4.5 or 6.3/105mm lens, Automat shutter.

R3*   **A**

STANDARD DE LUXE: c1930, 6 x 9cm folding camera; Agfa Anastigmat f6.3/105mm lens; 6 x 9cm plates.

R2*   **C+**

ANSCO MEMORY KIT: c1930, consists of No. 1 Readyset Royal camera in ostrich covering, instruction book, room for 4 rolls of film in walnut wood gift box.

R3*   **E+**

AGFA ANSCO READYSET MOROCCAN CAMERA: c1930's, 120 roll film folding camera; Antar lens; blue bellows, embossed blue Moroccan leather.

R3*   **D+**

AGFA ANSCO READYSET TRAVELER: c1930's. Antar lenses; cloth covered in combination stripes, grey bellows; two models for 120 and 115 roll film.

R2*   **C–**

ANSCO VEST POCKET READYSET 127 CAMERA: c1930's. Wollensak lens; 5 colours available; orange, blue, green, red and turquoise.

R2*   **C+**

AGFA ANSCO VIEW: c1939. 5" x 7" view camera; Wollensak Verito Portrait lens.

R3*   **E**

AGFA FLEXILETTE: 1960. 35mm twin lens reflex with waist-level finder. 45mm f2.8 Color Apotar lenses in Prontor shutter. 1-1/500s.

R2*   **D**

MEMO (1940): c1940. 35mm folding camera; Agfa Memar 50mm f3.5 lens;

Ansco shutter ½-¹⁄₂₀₀ s. Rapid shift film mechanism.

R2*   **C+**

SPEEDEX: c1940, 120 roll film folding camera; 85mm f4.5 lens; 12 exp, 2¼" x 2¼" on 120 roll film.

R2*   **B–**

AUTOMATIC REFLEX: c1947, 2¼" x 2¼" TLR; Ansco Anastigmat 83mm f3.5 coated lens; Ansco shutter 1-¹⁄₄₀₀ s; 12 exp, 2¼" x 2¼" on 120 roll film. Eye-level focusing, built-in magnifying lens for critical focus.

The Automatic Reflex was originally introduced in 1947 without flash synch. The 1949 version had factory installed flash synch for class F bulbs.

R3*   **D+**

ISOLAR: c1930s, Agfa Solinar 135mm f4.5 lens; Compur shutter; double extension bellows; ground glass back; 9 x 12cm plates.

R2*   **B**

KARAT 3.5: c1937, 35mm folding VFR camera, Solinar f3.5/5cm lens, Compur Rapid shutter, 12 exposures on special Agfa cartridges, also available post-war as the "Agfa 12/3.5".

R3*   **C–**

KARAT 4.5: c1935, 35mm folding VFR camera, Agfa Oppar 5.5cm f4.5 lens, Vario shutter ½5-¼25 s, 12 exposures on special Agfa cartridges.

R2*   **B+**

KARAT 6.3: c1934, 35mm folding VFR camera, Anastigmat-Igestar f6.3/5cm lens,Vario shutter, ½5-¼00s,12 exposures on special Agfa cartridges.

R2*   **C–**

KARAT 12/2.8: c1946, folding RFR camera for 12 exposures on special Agfa cartridges, Xenar f2.8/50mm lens, Compur Rapid shutter, this camera became the Karat 36 of 1949.

R3*   **C**

KARAT 36: c1949, 35mm folding RFR camera, Soligon, Heligon or Xenar f2.8/50mm coated lens; Synchro-Compur shutter 1-¼00s, CRF. Used orthodox 35mm in normal cassettes.

R2*   **D**

Karat 36

KARAT IV; c.1959, 35mm folding RFR camera; Agfa Solinar f2 or f2.8/50mm coated lens; prontor SVS shutter, 1 – ¼00s redesigned top plate, with centred accessory shoe.

R2*   **D**

AGFA OPTIMA I: c1961. 35mm camera. Auto exposure by red/green indicators in viewfinder. Metal body, leatherette covered. 45mm f2.8 Color Agnar and Prontorlux shutter, 1/30-1/500s.

R2*   **C**

AGFA OPTIMA II: c1961. Similar to first model with 45mm f2.8 Color Apotar and Prontormator shutter. First pressure of release automatically selects between 1/30s and 1/250s with the appropriate aperture.

R2*   **C**

AGFA OPTIMA III: c1961. Similar to second model with 45mm f2.8 Color Apotar and Compur shutter 1/30-1/500s. Apertures and speeds selected automatically.

R2*   **C**

AGFA OPTIMA IIIS: c1961. Similar to Optima III with rangefinder and parallax compensation in the viewfinder.

R2*   **C**

AGFA OPTIMA REFLEX: 1961. 35mm twin lens reflex with eye-level viewfinder. Twin 45mm f2.8 Color Apotar coated lenses in Prontor Special shutter, 1/30-1/250s. Autoexposure with low light indicator in viewfinder.

R2*   **D+**

AGFA SILETTE: c1957, metal 35mm VFR camera, Colour Apotar f2.8/45mm lens, Prontor SVS shutter, lever advance, top plate mounted shutter release, centred VFR and accessory shoe, also exists with off centre bright line finder.

R2*   **C+**

AGFA AMBI SILETTE: c1950s, metal 35mm RFR camera with interchangeable Colour Solinar f2.8/50mm lens, Synchro Compur shutter, VFR with fields of view for 35mm, 50mm, and 90mm.

R3*   **D**

LENSES FOR AMBI SILETTE:

Colour Ambion f4/35mm lens: **C–**

Colour Telinear f4/90mm lens: **C–**

AGFA SILETTE I: c1962, metal 35mm VFR camera, Colour Agnar f2.8/45mm lens, Prontor 125 shutter, off-centre VFR and accessory shoe, front mounted shutter release, new square cornered design.

R2*   **B–**

AGFA SILETTE L: c1957, metal 35mm VFR camera, Colour Solinar f2.8/50mm lens, Compur Rapid shutter, built-in light meter, lever advance, top plate mounted shutter release, off centre VFR and accessory shoe.

R2*   **B+**

AGFA SILETTE L: c1962, metal 35mm VFR camera, Colour Apotar f2.8/45mm lens, Prontor 125 shutter, built-in coupled light meter, off-centre VFR, centred accessory shoe, front mounted shutter release, new square cornered design.

R2*   **B–**

AGFA SILETTE SL: c1957, metal 35mm VFR camera, Colour Solinar f2.8/50mm lens, Compur Rapid shutter, built-in light meter for match needle metering, lever advance, top plate mounted shutter release, off centre VFR and accessory shoe.

R2*   **C–**

AGFA SILETTE LK: c1958, metal 35mm VFR camera, Colour Apotar f2.8/50mm lens, Prontor LK shutter, built-in coupled light meter, lever advance, top plate mounted shutter release, off centre VFR and accessory shoe.

R2*   **C–**

AGFA SUPER SILETTE: c1959, metal 35mm RFR camera, Colour-Solinar f2.8/50mm or Soligon f2/50mm lens, Synchro Compur shutter, built-in light meter, CRF, off-centre VFR, centred accessory shoe, front mounted shutter release, new square cornered design.

R3*   **C–**

AGFA SUPER SILETTE LK: c1960s, metal 35mm RFR camera, Colour Apotar f2.8/45mm lens, Prontor 125 shutter, built-in coupled light meter controls aperture, CRF, off-centre VFR, centred accessory shoe, front mounted shutter release, new square cornered design.

R2*   **C–**

AGFA SILETTE AUTOMATIC: metal 35mm RFR camera, Colour-Solinar f2.8/50mm lens, Prontor SLV shutter, built-in light meter for match needle metering, CRF, off-centre VFR and accessory shoe, top plate mounted shutter release.

R3* **C–**

AGFA SILETTE F: c1963, metal 35mm VFR camera, Colour Agnar f2.8/45mm lens, Prontor 125 shutter, flash for AG-1 bulbs, off-centre VFR , front mounted shutter release, square cornered design.

R2* **B–**

AGFA SILETTE RAPID I: c1965, metal 35mm VFR camera using special Agfa Rapid cassettes, Colour Agnar f2.8/45mm lens, Parator shutter, like (AS190).

R2* **B–**

AGFA SILETTE F: c1965, metal 35mm VFR camera using special Agfa Rapid cassettes, Colour Agnar f2.8/45mm lens, Parator shutter, built-in flash for AG-1 bulbs.

R2* **B–**

AGFA SILETTE RAPID L: c1962, metal 35mm VFR camera using special Agfa Rapid cassettes, Colour Apotar f2.8/45mm lens, Prontor 250 shutter, built-in coupled light meter.

R2* **B–**

AGFA SOLINETTE II:1954. 35mm folding camera. Light alloy die casting covered with grained plastic. 50mm f3.5 Apotar in Prontor SV shutter, 1-1/300s + B. Button on the back doubles as exp counter reset and to free sprockets for rewinding.

R2* **C+**

AGFA ISOLA: c1950s, horizontally styled metal VFR camera for 6 x 6cm frames on 120 roll film,collapsible Agnar f6.3/75mm lens, Singlo-2 shutter, body mounted shutter release.

R2* **B–**

AGFA ISOLA I: c1950s, horizontally styled metal VFR camera for 6 x 6cm frames on 120 roll film, collapsible meniscus lens and simple shutter, body mounted shutter release.

R2* **B–**

AGFA ISOLY I: c1960s, metal VFR camera for 4 x 4cm frames on 120 roll film, Achromat lens, simple shutter.

R2* **B–**

AGFA ISOLY II: c1960s, metal VFR camera for 4 x 4cm frames on 120 roll film, Agnar f6.3/55mm lens, Single shutter.

R2* **B–**

AGFA ISOLY III: c1960s, metal VFR camera for 4 x 4cm frames on 120 roll film, Colour Apotar f3.9/60mm lens, Pronto shutter.

R2* **B–**

AGFA-BOX: c1930s, metal box camera for 6 x 9cm frames on roll film, three position indicator for focusing.

R1* **B–**

AGFA TROLIX-BOX: c1938, plastic box camera for 6 x 9cm frames on roll film, meniscus lens, simple shutter, metal carrying handle, Produced at the same time as the Trolita folding camera, from "Trolit", a kind of thermo plastic.

R3* **C**

AGFA METALBOX-45: c1938, metal box camera for 6 x 9cm frames on roll film, meniscus lens, simple shutter.

R1* **B–**

AGFA CADET-A8: c1937, metal box camera for 6 x 4.5cm frames on roll film, meniscus lens, simple shutter.

R2* **B–**

AGFA SYNCHRO-BOX: c1949, metal box camera for 6 x 9cm frames on 120 roll film, built-in yellow filter.

R1*　　　　　　　　**B–**

AGFA CLACK: c1950s, horizontally styled metal VFR camera, 6 x 9cm frames on roll film, simple lens and shutter.

R2*　　　　　　　　**B–**

AGFA HELI-CLACK 9 X 12: c1930s, folding plate camera for 9 x 12cm plates, Heliar f4.5/10.5cm lens, Compur shutter.

R3*　　　　　　　　**C+**

AGFA HELI-CLACK 6.5 X 9: c1930's, horizontally styled folding plate camera for 6.5 x 9cm plates, Agfa Anastigmat f4.5/105mm lens, Agfa shutter.

R3*　　　　　　　　**B–**

AGFA ISORETTE: c1935, folding VFR camera for 6 x 6cm or 6 x 4.5cm frames on roll film, many lens/shutter combinations, among which are Igestar f6.3/70mm lens, Vario shutter and Apotar f4.5/70mm lens, Compur shutter. Not to be confused with the post-war "Isolette".

R3*　　　　　　　　**C**

AGFA ISOLETTE 6 X 6: c1949, folding VFR camera for 6 x 6cm frames on roll film, Apotar f4.5/85mm lens, Prontor shutter, centre mounted accessory shoe, body mounted shutter release.

R3*　　　　　　　　**B–**

AGFA ISOLETTE 4.5X6: c1949, folding VFR camera for 6 x 4.5cm frames on roll film, Solinar f4.5/80mm lens, Compur Rapid shutter, body mounted shutter release.

R3*　　　　　　　　**C+**

AGFA ISOLETTE II: c1950s, folding VFR camera for 6 x 6cm on roll film, Apotar f4.5/85mm lens, Prontor shutter, *new designed top plate*, body mounted release.

R2*　　　　　　　　**B–**

AGFA ISOLETTE III: c1950s, folding RFR camera for 6 x 6cm frames on roll film, *uncoupled* RFR, Apotar or Solinar f4.5/85mm lens, Prontor or Synchro Compur shutter, body mounted shutter release.

R3*　　　　　　　　**C+**

AGFA ISOLETTE V: c1950s, folding VFR camera for 6 x 6cm frames on roll film. Agnar f4.5/80mm lens, Vario shutter, *no body mounted shutter release, off-centre mounted accessory shoe.*

R3*　　　　　　　　**B–**

AGFA SUPER ISOLETTE: c1950s, folding RFR camera for 6 x 6cm frames on roll film, CRFR, Solinar f3.5/85mm lens, Synchro Compur shutter, body mounted shutter release, no more ruby window, automatic frame counting.

R3*　　　　　　　　**C–**

ISOLETTE L: c1950s, folding VFR camera for 6 x 6cm frames on roll film, or 24 x 36mm frames on special paperbacked Agfa film, Colour Apotar f4.5/85mm lens; Pronto shutter; built-in light meter.

R2*　　　　　　　　**C+**

AGFA SOLINETTE: c1952, folding 35mm VFR camera, Apotar f3.5/5cm lens, Prontor SV shutter, accessory shoe.

R2*　　　　　　　　**B–**

AGFA SOLINETTE II: 35mm folding camera. Light alloy die casting covered with grained plastic. 50mm f/3.5 Apotar in Prontor SV shutter, 1-1/300s+B. Button on the back doubles as exposure counter reset and to free sprockets for rewinding.

R2*　　　　　　　　**C+**

AGFA SUPER SOLINETTE: c1953, folding 35mm RFR camera, CRF, Solinar f3.5/50mm lens, Synchro Compur shutter, accessory shoe.

R3*　　　　　　　　**C+**

AGFA CLICK-I: c1959, plastic bodied horizontally styled box type camera, 6 x 6cm frames on 120 roll film, meniscus lens, simple shutter.

R1* **B–**

AGFA CLICK-II: c1959, plastic bodied horizontally styled box type camera, 6 x 6cm frames on 120 roll film, meniscus lens, simple shutter, built-in close-up lens.

R1* **B–**

MEMO AUTOMATIC (1964): c1964. Half-frame 35mm motor drive camera; Memar f2.8 coated lens; fixed shutter speed. Selenium photo-electric exp meter controls diaphragm for correct exp. Spring wound motor cycles 10-15 exp per wind at a rate of about 1 exp per s. Mfd. by Ricoh, Japan for G.A.F., New York.

R2* **C+**

AGFA FLEXILETTE: 35mm twin lens reflex with waist-level finder. 45mm f/2.8 Color Apotar lenses in Prontor shutter. 1-1/500s.

R2* **C+**

E. & H. T. Anthony & Company,
New York.

Edward Anthony opened his first daguerreotype studio in 1841, in New York City. In 1842, he and J. M. Edwards established a daguerreotype portrait studio in Washington D.C., where they photographed all the members of Congress, as well as many other prominent citizens. In 1843 Anthony established the National Miniature Gallery in New York City, where he operated a studio and sold photographic equipment and supplies. The company name changed many times: it was known as Edward Anthony and Howard Chilton from 1842 to 1843; as Anthony, Edwards & Chilton in 1843; as Anthony, Edwards & Co. from 1844 to 1845; Anthony, Edwards & Clark from 1844 to 1845; as Anthony Clark & Co. from 1845 to 1847; and as Edward Anthony from 1847 to 1862.

From 1849 to 1851, Edward Anthony operated his studio and manufactured equipment and supplies in New York City. During this time, Mathew Brady's studio was located in the same building. Anthony moved uptown in 1851, and opened his new offices and a warehouse at 308 Broadway. At the same time he also opened a factory in the city. The Anthony firm, at this time was one of the largest importers and manufacturers of photographic equipment and supplies in the United States.

Anthony's brother joined the company in 1853. In 1862, the name of the company was changed to Edward & Henry T. Anthony and Company, and later to E. & H. T. Anthony and Company. In 1869, the firm moved to 591 Broadway. In 1880, E. & H. T. Anthony and Company became agents to sell dry plates for George Eastman; in 1888, they began marketing the world's first flexible base film. The management of the company changed at this time, both Anthony brothers having died by 1888.

In 1902, E. & H. T. Anthony and Company merged with the Scovill and Adams Company, forming the Anthony and Scovill Company; the manufacturing facilities were transferred to Binghamton, New York. In 1907, the company name was shortened to Ansco.

ANTHONY 4 GEM TUBE CARTE DE VISITE CAMERA:

c1860, wet plate outfit with cherry wood stand; single early track. With plate holder with glass corners, dipper, dipping tank and box of early colouring dyes.

R4*   **I–**

ANTHONY VICTORIA FERROTYPE CAMERA:

c1879, four tube 5" x 7" multiple ferrotype camera; four Darlot lenses, 1, 2, 4 or 8 exp on a 5" x 7" plate. Patent perfection stand invented by L. H. Stoddard.

R4*   **H**

ANTHONY 8" X 10" UNIVERSAL PORTRAIT AND FERROTYPE CAMERA:

c1872; 4 Darlot Petzval 6½" f4 lenses; rubber bellows. 8" x 10" wet plate holder with glass corners specially fitted with 7" x 10" and 5" x 7" inserts: takes 1 or 4 exp on an 8" x 10" plate; 8 exp on a 7" x 10" plate; 4 or 8 exp on a 5" x 7" plate.

R4*   **E**

ANTHONY CLIMAX 8" X 10" VIEW AND PORTRAIT CAMERA:

c1872,; Darlot stereo lenses in adjustable lens board; lever focusing screw; double swing back; revolving 5" x 7" back. Ivory label, multiple attachments, separate ground glass frame. Early elevating stand.

R4*   **G+**

ANTHONY EQUIPMENT NO. 2:

c1881; 5" x 7" view camera; Prosh triplex lens and shutter; double dry plate holder. Early model was finished in black ebony. Rare.

R4*   **F**

ANTHONY EQUIPMENT NO. 3:

c1881; 5" x 8" dry plate camera for single or stereo exp; pair of E & A single achromatic lenses; 5" x 8" double dry plate holder; black ebony construction. Original price $15 with tripod and case.

R4*   **F+**

ANTHONY 11" X 14" NOVEL VIEW PLATE CAMERA:

c1885; (preceded Patent Novellette); E. & A. Universal finder; 10 sizes: 4" x 5" to 18" x 22". Anthony unjointed wood tripod. The bellows could rotate from a horizontal to vertical format. Patent February 20, 1883.

R3*   **G**

ANTHONY 5" X 8" NOVEL VIEW: c1885; 5" x 8" view camera; Prosh Duplex lens and shutter; double swing. Early version of revolving back. 10 sizes: 4" x 5" to 18" x 22".

R3*   **E+**

ANTHONY 4" X 5" PATENT NOVEL-LETTE VIEW CAMERA: c1887. 4" x 5" view camera; E.A. Rapid No. 1 lens; water-house stops; Anthony's drop shutter; solid wood bed..

R4*   **F**

ANTHONY PATENT BIJOU 3¼" X 4¼" CAMERA: c1884; 3¼" x 4¼" view camera; E. A. No. 1 Hemispherical lens; water-house stops. Available with or without swing back; polished mahogany with brass fittings. Camera in photograph is fitted with an optional guillotone shutter. Smallest Anthony camera: dimensions, 5" x 5" x 3½"; weight, 14½ ounces.

R4*   **F–**

ANTHONY ENGLISH STYLE COMPACT CAMERA: c1888, 5" x 8" compact view camera; reversible back; 16" bellows extension; telescopic bed for long focus lenses; folded size, 9⅛" x 9⅛" x 3⅛". 4 sizes: 5" x 7" to 8" x 10".

R3*   **F–**

ANTHONY COOPER UNIVERSAL ENLARGING LANTERN: c1887, used as an 8" x 10" enlarging camera, copying camera, portrait camera or magic lantern. The kerosene burner lamp and condensers were removed for daylight enlarging. Patent by Cooper & Lewis.

R4*   **F–**

ANTHONY'S PHANTOM CAMERA: 8" x 10" view camera; revolving back using key hole slots. 5 sizes: 4¼" x 6½" to 8" x 10". C 1888.

R4*   **E+**

ANTHONY VINCENT 8" X 10": c 1890, cone shaped Anthony single combination lens; reversible back; telescoping bed. 4 sizes: 5" x 7" to 8" x 10".

R3*   **F–**

SCHMID'S PATENT DETECTIVE CAMERA, ORIGINAL MODEL: c1883, box-type detective camera. 6 sizes: 8 x 10.5cm; 10.5 x 12.5cm; 11.5 x 16.5cm; 12.5 x 20cm; 16.5 x 21.5cm; 20 x 25cm on plates. c1882 non folding handle. First American camera designed to be hand held.

R5*   **I–**

SCHMID'S PATENT DETECTIVE CAMERA, SECOND MODEL: c1885, 3¼" x 4¼" detective camera; E. Anthony Rapid Rectilinear 6½" f8 lens; interchangeable waterhouse stops; variable speed rotary shutter; brass handle that folds down. 6 sizes, 3¼" x 4¼" to 8" x 10". Patent 1883.

R5* **I–**

SCHMID'S PATENT DETECTIVE CAMERA – THIRD CAMERA: c1886, 4" x 5" camera; removable back; side focusing lever; takes Eastman-Walker roll holder.

R5* **I–**

ANTHONY CLIMAX DETECTIVE CAMERA: c1885-89. wood finish detective camera; lenses of varying focal length used without removing shutter. Camera could be fitted in patent satchel handbag. 4" x 5" exp (larger sizes made to order).

R4* **G+**

ANTHONY'S CLIMAX DETECTIVE CAMERA: c1888. Leather covered detective camera; lenses of varying focal length; separate rear compartment was available

with 5 double holders; 4" x 5" exp (larger sizes made to order).

R4* **G–**

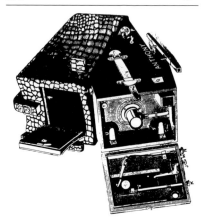

ANTHONY'S SATCHEL DETECTIVE CAMERA: c1887. Satchel-type detective camera; Dallmeyer Rapid Rectilinear lens; guillotine shutter. A satchel covered in alligator skin contained a Climax Detective Camera. 4" x 5" exp on plates.

R5* **J+**

ANTHONY PDQ (PHOTOGRAPHY DONE QUICKLY): c1890, 4" x 5" detective camera; E & A single achromatic No. 1 lens, rotating stops; variable speed shutter and focusing; removable ground glass; reversible finder.

R4* **F+**

ANTHONY LILLIPUT DETECTIVE CAMERA: c1886. Detective camera in small leather handbag; 65mm f8 lens; covers a 60 degree angle; variable speed sector shutter; 6 exp, 2½" x 2½" on glass plates or film; camera measures 4" x 4" x 6".

R4* **H**

ANTHONY MODEL MANHATTAN: c1886, 5" x 8" mahogany view camera; single achromatic EA nickel plated lens; Anthony nonpareil shutter. Inexpensive model: lacks rising front; does not fold, has

swings. 3 sizes: 4" x 5" to 5" x 8" and stereo.

R3*   **E**

the internal separation. Non stereo models are about 40%-50% less expensive.

R4*   **F+**

ANTHONY MODEL 2B: c1888, 5" x 8" view camera; Garland shutter; rising front; swing back; dark mahogany construction with brass fittings. 6 sizes: 4" x 5" to 8" x 10".

R4*   **E**

ANTHONY CHAMPION 8B: c1888. 8" x 10" view camera; E & A cone shaped single achromatic No. 4 lens; swing back; back bed lock, folding bed with patent clamps (pat. February 20, 1888); mahogany finish with brass fitting; holder, case.

R4*   **E**

ANTHONY CHAMPION MODEL 5" X 8" STEREO CAMERA: c1885. 5" x 8" stereo view camera; swing back; bed locks from rear; stereo patent lamp hooks. The Anthony Champion could also be used as a non-stereo camera by changing to a single center mounted lens and removing

ANTHONY CHAMPION MODEL 5" X 7" VIEW CAMERA: c1888. 5" x 7" view camera; Darlot lens; rotating stops; swing back; patent clamp hooks; rear bed locks. 6 sizes and stereo format.

R3*   **F+**

ANTHONY MODEL NPA: c1888. 5" x 8" stereo camera; EA wide angle nickel plated lens; rising front; patent swing back; patent clamp hooks; Anthony Climax tripod; Anthony Universal finder. Complete outfit:

R4*   **F–**

Antony Model NPA

ANTHONY PATENT NOVELETTE VIEW CAMERA c1890.
The Novelette used the same rotating bellows system as the Novel to change from horizontal to vertical format. Normally fitted with an achromatic lens. Cherry or walnut natural wood finish. Available in sizes from 4x5 to 11x14 inches. There were various models fitted with minimum to elaborate tilts and swings.

R3*   **F–**

ANTHONY PATENT NOVELLETTE VIEW CAMERA:
8" x 10" view camera; J. Dallmeyer R.R. lens; revolving bellows; E & A Universal finder; double swing back; patent clamp hooks; polished mahogany construction. 7 sizes: 4" x 5" to 11" x 14". Original price, $33. Patent February 20, 1888.

R4*   **E+**

ANTHONY PATENT NOVELETTE STEREO CAMERA c1890
This camera has been fitted with optional stereo lenses, and an internal separator. When removed

and a single lens installed, it was a regular view camera.

R4*   **G**

ANTHONY VICTOR CAMERA: c1888.
Anthony single combination wide angle lens; rising front; single swing; double rack and pinion movement; patent swing back. Eclipse double plate holder. 6 sizes: 4" x 5" to 8" x 10".

R4*   **E+**

ANTHONY FAIRY CAMERA:
c1890. 5" x 8" view camera; EA nickel lens; rack, cog wheel and pinion focusing; Anthony

Universal wood finder; reversible back; key hole slots for revolving back; polished Circassian walnut wood. 6 sizes: 4" x 5" to 8" x 10". Early wood stand.

R4* **E+**

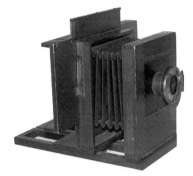

CLIMAX MULTIPLYING CAMERA: c1901. 5" x 7" camera; single Darlot portrait tube; multiple exp on 5" x 7" plate.

R4* **F–**

ANTHONY KNICKERBOCKER CAMERA: c1891. 5" x 7" view camera; EA single achromatic nickel plate lens; reversible back single swing; back focus; nickel plated fittings. 4 sizes: 5" x 7" to 8" x 10".

R3* **E+**

ANTHONY NORMANDIE CAMERA: c1890. 6½" x 8½" view camera; Darlot lens; back focus; revolving stops; single swing; reversible back. 9 sizes: 4" x 5" to 14" x 17".

R4* **E+**

THE KLONDIKE CAMERA: c1898, box plate camera; adjustable shutter speeds; adjustable diaphragm; dry plates, 3¼" x 4¼".

R4* **D+**

ANTHONY CLIMAX PORTRAIT CAMERA: c1888, brass lens; double swing back; bed extends to 49". Anthony Automatic Cabinet Attachment: sliding ground glass replaced by plate holder. c 1888. Complete with No. 1 New York Camera and stand:

R2* **F–**

ANTHONY 4" X 5" CLIMAX ENLARGING CAMERA: c1890, reducing or copying camera; reversible back; lens can be used inside or outside camera. 9 sizes: 4" x 5" to 20" x 24".

R3*   **E**

ANTHONY VIEW CAMERA: c1900, 6½" x 8½" view camera; homocentric lens; Kolios shutter; nickel plated fittings. Ivory label marked: E. & H. T. Anthony, New York, Chicago.

R3*   **E–**

Anthony Accesssories

Anthony CDV Albums: 2 versions. C 1860's. EACH   **C**

ANTHONY CLIFTON VIEW CAMERA: c1901. Anthony drop shutter; double swing back and front; front and back focus; reversible back; red bellows. 6 sizes: 5" x 7" to 14" x 17".

R4*   **E**

ANTHONY LANTERN SLIDE CAMERA: c1888, for copying negatives 4" x 5" or smaller on 3¼" x 4¼" plates. Revolving ground glass frame; folding extension bed.

R4*   **E**

FUMING BOX FOR ALBUMEN PAPER: c1875, mahogany construction with lead lined drawers. Used ammonia to increase the speed of albumen paper (first suggested by H. T. Anthony in 1862).

R4*   **H+**

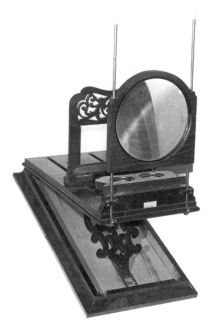

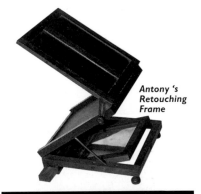

Antony 's Retouching Frame

ANTHONY GRAPHOSCOPE: c1870's, viewer for photos and stereo cards.

R3*   **E**

DRY PLATES: c1888, distributed by E. & H.T. Anthony for the Eastman Dry Plate Co.

R4*   **B**

ANTHONY'S CLIMAX KEROSENE DARK ROOM LANTERN: c1888, has three large illuminating surfaces with reflector.

R3*   **C+**

ANTHONY'S RETOUCHING FRAME: c1885, for retouching negatives; has drawer for brushes, stippling pencils and reflecting mirror.

R2*   **D**

Karl Arnold,
Marienberg, Germany.

KARMA FLEX 4 X 4 MODEL II: c1932, SLR type for 4cm x 4cm frames on roll film.Vidar or Victor or Regulyt f4.5/60mm lens, guillotine shutter ½25 -⅟100s.

R3*   **F–**

KARMA FLEX 4 X 4 MODEL I: c1932, TLR type box camera (fixed focus) for 4cm x 4cm frames on roll film "Spezial" f9 lens, simple shutter .

R3*   **F**

KARMA FLEX 6 X 6 MODEL II: c1932, TLR for 6cm x 6cm frames on roll film, Victar or Pololyt f3.5/75mm lens, CPFS to 1/500s.

R4*   **E–**

KARMA FLEX 6 X 6 MODEL I: c1932, TLR type box camera (fixed focus) for 6cm x 6cm frames on roll film, "Spezial" f7.7 lens, simple shutter, waistlevel VFR convertible to eyelevel VFR.

R4*   **E**

KARMA: c1932, RFR camera for 6cm x 6cm frames on roll film, Victar or Pololyt f3.5/75mm lens, CPFS to ⅟500s, basically the bottom half of a Karma Flex 6 x 6 model II, with tubular VFR and uncoupled RFR.

R4*   **E**

Apparate & Kamerabau
Friedrichshafen, Germany

AKAREX I: c1954, 35mm RFR camera, non-interchangeable Isco Westar f3.5/45mm lens in either Prontor, ½5 – ½00s or Prontor SVS 1 – ⅓00s shutters, lever wind.

R3*   **C**

AKAREX III; c1955 35mm RFR camera with interchangeable lens/VFR assemblies, Isco Westar f3.5/35mm or Schneider Xenon f2/50mm lens, Synchro Compur 1 – 500s shutter. Schnieider 35mm and 90mm accessory lenses with attached finders were available.

R3*   **C**

AKARETTE MODEL "O"; 1949-50, black metal bodied 35mm VFR camera with interchangeable lens, Schneider Xenar f3.5/50mm, Schneider Xenar f2.8/45mm or Schneider Xenon f2/50mm normal lens., behind the lens leaf shutter ½5 – ½00s, two viewfinders for fields of view corresponding to 35mm, 50mm, and 75mm, f4.5/35mm lens and f3.5/75mm lenses available, see (AP003) and (AP004).

R3*   **C+**

AKARETTE MODEL II 1950-54, metal bodied 35mm VFR camera with inter-changeable lens, Schneider Xenar f3.5/50mm, Schneider Xenar f2.8/45mm or Schneider Xenon f2/50mm normal lens, behind the lens leaf shutter ½5 – ½00s, two

viewfinders for fields of view corresponding to 35mm, 50mm, and 75mm, selector lever on the front of the camera marked "50mm" and "75mm" allows blocking one of the VFR windows. f4.5/35mm lens, and f3.5/75mm lenses available. Much like the model "O", with the addition of chrome trim, vrf selector lever and self timer.

R3*   **C+**

AKARELLE: 1954-55, metal bodied 35mm VFR camera with interchangeable lens, Schneider Xenar f3.5/50mm, Schneider Xenar f2.8/45mm or Schneider Xenon f2/50mm normal lens, Prontor S shutter ½5 – ½00s, two viewfinders for fields of view corresponding to 35mm, 50mm, and 90mm, selector lever on the front of the camera marked "50mm" and "90mm". f4.5/35mm lens, and f3.5/90mm lenses available. Much like the Akarette model II, with the addition of lever wind, front mounted strap lugs and 90mm field of view VFR. Late cameras have no selection lever, but rather fields marked in the VFR.

R3*   **C+**

AKARELLE AUTOMATIC S: c1960, 35mm VFR camera, non-interchangeable Isco Westanar f2.8/45mm lens, built-in light-meter coupled to shutter, providing auto-matic exposure, speed selected indicated in the VFR.

R2*   **C–**

Akarelle V: c1961, simple 35mm VFR camera, Arretar f2.8/45mm lens, Vario Shutter, ⅕ – ⅟₂₀₀s

R2*   **B**

AKARELLE W: c1963, 35mm VFR camera with interchangeable Colour-Wilon f2.8/50mm lens, Prontor SVS shutter, 1 – ⅟₃₀₀s, Lineogon f3.5/35mm WA accessory lens w/shoe mount wide angle viewer available. (price is for camera with two lenses and WA VFR.)

R3*   **C**

ARETTE 1A: 1956. 35mm VFR camera. 45mm f2.8 Westar Prontor-SVS shutter 1-1/300s + B. Synch for bulb and electronic flash.

R3*   **C**

ARETTE-IB: c1956, 35mm VFR camera with non interchangeable Westar or Xenar f2.8/45mm lens, Prontor SVS shutter, 1 – ⅟₃₀₀s, lever advance built-in light meter

R3*   **C–**

ARETTE IC: c1957, 35mm camera with coupled RFR and non interchangeable Westar or Xenar f2.8/45mm lens, Prontor SVS shutter, 1 – ⅟₃₀₀s, lever advance like the Arette IB, but with CRF, new body style, and without built-in light meter.

R3*   **C–**

ARETTE ID: c1957, 35mm camera with coupled RFR and non interchangeable Westar or Xenar f2.8/45mm lens, Prontor SVS shutter, 1 – ⅟₃₀₀s, lever advance like the Arette IC, but with built-in EV scale light meter.

R3*   **C–**

ARETTE-A: c1957, 35mm VFR camera with non-interchangeable Arettar 2.8/45mm, Isconar f2.8/45mm lenses, Vario shutter, ⅕ – ⅟₂₀₀s or Prontor SVS shutter, 1 – 300s, 1:1 optical VFR so both eyes could be open when using the camera.

R3*   **C–**

ARETTE BN: 1958. Replacement for the IB. Similar specification but with lever wind transferred to baseplate and a redesigned top plate, incorporating the exp meter. Rewind knob is flush with body and springs up at a touch.

R3*   **B+**

ARETTE-BW: c1959, 35mm VFR camera with interchangeable Schneider Xenon f2/50mm lens, Prontor SVS, 1 – 1/300s, field of view for 50mm and 90mm marked in VFR, built-in light meter. Late models (c1960), have the meter mounted in the front centre of the top plate, and Wilon f2.8/50mm lens. 90mm accessory lens available.

R3*   **C–**

ARETTE DN: c1958, 35mm camera with coupled RFR and non interchangeable Westar or Xenar f2.8/45mm lens, Prontor SVS shutter, 1 – 1/300s, built-in EV scale light meter, lever advance like the Arette ID, but lightmeter reading visible in the VFR.

R3*   **C–**

Schneider Xenagon f3.5/35mm lens and finder assembly: **C–**

Schneider Tele-Xenar f3.5/90mm lens and finder assembly: **C+**

Schneider Xenar f4.5/35mm lens: **C–**

Schneider Tele-Xenar f3.5/75mm lens: **D–**

Schneider Tele-Xenar f3.5/90mm lens: **D**

Telexon f5.6/90mm lens: **C**

Industria Argentina, (SIAF)

BISLENT: c1950, Bakelite stereo VFR camera for 2.5 x 3.5cm single frames or

stereo pairs vertically on 120 roll film, simple lens and shutters, each lens has its own release.

R4*   **D+**

REX-JUNIOR: c1950, Bakelite VFR camera for 6 x 6cm frames on 120 or 620 film, Lujo f10/8.5cm lens, simple shutter, made under license from Gevaert.

R4*   **C–**

REX: c1950, Bakelite VFR camera for 6 x 9cm or 6 x 4.5cm on 120 or 620 film, Lujo f10/9.1cm lens, simple shutter.

R3*   **B+**

GRADOSOL.

R4*   **C**

Argus Inc..
Ann Arbor, Michigan.

ARGUS K: c1939, 35mm camera; Argus Anastigmat 50mm f4.5 lens; Ilex shutter 1/25-1/200 s. Extinction meter coupled to lens diaphragm.. This camera represents the only attempt to couple an extinction meter to the diaphragm of a 35mm camera.

R3*   **D–**

Argus A (gold coloured version)

ARGUS A c1937. At the time of its introduction, the Argus A was the least expensive 35mm camera available. It was made in a number of colours these included black (most common), grey, brown, ivory, and gold. Coloured models, particularly the gold version, are considerably more valuable.

R3*   **D–**

ARGUS A2B: c1939-1950. 35mm camera; Argus Anastigmat 50mm f4.5 lens; Argus shutter 1/25-1/50 s.

R2* **B**

ARGUS C-3 C1940. 35mm RFR camera; Cintar Anastigmat 50mm f3.5 lens; five rivets on the back hinge indicates pre-war production. The Argus C-3 was arguably the most popular 35mm camera on the market from c1940-1955. It was rugged, inexpensive, and produced good results.

R1* **B**

ARGUS C3 MATCHMATIC: 35mm RFR camera, add-on non-coupled Selenium meter. Two tone colour design.

R1* **B**

ARGUS GOLDEN SHIELD: Chrome metal front plate, and "Golden Shield" emblem.

R2* **C–**

ARGUS A3: c1942, 35mm camera; Argus Anastigmatic 50mm f4 lens; Argus shutter 1/25-1/50 s. Built-in extinction exp meter.

R1* **B**

ARGUS C4: c1951,35mm RFR camera; Cintar 50mm f2.8 coated lens; Argus shutter ⅒-¹⁄₃₀₀ s, CRF.

R1* **B**

ARGUS C44: c1951, 35mm RFR camera, interchangeable Cintagon 50mm f2.8 coated lens, Argus shutter ½₅-¹⁄₃₀₀s, CRF.

R2* **C–**

ACCESSORIES AND LENSES FOR C44:

35mm f4 wide angle lens:	**B**
100mm f3.5 telephoto lens:	**B**
VFR for 50mm, 35mm, and 100mm:	**B**
light meter for C44:	**A**

ARGUS AUTRONIC 35: Cintar 50mm f3.5 lens; synch shutter ⅟₃₀ – ⅟₅₀₀ s. Selenium photo-electric cell controlled exp. c1960-1962.

R1* **C–**

Arsenal Zavod.
(Arsenal works), Kiev, Ukraine, (formerly USSR.)

Originally made with machinery removed from the Zeiss factory at the end of WWII, Kiev 35mm RFR cameras have been in production ever since. Like their Contax look-a-like relatives, they tend to have shutter problems which are very difficult to repair. For these cameras, at least, the first two digits of the snr give the year of production. As the Arsenal factory grew, other camera models came into production. Some cameras, especially the Kiev 88 are still available.They are included because of their origins and design, their relatively low price, is the reason they are in many collections.

KIEV 2: 1948-57; Vertical mfps, 1 – ¼₂₅₀ sec, combined RFR/VFR windows, interchangeable Contax bayonet type mount, earliest cameras have lenses marked "3K" (maybe meaning Sonnar/ Krasnogorsk) later cameras have f2.0/50mm Jupiter 8 lens.

R3*   **D+**

Kiev 2A: 1957-59; PC synch added, name written in Cyrilic and Latin letters.

R3*   **D+**

KIEV 3: 1951-57; Vertical mfps, 1 – ¼₂₅₀ sec, combined RFR/VFR windows, interchangeable Contax bayonet type mount, f2.0/50mm Jupiter 8 lens uncoupled built-in meter located on the top of the camera body.

R3*   **D**

KIEV 3A: 1957-59; Vertical mfps, 1 – 1/1250 sec, combined RFR/VFR windows, interchangeable Contax bayonet type mount, f2.0/50mm Jupiter 8 lens as the Kiev 3, but with PC synch added to the front of the camera body.

R2*   **D–**

KIEV 4: 1959-79, Vertical mfps, 1 – ¼₂₅₀ sec, combined RFR/VFR windows, interchangeable Contax bayonet type mount, f2.0/50mm Jupiter 8M lens uncoupled built-in meter located on the top of the camera body as the Kiev 3 (but smaller and more sensitive), PC synch added to the front of the camera body. Redesigned camera back like post-war Contax, film memo.

R2*   **D–**

KIEV 4A: 1959-79; Vertical mfps, 1 – ¼₂₅₀ sec, combined RFR/VFR windows, interchangeable Contax bayonet type mount, black f1.8/53mm Helios 103 lens as the Kiev 4, but with reduced top shutter speed and hot shoe in addition to the PC synch on the front of the camera body, no meter, black rewind and film advance knobs.

R2*   **D–**

KIEV 4AM: 1979-81; Vertical mfps, 1 – ¼₀₀₀ sec, combined RFR/VFR windows, interchangeable Contax bayonet type mount, black f1.8/53mm Helios-103 lens as the Kiev 2A, but with reduced top shutter speed and hot shoe in addition to the PC synch on the front of the camera body, self timer, no meter, black rewind crank and film advance knob.

R2*   **D–**

KIEV 4M:as Kiev4 AM, but for built-in uncoupled light meter

R2*   **D–**

"NO NAME" KIEV: c1963, Vertical mfps, 1 – ⅟₁₂₅₀ sec, combined RFR/VFR windows, Contax bayonet type mount. Often thought of as having been made at the post war Zeiss plant in East Germany, these cameras were really produced in the Soviet Union, concurrently with the Kiev 4A, for export to the West.

R4*   **F**

KIEV 5: c1968;, 35mm RFR camera, built-in lightmeter, interchangeable Jupitor-8M f2/50mm lens using Kiev/Contax mount, side mounted rewind crank, MFPS 1/2 – ⅟₁₀₀₀s, made in limited numbers.

R4*   **E-**

KIEV 35A: c1985, black plastic 35mm VFR camera, copy of Minox 35GT.

R2*   **C**

ACCESSORIES AND LENSES FOR KIEV 35MM RFR CAMERAS

Jupiter-12 35mm f2.8: in chrome   **D-**

Jupiter-12 35mm f2.8: in black   **D-**

Jupiter-9 85mm f2.0: in chrome   **D-**

Jupiter-9 85mm f2.0: in black   **C+**

Jupiter-11 135mm f4 lens (copy of Zeiss Sonnar):   **C+**

Jupiter-11 135mm f4 lens (fat barrel):   **D**

Kiev Stereo (copy of Zeiss Stereotar): **G-**

3.5cm accessory VFR: **C**

8.5cm accessory VFR: **C**

(Note: no 13.5cm finder was produced, and the only turret type finder made in the USSR was made by and for Zorki.)

KIEV-VEGA: c1965, subminiature camera for use with Minolta 16 cassettes, focusing f3.5/23mm Industar lens, shutter speeds ⅟₃₀, ⅟₆₀, & ⅟₂₀₀s. Grey or Brown.

R3*   **C**

KIEV-30: c1975, subminiature camera, as (KV111), but in black, often found in a complete set, including developing tank

adapter and unused film. (for outfit add 50%).

R3*   **C-**

KIEV-30M: c1989, subminiature camera. Stencilled name on the front.

R3*   **C-**

KIEV 30M 1949-89: 1989, as Kiev 30M, but no name, engraved "Kiev 1949-1989" on back, Red star with hammer and sickle engraved on front.

R4*   **D+**

KIEV 10 AUTOMAT: c1965, 35mm SLR with interchangeable bayonet mount Helios f2/50mm lens, unique metal rotary focal plane shutter, ½ – ⅟₁₀₀₀s, built-in non-TTL light meter, shutter speed preferred automatic to total manual operation, lever advance, bottom mounted rewind crank.

R4*   **E-**

LENSES FOR KIEV 10:

20mm f4 lens: **D-**

37mm f2.8 lens: **C**

85mm f2.8 lens: **D**

KIEV 6C: c1970, SLR for 6cm x 6cm frames on 120 or 220 film, horizontally styled much like a large 35mm SLR, interchangeable Volna f2.8/80mm lens in Pentacon Six breech mount., CFPS 1 – ⅟₁₀₀₀s, removable waist level finder.

R2*   **E-**

KIEV 60: c1980, SLR for 6cm x 6cm frames on 120 or 220 film. Improved film transport and "more convenient shutter release button position", often found with the TTL metering prism, sometimes found in hard leather outfit case with lens hood, and accessory shoe.

R2*   **E-**

LENSES FOR KIEV 6, 6C OR 60

Zodiak-8b 30mm f3,5 wide angle lens: **E**

Mir-26b 45mm f3.5 wide angle lens: **D+**

Mir-38b 65mm f3.5 wide angle lens: **D**

MC Vega-28b 120mm f2.8 telephoto lens: **D**

Kaleinar-3b 150mm f2.8 telephoto lens: **D+**

MC Telear-5b 250mm f5.6 telephoto lens: **D+**

SALYUT: c1965, 120 SLR for 6 x 6cm frames, copy of 1000F Hasselblad, f2.8/80mm lens in interchangeable mount, MFPS ½-1000s, interchangeable film backs, removable waistlevel finder, non-automatic lens aperture, usually found not working. *(Note: because of patent infringement problems, Salyut cameras were made for domestic consumption only.)*

R3*   **D+**

SALYUT S (C) : c1967, as (KV120) but for semi-automatic aperture – à la Exakta.

R3*   **D+**

KIEV 80: c1975, 120 SLR for 6cm x 6cm frames, interchangeable f2.8/80mm lens in bayonet mount, interchangeable backs, removable waist level finder, automatic lens aperture, MFPS ½ – ¹⁄₁₀₀₀s, these cameras are famous for being unreliable, and not up to hard use.

R2*   **D**

ZENITH 80: c1975, export version of the Kiev 80,but not very successful.

R3*   **D**

KIEV 88: c1984. Now with hot shoe synch, often found with the TTL metering prism, lens shade, extra film back in a hard leather case as a "Kiev 88TTL" outfit, MFPS ½ – ¹⁄₁₀₀₀s, as with the preceding Kiev 120 SLRs, these cameras are famous for being unreliable, easily broken, hard to repair. (complete "TTL" outfit adds 100%)

R2*   **E–**

CURRENT LENSES FOR ZENITH 80, KIEV 80 AND 88

Zodiak-8B 30mm f3,5 wide angle lens: **E**

Mir-26B 45mm f3.5 wide angle lens: **D**

Mir-38B 65mm f3.5 wide angle lens: **D**

MC Vega-28B 120mm f2.8 telephoto lens: **D–**

Kaleinar-3B 150mm f2.8 telephoto lens: **D+**

MC Telear-5B 250mm f5.6 telephoto lens: **E–**

Asahi Optical Co.,
Tokyo, Japan.

For further information see Pentax and Pentax SLR 35mm Cameras 1952-1989, by Danilo Cecchi, Hove Collectors Books, 1990.

Asahi Kogaku Goshi Kaisha Asahi was founded in 1919 to produce lenses for spectacles, telescopes, etc. In 1929 it started to produce photographic lenses for many other manufacturers. In 1952 they introduced their first camera, the SLR Asahiflex. In 1957 the Asahi Pentax was the first Japanese 35mm SLR camera with a pentaprism.

ASAHIFLEX I: c1952, 35mm SLR camera; Takumar 50mm f3.5 lens with interchangeable screw mount; CFPS ¹⁄₂₀-¹⁄₅₀₀ s. c1952. First Japanese 35mm SLR.

R3*   **F+**

ASAHIFLEX IA; 35mm SLR camera; as model I FPS ½₅ – ⅟₅₀₀s.; Second x terminal for flash; c.1953; called Ia by collectors.

R3* **F–**

ASAHIFLEX IIB: 35mm SLR camera; Takumar 58mm f2.8 preset lens with interchangeable screw mount; FPS ½₀-⅟₅₀₀s. Waist-level vf and eye-level optical vf. c1954. First 35mm SLR with combined focusing and viewing to use instant-return mirror.

R3* **E+**

ASAHIFLEX IIA; c. 1955 35mm SLR Camera; As IIb with slow speedss of ½ ⅕ ⅒ added by knob on the front.

R3* **E+**

PENTAX AUTO 110: c. 1979. SLR for 110 film, interchangeable f2.8/24mm normal lens, behind the lens automatic shutter,

lever wind. The Pentax Auto 110 was the only 110 format camera to be designed as a complete system with a variety of interchangeable lenses. When first marketed it came in a fitted box with lenses, filters, strobe, and auto winder. A completely intact boxed system increases value by 30-50%.

R2* **C+**

PENTAX AUTO 110 SUPER; c. 1982; as 110 with brighter viewing screen; self-timer; single stroke advance; slow speed indicator on screen; price with 24mm F2.8 lens.

R2* **D**

ACCESSORIES FOR THE PENTAX AUTO 110:

f2.8/18mm Wide angle lens:	**C+**
f2.8/50mm Telephoto lens:	**C+**
F2.8/70mm Telephoto Lens:	**D**
F2.8/40-70mm Zoom lens; **(SCARCE)**	**E**
1.7x Vivitar Converter	**C+**
Auto winder:	**B+**

ASAHI PENTAX; c.1958; 35mm SLR; FPS; slow speed knob on front 1-1/10s.fast speeds ⅟₂₅-⅟₅₀₀s.; 42 x 1mm Lens mount; lens 55mm f2.2 Takumar manual setting lens; Lever film advance.

R2* **E+**

ASAHI PENTAX S2; c1959; 35mm SLR; FPS;1-⅕₀₀S. B.T. All speeds on one knob on top plate; 55mm f/2 Auto Takumar lens; U.S.A. models "H2" logo replaced the "AO" on the pentaprism.

R1*   **D**

ASAHI PENTAX S3; c1960; 35mm SLR; FPS;1-⅕₀₀S.or 1-1000s.; f/1.8 Auto Takumar lens; few S3's had clip on exp meter facility; many variations of this camera; Sold in U.S. as Asahi Honeywell.

R1*   **D**

ASAHI PENTAX S1; c1961; 35mm SLR; FPS; 1-1/500; f/2 Auto Takumar lens;

shutter coupled to seperate exp meter at T setting.

R1*   **D**

ASAHI PENTAX SV; c1963-1967; 35mm SLR; FPS 1-⅟₁₀₀₀S.T. B.: 55mm f/1.8 Fully automatic Super Takumar lens; Delayed action self-timer under rewind knob; "H3v" logo in U.S.A..

R1*   **D**

ASAHI PENTAX SIA; c1963; 35mm SLR; FPS 1-⅕₀₀S. As SV model without self-timer; "HIa" logo in U.S.A.

R1*   **D**

ASAHI PENTAX S2 SUPER; c1959, 35mm SLR; Same as the SV model, mainly sold in Japan; The word SUPER was not engraved on any part of the camera.

R1*   **C+**

ASAHI PENTAX SPOTMATIC; C.1965; 35mm SLR; FPS 1-¹⁄₁₀₀₀s. & B.; Self-timer; First Pentax with TTL metering,with Cds cells, needle visible in finder, Powered by 1.5v batt in base; multi stroke film advance lever;ASA settings under speed dial; Exp. meter switch above FP and X flash contacts;

R1*   **D**

ASAHI PENTAX SL; c. 1968; 35mm camera as the Spotmatic without the exp meter.

R1*   **C+**

ASAHI PENTAX SPOTMATIC MOTOR DRIVE; c1966; Standard Spotmatic with modified base to take 12volt motor drive; Exp. 3 frames per sec. price camera and motor.

R2*   **F+**

ASAHI PENTAX SPOTMATIC II OR SPII; c1971; Reintroduced Standard Spotmatic; Hot-shoe added;Exp meter increased to ASA3200; New range of lenses Super Multi Coated Takumar (SMR) for metering at all apertures;Sold as Asahi Honeywell Pentax in USA.

R1*   **D**

ASAHI PENTAX SPOTMATIC SPF; c1973; As the SPII with shutter release lock; SMC Takumar lenses switch on exp meter when fitted; "F" on front "SPF" on top plate.

R1*   **D**

ASAHI PENTAX SPOTMATIC 1000; C.1973; 35mm SLR; FPS 1-¹⁄₁₀₀₀s.;full metering; no self-timer;no hot shoe; 50mm f/2 Lens;

R1*   **D**

ASAHI PENTAX ELECTRO SPOTMATIC; c. 1971; sold in Japan; the first electronic Pentax; Aperture priority; Electronic FPS ¹⁄₁₀₀₀ to slowest speed, set by light meter; some manual shutter speeds; ¹⁄₆₀s. max flash synch.;

R1*   **D**

ASAHI PENTAX ES; c. 1972; As the Electro Spotmatic; With 5 manual speeds ¹⁄₆₀ to ¹⁄₁₀₀₀ & B.; Switch for Automatic shutter 8sec. to ¹⁄₁₀₀₀s.and film speed ring under rewind button; 6volt batt; no self-timer; Takumar 50mm f/1.4 lens;

R1*   **D**

ASAHI PENTAX ESII; c. 1947; As the ES with shutter on eyepiece for use with self-timer; battery in base; safty lock on release; 55mm f/1.8 Lens; exp meter range ASA 3200; (Chrome Price plus 50%)

R1*   **D**

ASAHI PENTAX K2; c. 1975; 35mm Electronic SLR; vertical MFPS 8sec.-¹⁄₁₀₀₀s B.; K2 on front;self-timer;preview button; mirror lock; FP & X flash contacts next to rewind knob; full exp and shutter info on Screen;

R1*   **C+**

Asahi

ASAHI PENTAX KX; c. 1975; 35mm SLR; mechanical CFPS 1-¹⁄₁₀₀₀s.; Window in base of pentaprisim; self-timer; preview button; mirror lock; FP & X contacts on front; Silicon cell metering; K lens mount.

R1*   **D+**

ASAHI PENTAX KM; c. 1975; 35mm SLR; mechanical CFPS 1-¹⁄₁₀₀₀s.; Cds metering; as KX except; no shutter release lock; no mirror lock; no batt check; no apature window;no film label slot; no motor drive.

R1*   **D+**

ASAHI PENTAX K1000; c. 1976; 35mm SLR; K mount version of SP 1000; no self-timer;no view button; no film speed disc;no FP flash contact; 55mm f/2 SMC lens.

R1*   **D+**

ASAHI PENTAX K2 DMD; (Data Motor Drive) c.1976-1980; 35mm SLR; same as K2 with modified base to take motor drive and data back.

R1*   **E+**

PENTAX LX: 1980. Pentax's first professional SLR. Auto exp for aperture priority, shutter priority and program modes. Spot metering. Electronic and mechanical shutter 125s-1/2000s. Accepts all K-mount lenses. Part of a complete system that includes data backs motor drives and autowinders. Limited edition in gold also available.

R4*   **E**

PENTAX ME: 1977. Aperture priority automation only. Shutter speeds 8s-1/1000s. Also available as the ME SE, a special edition with brown leather covering.

R1*   **D**

PENTAX ME SUPER: 1980. Aperture priority and manual metering. Shutter 4s-1/2000s. Speeds set by dual push-button controls. Also available as the ME Super SE, a special edition with brown leather covering.

R1   **A**

PENTAX ME-F: 1981. Similar to the ME but with autofocus capability with the AF35-70mm f2.8 zoom, incorporating a focusing motor.

R1*   **D+**

Note: Pentax made many more SLRs in the 1970s and 1980s, some with only minor variations in specification. They included models such as the MG, MV, MV1 and MX, before moving onto the P range of cameras in 1985. Full details and specifications can be found in the book Japanese 35mm SLR Cameras by Bill Hansen and Michael Dierdorff, published by Hove Books.

Australian Camera Manufacturers, Australia
A.C.M.A., Australia.

SPORTSHOT: c1938, VFR bakelite camera for 6 x 9cm on 120 or 620 film, curved film plane, Lentar f13.5 lens, simple shutter, base of camera marked "British made", but this was common practice for Australian-made products before WWII. Available in black, brown, red, and green.

R3* **C–**

Automatic Radio Co..
Boston, Massachusetts.

TOM THUMB CAMERA RADIO: c1938, combination AM radio and detective camera; Maestar 57.5mm lens; reflex finder; 3 x 4cm exp on 127 film.

R3* **E**

Reference Notes

A.H. Baird,
Edinburgh, Scotland.

BAIRD SINGLE LENS STEREO CAMERA: c1910. Tessar 18cm f4.5 lens; rollerblind shutter; single or stereoscopic exposure by displacing the lensboard right, centre, or left. Mahogany tailboard with brass fittings.

R4*   **F**

Max Balbreck,
J. JOUX, Paris, France.

L'ALETHOSCOPE: c1925, stereo camera; Rapid Rectilinear lenses or Balbreck, Steinheil, Goerz, Zeiss Anastigmat; 5 speed guillotine shutter; changing magazine for 12 plates. 2 sizes: 6 x 13cm, 45 x 107mm.

R4*   **E–**

B. & W. Manufacturing Co.
Toronto, Canada.

PRESS KING: c1950. 4" x 5" press camera; Kodak Ektar 127mm f4.5 coated lens; Graphic MX shutter 1 – ¼₀₀ s. 4" x 5" exp on cut film.

R4*   **E–**

W. Bayer, Freital, Germany.

BAYERFLEX: c1936. Anastigmat 75mm f3.5 lens, Pololyt Laak, Rathenow; FPS ½s-1⁄₀₀ s.

R3*   **E–**

Ch. Bazin et L. Leroy,
Paris, France.

LE STEREOCYCLE: c1898. 6 x 13cm stereo camera; Koch Anastigmat 85mm f9 lens; guillotine shutter; 6 x 13cm plates; turning camera upside down activates plate changing mechanism.

R4*   **E+**

Balda Werke, Max Baldweg,
Dresden, German (pre 1945), then:

Balda-Kamerewerk-Bünde,
Westfalen, West Germany.

BALDA ROLL-BOX: c1934, metal box camera for 6 x 9cm frames on roll film, simple lens and shutter.

R2*   **A**

BALDA STAHLBOX: c1936, metal box camera for 6 x 9cm frames on roll film, simple lens and I and B shutter. The name means "Steelbox".

R2*   **A**

BALDA DREIBILD-BOX: c1935, box camera for 6 x 9cm, 6 x 6cm or 6 x 4.5cm frames on roll film, simple lens and shutter. The name means "Three picture box".

R2*   **A**

BALDA-BOX: c1935, metal box camera for 6 x 9cm frames on roll film.

R3*   **A**

BALDA POKA-DUPLEX: c1934, box camera for 6 x 9cm or 6 x 4.5cm frames on roll film, simple "close" and "distant" focusing.

R3*   **A**

BALDA POKA II: metal box camera for 6 x 9cm frames on roll film, built-in close-up lens. Later cameras offered in red, blue, grey, green and beige, and with 6 x 6cm capacity (coloured camera adds 200% to the price).

R3*   **A**

BALDA MICKEY ROLL-BOX: c1936, simple box camera using 127 film for 6.5 x 4cm frames, advertized as the "camera for everyone", available in three models, Model "O" with meniscus lens, Model I with "better" lens and provision for cable release, and Model II, with simple focusing.

R3*   **C–**

BALDA FRONTBOX: c1934, metal box camera for 6 x 9cm frames on roll film, marked "Balda Frontbox" on the camera front, in different styles.

R2*   **A**

BALDI: c1930, folding camera for 3 x 4cm frames on 127 film, many 50mm lenses were available, including f2.9 Xenar, f3.5 Vidanar, and f4.5 Tessar, in various Compur shutters.

R2*   **C–**

SUPER BALDINA (PRE-WAR): c1934 folding camera with coupled RFR for 24 x 36mm film, many 50mm lens were offered including f2.8 Tessar and f2 Xenon, in various Compur shutters with either front element focusing or helicoid focusing mount. Early cameras have black top housings and shutter mounted shutter releases, while later cameras have chromed top housings and body mounted releases.

R2*   **C**

BALDINA (PRE-WAR): c1933, folding camera, but without built-in RFR, late cameras have body mounted shutter release.

R2*   **B**

BALDINETTE: c1951, folding 35mm camera; Baldanar or radionar f2.8 or Baltar or Radionar f2.9 50mm lens; Prontor S, SV or Synchro Compur shutter.

R2*   **B**

SUPER-BALDINETTE: c1951, folding 35mm camera with CRF, Ennit f2.8/50mm lens in Prontor SV shutter, or Heligon f2/50mm lens in Compur shutter. (add 50% for Heligon lens).

R3*   **C+**

MESS-BALDINETTE: c1951, folding 35mm camera with uncoupled RFR, Baltar f2.9/5cm lens in Prontor shutter. This camera was intended as a less expensive alternative to the Super-Baldinette, but was priced only slightly higher than the Baldinette. Not sold in great quantities.

R3*   **C**

BALDAFIX: c1953, folding camera for 6 x 9, 6 x 6, or 6 x 4.5cm frames on rollfilm, non automatic frame counting, no double exposure prevention, Ennar f4.5/10.5cm lens in Pronto shutter.

R2*   **B**

BALDALUX: c1953, folding camera for 6 x 9, 6 x 6, or 6 x 4.5cm frames on rollfilm, automatic frame counting, double exposure prevention, Radionar f4.5 or Trinar f3.5 10.5cm lenses in Synchro Compur or Prontor SV shutter. The higher priced alternative to the Baldifix.

R3*   **C**

BALDAMATIC 1: Based on the Baldessa 1B, but with a new Prontormat shutter and a depth of field scale added to the 45mm f2.8 Color-Baldanar. Camera is automatic with two bands for daylight or flash on the aperture ring. Match needle metering. No shutter speeds or aperture settings are shown on the shutter control or the daylight section of aperture control. If turning the ring for exposure control takes it into the flash band, it means there is not enough natural light. The flash band then has f-numbers inscribed.

2*   **C–**

BALDAX: c1954, folding camera for 6 x 6cm frames on rollfilm, automatic frame counting, Ennagon f3.5/7.5cm lens or Radionar f2.9/8cm lens in Prontor Sv shutter.

R2*   **C–**

SUPER-BALDAX: c1959, folding camera for 6 x 6cm frames on rollfilm, automatic frame counting, CRF, Baldar f2.9/8cm in Prontor SVS shutter or Ennit f2.8/8cm lens in Synchro Compur shutter.

R2*   **C+**

BALDALETTE: c1949, folding 35mm camera with coated or uncoated Radionar

f2.9/5cm lens in Pronto, Prontor or Compur Rapid shutter.

R3*   **C–**

RIGONA (POST WAR): c1954, folding 35mm camera, Rigonar f3.5/50mm lens in Pronto shutter.

R3*   **C–**

RIGONA (PRE-WAR): c1936, folding camera for 3 x 4cm frames on 127 rollfilm, Radionar f2.9/5cm or Vidanar f4.5/5cm lens in Prontor II or Vario shutter. Chrome top plate and body release were offerred as options. Found with film wind on the top, or on the bottom!

R3*   **B+**

MESS-RIGONA: c1954, folding 35mm camera with uncoupled RFR, Rigonar f3.5/5cm lens in Pronto shutter.

R3*   **C**

BALDIX: c1953, folding camera for 6 x 6 frames on 120 rollfilm, Ennagon f3.5 or Baltar f2.9 7.5cm lens in Prontor SVS shutter.

R2*   **B**

MESS-BALDIX: c1954, folding camera for 6 x 6cm frames on 120 rollfilm, uncoupled RFR, many lens and shutter combinations were listed in catalogues, but the Ennagon f3.5/7.5cm lens in Prontor SV shutter is most often seen.

R3*   **C**

JUBILETTE: c1934, folding 35mm camera with Baltar f3.5/5cm lens in Compur shutter.

R3*   **C–**

VENUS: c1935, aluminium bodied folding 6.5 x 9 sheet film with Zeiss Tessar or other lens in Compur shutter.

R2*   **C–**

NIZZA: c1935, aluminium bodied folding 9 x 12cm sheet film camera with Zeiss Tessar or other lens in Compur shutter. Like so many other cameras of the same kind and era.

R2*   **C–**

JUWELLA: c1938, folding camera for 6 x 9 frames on rollfilm, Juwella Anastigmat f6.3 or f4.5/10.5cm lens in Balda or other shutter.

R2*   **C–**

JUWELLA II: c1938, folding camera for 6 x 9 or 6 x 4.5 frames on rollfilm, Juwella Anastigmat f6.3 or f4.5/10.5cm lens in Balda, Pronto or other shutter, for 6 x 4.5 format capability.

R2*   **C–**

PONTINA: c1936, folding camera for 6 x 9cm or 6 x 4.5cm frames on rollfilm, as with so many Balda cameras, the customer had a choice of several lens and shutter combinations, including Trioplan, Trinar, or Rarionar f4.5/10.5cm lens in Prontor I, Prontor II or Compur shutter.

R3*   **F–**

BALDAXETTE: c1935, black folding camera for 6 x 4.5cm frames on rollfilm, CRF, automatic parallax correction, Trioplan, Radionar, Tessar, or Xenar 7.5cm lens in Compur shutter. Chrome model brings 20% less.

R3*   **D–**

BALDAXETTE MODEL-II: c1935, chrome folding camera for 6 x 6cm frames on rollfilm, CRF, automatic parallax correction, Trioplan, Radionar, Tessar, or Xenar 7.5cm lens in Compur shutter.

R3*   **C+**

SUPER-PONTURA: c1939, folding camera for 6 x 9cm or 6 x 4.5cm frames on rollfilm, CRF, Trioplan f4.5 or f3.8/10.5cm lens or Tessar f4.5/10.5cm lens in Compur or Compur Rapid shutter. The lens assembly automatically returns to infinity when the camera is closed. The outbreak of war brought production to a standstill, and after 1945 no attempt was made to bring this camera back, few produced.

R4*   **F**

PICCOCHIC: vest pocket camera; Vidanar 50mm f2.9 lens; Compur shutter; 16 exp, 3 x 4cm on 127 roll film.

R2*   **C**

BALDINA (POST WAR): c1954, 35mm VFR camera with interchangeable Baldinar, Xenon, Xenar, or Radionar 50mm lens in Pronto, Prontor, Compur-Rapid or Synchro-Compur shutter, Schneider 70mm Longar accessory lens available.

R2*   **C–**

SUPER-BALDINA (POST WAR): c1954, 35mm camera with CRF and interchangeable Baldinar, Xenon, Xenar, or Radionar 50mm lens in Pronto, Prontor, Compur-Rapid or Synchro-Compur shutter, Schneider 70mm Longar accessory lens available.

R2*   **C+**

SUPER BALDAMATIC: 1961. 35mm automatic camera with manual override. 45mm f2.8 Xenar. Compur shutter 1/30-1/500s. Shutter release on the front of the body and a left-handed lever wind that requires only half a turn to advance the film and cock the shutter led the manufacturers to claim that shooting was possible at one frame per second or even more.

R3*   **D**

BALDIXETTE: c1960, metal VFR camera for 6 x 6cm frames in 120 roll film, front element focusing Baldar f9/7.2cm lens in collapsible tube mount, simple shutter.

R3*   **A**

BALDESSA: c1957, 35mm VFR camera with Westanar f2.8/50mm lens in Prontor SVS shutter, top mounted shutter release, after 1964 the body style changed, and the shutter release was mounted on the front of the camera body.

R2*   **A**

BALDESSA I: c1957, 35mm VFR camera with brightline finder, Isconar f2.8/45mm lens in Pronto or Prontor SVS shutter.

R2*   **A**

BALDESSA IA: c1957, 35mm camera with CRF, Baldanar f2.8/45mm lens in Priontor SVS shutter.

R2*   **B**

BALDESSA IB: c1957, 35mm camera with CRF, and built-in light meter, Baldanar f2.8/45mm lens in Priontor SVS shutter.

R2*   **B**

BALDESSA F: c1964, Built-in AG-1 flash lamp holder.

R2*   **A**

BALDESSA LF: c1964, with built-in light meter.

R2*   **A**

BALDESSA RF/LK: c1964, 35mm RFR camera, Westanar f2.8/45mm lens, Prontor shutter, CRF, but for built-in AG-1 flash lamp holder, built-in light meter with automatic aperture control.

R2*   **B**

BALDESSA F/LK: c1964, without CRF.

R2*   **A**

BALDESSA RF: c1964, without light meter.

R2*   **D+**

R. & J. Beck Ltd., *London, England.*

FRENA: c1897, box-type detective camera; Beck Achromatic single 4" f11 lens; rotating shutter ⅕-⅛₀ s; 50 exp, 6.5 x 9cm on sheet film in magazine.

R2*   **E**

FRENA DELUXE: c1897, box-type detective camera; 40 exp, 6.5 x 9cm on special sheet film. Covered with brown calveshide, gold metal-plated fittings.

R3*   **F–**

Kamera-Fabrik Woldemar Beier
Freital, Germany.

BEIER-BOX MODEL "O": c1929, metal box camera for 6 x 9 frames on rollfilm

R3*   **B**

BEIER-BOX MODEL "I": c1930, metal box camera for 6 x 9 frames on rollfilm, with the addition of a wire frame finder and better lens.

R3*   **C**

BEIER-BOX MODEL "II": c1930, metal box camera for 6 x 9 frames on rollfilm, with the addition of a built-in close-up lens.

R3*   **B**

BEIRA: c1931, folding strut type camera for 36 exp, 24 x 36mm.on 1.6m of "normal movie film". Early cameras were without RFR, later cameras added a coupled RFR. Many lens and shutter combinations were offerred, among them Meyer Trioplan f2.9/50mm lens in Compur shutter $^{1-1}\!/_{300}$s and Leitz Elmar f3.5/50mm in Compur Rapid shutter, 1 – $\frac{1}{500}$s, a Meyer Makro Plasmat f2.7/50mm lens was also offerred in catalogues of the day. Coupled RFR adds 100%, Elmar lens adds 100%, EST Makro Plasmat adds 100%.

R4*   **D**

BEIRETTE (PRE-WAR); c1938, folding 35mm VFR camera, Steinheil Cassar f2.9/5cm lens in Compur shutter, 1 – $\frac{1}{200}$s.

R3*   **C–**

BEIRETTE (POST WAR): c1965, simple metal 35mm camera from the East German firm of VEB Beier.

R2*   **A**

Belca Werke,
Dresden, Germany.

BELPLASCA: c1955. 35mm stereo camera; Tessar 37.5mm f3.5 lens; shutter 1-$\frac{1}{200}$s.

R3*   **E**

Bell & Howell Inc.,
Chicago, Illinois.

FOTON: c1948, 35mm spring-wind motor drive camera; Taylor & Hobson-Cooke Amotal 50mm f2.2 coated lens with interchangeable screw mount; additional three lug bayonet mount for accessory telephoto lens. Mfps 1 – $\frac{1}{1000}$ s; spring-wind motor drive advances film and cocks shutter at a maximum rate of 6 frames per sec. and cycles 9 – 15 exp per winding. Cook Telephoto 216mm f5.6 coated lens, **F+**. Cook Telephoto 4" coated lens, **E**. Prices higher in Japan.

R4*   **F+**

STEREO VIVID: c1951, 35mm stereo camera; Steinheil Cassar or Rodenstock Tridar f3.5 lens; guillotine shutter ¹⁄₁₀-¹⁄₁₀₀ s, CRF. Taking the film under a roller reduced the inter-lens separation to 65mm. Originally by Three Dimension Co.

R2*   **E–**

STEREO COLOURIST: c1952, 35mm stereo camera; Rodenstock Trinar f3.5 lens; Velio shutter ¹⁄₁₀-¹⁄₂₀₀ s, bulb, flash. Originally by Three Dimension Co, and manufactured in Germany by Bodenseewerk Apparate und Maschinenbau G.m.b.H, Uberlingen, Germany, and offered by them as the "Boden-Stereo."

R2*   **D+**

Bell Camera Co.,
Grinnell, Iowa.

BELL'S STRAIGHT WORKING PANORAM CAMERA: horizontal format, folding bellows camera; 5 panoramic exp, 11½" x 3¼" on roll film. C 1908.

R4*   **F–**

BELL 14: subminiature camera; 12 x 14mm exp on 16mm roll film. Mfg. in Japan. C 1960.

R3*   **B**

H. Belleni & Fils,
Nancy, France.

JUMELLE BELLIENI: c1899, 9 x 14cm stereo camera; Zeiss Protar 135mm f8 lenses; pneumatic, circular 5 speed shutter. Magazine for 12 plates.

R3*   **E**

JUMELLE BELLIENI: c1896, 12.9 x 18cm stereo camera; Zeiss Protar 110mm f8 lenses; 6 speed rotating shutter; changing mechanism for 12.9 x 18cm plates. Panoramic setting; rising and sliding lens panel.

R3*   **E–**

Curt Bentzin,
Görlitz, Germany.

After 1945 the factory was "nationalized" and became the Optik-Primar-Kamera-Werke VEB . Cameras from this factory are located at the end of this listing, and are considered a continuation of the pre-war production.

PRIMAR REFLEX 6.5 X 9: "Spiegel Camera Reflex" c1920s, SLR for 6.5cm x 9cm plates, several lenses offered including Biotessar f4.5/13.5cm lens, self capping CFPS ¹⁄₅ – ¹⁄₁₀₀₀s.

R3*   **F–**

PRIMAR REFLEX 9 X 12: c1920. "Spiegel Camera Reflex", SLR for 9cm x 12cm plates, several lenses offered including Tessar f4.5/18cm lens, self capping CFPS ¹⁄₃ – ¹⁄₁₀₀₀s.

R3*   **F–**

PRIMAR REFLEX 10 X 15: "SPIEGEL CAMERA REFLEX" c1920s, SLR for 10cm x 15cm plates, Tessar f4.5/21cm lens, self capping CFPS ¹⁄₃ – ¹⁄₁₀₀₀s.

R3*   **F–**

PRIMAR REFLEX 13 X 18: "SPIEGEL CAMERA REFLEX" c1920s, SLR for 13cm x 18cm plates, Tessar f4.5/25cm lens, self capping CFPS ¹⁄₄ – ¹⁄₁₀₀₀s.

R3*   **F–**

PRIMAR REFLEX 3¼ X 4¼: c1920s **"SPIEGEL CAMERA REFLEX"**, SLR for

3¼inch x 4¼ inch plates, Tessar f4.5/25cm lens, self capping CFPS ⅕ - ¹⁄₁₀₀₀s.

R3*   **F–**

PRIMARETTE: 1933. Twin lens camera that is not a twin lens reflex. 8 exp on 127. Viewing lens and taking lens each linked to the body by its own bellows. Top lens moves up and down during focusing for parallax correction. 75mm f3.5 Meyer Trioplan, Primotar or Tessa lenses. Rimset Compur shutter 1-¹⁄₂₅₀s + T & B. Rare.

R4*   **F+**

PRIMAR FOLDING REFLEX 6.5 X 9: c1920s, **"KLAPP REFLEX PRIMAR"** folding SLR camera for 6.5 x 9cm plates several lenses offered including Biotessar f2.8/13.5cm lens, CFPS ⅕ - ¹⁄₁₀₀₀s.

R3*   **D≠**

PRIMAR FOLDING REFLEX 9 X 12: c1920s, **"KLAPP REFLEX PRIMAR"** folding SLR camera for 9cm x 12cm plates several lenses offered including Tessar f4.5/18cm lens, CFPS ¼ - ¹⁄₁₀₀₀ s.

R3*   **D+**

PRIMAR FOLDING REFLEX 10 X 15: c1920s, **"KLAPP REFLEX PRIMAR"** folding SLR camera for 10 x 15cm plates, Tessar f2.8/13.5cm lens, CFPS ⅓ - ¹⁄₁₀₀₀ s.

R3*   **D+**

PRIMAR FOLDING REFLEX 3¼ X 4¼: c1920s, **KLAPP REFLEX PRIMAR** folding SLR camera for 3¼inch x 4¼inch plates, Boitessar f2.8/16.5cm lens, CFPS ⅓ - ¹⁄₁₀₀₀ s.

R3*   **D–**

PRIMAR 6.5 X 9: c1920s, **"FOKAL PRIMAR"** c1920s, folding VFR camera for 6.5 x 9cm plates, several lenses offered including Doppel Plasmat f4/12cm, CFPS 1/8-1/1000s.

R3*   **D**

PRIMAR 9 X 12: c1920s, **"FOKAL PRIMAR"** folding VFR camera for 9cm x 12cm plates several lenses offered including Makro Plasmat f2.9/15cm lens, CFPS ⅛-¹⁄₁₀₀₀ s.

R3*   **D**

PRIMAR 10 X 15: c1920s, **"FOKAL PRIMAR"** c1920s, folding VFR camera for 10 x 15cm plates, several lenses offered including Doppel Plasmat f4/18cm lens, CFPS ⅛-¹⁄₁₀₀₀s.

R3*   **D**

PRIMAR 13 X 18: c1920s, **"FOKAL PRIMAR"** folding VFR camera for 13 x 18cm plates, several lenses offered including Doppel Plasmat f4/21cm lens, CFPS ¼-¹⁄₁₀₀₀s.

R3*   **D+**

NIGHT PRIMAR: c1929, **"NACHT PRIMAR"** VFR camera for 6.5cm x 9cm plates, Plasmat f1.9/9cm lens , CFPS 8 - ¹⁄₁₀₀₀s.

R4*   **G**

STEREO PRIMAR: c1910, strut folding stereo VFR camera for 4.5cm x 10.7cm plates, Tessar f4.5/12cm lenses, CFPS 1 - ¹⁄₁₀₀₀s.

R3*   **E**

STEREO REFLEX PRIMAR: c1915, strut folding stereo reflex camera for 4.5cm x 10.7cm plates, Anastigmat f6.8/9cm lenses, both lenses used for reflex viewing.

R4*   **F+**

PLAN PRIMAR: c1930s, folding VFR camera for 6.5cm x 9cm plates, several lens and shutters offered including front element focusing Trioplan f6.3/10.5 lens, Vario shutter.

R3*   **C–**

HORIZONTAL PRIMAR: c1920s, **"QUER PRIMAR"**, horizontal format folding VFR camera, *available with and without CFPS*, triple extension bellows, Tessar f3.5/13.5cm lens, Compur shutter, (CFPS adds 50%).

R3*   **D–**

HORIZONTAL PRIMAR STEREO: c1920s, **"QUER PRIMAR"**, horizontal format folding stereo VFR camera, *available with and without CFPS*, triple extension bellows, Tessar f4.5/9cm lenses, Compur shutters, with stereo lenses, (CFPS adds 50%).

R3*   **E**

UNIVERSAL SQUARE PRIMAR 9 X 12: c1920s, Universal Quadrat Primar folding drop bed VFR camera for 9cm x 12cm plates, *available with and without CFPS, Plasmat f4/15cm lens*, Compur shutter, (CFPS adds 25%).

R3*   **C+**

UNIVERSAL SQUARE PRIMAR 10 X 15: c1920s. Universal Quadrat Primar folding drop bed VFR camera for 10cm x 15cm plates, *available with and without CFPS*, Satz Plasmat f4.5/17.3cm lens, Compur shutter, (CFPS adds 25%).

R3*   **D**

UNIVERSAL SQUARE PRIMAR 13 X 18: c1920s. Universal Quadrat Primar folding drop bed VFR camera for 13cm x 18cm plates, *available with and without CFPS*, Plasmat f4/21cm lens, Compur shutter, (CFPS adds 25%).

R3*   **D**

PRIMARFLEX 6X6: c1930's, SLR for 6x6cm frames on 120 roll film, glass plates in small holders could be used. Interchangeable Trioplan f2.8/10cm lens, CFPS 1-1/1000s. Rarely found with a properly functioning shutter. The Primarflex was a very

advanced camera for its time with a complete set of interchangeable lenses and a quick-change loading system. Its basic design in advanced form became the first Hasselblad in 1948. The late Dr. Victor Hasselblad once commented that the 6x6 Primarflex had strongly influenced him when he was designing the Hasselblad camera.

R3*   **E+**

Bermpohl & Co.
Berlin, Germany

BERMPOHL SINGLE EXPOSURE COLOUR CAMERA: (BN100)c1920 ; Meyer Plasmat 215mm f/4 lens; Compound shutter 1-1/75s, 9x12cm plate holders. The incoming light was split into three components by 2 internal semi-transparent mirrors. Three plates one each for red, green, and blue light were exposed.

R4*   **H–**

Berning- (see Robot listing)

Bertram, *Munich, Germany*

BERTRAM-KAMERA: 1954. Professional camera for press and sports photographers. Metal body, bellows, CRF for all lenses. Viewfinder automatically changes as lens is fitted. Focusing scale in viewfinder. Parallax corrected. Compur shutter 1-1/400s + T & B. Self timer. Swing back. Rollfilm and cut film holders. Image size: 2/4 x 3/4 inch. Xenar 105mm, Angulon 65mm and Tele Xenar 180mm.

R4*   **F**

Adolphe Bertsch, *Paris, France*

CHAMBRE AUTOMATIQUE DE BERTSCH: brass wet plate camera; Achromatic meniscus lens; lens cap controls exp. Single exp, 2½" x 2½" on wet collodion plate. C 1861. One of the first camera outfits to include materials necessary for the sensitizing and developing of wet plates.

R5*   **I–**

STEREO CHAMBRE AUTOMATIQUE DE BERTSCH: c1865 brass stereo version of Bertsch's Chambre Automatique; paired Petzval stereoscopic objectives, lens cap controls exp. Measures 3¾" x 4½" x 6⅜". Takes 2 exp, 2⅜" on wet collodion plates. This was one of the first camera outfits

which included materials necessary for the sensitizing and developing of wet plates.

R5*   **J**

BIFLEX 35: 35mm camera; Tritar 2cm f2.5 lens; 200 exp on 35mm roll film. Mfg. in Switzerland. C 1945. Possibly made for British intelligence.

R4*   **H**

BINOCA: c1950, subminiature binocular camera; camera is included in a 2.5x power binocular. Bicon 40mm f4.5 lens; variable speed shutter and bulb. 16mm film in cassette. Mfd in Japan..

White: R4*   **G**
Red/Bl: R4*   **G**

Blair Camera Co., *Boston, Massachusetts.*

In 1879, Thomas H. Blair founded the Blair Tourograph Co. in Connecticut. In 1881, he moved to Boston, Massachusetts, where he incorporated as the *Blair Tourograph and Dry Plate Company; on March 5, 1886 the company name was changed to the Blair Camera Company. The firm was purchased in 1899 by the Eastman Kodak Co; in 1907 the company assets were moved to Rochester, New York, where for a few years some cameras were inscribed "Blair, Division of the Eastman Kodak Co." George Eastman needed one of Blair's important patents - paper backed roll film. Without question this convenient daylight loading system was critical to the expansion of snapshot photography.*

BABY HAWKEYE: roll film box camera; 2" x 2" exp on roll film. C 1897.

R4*   **B–**

BLAIR 4" X 5" VIEW CAMERA: c1880, brass Dallmeyer No. 1 R.R. lens; front focus; tilting and reversible back; sliding bottom lock; mahogany with brass fittings.

R4*   **E**

BLAIR'S IMPROVED REVERSIBLE BACK CAMERA: c1890, 5" x 7" view camera; rack and pinion front focusing; bed mfg. in 3 sections. Sizes: 4" x 5" to 8" x 10".

R4*   **E**

DETECTIVE AND COMBINATION CAMERA (FIRST MODEL): c1888, 4" x 5" detective camera; glass focusing; front shutter cocking; side shutter adjustments;

oak finish, brass fittings. First model had removable knob for ground glass focusing.

R4*   **E**

DETECTIVE AND COMBINATION CAMERA (SECOND MODEL): c1890, 4" x 5" detective camera; removable rear panel for group glass focusing; counter on side for film or plates; oak finish, brass fittings; used with Eastman-Walker roll film holder.

R4* Wood: **E**
Leather: **E+**

DETECTIVE AND COMBINATION CAMERA (THIRD MODEL): c1890, 4" x 5" detective camera; focusing and shutter release on top with Eastman-Walker roll holder; separate ground glass for critical focusing by removing rear panel; nickel or brass plated fittings, dark mahogany finish.

R4* Wood: **E**
Leather: **E**

ENGLISH COMPACT VIEW CAMERA: c1890, 6½" x 8½" view camera; reversible back; double extension bellows; mahogany finish, brass fittings. 7 sizes: 3¼" x 4¼" to 10" x 12".

R3*   **E**

FOLDING HAWKEYE: c1890, 5" x 7" folding camera; Bausch & Lomb Rapid Rectilinear lens; Blair shutter. 4" x 5"

R4* 4x5" size: **D+**
5x7" size: **E+**

HAWKEYE DETECTIVE CAMERA: c1890, box-type detective camera.

R3*
Wood: E
Leather: E

Blair

KAMARET: c1891. Rapid Rectilinear lens; double exp prevention; 2 speed guillotine shutter; for 100 exp, 4" x 5" without reloading. First camera to place film spools in front instead of to rear of camera, thus shortening the camera, making it more compact. Original price $40. Distributed by E. & H.T. Anthony.

R4*   **F**

LUCIDOGRAPH: c1885, 4" x 5" view camera; Pantagraph R.R. 5 ¾" lens.

R4*   **F+**

NO. 3 COMBINATION HAWKEYE: c1905, 3¼" x 4¼" roll film and plate camera; roll holder lifts up for focusing, similar to No. 4 Screen Focus Kodak.

R4*   **E+**

NO. 4 WENO HAWKEYE: c1900, 3½" x 4½" box camera.

R2*   **B**

NO. 4 COMBINATION HAWKEYE: c1904, 4" x 5" roll film and plate camera; roll holder lifts up for focusing, similar to No. 4 Screen Focus Kodak.

R4*   **E+**

PETITE KAMARETTE: c1892, miniature box roll film camera. Round exp, 3½" diameter on roll film.

R3*   **F**

STEREO HAWKEYE MODEL NO. 4: c1890's, roll film stereo camera; Bausch & Lomb Optical Co. Rapid Rectilinear lenses U.S. 4; shutter 1 – ¹⁄₁₀₀ s. Red bellows; leather covered body.

R4*   **F–**

TOURIST HAWKEYE: c1900, wooden folding roll film camera; 2 speed shutter; 3½" x 3½" exp on roll film or plates; exp counter at back.

R4*   **D+**

TOURIST HAWKEYE SPECIAL CAMERA: c1897, 4" x 5" camera; Rapid Rectilinear

Unicum shutter. Sliding and rising front; fine focus; red bellows.

R3*   **E**

WENO: c1903. Rapid Rectilinear lens; Bausch & Lomb shutter; 9 x 18cm exp on roll film.

R3*   **E–**

WENO STEREO HAWKEYE: folding roll film stereo camera; 3½" x 6" exp on roll film.

R4*   **E+**

Bland & Co., *England.*

BLAND & CO. WET PLATE: c1850, brass lens L.F. Colas; wet plate holder; ground glass screen

R4*   **H**

Edmund Bloch, *Paris, France.*

PHOTO-CRAVATE (BLOCH'S DETECTIVE PHOTO SCARF): c1890, magazine camera concealed in cravate; periscopic lens,

25mm f16; single speed pneumatic shutter; 6 exp, 23mm diameter on dry plates. The buyer had a choice of colours, styles, and patterns. Original cost of the complete outfit was 60 francs.

R5*   **I+**

LE PHYSIOGRAPHE: c1910, monocular detective camera; Krauss Tessar 51mm f6.3 lens; 4.5 x 5cm exp on plates.

R5*   **G**

STEREO PHYSIOGRAPHE: c1896, stereo binocular-type detective camera; Krauss Tessar 51mm f6.3 lenses; single speed rotating shutter; 45 x 107mm exp on plates.

R5*   **H–**

Leon Bloch, *Paris, France.*

PHOTO BOUQUIN: c1904, stereo book-type detective camera; achromatic lenses; rotary shutter; central vf concealed in binding. 45 x 107mm exp on plates. The Photo Bouquin was the only stereoscopic book camera.

R5*   **I–**

PHYSIO POCKET: The Physio Pocket is identical to the Physiographe, the latter name was used after about 1909-10. Several different lenses were used including the Cooke Anastigmat to the Krauss Tessar.

R4*   **H–**

Bodenseewerk Aparate und Maschinenbau GmbH
Uberlingen, Germany.

BODEN-STEREO: c1953, 35mm stereo camera; Rodenstock Trinar f3.5 lens; Gauthier Velio shutter ¹⁄₁₀-¹⁄₂₀₀ s, bulb, flash.The same camera as the Stereo-Colourist, offered by Bell and Howell, but under the manufacturer's own name.

R3* **D+**

Bolsey

Bolsey Corp. of America
New York.

Jacques Bolsey was a Swiss designer who was responsible for the Bolex movie camera amongst several others. His American 35mm cameras were innovative, sturdy and inexpensive.

Bolsey B2

LA BELLE PAL: 35mm rf camera; Wollensak Anastigmat 44mm f4.5 coated lens.

R3* **D**

BOLSEY B: c1949 35mm RFR camera, Wollensak f3.2/44mm lens, shutter ¹⁄₂₅-¹⁄₂₀₀ s, CRF.

R2* **B**

Bolsey B2 US Army

BOLSEY B2: c1949. 35mm RFR camera, with double exposure prevention, and flash synch, Wollensak shutter ¹⁄₁₀ – ¹⁄₂₀₀.

R2* **B**

Bolsey B2 US Air Force

BOLSEY B2 (U.S. ARMY): c1949. similar to Model B2, except special plate on top with U.S. Army engraving, and olive drab paint.

R3* **E–**

BOLSEY B2 (U.S. AIR FORCE): c1949, similar to Model B2, except special plate on top with U.S.A.F. engraving.

R3*   **E–**

BOLSEY C: c1950, 35mm TLR; Wollensak Anastigmat f3.2/44mm lens, Wollensak Alphax shutter 1/10 – 1/200s, CRF. (prices much lower in the USA).

R3*   **D–**

BOLSEY C22 "SET-O-MATIC": c1953, 35mm TLR, with "Set-O-Matic" flash calculator. (prices much lower in the USA).

R2*   **D–**

BOLSEY 8: c1956, 8mm still and motion picture camera; Bolsey-Elgeet 10mm f1.8 Navitar lens; rotary shutter ⅟₅₀-⅟₆₀₀ s. Special cassette holds 25 ft of 8mm film. Single exp stop mechanism, variable shutter speeds, automatic footage counter.

R4*   **E**

BOLSEY JUBILEE: c1955, 35mm rf camera; Bolsey-Steinheil Anastigmat 45mm f2.8 lens; Bolsey Gauthier Auto-Synchro shutter ⅟₁₀-⅟₂₀₀ s, CRF.

R3*   **C+**

BOLTAVIT: Boltar 40mm f7.7 lens; shutter ½₅-⅟₅₀-⅟₁₀₀ s; 12 exp, 25 x 25mm on 35mm roll film. Metal cast body. C 1936.

R3*   **C–**

Boniforti & Balleno,
Milano, Italy

PERSEO: c1948, 35mm RFR camera with coupled interchangeable f3.5 or Heligon f2/50mm lens, CFPS ⅟₂₀ – ⅟₁₀₀₀s. front mounted shutter release, several variations exist with different shutter speed dials, film counters, and logo placements, in all around 200 units were produced.

R4*   **G+**

A. Boreaux,
Basle, Switzerland.

NANA: c1913, 45 x 107mm stereo camera; Suter 62mm f6.8 lenses; 6-speed guillotine shutter. Metal body covered with Morrocan leather.

R4*   **E**

Boston Camera Co, Boston, Massachusetts.

HAWKEYE DETECTIVE CAMERA: c1889, box-type detective camera.

R3*   **E**

Boumsel, Paris, France.

LONGCHAMP: c1935. Bakelite TLR for 3 x 4cm format on 127 film. Simple lens and single speed shutter. Probably made at the Norca factory for Boumsel. Also found in brown bakelite, from after the war.

R2*   **B**

AUTEUIL: c1948. Brown bakelite, based on the Longchamp body, but with 50mm/f3.5 Topaz lens in a Gitzo shutter, or a 50mm/f3.5 FAP Anistigmat in a Rapid-Synchro shutter. A real sales flop, left-over bodies were made into Longchamp cameras.

R4*   **C+**

AZUR: c1948. Folding roll film cameras for 6 x 9cm format. Available in several combinations of lens and shutters.

R3*   **B**

Carl Bralin Camerawerk, Nurnberg, Germany.

PAXETTE I: c1950, 35mm VFR camera, Pointar, Kataplast or Cassar f2.8/45mm

lens, Prontor S shutter; built-in extinction meter, lever wind on early cameras.

R2*   **B**

PAXETTE 1A: 1957. 35mm VFR camera, similar to the Paxette 1M with small modifications. Film speed indicator extended to 200ASA. Lens and shutter entirely new: four-element 50mm f2.8 Plastigon in a Prontor-SVS exposure value shutter.

R2   **C**

PAXETTE IM: c1951, 35mm camera with uncoupled RFR, Cassar or Kataplast f2.8/45mm lens; Pronto or Prontor S shutter.

R2*   **C–**

PAXETTE II: c1953, 35mm VFR cameras with interchangeable lenses, Cassar or Kata f2.8/45mm lens in Prontor S shutter, built-in extinction meter.

R3*   **C**

PAXETTE IIM: c1953, 35mm camera with uncoupled RFR, interchangeable Cassar or Kata f2.8/45mm lens; Pronto or Prontor S shutter.

R2*   **D–**

SUPER PAXETTE IB: c1958, 35mm camera with CFR; Kata f2.8/45mm lens; Pronto shutter.

R2*   **D**

SUPER PAXETTE I: c1958, 35mm camera with CFR, Prontor SVS shutter, Kata f2.8/45mm lens.

R2*   **D**

SUPER PAXETTE IL: c1958, 35mm camera with CRF and brightline finder, fixed f2.8/50mm Katagon lens in Pronto or Prontor SVS shutter.

R3*   **D**

SUPER PAXETTE IIL: c1958, 35mm camera with brightline finder and inter-changeable Tessar, Cassarit, or Xenar f2.8/50mm lens or Quinon f2/50mm lens in Prontor SVS shutter. All Super Paxette II cameras have in common accessory lenses from 35mm to 200mm coupled with the RFR, and built-in fields of view for 35mm-135mm.

R3*   **D**

SUPER PAXETTE II: c1956, 35mm camera with coupled RFR; interchangeable Cassarit, Tessar, or Xenar f2.8/45mm lens in Prontor SVS shutter.

R3*   **D**

SUPER PAXETTE IIB: c1957, 35mm camera with coupled RFR; interchange-able Cassarit, Tessar, or Xenar f2.8/45mm lens in Prontor SVS shutter.

R3*   **C+**

SUPER PAXETTE IIBL:c1958, 35mm camera with coupled RFR; interchange-able Cassarit, Tessar, or Xenar f2.8/45mm or Katagon f2.8/50mm lens in Prontor SVS shutter, built-in light meter.

R3*   **D–**

PAXETTE AUTOMATIC REFLEX: c1958, 35mm SLR with body mounted light meter coupled to interchangeable Ultralit f2.8/50mm lens, Synchro-Compur shutter 1 – ¹⁄₅₀₀s, several top styles and meter posi-tions.

R3*   **D–**

PAXETTE AUTOMATIC REFLEX IB: c1958, 35mm SLR with body mounted light meter not coupled to fix mounted Cassarit f2.8/50mm lens, Synchro-Compur shutter 1 – ¹⁄₅₀₀s, lightmeter reading visible in the VFR.

R3*   **D–**

PAXETTE AUTOMATIC: c1959, 35mm camera with CRF, VFR with fields of view for 35mm, 50mm, 85mm and 135mm, built-in light meter coupled to aperture and shutter speeds, interchangeable f2.8/ 50mm Colour-Ennit lens in Prontor-SLK shutter.

R3*   **C+**

PAXETTE ELECTROMATIC: c1960, simple 35mm VFR camera with single speed shutter, and automatic aperture control, f5.6/45mm fixed focus lens.

R2*   **B**

PAXETTE ELECTROMATIC IA: c1961, 35mm VFR camera, automatic aperture control, interchangeable Trinar f2.8/40mm lens, field of view for accessory 75mm lens marked in VFR, special elec-tronic flash offered as accessory.

R2*   **C**

PAXETTE ELECTROMATIC III: c1963, 35mm VFR camera with full automatic or manual control, Ultralit f2.8/40mm lens in Prontormatic shutter, 1 - 1/500s.

R2*   **C–**

ACCESSORIES FOR PAXETTE CAMERAS:

Optical VFR for 35mm and 85mm fields of view: **B+**

Optical VFR for 90mm field of view: **B+**

Optical VFR for 135mm field of view: **B+**

Optical VFR for 200mm field of view: **B**

Choroplast f4.5/35mm lens: **B**

Choroplast f3.5/38mm lens: **B**

Tele-Rotelar f4/75mm lens: **C–**

Neoplast f5.6 85mm lens: **C**

Telexon f5.6/85mm lens: **C–**

Telenar f3.8/90mm lens: **C**

Telexon f3.8/135mm lens: **C+**

Telenar f5.6/135mm lens: **C–**

Tele Ennalyt f4.5/200mm lens: **D–**

IMPERIAL BOX 6 X6: c1950, box camera for 6 x 6 frames on roll film, with and without synchro.

R2*	**A**

IMPERIAL BOX 6 X 9: c1950, box camera for 6 x 9 frames on roll film, with and without synchro.

R2*	**A**

NIMCO: c1952, 6 x 6 box camera produced by Braun for other retail sellers.

R3*	**A**

NORCA I: c1952, folding VFR camera for 6 x 9 frames on rollfilm, f8/105mm lens, Pronto shutter.

R2*	**B**

NORCA II: c1952, folding VFR camera for 6 x 9 frames on rollfilm, F6.3 Gotar lens in Prontor-s shutter.

R2*	**B**

NORCA III: c1952, folding VFR camera for 6 x 9 or 6 x 6 frames on rollfilm, f4.5 Gotar lens, Pronto shutter.

R2*	**B**

NORCA II SUPER: c1953, folding RFR camera for 6 x 9 or 6 x 6 frames on roll film, f6.3/105mm Cassar lens, Prontor-s shutter.

R3*	**C**

NORCA IV SUPER: c1953, folding RFR camera for 6 x 9 or 6 x 6 on roll film, f4.5/105mm Cassar lens, Prontor-S shutter.

R3*	**C**

PAXINA I: c1952, metal VFR camera for 6 x 6 frames on roll film, simple f7.7 lens in two speed shutter, square telescoping front.

R3*	**B**

PAXINA II: c1952, metal VFR camera for 6 x 6 frames on roll film, telescoping tube mounted Kata f3.5 or Steiner f3.5/75mm lens Vario shutter.

R2*	**B**

PAXINA 29: c1953, metal VFR camera for 6 x 6 frames on roll film, telescoping tube mounted Steiner f2.9/75mm lens, Vario shutter.

R2*	**B**

GLORIETTE: c1954-57, 35mm VFR camera, lever advance, Cassar f2.8/45mm lens, Vario, Pronto or Prontor shutter, different top plate styles.

R2*	**C–**

GLORIETTE B: c1955, 35mm VFR camera, lever advance, Cassar f2.8/45mm lens, Prontor-SVS shutter, built-in uncoupled light meter.

R3*   **C–**

GLORIA: c1958, metal RFR camera for 6 x 6 frames on rollfilm, uncoupled RFR, telescoping front, Praxar f2.9/75mm lens, Pronto or Prontor-SVS shutter.

R3*   **C**

COLOURETTE SUPER I: c1958, 35mm camera CRF, lever advance, Cassar f2.8/45mm lens, Compur-Rapid shutter.

R2*   **B**

COLOURETTE SUPER IB: c1958, 35mm camera CRF, lever advance, fixed mount Plastagon f2.8/45mm lens, Compur-Rapid shutter, Built-in light meter.

R3*   **C–**

COLOURETTE SUPER IBL: c1958, 35mm RFR camera, lever advance, fix mount Cassar, Culminar, Ysarex or Xenar f2.8/50mm lens, Synchro Compur shutter, built-in light meter.

R3*   **C–**

COLOURETTE SUPER II: c1958, 35mm camera CRF, lever advance, interchangeable Cassar, Culminar, Ysarex or Xenar f2.8/50mm lens, automatic depth of field indicator,Compur-Rapid shutter with EV values.

R3*   **C+**

COLOURETTE SUPER IIB: c1958, 35mm camera CRF, lever advance, interchangeable Cassar, Culminar, Ysarex or Xenar f2.8/50mm lens, automatic depth of field indicator,Compur-Rapid shutter with EV values, built-in light meter.

R3*   **E–**

BRINS PATENT CAMERA, LONDON, ENGLAND: c1891, 30mm f3.5 lens; simple shutter. Circular exp, 25mm diameter; lens at rear permits use as monocular. Mfd in London, England. This camera, if authentic reaches an R5 rarity level, almost unavailable. Beware of cleverly made fakes which are worth about 25% of an original.

R4*   **H+**

A. Briois,
Paris, France.

LE REVOLVER THOMPSON: C1862 revolver-type detective camera; Petzval-type 40mm f2 lens; rotary shutter. 4 exp, 23mm diameter on circular wet collodion plates, 75mm diameter.

R5*   **K–**

Andre Brizet,
Paris, France.

LE PHYSIOSCOPE: c1922, 6 x 13cm stereo camera; Tessar Krauss 74mm f6.3 lenses; Stereo Compur shutter 1-$\frac{1}{150}$ s. Rising lens panel; changing magazine for 12 plates.

R4*   **E**

Brooklyn Camera Co..,
Brooklyn, New York.

THE BROOKLYN CAMERA: c1885, 1/4 plate view camera; non-folding bed; collapsible bellows.

R3*   **E–**

Christian Bruns,
Munich, Germany.

BRUNS DETECTIVE CAMERA: c1893, 3¼" x 4¼" detective camera; 144mm f6.3 lens. Magazine holds 12 exp, 3¼" x 4¼". The camera has two Vfr: the first is a waist-level reflex viewer; the second consists of a separate bellows with ground glass, which

is assembled on top of the camera—the camera lens slides upward and is positioned on the Vrf.

R5*   **I–**

Bullard Camera Co., Springfield, Massachusetts.

BULLARD MAGAZINE CAMERA: c1898, plate-loading magazine folding camera; eighteen 4" x 5" plates.

R4*   **D**

Burleigh Brooks Optics, Hackensack, New Jersey.

BROOKS VERIWIDE: wide-angle panoram camera; Super-Angulon 47mm f8 coated

lens; Synchro-Compur shutter 1- ¹/₅₀₀ s; 8 exp, 6 x 9cm on 120 roll film. Users pay more than collectors for this.

R2*   **F+**

Busch Camera Co, Chicago, Illinois.

BUSCH VERASCOPE F40: c1950, 35mm stereo camera; Berthiot 40mm f3.5 coated lenses; CRF. Version of French made Richard Verascope F40 for U.S. market.

R4*   **F**

W. Butcher & Co., London, England.

William Butcher joined his father's pharmacy business in Blackheath in what is now south London in 1889. He had an obsessive interest in photography, and developing and printing rapidly became a major part of the business. In 1896 he leased a workshop nearby to make cheap cameras, d & p kits, etc., under the brand name "Primus". The photographic business developed so fast that in 1902 Butcher moved to a large building, in the centre of London. It was now a separate business under the name of W. Butcher & Sons, Ltd. The majority of cameras were now imported, or made from imported parts, mainly from Hüttig. The outbreak of war in 1914 cut off

Butcher's supplies, so a joint manufacturing company was formed with Houghton's, the Houghton Butcher Manufacturing Company, to make cameras for both companies. They continued to be marketed separately until complete amalgamation came in 1926 as Houghton-Butcher (Great Britain) Ltd. Ensign Ltd. was formed in 1930 to market the products. Some Butcher models continued into the Ensign era, which is covered in the Houghton section.

CLINCHER; c1913-1919. Magazine box camera; wood body; Leatherette covered; T&I shutter; No1, 6 plates 2¼ X 3¼; No2 6 plates 3¼ X 4¼; No3 12 plates 3¼ X 4¼; No4 6 plates 9 X 12cm.

R1* **B**

CORONET; c1913-1919. Folding field camera; Mahogany and brass fittings; Turntable in baseboard; No1.Single Achromatic lens; revolving shutter; No2.Primus RR-Beck Symmetrical or Aldis Uno lenses; in front of roller blind shutter; both models made in quarter,half and whole plate.

R2* **E**

THE LITTLE NIPPER: c1900. Made by Hüttig; 2½" x 3½" exp on plates of film; reversing finder; lens cap.

R2* **D**

MIDG; c1902-1920. Drop plate magazine box cameras; (Imported) quarter plate and postcard sizes; No 0 Built in shutter and lens; No's.1,2,3, and 4. Have better lens shutter combinations; protected by front cover.

R1* **B**

NATIONAL; c1900-1905. Half plate folding field camera; Mahogany finish; Tapered bellows;Reversing back; 7" Ross F/6.3 Homocentric lens; Thornton-Pickard roller blind shutter.

R2* **F–**

PILOT; c1904-1906. Falling plate magazine box camera;3½ x 2½ plates.

R1* **B**

ROYAL MAIL POSTAGE STAMP CAMERA: c1907. 15 postage stamp size photographs on a single plate.

R4* **H**

PRIMUS SO-LI-TO; c1897-1899. Collapsible box camera;morocco leather covered; Truncated pyramid; intended for cyclists and tourists.

R3* **F+**

THE STEREOLETTE: c1910. Made by Hüttig; 45 x 107mm stereo; meniscus lens; guillotine shutter; reflex viewer; spirit level; mahogany. 5 x 107mm exp on plates.

R4* **E+**

WATCH POCKET CARBINE, Tropical Model: 120 roll film camera, Tessar 9cm/f4.5 lens, Dial-set Compur shutter, copper toned metal body, brown bellows.

R3* **D**

A. Cadot,
Paris, France.

SCENOGRAPHE CADOT: c1900. 9 x 18cm stereo camera; Aplanatic 150mm f11 lenses; guillotine shutter. Rising front panel. The lens on one side can be shifted to the center to make a panoramic picture.
R4*   **E+**

E. Caillon,
Paris, France.

LE BIOSCOPE: c1915. 45 x 107mm stereo camera; Berthiot Saphir f6.3 or f4.5 lenses; shutter ½-¹⁄₂₀₀s. Leather covered; rising and falling front; panoramic movement.
R4*   **E–**

LE MEGASCOPE: c1915, 6 x 13cm stereo camera; Hermagis 85mm f6.3 lenses; guillotine shutter with variable speeds. Rising and falling front. Changing mechanism for 12 plates, 6 x 13cm.
R3*   **D+**

SCOPEA: c1915. 45 x 107mm stereo camera; Balbreck Rectilinear 54mm lenses; 5 speed guillotine shutter.
R4*   **D+**

CALYPSO: 1960, 35mm underwater camera; Berthiot 35mm f2.5 coated lens, interchangeable bayonet mount with watertight O rings. mfps ¹⁄₃₀-¹⁄₅₀₀s. This was the first underwater camera that did not require a separate waterproof pressure housing. Jacques Cousteau, co-inventor of the Aqualung was involved in its design. It is highly collectable. Nikon purchased the

rights to the design and re-introduced it as the Nikonos Underwater Camera.
R4*   **F+**

THE CAMEO: c1950, 8 x 17cm folding stereo camera; Beck Symmetrical lenses. Ground glass back. 8 x 17cm exp on plates. Mfd in Britain.
R3*   **D**

CAMERA-LITE: cigarette lighter-type detective camera; achromatic f8 lens. Similar to Echo 8, except has frame vfr instead of reflex vfr. C 1956.
R4*   **F+**

Camojet Ltd.,
Brentwood, Essex, England

CAMOJET: 1955. Subminiature for 14x14mm images on 16mm rollfilm. Made from molded plastic. Supplied with

a spare rollfilm back. Plastic projector also available.

R3*   **A**

The Canadian Camera and Optical Co.,
Toronto, Canada.

GEM GLENCO: c1910, 4" x 5" folding plate camera; red bellows with brass fittings.

R4*   **D**

Candid Camera Corp. of America

PERFEX 44: c1939-1940. 35mm RFR camera; Anastigmat 50mm f3.5 or f2.8 lens, interchangeable screw mount; CFPS 1-⅟₂₅₀ s, B, synch.

R2*   **C+**

PERFEX SPEED CANDID: c1938-1939. 35mm camera; Anastigmat 50mm f3.5 or f2.8 lens; CFPS ½₅-⅟₅₀₀ s; non-coupled RFR.

R2*   **C**

Canon Camera Company Inc.,
Tokyo, Japan.

For futher information see Canon Rangefinder Cameras 1933-1968 by Peter Dechert, Hove Collectors Books, 1985, and Canon Compendium, Handbook of the Canon System (for rangefinder and SLR cameras) by Bob Shell, Hove Books, 1994.

Most of the cameras manufactured in Japan between 1947 and (late) 1951 were marked "Made in Occupied Japan", usually on the baseplate, rear door, or top cover. Many cameras made after 1952 were marked with variations of the E-P symbol (usually within a diamond) which meant that the specific camera (or lens) was allocated for sale in the military post-exchange system. E-P markings are common – they do not designate any specific model of camera. An earlier variation of the diamond marking encloses a series of Japanese characters that translate to "CPO" in English. This practice dates to 1947 (approximately). A slightly later version encloses the English letters "CPO" within a diamond. Both of these markings are uncommon today; originally they designated cameras made for testing purposes. These cameras were supplied to the army of occupation and for early sale to military personnel.

GROUP 1: All cameras in this group have serial numbers below 45,000. The slowest instantaneous speed on the fast-speed dial is ⅟₂₀ s. All use 35mm film.

CANON/NK HANSA: c1935, Nikkor f3.5 lens in bayonet mount; CFPS ⅟₂₀-⅟₅₀₀ s. Pop-up vf; exp counter on front of body; top plate usually marked "Hansa" but sometimes not (if not the camera has sometimes been called "Canon Original"). This version was contemporaneously known simply as "the Canon Camera" and is distinguished by the engraved logo "Nippon Kogaku Tokyo" next to the serial number on its focusing mount, signifying that it was made under the supervision of Nippon Kogaku at Seiki Kogaku Kenkyujo. It therefore can be considered the earliest of both Canon and Nikon lines. Mfd 10/1935-8/1937, qty est 400-500. Price depending on the presence of parts designed for earlier unmarked Kwanons which are usually found on only a few cameras among the range under approximately serial 300.

R5* **J–**

CANON HANSA: Mfd 9/1937-6/1940, no "Nippon Kogaku Tokyo" engraving next to focusing mount serial number, signifying manufacture under Seiki Kogaku K. K. K. contol allowing reorganization and expansion of the company. Qty est 600-700.

R4* **I+**

CANON S: c1938-1944. Nikkor f4.5, f3.5, f2.8 or f2 lens in bayonet mount; CFPS 1-⅟₅₀₀ s. Pop-up vf, CRF; lever operated slow-speed dial on front of body; exp counter

under wind knob; serial no. on top plate. Qty 1600. This model shows several variations: in the slow-speed dial orientation, in the knob shape and markings and in the construction and markings of lens mounts. Some lenses may not fit all mounts. The earliest f2 lens with interior front diaphragm scale is the scarcest model; the f3.5 lens is the most common. With f3.5 lens, with f2.8 lens, with earliest interior-set f2 lens, with rimset f2.

With these lenses: **H+**

With Regno-Nikkor: **I–**

CANON NS: c1939-1944. Similar to Canon S, except does not have slow-speed dial. Nikkor f4.5 or f3.5 lens. Qty est 100.

R5* **I–**

CANON J: c.1939-1944. Nikkor f4.5 or f3.5 lens in threaded mount similar to, but not identical to Leica mount; CFPS ⅟₂₀-⅟₅₀₀ s. No RFR. No body plate patch over slow-speed dial area; vf in Leica-type top plate with straight edge near rewind knob. Qty est 200. C 1/1939-1944.

R5* **I+**

CANON JS: c1941-1945, similar to Canon S except has front mounted slow-speed dial. (1-⅟₂₀ s). Qty est 50.

R4* **I–**

SEIKI X-RAY CAMERA: c1939-1947. 35mm X-Ray recording camera; Nikkor f2 or Serenar f1.5 lens in massive bayonet mount; exp by darkslide. Wind knob has spring loaded chain. Qty unknown, possibly several thousand.

R4*   **F**

CANON X-RAY CAMERA: c1947-1951, similar to previous model, except marked "X-Ray Canon 35" on top. Qty unknown.

R4*   **G+**

CANON S-I: c 12/1945-11/1946. Nikkor f3.5 lens, post-war continuation of Canon S, and essentially identical to late wartime production; most serials should be later than 12386 but are mixed. Qty 97.

R5*   **H–**

CANON J-II: c1945-1946. Top cover resembles its Leica counterpart, curving around small rewind knob. Some have a metal patch over the slow-speed dial area. Nikkor or Serenar f3.5 lens in non-Leica type thread mount. Qty 525. With Nikkor lens, or Serenar lens.

R5*   **I–**

SEIKI CANON S-II: c1946. Nikkor f3.5 or Seiki Kogaku Serenar f3.5 or f2 lenses. Interchangeable lens mount, almost all with semi-Leica screw thread but a few early ones with Canon J-thread or in-between mounts. CFPS 1-1/500 s. Combined vf-RFR without variable magnification. "Seiki Kogaku Tokyo" maker's name on top. Qty 2000, more with J-thread

mount; With F3,5 Nikkor; $1.1k £800 DM2k

R4*   **F+**

CANON S-II: c8/1947-1952. Similar to previous model, except all have "Canon Camera Co." logo and Nikkor or Canon Serenar lenses. Qty 5550.

R3*   **F–**

CANON CX-35: c1951-1957. Late version of Canon X-Ray Camera. Canon f1.5 lens in bayonet mount. Marked "CX-35" on top cover. Qty unknown, probably several thousand.

R4*   **F**

CANON IIB: c1/1949-7/1952. Serenar f3.5 or f1.9 lens, CFPS 1-1/500 s. Combined vf-RFR with three-stage magnification. A few later had flash synch rails. Qty 14,400. Without flash synch rail, $100-$175; more with synch rail.

R3*   **E+**

GROUP 2: All models in this group have serial numbers between 45,000 and 169,990. The slowest instantaneous speed on the fast-speed dial is 1/25 s. All have combined vf-RFR with three-stage magni-

---

fication. Synched cameras all have side flash rail; they have no other flash outlet.

CANON 1950: Mfd 7/1950-10/1950. Serenar f1.9 lens, CFPS 1-⅟₁₀₀₀ s; flashbulb rail synch. Can quickly be distinguished by "Canon Camera Co. Ltd." maker's logo and serial between 50000 and 50199, and there are other differences. This version was briefly designated IIC by Canon, and most surviving examples have baseplates with "San Francisco" markings indicating sale (as model IIC or IVM) by C. R. Skinner in USA. Qty 50.

R5*   **H**

CANON IV: c4/1951-4/1952. Serenar f1.9 lens; CFPS 1-⅟₁₀₀₀ s, flashbulb synch. Two-piece vf magnification lever. Qty 1380. "Canon Camera Co. Inc." maker's logo.

R3*   **E+**

CANON IIC: c3/1951-8/1951. Serenar f3.5 or f1.9 lens; CFPS 1-⅟₅₀₀ s, no synch. Two piece magnification vf lever. Qty 800.

R4*   **F**

CANON III: c2/1951-12/1952. Serenar f3.5 or f1.9 lens; CFPS 1-⅟₁₀₀ s, no synch. Two piece magnification lever. Qty 10,175.

R3*   **E**

CANON IIIA: c12/1951-9/1953. Serenar f1.8 lens; CFPS 1-⅟₁₀₀₀ s, no synch. One piece magnification lever. Film reminder in wind knob. There were several variations in the interior construction, the manufacturer's logo, and the engraving. Qty 9025.

R3*   **E**

CANON IIA: c3/1952-9/1952. CFPS ½₅-⅟₅₀₀ s, no synch. Slow-speed dial area covered by patch. Qty 99. Verify authenticity before paying premium price.

R5*   **G+**

CANON IVF: c12/1951-1952. CFPS 1-⅟₁₀₀₀s, flash bulb synch. One piece magnification lever; film reminder; built-up interior wall next to film supply chamber. Qty 6880 includes Canon IVS**.

R3*   **E**

CANON IVS: c1952-5/1953. Has die-cast wall next to film supply chamber. Qty 6880 including Canon IVF.

R3*   **E+**

Canon IID1 with later f1.2/50mm lens

CANON IID1: c10/1952 – 6/1954. Has film reminder in wind knob. Qty 2400.

R3*   **E**

Canon IVSB with 135mm f3.5 lens and 135mm finder

CANON IVSB c12/1952-3/1955. Canon f1.8 lens was standard (rather than Serenar); CFPS 1-$\frac{1}{1000}$ s, flashbulb synch, X synch at C $\frac{1}{15}$ s setting on slow-speed dial. Slow-speed dial lock. Some other bodies were updated by Canon agencies to synch standards; these bodies show many variations. This model was often known overseas as IVS2, but IVSB is the factory designation. Qty 35,000.

R3*   **E+**

CANON IIAF: c6/1953 – 8/1953. CFPS $\frac{1}{25}$-$\frac{1}{500}$ s, flashbulb synch. Slow-speed dial area covered by patch. This is the scarcest Canon camera; buyers should authenticate any camera. This camera was never marketed in U.S. Qty 15.

R5*   **I–**

CANON IIF: c7/1953-3/1955. CFPS 1-$\frac{1}{500}$ s, flashbulb synch only. Some bodies are identified on the loading diagram inside the baseplate. Qty 12,000.

R3*   **E**

CANON IIS: c2/1954-3/1955. CFPS 1-$\frac{1}{500}$ s, flashbulb synch and X synch at $\frac{1}{15}$ s position on slow-speed dial. Qty 1850.

R3*   **E+**

CANON IID: c8/1952-2/1955. CFPS 1-$\frac{1}{500}$ s, no synch. No film reminder; one piece magnification lever. Qty 21,700.

R3*   **E–**

GROUP 3: All models in this group have serial numbers between 170,000 and 235,000 (bottom loading) or between 500,001 and 599,900 (back loading), except as noted. All have combined vf-RFR with three-stage magnification. The slowest instantaneous speed on the fast speed dial

is ⅟₃₀ s and all have front mounted slow-speed dials. The fast speed index is on top of the shaft in the centre of the dial and it rotates with the dial during winding and exp.

R3*   **C+**

CANON IVSB2: c7/1957/1956, 4-CFPS 1-⅟₁₀₀₀ s, flashbulb synch, X synch on slow-speed dial at ⅟₁₅ s and on fast-speed dial at ⅟₄₅ s. Bottom loading. Qty 17,000. serial numbers between 120,000 and 230,000.

R3*   **C+**

CANON IIS2: c2/1955-7/1956. CFPS 1-⅟₅₀₀ s. Qty 16,600.

R3*   **E**

CANON IID2: c1955-7/1956. No synch. Qty 16,200.

R3*   **E**

CANON IIF2: c6/1955-4/1956. Only has flashbulb synch, no X synch. Qty 2420.

R3*   **E+**

CANON VT: c4/1956-2/1957. Canon 50mm f1.2 lens and 35mm f1.8 lens were standard equipment on this camera,

however the Canon 50mm f1.8 (black focusing ring) and 50mm f1.5 were also available. Identified on front of baseplate; backloading; baseplate trigger-wind film advance. Prototype models were often marked "Model V" (instead of "Model VT") and early advertising used that designation; at least four other minor variations exist. Qty 15,600.

R3*   **E+**

CANON L2: c11/1956-12/1957. Identified on bottom of baseplate. Back loading; thumb-lever film advance. Qty 7,350.

R3*   **E+**

CANON L1: c2/1957-12/1957. Identified on bottom of baseplate. No self-timer. Qty 8,000.

R3*   **Black: G**
                              Chrome: E

CANON VT-DELUXE: c2/1957-9/1957. Identified on front of baseplate. Cloth shutter curtains; no baseplate magazine opening key. Qty 3500.

R3*   **Black: G+**
                              Chrome: E

CANON VT-DELUXE-Z: c4/1957-6/1958. Has baseplate magazine opening key. Qty 4875.

R3*   **Black: G+**
                              Chrome: F–

CANON VT-DELUXE-M: c1/1958-8/1958. Identified "VT-DeLuxe" on front of baseplate and has original factory-installed metal

shutter curtains; designated from the beginning as VT-DeLuxe-M in factory records. Qty 2550.

R4* **Black: G+**
Chrome: F

CANON L3: c10/1957-12/1958. Identified on bottom of baseplate. Qty 12,975.

R3* **E+**

CANON VL: c12/1957-12/1958. Metal FPS 1 – 1/1000 s, flashbulb and X synch. Back-loading; thumb-lever film advance, self-timer. No identification on body, although a few prototypes made to test the metal shutter design were probably marked "Model L1" on the baseplate. Qty 5450.

R3* **E+**

CANON VL2: c1/1958-12/1958. Lacks ⅟₁₀₀₀s. speed. Qty 8450.

R3* **E+**

GROUP 4: All models in this group have shutter speeds 1-⅟₁₀₀₀s. on a single non-spinning top-mounted dial, metal shutter curtains, full synch, back-loading, and combined vf-RFR with projected frame lines.

CANON VI-T: c6/1958-7/1960. Identified on front of baseplate. Baseplate trigger wind; three-stage vf magnification; shutter speed dial notched for accessory exp meter. Qty 8175.

R3* **Black: H–**
Chrome: E+

CANON VI-L: c6/1958-3/1961. Thumb-lever film advance instead of baseplate trigger. This was the last Canon to lack model identification on body. Qty 10,350. Very few were imported to the U.S.

R3* **Black: G**
Chrome: E+

CANON P: c12/1958-5/1961. Identified on top cover. Qty 88,000.

R3*   **Black: G+**
               Chrome: E

Canon 7 with f0.95 lens

CANON 7: c1961. Identified on top cover. Qty 138,000. c6/1961-11/1964. The Canon 50mm f0.95 lens was introduced with this model which had a Leica-type thread mount with an outer bayonet flange. The Mirror Box 2 accessory housing was also introduced at this time; it accepted long focal length telephoto lenses. ($375 £250 DM650 With 50mm f0.95 lens).

R3*   **Black: H–**
               Chrome: F

CANON 7S: c2/1965-8/1967. Identified on top cover. Several variations with minor cosmetic differences exist; Canon 7 vf optics. Qty est 16,000. No black bodies

known to date; Body only £275; Chrome with f0.95 lens.

R3*   **F**

CANON 7SZ: c8/1967-9/1968. Has revised finder optics differentiated by adjustment port above second "n" in topside "Canon" logo. Qty est 4000.

R3*   **F**
Body   **F+**

GROUP 5: Early Canon SLR cameras. All are identified on the camera body.

CANONFLEX: c 1/1959-7/1960., the first Canon SLR to be sold, with baseplate trigger wind, shutter to 1/1000 s, removable finder. Uses Canonmatic lenses. Qty 17,000.

R3*   **D**

CANONFLEX RP: c6/1960-1/1962. Fixed finder, Canomatic lenses. Qty 31,000.

R3*   **D**

CANONFLEX R2000: c6/1960-1/1962. Top speed 1/2000 s, Canomatic lenses. Qty 8800.

R3*   **D+**

CANONFLEX RM: c2/1961-3/1964. built-in selenium meter, Canomatic lenses. Qty 72,000.

R3*   **D+**

CANONEX: c10/1963-5/1964. SLR camera, leaf shutter, fixed lens.

R2*   **D–**

CANON FX: c4/1964-1966. CdS meter built-in FL lenses. This model did not have QL feature.

R2*   **D–**

CANON FP: c10/1964-3/1966. No meter, FL lenses, no QL.

R2*   **D–**

CANON PELLIX: 1964; 35mm SLR camera;Canon FL 50mm f1.8 lens, inter-changeable breech-lock mount; mfps 1-$^1/_{1000}$s, FP,M,X synch. Cds through-the-lens meter. Stationary pellicle mirror splits incoming light between the film plane and viewfinder. Approximately $^1/_3$ of a f stop less light falls on the film and the finder is $^1/_3$ less brilliant. The word Pellix is derived from pellicle, the thin semi-transparent membrane used in beam-splitting cameras. The advantage of a stationary mirror was the lack of vibration when the mirror flipped up and the silent operation.

R3*   **D+**

CANON PELLIX-QL: c1966-1970; The "Quick Load" version of the Pellix.

R2*   **E–**

CANON TL-QL: c1967-1972; Same as FT-QL except CFPS 1/500; no self-timer;

R2*   **C+**

CANON TLB: c1972; 35mm SLR camera; FPS 1-⅟₅₀₀s.budget version of the FTb ; no hot shoe;no mirror lock up; new style Cds meter.

R2*   **C+**

CANON EX-EE: c1968-1973; SLR camera; TTL Cds meter;fixed lens with interchangable front elements; shutter priority – manual;CFPS 1-⅟₅₀₀s,B.; 1/60s. X flash exp.

R2*   **C+**

CANON EX-AUTO: c1972-1976; Name variant of the EX-EE.

R2*   **C+**

CANON F-1: c1970-1976; 35mm SLR camera;Canon's first professional camera; MFPS 1-⅟₂₀₀₀s.B.; ⅟₆₀s.B. X. Flash exp; factory fitted motor drive to serial numbers under 200,001; interchangable finders, screens & pentaprism;TTL Cds meter;Meter needle display.

R2*   **E+**

CANON F-1 "ORIGINAL":c1972-1976; As F-1 with ability to accept add on motor drive MF.

R2*   **E+**

CANON F-1N: c1976; Slightly modified version of F-1; Identified by the plastic tipped film advance lever; film reminder frame on back.

R2*   **F**

CANON FT-QL: c1966-1972; 35mm SLR camera;CFPS 1-⅟₁₀₀₀s,B.; FP⅟₃₀s,X⅟₆₀s. flash exp.; Cds Meter Needle display; mirror lock;battery check; self timer.

R2*   **C**

CANON FTB: c1970-1973; 35mm SLR camera; CFPS 1-⅟₁₀₀₀s. B.; FD lens mount; Hot shoe;⅟₃₀s. FP. X⅟₆₀s. Flash exp.

R2*   **Black E–**

CANON FTBN: c1973-1977; 35mm SLR camera; FD lens mount;CDS meter needle display; CFPS 1-⅟₁₀₀₀s. B.;FP1/30s, X ⅟₆₀s. Flash exp;QL-system; mirror lock.

R2*   **Black E–**

CANON EF: c1973-1977; 35mm SLR camera;FD mount; SPC meter, needle

display; Exp warning; MFPS 30s,-¹⁄₁₀₀₀s.; X ¹⁄₁₂₅s. flash exp; mirror lock.

R2*   **D+**

CANON AT-1: c1976-1982; 35mm SLR camera; FD-N lens mount;SPC meter needle display Exp warning; CFPS 2s.-¹⁄₁₀₀₀s.; ¹⁄₆₀s. X flash exp.

R2*   **C+**

Canon A-1:c1978-1986, 35mm SLR camera, FD-N mount; SPC meter; digital displays; interchangeable screens; CFPS 30s, ¹⁄₁₀₀₀s. The Canon A-1 was the first to have a built-in computer chip that programmed the exposure functions of shutter speed and aperture setting. The A-1 is of interest to collectors who specialize in technical "firsts."

R2*   **E–**

CANON TX: c1974-1978; 35mm SLR camera;Cds meter; Exp warning; CFPS 1-¹⁄₅₀₀s. B.; FP¹⁄₃₀s, X¹⁄₆₀.flash exp.; Also marketed by Bell & howell as FD35.

R2*   **C**

CANON AV-1: c1979-1983; 35mm SLR camera.SPC meter needle display; analog speed display; CFPS 2s.-¹⁄₁₀₀₀s. B.; ¹⁄₆₀s. X Flash exp.

R2*   **D–**

CANON AE-1: c1976-1984; 35mm SLR camera; FD-N lens mount; SPC meter needle display; Exp. warning; CFPS 2s.-¹⁄₁₀₀₀s.B.; X¹⁄₆₀s. flash exp. self-timer; batt check.

R2*   **D–**

CANON AE-1 PROGRAM: c1981-1986; 35mm SLR camera; SPC meter;shutter or aperture priority & manual; digital display;

CFPS 2s.-¹⁄₁₀₀₀s.; 1⅟₆₀s, X flash exp.

R2*   **D**

CANON AL-1: c1983-1985; 35mm SLR camera; SPC meter; needle display; camera shake warning; CFPS 2s.-¹⁄₁₀₀₀s. B.; 1/60s. X flash exp; FD-N mount.

R2*   **C+**

Canon screw mount (unless otherwise indicated) lenses for cameras:

NB, lenses marked "Seiki Kogaku" should be for camera bodies also marked "Seiki Kogaku"

Serenar 28mm f3.5:	**D+**
Serenar 35mm f3.5:	**D**
Serenar 35mm f3.2: in Chrome,	**D–**
Serenar 35mm f2.8:	**E–**
Serenar 5cm f3.5:	**E**
Serenar 50mm f3.5: in Chrome	**C+**
Serenar 5cm f2.0:	**E+**

Serenar 5cm f1.5:	**E+**
Serenar 50mm f1.8: in Chrome	**C**
Serenar 85mm f2.0: in Chrome	**D**
Serenar 85mm f1.9: in Chrome	**D+**
Serenar 100mm f4.0: in Chrome	**D–**
Serenar in S-bayonet mount, 13.5cm f4.0:	**E**
Serenar 13.5cm f4.0:	**E+**
Serenar 135mm f4.0: in Chrome	**C+**
Serenar 20cm f4.0: very rare,	**H–**
Canon Lens 25mm f3.5: in Chrome, w/finder,	**F–**
Canon Lens 28mm f2.8: in Chrome	**D+**
Canon Lens 28mm f3.5:	**D**
Canon Lens 35mm f1.8: in Black	**D+**
Canon Lens 35mm f1.5: in Chrome	**E**
Canon Lens 35mm f2.0: in Black	**D+**
Canon Lens 35mm f3.5: in Chrome	**C+**
Canon Lens 50mm f0.95: in Black	**E+**
Canon Lens 50mm f1.2: in Black	**C+**
Canon Lens 50mm f1.4: in Black	**D+**
Canon Lens 50mm f1.5: in Chrome	**C–**
Canon Lens 50mm f1.8: in Black	**C–**
Canon Lens 50mm f2.8: in Black	**C–**

CANON LENS (SOME MARKED SERENAR)

85mm f1.5: in Chrome,	**F**
Canon Lens 85mm f1.8: in Black	**D+**
Canon Lens 85mm f2.0: in Chrome	**D**
Canon Lens 100mm f3.5: in Black	**D–**
Canon Lens 100mm f2.0 in Black	**E–**
Canon Lens 135mm f3.5: in Chrome, **C** in Black	**D–**
Canon Lens: (for use with Mirror Box 2), 135mm f2.5:	**C+**
Canon Lens (for use with Mirror Box), 200mm f3.5:	**D+**
Canon Lens (for use with Mirror Box), 400mm f4.0); w/finder	**G–**

CANON RANGEFINDER ACCESSORIES

Mirror Box 1 reflex housing: **E–**

CANON ACCESSORY VIEWFINDERS

35mm:	**B+**
85mm:	**C**
100mm:	**C**
135mm:	**B+**

CANONET: 1961. 35mm camera with large Selenium cell surrounding lens. Auto exposure controlled by Canon's 'Electric Eye' system, so called because the swing of the meter needle controls the opening and closing of the aperture – like the pupil of the eye. Exposure automatically adjusted between f1.9 and f16 with speeds from 1-1/500s. 45mm Canon lens. Film travel right to left. M & X synch. Lens hood reversible to form a lens protector.

R2* **B**

MAMIYA REFLEX WITH CANON LENS: (about 1960). Special SLR combination sold briefly by Olden Camera, New York . Body mfd by Mamiya with an Exakta lens mount – the standard lens was a Canon 50mm f1.9 (auto Exakta mount). This combination was unique in the U.S. (original price, $118.50); a curiosity item for Canon or Mamiya collectors.

R4* **E–**

CANON DIAL 35: c1963. Unusually designed half-frame 35mm camera. Produces 72 pictures on 36 exposure cassette. Clockwork mechanism advances film. f2.8, 28mm lens. Shutter 1/30-1/250s. The exposure meter which is wrapped around the lens looks rather like a telephone dial, the name of the camera.

R3* **C**

ION: 1989. The first commercially available electronic camera. The initials stand for Image Online Network. Up to 50 full-colour pictures on 54x60mm disc. Fixed focus lens, all other functions automatic. Built-in flash. Capable of three shots per second.

R2* **B+**

Carl Zeiss, Jena, Germany

WERRA: 1954-55, 35mm VFR camera with *olive green* body covering, f2.8/50mm coated Tessar in Compur Rapid shutter, 1 – ⅕₀₀s, knurled and knobbed aluminium film advance/shutter cocking ring, knob film rewind. (-75% without lens shade and/or screw in lens cap).

R3* **C**

WERRA IA: 1956-60, 35mm VFR camera with *black* body covering, f2.8/50mm coated Tessar in Synchro Compur Rapid shutter, 1 - ⅟₅₀₀s, knurled and knobbed aluminium film advance/shutter cocking ring, knob film rewind. (-75% without lens shade and/or screw in lens cap).

R2* **C**

WERRA IB: 1960-62, 35mm VFR camera with black body covering, f2.8/50mm coated Tessar in Synchro Compur Rapid shutter, 1 - ⅟₅₀₀s or Vebur 250 or Prestor RVS 500 shutters, after *1961 the RVS shutter indicated a top shutter speed of ⅟₇₅₀s* (putting this camera on the short list of cameras having leaf shutters with indicated speeds faster than ⅟₅₀₀s) *smooth covered* film advance/shutter cocking ring, knob film rewind, late cameras have a bright-line finder and round eye-piece. (-75% without lens shade and/or screw in lens cap, +50% for ⅟₇₅₀s shutter).

R3* **C-**

WERRA IC: 1962-64, 35mm VFR camera with black body covering, f2.8/50mm coated Tessar in Prestor RVS shutter 1-⅟₇₅₀s or Prestor RVS 500 shutter, smooth covered film advance/shutter cocking ring, *crank film rewind.* (-75% without lens shade and/or screw in lens cap).

R3* **C-**

WERRA IE: 1964-66, 35mm VFR camera with embossed black body covering, f2.8/50mm coated Tessar in Prestor RVS shutter 1-⅟₇₅₀s or Prestor RVS 500 shutter,

with *EV scale,* smooth covered film advance/shutter cocking ring, crank film rewind, re-designed rounder top plate, (-75% without lens shade and/or screw in lens cap).

R2* **C-**

WERRA II: 1960-64, 35mm VFR camera with black body covering, f2.8/50mm coated Tessar in Prestor RVS 500 shutter, 1 - ⅟₅₀₀s smooth covered film advance/ shutter cocking ring, knob film rewind. *built-in selenium meter* with hinged cover and an exposure calculator on the camera back. (-75% without lens shade and/or screw in lens cap).

R3* **C**

WERRA IIE: 1964, 35mm VFR camera with embossed black body covering, f2.8/50mm coated Tessar in Prestor RVS 750 shutter, 1 - ⅟₇₅₀s smooth covered film advance/ shutter cocking ring, crank film rewind. built-in selenium meter, *but no exposure calculator* on the camera back, *accessory shoe,* re-designed rounder top plate, (-75% without lens shade and/or screw in lens cap).

R2* **C-**

WERRAMAT: 1961-64, 35mm VFR camera with embossed black body covering, f2.8/50mm coated Tessar in RVS 500 shutter, 1 - ⅟₅₀₀s smooth covered film advance/shutter cocking ring, knob film rewind. built-in selenium meter *without* hinged cover indicator needle visible in the VFR, *without* accessory shoe, streamlined lens housing (-75% without lens shade and/or screw in lens cap.)

R3* **C**

WERRAMAT E: 1961-64, 35mm VFR camera with embossed black body covering, f2.8/50mm coated Tessar in RVS 500 shutter, 1 - ⅟₅₀₀s smooth covered film advance/shutter cocking ring, knob film rewind. built-in selenium meter *without* hinged cover indicator needle visible in the

VFR, *with* accessory shoe, streamlined lens housing (-75% without lens shade and/or screw in lens cap.)

R3*   **C**

WERRA III: 1959-64, 35mm camera with *coupled RFR* and *interchangeable lenses,* black body covering, bayonet mount f2.8/50mm Tessar in front of Prestor RVS shutter, 1 – ½₅₀s, crank rewind, field of view indicated for 35mm,50mm, and 100mm in the VFR.(-75% without lens shade and/or screw in lens cap.)

R3*   **D**

WERRA IIIE: 1964-66, 35mm camera with coupled RFR and interchangeable lenses, *rounder body style* with striated black body covering, bayonet mount f2.8/50mm Tessar in front of Prestor RVS shutter with EV scale, 1 – ½₅₀s, crank rewind, field of view indicated for 35mm,50mm, and 100mm in the VFR, (-75% without lens shade and/or screw in lens cap.)

R3*   **D**

WERRA IV: 1959-62, 35mm camera with coupled RFR and interchangeable lenses, black body covering, bayonet mount f2.8/50mm Tessar in front of Prestor 500 shutter, 1 – ½₅₀₀s, crank rewind, field of view indicated for 35mm,50mm, and 100mm in the VFR, *built-in selenium meter with hinged cover.* (-75% without lens shade and/or screw in lens cap.)

R3*   **D**

WERRA V: 1959, 35mm camera with coupled RFR and interchangeable lenses, rounded body with black covering, bayonet mount f2.8/50mm Tessar with Prestor 500 shutter, 1 – ½₅₀₀s, crank rewind, field of view indicated for 35mm, 50mm, and 100mm in the VFR, built-in selenium meter with hinged cover. (-75% without lens shade and/or screw in lens cap.)

R3*   **D**

WERRAMATIC: 1961-64, 35mm camera with coupled RFR and interchangeable lenses, rounded body with black covering, bayonet mount f2.8/50mm Tessar in front of Prestor 500 shutter, 1 – ½₅₀₀s (after 1962, Prestor RVS 750 shutter, 1 – ½₅₀s), crank rewind, field of view indicated for 35mm,50mm, and 100mm in the VFR, built-in selenium meter *without* hinged cover. (-75% without lens shade and/or screw in lens cap, +50% for Prestor 750 shutter.)

R3*   **D**

WERRAMATIC E: 1964-66, 35mm camera with coupled RFR and interchangeable lenses, rounded body with black covering, bayonet mount f2.8/50mm Tessar in front of Prestor RVS 750 shutter with EV scale, 1 – ½₅₀s, crank rewind, field of view indicated for 35mm,50mm, and 100mm in the VFR, built-in selenium meter *without* hinged cover, accessory shoe, re-designed rounder top plate with new decoration, (-75% without lens shade and/or screw in lens cap.)

R`3*   **D**

ACCESSORY LENSES FOR WERRA CAMERAS,

Flektogon f 2.8/35mm lens: **C+**

Cardinar f4/100mm lens: **C+**

Stereo attachment: EST   **D**

Jules Carpentier,
Paris, France.

JUMELLE CARPENTIER (4.5 X 6CM MODEL): c1892, binocular-type detective

camera; Rectilinear lens or Zeiss Anastigmat lens. 12 exp, 4.5 x 6cm on plates.

R2*   **D**

JUMELLE CARPENTIER (6.5 X 9CM MODEL): c1892, binocular-type detective camera; Zeiss Krauss Anastigmat lenses; 18 or 24 exp, 6.5 x 9cm on plates.

R2*   **D**

Chiyoda Optical Co.,
Osaka, Japan

MINOLTA AUTOCORD: c1955. Twin-Lens Reflex for 6x6cm images on 120 rollfilm. Rokkor f3.5, 75mm lens. Shutter 1-1/400s. Self cocking and auto-stop winding. This was the first in a series of very popular TLR's for about 10 years.

R3*   **C**

C.D. Chinaglia Domenico,
Belluno, Italy.

KRISTALL: 1952. Cfps, ¹⁄₂₀ - ¹⁄₁₀₀₀, Vfr only, no Rfr. flash synch, "E" for electronic flash, "V" for bulbs. Screw mount Krinar

F3.5/50mm, SOM Berthiot f2.8/50mm, or Schneider-Xenon f2.0/ 50mm lens. Less than 1000 cameras are thought to have been made.

R3*   **E+**

KRISTAL 2: c1949, 35mm RFR camera with interchangeable Trixor, Trigon, Vistor, or Steiner f3.5/50mm lens, among others, CFPS 1/20 - ¹⁄₁₀₀₀s, copy of Leica II.

Kristall 2a

KRISTALL 2A: c1950, as Model 2s, but for internal synchro selector, (Identical to that of the Wega IIa).

R4*   **F–**

KRISTALL 2S: c1950, Cfps, 1/20 - ¹⁄₁₀₀₀ sec, seperate Rfr/Vfr windows. Screw mount Steiner f3.5/50mm, SOM Berthiot f2.8/50mm, Schneider-Xenon f2.0/50mm, or Anastigmat Trixar f3.5/50mm lens. Both the top plate and the base plate are of polished steel, and are not chrome plated.

R4*   **F–**

KRISTALL 3: 1951. Cfps, 1 - ¹⁄₁₀₀₀ sec, seperate Rfr/Vfr windows. Screw mount Steiner f3.5/50mm, SOM Berthiot f2.8/50mm, Schneider-Xenon f2.0/ 50mm, or Anastigmat Trixar f3.5/50mm lens. This model is the same as the 2, with slow speeds added.

R4* **F**

KRISTALL 3S: Added PC synch on the front of the body.

R4* **F–**

KRISTAL 3S, TYPE 2: Redesigned top plate, looking more like the Kristall 53.

R4* **F**

Kristall 53 showing VFR selection lever

KRISTALL 53: 1953. Cpfs, 1 – ¹⁄₁₀₀₀ sec, seperate Rfr/Vfr windows, Vfr with fields of view for 28mm, 35mm, 50mm, 75mm, 90mm, and 105mm lenses. Screw mount Krinar f3.5/50mm, SOM Berthiot f2.8/50mm, or Schneider-Xenon f2.0/50mm lens. Less than 1000 cameras are thought to have been made.

R3* **F**

KRISTALL R: 1954. Cfps, ¹⁄₂₀ – ¹⁄₁₀₀₀, combined Rfr/Vfr window with built-in orange filter to improve Rfr contrast, flash synch. Screw mount Krinar f3.5/50mm, SOM Berthiot f2.8/50mm, or Schneider-Xenon f2.0/50mm lens.

R4* **F**

Century Camera Co.,
Rochester, New York.

The Century Camera Co. was founded in 1900 by five former employees of the Rochester Optical Co.; the company was located in Rochester, N.Y. In 1903 Eastman Kodak Co. bought controlling interest in the firm. In 1907 the name was changed to Century Camera Div., Eastman Kodak Co.; in 1917 it became part of the Folmer-Century Div., of Eastman Kodak Co.

CENTURY ENLARGING & REDUCING CAMERA: c1890s. 5" x 7" enlarging and reducing camera; extension bellows; lantern slide attachment. Polished wood finish, brass fittings.

R3* **D+**

CENTURY GRAND SR.: 5" x 7" c1902. Folding plate camera (top-of-the-line); Planatic Series III triple convertible lens. Red triple extension (24") bellows; front double sliding rack and pinion; back swings; dovetailed construction; covered with black cowhide. Sizes: 4" x 5" or 6½" x 8½" Original price, $45.

R3* **E–**

CENTURY PLATE CAMERA: c1910. 4" x 5" plate camera; Wollensak lens; Century shutter. Red bellows; brass fittings.

R3*   **D+**

CENTURY STEREO CAMERA: c1900s. 5" x 7" folding plate stereo camera; stereo shutter 1-$\frac{1}{100}$ s. 5" x 7" exp on dry plates.

R4*   **F**

CENTURY VIEW CAMERA: c1900. 5" x 7" view camera; rear focus; double extension bellows. Polished mahogany finish with brass fitting. Brass label: Century Camera Co., Rochester, N.Y. Several sizes from 4" x 5" to 11" x 14".

R3*   **E+**

Certo Kamerawerk,
Dresden, Germany.

Many models were around for years without great changes, note that dial set Compur shutters are found on cameras before 1928, afterwards, rimset Compur shutters were used. Sometimes this is the only difference between identical camera models made ten years apart.

DOLLY MODEL A: c1930, 3 x 4cm strut folding camera, front focusing Radionar f4.5/50mm lens, Compur shutter 1-$\frac{1}{300}$S.

R2*   **C–**

DOLLY MODEL B: c1930, 3 x 4cm strut folding camera, *lever focusing* Radionar f2.9/50mm lens, Compur shutter 1-$\frac{1}{300}$ s.

R2*   **C–**

DOLLY 4 X 6.5: c1935, 4 x 6.5cm bed folding camera, Tessar f3.5/70mm lens, Compur shutter.

R2*   **B**

SS DOLLY MODEL A: c1937, folding bed camera for 4.5 x 6cm or 6 x 6cm on 120 roll film, interchangeable Trioplan f2/75mm lens among others, Compur shutter.

R3*   **C–**

SS DOLLY MODEL C: c1937, folding bed camera, but for use with either rollfilm *or plates*, interchangeable Xenar f2.8/75mm lens among others, Compur shutter.

R3*   **C**

SUPER SPORT DOLLY MODEL A: c1936, folding bed camera for 6 x 4.5cm or 6 x 6cm frames on 120 roll film, coupled RFR, after 1939 with built-in extinction meter, interchangeable Tessar f2.8/75mm lens among others, Compur shutter, early cameras are all black, later ones have a chromed top plate.

R2*   **D–**

black than later versions, Cassar f2.9/50mm lens among others, Compur shutter.

R2*   **B+**

DOLLINA II: c1933, 35mm RFR strut folding camera for 24 x 36mm frames, CRF, Xenar f2/45mm lens among others, Compur shutter, available in either chrome or black.

R3*   **C+**

DOLLINA III: c1936, 35mm folding RFR camera, CRF, new body style, Xenon f2.50mm lens among others, Compur or Compur Rapid shutter.

R3*   **D+**

SUPER SPORT DOLLY MODEL C: c1936. For *plates or rollfilm.*

R3*   **D–**

DOLLINA: c1932, 35mm VFR strut bed folding camera for 24 x 36mm frames, many variations during production, early cameras lack body release and are more

SUPER DOLLINA: c1937, 35mm RFR camera, Cassar f2.9/50mm lens among others, Compur or Compur Rapid shutter 1-⅟₅₀₀ s.

R2*   **D+**

SUPER DOLLINA II: c1950, 35mm RFR camera, CRF, *coated Jena Tessar* f2.8/50mm lens, Compur Rapid shutter 1-$^1\!/_{500}$ s, *PC synch connection.*

R3*   **D+**

CERTO SUPER SIX: c1951, folding RFR camera for 6 x 6cm on 120 roll film, or 24 x 36mm on 35mm film with special adaptor, CRF, coated Jena Tessar f2.8/80mm lens, Synchro Compur shutter.

R3*   **D+**

CERTO-PHOT: c1955, all metal rollfilm camera for 6 x 6cm frames, simple focusing f8 lens, simple shutter $^1\!/_{50}$s.

R2*   **A**

CERTO-MATIC: c1960, Now with built-in uncoupled light meter.

R3*   **B–**

CERTOLOB O: c1925, leather bellows folding bed camera for 6.5 c 9cm film packs or plates, leather covered wooden body, Trioplan f4.5/105mm lens among others, Vario shutter.

R2*   **B+**

CERTOLOB : c1925, Xenar f2.9/105mm lens among others, Compur shutter, like (ER104) but with lens adjustments, and better finish.

R2*   **B+**

CERTORUF 9 X 12: c1925, leather bellows folding bed camera for 9 x 12cm film packs or plates, geared bed focusing Unofocal f4.5/135mm lens among others, Compur shutter, leather covered wooden body, waist lever finder mounted centrally on the front standard, double extension bellows.

R2*   **B+**

CERTORUF 10 X 15CM: c1925, 10 x 15cm plates or film packs. Xenar f4.5/165mm lens among others.

R2*   **B+**

CERTOREX: c1925, leather bellows folding bed camera for 9 x 12cm film packs or plates, *lever focusing* Unofocal f4.5/135mm lens among others, Vario shutter, leather covered wooden body, waist lever finder mounted centrally on the front standard.

R2*   **B+**

CERTOTROP 6.5 X 9: c1925, leather bellows folding bed camera for 6.5 x 9cm film packs or plates, *metal body,* geared bed focusing Trioplan f2.9/105mm lens, Compur shutter, *after 1930 with quick change lens/shutter mount.*

R2*   **B+**

CERTOTROP 9 X 12: c1925, 9 x 12cm film-packs or plates, Xenar f4.5/135mm lens among others, Compur shutter.

R2*   **B+**

CERTOTROP 10 X 15: c1925, 10 x 15cm filmpacks or plates, Xenar f4.5/165mm lens among others, Compur shutter.

R2*   **B+**

CERTORUHM: c1925, "Quer" format, simply put, the camera has a square body with removable back allowing horizontal or vertical framing without turning the whole camera, wooden body, drop bed for perspective control, Xenar f4.5/135mm lens among others, Compur shutter.

R3*   **B+**

CERTOCHROM 9 X 12: c1925, leather bellows folding bed camera for 9 x 12cm plates or filmpacks, drop bed, metal body, *interchangeable* Xenar f4.5/135mm lens among others, Compur shutter.

R2*   **B+**

CERTOCHROM 10 X 15: c1925, as previous model but for 10 x 15cm plates or filmpacks.

R2*   **B+**

CERTOPLAT: c1925, leather bellows folding bed camera for 9 x 12cm plates or filmpacks, specially made for use with Plasmat f4/15cm lens, Compur shutter, double extension bellows, otherwise as Certoruf 9 x 12.

R3*   **C**

CERTOKUNST: c1925, leather bellows folding bed camera for 9 x 12cm plates or filmpacks, interchangeable Xenar f4.5/135mm lens among others, drop bed, tilting lens standard, intended for architechtural or studio use.

R3*   **C–**

CERTOSPORT 9 X 12: c1925, leather bellows folding bed camera for 9 x 12cm plates or filmpacks, Xenar f4.5/135mm lens among others, Compur shutter, like Certoruf 9 x 12 but with wire frame finder.

R2*   **B+**

CERTOSPORT 6.5 X 9: c1930, leather folding bed camera for 6.5 x 9cm filmpacks or plates, interchangeable Eurynar f4.5/105mm lens among others, Compur shutter, *metal body,* wire frame finder.

R3*   **C–**

CERTONET O: c1925, folding VFR camera for 6 x 9cm frames on roll film, Radionar f4.5/120mm lens, Vario shutter.

R2*   **B**

CERTONET XIV: c1928, folding VFR camera for 6 x 9cm frames on roll film, Radionar f4.5/120mm lens, Vario shutter, *wire frame finder, bubble level* next to waist lever finder.

R2*   **B–**

CERTONET XV: c1927, folding VFR camera for 6 x 9cm frames on roll film, Radionar f4.5/120mm lens, Compur shutter, *wire frame finder.*

R2*   **B–**

DAMEN KAMERA: c1905, folding bed camera for 6 x 9cm plates, *in the form of an ornate ladies handbag. Beware of Eastern European forgeries!*

R5*   **I**

DOPPEL-BOX: c1935, Certomat lens; single speed shutter. 8 exp, 6 x 9cm or 16 exp, 4.5 x 6cm on 120 film. Format changed by turning dial.

R3*   **C**

CERTO-BOX A: c1930, metal box camera with fixed focus f11 lens, 6 x 9cm on roll film.

R2*   **B–**

W. I. Chadwick,
Manchester, England.

CHADWICK DETECTIVE CAMERA: c1890, box-type.

R4*   **E**

CHADWICK PATENT STEREOSCOPIC CAMERA: c1892, ¼ plate stereoscopic camera; single or stereo achromat lenses. Folding rectangular bellows; rotating waterhouse stops. Stereo exp on two ¼ plates.

R4*   **F–**

J. T. Chapman,
Manchester, England.

THE BRITISH DETECTIVE CAMERA: c1890, box-type detective camera; Wray lens (brass barrel) with waterhouse stops; Thornton Pickard string-set shutter. 2¼" x 3¼" exp on dry plates.

R3*   **E–**

Chase Magazine Camera
Newburyport, Massachusetts.

CHASE MAGAZINE CAMERA: c1899, box-type magazine camera. 12 exp, 4" x 5" loaded in a magazine.
R3*   **D**

CHEVILLON DROP-PLATE MAGAZINE CAMERA: c1905. Rapid Rectilinear lens; rotating shutter.
R3*   **C–**

Chicago Camera Co.,
Chicago, Illinois.

PHOTAKE CAMERA: c1896, achromat 120mm f14 lens; guillotine shutter; 5 exp, 2" x 2" on dry plates.
R4*   **G–**

Chicago Ferrotype Co.,
Chicago, Illinois.

MANDELETTE POSTCARD CAMERA: c1915, direct positive ferrotype camera. 2¼" x 3¼" direct positive exp on paper.
R3*   **D**

MANDEL PHOTO POSTCARD CAMERA: c1915, street camera. Direct positives, rectangular (2" x 3") or small circular images.
R3*   **D+**

WONDER AUTOMATIC CANNON PHOTO BUTTON MACHINE: c1913, cannon-shaped street detective camera; round exp, 25mm diameter on ferrotype plates. Produced button-size tintypes to insert in breast pins. The camera came complete with tripod, 300 plates, pins, and developing chemicals.
R4*   **F+**

Child Guidance Products Inc. Los Angeles, Ca.

Mick-A-Matic c1969; Toy camera in the shape of Mickey's head. Meniscus lens in nose; simple sector shutter; flash synch using flash cubes; 126 Instamatic film. There were two models. On the first model, the shutter was tripped by pulling down Mickey's right ear. This caused a problem with camera movement so a more conventional shutter release was used on the second version.
R3*   **C+**

Model I is worth TWICE the amount. On occasion the camera is found unused complete in its original bubble-wrapped box adding substantially to its value.
R4*   **D+**

Chiyotax Camera Company.
Japan.

All cameras listed here were made under contract by the Reise Camera Company

CHIYOCA 35:c1951, 35mm VFR camera with interchangeable rigid Hexar f3.5/50mm lens, CFPS 1/20 - 1/500s, Leica

Standard copy.

R4* G–

CHIYOCA 35-1F: c1952, Added synch, collapsible Lena QC f3.5/50mm lens.

R4* G–

CHIYOCA IIF: c1953, 35mm RFR camera with interchangeable screw mount Reise or Lena QC f3.5/50mm lens, CFPS 1/20 – 1/500s, copy of Leica II.

R3* F+

CHIYOTAX IIIF: 1954, 35mm RFR camera with screw mount Lena QC F3.5/5cm lens, 1 – ⅕₀₀ sec CFPS, seperate RFR/VFR windows, diopter adjustment, double male pin type flash synch. Later cameras marked "Reise Camera Company", are identical to this earlier version, and are valued the same. Prices are higher in Japan.

R3* F+

La Cinescopie, S.A.
Brussels, Belgium

LE PHOTOSCOPIQUE: c1930; OIP Gand Labor 45mm, f3.5 lenses; Ibsor shutter 1-150s. 50exp, 24dx24mm with special cassettes.

R3* G–

Cincinatti Clock and Man. Co.,
Cincinnati, Ohio.

CINCLOX CAMERA 16MM MODEL 3-S: 1930, oval shaped 16mm movie camera; Cine Wollensak Velostigmat 1" f2.5 lens. Optical finder; footage indicator; variable speed mechanism; key wind operation.

R2* B

CINE 8 EMEL: c1935-1936. 8mm movie camera; 3 lens turret for Berthiot 12.5, 116mm and 35mm lenses; 5 speeds from

8 to 64 frames per s. First 8mm camera with back-wind capability.

R3* D–

Ciro Cameras Inc.,
Delaware, Ohio.

CIRO 35R: c1950. 35m RFR camera; Wollensak Anastigmat 50mm f4.5 coated lens; Alphax shutter ¹⁄₁₀-¹⁄₂₀₀ s, CRF.

R2* B–

CIRO 35S: c1950. 35mm RFR camera; Wollensak Anastigmat 50mm f3.5 coated lens.

R2* B–

CIRO 35T: c1950. 35mm RFR camera; Wollensak Anastigmat 50mm f2.8 coated lens; Rapax shutter 1-¹⁄₄₀₀ s.

R2* B+

CIROFLEX A: c1942. 2¼" x 2¼" TLR camera; Wollensak Velostigmat 85mm f3.5 lens; Alphax shutter ¹⁄₁₀-¹⁄₂₀₀ s. 12 exp, on 120 roll film.

R2* A

CIROFLEX B: c1948. 2¼" x 2¼" TLR camera.

R2* 　　　　　　　　　　　　　**A**

CIROFLEX C: c1948. 2¼" x 2¼" TLR camera.

R2* 　　　　　　　　　　　　　**A**

CIROFLEX D: c1950. 2¼" x 2¼" TLR camera.

R2* 　　　　　　　　　　　　　**B–**

CIROFLEX E: c1950. 2¼" x 2¼" TLR camera.

R2* 　　　　　　　　　　　　　**B≠**

CIROFLEX F: c1950. 2¼" x 2¼" TLR camera; Raptar f3.2 lens; Rapax shutter 1-¼₀₀ s. 12 exp on 120 roll film.

R2* 　　　　　　　　　　　　　**B+**

Latimer Clarke

LATIMER CLARKE: c1857. pantograph movement for sequential exp with single lens camera.

R5* 　　　　　　　　　　　　　**H**

Clarus Camera Co., Minneapolis, Minnesota.

CLARUS MS-35: c1950, 35mm RFR camera, Wollensak Velostigmat f2.8/50mm coated lens, CFPS ½₅-¼₀₀₀ s, CRF, first version with flash synch, and accessory shoe built-into the top plate. These cameras sell for 50% more in Europe.

R2* 　　　　　　　　　　　　　**D–**

CLARUS MS-35: c1954. Without flash synch, and with simple added on accessory shoe. This was an attempt to cut the cost of manufacturing the camera. Eventually, the Clarus Company went out of business, and the remaining camera parts *were probably* bought by the Wescon Company.

R2* 　　　　　　　　　　　　　**C+**

CLEMENT AND GILMER: c1908, tailboard stereo camera. Mahogany finish with red bellows. Mfd in Paris, France.

R3* 　　　　　　　　　　　　　**F–**

LE CLOPIC: c1903, Zeiss Krauss 136mm f8 lens; shutter 2 – ½₀₀₀ s. 6.5 x 9cm exp on plates. Mfd in Paris, France.

R3* 　　　　　　　　　　　　　**E**

LE CLOPIC REPORTER: c1903. 9 x 12cm camera; Berthiot Flor 135mm f4.5 lens; FPS ½-½₀₀₀ s. Mfd in Paris, France.

R3* 　　　　　　　　　　　　　**E–**

Close & Cone, New York, USA.

QUAD CAMERA: c1896. leather covered box camera; rotary wind shutter. 4 exp, 3½" x 3½" on plates.

R3* 　　　　　　　　　　　　　**C+**

CLUNY: c1910, box-type stereo camera; Protar 75mm f9 lenses; 3 speed guillotine shutter. Leather covered wooden body. Two models: 45 x 107mm and 6 x 13cm.

R4* 　　　　　　　　　　　　　**E**

Company Francaise de Photographie, Paris, France

PHOTOSPHERE: 1988. This is an unusual all-metal dry plate camera. A push-pull magazine contained 12 dry plates each 8x9cm. Early models were first available with individual double plate holders. Later, a variety of sizes were available. The lens was mounted in front of a half-sphere, and the shutter was mounted within the sphere. Lens periscope f13, focal length 95mm. Varying tension on a coil spring allowed approximate changes in shutter speed. Rarity R4 – the very unusual stereo model R5

R4* 　　　　　　　　　　　　　**H**

Compco, *USA*

COMPCO REFLEX II: c1950, metal and plastic TLR type box camera for 6 x 6cm frames on roll film, simple lens and shutter. (prices higher in Europe).

R2* **A**

Concava S.A. *Switzerland*

TESSINA: c1960. Horizontal twin lens sub-miniature reflex camera. Exp. 14x21mm on 35mm film in special cassettes; f2.8 - 25mm lens, shutter $^1/_2$ - $^1/_{500}$s. The Tessina uses a clockworks mechanism to automatically advance the film. A silenced version which used a manual film advance was also available. The Tessina received some notoriety in the US as the spy camera used by the Watergate break-in group.

R4* **F**

Tessina

ACCESSORIES;

Watch strap	**D+**
Exp meter	**D+**
Watch	**F**
Prism finder	**D+**
Magnifier	**D**
Neck chain	**C+**
Daylight loader	**C+**

C.O.M.I.
Construzioni Ottico Meccaniche Italia, Rome, Itali

LUXIA: 1949. 35mm half frame camera, available in silver or gold-plate with reptile or pigskin covering. Models in black, red, green, blue and beige. 27mm f2.9 Delmak lens. Shutter 1/25-1/250s. Similar to, but rival with the Ducati, made by Societa Scientifica Radio Brevitti in Milan.

R4* **G**

Conley Camera Co.,
Rochester, Minnesota.

CONLEY 4" X 5" FOLDING PLATE CAMERA: c1900. R.R. lens; Conley Safety shutter. Polished wood interior with nickel plated fittings; red bellows.

R3* **D+**

CONLEY 5″ X 7″ FOLDING PLATE
CAMERA: c1890. Gundlach Triple Convertible lens; double extension bellows; rear swings and tilts; shifting, rising and falling front. Polished mahogany with nickel plated fittings; red bellows.

R3*   **E–**

CONLEY MAGAZINE CAMERA: c1904. Simple lens; rotary shutter. Twelve 4″ x 5″ exp on dry plates – drop plate changing mechanism.

R3*   **C+**

CONLEY POSTCARD CAMERA: c1905. 3½″ x 5″ folding plate camera; Rapid Rectilinear lens; Klito shutter; vertical format; black bellows. Polished wood interior with nickel fittings.

R3*   **C+**

CONLEY STEREOSCOPIC BOX CAMERA: c1906. Meniscus lenses; single speed shutter. Stereo exp on 5″ x 7″ dry plates.

R4*   **E+**

KEWPIE NO. 2: side loading box camera; rotating waterhouse stops.

R3*   **B–**

Contessa Nettel,
Stuttgart, Germany.

ADORO TROPICAL CAMERA: c1925, 9 x 12cm tropical plate camera; Zeiss Tessar

15cm f4.5 lens; Compur shutter 1-$\frac{1}{150}$ s.

R4*   **F**

CLARISSA TROPICAL: c1919, 4.5 x 6cm tropical plate camera; Hugo Meyer Trioplan 7.5mm f3.5 lens; CFPS $\frac{1}{20}$-$\frac{1}{500}$

R4*   **G+**

CITOSKOP: C 1924, 45 x 107mm stereo camera; Tessar 65mm f4.5 lenses; Stereo Compur shutter, 1-$\frac{1}{500}$s.

R4*   **E**

CONTESSA NETTEL SONNET: c1921, 4.5 x 6cm tropical camera; Tessar 7.5cm f4.5 lens; Compound shutter, 1-⅓₀₀ s.

R4*   **G–**

DECKRULLO TROPICAL: c1925, 9 x 12cm tropical plate camera; Tessar 120mm f4.5 lens; teak construction, partially covered with brown leather, light brown leather bellows.

R4*   **G–**

DUCHESSA: c1926, 45 x 107mm folding stereo camera; Teronar f5.4 or Tessar f6.3 or f4.5 lenses; Compur shutter 1-½₅₀ s. 45 x 107mm exp on plates.

R4*   **F–**

ERGO: c1924, monocular-type detective camera; Tessar 55mm f4.5 lens; Compur 1/25-1/100 s. 4.5 x 6cm exp on plates. Sold originally as the Argus by Contessa Nettel (see Nettel Kamerawerk listing); later sold as the Ergo by Zeiss Ikon.

R4*   **G**

PICCOLETTE: c1920, 127 roll film folding camera; Carl Zeiss Series IIb 7.5cm f6.3 lens; Compur shutter 1-1/300 s. 8 exp, 4 x 6.5cm on 127 roll film.

R3*   **C+**

WESTCA: c1914, all metal strut folding camera for 4.5 c 6cm plates, Aplanat f6.8/75mm lens.

R3*   **D+**

ATLANTA: c1915, plate camera for extra long (500mm or 800mm lens) for use as an aerial camera.CFPS, with either Aeroplast f6.8/500mm or f9/800mm lens.

R5*   **G–**

PIXIE: c1910, strut folding camera for 4 x 6cm frames on roll film, Tessar f6.3/70mm lens among others, various shutters.

R3*   **D+**

RECTO: c1925, strut folding camera for 4.5 x 6cm plates or film packs, various lenses and shutters, waist level reflex finder.

R3*   **D+**

NETTIX: c1920, strut folding camera for 4.5 x 6cm plates or film packs, various lenses and shutters, wire frame finder.

R3*   **D**

FIDUCA 6.5 X 9: c1920, metal bodied bed folding camera for 6.5 x 9cm plates or film packs, various lenses, Compur or Vario shutter.

R3*   **C–**

FIDUCA 9 X 12: c1920, metal bodied bed folding camera for 9 x 12cm plates or film packs, various lenses, Compur or Vario shutter.

R3*   **C–**

ALINO: c1920, metal bodied bed folding camera for 6.5 x 9cm plates or film packs, double extension bellows, various lenses and shutters.

R3*   **C**

SUEVIA: c1920, metal bodied bed folding camera for 6.5 x 9cm plates or film packs, various lenses and shutters, economy version.

R3*   **B+**

TAXO: c1920, metal bodied bed folding camera for 9 x 12cm plates or film packs, various lenses and shutters, economy version.

R2*   **B+**

TESSCO: c1920, metal bodied bed folding camera for 9 x 12cm plates or film packs, double extension bellows, various lenses and shutters.

R2*   **B+**

DONATA: c1920, bed folding camera for 9 x 12cm plates or film packs, various lenses and shutters, double extension bellows.

R2*   **B+**

ADORO 9 X 12: c1920, metal bodied folding bed camera for 9 x 12cm plates or film packs, various lenses and shutters, double extension bellows.

R2*   **B+**

ADORO 10 X 15: c1920, metal bodied folding bed camera for 10 x 15cm plates or film packs, various lenses and shutters, double extension bellows.

R2*   **B+**

ONITO 9 X 12: c1920, folding bed camera for 9 x 12cm plates or film packs, various lenses and shutters, economy version.

R2*   **B**

ONITO 10 X 15: c1920, folding bed camera for 10 x 15cm plates or film packs, various lenses and shutters, economy version.

R2*   **B**

ALTURA 9 X 12: c1920, folding bed camera for 9 x 12cm plates or film packs, various lenses and shutters.

R2*   **B+**

ALTURA 10 X 15: c1920, folding bed camera for 10 x 15cm plates or film packs, various lenses and shutters.

R2*   **B+**

SONTO: c1920, folding bed camera for 13 x 18cm plates or filmpacks, various lenses and shutters, double extension bellows.

R3*   **C–**

VOLUPA: c1920, folding bed camera for 10 x 15cm plates or filmpacks, double extension bellows, various lenses and shutters.

R3*   **B+**

MIROFLEX 6.5 X 9: c1919, strut folding SLR for 6.5 x 9cm plates or filmpacks, Tessar f4.5/120mm lens among others, CFPS, later cameras are from Zeiss-Ikon are more often found.

R4*   **F**

MIROFLEX 9 X 12: c1919, strut folding SLR for 6.5 x 9cm plates or filmpacks, Tessar f4.5/135mm lens among others, CFPS, later cameras are from Zeiss-Ikon are more often found.

R4*   **F**

Corfield,
England.

CORFIELD 66: 1961. Cfps, 1/10 - 1/500 sec. Interchangeable ground glass focusing, 6 X 6cm on 120 roll film using film back, or sheet film holders, interchangeable finders, 4 element Lumax f3.5/95mm lens. About three hundred cameras were made before production was halted.

R4*   **F**

PERIFLEX 1:1953-1958. Cfps, 1/30 - 1/1000 sec. The Corfield 35mm cameras used an unusual and unique focussing system. A small mirror could be inserted into the optical path manually on some models, automatically on others enabling the user to focus. Standard lenses were either f1.9/50mm, f3.5/45mm, or f2.8/50mm. Black top and bottom plates replaced by silver satin anodized finish in 1955.

R2*   **E**

PERIFLEX ORIGINAL: 1953. Cfps, 1/30 - 1/1000 sec, reflex focusing using a small periscope which intercepts the aerial image before it reaches the film plane, interchangeable viewfinders, screw mount f3.5/50mm Lumar, front cell focusing, coated from 1954. Aluminium body, covered with light brown pigskin, black top and bottom plates. Glass pressure plate, sprocketless film advance.

R4*   **F+**

PERIFLEX 2: 1958. Cfps, $^1/_{30}$ - $^1/_{500}$ sec, reflex focusing using a small periscope which intercepts the aerial image before it reaches the film plane, interchangeable viewfinders, screw mount Lumax f1.9/50mm, f3.5/45mm or f2.8/50mm lens. Simplified version of Periflex 3 with the EV scale and film reminder omitted. Introduced after the more expensive Periflex 3.

R2*   **F–**

PERIFLEX 3A: 1959. Cfps, 1 - $^1/_{1000}$ sec, lever wind, reflex focusing using a small periscope which decends automatically when the film is advanced, to intercept the aerial image from the centre of the frame before it reaches the film plane. Interchangeable viewfinders, screw mount f3.5, 2.8, or 1.9/50mm Lumax lenses, focusing to 9 inches. Frame counter counts backward during rewind, showing number of frames rewound into the film cassette.

R3*   **F**

PERIFLEX 3B: 1960. Cfps, 1 - $^1/_{1000}$ sec, lever wind, reflex focusing using a small periscope which decends automatically when the film is advanced, to intercept the aerial image from the centre of the frame before it reaches the film plane. Interchangeable viewfinders, screw mount f2.8 (four element), f2.4 (six element), f1.9 (six element) Lumax lenses. Distinguished by its three flash synch sockets, this camera represents the peak of the periflex range in features and complexity.

R3*   **E+**

PERIFLEX 3: 1957. Cfps, 1 - $^1/_{1000}$ sec, reflex focusing using a small periscope which decends automatically when the film is advanced, to intercept the aerial image from the centre of the frame before it reaches the film plane. Interchangeable viewfinders, screw mount f3.5, 2.8, or 1.9/50mm Lumax lenses, focusing to 9 inches.

R3*   **E**

PERIFLEX GOLD STAR: 1961. Cfps, 1 - $^1/_{500}$ sec using the same mechanism as the Prontor leaf shutter in order to give consistant and accurate exposure, lever wind, reflex focusing using a small periscope which decends automatically when the film is advanced, to intercept the aerial image from the centre of the frame before it reaches the film plane. Interchangeable viewfinders, screw mount f2.8 (four

element), f2.4 (six element), f1.9 (six element) Lumax lenses. Usually found in quite good working order, quite usable even today.

R2*   **D+**

INTERPLAN: 1960s. Cfps, 1 – $^1/_{300}$ sec using the same mechanism as the Prontor leaf shutter in order to give consistant and accurate exposure, lever wind. Sold without lens, for use with Leica screw mount lenses (Interplan A), or Edixa/Pentax screw mount lenses (Interplan B), or Exakta bayonet (Interplan C). Based on the Periflex Gold Star, but simpler, without reflex focusing.

R3*   **E–**

LENSES MADE FOR THE PERIFLEX SYSTEM: 1950-60s

28mm, f3.5, Retro-Lumax, 1959   **D–**

35mm, f3.5, Retro-Lumax, 1957   **C–**

85mm, f1.5, Super Lumax, 1960,
RARE   **E**

90mm, f2.8, Tele Lumax, 1961,
RARE   **D**

95mm, f2.8, Lumax, 1960   **D–**

100mm, f4.0, Lumar, 1956   **C+**

135mm, f3.5, Tele Lumax, 1958
(leather banded mount)   **C+**

135mm, f3.5, Tele Lumax, 1961(diamond turned mount) rare.   **D**

150mm, f3.5, Lumar,1954, only one known to exist

240mm, f4.5, Tele Lumax, 1960, special viewfinder,rare.   **E+**

400mm, f4.5, Tele Lumax, 1960, same Vfr as 240mm lens,
RARE   **E+**

Cornu, *Paris, France.*

ONTOFLEX: c1939. TLR camera; Tessar 90mm f3.5 lens; Compur Rapid shutter 1-1/400 s. 6 x 9cm exp, horizontal or vertical format.

R4*   **E+**

ONTOSCOPE: c1925, 35mm stereo camera; Berthiot 40mm f3.5 lenses; shutter 1-$^1/_{400}$ s. Pair of stereo exp, 24 x 30mm on 35mm film.

R4*   **E**

ONTOSCOPE: c1925. 45 x 107mm stereo camera; Tessar 55mm f4.5 lenses; guillotine shutter 1/5-1/400 s. Changing magazine for 12 plates, 45 x 107mm.

R3*   **D+**

ONTOSCOPE: c1925, 6 x 13cm stereo camera; Berthiot 85mm f4.5 lenses; guillotine shutter 1/5-1/300 s. Panoramic settings; rising and falling front.

R3*   **D+**

REYNA: 1941, 35mm camera with cast aluminium body, 50mm/f3.5 Flor Berthiot or Saphir Boyer lens, Gitzo shutter 1/25-1/200s, no automatic stop when winding the film.

R4*   **D–**

REYNA II: 1942, 35mm camera with cast aluminium body, 50mm/f3.5 Flor Berthiot lens, Vario Reyna shutter, 1/25-1/100s, In Black or shiny Brown. With addition of automatic film stop.

R3*   **D–**

ONTOBLOC I: c1947, 35mm camera with cast aluminium body, 50mm/f3.5 Saphir Boyer lens, Coronto shutter, 1-1/300s, owners of Reyna II cameras could have them fitted with the Coronto shutter by sending them back to the factory.

R3*   **C+**

ONTOBLOC II: c1948, 35mm camera with cast aluminium body, 50mm/f3.5 Saphir Boyer lens, Coronto shutter, 1-1/300s, with chrome top plate.

R3*   **C+**

ONTOBLOC III: c1948, 35mm camera with cast aluminium body, 50mm/f2.8 Flor Berthiot lens, Coronto-Rapid shutter, 1-1/400s, like previous model, but with faster shutter and lens.

R3*   **C+**

WEEK-END BOB: c1946, 35mm camera with cast aluminium body, the same style as the Reyna cameras previously listed, but with simple shutter and lens. Grey body with gold coloured metal work.

R3*   **C+**

FAMA-FLOR: c1940, 35mm camera with cast aluminium body, distributed by the Maillard company, Fama shutter 1-1/300s, 50mm/f2.8 lens in interchangeable mount. Built-in blind which protects the film from light when the lens/shutter are changed.

R3*   **D**

FAMA-FLOR II: c1940, 35mm camera with cast aluminium body, with built-in vrf adjustable for 35mm, 50mm, and 90mm fields of view. A 35mm/f3.5 wide angle lens and a 90mm/f4.5 Telephoto lens were available for this, and the Fama-Flor camera. A complete set, including both accessory lenses adds 200% to the price.

R3*   **D**

ONTOSCOPE c1920. 6x13cm stereo camera with matched Tessar 8.5cm f4.5 lenses. Entire body nickle plated. Shutter 1/5 to 1/300s. Lens board may be shifted to center for panoramic picture. Interchangeable magazines for glass plates or roll film.

R2*   **D–**

Coronet
Birmingham, England.

CADET: 1957. Similar to Flashmaster (see below), with modifications to the film wind mechanism. Shutter release also shifted to front right of lens moulding. Camera not synchronised for flash.

R1   **A**

CORONET CAMEO: c1935, plastic sub-miniature camera; 13 x 17cm exp on 16mm roll film.

R2*   **D–**

CUB: 1947. Light-weight Bakelite camera for 40x27mm images on Kodak's 828 film (also sold by Coronet as 888 and Ilford as 88). Fixed focus lens, instantaneous shutter. Lens extends from the body on metal tube. Folding eye-level viewfinder.

R1*   **B**

Coronet Cameo

CUB FLASH: Similar to the cub but synchronised for flash. 'T' setting added to shutter, f11 and f16 apertures. Non folding viewfinder.

R1*   **B**

CORONET MIDGET C1934-35. During the 1930's this firm manufactured a large variety of simple cameras, the most famous o which was the Coronet Midget. Molded out of bakelite, the midget was available in a variety of colours (black, red brown, blue, & green). The price varies greatly between colours.

Black:

R2*   **D**

Brown/red:

R2*   **D+**

Green:

R2*   **D+**

Blue:

R3*   **C+**

CORONET "3D" STEREO CAMERA: c1954, plastic stereo camera, available in different colours; meniscus lens; single speed shutter. 4 stereo pairs or 8 single exp, 4.5cm on 127 film.

R2*   **C+**

CORONET "VOGUE"; Streamlined plastic; front opening camera; 6 exp 50x30mm on special film; f10 meniscus lens. Instantaneous or B shutter.

R3*   **D+**

CORONET "CAMEO"; c.1948; Moulded Bakelite camera 2" x 1" x 1¼" Dim.;Fixed focus f11 Lens; 1/25 shutter; front of Vfr.slides into camera, rear of Vfr.folds over back.

R3*   **D+**

FLASHMASTER: 1955. Beginners' camera for 12 exp on 120. Black plastic with chrome trim. Meniscus lens, everset shutter in an extension from the main body, direct vision viewfinder. Takes its name from being unusual in a camera of its type and price being flash synchronised.

R1*   **A**

Cosina Company Ltd.,
Nagano, Japan

EXACTA TWIN TL: 1970. Eye-level 35mm SLR. Made under contract for Ihagee, in West Germany. It used all existing Exacta lenses which were in generous supply. Schneider-Kreuznach Xenon lens f1.9, 50mm lens. Many of the features of the original Exacta appeared on the Exacta Twin TL in sophisticated form.

R4* **NSR**

Jean Cros,
St. Etienne, France.

REYNA-CROSS II: 1942, 35mm camera with cast aluminium body, 50mm/f3.5 Flor Berthiot lens, Reyna/Cross shutter,1/25-1/200s. Made in the "free" zone of France.

R4* **D–**

REYNA CROSS III: 35mm camera with cast aluminium body, now equipped with a 45mm/f2.9 lens, and Micromanic shutter, 1/25-1/200s.

R4* **D–**

Crown Camera Co,
New York.

CROWN CAMERA: c1910, cardboard box camera; meniscus lens; simple shutter. 1¼" x 1½" exp on dry plates.

R3* **D+**

Curtis Colour Lab.

CURTIS COLOUR SCOUT: c1942, 2¼" x 3⅛" colour camera; Goerz Dogmar 7½" f4.5 lens; Compur shutter.

R5* **F–**

CYCLOPS: c1950, binocular-type detective camera; Telesigmar f4.5 lens; shutter 1/25-1/100 s. 16mm film in special cassettes. Similar to Teleca Camera. Mfd in Japan.

R4* **F+**

Reference Notes

THE DAGUERREOTYPE PROCESS

Daguerreotypes are highly prized by collectors. Ordinary portraits sell for up to £50 depending on the size, quality and beauty of the image. Daguerreotypes of famous people by an identified portraitist can sell for several thousand pounds. An occupational — that is a daguerreotype of a worker with his tools — is especially valued. A 1/6th-plate or a 1/4-plate occupational will usually bring between £300 and £1,000. Outdoor scenes are rare and very desirable; they usually sell for between £500 and £1,500.

DAGUERRIAN SENSITIZING BOX: c1845. American-style of sensitizing box using either iodine or bromine for preparing quarter, sixth or ninth daguerreotype plates.

R5*   **H**

DAGUERREOTYPE POSING STAND: c1845, cast-iron fluted stand; original paint.

R5*   **H**

DAGUERREOTYPE CAMERA: c1848. ¼ plate chamfered-box type daguerreotype camera. Mfr unknown; American construction.

R5*   **Complete: J+**
Stand alone: G–

Dai-Ichi Optical Works, Japan.

CHICON 35: 1954. Cfps, 1 - ¹⁄₅₀₀ sec, separate Rfr/Vfr windows, diopter adjustment. Screw mount Hexanon f3.5/50mm lens. Made in very small quantities, this camera was the forerunner of the Honor cameras from Mejiro Optical Works. Very Rare.

R5*   **H–**

ZENOBIA: 1949-53. 16 exposures on 120 film, folding camera with between the lens shutter 1 - ¹⁄₅₀₀S, 75mm f3.5 Hesper Anastigmat lens.

R3*   **B**

ZENOBIAFLEX: c1953; 6 X 6cm TLR; Neo-Hespar 75mm f3.5 lens in Daiichi Rapid shutter 1-¹⁄₅₀₀S. B.;

R3*   **D**

Dalka Industries Pty. Ltd., Australia.

CANDID: c1939, plastic VFR camera for 6 x 6cm on 120 or 620 film, simple lens and shutter, believed to be a very early example of rigid polystyrene injection molding. very rare.

R4*   **C–**

J. H. Dallmeyer, London, England.

DALLMEYER STEREOSCOPIC WET-PLATE CAMERA: c1861. Petzval lens rarer than later Rapid Rectilinear; flap shutter;

rack and pinion focusing; mahogany wood with brass fittings.

R4*   **I+**

DALLMEYER SPEED CAMERA: C.1923-1930's; Dropped baseboard formed side panel when in use; N&G FPS ⅛-¹⁄₁₀₀₀s.; F 2.9 Pentac lens; Price given for 4.5 x 6cm, larger sizes quarter-plate, 3½ x 2½ less 40%

R3*   **F–**

DALLMEYER SNAPSHOT CAMERA: c1928. Simple folding camera using struts. 12 exposures in filmpack each 6.5x9cm. f6 Dallmeyer Anastigmat triplet. Simple single-speed shutter, T&B. Three position focusing.

R3*   **C+**

J. Damoizeau,
Paris, France.

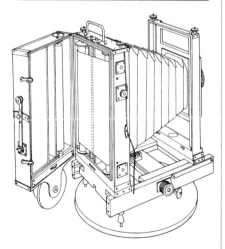

LE CYCLOGRAPHE A FOYER FIXE: panoramic camera which can cover a full 360 degrees. Clockworks motor drives film past a slit. This model Cyclographe has a fixed focus lens and is rigid.

R5*   **I–**

VARIABLE FOCUS CYCLOGRAPHE (DA500), Panoramic camera covering 360 degrees driven by a clockworks motor. Unlike the fixed focus model, the focusing Cyclographe is considerably larger and uses a bellows. There were two models, one for 7" film (178mm) and one for 9" (229mm) film.

R5 to unavail.   **NSR**

Dan Camera Works
Tokyo, Japan

DAN 35 MODEL I: 1946. 15 24x24mm exposures on 35mm size rollfilm. 50mm f4 Dan Anastigmat. Shutter speeds 1/25-1/100 + B.

R2*   **E**

DAN 35 MODEL II: 1948. Similar to Model I but with auto frame counter.

R2*   **E**

DAN 35 MODEL III: 1949. Similar to Models I and II, but with image size changed to 24x32mm and 40mm f3.5 Dan Anastigmat.

R2*   **E**

DAN SUPER 35: c. 1950. Similar to previous models with built-in rangefinder. 40mm f3.5 Eria Anastigmat lens. Shutter 1/25-1/200s + B. Flash synchronised.

R2   **F**

J. B. Dancer,
Manchester, England.

J. B. DANCER'S STEREO WET-PLATE CAMERA: c1856. This camera was probably the first commercially produced stereo wet-plate camera.

R5 to unavail.   **J**

Dangelmaier & Co.,
Reutlingen, Germany

This company changed names and address more than a few times in the 1950s and 60s, ending up in the mid 1970s as the Dacora/Weber company in Nürnberg. For simplicity all cameras are listed here, whether made in Reutlingen, Munich or Nürnberg.

DACO: c1949, bakelite box camera for 6 x 6 frames on roll film, simple lens, two position focusing, three lens openings, f11, f16, and f 22, single speed shutter, no built-in handle!

R3*   **B+**

DACI ROYAL: c1950, metal box camera for 6 x 6 frames on roll film, simple f9 lens, single speed shutter, synch connection.

R2*   **A**

DACI ROYAL I: c1950, metal box camera for 6 x 6 frames on roll film, simple f9 lens, single speed shutter, without synch connection.

R2*   **A**

SUBITA: c1953, folding VFR camera for 6 x 6 frames on roll film, Astigmat f6.3/75mm lens, simple Singlo two speed shutter,*without* double exposure prevention or body release. A cheap version of the Dacora camera .

R2*   **B–**

DACORA: c1953, folding VFR camera for 6 x 6 frames on roll film, Dacora f5.6/75mm lens, Vario shutter *without* double exposure prevention, or coated Dacora F3.5/75mm lens in Pronto or Prontor shutter *with* double exposure prevention!

R2*   **B+**

DACORA-RECORD: c1954, folding camera for 6 x 6 frames on roll film, uncoupled RFR, lever film advance, Dignar f4.5/75mm lens or Ennar or Westar f3.5/75mm lens in Prontor-s or Prontor SVS shutter.

R3*   **C–**

DACORA-RECORD-ROYAL: c1954, folding camera for 6 x 6 frames on roll film, *coupled RFR*, lever film advance, Dignar f4.5/75mm lens or Ennar or Westar f3.5/75mm lens in Prontor-S or Prontor SVS shutter.

R3*   **C+**

DIGNETTE: c1954-60, 35mm VFR camera, several body styles, several lens and shutter combinations, typically, Dignar f2.8/45mm lens in Vario shutter.

R2*   **B–**

SUPER DIGNETTE: c1955-60, 35mm VFR camera with built-in light meter, several body styles, several lens available, typically, Dignar f2.8/45mm lens in Vario or Pronto shutter.

R2*   **B–**

DIGNA 6 X 6: c1954, metal VFR camera for 6 x 6 frames on roll film, several lens and shutter combinations available, typically Westar f2.9/75mm, Prontor shutter

R2*   **B–**

DIGNA I: c1954, metal VFR camera for 6 x 6 frames on roll film, Achromat lens in single speed shutter, cheap version of the Digna 6 x 6 .

R2*   **B–**

COLOUR DIGNA 6 X 6: c1956, metal VFR camera for 6 x 6 frames on roll film, several lens and shutter combinations available, typically Achromat f4.5/75mm, Vario shutter, built-in extinction light meter.

R2*   **B–**

DACORA CC: c1960, full automatic 35mm VFR camera, with manual possible, Ysarex f2.8/45mm lens, Prontormatic shutter.

R2*   **B–**

DAKORA 66: c1964, simple metal VFR camera for 6 x 6 frames on 120 roll film.
R2*   **B–**

DAKORA 44: c1964, simple metal VFR camera for 4 x 4 frames on 127 roll film.
R3*   **B–**

Albert Darier
Geneva, Switzerland.

L'ESCOPETTE DE DARIER: gun-type detective camera; Steinheil Antiplanet 90mm f6 lens; spherical shutter 1/25-1/100 s. One of the first cameras to use Eastman roll film for 100 exp. 6.8 x 7.2cm. C 1888.
R5*   **J**

DARLING: sub-miniature camera; 16mm film in special cassette.
R4*   **F–**

A. Darlot
Paris, France.

LE RAPIDE: c1887. Darlot rectilinear 135mm f8 lens; rotary between-the-lens shutter; 12 plates, 9 x 12cm in gravity-fed magazine.
R4*   **I**

L. F. Deardorff & Sons
Chicago, Illinois.

L.F. DEARDORFF & SONS VIEW CAMERA: c1960. 5" x 7" view camera; front and rear swings and tilts; double extension bellows. Seasoned mahogany wood with nickel plated fittings. 4" x 5", 8" x 10". Users are willing to pay more than collectors.
R4*   **G**

Andre Debrie
Paris, France.

SEPT: c1923, half-frame 35mm still camera, movie camera, projector, contact printer. Berthiot Stylor 50mm f3.5 lens. 250 exp on perforated 35mm film, 18x24mm images.

Sept First Model

Sept
Second Model

Special cartridges held 17 feet of film. Sold by Societe Francais Sept. Two basic models. Flat front on first. Second model with a larger spring has rounded front. The Sept was frequently used by Hollywood cameramen during the silent film era for tricky shots requiring a very compact instrument.

R2* **E**

Delaye
Paris, France.

LE PRISMAC: c1906, stereo camera; Kenngott anastigmatic 54mm lenses; variable speed guillotine shutter. Le Prismac is fitted with internal prisms which eliminated the need to transpose stereo views when printing to positive.

R5* **H–**

Demarie-Lapierre-Mollier
Paris, France

DEHEL: 1940, 6 x 9cm folding roll film camera with various lenses and shutters, among which the Manar 90mm/f3.5 and f4.5 use a slightly curved film plane and pressure plate.

R2* **B–**

DEHEL PRIMAR: 1940, 6 x 4.5cm roll film camera, with various lens and shutter combinations. Called "The Soldier's Camera" when first introduced in the Spring of 1940.

R2* **B+**

TELKA-III (DEHEL SUPER): 1948, 6 x 9cm folding roll film camera with CRF, 95mm/f3.5 Sagittar in Prontor shutter, speeds of 1-⅟₂₀₀s, early cameras have a black face plate on the shutter, while later ones have a chrome plate. Delivered with a test film taken with the camera at the factory to show the quality of the lens!

R2* **C+**

TELKA-IIIA: 1951, 6 x 9cm folding roll film camera with CRF, 95mm/f3.5 Sagittar in Prontor SV shutter, speeds of 1-⅟₂₀₀s, bright yellow VFR window to increase the contrast of the rangefinder image.

R3* **C+**

TELKA-IIIB: 1952, 6 x 9cm folding roll film camera with CRF, 95mm/f3.5 Sagittar in Prontor SV shutter with "EV" markings, speeds of 1-⅟₃₀₀s, special adaptor for using Bantam 828 colour film.

R2* **D–**

TELKA-III "PROFESSIONAL": 1953, 6 x 9cm folding roll film camera with CRF, 95mm/f3.5 Sagittar in Prontor SV shutter, speeds of 1-⅟₃₀₀s, entirely black for that "professional look".

R4* **E–**

TELKA-X: 1950, 6 x 9cm folding roll film camera with simple lens and shutter, folding VFR, name marked on the shutter.

R2* **B+**

TELKA-XX: 1951, 6 x 9cm folding roll film camera with 110mm/f4.5 Manar lens in Gitzo shutter. Early cameras have a folding VFR, while later ones have a top plate similar to the Telka-III without CRF.

R2* **B+**

TELKA-I: 1954, 6 x 9cm folding roll film camera without CRF, 95mm/f3.5 Sagittar in Prontor shutter, speeds of 1-¼₀₀s, essentially the same camera as the Telka-III, but without CRF.

R3*   **B+**

SUMMA: 1953, 6 x 9cm folding roll film camera with simple lens and shutter, or 110mm/f4.5 Manar lens in Gitzo shutter, folding VFR, name marked on the shutter. The same camera as the Telka-X, and Telka-XX, but delivered for a company in Monte Carlo. The name was quickly dropped, as an Italian camera already had the registered rights to the name.

R3*   **C–**

TELKA-II: 1955, 6 x 4.5cm roll film camera, front focusing 75mm/f3.5 Manar lens, Prontor S shutter, speeds of 1 - ½₀₀s, folding VFR.

R3*   **C**

TELKA-SPORT: 1960, 6 x 4.5cm roll film camera, CRF 70mm/f3.5 Sagittar lens in an Atos shutter, speeds of 1-¼₀₀s. Provided with adaptors for using Bantam 828 film. About 1000 cameras are said to have been made. The last camera made by Demarie-Lapierre-Mollier, a house which was originally founded in 1848.

R4*   **E–**

Detrola Corp.
Detroit, Michigan.

DETROLA 400: c1938, 35mm rf camera; Wollensak Velostigmat 50mm f3.5 lens,

interchangeable screw mount; CFPS 1-¼₀₀s, CRF.

R3*   **F**

DETROLA A: c1938, Bakelite VFR camera for 3 x 4cm frames on 127 film, fixed focus lens and shutter in collapsible tube mount. (prices less in the USA).

R2*   **B–**

DETROLA B: c1938, with built-in extinction meter. (prices less in the USA).

R2*   **B+**

DETROLA D: c1938, with f4.5 lens. (prices less in the USA).

R3*   **B–**

DETROLA E: c1938, with f3.5 lens. (prices less in the USA).

R3*   **B–**

DETROLA G : c1938, Bakelite VFR camera for 3 x 4cm frames on 127 film, Detrola f4.5/2" lens, shutter ½₅ - ½₀₀s, collapsible tube mount, helociod focusing. (prices less in the USA).

R2*   **B–**

Devin Colorgraph Co.
New York.

DEVIN ONE-SHOT COLOUR CAMERA: c1940. 6.5 x 9cm sheet film one-shot

colour camera; Goerz Dogmar 5½" f4.5 lens; Compur dial-set shutter 1-½₅₀ s, CRF. c1940.

R5*   **F+**

QRS KAMRA:
c1928, 35mm bakelite camera; Graf Anastigmat f7.7 lens; single shutter speed. 40 exp on 35mm film in special cassette.

R3*   **D**

E. Deyrolle Fils
Paris, France.

LE SCENOGRAPHE OF DR. CANDEZE:
c1874, landscape lens mounted on sliding panel – stereo pictures in two exp. 10 x 15cm on dry plates. Le Scenographe was an extremely early example of a compact and inexpensive dry-plate camera.

R5*   **H**

DICK TRACY CAMERA: toy plastic camera; 127 roll film.

R2*   **C**

Diax Kamerawerk
Walter Voss, Ulm, Germany

DIAX: c1948-52, metal 35mm VFR camera, Xenar f2.8/4.5cm lens, Compur Rapid shutter.

R3*   **B+**

DIAX IA: c1950, metal 35mm VFR camera with three finders, one each for 35mm, 50mm, and 90mm fields of view, interchangeable Xenar f2.8/45mm, Xenon f2/50mm, Westar, or Isconar f3.5/50mm lens, Synchro Compur shutter.

R2*   **C**

DIAX II: c1950, metal 35mm camera with *coupled* RFR, *non*-changeable Xenar f2.8, Xenon f2, or Heligon f2/45mm lens, Synchro Compur shutter.

R2*   **C**

DIAX IIA: c1955, metal 35mm camera with coupled RFR, interchangeable Xenar f2.8/45mm, Xenon f2/50mm, Westar f3.5/50mm, or Isconar f3.5/50mm lens, Synchro Compur shutter. Built-in finder for 90mm lens located next to 50mm combined RFR/VFR.

R2*   **C+**

DIAX IB: c1956, metal 35mm VFR camera with three finders, one each for 35mm, 50mm, and 90mm fields of view, Westar f3.5, Isconar f3.5, Xenar f2.8 or Xenon f2/50mm lens, Synchro Compur shutter, lever advance, new body style compared with Diax Ia .

R3*   **C**

DIAX IIB: c1956, 35mm camera with coupled RFR for all lenses from 35mm to 135mm, seperate VFR for 90mm lens located next to combined RFR/VFR,

Isconar f3.5, Xenar f2.8 or Xenon f2/50mm lens, Synchro Compur shutter, lever advance, new body style compared with Diax IIa.

R2*   **D**

DIAXETTE: c1953, simple metal 35mm VFR camera, Cassar f2.8/45mm lens, Prontor shutter.

R3*   **B–**

ACCESSORIES FOR DIAX CAMERAS

Xenagon f3.5/35mm lens: **C–**

Isconar f4.5/85mm lens: **C+**

Tele-Xenar f3.5/90mm lens: **C+**

Tele-Xenar f4/135mm lens: **C+**

DAN 35: Dan 40mm f4.5 lens; single speed shutter; 12 exp on special cassettes, 24 x 24mm exp. c1950.

R3*   **C+**

Ditmar
Vienna, Austria

DITMAR: c1939, 9.5mm movie camera; Cinor Berthiot 25mm f1.8 lens; 2 speeds: 16 and 32 frames per s; non-coupled photo-electric cell; 15mm cassettes. Mfd in Austria.

R3*   **C–**

Dom-Martin
Paris, France.

DOM-MARTIN: c1903, press-type stereo camera; aluminium body. 2 sizes: 6 x 13cm, 8 x 16cm.

R4*   **F+**

Doryu Camera Co.
Japan.

DORYU-2: c1890, pistol-type detective camera; Dorimar 17mm f2.5 lens; 3 speed shutter. 10 x 10mm exp on special 16mm film. bullet shaped flash cartridges. In 1955, an improved model was produced with a 15mm f2.2 lens and a faster shutter.

R5*   **J+**

DORYU FLASH CARTRIDGES: Packages of six bullet shaped flash cartridges have recently made their way into the market. They would be of more value to a Doryu owner, who might be willing to pay above the going price for a package to try out in his camera!

R3*   **D+**

Dossert Detective Camera Co.
New York, New York.

DOSSERT DETECTIVE CAMERA: c1890, 4" x 5" leather covered, box-type detective camera; 4" x 5" exp on dry plates; sliding panels to mask lens openings and ground glass opening.

R4*   **F+**

007 ATTACHE CASE CAMERA: c1970, toy camera; radio, coding device, and tele-scope in attache case.

R4*   **E+**

Dr. Doyer, M. Gillon
France.

LA DIPLIDE: c1904, eye-level reflex camera; helicoid focusing to 0.5m. 6 x 13cm exp on roll film.

R4*   **F–**

Dubroni
Paris, France.

DUBRONI APPARATUS NO. 1: c1865. Rigid bodied camera for in-camera processing of single wet collodion plate. Lens cap controls exposure. Invented by Bourdin, Paris, France. (Dubroni is an anagram of Bourdin). Mfd. by Maison Dubroni, Paris, France. The first model shows the exposed bottle in which all the processing takes place.

R5*   **H+**

DUBRONI APPARATUS NO. 1 (SECOND VERSION): c1866. Sides are enclosed and the internal bottle is ceramic. Both cameras were sold with a complete case containing all necessary chemicals for sensitizing and

Dubroni Apparatus No. 1

processing the plate. They are very rarely found with the complete system.

R5*   **G+**

LE PHOTO SPORT: c1889, Darlot Planigraphe 210mm f9 lens; simple rotary shutter. 9 x 12cm plates.

R5*   **J–**

Ducati
Milan, Italy.

Ducati Simplex with rangefinder

DUCATI SIMPLEX: c1938, half-frame 35mm camera; Ducati Etar f3.5/35mm lens; CFPS $\frac{1}{25}$-$\frac{1}{250}$ s.

R3*   **F–**

DUCATI (WITH RANGEFINDER): c1938, half-frame 35mm camera, Vitor f3.5/35mm lens; CFPS $\frac{1}{20}$-$\frac{1}{500}$ s, CRF.

R3*   **F**

DURST S.A.
Switzerland.

AUTOMATICA: 1961. Automatic 35mm camera. Setting the film speed also sets the aperture and the built-in meter selects the shutter speed, indicated by a needle in a top plate window. Override allows both shutter speeds and apertures to be set manually. 45mm f2.8 Schneider Durst Radionar and Prontor-SVS shutter 1-1/300s + B.

R2*   **A**

DUCA: c1946, 35mm camera; Ducar 50mm f11 lens; shutter, T and I. 12 exp, 24 x 36mm on Agfa Rapid cassettes.

R3*   **D–**

Duca

Reference Notes

Earth KK
Japan

GUZZI: c.1938. Subminiature, cast metal camera for 20x20mm images on miniature rollfilm. Unmarked fixed focus lens, everset shutter for I & B. Similar to the post-war Top from the Top Camera Works.

R4   **A**

Eastern Speciality Mfg. Co.
Boston, Massachusetts.

SPRINGFIELD UNION CAMERA: c1899, plate brought into plane of focus by rotating block inside camera; 4 exp, 3½" x 3½" on dry plates.

R4*   **F–**

Albert Ebner & C0.
Stuttgart, Germany.

EBNER: c1938, plastic folding camera; Rodenstock-Trinar-Anastigmat 10.5cm f4.5 lens; Compur shutter 1-¹⁄₂₅₀ s; 8 exp, 2¼" x 3¼" on 120 roll film.

R3*   **D+**

EDER PATENT CAMERA: c1930. German folding plate camera; viewing lens and bellows paired horizontally with taking lens; 6 x 6cm exp on plate or film.

R4*   **F**

Eho Kamerafabrik
Dresden, Germany

After July 1939, known as the Amca Kamerawerk, Berthold Altman prop, Altmann lent the first three letters of his family name to Altissa, Altix, Altiflex and Altiscope line of cameras. See Altissa Kamerawerk for post-war cameras.

ALTISSA: c1939. Simple fixed focus box camera design with I and B speed shutter. Large optical finder in top with some models having reflex viewing adds 100% to the price. Not to be confused with the post-war Altissa, though looking very similar!

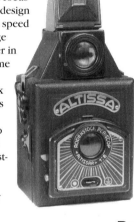

R2*   **D+**

Ebner

EHO BOX: 1932-39, line of inexpensive box cameras in 6 x 6cm, 6 x 9cm, 6 x 4.5cm and 3 x 4cm formats with meniscus or better lenses, some with wire frame finders in addition to the typical waistlevel reflex finders. All are about the same price, though the smaller format cameras are rarer and go for 100% more.

R2*   **A**

EHO STEREO BOX: c1936, simple box camera for stereo pairs 6 x 13cm on roll film, wire frame finder and reflex finder.

R2*   **D–**

ALTIFLEX: c1936-39, TLR for 6 x 6 frames on roll film with Victar or Trinar 75mm lens in Automat, Prontor II or Compur shutter, side mounted focusing handle.

R3*   **C–**

ALTISCOPE: c1936, stereo camera for 6 x 13cm stereo pairs, or 6 x 6 single non-stereo frames, Victor f4.5/75mm lenses, simple three speed shutter, the same optical finder as used on the Altissa box camera.

R4*   **D**

ALTIX: c1937, 35mm VFR camera for 24 x 24mm frames on regular 35mm film, Laack f3.5/3.5cm lens, simple shutter. The first of the Altix cameras. (See **ALTISSA** listing for post-war cameras).

R3*   **B+**

Eiho Company
Taiwan

DRINKS CANS CAMERAS: c.1977. All of the same basic design, but with different trade names on them. 110 cameras with fixed focus, aperture and shutter speeds. Designs include Coca Cola, Pepsi Cola, Miller Lite, 7-Up, Budweiser, Crown Paint and more.

R1*   **A**

L'Electra Plastica Industria S.A.
(L.E.P.I.S.A.) Barcelona, Spain

FOTEX: c1960, bakelite VFR camera for 6 x 9cm on roll film, simple lens and shutter, delivered with a bakelite lens/shutter cover just like the Photax by MIOM.

R4*   **C**

Elop Kamerawerk Flansburg
Germany

ELCA II c1950; 35mm camera; 50 exp 24 X 24mm; 3.5cm f4.5 Elocn lens; Prontor shutter;

R3*   **D**

E. Enjalbert
Paris, France.

L'ALPINISTE: c1886. Aplanatic lens; guillotine shutter. Magazine held 9 x 12cm plates which were changed manually through a leather pouch.

R5*   **G–**

PHOTO REVOLVER (DE POCHE): c1883, revolver-type detective camera; achromatized periscopic 70mm f10 lens; between

the lens rotary sector shutter. 10 exp, 2 x 2cm on dry plates. Rotation of barrel (magazine) simultaneously changed the plate and cocked the shutter. The trigger acted as the shutter release.

R5* **J+**

LE TOURIST D'ENJALBERT: Steinheil lens with waterhouse stops; 8 exp on 13 x 18cm plates. C 1880.

R5* **F+**

Erac Selling Co.
London, England

ERAC: c1931, pistol-type detective camera; fixed focus meniscus lens; 18 x 18mm exp on 20mm roll film. Film advance coupled to trigger and shutter. Invented by H. Covill and H. Steward.

R4* **F+**

Erica S.R.L
Argentina.

ATLAS: c1950, metal box camera for 6 x 9cm frames on roll film, simple lens and shutter.

R4* **B+**

Heinrich Ernemann Werke A.G.
Dresden, Germany

BOB 0: c1924. Ernemann Double Erid 5" f8 lens; 4⅛" x 3¼" exp on roll film.

R2* **B**

BOB I: c1924. Ernemann Ernastigmat 5¼" f 6.8* lens; Cronos shutter; 4⅛" x 3¼" exp on roll film.

R2* **B**

BOB II: c1924. Ernemann Ernastigmat 5¼" f6.8* lens; Cronos shutter; 4⅛" x 3¼" exp on roll film.

R2* **B**

BOB III: Ernemann Ernastigmat 4⅛" f6.8* lens; Cronos shutter; 3⅛" x 2⅛" exp on roll film. c1924.

R2* **B+**

BOB IV: c1924. Ernemann Ernastigmat 4⅜" f6.8* lens; Cronos shutter; 3¼" x 2¼" exp on roll film.

R2* **C**

BOB V: c1910-1913. Ernemann Ernastigmat 3" f6.8* lens; Cronos shutter; 2½" x 1⅝" exp on roll film.

R2* **C**

BOB X: c1922, roll film stereo camera; Ernon 65mm f6.8 lenses; 45 x 107mm exp on roll film.

R4* **F–**

BOB XV: c1924, roll film stereo camera; Ernemann Doppel-Anastigmat (Ernon) 65mm f6.8 lenses; interleaf shutter 1 - ¹⁄₁₉₀₀ s, optical vf, reflecting waist level vf. 45 x 107mm exp on roll film. c1924.

R4*   **F**

ERMANOX F1.8: c1926. 4.5 x 6cm miniature plate camera; Ernostar 85mm f1.8 lens; CFPS ¹⁄₂₀-¹⁄₁₀₀₀ s.

R4*   **G+**

BOBETTE I: c1923-1925. Ernoplast 50mm f4.5 lens; Automatic central shutter ¹⁄₂₅-¹⁄₁₀₀ s; 22 x 33cm exp on special 40mm wide roll film.

R3*   **D**

ERMANOX (6.5 X 9CM): c1925, 6.5 x 9cm plate camera; Ernostar 125mm f1.8 lens; CFPS ¹⁄₂₀-¹⁄₁₀₀₀ s.

R4*   **G+**

ERNI: c1920. Achromatic f12.5 lens; 2⁵⁄₁₆" x 1⅜" exp on plates.

R3*   **E**

ERMANOX F2.0 (ORIGINAL): c1924, 4.5 x 6cm miniature plate camera; Ernostar 100mm f2.0 lens; CFPS ¹⁄₂₀ - ¹⁄₁₀₀₀ s.

R4*   **G+**

ERNOFLEX: c1920. 4.5 x 6cm SLR camera; Ernon 75mm f3.5 lens; CFPS ¹⁄₂₀-¹⁄₁₀₀₀ s.

R3*　　　　　　　　　**G**

FILM K BOX CAMERA: c1914-1927; taking 4 X 6.5cm, 6 X 6cm, 5 X 7.5cm, 6 X 9cm, 6.5 X 11cm exp on roll film; lens f12.5; shutter 'T' & 'I';

R3*　　　　　　　　　**C+**

GLOBUS FIELD VIEW CAMERA: c1900, 13" x 18" view camera; Any number of brass lenses can be found mounted on this camera; FPS; double extension bellows; polished wood with brass fittings; black cloth-covered holders. Brass importer's label: Allison & Hadaway Corp., N.Y.

R4*　　　　　　　　　**F–**

ERNOFLEX, MODEL II WITH TRIPLE EXTENSION: c1925. 3¼" x 4" folding SLR camera; Ernemann Ernon 7⅛" f3.5 lens; CFPS to ¹⁄₁₀₀₀ s. Probably the first SLR to couple the revolving back to movable masks in the vf area.

R4*　　　　　　　　　**F**

STEREO ERNOFLEX: c1925, 45 x 107mm stereo camera; Ernostar 75mm f4.5 lenses; CFPS ½₅-¹⁄₁₂₀₀ s.

R5*　　　　　　　　　**H–**

Stereo Ernoflex

HEAG I: c1924. Ernemann Erid 3¹⁵⁄₁₆" f8 lens; 3½" x 2½" exp on plates.

R2*   **B+**

HEAG II: c1924. Ernemann Ernoplast 5¼" f4.5* lens; Cronos shutter; 4¼" x 3¼" exp on plates.

R2*   **B+**

HEAG III: c1924. Ernemann Erid 4¹⁄₈" f8 lens; Cronos shutter 3½" x 2½" exp on plates.

R2*   **B+**

HEAG IV: c1924. Ernemann Ernastigmat 5¼" f6.8 lens; Cronos shutter; 4¼" x 3¼" exp on plates.

R2*   **B+**

HEAG V: (EW124): c1924. Zeiss Tessar 5¼" f6.3* lens; Cronos shutter; 4¼" x 3¼" exp on plates.

R2*   **F−**

HEAG VII: c1924. Zeiss Tessar ¼" f6.3* lens; Cronos shutter; 4¼" x 3¼" exp on plates.

R2*   **B+**

HEAG XI: c1924. Zeiss Tessar 7⅛" f6.3* lens; Cronos shutter; 6½" x 4¾" exp on plates.

R2*   **C−**

TROPICAL HEAG XI: c1920. 9 x 12cm tropical plate camera; Tessar 13.5cm f6.3 lens; Compur 1-¹⁄₂₅₀ s. Mahogany finish, brown bellows and brass fittings. 9 x 12cm exp on plates.

R4*   **G+**

HEAG XII: c1911. 10 x 15cm camera; Ernon 150mm f6.8 lens; Ernemann central shutter.

R3*   **C**

HEAG XII: c1907, model 3; 9 x 14cm stereo camera; Ernemann Double Anastigmat 15cm lens; shutter 1-¹⁄₃₀₀ s.

R4*   **E+**

HEAG XI: c1914. 45 x 107mm folding stereo camera; Ernemann Aplanat 65mm f6.8 lens; between lens shutter to ¹⁄₃₀₀ s.

R4*   **E**

HEAG XV: c1913-14. Folding camera; 4.5 X 6cm size; 80mm f6.8 Detective Aplomat lens; dial-set shutter; 1s,½,⅕,½5,½0 ½00s.; Two fixed brilliant Vfr on baseboard. Stereo version, quadruple prices.

R4*   **C+**

KLAPP; c1920. Folding press camera (strut type); CFPS; various lenses from Bush Aplanat to Tessars and f2.7 Ernostar. Early models (illustrated) had single fold bellows; open viewfinder; later models had conven-

tional bellows; protected viewfinder; Made in 6.5 X 9cm, 9 X 12cm, 10 X 15cm, 13 X 18cm.

R3*   **E–**

KLAPP STEREO: c1911. Tessar 55mm f4.5 lenses; FPS; changing mechanism for 12 plates.

R4*   **G**

TROPICAL KLAPP: c1914. 10 x 15cm plate camera; Tessar 165cm f4.5 lens; CFPS. Teak construction with brown leather bellows and brass fittings.

R4*   **G+**

MINIATURE KLAPP: c1914-1925. 4.5 x 6cm folding camera; Anastigmat 75mm f4.5 lens; FPS to ½000 s. 4.5 x 6cm exp on plates.

R4*   **F+**

ROLF I: Ernemann Ernastigmat 3" f6.8* lens; Cronos shutter to ¹⁄₁₀₀ s; 2½" x 15/8" 8 exp on roll film. c1924.

R2*   **B+**

UNETTE: c1924, leather covered wooden bodied box camera for 22 x 33mm exp on special 40mm roll film, meniscus lens; guillotine shutter.

R4*   **D**

LILIPUT: c1913. Simple folding camera with achromatic lens, the least expensive camera made by Ernemann. 4.5x6cm images on glass plates.

R4*   **F**

STEREO LILIPUT: c1914. Simple stereo camera, with achromatic lens which made 45x107mm stereo pairs on single glass plates.

R4*   **F**

SIMPLEX: c1924. Double Erid 5½" f11 lens; 3½" x 2½" exp on plates.

R2*   **C+**

STEREO-SIMPLEX: c1924. Ernemann Erid 2⅜" f8 lenses; 45 x 107mm exp on plates.

R3*   **D**

Edward Eves Ltd.
Leamingtom Spa, England

EDWARD EVES ONE SHOT COLOR CAMERA: 1949. Beam-splitting colour camera made for 5x4-inch plates in standard Speed Graphic or MPP holders. Pellicle reflectors split the image through tri-colour set of filters mounted in glass. Body of Elektron casting. Lens panel with swing and tilt. 10½-inch f6 Taylor Taylor & Hobson Aviar lens as standard, 10-inch f8 Aldis lens offered as a cheaper alternative. Rack and pinion focusing. Took the Kodak P 1200 plate.

R4*   **G**

EDWARD EVES COLOR CAMERA: 1951. Similar to the One Shot Color Camera, but made for 3/2 x 2½ inch negative size. 13.5cm f4.8 Wray Lustrar lens in Epsilon shutter.

R4*   **G**

Expo Camera Co.
New York, New York

EXPO: (1905-1939) Watch style detective camera. Meniscus lens; 16x22mm images on roll film in daylight loading cassette. The

Expo

Expo was also manufactured in England using the name Ticka.

R3*   **E+**

EXPO POLICE CAMERA: c1911. Miniature detective camera; meniscus f16 lens, adjustable diaphragm; CFPS; 12 exp, 12 x 26mm on roll film in special cassette.

R4*   **F**

Expo (also manufactured in England using the name Ticka)

Reference Notes

_____

_____

_____

_____

_____

_____

_____

_____

_____

_____

_____

_____

_____

_____

_____

_____

Fabrik Fotografsches Apparats
Lübeck, Germany

FOTAL: c.1950-54. Unusual cylindrical shape body with fixed focus 20mm f2.8 Optar lens. Prontor shutter. Made for 9.5mm size and 16mm rollfilm. Made in green, black, blue and reptile skin body covering.

R4*   **A**

FAP, Fabrique d'Appareils Photographique
Suresnes, France

NORCA "A": c1938, Bakelite 35mm VFR camera, with leather covering, 50mm/f3.5 Saphir or Flor lens in spring loaded collapsible tube, Gitzo btl shutter, speeds ½s-⅓₀₀s, very like the Argus "A" camera.

R3*   **E–**

NORCA "B": c1946, Bakelite bodied 35mm VFR camera, 50mm/f3.5 Saphir or Flor lens in collapsible tube, *not* spring loaded as the Norca "A", "Rapid-Synchro" copy of Compur Rapid shutter or simpler Norca shutter, speeds ½s-⅓₀₀s. The story goes that the director of FAB was held in a German prisoner of war camp for 5 long years. Upon his release, he quickly picked up where he left off back in 1939. As a result, the Norca "B" was one of the first French cameras on the market in quantity after WWII.

R3*   **C+**

NORCA "CMT": c1948. Metal bodied 35mm VFR camera, keeping the same design as the Norca "A" and "B" cameras, black leather covering, top mounted accessory shoe, 50mm/f3.5 FAP Anistigmat lens in Rapid-Synchro Shutter, speeds 1-1/500s. Some dark brown cameras were made (worth 50% more).

R3*   **C+**

LE ROWER: c1948. Black bakelite VFR camera for 3 x 4cm format on special Gevaert film. Very like the Univex model A camera.

R3*   **B+**

NORCA PIN UP: based on the bakelite bodied Rower camera, 24 x 36mm format on 35mm film in special cassettes, 50mm/f3.5 FAP Anistigmat lens in Atos shutter, ⅒-⅓₀₀s, Optical VFR. Announced as the Norca PM (for petite module) then Norca Atomic, the name Pin Up was finally chosen. Only a few hundred made.

R4*   **D**
R2*   **D–**

Gilles Faller
Paris, France

CHAPEAU PHOTOGRAPHIQUE: c1884, hat-type detective camera; aplanatic lens covered by button at top of hat; 9 x 12cm plates loaded in double frame. Tripod folds into cane; camera could also be mounted in a hat provided by the buyer. Original price was 90 francs.

R5*   **J**

GILFA (7 X 9CM): c1920. Anastigmat 105mm f4.5 Virlot lens; Gitzo central shutter. Mahogany finish.

R4*   **D+**

J. Fallowfield Ltd.
London, England

FALLOWFIELD FACILE: c1890, box-type detective camera; 12 exp, 3¼" x 4¼" on plates, Miall's patent.

R4*   **F+**

FALLOWFIELD HAND CAMERA: c1892, valise-type detective camera; similar to Hand Camera – a small valise covered in Moroccan crocodile skin.

R4*   **F–**

MIALL HAND CAMERA: vc1891, valise-type detective camera; 8 x 10cm exp on plates (daylight loading). Size: 15 x 18 x 25cm; weight 2.3kg.

R4*   **H+**

Fauvel
Paris, France

FAUVEL: c1889, 8 x 16cm stereo camera; rising front.

R4*   **E+**

FAUVEL: c1912, 45 x 107mm stereo camera; Rapid Rectilinear lens; iris diaphragm; FPS.

R3*   **F–**

FAUVEL POST CARD: c1899, 9 x 14cm stereo camera; cpfs; covered with Moroccan leather.

R4*   **F–**

FED Machine Works
Kharkov, Ukraine (formerly USSR)

Early FED and fake Leica

FED: 1934-55. Cfps, ½₀ – ⅟₅₀₀ s, no slow speeds, no synch, CRF. Interchangeable Leica-type screw mount lens. The original FED camera was a copy of the Leica II camera. The history of the factory is quite interesting. About 700,000 FED cameras were made with no technical changes. At least six different engraving styles are known to exist. A table showing serial number information is located in the ID section, and will help you in establishing the year of manufacture of a FED camera. Early cameras, first 1000=**G**, *serial numbered 31-4000* bring **F**, *numbers 4000-20,000*, **E**. Numbers above 10,000 are quite common.

R2*   **D+**

FED-2 (FIRST VERSION): 1955-57. Cfps, ½₀ to ⅟₅₀₀ s, no slow speeds, no synch, CRF.

Interchangeable Leica-type screw mount lens. Not a true Leica copy, the first version FED-2 uses a combined rangefinder/viewfinder window, removeable back, and long base rangefinder. It kept, however the collapsible FED f3.5/50mm lens of its predecessor. US prices 50% higher.

R2*   **D+**

FED-2 (SECOND VERSION): 1957-64. Like the first version FED-2, except with flash synch and self timer. Cfps, ½₀ to ⅟₅₀₀s, no slow speeds, no synch, CRF. Interchangeable Leica-type screw mount lens. Rigid FED/Industar 26M f2.8/52mm lens. Like the first version FED-2, except with flash synch and self timer. US prices 50% higher. (Red Blue and Green covered versions have been found, but they seem to have been recovered *outside* the factory, probably in Poland.)

R2*   **D**

FED-2L: 1964-70s. Cfps, ½₀ to ⅟₅₀₀s, no slow speeds, synch, CRF. Interchangeable Leica-type screw mount lens, Like the second version FED-2, but now with an improved f2.8, 52mm Industar-61 lens, made with rare earth glass containing Lanthanum, and self timer. US prices 50% higher.

R2*   **D**

FED-3 (FIRST VERSION): 1962-64. Cfps, 1 to ⅟₅₀₀ s, slow speeds, synch, CRF. Interchangeable Leica-type screw mount lens, self timer and f2.8/52mm Industar lens. Slow speeds, different diopter adjustment system, and a changed top plate came with this model. Very few were made before the introduction of the improved second version, though prices for each are the same. US prices 50% higher.

R3*   **D**

FED-3 (SECOND VERSION): 1964-80s. Cfps, 1 to ⅟₅₀₀ s, slow speeds, synch, CRF. Interchangeable Leica-type screw mount lens, self timer. Using the f2.8, 52mm Industar-61 lens, and having a single-level

top plate, the second version FED-3 also incorporated a rapid advance lever instead of the round knob used on all earlier FED cameras. Also sold as the Revue-3, this camera was made in quite large quantities. The "Olympic" model adds about 30% to the value of the camera. US prices 50% higher.

R2*   **D**

FED-4: c1964. Cfps, 1 to ⅟₅₀₀ s, slow speeds, synch, CRF. Interchangeable Leica-type screw mount lens, self timer. Like the FED-3, with Industar-61 f2.8, 52mm lens, but with the addition of a built-in light meter. Also sold as the Revue-4. More common in Europe. US prices 50% higher.

R2*   **D**

FED-5A: after 1978. Cfps, 1 to ⅟₅₀₀ s, slow speeds, synch, CRF. Interchangeable Leica-type screw mount lens, self timer. An improved version of the FED-4, with the same features. US prices about 50% higher.

R2*   **D**

FED-5B: after 1978. Cfps, 1 to 1/500 s, slow speeds, synch, CRF. Interchangeable Leica-type screw mount lens, self timer. The same as the FED-5A, but without the built-in light meter. Not made for the export market. "Olympic" model adds 30% to the price. US prices about 50% higher.

R2*   **D**

FED-5C: after 1978. Cfps, 1 to ⅟₅₀₀ s, slow speeds, synch, CRF. Interchangeable Leica-type screw mount lens, self timer. The

same as the FED-5A with the addition of a bright line viewfinder frame. US prices about 50% higher.

R2*   **D**

ZARYA: 1958-59. Cfps, $^{1}/_{20}$ to $^{1}/_{500}$ s, no slow speeds, synch. Interchangeable Leica-type screw mount lens. f3.5/52mm rigid mount Industar lens. Not a true Leica copy, and the only Russian Leica-type camera without a rangefinder. Very few were made, and since its original price was not much lower than the FED-2, it was not very successful on the market place. The current price does not reflect its rarity.

R3*   **D**

FED V (B): 1938. The same camera as other early FEDs, but with the addition of slow speeds and $^{1}/_{1000}$ s. It is said only 40 cameras were made.

R5*   **NSR**

FED S(C): 1938. The same as other early FEDs, except with the addition of $^{1}/_{1000}$ s.

R4*   **E+**

COUNTERFEIT LEICA: Some FED cameras are found with top plates engraved with Leitz markings. These cameras show very poor quality plating, and generally inferior workmanship when compared to the Leica's which they were attempting to mimic. On many cameras the top plate remains un-drilled where the accessory shoe would normally be placed.

R3*   **F–**

FED STEREO: c1989, 35mm stereo camera with Industar-81 f2.8.38mm lenses, simple shutter $^{1}/_{30}$ – $^{1}/_{650}$s, automatic exposure control. Though a new product, this camera has become an "instant" collectable.

R3*   **F**

Feinwerktechnik GmbH
Lahr, Germany

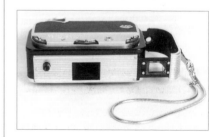

MEC 16: c1956, subminiature camera, f2.8/20mm lens, shutter $^{1}/_{25}$ – $^{1}/_{1000}$s. 24 exp, 10 x 14mm on 16mm film, in brown, black

or gold. (complete presentation case adds 200%).

R2*   **C**

MEC 16SB: c1957. Coupled TTL light meter and Heligon f2/22mm lens, shutter ⅕₀ – ¹⁄₁₀₀₀s. "SB" stands for *Simultan-Belichtungsmesser*. This was the first non-SLR to offer TTL metering. (complete presentation case adds 200%).

R2*   **D–**

Ferannia
Milan, Italy

EURA 66: 1959. 12 exp on 120. Black plastic body with metal lens panel and chrome trim. Coated meniscus f8 lens. Everset shutter at 1/50s. Flash synch.

R2*   **B+**

ASTOR: 1953. 12 exp on 120. Alloy die cast. Double telescopic metal tube links lens to body. 75mm f4.5 lens made by Officine Galileo. Prontor-SV shutter 1-1/300s + B. X & M synch. Viewfinder indicator appears after exposure to act as film wind reminder.

R2*   **B+**

ELIOFLEX: 1951. TLR for 12 exp on 120. Apertures f8-f22. Speeds 1/25-1/200s + B. Finished in black imitation leather and chrome.

R2   **B+**

Joseph Fetter

PHOTO ECLAIR: c1886, concealed vest detective camera; rectilinear 40mm f8 lens; rotary sector shutter; 5 exp on 4 x 4cm plates. Plate changed by rotating camera back. Shutter differentiates this from the Gray and Stirn models. Later model had lens

at base of camera, to allow addition of a 45 degree angle vf.

R5*   **H**

FEX
Lyon, France

COMPA FEX: c1942; simple black wooden box camera with frame finder made during the German occupation of France. Very few have survived.

FEX: c1944; simple bakelite camera for 4.5x6cm pictures on roll film. Replaced by Super Fex in 1945. Fexar lens, single speed shutter. The company made a large number of simple plastic cameras frequently found in French flee markets. Curiously a nearly identical camera was made in Czechoslovakia for several years after the war. Both are clearly identified as Made in France or Made in Czechoslovakia.

R4*   **B+**

SUPER-FEX: Simple black bakelite camera for 6 x 4.5 format on roll film. Metal wind knob. Made in large quantities.

R2*   **B–**

ULTRA-FEX: Simple black bakelite camera for 6 x 9 format on roll film. Made in many, many versions, among which are the Sport-Fex, the Uni-Fex, and the Delta, all having the lens in a rectangular collapsible mount.

One of the most commonly found French cameras.

R1*   **A**

ELITE: One of the Ultra-Fex versions, but with built-in extinction meter, and through the use of a metal mask both 6 x 9cm and 6 x 6cm formats were possible. Often found with Colour-Fexar lens in Atos shutter.

R2*   **B–**

Finetta Werk, P. Saraber
Goslar, Germany

FINETTE: c1947, 35mm VFR camera, Fenar f6.3/43mm lens, simple shutter.

R3*   **B+**

FINETTA: c1950, 35mm VFR camera, Finetar f2.8/45mm lens, interchangeable mount, FPS ½₅-¼₀₀₀ s.

R2*   **B+**

FINETTA SUPER: c1951, 35mm VFR camera, interchangeable Finetar f2.8/45mm lens, simple shutter, ½₅ – ¼₀₀S, flat top plate.

R2*   **B+**

FINETTA 88: c1954, with ½₅ – ½₀₀S shutter.

R2*   **C–**

FINETTA 99: c1955, 35mm VFR camera, Finetar f2.8/45mm or Staeble-Finon f2.8/45mm lens, interchangeable mount; FPS 1-⅟₁₀₀₀ s. Built-in spring motor drive – 20

exp in 10 sec. possible when fully wound; Earlier version had no slow speeds.

R3*   **E–**

ACCESSORY LENSES FOR FINETTA CAMERAS

Finettare f4.5/35mm wide angle lens: **C**

Finettare f4.5/70mm telephoto lens: **C**

Finettare f6.3/105mm telephoto lens: **C**

Dr. Foi,
Geneva, Switzerland

DR. FOL'S PHOTOGRAPHIC RIFLE: c1984, rifle-type detective camera; Steinheil Antiplanet lens; Thury & Amey shutter. 11 plates, 9 x 10cm in magazine.

R5*   **J**

Foster Instruments Pty. Ltd.
Sydney, Australia

SWIFTSHOT: c1951, metal box camera for 6 x 9 frames on 120 or 620 roll film, simple lens and shutter, built-in yellow filter, marked either "Model A" or "made in Australia" on the camera front, in red, black, blue, beige, grey, green or crocodile!

R2*   **B–**

Swiftshot

Foth & Co.
Berlin, Germany (also see Gallus)

FOTH DERBY I: c1930, 127 roll film folding camera; Foth Anastigmat 50mm f3.5 lens; CFPS ½₂₅-½₀₀ s; The first model made 1" x 1½" negatives; later 16 exp, 1¼" x 1¼" on 127 roll film.

R2*　　　　　　　　　　　　　**B+**

FOTH DERBY II: c1934, 127 roll film folding camera; Foth Anastigmat 50mm

f3.5 lens; CFPS ½₂₅-½₀₀ s, CRF. 16 exp, 11/4" x 1½" on 127 roll film.

R2*　　　　　　　　　　　　　**D–**

FOTH-FLEX: c1935, 2¼" x 2¼" TLR; Foth Anastigmat 75mm f3.5 lens; CFPS 1-½₀₀s; 12 exp, 2¼" x 2¼" on 120 roll film. The Foth-Flex was the only medium format twin-lens reflex fitted with a focal plane shutter.

R3*　　　　　　　　　　　　　**D**

FOTH FOLDING CAMERA: c1930, 120 roll film folding camera; Foth Doppel Anastigmat 105mm f4.5 lens; Compound 1/25-¹⁄₁₀₀ s. Some covered in alligator skin valued 50% higher.

R4*   **D**

Fotobras S.A. Ind. & Com.
Curtiba-Parana, Brazil

BRASILMATIC CAMERA: c1950, metal box camera for 6 x 9cm frames on roll film, simple lens and shutter.

R3*   **B**

Foto-Fex Kamerawerk
Fritz Kraftanski Berlin, Germany

MINI-FEX: c1930, subminiature VFR camera for 13mm x 18mm frames on 16mm perforated film, various lens and

shutters offered including Astrar f2.7 or "ultra fast" Pan-Tachar f1.8/25mm lens, Compur or Pronto shutter; Earlest cheapest model.

R4*   **F**

MINI-FEX MG: c1939, sub-miniature VFR camera for 13mm x 18mm frames on 16mm perforated film, Trioplan f3.5 or "ultra fast" Pan-Tachar f1.8/25mm lens, Pronto shutter. The "MG" in the name refers to the German *"MaschinenGewahr"*, meaning machine gun. One sliding movement of a button located on the camera side armed the shutter, released the shutter, and transported the film.

R4*   **G**

SCHOOLBOY-BOX: c1929, metal box camera for 4cm x 6cm plates, meniscus lens, two speed shutter.

R3*   **A**

FRAMA – Franz Matthias
Dresden, Germany

This photo retailer sold cameras under its house brand names. They were actually made by companies like Balda and Agfa.

FRAMAX: c1930, metal folding camera for 6 x 9cm frames on roll film, f4.5 or 6.3 lens, Prontor shutter among others.

R2*   **A**

FRAMAFIX: c1930, metal folding camera for 6 x 9cm *or* 6 x 4.5 on roll film, Xenar f4.5/105mm lens among others.

R2*   **A**

KNIPSY: c1930, metal folding camera for 6 x 9cm frames on roll film, front lens focusing Trioplan f6.3 or f4.5/105mm lens, Vario or other shutter.

R2*   **A**

PLANA: c1930, folding bed camera for 6 x 9cm plates or film packs, Xenar f4.5/105mm lens among others, Vario, Prontor or Compur shutter, wire frame finder.

R3*   **B+**

ROLLY: c1930, metal folding camera for 6 x 9cm on roll film, Anastigmat f4.5/105mm lens among others, Vario or Pronto shutter, wire frame finder.

R2*   **A**

Francais
Paris, France

LE COSMOPOLITE: c1887. 2 Francais Rectilinear lenses (bayonet mounts) with waterhouse stops; behind the lens shutter. 9 x 12cm exp on plates.

R4*   **E+**

Franka Camera Werke
Bayreuth, Germany

BUBI: c1915, strut folding camera for 6 x 4.5 plates or film packs, simple shutter and lens, wire frame finder.

R3*   **C+**

BUBI VELO: c1915, strut folding camera for 6 x 4,5cm plates of film packs, Velonar f6.8/75mm lens, Compound shutter, wire frame finder.

R3*   **D**

BUBI 3 X 4: c1930, metal folding camera for 3 x 4cm frames on 127 film, Victar f4.5/75mm lens among others, Prontor shutter.

R2*   **A**

VEST POCKET MODEL 50: c1921, strut folding camera for 6 x 4.5 plates or film-packs, with waist level finder and dialset Compur.

R3*   **D**

BONAFIX: c1930-1955, metal folding camera for 6 x 9cm or 6 x 4.5 frames on roll film, f6.3/105mm lens, Vario shutter, *most* cameras after 1950 have chrome top plate, and allow 6 x 6cm instead of the 6 x 4.5cm format.

R2*   **A**

IDAFIX: c1930, metal folding camera for 6.5 x 11 frames on 130 roll film, Velostigmat f6.3/135mm lens, Pronto shutter.

R3*   **A**

ROLFIX: c1936-56, metal folding camera for 6 x 9cm or 6 x 6cm on 120 roll film, Trioplan f4.5/105mm lens among others, Compur shutter, several different variations.

R2*   **A**

SOLIDA: c1934-56, metal folding camera for 6 x 4.5 frames on roll film, optical VFR, Victar f2.9/70mm lens among others, Compur shutter, several different variations.

R2*   **B**

SOLIDA I: c1955, folding camera for 6 x 6cm or 4 x 4cm frames on 120 roll film, f4.5/75mm lens among others, Vario shutter.

R2*   **B–**

SOLIDA II: c1955, folding camera for 6 x 6cm or 4 x 4cm frames on 120 roll film, duel VFR for 4 x 4 and 4 x 6, Ennagon f4.5/75mm lens among others, Pronto or Prontor shutter, variations made with lever advance and automatic frame counting.

R3*   **B+**

SOLIDA IIL: c1955, with built-in uncoupled EV light meter, 6 x 6cm only.

R3*   **E–**

SOLIDA III: c1955, with faster Radionar f2.9/80mm lens, 6 x 6cm only.

R2*   **B**

SOLIDA IIIL: c1955. Now with uncoupled rangefinder.

R3*   **C**

SOLIDA JUNIOR: 1953. Folding rollfilm camera. 12 exp on 120. 75mm f3.5 Frankar. Vario shutter, synch for bulbs. Retractable spool chamber for easy loading.

R2*   **A**

SOLIDA RECORD B: c1960. Available with or without lever advance or automatic frame counting. f8/80mm lens, simple shutter.

R2*   **A**

SOLIDA RECORD T: c1963, all metal VFR camera for 6 x 6cm or 4 x 4cm on 120 roll film, f8/70mm lens with front lens focusing, simple shutter, available with lever advance and automatic frame counting for 6 x 6cm frames only.

R2*   **A**

FRANKA: c1950, 35mm VFR camera, Radonar f2.9/50mm lens, Compur shutter, lever wind, exposure table on top plate.

R3*   **B+**

FRANKANETTE: c1958, 35mm VFR camera, Isconar f2.8/45mm lens among others, Pronto shutter.

R2*   **A**

FRANKANETTE L: c1958, 35mm VFR, Ennagon f2.8/45mm lens among others, Pronto shutter, built-in meter.

R2*   **A**

SUPER FRANKANETTE: c1958, 35mm VFR camera, Xenar f2.8/45mm lens among others, Prontor-SVS shutter.

R   **B**

SUPER FRANKANETTE L: c1958, 35mm VFR camera with built-in light meter, Westanar f2.8/45mm lens among others, Prontor shutter, lever wind.

R2*   **B+**

SUPER FRANKANETTE E: c1958, 35mm RFR camera, Xenar f2.8/45mm lens, Printor-SVS shutter, CRF.

R2*   **B+**

SUPER FRANKANETTE EL: c1958, 35mm VFR with built-in meter and CRF, Xenar f2.8/45mm l Prontor -SVS shutter.

R2*   **C–**

SUPER FRANKANETTE SLK: c1958, 35mm VFR camera with built-in *coupled* light meter, Xenar f2.8/45mm lens, Prontor-SLK shutter.

R2*   **B**

FRANCOLOUR: c1960, 35mm VFR camera with Frankar f2.8/45mm lens, Pronto or Vario shutter, lever wind.

R2*   **A**

G. Frank & Pearsall
Brooklyn, New York

THE COMPACT CAMERA: c1883, $6^{1}/_{2}$" x $8^{1}/_{2}$" view camera; $6^{1}/_{2}$" x $8^{1}/_{2}$" exp on dry plates.

R5*   **G+**

Franke & Heidecke
Braunschweig, Germany

HEIDOSCOP: c1921. 45 x 107mm reflex stereo camera; Zeiss Tessar 55mm f4.5

ROLLEI 16S: 1966, subminiature camera; Tessar 25mm f2.8 lens; 12 x 17mm exp on 16mm film.

R3*   **Black: D–**

Red/green: D+

lens; Compound 1-⅟₅₀₀ s; 45 x 107mm exp on plates.

R3*   **F–**

HEIDOSCOP: c1921. 6 x 13cm plate and cut-film reflex stereo camera; Zeiss Tessar 75mm f4.5 lenses; Compound shutter 1- ⅟₃₀₀ s; 6 x 13cm exp on plates or cut-film.

R3*   **F–**

ROLLEI A110: 1974. 110 film. Metal bodied camera with open-shut film wind. 23mm f2.8 Tessar. Automatic programmed exposure. Usually found in black. Rarer in brushed chrome and gold.

R3*   **C+**

ROLLEIDOSCOP: c1925. 45 x 107mm reflex stereo camera; Zeiss Tessar 75mm f4.5 lenses; Compur 1-1/300 s; 45 x 107mm exp on roll film.

R3*   **G+**

ROLLEIDOSCOP: c1926. 6 x 13cm reflex stereo camera; Zeiss Tessar 75mm f4.5 lenses; Compur 1-⅟₅₀₀ s; 6 x 13cm exp on roll film.

R3*   **G+**

ROLLEI 35: c1970, 35mm camera; Tessar 40mm f3.5 coated lens; shutter ½-⅟₅₀₀s. Black German model add 75% c1970.

R2*   **E+**

R3*   **F–**

ROLLEI 35: With Schneider lens, (gold-plated model): c1970, 35mm camera; Carl Zeiss Tessar 40mm f3.5 coated lens; shutter ½-¹⁄₅₀₀ S.

R4*   **F+**

35B: c1979-1978, 35mm camera;40mm Triotar F3.5 lens;Prontor shutter ¹⁄₃₀ – 1/500s. B; uncoupled Selenium meter; ident. "B35" or "35B" on camera face.

R1*   **D+**

35C: c1969-1971. 35mm camera; Triotar F3.5/40mm lens; Prontor ¹⁄₃₀-¹⁄₅₀₀s. B shutter; no light meter.

R4*   **(Rare) F–**

35S: C1947-1980. 35mm camera; 40mm f2.8 Rollei HFT Sonnar lens; Rollei Compur 1/2 – ¹⁄₅₀₀s. B. shutter; Serial No. under take up spool;Inscribed "Rollei 35S" on camera face.

R2*   **F–**

35S SILVER: c1978. 35mm camera;40mm f2.8 Rolli Sonnar lens; Rollei Compur 1/2 – ¹⁄₅₀₀s. B. Ident. "Rollei 35 S" followed by a wreath; Silver plate and Silver coloured leather.

R4*   **G**

35S GOLD: c1974-1976. 35mm camera; 40mm F2,8 Rollei Sonnar lens; Rollei Compur 1/2 – ¹⁄₅₀₀s.B. shutter; Serial No on back plate, also ident's Gold content; covered in Lizard or Alligator skin.

R4*   **G**

35T: c1974-1980. 35mm camera; 40mm f3.5 Tessar lens; Rollei Compur ½ – ¹⁄₅₀₀s. B. shutter; "Rollei 35 T" on face; Serial No's under take up spool. Features other than the name, same as Rollei 35.

R2*   **E+**

35 LED: c1978-1982. 35mm camera; 40mm f3.5 Rolli Triotar lens; Rollei prontor ¹⁄₃₀ – 1/500s. shutter; Silicon photo diode cell light meter;coupled exp indicated in finder with red and green LED's; Hot shoe; "Rollei 35 LED" on face.

R1*   **D**

35SE: c1980-1982. 35mm camera; 40mm f2.8 Rolli HFT Sonnar lens; Rollei Compur

½ – ⅟₅₀₀s. B. Shutter; Serial no's under feed spool; "35 SE" on face.

R2*   **F–**

35TE: c1980-1982. 35mm camera;40mm f3.5 Tessar lens; Compur ½ – ⅟₅₀₀s. B. Shutter; Serial No's under feed spool; Cds meter with LED indicators coupled to aperture, shutter, film speed; Hot shoe; "35 TE" on camera face.

R2*   **E+**

35 PLATIN:(SPECIAL EDITION 1986); (FH150) 35mm Camera; 40mm F2.8 Rollei Sonnar lens;

R4*   **G+**

35 CLASSIC: c1990. 35mm camera; 40mm F2.8 Zeiss Sonnar HFT lens; Coupled Cds exp meter.

R1*   **F+**

NOTE: Several Rollie 35mm Cameras have Tan Leather covering, these would be classed as R4* rarity.

ROLLEICORD I: c1933-1935. Zeiss Triotar 75mm f4.5 lens; Compur shutter 1-⅟₃₀₀ s. Original camera body, nickel plated art-deco design. Later version (after 1934) was covered with leather. Difficult to find in excellent condition.

R3*   **E–**

ROLLEICORD IA: c1935-1941. Zeiss Triotar 75mm f4.5 or f3.8 lens; Compur shutter 1-⅟₃₀₀ s.

R3*   **C+**

Rolleicord I

Rolleicord IA

ROLLEICORD II: 1950. Zeiss Triotar 75mm f3.5 lens – equipped with factory coated 75mm f3.5 Triotar or Xenar lens after 1950. Compur shutter 1-1/300 s (1938-1945); Compur-Rapid shutter 1-1/500 s (1945-1951) – flash synch (1950-1951). Snr 612,000-1,135,999.

R3*   **C+**

ROLLEICORD III: c1950-1953. Zeiss Triotar or Xenar 75mm f3.5 lens; Compur-Rapid shutter 1-1/500 s. Snr 1,137,000-1,344,050. c1950-1953.

R3*   **C+**

ROLLEICORD IV: c1953-1955. Xenar 75mm f3.5 lens; Synchro-Compur shutter 1-⅟₅₀₀ s. Snr 1,344,051-1,390,999.

R3*   **D–**

ROLLEICORD V: c1955-1957. Xenar 75mm f3.5 lens; Synchro-Compur shutter IVS 1-⅟₅₀₀ s. Snr 1,500,000-(?).

R3*   **D–**

ROLLEICORD VA: c1957-1960. Xenar 75mm f3.5 lens; Synchro-Compur MXV shutter 1-⅟₅₀₀ s. Snr 1,584,000-1,940,999.

R3* D   **Vb= E–**

ROLLEIFLEX (ORIGINAL): c1929-1932. Zeiss Tessar 75mm f4.5 lens until 1929; Zeiss Tessar 75mm f3.8 lens after 1929; Compur shutter 1-⅟₃₀₀ s. Snr up to 200,000.

R4*   **E–**

ROLLEIFLEX STANDARD 1932: c1932-1937. Zeiss Tessar 75mm f4.5, f3.8 or f3.5 lens; Compur shutter 1-⅟₃₀₀ s. Snr 200,000-567,550.

R4*   **D**

ROLLEIFLEX 1937: c1937-1949. Zeiss Tessar 75mm f3.5 lens until 1945; Zeiss Tessar or Xenar 75mm f3.5 after 1945. Snr 280,000-1,000,000.

R3*   **D–**

ROLLEIFLEX NEW STANDARD 1939: c1939-1941. Zeiss Tessar 75mm f3.5 lens; Synchro-Compur shutter 1-⅟₅₀₀ s. Snr 805,000-928,999.

R3*   **D–**

ROLLEIFLEX 1950: c1949-1951. Zeiss Tessar 75mm f3.5 (coated lenses marked "T" or Schneider Xenar 75mm f3.5 (coated lenses marked with red triangle) lens; Compur shutter 1-1/500 s. Snr 1,100,000-1,168,000.

R2*   **D**

ROLLEIFLEX AUTOMAT: 1951. One of the first Rolleiflexes to reach the UK after WWII. TLR for 12 exp on 120. Red window replaced by auto film wind. Made to take Rolleikin 35mm back and panoramic head. f3.5 Xenar lens. Synchro-Compur shutter.

R2   **D**

ROLLEIFLEX "MX": c1951-1954. Zeiss Tessar or Xenar 75mm f3.5 lens; Synchro-Compur shutter 1-⅟₅₀₀ s. Snr 11,000-1,427,999.

R2*   **D**

ROLLEIFLEX 2.8A: c1950-1953. Zeiss Tessar 80mm f2.8 lens; (a few cameras were mfd with Biometar 80mm f2.8 lens, and are much sought after, worth 150% or more); Compur-Rapid shutter 1-1/500 s. Snr 1,101,000-(?).

R2*   **E–**
2.8B WITH BIOTAR LENS   **G+**

ROLLEIFLEX 2.8C: c1953-1956. Xenotar 80mm f2.8 lens; Synchro-Compur shutter 1-1/500 s. Snr 1,260,250-1,475,278.

R3*   **E**

ROLLEIFLEX "MX" (EVS): c1954-1956. Zeiss Tessar or Xenar 75mm f3.5 lens; Synchro-Compur shutter LVS 1-⅟₅₀₀s. Snr 1,428,000-1,729,999.

R2*   **E–**

ROLLEIFLEX 2.8D: c1955-1956. Zeiss Tessar or Xenotar 80mm f2.8 lens; Synchro-Compur EVS shutter 1-⅟₅₀₀ s. Snr 1,600,000-1,620,999.

R3*   **E**

Rolleiflex 3.5E

ROLLEIFLEX 2.8E: c1962-1965. Zeiss Planar or Xenotar 80mm f2.8 lens; Synchro-Compur MXV shutter 1-⅟₅₀₀ s. Snr 1,621,000-1,665,999. c1958-1959. Rolleiflex 2.8E-2; Snr 2,350,000-2,357,999. c1959-1962. Rolleiflex 2.8E-3; Snr 2,360,000-(?).

R3*   **F**

ROLLEIFLEX 3.5E: c1962-1965. Zeiss Planar or Xenotar 75mm f3.5 lens; Synchro-Compur LVS shutter 1-⅟₅₀₀ s. Snr 1,740,000-1,869,000. c1957-1959. Rolleiflex 3.5E-2; Snr 2,480,000-2,482,099. c1960-1962. Rolleiflex 35.E-3; Snr 2,380,000-(?).

R3*   **F–**

ROLLEIFLEX 3.5 F: 1958. Zeiss Planar 75mm f3.5 coated lens; Synchro-Compur LVS shutter 1-⅟₅₀₀ s.

R3*   **F**

Rolleiflex 3.5F

Compur-Rapid shutter 1-$\frac{1}{500}$ s. Snr 622,000-733,000.

R3*   **F–**

ROLLEIFLEX 2.8F: 1960. Zeiss Planar 75mm f2.8 coated lens; Synchro-Compur LVS shutter 1-1/500 s.

R4*   **F+**

ROLLEIFLEX T: 1959. TLR for 12 exp on 120. Can be adapted to take 16 exp. 4x4cm or 16 exp 4x6.5cm. Aperture and speed settings can be linked and set by exposure values. 77mm f3.5 Tessar lens. Synchro-Compur shutter 1-1/500s.

R3*   **D+**

ROLLEIFLEX 4 X 4CM: 1931. c1931-1939. Zeiss Tessar 60mm f3.5 or f2.8 lens; Compur shutter 1-1/300 s; Compur-Rapid shutter 1-1/500 s, after 1935. Snr 200,000-600,000.

R3*   **E–**

ROLLEIFLEX 4 X 4CM SPORTS (1938): c1938-1941. Zeiss Tessar 60mm f2.8 lens;

ROLLEIMAGIC: 1961. The first fully auto TLR. 12 or 16 exp on 120. Photo cell mounted behind plastic window about viewing lens. Meter needle appears between two red markers when light is

sufficient. Manual override of automation for flash or time exposures. 75mm f/3.5 Xenar lens. Prontormat-S shutter. Unpopular when launched due to ugly styling to incorporate auto exposure functions.

R3* 　　　　　　　　　　　　**D**

ROLLEIFLEX 4 X 4CM (1957): c1957. Zeiss Tessar 60mm f2.8 lens; Synchro-Compur shutter 1-⅟₅₀₀ s.

R2* 　　　　　　　　　　　　**E–**
Black 　　　　　　　　　　　　**F+**

SL26: c1970. SLR Instamatic camera; Tessar 40mm f2.8 lens, interchangeable front element; behind-the-lens shutter 1/2-⅟₅₀₀ s. Instamatic film cartridge.

R3* 　　　　　　　　　　　　**D+**

TELE ROLLEIFLEX: 1959. Made mostly for portraiture. TLR, based on the Rolleiflex 2.8E, but using 135mm f4 Sonnar taking lens and Heidosmat viewing lens of same focal length and aperture. Synchro-Compur shutter 1-1/500s. Apertures and shutter exposure value coupled. Removable optical flat in the film gate ensures perfect flatness of film for critical focusing.

R3* 　　　　　　　　　　　　**G**

WIDEANGLE ROLLEI: 1961. Wideangle lens version of the Rolleiflex. 55mm f4 Distagon lens, focusing down to 24 in. Synchro-Compur shutter 1-1/500s.

R4* 　　　　　　　　　　　　**H–**

Franklin Photographic Industries Inc.
Chicago, Illinois

FRANKLIN MAGAZINE 8: c1942. 8mm movie camera; mfd under Kodak license; Cine Raptar Wollensak 2" f2.5 lens.

R2*   **B–**

FRENCH DETECTIVE CAMERA: c1895. H. Duplovich 120mm f6.8 lens; 6 x 9cm exp; plates changed by chain mechanism. Mfd in France.

R5*   **G+**

FRENCH DRY PLATE CAMERA: c1880. 7 x 9cm format rigid wooden camera; insertable disc stops. Mfd in France.

R3*   **E+**

FRENCH SLIDING BOX DAGUERREO-TYPE CAMERA: c1845. Photographe a verres combines, 190mm f6 lens; pivoting plate shutter. Interchangeable front lens elements for various focal lengths; 6.5 x 7.5cm image. Mfd in France.

R5*   **I+**

FRENCH ESPIONAGE CAMERA: c1940, pre-war subminiature detective camera; mfps $\frac{1}{20}$-$\frac{1}{250}$ s; 45 exp. Mfd in France. Invariably found without lens.

R5*   **F+**

FRENCH TAILBOARD CAMERA: c1890s. 13" x 18" tailboard camera; wide angle lens; removable ground glass back; shifting front lens standard (stereo); brass handle; red bellows. Mfd in France.

R3*   **E+**

Fuji Photo Film Industry
Tokyo, Japan

FUJI INSTANT CAMERA – MODELS F50-S & F10: c1981. Two instant cameras made in Japan under license from Eastman Kodak using the Kodak Instant system. After a famous lawsuit, Kodak was forced to discontinue making instant products in the U.S. although Fuji reached a separate agreement with Polaroid and continued to market the products in Japan. The F10 is a simple rigid camera with auto exposure – an electronic flash was optional. The F50-S was folding, had a built-in flash and had programmed exposure control. R1 in Japan, R3 elsewhere. The camera was not officially exported.

R3*   **B**

Fuji Photo Film Ltd.
Tokyo, Japan

FUJICAFLEX: c1954. Marketed as a premium TLR. Fujinar f2.8 83mm lens. Seikosha-Rapid shutter 1-1/400s. 6x6cm images on 120 film. Camera incorporated a number of innovations including a single knob for both film advance and focusing. Taking lens had a special close focusing position (2.3feet), without need of accessory lens.

R3*   **E**

FUJICA GW690 PROFESSIONAL: c1978. Eye-level medium format rf camera. 120/220 rollfilm, producing 6x9cm images. Fujinon f3.5, 90mm interchangeable lens.

R3*   **NSR**

Galileo Optical
Milan, Italy

CONDOR I: c1954. 35mm RFR camera; Galileo Eliog 560mm f3.5 lens; Galileo Iscus Rapid shutter 1-⅕₀₀s, CRF.

R3*   **E–**

GAMI 16: c1955, subminiature camera; Esanitar 25mm f1.9 lens; shutter ½-¼₀₀₀ s; 12 x 17mm exp on 17mm film in special cassettes; CRF.

R4*   **F**

Gamma Precision Machine
Rome, Italy

GAMMA-I: 1947. Cpfs, ½₀- 1000 s, CRF, special bayonet mount Koristka Victor f3.5/55mm lens. Internal film cutter, allowed exposed 35mm roll film in special cassettes to be removed from the camera for processing in mid roll. Odd shaped camera body. Quite rare.

R4*   **F+**

GAMMA (SPECIAL): 1948. The same body style as the Gamma-I, but without RFR or VFR.Cpfs, ½₀-1000s, special bayonet mount Koristka Victor f3.5/55mm lens. Internal film cutter allowed exposed 35mm roll film in special casettes removed from the camera for processing in mid roll. Odd shaped camera body. Extremely rare.

R5*   **G+**

GAMMA-III: 1950-51. The same body style as the Gamma-I, but with slow speeds.Cpfs, 1-1000 s, interchangeable Leica-type screw mount Koristka Victor f3.5/55mm lens or Beta f3.5/50mm lens. Internal film cutter allowed exposed 35mm roll film in special cassettes to be removed from the camera for processing in mid roll. Shares the same odd shaped camera body as the other Gamma cameras, but has a different frame counter than Gamma-II.

R4*   **F+**

GAMMA-II: 1950. The same body style as the Gamma-I, but with slow speeds. Cpfs,

1-1000 s, interchangeable Leica-type screw mount Koristka Victor f3.5/55mm lens or Beta f3.5/50mm lens. Internal film cutter allowed exposed 35mm roll film in special casettes removed from the camera for processing in mid roll. Quite rare. Even rarer Airforce version with f2.0/50mm Epitamitar lens valued at about 300% higher.

R4*   **F+**

Gamma Works
Budapest, Hungary

DUFLEX: c1947, 35mm SLR which incorporated a number of advanced features for its time. Framing of different focal length lenses (although none were available), instant return mirror etc. As few as 500 were made and the Duflex is rarely found.

R5*   **H–**

GANDOLFI LTD.
Hampshire, England

Louis Gandolfi, later Louis Gandolfi & Sons, was founded in 1885, and is still in production. The earliest Gandolfi cameras were named The Compactum, The Collapsible, and The Special, all dating from 1895. The Compactum was made in sizes from half plate to 12" x10". The Premier and the Simplex followed and all were predecessors of the Imperial. which became the mainstay of the tapered bellows field camera designs from Gandolfi. These cameras are rare and no price indications are available. At times from 1902 Gandolfi offered magazine box type cameras and a range of tripods, stands, shutters and lenses. Mostly, sold over relatively short periods but the hand and stand cameras remained until the late thirties.

Universal

UNIVERSAL SQUARE BELLOWS CAMERA: 1899. The first regular production model made in six sizes: Half-plate, to 18" x 16"; later 5" x 4" and 5" x 7" models were added. Made from mahogany with solid brass fittings, this was a tailboard camera with fixed front and rear focusing. It had double swing reversible back, rise and cross front parallel bellows. Approximately 1,000 of these cameras were produced. Prices range from **F** to **H** depending on size and condition.

IMPERIAL CAMERA: A tapered bellows camera having focusing front and rear standards with swing and tilt movements making it the predecessor of the present day Precision camera. The Imperial was made in half-plate, whole plate, 10" x 8" and 12" x 10" sizes and continued with minor changes until World War 2.

UNIVERSAL FOLDING HAND AND STAND CAMERA: This was a de luxe camera covered with Morocco leather, bearing some similarities to the Sanderson design. First introduced about 1907 in ¼ plate and 5" x 4" sizes and in postcard, half-plate and 7"x 5" by 1910.

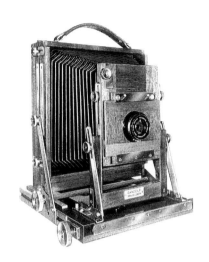

PRECISION TAPERED BELLOWS CAMERA: Introduced in 1945 and continued in manufacture to the present time, this is a truly universal camera with a wide range of movements. Convenient in the studio and on location, where weight and bulk are important. Usually constructed in mahogany or teak, occasionally rosewood examples are found. The woodwork is deeply French polished and the solid heavy gauge brass fittings are hard lacquered. Black polished wood and satin chrome plated examples are occasionally found. Early models have hinged focusing screens and use double book form plateholders in wood and brass to match the camera. Since the early 1960s, international standard spring backs have been available. Cameras individually made to such high standards of craftsmanship are expensive, whether old or new, and constitute a sound investment as well as a universal tool. New prices range from about **G** for 4" x 5" to **H** for 8" x 10" models. Older used models may be found from **F** to **H** depending on size and condition.

PRISON CAMERA: Gandolfi produced a number of specialised cameras for Govern-ment departments. The prison service used Gandolfi equipment for identification records.

WIDE ANGLE CAMERAS: Box type wide-angle cameras fitted with the Goerz Hypergon lens. With extreme angles of view, the 75mm lens covering 8" x 10", at small apertures, no focusing was required and no bellows provided. These cameras are much sought after and complete with lens in good condition trade at **G** to **H–** depending on size.

Antonio Gatto
Pordenone, Italy

SONNE-IV: 1948. Cfps, ¹⁄₂₀ to 1/1000s, CRF, interchangeable Leica-type screw mount Adlenar f3.5/50mm lens. On the earliest versions a rising sun is engraved next to the rangefinder window. No models I, II, or III seem to have been made. Quite rare.

R4* **F**

SONNE-V: 1950. Cfps, 1 -¹⁄₁₀₀₀s, flash synch, interchangeable Leica-type screw mount Schneider Xenar f3.5/50mm lens, or f2.8/50mm lens. Also found with "T" Elionar f3.5/50mm lens. Quite rare.

R4* **F**

SONNE-C: 1951. Cfps, 1 -¹⁄₁₀₀₀ sec, flash synch, interchangeable Leica-type screw mount Schneider Xenar f3.5/50mm lens, or f2.8/50mm lens. Also found with "T"

Elionar f3.5/50mm lens. Similar to the Sonne-V, but with changed top cover.

R4*   **F**

SONNE-C4: 1953. Cfps, 1-¹⁄₁₀₀₀s, flash synch, interchangeable Leica-type screw mount Schneider Xenar f3.5/50mm lens, or f2.8/50mm lens. Also found with "T" Elionar f3.5/50mm lens. Seperate slow speed control, and combines RFR/VFR window. Also known as the Sonne-Colour camera. Quite rare. It is difficult to find any Sonne cameras in condition "C" or better.

R4*   **F**

L. Gaumont & Cie
Paris, France

BLOCK-NOTES: c1903. 4.5 x 6cm vest pocket camera; Tessar f6.8 lens. 4.5 x 6cm model, $90-$175. 6 x 9cm model.

R3*   **E–**

STEREO BLOCK-NOTES: c1903. 45 x 107mm stereo camera; Tessar f6.3 lenses.

R3*   **E+**

STEREO BLOCK-NOTES: 1904. Compact folding stereo camera for 6x13cm glass plates in individual holders. Fixed focus

anastigmat lenses f5.5, 60mm. Six speed guillotine shutter.

R3*   **E**

"REPORTER" TROPICAL CAMERA: c1924. 135mm f4.5 lens; FPS; 9 x 12cm exp on cut film.

R5*   **G–**

SPIDO: c1899. 9 x 12cm; Zeiss Krauss Protar 136mm f8 lens; Decaux pneumatic shutter; 12 plates.

R3*   **E–**

SPIDO STEREO: c1922, 6 x 13cm stereo camera; Hermagis Anastigmatic 85mm f6.3 lenses; variable speed guillotine shutter.

R3*   **E+**

SPIDO STEREO (9 X 18CM MODEL): c1900, black leather covered jumelle style camera; Goerz Dagor 110mm f6.8 lenses; Decaux 6 speed shutter. Changing mechanism for 12 plates, 9 x 18cm. Panoramic setting; rising and sliding lens panel.

R3*   **E+**

G. B. MULTIPLYING CAMERA: c1900. F. L. Chevalier lens; 12 exp, 25 x 25mm on 6 x 13cm plates by sliding and turning the plate holder. Mfd in France.

R4*   **F–**

Genie Camera Co.
Philadelphia, Pennsylvania

GENIE: c1890, box-type detective camera; push-pull movement changes plates and advances exp counter on brass magazine. 3¼" x 4¼" exp on plates in magazine.

R4*   **F**

G. Gennert
New York, New York

LONG FOCUS MONTAUK: c1890, brass shutter; red bellows; polished wood interior. Front and rear bellows extension for long focus (close-up photography).

R4*   **E–**

MONTAUK: c1890. 4" x 5" box-type detective camera.

R4*   **D+**

MONTAUK MULTIPLYING CAMERA: c1890, shifting lens standard; sliding back. 32 exp on 5" x 7" plate. C.

R4*   **F–**

MONTAUK STEREO: c1889, hand/stand-type stereo camera; Beck Symmetrical Rapid Rectilinear 5" lens or Bausch & Lomb; Bausch & Lomb iris diaphragm-type between lens shutter; short baseboard; rising front; reflecting finder. 3 sizes: 4¾" x 6½, 5" x 7" and 5" x 8".

R4*   **F–**

Kamerawerk Adolf Gerlach
Wuppertal, Germany

IDEAL: c1952-56, metal camera for 6 x 6 frames on roll film, simple f7.7 lens mounted in a collapsible tube, simple one speed shutter, cheap construction.

R3*   **A**

TRIXETTE: c1954, metal camera for 6 x 6 frames on roll film, coated f5.6/75mm Supra-Anastigmat lens in "Spezial" shutter, ½₅ – ½₀₀S.

R3*   **B+**

TRIXETTE I: c1956, metal camera for 6 x 6 frames on roll film, coated f5.6/75mm Supra-Anastigmat lens in "Spezial" shutter, ½₅ – ½₀₀S, basically the same camera as Triyelte but with improved spring system for folding the lens, still interesting.

R3*   **B+**

IDEAL BOX: c1955, metal box camera for 6 x 9 frames on roll film, simple lens and shutter.

R2*   **A**

IDEAL COLOUR 35: 35mm VFR camera with coated Nixon or Nixonar f3.5/4.5cm lens "Spezial" shutter ½₅ – ½₀₀S. collected more for the "Nixon" name on the lens than for any other reason!

R3*   **B–**

Geyer Maschinen
Berlin, Germany

GEYER CAMERA: c1929, 16mm movie camera; Carl Zeiss Triotar 25mm f2.9 lens. Hand crank or spring motor drive.

R4*   **D–**

Geymet and Alker
Paris, France

JUMELLE PHOTOGRAPHIQUE (JUMELLE DE NICOUR): c1867, binocular-type detective camera; 50 exp, 4 x 4cm in removable magazine. Patented by Octave Nicour. The first camera to use this disguise.

R5*   **I+**

G.G.S.
Milan, Italy

LUCKY: 1948. Small 35mm VFR camera. 50mm f/3.2 Solar Anastigmat lens. Carica shutter 1/20-1/200s. Some models also have 1/25s added. Only around 3,000 made.

R5*   **E**

LUCKYFLEX: c1948, metal TLR for 35mm film, focusing Solar f3.2/50mm lens, GGS shutter, ¹⁄₂₀ – ¹⁄₃₀₀s, very small production, maybe 2000 units.

R3*   **F+**

Globus Brothers
New York, N.Y.

GLOBUSCOPE: c1981, 35mm panoramic camera capable of 360 degree images using standard 35mm film cassettes. f3, 22mm lens. Effective shutter speed 1/400s. Camera rotational action is very smooth via a viscous damped spring motor.

R3*   **NSR**

A. & B. Glock

GLOCK: c1890, field-type stereo camera; single lens on sliding panel for sequential exp; rising front; 18 x 24cm.

R4*   **F–**

Gnome Photographic Products
England

BABY PIXIE: c. 1950. Metal box camera. 16 exp on 620. Unmarked lens. Shutter for B & I only. Large metal viewfinder folds up from top. Leatherette covered. Chrome trim.

R1*   **B**

C. P. Goerz, *Berlin, Germany*

STEREO ANGO: c1906. Goerz Dagor 120mm f6.8 lens; FPS 1/10-¹⁄₁₀₀₀ s. Paired exp on 9 x 18cm dry plates; film pack adapter; rising and sliding lens panel. c1906.

R4*   **E–**

ANSCHUTZ CAMERA: c1890. Clement & Gilmer Wide Angle 25cm f15 lens, but usually found with original Goerz lens; eye level finder; CFPS. Introduced by Ottomar Anschutz, Prussia. The Anschutz Camera is of great historical interest because of its cloth focal plane shutter. Anschutz used this camera for early high-speed photography.

R4*   **G+**

ANSCHUTZ: c1895, 9 x 12cm folding camera; Goerz Double Anastigmatic Series III No. 0, 120mm ;lens, CFPS. It utilized the dry collodion process.

R3*   **D+**

ANSCHUTZ: c1912. 9 x 12cm folding camera; Dagor 135mm f6.8 lens; CFPS.

R3*   **D+**

ANSCHUTZ DE LUXE: c1910. 9 x 12cm folding camera; Goerz Doppel Anastigmat 180mm f6.8 lens; covered in dark green leather; CFPS.

R3*   **F–**

ANSCHUTZ STEREO: c1912. 9 x 18 stereo camera; Goerz Doppel-Anastigmat 130mm lenses; Anschutz CFPS; 9 x 18cm exp on plates. CFPS.

R4*   **E+**

COAT POCKET TENAX: c1912; Strut type folding camera; exp 6.5 X 9cm on film packs or plates; 90mm f4.5 Dogmar lens.

R3*   **C+**

FOLDING REFLEX: c1912, 4" x 5" SLR camera; Goerz Doppel-Anastigmat f4.8 lens; Goerz Anschutz CFPS. 4" x 5" exp on plates.

R4*   **F–**

HYPERGON-DOPPEL-ANASTIGMAT WIDE ANGLE LENS: c1900. Series X, 75mm f22 lens. Rotating fan blade in centre to permit uniform exp. The Hypergon was available in various focal lengths, covering 4 x 5 to 11 x 14". On rare occasions they are found with the original tube and bulb used to spin the propeller (usually dried out).

R5*   **G+**

REPORTER: c1889, book-type detective camera; Goerz Aplanat 60 degree angle coverage lens; gravity shutter; 4 x 5.5cm exp on roll film.

R5*   **H+**

STEREO PHOTO BINOCLE: c1899, binocular-type detective camera; Dagor 75mm f6.8 lens; guillotine shutter; 45 x 107mm exp on plates. Could function as a mono or a stereo camera.

R5*   **H**

TENAX: c1922, 6 x 9cm roll film and plate camera; Goerz Anastigmat 12.5mm f6.3 lens; Goerz dial-set shutter 1-$\frac{1}{200}$s. 6 x 9cm exp on roll film and cut film.

R2*   **C+**

ROLL TENAX: c1921; Folding roll film camera; exp 4 X 6.5cm; Compur shutter; 7.5cm Dogmar f4.5 lens.

R2*   **C+**

VEST POCKET TENAX: c1909. 4.5 x 6cm camera; Dogmar 75mm f4.5 lens; shutter 1-1/250 s.

R3*   **D+**

Roll Tenax

STEREO VEST POCKET TENAX: c1920. 45 x 107mm stereo plate camera; Dopp-Anastigmat Celor 60mm f4.5 lens; shutter ½-¹⁄₂₅₀ S.

R3*   **E+**

C.P. Goerz, *Vienna, Austria*

MINICORD: c1951. 16mm subminiature TLR camera; Helgor 25mm f2.0 lens; mfps

¹⁄₁₀ – ¹⁄₄₀₀ s; 10 x 10mm exp on 16mm film in special cassettes; eye level viewing through roof prism. Standard model black and chrome. Red leather and gold trim rare and much more valuable.

R4*   **F–**

GOLDECK 16: c.1960. Subminiature for 16mm film. 10x14mm images. Lever film wind. Bright frame finder. 20mm f2.8 Color Ennit. Interchangeable 50mm and 75mm advertised. 'C'-mount also allowed 16mm cine lenses to be fitted. Early model with fixed focus lens, later models offered focusing mount. Super model has 9-speed shutter.

R3*   **D**

GUGO II: 1952. Metal bodied camera with lens extended on metal tube. 12 exp on 120. 3 inch f4.5 Kesar. Three-speed shutter, synch for flash.

R4*   **D+**

R.R. Goldmann
Vienna, Austria

UNIVERSAL DETECTIVE CAMERA:
c1890. Early hand-held dry plate camera for
plates 13x18cm. Lens, anastigmat f6.3 by
E. Francais of Paris. Unusual front mounted
shutter for exposures 1/2-1/1000s. Several
sizes and a stereo model were available. It
was finished in black lacquer.
R5*   **E**

Goldschmid Switzerland.

BINOCLE: c1890, binocular-type detective
camera; Steinheil 15cm f6.3 lens; guillotine
shutter; frame loaded plates, 5 x 6cm. One
eye-piece was attached to the lens; the
other to the plate loader.
R5*   **H+**

Goltz & Breutmann
Dresden, Germany

MENTOR-COMPUR-REFLEX: c1928. 6 x
9cm SLR; Tessar 105mm f4.5 lens; Compur
1-$\frac{1}{250}$ s; 6 x 9cm exp on plates.
R3*   **E–**

MENTOR FOLDING REFLEX: c1914. 3$\frac{1}{4}$
x 4$\frac{1}{4}$" folding reflex camera; Tessar 150mm
f4.5 lens; CFPS $\frac{1}{20}$ – $\frac{1}{1000}$ s.
R3*   **E–**

MENTOR SPORT REFLEX CAMERA:
c1927. 3$\frac{1}{4}$ x 4$\frac{1}{4}$" reflex camera; Tessar
150mm f4.5 lens; FPS 1/8-1/300s.
R3*   **E–**

MENTOR STEREO REFLEX: c1914. 45 x
107mm stereo SLR camera; Zeiss Tessar
105mm f4.5 lenses; CFPS $\frac{1}{15}$-$\frac{1}{1000}$ s. 45 x
107mm exp on plates.
R4*   **F**

MENTORETTE: c1936. 6 x 6cm TLR;
Mentor 75mm f3.5 lens; CFPS $\frac{1}{15}$-$\frac{1}{600}$ s; 12
exp, 2$\frac{1}{4}$ x 2$\frac{1}{4}$" on 120 roll film.
R4*   **D**

LE GOUSSET: c1910, achromatic lens; one
speed shutter; 4.5 x 6cm film pack. Mfd in
Paris, France.
R4*   **D+**

GRAPH-CHECK SEQUENTIAL CAMERA:
c1975, 8 lens camera takes eight sequential photos on one sheet of 4" x 5" Polaroid

film; each image is delayed incrementally from $\frac{1}{10}$ – 4s. For analyzing physical and mechanical motion. Still in frequent use.

R3*   **F–**

Gomz
(State Optical Mechanical Works),

After WWII. known as LOMO (Leningrad Optical Mechanical Works)

Leningrad, USSR. (now St Petersburg, Russia).

LENINGRAD: (In Cyrillic or Roman letters): 1953-59. Cfps, 1 – $\frac{1}{1000}$s, adjustable flash synch, combined RFR/VFR, with frame lines for 35mm, 50mm, 85mm, and 135mm fields of view. Built-in spring drive for film transport. 10 exposures at 2-3 per second are possible when the spring is fully wound. Jupitor-8 f2.0/50mm lens. This camera was not made especially for the secret police as is sometimes mentioned. At 900 Rubels, it was the most expensive domestic 35mm camera offered in the

USSR. Prices are 25-50% higher for this camera in Japan.

R3*   **E+**

SPORT (CNOPM): 1936? CFPS, 50mm f3.5 lens. This may be the first 35mm single lens reflex ever placed on the market. There is some question as to its date of introduction. 24x36mm images on regular 35mm film in special cassettes. Certain similarities suggest that its overall design may have been influenced by expatriate Zeiss engineers, but there is no hard evidence.

R4*   **F+**

SPUTNIK: c1957, Bakelite stereo camera, for 6 x 13cm frames on 120 roll film f4.5/75mm lenses, ground glass focusing on reflex waistlevel VFR, betwen-the-lens shutter $\frac{1}{10}$ – $\frac{1}{100}$s, later cameras have $\frac{1}{5}$s – 1-150s. (complete outfit with viewer adds 40%).

R3*   **F+**

SMENA: c1953, Bakelite 35mm VFR camera, f4.5/40mm lens, shutter ⅒ – ¹⁄₁₀₀S.

R3*   **Black;C– Red; C+**

SMENA 2: c1956, Bakelite 35mm VFR camera, f4.5/40mm lens, shutter ⅒ – ¹⁄₂₀₀S, accessory shoe. This camera was copied by the Chinese in their "Yangtze River" and "Hua Mountain" cameras.

R3*   **C–**

LUBITEL: c1954, bakelite TLR for 6 x 6cm on roll film, focusing f4.5/75mm lens, shutter ⅒ – ¹⁄₂₀₀S, copy of Voigtländer Brilliant.

R2*   **B–**

LUBITEL 2: c1956, with flash synch.
R2*   **B–**

Gerhard Goldammer
Frankfurt, Germany

GOLDECK 16. c1960. Subminiature for 16mm film. 10x14mm images. Lever film wind. Bright frame finder. 20mm f/2.8

Color Ennit. Interchangeable 50mm and 75mm advertised. 'C'-mount also allowed 16mm cine lenses to be fitted. Early model with fixed focus lens, later models offered focusing mount. Super model has 9-speed shutter.

R3*   **C+**

GOLDA: c1950, 35mm RFR camera, uncoupled RFR, Trinar f3.5/45mm lens and Prontor shutter in collapsible tube mount.

R3*   **C–**

GUGO-KNIPS: c1950, VFR camera for 6 x 6cm frames on 120 roll film, f8, f4.5, f3.5, or f2.9 lens and Vario or Pronto shutter in collapsible tube mount.

R2*   **B–**

GUGO II. c1952. Metal bodied camera with lens extended on metal tube. 12 exp. on 120. 3 inch. f/4.5 Kesar. Three-speed shutter, sunch for flash.

R4*   **B**

GOLDIX: c1960, VFR camera for 4 x 4cm frames on 127 film, Goldeck f7.7/60mm lens, simple shutter.

R2*   **B–**

(Graflex) The Folmer & Schwing Mfg. CO.
New York

DECEPTIVE ANGLE GRAPHIC: c1901-04, rapid rectilinear 12.5cm, f6.3 lens. 3¼ x 4¼" plates. Right-angle detective type finder. False lenses on apparent front of camera made it look like a stereo camera, whilst the taking lens was on the side. When George Eastman purchased the company several years later the inventory showed only a few in stock.

R5*   **H+**

THE FOLDING POCKET GRAPHIC:
Graphic R.R. lens; Automatic shutter; 3¼"
x 4¼" exp. c1904.

R3*   **D+**

THE GRAFLEX CAMERA: c1904. Zeiss
Series VIIA f6.3* lens; CFPS ¹⁄₁₀-¹⁄₁₂₀₀ s. 4
models: 4" x 5", 5" x 5", 6½" x 8¼", 10 x 8
$500.

R4*   **F+**

THE GRAPHIC CAMERA: c1904. Goerz
Series III* lens; sector shutter; leather
covered mahogany. 3 models: 4" x 5", 5"
x 7", 8" x 10"   **E-F**

THE GRAPHIC SR: c1904. Bausch & Lomb
Zeiss Convertible Series VIIa* lens;
Diaphragm shutter. 2 models: 4" x 5",
5" x 7".

R4*   **E–**

THE GRAPHIC TWIN LENS SPECIAL:
c1904. Zeiss Convertible No. 7 Series VIIa*
lens; diaphragm shutter; 4" x 5" exp.

R5*   **G+**

REVERSIBLE BACK CYCLE GRAPHIC
SPECIAL: c1904. Goerz Series III* lens;
sector shutter; optional CFPS. 4 models: 4"
x 5", 5" x 7", 6 ¼ x 8½", 8" x 10".

R3*   **E–**

THE REVERSIBLE BACK GRAFLEX
CAMERA: c1904. Zeiss Series VIIA f6.3*
lens; CFPS ¹⁄₁₀-¹⁄₁₂₀₀s. 2 models: 4" x 5", 5" x
7".

R3*   **F–**

REVERSIBLE BACK GRAPHIC: c1904.
Bausch & Lomb Zeiss Convertible Series
VIIA* lens; diaphragm shutter. 4 models
were sold: 4" x 5", 5" x 7", 6½ x 8½", 8" x
10".

R3*   **E–**

REVERSIBLE BACK GRAPHIC SPECIAL:
c1904. Plastigmat* lens; diaphragm shutter.
3 models: 4" x 5", 5" x 7", 6½" x 8½".

R3*   **E–**

THE SKY SCRAPER CAMERA –
REVERSIBLE BACK – DOUBLE SWING:
c1904. Century Rapid Convertible lens;
Wollensak shutter; maroon leather bellows,
brass fittings. Walnut construction; rising
front panel; extreme tilting back. 3 models:
8" x 10", 11" x 14", 14" x 17".

R4*   **F–**

THE SKY SCRAPER SPECIAL CAMERA:
c1904.   Hypergon-Doppel-Anastigmat
75mm f22 lens; special recessed lens board
permits use of extremely short focus
lenses. 2 models: 8" x 10", 11" x 14".

R4*   **F+**

STEREOSCOPIC   GRAPHIC: c1904.
Graphic R.R. lens; CFPS ⅒-¹⁄₁₂₀₀ s, 5" x 7" exp.

R4*   **G–**

THE TELESCOPIC GRAPHIC CAMERA:
c1904. Graphic R.R.* lens; Automatic*
shutter; 5" x 7" exp.

R4*   **F**

THE TELESCOPIC STEREO GRAPHIC:
c1904, matched Graphic R.R. lenses; CFPS
⅒-¹⁄₁₂₀₀s.

R5*   **G+**

THE TOURIST GRAFLEX: c1904. Cooke
Series III f6.5* lens; CFPS. 2 models:
4" x 5", 5" x 7".

R3*   **F–**

THE TRIPLE LENS STEREO GRAPHIC:
c1904. Matched pair of No. 7 Series VIIa
Bausch & Lomb Zeiss Convertible lenses;
CFPS ⅒-¹⁄₁₂₀₀s. 5" x 7" exp.

R5*   **G+**

(Graflex) Folmer & Schwing Div.
Eastman Kodak Co., New York

*The Eastman Kodak Company
acquired the Folmer and Schwing
manufacturing company in 1905. It
was operated as a division of Eastman
Kodak making a premium line of
cameras until it became an
independent company in 1926. A
number of instruments were made
both before and after the ownership
change with only minor design
differences.*

THE AUTO GRAFLEX: c1907-1923.
Bausch & Lomb Zeiss Tessar Series IIb f6.3*
lens; CFPS ⅒-¹⁄₁₀₀₀ s. 3 models: 3¼" x 4¼",
4" x 5", 5" x 7".

R3*   **D**

**BANQUET   PANORAMIC   VIEW
CAMERA:** c1920. 7 x 17; tilting front; front
and rear rack and pinion focusing.
Mahogany finish, brass fittings.

R4*   **F+**

CIRKUT CAMERA: Turner-Reich Convertible Anastigmat Series II* lens; Century No.
4 shutter. No. 5 Cirkut Camera, $1500 No.
6 Cirkut Camera , $2000.

R4*   **G–**

Graphic No. 0

NO 10 CIRKUT CAMERA: c1900; The early models, those made by the firm before it was purchased by Eastman Kodak used a small fan and air friction to control rotational speed. Later they used a mechanical governor. The #10 (meaning 10 inch wide film) is still used by panoramic enthusiasts today and was actually in production until just before the Second World War. The entire system consisted of a special geared tripod head, and a selection of gears to control speed. The absence of any of these critical components will lower the price.

R4*   **H–**

NO. 16 CIRKUT CAMERA.

R4*   **H**

THE CIRKUT OUTFIT: c1908, panoramic camera; consists of R.B. Cycle Graphic with Cirkut Panorama attachment. Prices include a complete set of gears.No. 6 Cirkut Outfit. No. 8 Cirkut Outfit.

R4*   **H–**

GRAPHIC NO. 0: c1909-1920. Zeiss Kodak Anastigmat f6.3 lens; CFPS ¼-⅕₀₀ s; 6 or 12 exp, 4.5 x 6cm on roll film.

R3*   **E–**

THE NATURALIST'S GRAFLEX: c1907-1921. Bausch & Lomb Zeiss Protar lens, Series VIIa, No. 19 f6.3* lens; CFPS ¹⁄₁₀-¹⁄₁₀₀₀ s; 4" x 5" exp.

R5*   **H+**

THE 1A GRAFLEX: c1909-1925. Kodak Anastigmat f4.5* lens; CFPS ¹⁄₁₀-¹⁄₁₀₀₀ s; 2½" x 5¼" exp on 116 roll film.

R3*   **E–**

THE PRESS GRAFLEX: c1908. Bausch & Lomb Zeiss Tessar Series Ic No. 16 f4.5* lens; CFPS ⅕-¹⁄₁₅₀₀ s; 5" x 7" exp.

R4*   **E+**

R.B. TELE GRAFLEX: c1912-1923. CFPS ¹⁄₁₀-¹⁄₁₀₀₀S. 3¼ x 4¼", c1915-1923, **C**. 4" x 5".

R4*   **E–**

The Press Graflex

THE REVOLVING BACK AUTO GRAFLEX:
c1909-1940. Bausch & Lomb Zeiss Tessar Series IIb No. 6 f6.3* lens; CFPS ¹⁄₁₀-¹⁄₁₀₀₀s. 2 models: 3¼" x 4¼", 4" x 5".

R3*   **D+**

THE REVOLVING BACK CYCLE GRAPHIC: c1908.
Bausch & Lomb Plastigmat* lens; Volute shutter. (Graflex Focal Plane Shutter available as an accessory). 4 models: 4" x 5", 5" x 7", 6½" x 8½", 8" x 10".

R3*   **D+**

SPEED GRAPHIC (ORIGINAL): c1912-1940.
Kodak Anastigmat f4.5* lens; cpfs ¹⁄₁₀-¹⁄₁₀₀₀ s. 3¼" x 4¼", c1913, 4" x 5", c1912-1927, 3¼" x 5½", c1912, 5" x 7", c1913-1940.

R3*   **D+**

STEREO GRAFLEX: c1904.
Zeiss Series VIIa No. 7* lens; CFPS ¹⁄₁₀-¹⁄₁₀₀₀ s; 5" x 7" exp.

R4*   **G–**

THE STEREO AUTO GRAFLEX: c1907-28.
Bausch & Lomb Zeiss Tessar f6.3* lenses; CFPS ¹⁄₁₀-¹⁄₁₀₀₀ s; 5" x 7" exp.

R4*   **G–**

THE STEREOSCOPIC GRAPHIC: c1908.
Bausch & Lomb Protar VIIa No. 7 f6.3* lenses; CFPS ¹⁄₁₀-¹⁄₁₀₀₀ s; 5" x 7" exp.

R5*   **G**

THE 3A GRAFLEX: c1907-1926.
Bausch & Lomb Zeiss Tessar Series IIb No. 5A f6.3* lens; CFPS ¹⁄₁₀-¹⁄₁₀₀₀ s; 3¼" x 5½" exp on 122 roll film.

R3*   **D–**

(Graflex) Folmer Graflex Corp.
Rochester, New York

ANNIVERSARY SPEED GRAPHIC: c1940-1947. Kodak Anastigmat 5½" f4.5 lens; Compur 1-½₅₀ s; CFPS ⅒-¼₀₀₀ s. 3¼" x 4¼", c1940-1947, 4" x 5".

R2*   **E–**

National Graflex – Series II

GRAFLEX FINGERPRINT CAMERA: c1930, pre-focused lens for making 1:1 photos of fingerprints or small objects; built-in illumination.

R3*   **D+**

NATIONAL GRAFLEX – SERIES I: c1933-1935. Bausch & Lomb Tessar 75mm f3.5 lens, non-interchangeable mount; CFPS 1/30 – ⅕₀₀s. Ten exp, 2¼" x 3¼" on 120 roll film.

R3*   **D+**

NATIONAL GRAFLEX – SERIES II: c1934-41. Bausch & Lomb Tessar 75mm f3.5 lens, interchangeable mount; CFPS ½₀-½₀₀s. 10 exposures, 2¼" x 3¼" on 120 roll film.

R3*   **E–**

BAUSCH & LOMB 140MM F6.3 TELE-PHOTO LENS.
R3*   **D**

R.B. GRAFLEX, SERIES B: c1925-1942. Kodak Anastigmat f4.5 lens, screw thread interchangeable mount; CFPS ⅒-¼₀₀₀ s. 2¼" x 3¼", c1925-1951, 3¼" x 4¼", c1925 - 1942, 4" x 5".

R2*   **D**

R.B. GRAFLEX, SERIES C: c1926-1935. Cooke 6½" f2.5 lens; CFPS ⅒-¹⁄₁₀₀₀ s; 3¼" x 4¼" exp.

R2*   **D**

R.B. GRAFLEX, SERIES D: c1928-1945. CFPS ⅒-¹⁄₁₀₀₀ s; 3¼" x 4¼", c1928-1941, 4" x 5".

R2*   **D**

R.B. Super D Graflex

R.B. HOME PORTRAIT GRAFLEX: c1912-1942. Zeiss Tessar 10"* lens; CFPS 1-¹⁄₅₀₀ s; 5" x 7" exp.

R4*   **E**

R.B. SUPER D GRAFLEX: c1948-1958. Kodak Ektar 152mm f4.5* lens with semi-auto diaphragm; CFPS ⅕-¹⁄₁₀₀₀ s. 3¼" x 4¼", c1941-1963, 4" x 5".

R3*   **E+**

SPEED GRAPHIC: – 4" X 5": c1928-1939. Zeiss Tessar f4.5* lens; Dial-set Compur 1-¹⁄₃₀₀ s; CFPS ⅒-¹⁄₁₀₀₀ s; 4" x 5" exp.

R3*   **D+**

Graflex Inc.
Rochester, New York

COMBAT GRAPHIC (70MM): 1947-48. 70mm perforated film in cassettes; Kodak Ektar 100mm f2.8 coated lens; CFPS 1 – 1/500s; 2¼ x 3¼ inch images. Interchangeable lenses. Spring-wound film advance. Manufactured by Graflex for the

US Army and was supplied in a fitted case with 3 lenses, flashgun, and filters. Price is doubled if complete . The 70mm Combat Graphic was designed by Hubert Nerwin Snr. who had designed the Contax II for Zeiss. It shows a startling resemblance to the Contax, although much much larger. Mr. Nerwin had gone to the US in 1946 as a part of "Operation Paperclip." This was a US Army project that transferred to the United States a large number of German scientists and engineers. Werner von Braun of rocket fame was part of this group.A civilian version of the 70mm Combat Graphic was marketed briefly with little success. Not more than 50 of them were made. The retail price of $1800.00 in 1950 was very high.

R4* **F+**

COMBAT GRAPHIC: 4" x 5" sheet film combat camera; Kodak Anastigmat Special 127mm f4.7 lens; Graphic shutter 1-¼₀₀ s, CFPS ¹⁄₃₀ – ¹⁄₁₀₀₀s; 4" x 5" exp on cut film and film pack. Water and dust resistant wooden construction with olive drab paint. c1942. Standard camera used by the U.S. Armed Forces in WWII.

R3* **F−**

GRAPHIC JET: c1961. 35mm motor drive camera; Graflex Optar 50mm f2 coated lens; Copal SVK, 1-¹⁄₅₀₀ s, CRF. "Jet-O-Matic" motor consists of CO_2 charger – drive motor automatically advances film and cocks shutter after each exp. Each CO_2 charger cycles 6 to 8 rolls of 20 exp 35mm film, at a maximum rate of 2 exp per s. Rapid wind film advance and shutter cocking may also be operated manually. Push button focusing moves film plane while lens remains stationary. Selenium photo-electric exp meter coupled to shutter. Mfd. in Japan, for Graflex Inc., Rochester. The CO_2 powered drive system of the Graphic Jet was not a design success and most of the cameras were used with the manual film advance. On rare occasions they are found with the original box and several CO_2 cartridges. The camera was made by Kowa Co. in Japan.

R4* **E**

GRAPHIC 35: c1956. 35mm rf camera; Graflex 50mm f3.5 coated lens; Prontor 1-¹⁄₅₀₀ s.

R2* **C−**

STEREO GRAPHIC: c1955. 35mm stereo camera, optical VFR, fixed focus Graflar 35mm/f4 lenses, single shutter speed, 1/50s, each lens was set for a slightly different point of focus, thereby ensuring at least one of the stereo pair to have the major subject in sharp focus. This was known as the "Depthmaster" system. The same camera was sold as the "Wray Stereo Camera" in England.

R2* **D**

GRAPHIC VIEW CAMERA: c1941-1950. 4" x 5" metal view camera.

R3* **E–**

MINIATURE SPEED GRAPHIC: c1938-1947. Kodak Anastigmat Ektar 107mm f3.7 lens; Compur shutter 1 - 1/250s, CFPS 1/10-1/1000s; 21/4" x 3¼" exp.

R3* **E**

PACEMAKER CROWN GRAPHIC: c1947-65. Kodak Ektar 101mm f4.5* coated lens; Kodak Flash Supermatic shutter 1-1/400 s. No FPS. 2¼" x 3¼", **D+**; 3¼" x 4¼", **D+**; 4" x 5", **E**. Still used by enthusiasts.

R3* 2¼ X 3¼ **E+**
5X4 **E+**

PACEMAKER SPEED GRAPHIC: c1947-1970. Kodak Ektar 101mm f4.5* coated lens; Kodak Flash Supermatic shutter 1-1/400 s, CFPS 1/30-1/1000 s. The Pacemaker is the only Graphic model with a single body release for both front and FPS. 2¼" x 3¼", c1947-1958, 3¼" x 4¼, c1947-1962. 4" x 5".

R3* **E+**

SUPER SPEED GRAPHIC: 1950-1970. 4" x 5" press camera; Graflex Optar 135mm f4.7 coated lens; special high speed between the lens Graflex shutter 1-1/1000s, without FPS , CRF.

R2* **F–**

Great Wall Camera Factory

Beijing, China.

GREAT WALL DF-2: 1970's. 120 roll film SLR, metal behind the lens shutter, 1/30 - 1/200s, ruby windows for frame counting, removable metal mask for 6 x 4.5 size negatives. Waist level VFR, coated 90mm screw mount lens. Later models incorporated self timer, and flash synch. This copy of the

spring motor film advance. As the Great Wall SZ-1, but with internal changes.

R3*   **C+**

1930's "Super Pilot" is no longer in production.

R3*   **C+**

J.J. Griffin and Son
London, England

CYKO NO. 1: c1902. 6.5 x 9cm all aluminium camera; Aplanatic 12cm lens; guillotine shutter.

R4*   **F**

POCKET CYKO: c1902, all aluminium folding camera; 6.5 x 9cm exp.

R4*   **F**

GREAT WALL SZ-1: 1970's. Between the lens leaf shutter, 1 - ¹⁄₃₀₀s, combined RFR/VFR, fixed f2.8/45mm lens, built-in spring motor film advance. A copy of a Ricoh camera, early cameras sometimes had the political slogan "Serve the People" in Mao's handwriting on the top plate, and are quite rare, even in China. This adds 200% to the value.

R3*   **C+**

GREAT WALL SZ-2: 1970's. Between the lens leaf shutter, 1 - ¹⁄₃₀₀s, combined RFR/VFR, fixed f2.8/45mm lens, built-in

W. Griffiths & Co.
Birmingham, England

THE GUINEA DETECTIVE OR HAND CAMERA: c1891. Valise type detective camera; single achromatic f9 lens; T and I settings. Original cost was one guinea.

R5*   **E+**

Grundmann, Leipzig

DETECTIVE CAMERA: wooden box detective camera; focusing lens tube; string set shutter; 9 x 12cm plates.

R4*   **F+**

Guangdong Camera Factory,
Guangdong, China.

PEARL RIVER: c1965. 2¼" x 2¼" TLR; Pearl River 75mm f3.5 coated lens; Pearl River shutter ½₅-½₅₀ s. 12 exp, 2¼" x 2¼" on 20 roll film. Mfd in China.

R3*   **C+**

Ets. E. Guerin & Co.
Paris, France

LE FURET (THE FERRET): c1923-1929. 35mm camera; Hermagis Anastigmatic 40mm f4.5 lens; 3 speed rotary shutter; 25 exp on 35mm film. Designed in 1913; marketed. Smallest pre-Leica 35mm camera. Invented by M. Maroniez.

R4*   **G+**

THE GUILFORD: view camera; Ross Extra Rapid brass lens; Walnut finish, brass fittings and black bellows. Mfd in England.

R3*   **D+**

Guilleminot Roux & Cie
Paris, France

GUILLEMINOT DETECTIVE CAMERA: c1900, detective camera; Aplanat 150mm f9 lens; rotary sector shutter with 8 speeds. Ground glass viewing. Walnut finish, brass fittings.

R4*   **F+**

LE SPHINX: c1891. Aplanat lens; rotary sector shutter. 9x12 cm glass plates. This camera was fitted with a clockwork powered plate changing mechanism. The beginning of this type of camera automation.

R5*   **G–**

Gundlach-Manhattan Optical Co.
New York

BO PEEP CAMERA: c1898. 4" x 5" folding plate camera; reversible finder; red bellows; solid wood front; wood interior.

R3*   **E–**

Bo Peep Camera

Korona IV

KORONA I: c1900. 4" x 5" folding camera; Gundlach Optical Triple Convertible lens and shutter; long focus bed; side, rear, top and front open for red double extension bellows.

R4*   **E-**

KORONA IV: 4" x 5" folding camera; Rapid Convertible lens; Gundlach Manhattan shutter 1-¹⁄₁₀₀s; 4" x 5" exp on dry plates.

R3*   **D**

KORONA PANORAMIC VIEW: 4" x 12" panoramic view camera; Triple Convertible Turner Reich lens. 4 sizes: 5" x 12", 7" x 17", 8" x 20", 12" x 20".

R4*   **G-**

KORONA ROYAL STEREO: c1920s, 5" x 7" stereo camera; rear tilts; front shift. Polished wood interior with nickel plated fittings.

R4*   **F**

Korona Panoramic View

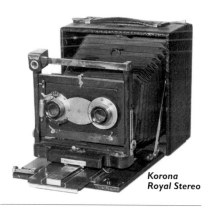

Korona Royal Stereo

NIGHT-HAWK DETECTIVE CAMERA:

c1905, box type detective camera; string set shutter; 4" x 5" exp on plates. Leather and wood finished versions.

R4*   **E+**

WIZARD DUPLEX NO. 1:

c1904, folding 3¼" x 4¼" combination plate and roll film camera; roll holder for No. 3 Folding Pocket Kodak Film made by Eastman Kodak is removable for plate use.

R4*   **E+**

WIZARD DUPLEX NO. 2:

c1904, combination roll film and plate folding camera. Hinged back is removable to permit accurate ground glass focusing.

R4*   **E+**

Guthe & Thorsch
Dresden, Germany.

Later Kamera Wertstätten and in 1959 VEB Kamera und Kinowerke Dresden, finally becoming part of the giant VEB Pentacon. For simplicity cameras are grouped by name with no regard as to which named company produced them.

JOLLY: 1950. Subminiature for 10x15mm images from the KW works and made from stamped sheet metal. Fixed focus lens. I & B shutter.

R3*   **C**

KW PATENT ETUI 6.5 X 9: c1930, 6.5x 9cm folding plate camera, Tessar 120mm f4.5 lens among others, (earliest cameras have dial set, later ones have rim set)

Compur shutter 1-½₅₀s among others, double or single extension bellows, known for its ultra slim design.

R3*   **C+**

KW PATENT ETUI 9 X 12: c1930, 9 x 12cm folding plate camera, Trioplan f3.8/135mm lens among others, (earliest cameras have dial set, later ones have rim set) Compur shutter 1 - ½₅₀s among others, known for its ultra slim design.

R3*   **C+**

KW PATENT ETUI DELUXE: c1932, 6.5 x 9cm *or* 9 x 12cm folding plate camera, Tessar lens among others, Compur shutter 1 - ½₅₀s. Brown or blue or red leather covering with matching bellows.

R4*   **E+**

PILOT TWIN LENS REFLEX: c1931, 127 roll film TLR camera, Schneider Xenar 5cm f3.5 lens among others, Compur, shutter 1-¹⁄₃₀₀s; 3 x 4cm exp on 127 roll film, early cameras have the "Pilot" name in script, after 1935 "Pilot" is in all upper case printing.

R4*   **F–**

PILOT 6: c1934, roll film SLR for 6 x 6cm frames on 120 film, KW Anastigmat f2.9,

Pilot Twin Lens Reflex

Pilot Super

f3.5, f4.5 or f6.3/75mm lens, FPS, early models ⅟₂₅ – ⅟₁₀₀S, later models ⅟₁₅-⅟₁₅₀S.

R2* **C+**

PILOT SUPER: c1936, roll film SLR for 6 x 6cm or 6 x 4.5cm frames on roll film, screw mount Laack f2.9/75mm lens among others, FPS ⅟₂₀-⅟₂₀₀S, built-in extinction meter.

R3* **D**

KW REFLEX BOX: c1936, roll film SLR for 6 x 9cm frames on 120 film, f6.3 or 4.5/105mm lens, FPS ⅟₂₅ – ⅟₁₀₀S.

R3* **D**

POCKET DALCO: c.1932. Name variation for Patent Etui Deluxe.

R3* **C+**

Pocket Dalco

PRAKTIFLEX: c1937, 35mm SLR interchangeable Xenar f3.5/50mm lens among others, CFPS ⅟₂₀ – ⅟₅₀₀S, top mounted shutter release, fixed waist level finder.

R3* **C+**

PRAKTIFLEX II: c1940, 35mm SLR interchangeable Xenar f3.5/50mm lens among others, CFPS ½₀ - ⅕₀₀s, *front* mounted shutter release, fixed waist level finder.

R3*   **C+**

PRAKTICA: c1948, 35mm SLR, post-war version of the Praktiflex, different in name and shutter speeds (1 - ⅕₀₀s) only.

R2*   **B+**

PRAKTICA FX: c1954, with F and X synch connections on the camera front.

R2*   **C−**

PRAKTICA FX 2: c1956, with new finder hood and PC type synch.

R2*   **C−**

PRAKTICA FX 3: c1958, with automatic aperture.

R2*   **C−**

PRAKTINA FX: c1954, 35mm SLR with interchangeable Biotar f2/50mm lens among others, CFPS 1 - ⅟₁₀₀₀s, built-in direct vision VFR, often found with spring motor and 250 exposure back (motor and back each add 100%).

R2*   **C**

PRAKTISIX: c1955, roll film SLR for 6 x 6cm frames on 120 film, interchangeable Tessar or Biometer f2.8/80mm lens, CFPS 1 - ⅟₁₀₀₀s, interchangeable waistlevel VFR, often found with shutter problems.

R3*   **D+**

PRAKTISIX II: c1969, as (GT114) but with brighter finder and the same shutter problems.

R2*   **D+**

PENTACON SIX: c1970, as (GT115) but now made by VEB Pentacon, and capable of 120 (twelve exposures 6 x 6cm) or 220 (twenty four exposures 6 x 6cm) film operation.

R3*   **E−**

PENTACON SIX TL: c1975-90, the last in the line of 120 SLRs from Dresden, finally the shutter is more reliable, and the film advance is redesigned. This camera is often bought by someone who wants to start on medium format with a small budget, or by a collector looking for an interesting usable piece at a bargain price.

R2*   **E−**

LENSES AND ACCESSORIES FOR PRAKTISIX/PENTACON SIX

Flektagon 50mm f4.0 w/angle lens:	**E−**
Flektagon 65mm f2.8 w/angle lens:	**D**
Biometer 120mm f2.8 telephoto lens:	**D**
Sonnar 180mm f2.8 telephoto lens:	**E−**
Sonnar 300mm f4.0 telephoto lens:	**E−**
Orestegor 300mm f4.0 telephoto lens:	**D**
Orestegor 500mm f4.0 telephoto lens:	**E+**
TTL prism meter:	**C**
Magnifying finder:	**B+**
Prism finder:	**B+**

Reference Notes

Haake et Albert
Frankfurt a/M, Germany

BADECKER: c1892, book type detective camera; Voigtlander Euryscop 80mm lens; 24 exp on 4.5 x 6cm plates.

R5*   **H+**

Haglund, Germany

L'ALBUM CAMERA: c1889, book type detective camera; guillotine shutter. 2 plates, 10 x 12.5cm in pivoting magazine.

R5*   **H+**

W. Haking
Hong Kong

HALINA 35X: 1959. 35mm camera resembling a scaled down Leica screw model. Metal body with black grained leathercloth. 45mm f3.5 Halina Anastigmat lens. Shutter 1/25-1/200 + B.

R1*   **B**

HALINA: 6-4: 1961. Dual format camera for 12 or 16 exp on 120. Twin viewfinders to cover each format. f8 Halina Achromat, apertures punched out of metal plate. Shutter 1/50s + B. Warning sign on top plate states: "When testing the camera without a film, it is important that the Transport Knob is transported NOT less than half a turn before the body release is depressed"!

R1*   **B**

HALINA: A1: 1957. TLR with two lenses linked by gear rings on edges for focusing. 80mm f3.5 Halina Anastigmat. Shutter 1/25-1/100s + B.

R1*   **C**

HALINA: PREFECT: 1957. TLR look-alike box camera for 12 exp on 120. f8 double meniscus lens. Everset shutter.

R?   **B**

PET: 1961. Modestly specified 35mm camera. Halina Achromat lens. Shutter for I & B. Aperture scale for dull, bright and sunny. Synch for flash.

R1*   **B**

VICEROY: 1959. 12 exp on 120. Similar to the Prefect but with addition of masking plates to take 24 24x36mm images on 120. TLR-style box camera. Non focusing f8 double meniscus lens. Shutter for I & T (not B).

R1*   **A**

Hanimex (HANnes IMport and EXport) *Australia*

Though not actually a manufacturer of cameras, Hanimex is a very large dealer in photographic equipment. Like so many other large photographic houses, HANIMEX contracted with camera manufacturers for "house brands".

ELECTRA II: c1961, 35mm VFR camera, Hanimar f2.8/45mm lens, automatic aperture and shutter control by means of a built-in Selenium light meter, focusing by use of four separate shutter release buttons, actually a Dacoramatic 4D.

R2*   **B–**

HANIMAR: c1953, 35mm VFR camera with interchangeable Finetar f2.8/45mm lens, shutter ½s – ⅟₂₀₀S, actually a Finetta 88.

R2*   **B–**

HOLIDAY 35: c1957, 35mm RFR camera, Kominar f3.5/4.5cm lens, leaf shutter 1 – ⅟₅₀₀S, CRF, looking like the Petrie 35.

R2*   **B–**

EAGLET: c1951, metal box camera for 6 x 6cm or 6 x 4.5cm on 120 rollfilm, simple lens and shutter, made in Italy by Fototecnica.

R2*   **B–**

HANIMEX BOX: c1955, metal box camera for 6 x 9cm frames on roll film, simple lens and shutter, built-in yellow filter, actually an Alka box camera made by Vredeborch in West Germany.

R2*   **B–**

HANIMEX RF35D: c1970s. The first 35mm SLR with a built-in flashgun. Styled more like a compact of the day with the addition of a pentaprism.

R4*   **C**

E. Hanau, Paris, France

L'OMNIGRAPHE: c1887-1906, guillotine shutter. 12 plates, 9 x 12cm.

R5*   **G+**

LE MARSOUIN: c1900, 45 x 107mm stereo camera; Tessar 55mm f6.3 lenses; 3 speed guillotine shutter. 12 stereo exp on 45 x 107mm dry plates in push-pull magazine #1 used 45 x 107cm plates, #2 6 x 13cm plates about equal in value.

R4*   **F–**

LE HANDY: c1900, Lemardley 135mm f7.7 lens; guillotine shutter ½s-¹⁄₁₀₀s. 9 x 12cm exp; helical focusing. Mfg in Paris, France.

R4*   **F**

George Hare
London, England

GEORGE HARE STEREOSCOPIC WET PLATE: c1865-1870, brass bound mahogany camera; Petzval lenses; 2 sets of waterhouse stops in leather cases; flap shutter; rack focusing from rear.

R5*   **H**

TOURIST STEREO CAMERA: c1860, 8 x 17cm stereo camera; Dallmeyer 110mm f11 lens; sliding lens panel; 8 x 17cm exp in Berry system magazine.

R5*   **H–**

TAILBOARD CAMERA: c1865; Brass and Mahogany constructon; Rack focusing; Dallmeyer Landscape lens;Half-plate, qurter-plate and 12" x 10" sizes.

R2*   **F**

Victor Hasselblad, *Sweden*

HASSELBLAD 1600F: c1948-1954, 120 roll film SLR; Kodak Ektar 80mm f2.8 coated lens, interchangeable mount; CFPS 1- ¹⁄₁₆₀₀s. 12 exp, 2¼" x 2¼" on 120 roll film in special magazine.

R3*   **F–**

HASSELBLAD 1000F: c1954-1960, 120 roll film SLR; Zeiss Tessar 80mm f2.8 coated lens, interchangeable bayonet mount; CFPS 1- ¹⁄₁₀₀₀s. 12 exp, 2¼" x 2¼" in special magazine.

R3*   **F–**

HASSELBLAD SUPER WIDE CAMERA: c1956-1960, 120 roll film SLR; Carl Zeiss

Biogon 38mm f4.5 coated non-removable lens with 90 degree field of view; Synchro-Compur shutter 1-⅟₅₀₀s. 12 exp, 2¼" x 2¼" in special magazine.

R4*   **G**

Dr. Hans Hensold *see ISO*

Herco, Herbert George & Co.

DONALD DUCK CAMERA: c1946-47, plastic camera; 127 roll film.

R3*   **B+**

ROY ROGERS AND TRIGGER 620 SNAP SHOT CAMERA: c1947, plastic box camera. 8 exp on 620 roll film.

R2*   **B+**

J. Fleury Hermagis
Paris, France.

HERMAGIS FIELD CAMERA: c1890. Hermagis Aplanastigmat 210mm f6.8 lens; Thornton Pickard roller blind shutter. 5" x 7" exp on plates. Rotating maroon bellows; polished walnut with brass fittings.

R4*   **E–**

INSTANTANEOUS STEREOSCOPIC CAMERA: c1888. Hermagis Aplanat f8 lens; 8 speed guillotine shutter. 12 stereo exp on 8 x 16cm dry plates.

R5*   **H**

JUMELLE HERMAGIS: c1895, 6.5 x 9cm camera; Aplanastigmatic lens.

R4*   **E–**

VELOCIGRAPHE: c1891, satchel type detective camera; Hermagis rapid rectilinear lens; central rotary shutter. 12¼ plates or 25 exp on film. Invented by Ricard et Lacroix.

R5*   **G–**

A. Herzog, *New York*

HERZOG CAMERA: c1876, periscopic 100mm f8 lens; 3¼" x 4¼" plates.

R5*   **G+**

Dr. Adolf Hesekiel & Co.E
Berlin, Germany

ARCHIMEDES STEREOSCOP CAMERA: c1904, 35mm stereo camera; Aplanat; Zeiss Anastigmat; Goerz Double Anastigmat lenses; B & I shutter, pneumatic release; 8¼" x 17cm exp.

R5*   **H–**

DR. A. HESEKIEL'S QUARTER-PLATE: c1895. Goerz 140mm f6.3 double anastigmat lens; FPS (no markings). Mahogany, nickel fittings.

R5*   **G+**

POMPADOUR: c1907, pocket book-type detective camera; Certomat 105mm f8 lens; 3 speed shutter. 6.5 x 9cm exp on plates. Consists of folding Certo in crocodile skin covered pocketbook.

R5*   **I+**

Hess-Ives Corp.
Philadelphia, Pennsylvania

HICRO COLOUR CAMERA c1915 Achromatic lens. Simple tri-colour camera using a film system designed by Dr. Ives. Manufactured by Eastman Kodak under contract to the Hess-Ives Corporation.

R3*   **D**

Hetherington & Hibben
Indianapolis, Indiana

HETHERINGTON MAGAZINE CAMERA: c1890. 4" x 5" box-type detective camera. All operations such as: plate changing, aperture changing and shutter tensioning are accomplished by means of key inserted from outside the camera box.

R4*   **F–**

Emil Hofert, Eho Kamera Fabrik
Dresden, Germany

See Altissa for post war camera production.

BABY BOX EHO: c1930. Duplar f11 lens; 3 x 4cm frames on 127 roll film.

R2*   **B+**

EHO: c1932, box camera, Duplar f11/50mm lens; single speed shutter; 3 x 4cm frames on 127 roll film.

R2*   **C–**

STEREO BOX EHO: c1930, box camera, Duplar 80mm f11 lens; 5 stereo exp, 6 x 13cm or 10 single exp, 6 x 6cm frames on 120 film.

R3*   **D**

EHO BOX 110: c1930, metal box camera, f11 lens, simple shutter, 6 x 9cm frames on roll film.

R2*   **A**

ALTISSA BOX: c1930, box camera for 6 x 6 frames on roll film, optical VFR on early cameras is a simple squared tube affair, later cameras used a large distinctive VFR, simple f10 lens, simple shutter. This same camera was continued after 1945 with little outward change and is not so rare. It was copied by the Chinese in the 1950s and called the "Xing Fu".

R2*   **A**

SUPER ALTISSA: c1930, with focusing f4.5 lens.

R2*   **B–**

ALTIFLEX: c1935, metal TLR for 6 x 6cm frames on roll film, lever focusing Victor f4.5/75mm lens among others, Automat, Prontor or Compur shutter.

R3*   **B+**

ALTISCOPE: c1935, stereo camera for 6 x 13 frames on roll film, Victor f4.5 lenses, simple shutter, lever focusing.

R3*   **D**

Horne & Thornthwaite
England

WET PLATE CAMERA: c1850. Petzval lens.

R5*   **G+**

E. I. Horsman & Co.
New York

NO. 3 ECLIPSE CAMERA: c1896, folding view camera; meniscus lens – 3 insertable metal circular stops; 4¼" x 6½" exp on dry plates.

R4*   **E–**

George Houghton & Son Ltd.
London, England

Houghton-Butcher Ltd from 1926
Ensign Ltd from 1930

George Houghton was in the photographic business from the beginning when he became the sole importer into Great Britain of Daguerreotype cameras, equipment and pictures. Great expansion took place under his son and the firm became a major manufacturer and wholesaler of cameras. In the first few years of the new century Houghton's absorbed a number of small firms that had made cameras for them. These included Holmes Bros, who made the famous Sanderson. Like Butcher, Houghton's also imported many of their cameras from Germany, a supply which abruptly ended in 1914 on the outbreak of war. Together with Butcher, the Houghton Butcher Manufacturing Company Ltd. was formed to make cameras for both companies. Houghton's were the senior partners because they already had a much stronger manufacturing base. Each company continued to sell its own models under its own name until complete amalgamation came in 1926 with the formation of Houghton-Butcher (Great Britain) Ltd. Ensign Limited (Ensign was an old Houghton brand name) was formed in 1930 as the selling company. A new series of modern cameras was introduced

under Ensign, but many Houghton and Butcher models continued into the early years of the Ensign era. Name changes after WWII reflected further amalgamations: Barnet Ensign in 1945, Barnet Ensign Ross in 1948, and Ross Ensign Ltd, in 1954. A few years later the company disappeared into the Rank Organisation, which already owned Ensign's rivals, Kershaw (Soho) and Ross' rivals, Taylor, Taylor and Hobson, and camera production ceased.

ALL-DISTANCE ENSIGN BOX: c1928; 6 x 9cm T.B.I. shutter

R1* Black   **A**

Red blue or brown c1931;

R1*   **B–**

ALL-DISTANCE ENSIGN FOLDING CAMERA: c1928, 6 x 9cm; T.B.I. shutter.

R2*   **C+**

COMMANDO: c1946. Ensar 75mm f3.5 lens; Epsilon shutter 1-1/200s, crf; 6 x 6cm exp on roll film. 12 or 16 exp on 120 film-format selected by adjusting internal baffles prior to loading film. Camera is unusual in that rfr was coupled to the film plane; lens and mount were fixed. The pressure plate was spring loaded to adjust to film plane movement.

R2*   **D–**

CUPID: c1922. Meniscus 70mm f12 lens; guillotine shutter; 36 x 56mm exp on 120 roll film.

R2*   **C**

ENSIGN ALL-DISTANCE "TWENTY" BOX: c1934; 6 X 9cm Box camera; Black;

R1*   **A**

ENSIGN ALL-DISTANCE"TWENTY" NO.2 BOX: c1936; As (HO136)with filter;

R1*   **A**

ENSIGN AUTORANGE 820: c1953; 8/12 exp on 120 roll film; Coupled RFR; Ross Xpres F3.8 in Epsilon shutter;

R3*   **E+**

ENSIGN AUTORANGE 16/20: c1953; 16 exp on 120 roll film; Ross xpres F3.8 lens; 9 speed Epsilon shutter;

R2*   **E–**

ENSIGN AUTORANGE CAMERA: c1934; 9X6cm exp on 120 roll film; Ten models with various lens shutter combinations;

coupled range-finder; Model prefix A7 changed in 1936 to AR.

R2*   **E–**

R2*   **E+**

ENSIGN AUTORANGE CAMERA: c1936; With Focal Plain Shutter 1-⅕₀₀s.; Various lenses.

R2*   **E+**

ENSIGN CAMEO: c1936. Camera takes plates or film; 9 x 6cm. Quarter plate and Postcard sizes; several lens shutter combinations.

R2*   **C+**

ENSIGN CARBINE FOLDING CAMERA: c1932-1936. Eleven models.

R1*   **C**

ENSIGN CARBINE NO. 6 TROPICAL MODEL: c1925. Zeiss Tessar 10.5cm f4.5 lens; Compur shutter ½₅₀s. Brass body; tan bellows.

R2*   **E**

Ensign Ful-Vue

ENSIGN DOUBLE-8: c1930; Folding camera; 3 x 4cm on 127 roll film; F4.5 Ensar lens; 1/25-1/100 shutter;

R1*   **D–**

ENSIGN FUL-VUE: c1939-1943. 12 exp on 120 roll film; All distance lens; T & I shutter.

R2*   **B+**

ENSIGN FOCAL PLANE CAMERA: c.1920. Unusual design of folding camera for quarter plates, film packs or cut film. Lens cover doubles as fold-up lens hood. Direct vision wire viewfinder. Non-pleated bellows. Helical focusing. Self-capping focal plane shutter, 1/15-1/1000s. Choice of standard lenses – 5½-inch f4.5 Ross Xpres Anastigmat, 5¼-inch Cooke Aviar Anastigmat, 5¼-inch Zeiss Tessar Anastigmat,

R5*   **I**

ENSIGN FUL-VUE: c1946-1949. First post-war model. Classic curved shape.

R1*   **A**

ENSIGN FUL-VUE A LA MONDE: As previous model in red, blue or grey.

R2*   **B+**

ENSIGN FUL-VUE SUPER: c1954; This model was a little more angular in shape; pull up hood on view-finder carring the

Ross-Ensign logo; removable back; die-cast aluminium body; flash sockets; T.& I. shutter; 12 exp 6 x 6cm on 620 roll film. Also found with ruby red body. Found in black and rarer in red.

R2*   **B+**

ENSIGN FULVUEFLEX: c1957-1959. All plastic box; 120 roll film.

R1*   **A**

ENSIGN MIDGET: c1934. 3.5 x 4.5cm exp on E-10 roll film; models 22 & 33; three speed shutter T.I.;

R1*   **C+**

ENSIGN MIDGET MODEL 55; f6.3 lens in three speed shutter;

R1*   **D−**

ENSIGN MIDGET SILVER PRESENTA-TION MODEL 1936;

R3*   **D+**

ENSIGN MULTEX: c1936; 14 exp on 127 roll film; coupled rangefinder; FPS 1-1/1000s. T.; Ross Xpres f 3.5 or 2.9 lens;

R3*   **F−**

ENSIGN POPULAR TROPICAL REFLEX: c1917. 3¼" x 4¼" tropical SLR; Ross Xpres 6" f4.5 lens; CFPS. Teak wood and brown leather bellows, brass fittings.

R4*   **E**

ENSIGN POCKET "TWENTY" FOLDING CAMERA: c1934, 6x9cm; T & I shutter

R1*   **A**

ENSIGN POCKET E20: c1939. Self erecting cmaera; 6x9 cm.

R1*   **A**

ENSIGN RANGER: c1952, 8exp on 120 roll film; Esnar f6.3 lens; Trikon 3 spd. shutter.

R1*   **B+**

ENSIGN ROLL-FILM REFLEX: c1926; 8 exp on 120 roll film 6x9cm.several models;

R2*   **E−**

ENSIGN ROLL FILM REFLEX TROPICAL MODEL: c1925, 6 x 9cm roll film SLR camera; Aldis 4¼" f7.7 lens; single speed shutter.

R4*   **F**

ENSIGN SELFIX "20" FOLDING CAMERA: c1926, 6 x 9cm; Several lens shutter combinations.

R2*   **C–**

ENSIGN SELFIX 220: c1938, 12/16 on 120 roll film; Optical finder; film counter. Several lens shutter combinations.

R2*   **C–**

With Tessar or Schneider lens.

R3*   **C+**

ENSIGN SELFIX 320: c1946, 8/16 on 120 roll film; Four shutter/lens combinations; two with body release; chrome trim;

R2*   **C**

ENSIGN SELFIX 420: c1946, 8/12 on 120 roll film; Six shutter/lens combinations.

R2*   **C**

ENSIGN SELFIX 820: c1950; 12 or 16 exp on 120 roll film; various lens shutter combinations;

R2*   **C+**

ENSIGN SELFIX 820 SPECIAL: c1954; As model above with built-in un-coupled rangefinder.

R3*   **D+**

ENSIGN SELFIX 16/20: c1950; 16exp on 120 or 620 roll film; Model I f4.5 Ensar lens; 4 speed Epsilon shutter; optical finder; Model II f3.5 Ross Xpres in 8 speed Epsilon shutter; Albada finder; Model IV f4.5 Rosstar lens; Epsilon 8 speed shutter;

R2*   **D**

Ensign Selfix 16/20

ENSIGN SELFIX 12/20: c1953; 12 exp on 120 or 620 roll film; 4 models with Rossitar or Ross Xpres lens in 4 or 8 speed Epsilon shutters; with Optical or Albada finders;

R2*   **C+**

ENSIGN SELFIX 12/20 SPECIAL: c1955; As model above with un-coupled rangefinder;

R2*   **D+**

ENSIGN SNAPPER: c1955, plastic folding camera; f11 lens; focusing; T & I shutter.

R1*   **A**

ENSIGN SPECIAL REFLEX CAMERA: c1935; various models in 9x6cm, 9x12cm, quarter plate; FP shutter ⅛ – ¹⁄₁₀₀₀s; leather covered.

R2*   **E–**

ENSIGNETTE: c1910-1920's. Aluminium bodied folding roll film camera; Zeiss Tessar 75mm f6.8 lens; single speed shutter. No 1: 1½" x 2¼" exp, No. 2: 2" x 3" exp, No. 2 Junior: 2¼" x 3¼".

R2*   **C+**

ENSIGNETTE DE-LUXE: c1914; same as the Ensignette No1 and No2 with Goerz f6.3 or Tessar f5.6 lenses.

R2*   **D+**

Ensignette

ENSIGNETTE SILVER: Very rare silver-plated version of the No. 1 Ensignette. It is thought that only four exist, probably having been made to special order and for presentation purposes. At least one of them has a Taylor Taylor and Hobson Cooke f5.8 anasigmat lens. Never listed in the Houghton catalogues.

R5　　　　　　　　　　　　　**G**

FOLDING KLITO: c1912, 6 x 9cm folding plate camera; Symmetrical 'Rectimat' f11 lens; Ensign-Simplex shutter ½₂₅-¹⁄₁₀₀s.

R2*　　　　　　　　　　　**B+**

"HOLBORN" POSTAGE STAMP CAMERA: c1900, 9 postage stamp size exp.

R4*　　　　　　　　　　　**F+**

KLITO HAND CAMERAS: c1904-1919; a range of 13 models most having rise and cross fronts; compact well constructed; some with double extension; quarter-plate, half-plate and 5 x 4 sizes;

R1*　　　　　　　　　　　**B+**

KLITO NO. 0: c1906. Rapid Rectilinear lens, adjustable focus with supplementary lenses; guillotine shutter. 3¼" x 4¼" dry plates; drop plate changing mechanism.

R2*　　　　　　　　　　　**C−**

KLITO NO. 3: c1908. Beck Symmetrical f8 lens; rack and pinion focusing; guillotine shutter 2-¹⁄₁₀₀ s; 3¼" x 4¼" dry plates, drop plate changing mechanism.

R2*　　　　　　　　　　　**C−**

TICKA: c1907, pocket-watch camera (similar to Expo); Meniscus 30mm f16 lens; 25 exp, 22 x 16mm on roll film in special cassette. The Ticka and Expo were made under licence by separate manufacturers, from the Swedish inventor Magnus Niell.

R4*　　　　　　　　　　　**E+**

FOCAL PLANE TICKA: 1908. Improved version of the original Ticka, made in a limited edition. Cooke f6.5 lens. Focal plane shutter 1/75-1/400s + T.

R4*   **H**

Tropical Watch Pocket Carbine No. 4

WATCHFACE TICKA: 1912. Rare version of the original Ticka, incorporating a fake watchface. The hands stand at 7 minutes past 11 and their angle indicates the field of view, to form a crude viewfinder.

R4*   **H**

TROPICAL WATCH POCKET CARBINE NO. 4: c1925. Aldis Butcher f4.5 lens; Compur $^{1-1}\!/_{250}$ s.

R3*   **D+**

THE MASCOT: c1909-1920; Magazine plate camera; several models; 3½ x 2½ & quarter plate; taking 6 or 12 plates; supplementary lenses for 3 and 6 ft focusing;

R1*   **B+**

VEST POCKET ENSIGN: c1924; VP film giving 4 x 6.5cm exp on 127 roll film; f11 lens in a three speed shutter;

R1*   **B+**

Sanderson Cameras
In connection with Houghton

F.H.Sanderson was a cabinet maker and keen photographer whose principal interest was architectural photography. He was granted a patent in 1895 for his design of a unique strut system, consisting of two pairs of slotted arms, for the support of the lens panel of a camera, giving a high degree of freedom in rise, tilt and swing. He licenced the design to Houghton's for manufacture and the basic design remained in production from 1896 until the beginning of the Second World War. Sandersons were produced both as field (view) cameras and hand-and-stand cameras. The original slotted arms had been straight, but in 1902 the forward pair were angled below the slot.

SANDERSON REGULAR MODEL: c1900's. 5" x 8" view camera; Rapid Rectilinear 5" x 8" brass lens; behind-lens

Thornton Pickard shutter. Black leather bellows; Sanderson patent movements; British Ensign trademark.

R3* **E–**

SANDERSON REGULAR MODEL HAND CAMERA: c1900's, 3¼" x 4¼" hand camera; Beck Symmetrical lens; Unicum shutter.

R3* **E–**

SANDERSON TROPICAL: c1905. 3¼" x 4¼" tropical camera; Beck Convertible f7.7 lens; teak with brass fittings.

R4* **G**

SANDERSON HAND AND STAND "REGULAR" CAMERA: c1896-1901; Quarter-plate, Half-plate, 5" x 4" and 5" x 7"; wide range of movements; Seven lenses available; Wood constuction leather

bound; C. 1902-1909; new angular front struts introduced;

R2* **E–**

SANDERSON DE-LUXE HAND AND STAND CAMERA; c1902; As the Regular but superior finish; Rack and pinion focusing also lens panel movements and rear focusing when the baseboard is dropped for wide angle lens; same lens combinations as the Regular; detachable focusing chamber in place of a cloth.

R3* **F–**

SANDERSON JUNIOR: c1904; Folding plate camera; lower priced version of the Regular; Half-plate and 5" x 4" sizes; Beck Symmetrical lens in Unicum shutter;

R2* **E+**

SANDERSON TROPICAL: c1905; Folding plate camera; same sizes as the Regular; made of polished teak; brass bound; lenses were Beck Double Aplanat f7.7 or Bausch & Lomb RR;

R3*   **G**

SANDERSON TROPICAL: c1909; As previous model with rear rack and pinion focusing for w/a lens; rise & fall rack and pinion controled; improved reversing back.

R4*   **D**

SANDERSON TROPICAL: c1925, 4" x 5"; Homocentric f6.3 lens; Compur 1-1/200s. 4" x 5" exp on cut film.

R4*   **G+**

SANDERSON VIEW CAMERA: c1920. Suter B. No. 5 Aplanat lens; 8" x 10" plates. Mahogany wood, brass fittings.

R4*   **F–**

R.F. Hunter Ltd. London, England

PURMA SPECIAL: c1938; Black plastic miniature camera. Beck anastigmat $2^1/_4$" f6.3 lens 16 exp, $1^1/_4$ x $1^1/_4$ inch on 127 roll film. Unusual shutter design, very likely unique. Position of camera (horizontal or vertical) determined shutter speed. Reintroduced briefly after WWII.

R2*   **B**

PURMA PLUS: 1951. Metal version of the Purma Special. 55mm f6.3 Purma Anastigmat. Three speed shutter identified as 'slow', 'medium' and 'fast', engraved around viewfinder eyepiece. Shutter controlled by gravity. Takes 16 32x32 exp on 127.

R2*   **B+**

Hurlbut Manufacturing Co.
Belvidere, Illinois

HURLBUT VELOX MAGAZINE DETECTIVE CAMERA: c1890, magazine-type

detective camera. Plates are gravity fed into position; then returned to storage by inverting the camera.

R4*   **F**

R. Huttig A.G.
Dresden, Germany

ATOM: c1908. 90mm f8 lens; Compound shutter 1-$\frac{1}{250}$s; 4.5 x 6cm plates.

R4*   **E–**

CUPIDO: c1906. Helios Rapid Rectilinear lens; Lloyd central shutter 1-$\frac{1}{100}$s; 9 x 12cm exp.

R2*   **C**

FICHTER'S EXCELSIOR DETECTIVE: c1893, drop plate magazine camera; rectilinear lens; rotating shutter; 12 exp, 9 x 12cm.

R4*   **F+**

AVISO: c1920, plate box camera; 4.5 x 6cm exp, magazine load. Sold in England as the Gnome camera.

R4*   **E**

LLOYD STEREO CAMERA: c1906. Busch Aplanatic 90mm f8 lenses; Stereo Compound shutter 1-$\frac{1}{200}$ s. 9 x 18cm exp on plates or roll film. 2 sizes: 8 x 14cm, 9 x 18cm.

R4*   **E–**

MONOPOL: c1895, rectilinear lens; variable speed rotary sector shutter; 9 x 12cm dry plates in magazine.

R4*   **D+**

STEREO IDEAL: c1906, 6 x 13cm stereo camera; Lloyd Anastigmatic 90mm f6.8 lenses; pneumatic central shutter 1-$\frac{1}{100}$s.

R4*   **E–**

ICA A.G., Dresden, Germany

ARTIST REFLEX: c1910, Zeiss Tessar 15cm f4.5 lens; FPS ¼₁-¼₀₀₀s; 3¼" x 4¼" exp. Sliding lens panel.

R3*   **E–**

AVISO: c1920, box camera for 4.5cm x 6cm plates or sheet film with internal changing mechanism, meniscus lens, simple shutter, which is quite visible on the front of the camera.

R3*   **C–**

AVISO NR.4: c1920, box camera for 4.5cm x 6cm single plates, meniscus lens, simple shutter, which is quite visible on the front of the camera.

R3*   **C–**

ATOM NR. 53: c1913, *horizontal format,* folding VFR camera, for 4.5cm x 6cm plates, several lens and shutter combinations including Tessar f6.3 or f4.5/65mm lens Compur shutter 1-⅓₀₀s.

R3*   **E+**

ATOM NR. 51: c1913, *vertical format* folding VFR camera, for 4.5cm x 6cm

plates, several lens and shutter combinations including Maximar f5.4/9cm lens, Automat or Compur shutter, VFR mounted below the lens.

R3*   **D+**

BEBE NR. 40: c1920, strut folding VFR camera for 4.5cm x 6cm film packs or plates, several lens and shutter combinations, including Tessar f6.3 or f4.5/7.5cm lens, Compur shutter.

R3*   **E–**

BEBE NR. 41: c1920, strut folding VFR camera for 6.5 x 9cm film packs or plates, several lens and shutter combinations, including Maximar f6.8/12cm lens, Compur shutter.

R3*   **D–**

CORRIDA NR. 156: c1920s, folding camera for 9cm x 12cm plates or film packs, lever focusing, several lens and shutter combinations offered including Icar f6.3/13.5cm lens, Automat shutter.

R3*   **B+**

CUPIDO NR. 75: c1920s, self erecting folding VFR camera for 6cm x 9cm or 6.5cm x 9cm plates or film packs, several lens and shutter combinations including Tessar f4.5/12cm lens, Compur shutter.

R3*   **C**

CUPIDO NR. 77: c1915, horizontal self-erecting folding VFR camera for 7.5cm x 10.8cm or roll film, several lens and shutter combinations offered including Hekla f6.8-10.5cm lens, Automat shutter.

R3* **C**

CUPIDO NR. 79: c1918, vertical self-erecting folding VFR camera for 7.5cm x 10.8cm or roll film, several lens and shutter combinations offered including Tessar f6.3-13.5cm lens, Automat shutter.

R3* **B+**

FOLDING REFLEX: compact folding SLR camera; Zeiss Tessar f4.5 lens; CFPS ⅛-¹⁄₁₀₀₀s. c1925. Model A: 2¼" x 3¼" exp on film packs, $150. Model B: 9 x 12cm exp on plates or film packs.

R4* **E–**

Icarette 501

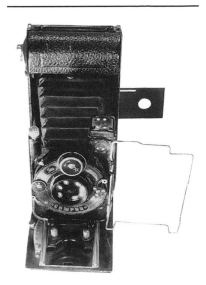

ICARETTE A: c1925, folding roll film camera; f6.3 lens; 12 exp, 2¼" x 2¼".

R2* **B+**

ICARETTE 501: Folding pocket camera; 6 exp 4½ X 2½; Tessar f6.3 lens in compound shutter;

R2* **C–**

ICARETTE II: Folding pocket camera; 6 x 9cm exp on roll film, film pack or plates; Tessar f4.5 in Compur shutter.

R2* **C–**

IDEAL NR. 111: c1925, folding plate camera for 6cm x 9cm or 6.5 x 9cm, several lens and shutter combinations available including Protar f6.3/10.5cm lens, Compur shutter.

R2*   **C–**

IDEAL NR. 205: c1925, folding plate camera for 9cm x12cm plates, several lens and shutter combinations available including Tessar f4.5/13.5cm lens, Compur shutter.

R2*   **C–**

IDEAL NR. 246: c1925, folding plate camera for 9cm x12cm plates, double extension bellows, several lens and shutter combinations available including Tessar f6.3/15cm lens, Compur shutter.

R2*   **C–**

LLOYD STEREO NR. 675: c1910, folding stereo/panoramic camera for 8 x 14cm exp on plates or roll film, several lens and shutter combinations offered including Maximar Double Anastigmatic f6.8/90mm lens, Stereo Compur shutter 1-$\frac{1}{100}$s. Rising and sliding front, panoramic setting.

R4*   **E–**

MINIMUM PALMOS NR. 453: c1920s, strut type folding VFR camera for 4.5 x 6cm exp on plates, several lens and shutter combinations offered including Tessar f4.5/8cm lens, CFPS 1 - $\frac{1}{1000}$s.

R4*   **E**

MINIMUM PALMOS NR. 454: c1920s, strut type folding VFR camera for 6 x 9cm or 6.5cm x 9cm plates, several lens and shutter combinations were available, including Tessar f6.3/12cm lens, CFPS 1 - $\frac{1}{1000}$s.

R3*   **D+**

MINIMUM PALMOS NR. 456: c1920s, strut type folding VFR camera for 9cm x12cm plates, several lens and shutter combinations offered including Tessar f4.5/15cm lens, CFPS 1 - $\frac{1}{1000}$s.

R3*   **D+**

MINIMUM PALMOS NR. 457: c1920s, strut type folding VFR camera for 10cm x 15cm plates, several lens and shutter combinations offered including Amatar f6.8/16.5cm lens, CFPS 1 - $\frac{1}{1000}$s.

R3*   **D+**

NIKLAS NR. 109: c1920s, folding bed plate camera for 6 x 9cm exp on plates, Ica Doppel Anastigmat 12cm f6.8 lens, Dial-set Compur shutter.

R3*   **B+**

POLYSCOP NR. 603: c1920s, box type stereo camera for single 4.5cm x 10.7cm plates, fixed focus achromat lenses, simple single speed shutter.

R4*   **D–**

POLYSCOPE NR, 605: c1920s, box type stereo camera for single 4.5cm x 10.7cm plates,several lens and shutter combinations available including Hekla f6.8/6cm lenses, shutter to $\frac{1}{250}$s.

R3*   **D+**

POLYSCOPE NR, 605/1: c1920s, box type stereo camera for 4.5cm x 10.7cm plates, delivered with magazine back for 12 plates, several lens and shutter combinations available including Maximar f6.8/6cm lenses, simple shutter.

R3*   **D+**

POLYSCOPE NR, 606: c1920s, close focusing box type stereo camera for single 4.5cm x 10.7cm plates,several lens and shutter combinations available including Hekla f6.8/6cm lenses, shutter to $\frac{1}{250}$s.

R3*   **D**

POLYSCOPE NR, 606/1: c1920s, close focusing box type stereo camera for 4.5cm x 10.7cm plates, delivered with magazine back for 12 plates, several lens and shutter combinations available including Maximar f6.8/6cm lenses, simple shutter.

R3*   **D+**

POLYSCOPE NR, 607: c1920s, box type stereo camera for single 4.5cm x 10.7cm plates, focusing and close focusing capability, several lens and shutter combinations available including Tessar f6.3/6.5cm lenses, shutter to ½₅₀s.

R3*   **E–**

POLYSCOPE NR, 607/1: c1920s, box type stereo camera for 4.5cm x 10.7cm plates, focusing and close focusing capability, delivered with magazine back for 12 plates, several lens and shutter combinations available including Tessar f4.5/6.5cm lenses, shutter to ½₅₀s.

R3*   **E–**

POLYSCOPE NR, 608: c1920s, close focusing folding strut type stereo camera for single 4.5cm x 10.7cm plates, several lens and shutter combinations available including Hekla f6.8/6cm lenses, shutter to ½₅₀s.

R3*   **D+**

POLYSCOPE NR, 608/1: c1920s, folding strut type stereo camera for single 4.5cm x 10.7cm plates, several fixed focus lens and shutter combinations available including Hekla f6.8/6cm lenses, shutter to ½₅₀s.

R3*   **D+**

POLYSCOPE NR, 608/2: c1920s, close focusing folding strut type stereo camera for 4.5cm x 10.7cm plates, delivered with magazine back for 12 plates, several lens and shutter combinations available including Novar f6.8/6cm lenses, shutter to ½₅₀s.

R3*   **F**

POLYSCOPE NR, 608/3: c1920s, folding strut type stereo camera for 4.5cm x 10.7cm plates, delivered with magazine back for 12 plates, several fixed focus lens and shutter combinations available including Tessar f4.5/6.5cm lenses, shutter to ½₅₀s.

R3*   **E–**

POLYSCOPE NR, 609: c1920s, box type stereo/panoramic camera for single 6cm x 13cm plates, focusing lenses, several lens and shutter combinations available including Tessar f6.3/9cm lenses, Compur shutter to ⅟₁₅₀s.

R3*   **E–**

POLYSCOPE NR, 609/1: c1920s, box type stereo/panoramic camera for 6cm x 13cm plates, delivered with magazine back for 12 plates, focusing lenses, several lens and shutter combinations available including Tessar f4.5/10.5cm lenses, Compur shutter to ⅟₁₅₀s.

R3*   **E–**

STEREOFIX NR. 604: c1920s, truncated box type stereo camera for 4.5cm x 10.5cm plates or film packs, several lens and shutter combinations available including Tessar f6.3/6.5cm lenses, Compur shutter, with close up focusing.

R4*   **D+**

STEREOFIX NR. 604/1: c1920s, truncated box type stereo camera for 4.5cm x 10.5cm plates or film packs, several lens and shutter combinations available including Tessar f6.3/6.5cm lenses, Compur shutter, without close up focusing.

R4*   **D+**

STEREO IDEAL: c1920s, 6 x 13cm stereo camera; Zeiss Tessar 9cm f6.5 lenses; Compur shutter 1-$\frac{1}{250}$s.

R4*   **E**

STEREOLETTE: c1912, compact folding stereo camera for 4.5cm x 10.7cm plates, Anastigmatic 60mm f6.8 lenses; Stereo Compur shutter 1-$\frac{1}{250}$s.

R3*   **E–**

STEREO PALMOS: c1920s, folding stereo camera for 6cm x 13cm plates, Zeiss Tessar 80mm f4.5 lenses, CFPS $\frac{1}{30}$-$\frac{1}{1000}$s.

R4*   **E**

TRILBY NR. 5: c1919, metal box camera for 6cm x 9cm plates with internal changing mechanism for 6 plates, meniscus lens, simple shutter, single waist level VFR.

R3*   **C+**

TRILBY NR. 11: c1919, metal box camera for 6cm x 9cm plates with internal changing mechanism for 6 plates, achromat 12cm lens, simple shutter, double waist level VFR.

R3*   **C+**

TRILBY NR. 12: c1919, metal box camera for 6.5cm x 9cm plates with internal changing mechanism for 6 plates, achromat 12cm lens, simple shutter, double waist level VFR.

R3*   **C+**

TRILBY NR. 13: c1919, metal box camera for 6cm x 9cm plates with internal changing mechanism for 12 plates, achromat 12cm lens, simple shutter, double waist level VFR.

R3*   **C+**

TRILBY NR. 14: c1919, metal box camera for 6.5cm x 9cm plates with internal changing mechanism for 12 plates, achromat 12cm lens, simple shutter, double waist level VFR.

R3*   **C+**

TRILBY NR. 17: c1919, metal box camera for 9cm x 12cm plates with internal changing mechanism for 6 plates, meniscus lens, simple shutter, waist level VFR.

R3*   **C+**

TRILBY NR. 18: c1919, metal box camera for 9cm x 12cm plates with internal changing mechanism for 12 plates, achromat 14cm lens, simple shutter, double waist level VFR.

R3*   **C**

TRILBY NR. 20: c1919, metal box camera for 9cm x 12cm plates with internal changing mechanism for 12 plates or 24 sheet film holders, achromat 14cm lens, simple shutter, double waist level VFR.

R3*   **C+**

TRILBY NR. 29: c1919, leather covered wooden box camera for 9cm x 12cm plates with internal changing mechanism for 12 plates or 24 sheet film holders, achromat 14cm lens and three built-in auxilliary lenses for focusing at 1, 3, and 5 meters, 1 - $\frac{1}{100}$s shutter, double waist level VFR.

R3*   **D–**

TRILBY NR. 31: c1919, leather covered wooden box camera with polished mahogany interior for 9cm x 12cm plates with internal changing mechanism for 12 plates or 24 sheet film holders, achromat 13.5cm lens and three built-in auxilliary lenses for focusing at 1, 3, and 5 meters,

1 - ¹⁄₁₀₀s shutter, double waist level VFR, opening front.

R3*   **D–**

TRILBY NR. 33: c1919, leather covered wooden box camera with polished mahogany interior for 9cm x 12cm plates with internal changing mechanism for 24 plates or 24 sheet film holders, focusing Alpha f11/14.5cm or Helios f8/13cm lens, Ica Automat shutter 1 - ¹⁄₁₀₀s shutter, double waist level VFR, opening front.

R3*   **D–**

TRONA NR. 210: c1920s, folding camera for 9cm x 12cm plates or film packs, double extension bellows, several lens and shutter combinations available including Novar f6.8/13.5cm lens, Automat shutter.

R2*   **B+**

TROPICA: c1925, 5" x 7" tropical camera; Carl Zeiss f4.5 lens; Compur shutter 1-¹⁄₂₅₀s; 5" x 7" exp on plates, teak construction with enamelled or nickel plated fittings.

R4*   **G+**

UNIVERSAL JUWEL: c1925, Tessar 165mm f4.5 lens; Compur shutter 1-1/250s; double extension, rotating back, wide-angle feature, rising and sliding panel.

R4*   **D–**

VICTRIX NR. 48: c1925, 4.5 x 6cm folding plate camera, several lens and shutter combination including Ica Dominar f4.5/75mm lens, Compur shutter.

R3*   **D**

VOLTA NR. 105: c1920, folding VFR camera for 6cm x cm or 6.5cm x 9cm plates or film packs, Alpha f11/12cm or Novar f6.8/10.5cm lens, Automat shutter.

R3*   **B+**

Victrix Nr 48

Ideal Toy Corp.
Hollis, New York

KOOKIE KAMERA: comic plastic novelty camera; plastic meniscus 80mm f11 lens; single speed shutter; 4.5 x 4.5cm exp on "in-camera" processed positive paper. c1968.

R3*   **D+**

Ihagee Kamerawerk
A.G., Dresden, Germany

For further information on Exakta cameras see Exakta Cameras 1933-1976 by Clament Aguila and Michel Rouah, Hove Collectors Books, 1987.

EXAKTA A: c1933; 127 roll film SLR camera; CFPS ¹⁄₂₅-¹⁄₁₀₀₀s; 8 exp, 1⅝" x 2½" on 127 film.. Lens fitted to model A had thread dia.39.5mm pitch 0.5mm Ihagee Exaktar

75mm-F 3.5 Meyer Primotar 75mm-F 3.5; Schneider Xenar 75mm-F2.9; Zeiss Tessar 75mm-F 3.5; Zeiss Tessar 75mm-F2.8; all the lenses available in both mount sizes for the range of cameras; Lenses not inter-changable on model "A"; Five versions available; No.2. c1933; Lens mount changed to 39.8mm pitch 0.75mm; No.3. c1934; Winder lever replaced knob;red window cover; Ihagee logo added to hood cover; No.4. c1934; As No.3 with Vacublitz 2 or 3 pin flash socket; No.5.c1939; As No.4 with top plate & front logo plate in matt chrome;

R3* **E–**

EXAKTA B: c1937, 127 roll film SLR camera; Zeiss Tessar 75mm f3.5 lens, non-interchangeable mount; CFPS 12-¹⁄₁₀₀₀s.; second speed knob for slow speeds;delayed speeds 6s.-¹⁄₁₀s.; 8 exp, 15/8" x 2½" on 127 roll film. c1933. Seven versions of the camera; No.2. c1934; as No. 1 with Ihagee logo on Vfr cover; No. 3. c1934; red window cover; film advance lever;infinity lock; lens mount 0.75mm

pitch; No.4.c1935 ;Vacublitz flash socket; No.5.; threaded socket for flash gun; No.6. c1938; No.6. c1938; first chrome Exacta B; No.7.c1938; as model No,6.painted black.

R2* **E–**

PARVOLA: c1930s. Characterised by large helical focusing mount. First turn brings lens to infinity setting. Further turning allows closer focusing. Models for 8 and 16 exp. on 127 plus a third dual format model for both. 7cm f4.5 Ihagee Anastigmat. Pronto shutter 1/25-1/100s + B&T. Also known as Klein Ultrix.

R3* **C+**

NIGHT EXAKTA: 1934-1937, 127 roll film SLR camera; Dallmeyer Super-Six 80mm

f1.9 lens, interchangeable mount; CFPS 12-¹⁄₁₀₀₀ s. Similar to Exakta B except for modified large size outer diameter focusing ring. Contrary to popular belief, ordinary Exakta lenses and Night Exacta lenses were perfectly interchangeable!; Serial numbers on finder frame; Four versions of this camera;No.1. c1934;Black body; no flash contacts; No.2. c1934;no slow speeds;flash socket added; No.3. c1937; Chrome top plate and front; No.4. c1937; as Exakta model "A";CFPS ½s-¹⁄₁₀₀₀s, B.T.;lever wind; flash sockets;

R3* **F+**

EXAKTA C: c1935. Similar to Model B with addition of plate back adapter for plates and cut film, with rear ground glass focusing. When plate back is used, reflex finder cannot be utilized. Lens spacing ring used with film; C. 1935. Three versions of the camera; No.1. ; black body: No.2.c1937; as No.1.chrome finish: No.3. c1939; as No.2.shutter speeds ½s-¹⁄₁₀₀₀s.T.B. full range of lenses;

R2* **D+**

EXAKTA JUNIOR: C. 1936;Simple version of the model "B"; CFPS½s-¹⁄₅₀₀s. T.B.; non-interchangable, telescopic tube, Ihagee anastigmat 75mm F 4,5 lens, front cell focusing; Three versions; No.1. c1936; black leather covering;no flash socket; knob film advance; No.2. c1937; as No.2 with flash socket;lever wind; No.3. c1938; as No.3. chrome finish:

R3* **F–**

ZEISS LENSES FOR VP EXAKTA

55mm f8.0 Tessar	**C–**
120mm f6.3 Tele-Tessar	**D+**
180mm f6.3 Tele-Tessar	**E–**
250mm f5.5 Tele-Tessar	**E–**

KINE EXAKTA: c1936; The first Ihagee 35mm SLR; a scaled down version of the VP model B.;CFPS 12s.-1/1000s. T.B.; delayed speeds 6s.-1/10s.; Ziess Tessar 50mm F 3.5 lens.; frame counter; lever

wind; flash sockets;folding Vfr; film cutter; removable back; Five versions; No.2. c1937; as No.1 with larger screen magnifier; No.3. c1937; as No,2. with name "Exacta" spelt with a "C" in place of the "K"; No.4. c1938; threaded flash attattchment; No.5. c1948; as No.4. strap lugs fixed;new slow speed dial; mirror chamber changed;some bodies marked "Made in Germany": price with round Vfr £500; with square Vfr as below;

R4* **E+**

ZEISS LENSES FOR THE KINE EXAKTA

35mm f2.8 Flektogon	**B**
40mm f4.5 Tessar	**B**
75mm f1.5 Biotar	**E–**
80mm f2.8 Tessar	**D**
85mm f4.0 Triotar	**C+**
105mm f3.5 Tessar	**D–**
135mm f4.0 Triotar (uncoated)	**C**
135mm f4.0 Triotar (coated)	**D–**
165mm f3.5 Tessar	**D–**
180mm f6.3 Tele-Tessar	**D+**
180mm f2.8 Sonnar	**E–**
250mm f6.3 Tele-Tessar	**E–**
300mm f4.0 Sonnar	**E**
Stereflex set for use on – normal lenses	**F+**

KINE EXAKTA II: c1948; 35mm SLR; As the Kine Exakta with; cover on Vfr; frame counter window; rewind knob; ribbed film pressure plate; Version No.2. c1949; as No1.; Two socket flash;

R2*   **E–**

EXAKTA VAREX: c1950; 35mm SLR camera; as Kine Exakta; with removable Vfr. & hood; Pentaprism right-way-round viewing with lock button on front plate;two sets of flash contacts for X & PF synch; takes full range of lenses;

R2*   **D–**

EXAKTA V: c1950, 35mm SLR camera; Xenon 50mm f2 lens, interchangeable bayonet mount; CFPS 12-¹⁄₁₀₀₀s. Snr 665,000-695,000(?). First 35mm SLR with interchangeable finder. Known as the Varex in the USA.

R3*   **D–**

EXAKTA VX: c1950; 35mm SLR camera; as the Varex with hinged & removable back; curved wind lever; X & PF flash contacts; milled knob rewind; film speed reminder in Weston & ASA; Meyer Primoplan 58mm F 1.9 lens; Five versions; No.2. c1954; Straight film tensioning lever; second lens baynot for tele lens; full apEture focusing with auto closing, first of the Automatic lenses; No.3. c1954; as No.2.Called Exakta Automatic in the U.S.A.; No.4. c1965; as No.4. Co-ax flash socket;shutter release cover; No.5. c1956; as No.4. film speed in DIN;

R2*   **D–**

EXAKTA VX: c1955; 35mm SLR camera; Tessar 50mm f2.8 lens, interchangeable bayonet mount; CFPS 12-¹⁄₁₀₀₀s. Snr 695,000-(?). Similar to Exakta V except has preset lens. Known as the Varex VX in the USA. c1955.

R2*   **D–**

EXAKTA VAREX IIA: c1957; 35mm SLR camera.VarexIIa engraved on front plate; CFPS; 12s.-¹⁄₅s.octagonal slow speed dial; ¹⁄₁₀-¹⁄₁₀₀₀s.fast speeds; three flash sockets "M" ¹⁄₅₀-¹⁄₁₀₀₀, "F" to ¹⁄₂₅, "X" ¹⁄₅₀ or slower; full range of lenses; Eight versions; No.2. c1957; no 1/150s, shutter speed; No.3. C. 1958; as No2.name plate in relief; No.4. c1958; as No.3 engraved "VXII" some also USSR OCCUP Germany; No's.6,7 and 8; c1961-1962; as Varex IIa; wider front panel;Exakta in upper case letters in white on black; Ihagee Dreden in upper case engraving on front plate;

R2*   **D**

EXAKTA VXIIA: c1957. 35mm SLR camera; Zeiss Pancolar 50mm f2 lens, interchangeable bayonet mount; CFPS 12-¹⁄₁₀₀₀s. Similar to Exakta VX, but has quieter slow speed shutter mechanism, and a third, "F" type flash socket was added.

R2*   **D+**

EXAKTA VAREX IIB: c1963; 35mm SLR camera;Same as the Varex IIa with slow speed knob round with milled edge; better

Exakta VXIIa

Exakta VXIIa

slow speed regulation 1/8s.-10sec.; fast speeds ⅟₃₀s.-⅟₁₀₀₀s. T.B.; PF & X flash sockets; simple Vfr removal; accepts all lenses in the Exakta range.

R2*   **D+**

EXAKTA VX 1000: c1967; 35mm SLR camera; same as Varex IIb with few changes except for the instant return mirror; non interchangable back.

R1*   **C+**

EXAKTA VX 500: c1969; 35mm SLR camera; CFPS ⅟₃₀-⅟₅₀₀s, B.; no slow speeds; no FP flash socket; accepts full range of lenses; low cost version of the VX1000.

R1*   **C**

EXAKTA RTL 1000: c1970; 35mm SLR camera; Slightly modified version of the

Praktika VLC; produced when Ihagee was absorbed by Pentacon; MFPS 8s.-¹⁄₁₀₀₀s,; instant return mirror; X flash ¹⁄₁₂₅s, PF ¹⁄₃₀; full range of auto lenses; interchangable Vfr's; TTL meter;

R1*   **C+**

EXAKTA TWIN TL: c1970. 35mm SLR camera; Made in Japan for IHagee;MFPS 1-¹⁄₁₀₀₀s.; two shutter releases; X & M flash ¹⁄₁₂₅s. auto return mirror;

R1*   **C**

EXAKTA 66: c1938, 6 x 6cm SLR camera; Tessar 8cm f2.8 lens; CFPS 12-¹⁄₁₀₀₀s. 12 exp on 120 roll film.

R4*   **G**

EXAKTA 66: c1954, 6 x 6cm SLR camera; CFPS 12-¹⁄₁₀₀₀s. Tessar 80mm f2.8 lens. 12 exp on 120 roll film. Originally announced at the 1952 Leipzig Fair, this camera was finally delivered in 1954. About 2000 were made, and it seems that all of them were exported to the USA. Not at all like the Exakta 66, and should not be considered as just another body style, but as a rarity in its own right!

R4*   **G**

EXA: c1952, 35mm SLR taking Exakta mount lenses, but with a very simple shutter, removable waist level finder, and limited range of shutter speeds.

R2*   **C**

EXA I: c1963; 35mm SLR new body shape; sector shutter; single flash socket.

R1*   **c**

EXA IA: C. 1965. redesigned body with lever advance.

R1*   **C**

EXA II: c1950; 35mm SLR camera;CFPS ¹⁄₂-¹⁄₂₅₀s.; two flash sockets PF ¹⁄₁s. X¹⁄₃₀s.; split image rangefinder screen.

R1*   **C**

EXA IIA: c1964: 35mm SLR camera; Same as Exa II; except for plain ground glass screen or split-image rangefinder;

R1*   **C**

EXA 500: c1966; 35mmSLR camera; same as IIa; fastest shutter speed ¹⁄₅₀₀; Fresnal lens focusing screen.

R1*   **C+**

EXA VX 100: c1968, now with external automatic aperture.

R1*   **C–**

EXA IB: c1975, now with internal automatic aperture.

R1*   **C–**

EXA IIB: c1965, with built-in, permanent pentaprism.

R1*   **C–**

ROLL-PAFF: c1922, 6 x 6cm SLR box camera; f6,8 Trioplan lens; single speed mirror shutter; 12 exp on 120 roll film.

R4* **D–**

PATENT KLAPP REFLEX: c1925, compact folding SLR camera; Dogmar 125mm f4.5 lens; CFPS ⅒₅-¹⁄₁₀₀₀s. 6.5 x 9cm exp.

R4* **E+**

ULTRIX AUTO: c1934, 4 x 6.5cm roll film folding camera for 127 film; Schneider Xenar 70mm f4.5 lens; Compur shutter 1-¹⁄₃₀₀s.

R2* **C–**

Ikko Sha Co., Ltd.
Japan

START 35: c.1948-1950. Simple Bakelite camera for Bolta size film, taking 24x24 negatives. Fixed focus, fixed aperture f8 lens. I & B shutter. Later models had hinged back. Later still, c 1958, metal was added to the body and the camera was synchronised for flash. Original model similar in style to the Rich-Ray Junior and Ebony, probably made by the same manufacturer.

R2* **D**

Ilford Ltd. *London, England*

ADVOCAT: 1949. Made for Ilford by Kennedy Instruments. Unusual for its 35mm focal length on standard 35mm image size, and for its white body, made from pressure die casting of aluminium silicon alloy, finished in a hard-stoved ivory enamel. f4.5 Dallmeyer. Shutter 1/25-1/200s.

R2* **C**

ADVOCAT SERIES II: 1952. Similar to original model but with f3.5 Dallmeyer. 35mm focal length retained. Focusing engravings changed to make easier reading, hinge and lock mechanism modified.

R2* **B+**

ILFOFLEX: Cheap plastic camera made to resemble a small format TLR. f8 Brytex lens. Fixed focus and aperture. I & B shutter. 12 exp on 127. Similar in style to the Bedfordflex.

R1* **B**

Ilfoflex

P.I.M. MONORAIL CAMERA: 1953. 5x4-inch monorail camera. Monorail in aluminium alloy, rack in plated brass. Lens panel and back supported in U-shaped brackets. Full range of camera movements. Square leather bellows with extension and movements.

R3*   **NSR**

PRENTICE: 1951. Folding camera for 8 exp on 120. Three-point focusing scale. f11 and f16 apertures, I & B shutter.

R2*   **A**

SPORTI 4: 1960. Made for Ilford by Dacora Kamerawerk. Aimed at children. 12 exp on 127. Made for use with Selochrome Pan film, with apertures for 'sunny' or 'cloudy'. Body made of polystyrene. Sold in 1961 as part of a kit containing camera, flashgun, film and flashbulbs.

R1*   **B**

SPORTSMAN: 1957. Made for Ilford by Dacora Kamerawerk. Inexpensive but well specified 35mm camera. 45mm f3.5 Dacora Dignar lens Vario shutter 1/25-1/200s + B. Shutter release on front of body. All metal construction.

R1*   **B**

SPORTSMAN RANGEFINDER: 1960. Similar to other Sportsman cameras, with addition of coupled rangefinder. Symbol focusing also allows manual focus. 45mm f2.8 Dacora Dignar lens. Pronto shutter 1/30-1/250s + B.

R1*   **B**

SPORTSMASTER: 1961. Unusual version of the Sportsman with four shutter releases, each linked to the focusing mechanism. Setting the appropriate shutter sets the focus in one of four zones. Prontor-lux shutter coupled with auto-exposure control, speeds governed by speed setting of film: 1/30s for 10ASA to 1/500s for 200ASA. 45mm f2.8 Dacora. Apertures set automatically or manually for flash photography.

R2*   **B+**

SUPER SPORTI: 1960. Similar to original model, with film wind and shutter interlocked. Shutter and aperture interlocked for three settings; 'sunny,' 'cloudy' and 'cloudy-dull'. Two apertures, f11 & f9. Two shutter speeds.

R1+   **B**

WITNESS: 1951. High quality 35mm CRF camera, showing strong influences from both Leitz and Zeiss. Witness lenses can be fitted quickly on bayonet, but mount also incorporates 39mm screw to take Leica lenses. Dust cover on accessory shoe. 5cm f2.9 collapsible Daron or 2-in f1.9 Dallmeyer Super-Six. FP shutter 1-1/1000s.

R5*   **G**

Ingersoll & Bros. *New York*

SHUR-SHOT CAMERA: c1897. Small all-wood plate camera; meniscus lens; guillotine shutter. Single exp on 2½" square, glass plates.

R4*   **E–**

International Metal & Ferrotype Co.
Chicago, Illinois

THE DIAMOND GUN FERROTYPE CAMERA: c1910. Large nickel plated all metal ferrotype camera in shape of a cannon, constructed so as to attract attention to a street operator. Has internal masks

for formats down to button tintypes. Camera is 18" in length and 8" in diameter.

R5*   **G+**

I.O.R., *Bucharest, Romania*

ORIZONT: c1960, metal 35mm VFR camera, Tricolar f3.2/50mm lens, simple shutter ⅒ – ⅟₁₂₅s.

R4*   **C–**

ORIZONT AMATOR: c1970. plastic and metal 35mm VFR camera, Fotoclar f2.8/40mm lens, combined aperture/shutter f2.8 at ⅟₃₀s – f16 at ⅟₃₀₀s.

R4*   **A**

ISO, Industria Scientifica Ottica S.R.L.
Milan, Italy

DUPLEX 120 c1950 Unusual stereo camera using 120 roll film. A pair of stereo images are made on each side of the film. The interocular separation of the lenses limits the depth sensation at any distance beyond about 8 feet. The camera is important for a stereo collector. A special viewer was available. Iperang 25mm f/6.3 fixed focus lenses.

R3*   **E**

DUPLEX SUPER 120 c1965. Similar to IS100 but fitted with Iriar 35mm, f3.5 lenses.

R3*   **E+**

ISO STANDARD: c1953, 35mm RFR camera, Leica copy, interchangeable Iriar f3.5 or 2.8/50mm lens, among others, CFPS shutter speeds ⅟₂₀ – ⅟₁₀₀₀s, interchangeable eyepieces for use with different focal length lenses, no strap lugs.

R4*   **G–**

Duplex Super 120

ISO METER LUX: c1947, 35mm RFR camera, Leica copy, interchangeable Trixar f3.5/50mm lens, CFPS 1 - ⅟₁₀₀₀s, coupled vertical RFR, built-in light meter.
R4*   **G+**

ISO BILUX: c1950, 35mm RFR camera, Leica copy, interchangeable Trixar f3.5/50mm lens, CFPS 1 - ⅟₁₀₀₀s, bottom trigger wind.
R4*   **G+**

ISO REPORTER: c1954, with improvements.
R4*   **G+**

HENSOLD REPORTER: c1955. Made for Dr. Hans Hensold of Wetzlar, and engraved with the Hensold name. Arion f1.9/5cm lens among others.
R4*   **G+**

Eugen Ising, *Germany*

ISIS: Metal body with lens drawn out on tube. 120 film. Direct vision finder. f3.5 Westar, Prontor S shutter 1-1/300s.
R2*   **B+**

Ives Corp.
Philadelphia, Pennsylvania

IVES' KROMSCOPE VIEWER; The wooden bodies were made by an English firm. Name unknown. Filters etc, installed in Philadelphia.
R4*   **F**

Reference Notes

Japy & Cie, *Paris, France*

LE PASCAL: c1898, Le Pascal was fitted with a clockwork mechanism which advanced the paper-backed roll film after each exposure. This was the first such camera on the market. There were two models identical in outside appearance. Model I was all wood with a leather hinged back. The second model had a removable metal back. A landmark first camera.

R4* **F–**

Jeanneret & Co. *Paris, France*

MONOBLOC: c1925, 6 x 16cm stereo camera; Boyer Saphir 75mm f4.5 lenses; Stereo Compur shutter 1-¼₅₀s. Interchangeable (rising) lens panel. Converts to take single panoramic pictures, 6 x 13cm.

R3* **E–**

Johnson & Harrison
England

PANTASCOPIC CAMERA: Unusual panoramic wet plate camera; Grubb 20cm lens. Clockwork mechanism moves a flat wet plate past a slit as the lens and camera body rotates. So rare as to be for all practical purposes unavailable.

R5* **J–**

F. Jonte, *Paris, France.*

F. JONTE FIELD CAMERA: 5" x 7" field camera; Rapid Rectilinear lens. Bellows rotate for format change. Polished mahogany finish, brass fittings. Mother-of-pearl label with mfr. name.

R4* **E+**

Joseph Peter
Hamburg, Germany

JOS-PE: c1925. Single shot, tri-colour camera; Steinheil Munchen Anastigmat Quinar 10.5cm f2.5 lens; Compound shutter ½-¼₀₀s; 3¼" x 4¼" exp on plates.

R5* **H**

L.Joux, *Paris, France*

STENO JUMELLE: c1894. Goerz 130mm f8 Anastigmat lens; 5-speed guillotine shutter; 12 exp, 9 x 12cm on plates.

R3* **E+**

STEREO JUMELLE DE JOUX: c1898. Zeiss Krauss 110mm, f8 Anastigmatic lense; guillotine shutter. Special rotating magazine for 12 plates, 8 x 17cm. Mfd in Paris, France.

R4* **E+**

Stereo Jumelle de Joux

Max Jurnick

JUMELLE BERTONI: c1900. Stereo camera; Elio 7cm f5.5 lens; shutter 1-½₀₀s; leather covered wooden body; magazine; 45 x 107mm.

R4*   **E+**

Max Jurnick

TOM THUMB CAMERA: c1889. Detective camera concealed in wooden box; Rapid Rectilinear lens; spherical shutter.

R5*   **H–**

Jumeau & Jannin
Paris, France.

LE CRISTALLOS: c1890. Meniscus lens; rotary shutter. 6 x 9cm exp on film.

R4*   **E–**

Reference Notes

Kalart Co.
New York, New York

KALART: c1948-1950, 3¼" x 4½" press camera; Wollensak Raptar 127mm f4.5 coated lens; Rapax shutter 1 – ⅟₄₀₀s. Dual left and right RFR windows for left-eye or right-eye operation. Has die-cast aluminium body with all built-in parts. Rising and lateral lens movements. The "Electric Brain" controls dual shutter release triggers; safety interlock requires holder to be inserted and the slide withdrawn to release the shutter. Two plug-in flash reflectors for midget lamps can be mounted on top of camera; interlocks prevent lamps from firing unless shutter has been cocked, film holder inserted and slide pulled. Built-in "Focuspot"

R3*   **E**

Kalos Kamerabau
Germany

KALOS: c.1950. 24 exp 9x12mm on 16mm rollfilm in a camera the size of a matchbox. 20mm f4.5 Mikro-Anastigmat. Shutter 1/30-1/100s + B.
R3*   **E**

PETITUX IV: c.1960. Design based on the Kalos. Changes included a focusing 25mm f2.8 Röschlein Supronar and shutter speeds 1/2-1/125s. Image size changed to 14x14mm.
R3*   **E**

Kamera Werkstütten
see – Guthe & Thorsch

Kashiwa Seiko Co.
Japan

COOKY 35: 1949. One of the smallest 35mm cameras made. Two models, one with a 40mm f2.8 Runer Anastigmat, the other with a 40mm f3.5 Zephyr. Shutter on both 1/25-1/100s. Auto frame counter on top plate.
R3*   **F**

Alfred C. Kemper
Chicago, Illinois.

KOMBI: Miniature metal-bodied camera and graphoscope (viewer) combination; biconvex single element lens. Permanently fixed pinhole diaphragm.; single speed shutter, 25 exposures 1⅛ inch round on special film made by Eastman Kodak. After exposure the film was processed to a positive transparency and reloaded into the camera. The back was removed and the image viewed through the lens which

acted as a 3X magnifier. Very collectable and still found in the US without too much difficulty.

R3*   **F**

Keio Department Store
Tokyo, Japan

TYRE CAMERA (POTENZA): c1981; 110 camera in the shape of an automobile tyre. Meniscus lens, f11, 26mm. Shutter 100s.

R1   **A**

Kennedy Instruments
London, England

KI MONOBAR: 1954 35mm monorail view camera, using cut film holders, ground glass focusing, very unusual.

R3*   **G**

Kern, *Aarau, Switzerland*

KERN FOLDING CAMERA: Kern Anastigmat 120mm f4.5 lens; Compur shutter 1 - ½₀₀s. 3¼" x 4¼" exp. Aluminium construction. c1920.

R4*   **F**

STEREO KERN: c1920. 35mm stereo camera; Kernon 35mm f3.5 lenses; guillotine shutter ½₅-½₀₀s.

R4*   **G**

SUPER STEREO: c1930. 35mm stereo camera; Kern f3.5 lens. 20 x 20mm format. Interlens separation increased to 64mm.

R4*   **G**

Thomas Kerr
Walthamstow, England

ABRAHAM'S DETECTIVE CAMERA:
c1888, wooden box-type detective camera;
plate changing by lever.

R4*   **F**

Keys Stereo Products,
U.S.A.

TRIVISION CAMERA: c1946, fixed focus
f8 lenses; single speed shutter ⅕₀s. 6 stereo
or 12 single exp on 828 film.

R3*   **C**

Odon Keyžlar
Slatinany, Czechoslovakia

OKAM: 1925; Trioplan 75mm f4.5 lens; 4.5
x 6cm dry plates, shutter ¹/₅ to ¹/₁₀₀₀ s.
Unusual focal plane shutter design varied
slit width and transit speed to reach high
speeds.

R3*   **NSR**

**Okam:
Back view**

KGB –
(Manufactured for former Russian Intelligence Services)

F21: c1980, metal 35mm VFR camera for
18x24mm frames with film loaded in
special cassettes. Built-in spring motor, f2.0
28mm fixed focus lens. The first model of
the F-21 appeared about 1950 and was
available only to the KGB. Much later a
civilian version was available on a limited
basis. Focusing version, f2.8 fixed focus
lens, f2.9 lens with automatic exposure
control. These cameras started bringing
very high prices, upwards of $3500. Now
the market has calmed a bit, and recently
one changed hands for $700. It is rumoured

that a large stock of cameras exists. It will be interesting to see what happens to the price.
R3*   **F**

Kiddie Kamera
Taiwan

This company made a number of cameras during the 1980s based on the faces of clowns and animals. All were for 110 film, all had fixed focus, aperture and shutter speeds. Styles included a bear, panda, Father Christmas, man clown and girl clown. The latter was the last made in the early 1990s and is the most common of the various models.
R2*   **B**

Kiev, *Ukraine*

JOHN PLAYER SPECIAL: c.1970. Disguised version of the Kiev Vega 16mm camera. Outer body designed to look like a pack of cigarettes and actually held two real cigarettes. The false cigarettes poking out the top are the camera's controls. Might have been a true spy camera, but the more likely origin is as a fake, manufactured in Poland.
R4*   **F**

KIEV: 1947. Copy of Contax II. CRF camera made with Zeiss parts following the seizure of the Contax plant by the Russian Army at the end of WWII. Equipment taken from Jena made lenses and production was shifted to Kiev. More Contax copies followed...
R2*   **C**

KIEV 2: 1947. 50mm f2 Jupiter 8 Shutter 1/2-1/250s.
R2*   **C+**

KIEV 2A: 1956. Similar to Kiev 2 with flash synch added.
R2*   **C+**

KIEV 3: 1952. Similar to Kiev 2 with uncoupled Selenium meter
R2*   **D**

KIEV 3A: 1956. Similar to Kiev 3 with flash synch added.
R2*   **D**

KIEV 4: 1957. A Kiev 3A with minor body changes.
R2*   **D**

KIEV 4A: 1958. Similar to Kiev 2A with small body changes.
R2*   **D**

KIEV 5: 1970. Updated and restyled version of the Kiev 4A with meter incorporated into body.
R2*   **D+**

More details of Kiev cameras and their association with Contax can be found in *The Zeiss Compendium* by Charles M. Barringer and Marc James Small, published by Hove Books.

Benjamin Kilburn

KILBURN PHOTOGRAPHIC GUN: c1884, gun-type detective camera. 10.5 x 12.5cm exp on plates; trigger released shutter.

R5*   **NSR**

Kin-Dar Corporation

KINDAR STEREO CAMERA: c1953, 35mm stereo camera; Steinheil Cassar f3.5 coated lenses; shutter ⅒-½₀₀s. Designed by Seton Rochwhite.

R3*   **D+**

K.K.W. LIGHTER CAMERA: c1975, cigarette lighter and compass. Pressing shutter release on this toy trips a lighter. Mfd in Japan.

R2*   **B**

King KG, *Germany*

MASTRA V35: 1958. Inexpensive 35mm VFR camera in a slim, die-cast body. 45mm f2.8 Cassar lens in Verio shutter 1/25-1/200s + B.

R1*   **A**

REGULA II: 1951. Basic 35mm VFR camera in chrome and black plastic fabric finish. 50mm f3.5 Staeble-Werk Kataplast lens in Prontor S shutter 1-1/300s + B.

R1*   **A**

Kilfit, *Munich, Germany*

MECAFLEX: 1953. Rare and unusual 35mm SLR for 24x24mm negatives. Waist-level finder covered by snap-up magnifier. 40mm f2.8 or f3.5 Kilar standard lenses in interchangeable bayonet mount. Shutter release, film, rewind and viewfinder found under hinged top plate. Matte chrome body with black leather covering. A few models made with brown covering. Rare 105mm f4 Teke-Kinar can sometimes be found. Even rarer accessory for converting viewfinder for eye-level use (mirror type, not pentaprism).

R4*   **F+**

Kinn, *France*

BABY KINAX: 1951. Folding camera for 8 exp on 620. All metal body in black grained finish, chrome fittings. Three numbered stop on lens for f16, f22 & f32. I & B shutter. Flash synch.

R2*   **B**

KINAFLEX: 1952. TLR for 12 exp on 120 or 620. Twin lenses geared together for focusing. 75mm Som Berthiot Flor lenses f3.5 for taking, f3 for focusing. Inter-lens shutter 1-1/300s + B. Flash synch at 1/25s or 1/50s.

R2*   **C**

KINAX-CADET: 1950. Folding camera for 8 exp on 620. Self erecting. 10cm Kior Anastigmat. Shutter 1/25-1/100s + B. Synch for flash. Red spot on focusing and aperture scales give a snapshot setting and depth of field of 10ft to infinity.

R2*   **C**

KINAX I: 1948. All metal folding camera. 105mm f4.5 Angenieux. Shutter 1/10-1/50s + B.

R2*   **B**

KINAX II: 1948. Essentially the same as the Kinax I but with a smoother shutter and better pressure pad.

R2*   **B**

KINAX III: 1951. Similar to Kinax I & II, but with masking frames to take 8, 12 or 16 exp on 620. 105mm f4.5 Berthiot Special lens, nine speed shutter 1-1/300s + B. An aluminium frame pulls up from behind the lens and swings in front of the optical viewfinder, two horizontal bars dissecting the view to give the fields for the smaller formats. Three red windows for three different formats.

R3*   **A**

Franz Kochmann
Korellewerk Dresden, Germany

After 1945 this factory was "nationalized" and became part of the Werkestette für Feinmechanik und Optik (WEFO), VEB, Dresden, East Germany. Post-war cameras made by this firm are treated as a continuation of the pre-war line, and are found at the end of this listing.

KORELLE: c1932, 4 x 6.5cm roll film camera, various lens and shutter combinations including Radionar 75mm f3.5 lens, Compur shutter 1-½₂₅₀s.

R2*   **C–**

KORELLE P: 4.5 x 6cm folding plate camera, various lens and shutter combinations including Xenar f2.9 lens, Compur shutter 1-½₂₅₀s.

R3*   **E+**

REFLEX-KORELLE: c1932, SLR camera for 6 x 6cm frames on 120 roll film, Ludwig-Dresden Victar f2.9 or f3.5/75mm lens, interchangeable screw mount, CFPS, ½₂₅-½₅₀₀s, black painted name plate, external selftimer, double stroke lever advance.

R3*   **D+**

REFLEX-KORELLE II: c1934, SLR camera for 6 x 6cm frames on 120 roll film, Ludwig-Dresden Victar f2.9 or f3.5/75mm lens, interchangeable screw mount,CFPS, 2 – ⅟₅₀₀s, *chrome name plate*, external self-timer, double stroke lever advance.

R3*   **D+**

REFLEX-KORELLE CHROME III: c1936, SLR camera for 6 x 6cm frames on 120 roll film, Radionar or Xenar f3.5 or Radionar f2.9/75mm lens, interchangeable bayonet mount, CFPS, 2 – ⅟₁₀₀₀s, chrome name plate, VFR hood, and front plate, internal self-timer, single stroke lever advance.

R3*   **E**

SPORT KORELLE 66: c1939, folding VFR camera for 6 x 6cm frames on 120 roll film, Tessar f2.8/8cm lens, interchangeable mount, CFPS to ⅟₁₀₀₀s.

R4*   **E**

KORELLE K: c1933, Bakelite 35mm half frame VFR camera 18mm x 24mm frames on standard 35mm film, various lens were available including Tessar f3.5 or f2.8/35mm lens, Compur shutter (dark brown body brings 100% more, as does Leitz Elmar f3.5/3.5cm lens.)

R3*   **F**

KORELLE 6X6: c1932, folding VFR camera for 6 x 6cm frames on 120 roll film, various lens and shutter combinations available including Radionar f2.9 or f3.5/75mm lens, Prontor or Compur shutter.

R3*   **C**

KORELLE 6X9: c1932, folding VFR camera for 6 x 9cm frames on 120 roll film, various lens and shutter combinations available including Radionar f4.5/105mm lens, Prontor or Compur shutter.

R3*   **C**

ENOLDE A, I, IA, II, III, IV, V, VI: c1918, folding plate or sheet film cameras in 6.5cm x 9 cm, 9cm x 12cm, and 10cm x 15cm sizes, leather covered wooden or metal bodies, rising and shifting fronts, more expensive models have double extension bellows, many lens and shutter combinations including Meyer, Steinheil, Rodenstock, and Schneider lenses and Vario, Ibsor and Compur shutters, models include I, Ia, A, II, III, IV, V and VI, all of which differ only slightly. (+30% for 6.5cm x 9cm size and double extension bellows).

R3*   **B**

ENOLDE: c1930, folding camera for 6cm x 9cm frames on roll film, unusual focusing tube/viewfinder swings away from the camera body and attaches to the lens standard when the camera is opened in the working position, moving the lens thereby focuses the image in the VFR, Zeiss Tessar f4.5/105mm lens, Compur shutter.

R4*   **E**

MEISTER-KORELLE: c1950, SLR for 6cm x 6cm frames on roll film, interchangeable Tessar f3.5/9cm Primotar f3.5/85mm lens, CFPS 1 – ⅟₁₀₀₀s.

R3*   **E**

Eastman Kodak Co.
Rochester, New York

George Eastman began the manufacture of dry plates in 1880, supplying all the needed capital for the new enterprise out of his own pocket. Henry Strong, a Rochester businessman loaned him some money and then in 1881 they formally founded the Eastman Dry Plate Company, with Strong as President and Eastman Treasurer. Dry Plates which were the company's main source of income were distributed by the E. & H.T. Anthony Co, at that time the largest jobber of photographic supplies in the U.S. In 1884 when the firm added flexible stripping film to the product line, they changed the corporate name to the Eastman Dry Plate and Film

Company. The film was for use in the recently introduced Eastman-Walker Roll Holder, a product designed primarily as an accessory for use with cameras made by a number of domestic U.S. and foreign manufacturers. The corporate name was shortened to the Eastman Company in 1889 and then lengthened to the Eastman Kodak Company early in the 1890's.

One of the most important cameras ever produced, called simply The Kodak had been introduced in 1888. At the same time, George Eastman created the photofinishing industry. The purchaser of the $25.00 camera mailed it back to the company where the 100 pictures were developed, printed, mounted and the camera reloaded for $10.00. The original sales slogan of "You Press the Button, We Do the Rest" was fully justified. By this division of labour, Eastman had revolutionized photography extending it to vast untouched markets.

By the mid 1920's, despite the postwar WWI economic boom we call the "roaring twenties" camera sales had become somewhat sluggish. Photographic technology hadn't changed much in the past two decades so there was little reason to replace a perfectly good camera. The company did not have a formal design department relying instead on the services of engineers who had some "flare" for product design. This policy had mixed success. In 1927 they hired the industrial designer Walter Dorwin Teague to upgrade the design of existing products and ultimately to create entirely new designs. Teague designed both the cameras and the packaging in which they were sold. Teague's packaging designs are of special interest to collectors because of their classic art-deco appearance adding considerably to its contents value.

Several of his designs include: the Gift Kodak for the 1930 Christmas market, an otherwise standard folding camera but fitted with a re-designed front and sold in a cedar box which could be used for cigarettes, and the Kodak Bantam Special which has been called the most beautiful small hand camera ever made. It is safe to say that all Kodak cameras made in the decade of the 1930's were either of his design or strongly influenced by him.

Note: Most of the more expensive Kodak cameras were supplied with a variety of lens and shutter combinations during their production spans. Usually we have listed the most readily available.

THE KODAK 1888; Small simple box camera loaded with film for 100 round pictures each 2½" in diameter. Periscopic lens, barrel shutter. Camera was returned to factory in Rochester, NY where the film was processed, printed and the camera reloaded and returned. No viewfinder, lines embossed in the top of the camera served

The Kodak (Original Kodak)

as a guide to give an approximate angle of view.

R5*   **H+**

NO. 1 KODAK: c1889-1895. Rapid Rectilinear lens; sector shutter; 100 exp, 2" diameter.

R4*   **G–**

NO 2 KODAK 1889; Round pictures as original Kodak and #1 but for 3^1/$_2$" pictures, other technical features are identical to Kodak #1 but scaled up and, of course, the camera is larger. Only the first of the production run did not have a viewfinder. Later a round viewfinder was added. A number 2 without a viewfinder is somewhat more valuable.

R4*   **F**

NO. 3 KODAK: c1890-1897, focusing box roll film camera; Bausch & Lomb Universal lens; sector shutter; 100 exp, 3¼" x 4¼".

R4*   **F–**

NO. 3 KODAK JUNIOR: c1890-1897. Bausch & Lomb Universal lens; sector shutter; 60 exp 3¼" x 4¼".

R4*   **F–**

NO. 4 KODAK: c1890-1898. Bausch & Lomb Universal lens; sector shutter; 48 exp, 4" x 5".

R4*   **F–**

NO. 4 KODAK JUNIOR: c1890-1897. Bausch & Lomb Universal lens; sector shutter; 48 exp, 4" x 5".

R4*   **E+**

NO. 4 FOLDING KODAK: Bausch & Lomb Universal lens; special Kodak sector shutter*; 48 exp, 4" x 5". C 1890-1892.

R4*   **F–**

EASTMAN INTERCHANGEABLE VIEW 5" X 8": c1885. Brass Rapid Rectilinear lens; waterhouse stops; behind-the-lens shutter. Tilting back; rising and falling front; ground glass back; side tripod holder attachment; ivory label.

R4*   **F–**

NO. 4 FOLDING KODAK IMPROVED: c1893-1897. Bausch & Lomb Universal lens; Bausch & Lomb Iris Diaphragm shutter; 48 exp, 4" x 5".

R4*   **F–**

NO. 5 FOLDING KODAK IMPROVED: c1893-97. Bausch & Lomb Universal lens; Bausch & Lomb Iris Diaphragm shutter; double swing, sliding front. Eastman-Walker roll holder for 54 exp, 5" x 7" on roll film or plates. Provisions for stereo.

R5*   **F–**

NO. 5 FOLDING KODAK (FIRST MODEL): c1890. Special Kodak sector shutter; film or plates; Eastman-Walker roll holder for 54 exp, 5" x 7" on roll film.

R5*   **F–**

NO. 6 FOLDING KODAK IMPROVED: c1893-1895. Bausch & Lomb Universal lens; Bausch & Lomb Iris Diaphragm shutter; 48 exp, 6½ x 8½".

R5*   **G–**

NO. 5 FOLDING KODAK (SECOND MODEL): c1892. Barker shutter; Eastman-Walker roll holder for 54 exp, 5" x 7" on roll film.

R5*   **F**

"A" ORDINARY KODAK: c1891-1895. Single lens; Special sector shutter; 24 exp, 2¾"x 3¼".

R5*   **G–**

"A" DAYLIGHT KODAK: c1891-1895.

Single lens; fixed diaphragm; Special sector shutter; 24 exp, 2¾"x 3¼". C 1891-1895.

R5*   **G–**

"B" ORDINARY KODAK: c1891-1895.

Single lens; revolving waterhouse diaphragm. Special sector shutter; 24 exp, 3 ½ x 4".

R5*   **F**

EASTMAN INTERCHANGEABLE VIEW 8" X 10": c1888. 8" x 10" view camera;

Prosh triple model shutter and lens. Separate front extension; ivory label.

R3*   **F–**

"B" DAYLIGHT KODAK: c1891-95.

Double lens; revolving waterhouse diaphragm. Special sector shutter; 24 exp, 3½" x 4".

R4*   **F–**

"C" ORDINARY KODAK: c1891-1895.

Single lens; revolving waterhouse diaphragm. Special sector shutter; 24 exp, 4" x 5".

R4*   **F+**

"C" DAYLIGHT KODAK: c1891-1895.

Double lens; revolving waterhouse diaphragm. Special sector shutter; 24 exp, 4" x 5".

R4*   **F–**

NO. 4 KODAK: c1894-1897. Leather

covered box camera; Achromatic lens; rotating waterhouse stops; Kodet (built-in) shutter. 4" x 5" plate or roll holder.

R4*   **F–**

NO. 4 FOLDING KODET: c1894. 4" x 5"

folding camera; 6⅜" lens; finder for horizontal or vertical photos on 4" x 5" plates or film; leather covered mahogany construction.

R4*   **F–**

NO. 4 FOLDING KODET SPECIAL: c1895-1897. Achromatic lens; Kodet (built-in)

shutter*. 4" x 5" plate or roll holder.

R4*   **F–**

NO. 4 FOLDING KODET JUNIOR: c1894-1897. Achromatic lens; Kodet (built-in)

shutter. 4" x 5" plate or roll holder.

R4*   **F–**

NO. 5 FOLDING KODET: c1895-1897.

Achromatic lens*; Kodak (built-in) shutter. 5" x 7" plate or roll holder.

R5*   **F–**

NO. 5 FOLDING KODAK SPECIAL: c1895-1897. Rapid Rectilinear lens; Kodet (built-

in) shutter*. 5" x 7" plate or roll holder.

R4*   **F–**

POCKET KODAK: c1896-1900. Single lens;

rotary shutter; 1½"x 2" exp on 102 roll film. First model had round vf. C 1895-1896, $80-$115. Second model has rectangular vf.

R3*   **D**

NO. 3 FOLDING POCKET KODAK DE LUXE: c1907.

R4*   **E+**

NO. 4 FOLDING POCKET KODAK: c1899. Suter Anastigmatic 150mm f6.3 lens; Ibsor shutter 1-¹⁄₁₀₀ s; 4" x 5" exp.

R2* **C–**

NO. 1A FOLDING HAWK EYE: c1905. Bausch & Lomb Rapid Rectilinear lens; ball-bearing shutter; 6.5 x 11cm exp.

R2* **B+**

NO. 2 BULLET: c1895-1896. Achromatic lens; rotary shutter; 3½" x 3½" exp on 101 roll film.

R2* **C–**

NO. 2 BULLET IMPROVED: c1896-1900. Achromatic lens; rotary shutter 3½" x 3½" exp on 101 roll film or single plate holder.

R2* **C**

NO. 2 BULLET SPECIAL KODAK: c1899, covered box camera; Rapid Rectilinear lens; Triple-Action shutter; for plates or roll film; 3½" x 3½" exp.

R3* **D–**

NO. 2 BULLS-EYE: c1896-1913, fixed focus achromatic lens; rotary shutter; 12 exp, 2 ½" x 3 ½" on 101 roll film.

R2* **D–**

NO. 2 BULLS-EYE IMPROVED: c1896-1913. Achromatic lens; Rotary shutter; 3½" x 3½" exp on 101 roll film.

R2* **C–**

NO. 2 BULLS-EYE SPECIAL: c1898-1904. Rapid Rectilinear lens; Eastman Triple Action shutter; 3½" x 3½" exp on 101 roll film.

R2* **C+**

NO. 4 BULLET: c1896, box camera for film or plates.

R3* **D–**

NO. 4 BULLS-EYE: c1896, roll film camera; rotary shutter; focused by external sliding lever.

R3* **D–**

NO. 4 BULLS-EYE IMPROVED: c1896-1904. Achromatic lens; Rotary shutter; 4" x 5" exp on 103 roll film.

R2* **C–**

NO. 4 BULLS-EYE SPECIAL: c1898-1904. Rapid Rectilinear lens; Eastman Triple Action shutter; 4" x 5" exp on 103 roll film.

R2* **C+**

NO. 2 FOLDING BULLS-EYE: c1899-1901. Achromatic lens; Rotary shutter; 3½" x 3½" exp on 101 roll film.

R2*   **C+**

NO. 2 FALCON: c1897-1899. Box camera; 4 1/2" Achromatic lens; rotary 3 stop shutter; 12 exp, 3½" x 3½" on 101 roll film.

R3*   **C+**

NO. 2 EUREKA: c1898-1899. Leather covered box camera; Achromatic lens; Rotary shutter; 3½" x 3½" exp on 106 roll film.

R3*   **D**

NO. 2 EUREKA , MODEL B: c1899, leather covered box camera; rotary shutter; 3½" x 3½" exp on plates or roll film.

R3*   **D**

NO. 2 EUREKA JUNIOR: c1899, leatherette covered box camera; 3½" x 3½" plates.

R3*   **D**

NO. 4 EUREKA: c1899. Achromatic lens; Rotary shutter 4"x 5" exp on 109 roll film.

R3*   **D**

NO. 1 PANORAM KODAK: c1900-1901. Rapid Rectilinear lens; swinging lens and focal plane slit; 2¼" x 7" exp on 105 roll film.

R3*   **E+**

NO. 1 PANORAM KODAK, MODEL B: c1901-1903. Meniscus lens; swinging lens and focal plane slit; 2¼" x 7" exp on 105 roll film.

R3*   **E+**

NO. 1 PANORAM KODAK, MODEL C: c1903-1907. Meniscus lens; swinging lens and focal plane slit; 2¼" x 7" exp on 105 roll film.

R3*   **E+**

NO. 1 PANORAM KODAK, MODEL D: c1907-1926. Meniscus lens; swinging lens and focal plane slit; 2¼" x 7" exp on 105 roll film.

R3*   **G+**

NO. 3A PANORAM KODAK: c1926-1928. Meniscus lens; swinging lens and focal plane slit; 3¼" x 10 3/8" exp on 122 roll film.

R3* **F–**

NO. 4 PANORAM KODAK: c1899-1900. Rapid Rectilinear lens; swinging lens and focal plane slit; 3½" x 12" exp on 103 roll film.

R3* **E+**

NO. 4 PANORAM KODAK , MODEL D: c1907-1924. Meniscus lens; swinging lens and focal plane slit; 3½" x 12" on 103 roll film.

R3* **E+**

NO. 2 FLEXO KODAK: c1899-1913. Achromatic lens; Rotary shutter; 3½" x 3½" exp on 101 roll film.

R3* **C+**

NO. 3 CARTRIDGE KODAK: c1900-1907. Rapid Rectilinear lens*; Eastman Triple Action shutter; 4¼" x 3¼" exp on 119 roll film.

R3* **D**

NO. 4 CARTRIDGE KODAK: c1897-1907. Rapid Rectilinear lens; Eastman Triple Action shutter; 4" x 5" exp on 104 roll film.

R3* **D**

NO. 5 CARTRIDGE KODAK: c1898-1901. Rapid Rectilinear lens; Eastman Triple Action shutter; 5" x 7" exp on 115 roll film or plates.

R3* **D**

NO. 0 FOLDING POCKET KODAK: c1902-1906. Meniscus lens; Automatic shutter; 2½" x 1⅞" exp on 121 roll film.

R3* **D–**

NO. 0 BROWNIE: c1914. Meniscus lens; Rotary shutter; 4 x 6cm on roll film.

R2* **B–**

NO. 1 BROWNIE; 1900. The camera that truly brought photography to everyone. It cost just $1.00 when introduced in 1900. The viewfinder was extra and not available immediately. It cost 25 cents. The box was covered with Brownies, little figures popularized by Palmer Cox in his children's stories. The boxes are very rare since they were used for only a few years and can easily double the price of the camera. Curiously the rollfilm, first made for this ultimate snapshot camera became #120, the only paper-backed film still made by Kodak and very nearly a professional only product.

In Japan 120 film is still called "Brownie Film."

R2* **A**

NO. 2 BROWNIE; 1901. The image size was increased to 2 ¼ x 3 ¼ and it now had a built-in viewer for both vertical and horizontal pictures.

R2* **A**

NO. 2 FOLDING BROWNIE , MODEL A: c1904. Achromatic meniscus lens; Pocket Automatic shutter; 6 x 9cm exp.

R2* **A**

NO. 2 STEREO BROWNIE: c1905, folding roll film stereo camera; paired exp, 3¼" x 2½" each; shutter adjustable for I, B & T; four lens openings.

R4* **F–**

NO. 2 BROWNIE , MODEL C: c1905, box roll film camera; 2¼" x 3¼ exp.

R2* **A**

NO. 2A FOLDING AUTOGRAPHIC BROWNIE: c1915. Achromatic lens; ball-bearing shutter; 2½ x 4¼ exp.

R2* **A**

Brownie Reflex

NO. 3 BROWNIE: c1908. Meniscus lens; Rotary shutter; Took 3¼ x 4¼ size exp.

R2* **A**

BROWNIE REFLEX: 1946. Elegant plastic camera for 12 exp on 127. Not a true reflex, but a TLR look-alike with fixed focus lens and viewfinder. I & B shutter. Synch for flash.

R1* **A**

DUAFLEX II: 1955. Box camera specification in a TLR-like design. Mirror in viewfinder hood allows eye-level viewing. Kodet meniscus lens. I & B shutter.

R1* **A**

Dualflex II

OO CARTRIDGE PREMO (KODAK) 1916; Meniscus lens, Kodak Rotary shutter. Smallest Kodak box camera it produced an image 1¼ x 1¾. Although this was the first Kodak camera to use 35mm wide film, it was unsprocketed and paper-backed. The film made for the OO Premo (Kodak) was nearly identical to Bantam film produced several decades later.

R3*   **C–**

NO. 1 FOLDING POCKET KODAK: c1898-1915. Achromatic lens; Rotary shutter*; 2¼ x 3¼ exp on 105 roll film.

R3*   **D**

NO. 1A FOLDING POCKET KODAK: c1899-1915. Achromatic lens; Pocket Automatic shutter; 2½" x 4½" exp on 116 roll film. Version no. 1 – 2 vfs. Version no. 2 – 1 vf.

R3*   **C–**

NO. 1A FOLDING POCKET KODAK SPECIAL: c1908-1912. Rapid Rectilinear lens; F.P.K. Automatic shutter; 2½" x 4¼" exp on 116 roll film.

R3*   **C–**

NO. 1A FOLDING POCKET "RR" KODAK: c1912-1915. Similar to No. 1A Folding Pocket Kodak Special . Kodak Ball Bearing shutter.

R2*   **C–**

NO. 2 FOLDING POCKET KODAK: c1899-1903. Achromatic lens; Eastman Automatic shutter; 3½" x 3½" exp on 101 roll film.

R2*   **B–**

NO. 3 FOLDING POCKET KODAK: c1900-1915. Rapid Rectilinear* lens; Unicum shutter; 3¼" x 4¼" exp on 118 roll film.

R2*   **B–**

No. 3 Folding Pocket Kodak

NO. 3A FOLDING POCKET KODAK: c1903-1915. Rapid Rectilinear lens; F.P.K. Automatic shutter; 3¼" x 5½" exp on 122 roll film.

R2*   **B–**

NO. 1A SPECIAL KODAK: c1912-1914. Zeiss Kodak Anastigmat f6.3 lens; Bausch & Lomb Compound* shutter; 2½" x 4¼" exp on 116 roll film.

R3*   **B+**

NO. 3 SPECIAL KODAK: c1911-1914. Zeiss Kodak Anastigmat f6.3 lens; Bausch & Lomb Compound shutter; 3¼" x 4¼" exp on 118 roll film.

R3*   **C–**

NO. 3A SPECIAL KODAK: c1910-1914. Zeiss Kodak Anastigmat f6.3 lens; Bausch & Lomb Compound*; 3¼" x 5½" exp on 122 roll film.

R3*   **C**

NO. 4 FOLDING KODAK: c1907-1912. Rapid Rectilinear lens; F.P.K. Automatic shutter; 4" x 5" exp on 123 roll film.

R3*   **C**

NO. 4A FOLDING KODAK: c1906-1912. Rapid Rectilinear lens; Bausch & Lomb Automatic shutter; 4 ¼" x 6½" exp on 126 roll film.

R2*   **C**

NO. 4 SCREEN FOCUS KODAK: c1904-1909. Rapid Rectilinear lens; Kodak Automatic shutter; 4" x 5" exp on 123 roll film.

R4*   **E**

3B QUICK FOCUS KODAK: c1906-1911. Meniscus Achromatic lens, Rotary shutter; 3¼ x 5½" exp on 125 roll film.

R4*   **E–**

STEREO KODAK MODEL 1: c1917-1925. Kodak Anastigmat f7.7 lenses; Stereo Automatic shutter; pair of 3⅛" x 3³⁄₁₆" exp on 101 roll film.

R4*   **E+**

NO. 2 STEREO KODAK: c1901-1905. Box-type stereoscopic camera; periscopic 5" f14 lenses; wl finder; oscillating sector between-the-lens shutter. 2, 3 or 5 paired exp, 3 3/8" x 3 3/8" on roll film. The only box-type stereo camera for roll film produced in America.

R4*   **F–**

NO. 4A SPEED KODAK: c1908-13. Bausch & Lomb Zeiss Tessar f6.3 lens; Kodak fps; 4¼" x 6 1/2" exp on 126 roll film.

R4*   **F–**

**No. 4
Speed Kodak**

NO. 1A SPEED KODAK: c1909-1913. Zeiss Kodak Anastigmat f6.3 lens; Graflex fps; 2½" x 4¼" exp on 116 roll film.

R4*   **E**

KODAK ENLARGING OUTFIT: c1920, for 4" x 5" or smaller; ground glass back; accessory for lantern slide camera; monorail; polished oak finish. With original box.

R3*   **D**

NO. 1 AUTOGRAPHIC KODAK JUNIOR: c1914-1926. Achromatic lens; Kodak Ball Bearing shutter; 2¼" x 3¼" exp on 120 roll film.

R1*   **B–**

NO. 1 AUTOGRAPHIC KODAK SPECIAL: c1921. Zeiss Kodak Anastigmat f6.3 lens; Optimo shutter; 2¼" x 3¼" exp on A120 roll film. c1915-1920. New model: Kodak Anastigmat f6.3 lens; Kodamatic shutter.

R3*   **B+**

NO. 1 AUTOGRAPHIC KODAK SPECIAL, MODEL B: c1922-1926. Kodak Anastigmat f6.3 lens; Kodamatic shutter 2¼" x 3¼" exp on A120 film.

R2*   **C–**

NO. 1A AUTOGRAPHIC KODAK: c1917-1924. Rapid Rectilinear lens; Kodak Ball Bearing shutter; 2½" x 4¼" exp on 116 roll film. New model: Kodak Anastigmat f7.7 lens; Kodak Ball Bearing shutter.

R1*   **A**

NO. 1A AUTOGRAPHIC KODAK JUNIOR: c1914-1926. Achromatic lens; Kodak Ball Bearing shutter; 2½" x 4¼" exp on A116 roll film.

R1*   **A**

NO. 1A AUTOGRAPHIC KODAK SPECIAL: c1914-1916. Zeiss Kodak f6.3 lens; Bausch & Lomb Compound shutter; 2½" x 4¼" exp on A116 roll film.

R2*   **B–**

NO. 1A AUTOGRAPHIC KODAK SPECIAL WITH COUPLED RANGE-FINDER: c1923-1926. Kodak Anastigmat f6.3 lens; Optimo shutter; 2½" x 4¼" exp on A116 roll film. c1917-1923. New model: Kodak Anastigmat f6.3 lens; Kodamatic shutter.

R3*   **D–**

NO. 2C AUTOGRAPHIC KODAK JUNIOR: c1916-1927. Achromatic lens; Kodak Ball Bearing shutter; 2⅞" x 4⅞" exp on A130 roll film.

R1*   **A**

NO. 2C AUTOGRAPHIC KODAK SPECIAL: c1923-1928. Kodak Anastigmat lens; Kodamatic shutter; 2⅞" x 4⅞" exp on A130 roll film.

R2*   **E**

NO. 3 AUTOGRAPHIC KODAK: c1914-1926. Rapid Rectilinear lens; Kodak Ball Bearing* shutter; 3¼" x 4¼" exp on A118 roll film.

R1*   **A**

NO. 3 AUTOGRAPHIC KODAK SPECIAL:
c1914-1924. Zeiss Kodak Anastigmat f6.3 lens; Bausch & Lomb Compound shutter; 3¼" x 4¼" exp on A118 roll film.

R2*   **B+**

NO. 3A AUTOGRAPHIC KODAK: c1918-1927. Rapid Rectilinear lens; Kodak Ball Bearing shutter; 3¼" x 5½" exp on A122 roll film.

R3*   **A**

NO. 3A AUTOGRAPHIC KODAK JUNIOR: c1918-1927. Achromatic lens; Kodak Ball Bearing shutter; 3¼" x 5½" exp on A122 roll film.

R1*   **A**

NO. 3A AUTOGRAPHIC KODAK SPECIAL: c1914. Zeiss Kodak Anastigmat f6.3lens; Bausch & Lomb Compound shutter; 3¼" x 5½" exp on A122 roll film.

R3*   **C**

NO. 3A AUTOGRAPHIC KODAK SPECIAL WITH COUPLED RANGE-FINDER: c1916-1924. Zeiss Kodak Anastigmat f6.3 lens; Optimo shutter; 3¼" x 5½"

exp on A122 roll film. First mfd camera withCRF.

R3*   **D+**

STERLING II: 1954. Folding design for 8 exp on 620. Die-cast body finished in black grained plastic. Top plate in grey plastic. 105mm f4.5 Anaston lens. Pronto shutter 1/25-1/200s + B.

R1*   **B**

VEST POCKET KODAK SPECIAL: c1912-1914. Zeiss Kodak Anastigmat f6.3lens; Kodak Ball Bearing shutter; 1⅝" x ½" exp on 127 roll film.

R2*   **B–**

VEST POCKET AUTOGRAPHIC KODAK SPECIAL: c1915-1926. Zeiss Kodak Anastigmat f6.9 lens; Kodak Ball Bearing shutter.

R2*   **B+**

VEST POCKET KODAK MODEL B: c1925-1934. Meniscus lens; Rotary shutter; 1⅝" x 2½" exp on 127 roll film.

R2*   **B+**

VEST POCKET KODAK SERIES III: c1926-34. Kodak Anastigmat f6.3 lens; Diomatic shutter; 1⅝" x 2½" exp on 127 film.

R2*   **B+**

NO 1A GIFT KODAK: c1930. 116 roll film, folding camera. Achromatic lens, Kodex shutter, 21/4" x 41/14" on 116 roll film. Art Deco design. (Add 30% for complete set with instructions and box).

R4*   **E+**

BEAU BROWNIE: c1930, box camera; Doublet lens; 116 roll film. c1930-1932. Black, Blue, Brown and Rose.

R4*   **C+**

Vest Pocket Kodak Series III

No. 1A Gift Kodak

Beau Brownie

BOY SCOUT KODAK: c1932. Meniscus lens; Rotary shutter; 1⅜" x 2½" exp on 127 roll film. With case add 25%

R3*   **E–**

GIRL SCOUT KODAK: c1929-1934. Meniscus lens; Rotary shutter 1⅝" x 2½" exp on roll film. Engraved with the official Girl Scout emblem. With case add 25%

R3*   **E–**

CAMP FIRE GIRLS' KODAK: c1931-1934. Meniscus lens; Rotary shutter. With case add 25%

R4*   **E**

KODAK ENSEMBLE: c1929-1933. (Kodak Petite in suede leather case with mirror, compact and lipstick).

R4*   **G–**

KODAK PETITE: c1929-1933. Vest Pocket Kodak Model B Camera, in blue, brown, gray, green or red. Black bellows are not original, and sell for 50% less. Meniscus lens; Rotary shutter; 1⅜" x 2½" exp on 127 roll film.

R3*   **D+**

VANITY KODAK: c1928-1931. Similar to Vest Pocket Kodak Series III Camera in blue, brown, gray, green or red. (see above) c1928-1933. Vanity Kodak Ensemble: Art-deco case includes lipstick, compact with face powder, mirror and change pocket, with Vest Pocket Kodak Series III, Model B.

R4*   **E+**

KODAK COQUETTE: c1930-1931. (Kodak Petite with matching lipstick holder and compact.)

R4*   **F+**

NO. 1 POCKET KODAK SPECIAL: c1926-1929. Kodak Anastigmat f6.3 lens; Kodamatic shutter; 2¼" x 3¼" exp on 120 roll film.

R2*   **B−**

NO. 1A POCKET KODAK SERIES II: c1928-1931. Achromatic lens; Kodex shutter 2½" x 4¼" exp on 116 roll film. In blue, brown, gray, green or red.

R2*   **B**

NO. 1A POCKET KODAK: c1926-1931. Achromatic lens; Kodex shutter; 2½" x 4¼" exp on 116 roll film.

R2*   **A**

NO. 2C POCKET KODAK SERIES III: c1924-1931. Kodak Anastigmat f7.7 lens; Diomatic shutter; 2⅞" x 4⅞" exp on 130 roll film.

R2*   **A**

NO. 3 POCKET KODAK SERIES III: c1926-1933. Kodak f7.9 lens; Kodex shutter; 3¼" x 4¼" exp on 118 roll film.

R2*   **B−**

PRIMOETTE JUNIOR: 1913. Unusual folding camera in which the baseboard rests at an angle to the body. Apertures numbered 1-4. Kodak Ball Bearing Shutter 1/25, 1/50, T & B. 2¼ x3¼-inch format on film pack.

R2*   **A+**

KODAK BULLET: c1935. 127 roll film camera; meniscus lens; sector shutter.

R2*   **A**

KODAK 50TH ANNIVERSARY BOX CAMERA: 1930; Brown with silver seal. The camera was given free to any child turning 12 in 1930 to celebrate Kodak's corporate half-century (1880-1930).

R2*   **C−**

No 2C Pocket Kodak Series III cameras

Kodak 50th
Anniversary Box

KODAK BABY BROWNIE SPECIAL:
c1939. 127 roll film camera; meniscus lens;
sector shutter; 8 exp on 127 roll film.

R1* **A**

KODAK REGENT: c1935. Tessar 105mm
f4.5 lens; Compur Rapid shutter 1-½₅₀ s;
compact RFR; 6 x 9cm on 620 roll film.

R3* **D**

KODAK REGENT II: c1939. Schneider
Xenar 105mm f3.5 lens; Compur Rapid
shutter 1-¼₀₀ s, CRF; 6 x 9cm exp.

R4* **F–**

SUPREMA: c1939. Schneider Xenar 80mm
f3.5 lens; Compur Rapid shutter 1-¼₀₀ s; 6
x 6cm exp on 620 roll film.

R4* **E+**

KODAK SIX-16: c1932-1936. Meniscus
Achromatic lens; Kodak shutter; 2½" x 4 ¼"
exp on 616 roll film.

R1* **A**

Kodak Six-20 (left) and Six-20
with Compur shutter (right)

KODAK SIX-20: c1934-1937, 620 roll film
camera; Kodak Anastigmat 100mm f4.5
coated lens; No. 1 Diodak shutter ¹⁄₁₀ – ¹⁄₁₀₀s;
2¼" x 3¼" exp on 620 roll film.

R2* **B**

KODAK SIX-20: c1932-1937. 620 roll film
camera; Kodak Anastigmat 105mm f4.5

lens; Compur shutter 1-1/250 s; 2¼" x 3¼" exp on 620 roll film.

R2*   **C–**

KODAK JUNIOR II: 1954. Folding design for 8 exp on 620. Die-cast light alloy body, top plate in grey plastic moulding, the whole covered in black grained leathercloth. 105mm f6.3 Anaston lens, Dakon II shutter 1/25s & 1/50s.

R2*   **A**

KODAK SENIOR SIX-20: c 1937-1939. Kodak Anastigmat f6.3 lens; Kodex shutter; 2¼" x 3¼" exp on 620 roll film.

R2*   **A**

JIFFY KODAK SIX-20: c1933-1937. Twindar lens; Sector shutter; 2¼" x 3¼" exp on 620 film.

R1*   **A–**

KODAK VIGILANT 616 SPECIAL: c1940, 616 roll film folding camera; Kodak Anastigmat 12mm f4.5 lens; No. 2 Supermatic shutter 1-¼₀₀ s; 8 exp on 616 roll film.

R1*   **A**

KODAK VIGILANT SIX-20: Kodak Anastigmat f6.3 lens; Diomatic shutter; 2¼" x 3¼" exp on 620 roll film. c1939-1948.

R1*   **A**

KODAK MONITOR SIX-20: c1939-1948. Kodak Anastigmat Special f4.5 lens; Supermatic shutter; 2¼" x 3¼" exp on 620 roll film.

R1*   **A**

KODAK MONITOR SIX-16: c1939-1946. Kodak Anastigmat Special f4.5 lens; Supermatic shutter; 2½" x 4 ¼" exp on 616 roll film.

R1*   **A**

SUPER KODAK SIX-20: c1938-1945. Kodak Anastigmat Special f3.5 lens; Kodak shutter controlled by Selenium photo-electric exp meter, CRF. 2¼" x ¼" exp on 620

roll film. First camera with built-in photo-electric exp control

R4*   **G**

KODAK DUEX: c1940-1946. 620 roll film camera; 16 exp on 620 roll film.

R3*   **A**

KODAK BANTAM: c1938. 828 roll film camera; Kodak Anastigmat 53mm f6.3 lens; shutter, T, I.

R1*   **A**

Kodak Flash
Bantam

KODAK BANTAM SPECIAL: c1936-1940.
Kodak Anastigmat Ektar f2 lens; Compur
Rapid shutter 1-$\frac{1}{500}$ s, CRF. 28 x 40mm exp
on 828 roll film. After World War II the
Bantam Special was sold with a Kodak
EKTAR f/2.0 in a Supermatic shutter.

R3* **E+**

KODAK BANTAM F5.6: c1938-1941.
Kodak Anastigmat Special lens; Kodak
shutter.

R2* **A**

KODAK BANTAM F8: c1938-1946. Koda-
linear f8 lens; sector shutter; 28 x 40mm
exp on 828 roll film.

R1* **A**

KODAK BANTAM F4.5: c1938-1948.
Kodak Anastigmat Special f4.5 lens; Kodak
shutter.

R1* **A**

KODAK FLASH BANTAM: c1947-1953.
Kodak Anastigmat Special f4.5 lens; Kodak
Flash Synch shutter

R1* **A**

BANTAM COLORSNAP: 1955. 8 exp on
828 film. Made to make colour photography easy for the beginner. Exposure
control by light value numbers on aperture scale, recommended settings given
by scale built into camera back. Exposure
system sets the shutter at 1/50s or 1/25s
according to subject.

R1* **A**

COLORSNAP 35: 1959. Update of the
Bantam Colorsnap, made to take standard
35mm cassettes in place of 828 rollfilm.
Single speed shutter at 1/40s. Exposure
control by weather symbols on aperture
scale. Synch for flash with Brownie
Flasholder.

R1* **A**

**KODAK RETINA – STUTTGART TYPE
NO. 117:** C July 1934-July 1935. 35mm vf

camera; Schneider-Kreuznach Xenar Anastigmat 5cm f3.5 lens; Compur 00 1-¹⁄₃₀₀ s. Large nickel plated knobs for film wind and rewind; rewind clutch lever positioned in film wind knob. Single film sprocket on top of camera with short shaft. Black lacquer with nickel trim.

R3*   **D+**

KODAK RETINA – STUTTGART TYPE NO. 118:
c July 1935-April 1936. 35mm vf camera. Similar to Stuttgart type no. 117 except: the rewind clutch lever was moved from film wind knob to the back of top cover, the film sprocket shaft extends across camera body. Black lacquer, nickel trim.

R3*   **D**

KODAK RETINA – STUTTGART TYPE NO. 119:
c April 1936-January 1938. 35mm RFR camera; Schneider Xenar 5cm f3.5 or Kodak Anastigmat Ektar 5cm f3.5 lens; Compur 00 1-¹⁄₃₀₀ s. Wind and rewind knobs reduced in diameter; exp counter moved to raised housing on right side of camera. Black lacquer, nickel trim. C April 1936-January 1938.

R2*   **D**

KODAK RETINA – STUTTGART TYPE NO. 126:
c March 1936-October 1937. 35mm vf camera; Kodak Ektar 5cm f3.5 lens (also Tessar, Alcor, Angenieux and Ysar lenses); Compur-Rapid shutter 1-¹⁄₃₀₀ s. Chrome or black lacquer with polished aluminium trim. Some cameras provided with accessory shoe.

R2*   **C**

KODAK RETINA I – STUTTGART TYPE NO. 141:
c October 1937-March 1939. 35mm vf camera; Kodak Ektar 5cm f3.5 lens (also Xenar); Compur or Compur-Rapid 1-¹⁄₃₀₀s. Body shutter release in front edge of enlarged exp counter. Wind and rewind knobs taller than previous model.

R2*   **D**

Retina I
(black finish)

KODAK RETINA I – STUTTGART TYPE NO. 143:
c January 1938-March 1939. 35mm vf camera; Schneider Xenar 5cm f3.5 lens; Compur shutter 1-¹⁄₃₀₀s. Similar to Stuttgart type no. 141 except: black lacquer finish, chrome wind and rewind knobs.

R2*   **D**

KODAK RETINA I – STUTTGART TYPE NO. 148:
c March 1939-Decmeber 1940. 35mm vf camera; Kodak Ektar 5cm f3.5 lens; Compur-Rapid shutter 1-1/300s. Exp counter reduced in size and moved closer to vf. First Retina to have film transport coupled to shutter to prevent double exp. Chrome finish.

R2*   **D**

KODAK RETINA I – STUTTGART TYPE NO. 149:
c March 1939-December 1940. 35mm vf camera; Schneider Xenar 5cm f3.5 lens; Compur-Rapid shutter 1-1/300s.

Retina I

**Kodak Retina I
(Compur Rapid
shutter)**

**Kodak Retina Ia
– Stuttgart type No 15**

Similar to Stuttgart type no. 148 except, black lacquer finish and trim.

R2*   **D**

KODAK RETINA I – STUTTGART TYPE NO. 010:
c May 1946-April 1949. 35mm vf camera; Retina Xenar 50mm f3.5 coated lens (also Ektar, Xenar, Zenar, Rodenstock lenses); Compur-Rapid shutter 1-¹⁄₅₀₀s. Mfd from combination of prewar and postwar parts. Same body and interlock as Stuttgart type no. 011, otherwise similar to Stuttgart type no. 148. Chrome finish.

R2*   **D**

KODAK RETINA I – STUTTGART TYPE NO. 013:
c April 1949-January 1951. 35mm vf camera; Retina Xenar 5cm f3.5 or f2.8 coated lens; Compur-Rapid shutter 1-¹⁄₅₀₀s (X synch was added to some cameras in 1949; after 1950 it was added to all production cameras.) One piece chrome top cover with integral vf.

R2*   **D**

KODAK RETINA IA – STUTTGART TYPE NO. 015:
c January 1951-July 1951. 35mm vf camera; Retina Xenar 50mm f3.5 or f2.8 coated lens (also Rodenstock, Heligon, Ektar lenses); Compur-Rapid shutter 1-¹⁄₅₀₀ s, X flash synch. First Retina with top

mounted rapid-wind film-advance coupled to shutter cocking.

R2*   **D**

KODAK RETINA IA – STUTTGART TYPE NO. 015:
c July 1951-April 1954. 35mm vf camera; Retina-Xenar 50mm f3.5 or f2.8 coated lens (also Kodak Ektar lens); Synchro-Compur shutter 1-¹⁄₅₀₀s, X-M flash synch. Similar to Stuttgart type no. 015 except for film indicator dial on top of rewind knob instead of under camera.

R2*   **D**

KODAK RETINA IB – STUTTGART TYPE NO. 018:
c1954-1958. 35mm vf camera; Xenar 50mm f2.8 coated lens, interchangeable front component; Synchro-Compur LVS 1-¹⁄₅₀₀s, VXM flash synch. New body design with rounded contours,

concealed bellows, first bright frame vf in Retina camera.

R2* **D**

KODAK RETINA IB – STUTTGART TYPE NO. 019: c1957-1960. 35mm vf camera; Xenar 50mm f2.8 coated lens, interchangeable front component; Synchro-Compur LVS 1-⅟₅₀₀s, VXM flash synch. Similar to Stuttgart type no. 018 except, top cover enlarged vertically to accept built-in, non-coupled selenium single-range exp meter. Enlarged vf with second window added in 1958 to permit projected frame line.

R2* **D**

KODAK RETINA II – STUTTGART TYPE NO. 122: c October 1936-June 1937. 35mm RFR camera; Schneider-Kreuznach Anastigmat Ektar 5cm f3.5 lens (also 5cm f2 Xenon lens); Compur-Rapid shutter 1-⅟₅₀₀s. First Retina with separate optical vf and CRF. Retractable body release, rewind knob brake lever.

R2* **D+**

KODAK RETINA II – STUTTGART TYPE NO. 142: c June 1937-May 1939. 35mm RFR camera; Schneider-Kreuznach Xenon 5cm f2.8 lens (also other lenses); Compur-Rapid shutter 1-⅟₅₀₀s, CRF. Similar to Stuttgart type no. 122, except film wind

knob instead of slow wind lever; top cover redesigned.

R2* **D+**

KODAK RETINA IIA – STUTTGART TYPE NO. 150: c May 1939-December 1940. 35mm RFR camera; Schneider Kreuznach Xenon 5cm f2.8 lens; Compur-Rapid shutter 1-⅟₅₀₀s. Redesigned top cover. First Retina with combined vf and CRF. Smaller (extensible) rewind knob.

R2* **D+**

KODAK RETINA II – STUTTGART TYPE NO. 011: c Summer 1946-Spring 1949. 35mm RFR camera; Retina-Xenon 50mm f2.0 coated lens (also Heligon and 47mm Kodak Ektar lenses); Compur-Rapid shutter 1-⅟₅₀₀ s, CRF. First RFR Retina with coated lenses (although variations exist with uncoated lenses). Serial no. inside back; Rochester imports prefixed with letters "EK".

R2* **D+**

KODAK RETINA II – STUTTGART TYPE NO. 014: c Summer 1949-January 1951. 35mm RFR camera; Retina-Xenon 50mm f2 or Retina-Heligon 50mm f2 coated lenses; Compur- Rapid shutter 1-⅟₅₀₀s, X synch, CRF. Similar to Stuttgart type no. 011 except has redesigned sloping front plate on front of shutter, also X flash synch.

R2* **D+**

KODAK RETINA IIA – STUTTGART TYPE NO. 016: c January 1951-July 1951. 35mm RFR camera; Retina-Xenon 50mm f2 coated lens; Compur-Rapid shutter 1-⅟₅₀₀s, X flash synch, CRF. Similar to Stuttgart type no. 014 except rapid-wind film-advance lever coupled to shutter cocking mechanism. Synchro-Compur with XM flash synch installed between July 1951-August 1954.

R2* **D+**

KODAK RETINA IIC – STUTTGART TYPE NO. 020: c1954-1958. 35mm RFR camera; Xenon-C 50mm f2.8 coated lens, interchangeable front component (also Heligon-C lens); Synchro-Compur LVS 1-⅟₅₀₀s, VXM flash sunch, CRF. Redesigned body with rounded contours and concealed bellows. Accepts either 80mm f4 telephoto or 35mm f5.6 wide-angle lens components.

R2*   **D+**

KODAK RETINA IIC – STUTTGART TYPE NO. 029:
c1958. 35mm RFR camera; Xenon-C 50mm f2.8 coated lens, interchangeable front component (also Heligon-C lens); Synchro-Compur LVS 1-⅟₅₀₀s, VXM flash synch, CRF. This camera is similar to Stuttgart type no. 020 except enlarged vf has bright frame lines for 50mm, 35, and 80mm lenses.

R2*   **E**

KODAK RETINA IIIC – STUTTGART TYPE NO. 021:
c1954. 35mm RFR camera; Xenon-C 50mm f2 coated lens, interchangeable front component; Synchro-Compur LVS 1-⅟₅₀₀s, VXM flash synch, CRF. Similar to Stuttgart type no. 020 except non-coupled selenium photo-electric exp meter with hinged cover, built into top cover.

R2*   **E**

KODAK RETINA IIIC – STUTTGART TYPE NO. 028:
c1958-1961. 35mm RFR camera; Xenon-C 50mm f2 coated lens, inter-

Kodak Retina IIIc

changeable lens component (also Heligon-C lens); Synchro-Compur LVS 1-⅟₅₀₀s, VXM flash, synch, CRF. Similar to Stuttgart type no. 021 except selenium meter redesigned. Has plastic honeycomb with non hinged cover; enlarged vf has bright frame lines for 50mm, 35mm and 80mm lenses.

R3*   **F–**

RETINA LENSES AND ACCESSORIES

Kodak Retina IIc, IIIc and IIIC cameras with Retina-Xenon C lens are matched for use with the Retina-Longar-Xenon C 80mm f4 and Retina Curtar-Xenon C 35mm f5.6 lenses; Kodak Retina cameras with Retina-Heligon lenses are matched for use with the Retina-Heligon C 80mm f4 and the Retina-Heligon C 35mm f4.5 lenses. Cameras with Xenon lenses were originally distributed in the US market, while cameras with Heligon lenses were distributed in the overseas market, both lenses are optically equivalent.

35-80 Multi finder: **B+**

Xenon or Heligon f5.6/35mm lens: **B+**

Xenon or Heligon f4/80mm lens: **C**

KODAK RETINA IIIS: c1959-1961. Retina-Xenon 50mm f1.9 lens; Synchro-Compur shutter 1-1/500s. c1959-1961.

R2*   **D**

KODAK INSTAMATIC REFLEX: 35mm SLR, interchangeable Xenon 50mm f1.9 lens or Xenar 50mm f2.8 lens.

R2*   **D**

KODAK RETINA REFLEX: c1958-1959, 35mm SLR, interchangeable Retina-Xenon 50mm f2 lens; Synchro-Compur shutter 1 – ⅟₅₀₀s.

R2*   **D**

Kodak

Kodak Retina Reflex

KODAK RETINA REFLEX S: c1959-60, 35mm SLR, interchangeable Xenar f2.8/50mm lens, Synchro Compur shutter, coupled light meter.

R2*   **D**

KODAK RETINA REFLEX III: c1961-1964, 35mm SLR, interchangeable Xenon f1.9/50mm lens; Synchro-Compur shutter 1-$\frac{1}{500}$S.

R2*   **D**

KODAK RETINA REFLEX IV: c1964-67, 35mm SLR, interchangeable Xenar or Ysarex f2.8/50mm lens, or Xenon or Heligon f1.9/50mm lens, Synchro Compur, shutter speed and lens opening visible in the VFR.

R2*   **D**

KODAK RETINETTE: c1952-1954. Recomar f4.5/45mm lens; Pronto SV shutter 1-$\frac{1}{300}$S.

R2*   **B+**

MATCH-BOX (-X): c1945, match-box detective camera; 25mm f5 lens; $\frac{1}{50}$ s shutter; 10 x 10mm exp on 16mm film. About the size of a small wooden matchbox, hence its name. It was made by Eastman Kodak for the O.S.S. as an espionage camera.

R5*   **H**

KODAK PONY 828: c1949-q959. Kodak Anaston f4.5 lens; Kodak Flash 200 shutter; 28 x 40mm exp on 828 roll film. c1949-1959.

R1*   **A**

KODAK PONY 135: c1950-1954. Kodak Anaston f4.5 lens; Kodak Flash 200 shutter; 36 exp on 35mm film.

R1*   **A**

KODAK 35: 1938-1948: 35mm VFR camera. Camera was available with three different lenses when first introduced, Kodak Anastigmat f/5.6, Kodak Anastigmat f/4.5, and Kodak Anastigmat Special f/3.5. In 1946, flash synchronization was added.

R2*   **B**

KODAK 35 (MILITARY): c1938-1951, 35mm VFR camera, Kodak Anastigmat f4.5 lens/51mm Kodak No.1 Diomatic shutter $\frac{1}{25}$-$\frac{1}{150}$ s, B. T. C .

R3*   **E**

The HOVE *International*
BLUE BOOK
Millennium Edition

Price & Rarity Codes

HOVE
COLLECTORS
BOOKS

30, The Industrial Estate
Small Dole
West Sussex, BN5 9XR, UK
Fax: +44(0)273-494992

Price & Rarity Codes

PRICE CODES

Price codes are new to the Millennium Edition. These are now shown under each camera on the right hand side.

The price code will *guide* you to the most likely price bracket for each camera.

To help refine the above code we add a + or – to indicate the lower or higher end of the group, for example **G+** would indicate a camera nearer £900, **G** would be the middle amount and **G–** would be closer to £500.

		UK	US	
A	Cameras valued to	£10	$15	€30
B	Valued between	£12-20	$17-40	€16-30
C	Valued between	£25-45	$50-75	€35-60
D	Valued between	£50-90	$80-150	€60-125
E	Valued between	£100-125	$160-350	€140-315
F	Valued between	£250-450	$375-750	€350-630
G	Valued between	£500-900	$800-1,400	€700-1,330
H	Valued between	£1,000-2,250	$1,500-3,500	€1,400-3,150
I	Valued between	£2,500-4,500	$4,000-7,500	€3,500-6,300
J	Valued between	£5,000-9,000	$8,000-15,000	€7,000-12,600
K	Valued between	£10,000-24,000	$17,000-35,000	€ 14,000-34,000
L	Above	£25,000	$45,000	€35,000

RARITY CODES

Rarity codes are below each camera on the left hand side, these will give you a *guide* to the likelihood of finding each item.

R1* These items will be easily found, giving a good choice.

R2* Slightly more difficult to find than **R1*** and usually in a higher price bracket.

R3* These items will take a little more searching out, usually in specialised markets.

R4* Much more difficult to locate and will involve more time and certainly more cost.

R5* Very difficult to locate, maybe only a few in a decade, and very costly.

U Usually unavailable, you may only see them in museums or select collections.

NSR Indicates that the camera has not sold recently.

CONDITION

Always buy the best condition item your pocket will allow. Condition and originality are most important.

Please read comments under each heading in the Introduction

Kodak 35

Kodak 35
(Military)

Kodak 35
Kodamatic shutter

Kodak 35 Rangefinder

Kodak 35
Flash Kadamatic
shutter

Kodak Ektra

Kodak 35
(Kodex shutter)

KODAK 35 RANGEFINDER: c1940-1951, Kodak Anastigmat Special f3.5 lens, Flash Kodamatic shutter, CRF.

R2* **C**

KODAK EKTRA: c1941-1948. Kodak Ektar 50mm f1.9 lens; cfps 1-$\frac{1}{1000}$ s; 36 exp on 35mm roll film. Features interchangeable magazine back, rapid film advance, CRF.

R4* **G**

INTERCHANGEABLE LENSES FOR EKTRA CAMERA.

Ektar 50mm f3.5 lens	**E–**
Ektar 50mm f1.9 lens	**E–**
Ektar 35mm f3.3 lens	**E–**
Ektar 90mm f3.5 lens	**E–**
Ektar 135mm f3.8 lens	**E–**
Ektar 153mm f4.5 lens	**G**

Kodak KE-7

KODAK SIGNET 35: Kodak Ektar 50mm f3.5 lens; Kodak Synchro 300 shutter. c1951-1958.

R2*   **B–**

KODAK SIGNET 40: c1956-1959. Kodak Ektanon 50mm f3.5 lens; Kodak Synchro 400 shutter.

R2*   **B–**

KODAK SIGNET 30: c1957-1959. Kodak Ektanar 50mm f2.8 lens; Kodak Synchro 250 shutter.

R2*   **B–**

Kodak Signet – "Signal Corps, U.S. Army Camera, Still picture

KE-7(1)": c1955. 35mm RFR camera; Kodak Ektar 44mm f3.5 lens; Kodak Synchro 300 shutter. Black finish.

R3*   **E**

KODAK SIGNET 50: c1957-1960. Kodak Ektanar 50mm f2.8 lens; Kodak Synchro 250 shutter.

R2*   **C–**

KODAK SIGNET 80: c1958-1962, interchangeable Kodak Ektanar f2.8/50mm lens; behind the lens shutter, built-in light meter.

R3*   **C**

Signet Multi Frame Finder	**B–**
Signet Wide Angle lens f3.5/35mm	**C**
Signet Telephoto lens f4/90mm	**C**

KODAK AUTOMATIC 35: c1959. Kodak Ektanar 50mm f2.8 lens; Kodak Synchro 80 shutter. Auto exp control.

R2*   **B+**

KODAK MOTORMATIC 35F: c1962. Kodak Ektanar 50mm f2.8 lens; Kodak

Kodak Automatic 35

Automatic Flash shutter. Spring-wound motor drive.

R3*   **C–**

The Kodak Pupille, Ranca and Vollendas were Nagel cameras which continued in production after Eastman Kodak bought Dr. August Nagel Camerawerk, Stuttgart, in 1932. See Nagel.

KODAK PUPILLE: c1932. Schneider Xenon 50mm f2 lens; Compur shutter 1⅟₁₆" x 1⅟₁₆" exp on 127 roll film.

R4*   **E**

WITH ELMAR LENS +100%

KODAK RANCA: c1932-1934. Nagel Anastigmat f4.5 lens; Pronto shutter; 1⅟₁₆" x 1⅟₁₆" exp on 127 roll film.

R4*   **E**

WITH ELMAR LENS +100%

KODAK VOLLENDA: c1932-1937. Radionar Anastigmat 50mm f3.5 lens; Compur shutter; 1⅟₁₆" x 1⅟₁₆" exp on 127 roll film.

R4*   **F–**

WITH ELMAR LENS +100%

KODAK VOLLENDA (6 X 9CM MODEL): c1939, folding camera; Elmar 10.5cm f4.5 lens; Compur shutter 1 – ½₅₀s; 8 exp, 6 x 9cm on 120 roll film.

R3*   **E–**

KODAK DUO SIX-20: c1934-1937. Kodak Anastigmat 75mm f3.5 lens; Compur shutter; 1⅜" x 2¼" exp on 620 roll film.

R3*   **C–**

KODAK DUO SIX-20 (RANGEFINDER MODEL): c1937. Schneider Kreuznach Xenar 75mm f3.5 lens; Compur Rapid

**Kodak
Duo-Six-20**

**Kodak Duo Six-20
(rangefinder model)**

shutter 1-¹/₅₀₀s, CRF; 1⅝" x 2¼" exp on 620
roll film.

R3*   **E+**

KODAK RECOMAR 18: c1932-1940.
Kodak Anastigmat f4.5 lens; Compur
shutter; 2¼" x 3¼" exp on film pack.

R3*   **B+**

KODAK RECOMAR 33: c1932-1940.
Kodak Anastigmat f4.5 lens; Compur
shutter; 3¼" x 4¼" exp on film pack.

R3*   **C−**

KODAK MEDALIST I: c1941-1946. Kodak
Ektar 100mm f3.5 lens; Supermatic shutter
1 – ¹/₄₀₀ s, CRF; 8 exp, 2¼" x 3¼" on 620 roll
film.

R3*   **D+**

**Kodak
Medalist II
(black)**

Kodak Medalist II

KODAK MEDALIST II: c1946-1952. Kodak
Ektar 100mm f3.5 lens; Flash Supermatic 1
– ¹/₄₀₀ s, CRF; 8 exp, 2¼" x 3¼" on 620 roll
film.

R3*   **E**

SPECIALIST MODEL 2: 1950. Half plate
stand camera. Wood and chrome-plated
brass. Recommended lens shutter
assembly was 203mm f7.7 Kodak Ektar in
8-speed Epsilon shutter 1-1/150s

Accessory gave double extension of bellows for close-ups.

R3* D+

KODAK REFLEX: c1946. TLR; Kodak Anastigmat 75mm f3.5 lens; Flash Kodamatic shutter; 12 exp, 2¼" x 2¼" on 620 roll film.

R2* B

KODAK TOURIST: c1948-1951. Kodak Anaston f4.5 lens; Flash Kodamatic shutter; 8 exp, 2¼" x 3¼" on 620 roll film.

KODAK CHEVRON: c1953-1956. Kodak Ektar 78mm f3.5 lens; Synchro-Rapid shutter 1-⅛₀₀ s; 12 exp, 2¼" x 2¼"on 620 roll film.

R3* D+

R1* A

KODAK STEREO: c1954-1959. 35mm stereo camera; Kodak Anastigmat 35mm f3.5 lenses; Kodak Flash 200 shutter ½₅-¹⁄₂₀₀s. 29 stereo pairs, 23 x 24mm on 35mm film.

In 1963 Eastman Kodak brought out the #126 Instamatic System. The film was pre-loaded into a plastic cassette that in turn dropped easily into a camera eliminating the "nuisance" of spool-to-spool loading. The system was very successful, and a number of manufacturers purchased licenses from Kodak to make both the cameras and special cassettes.

INSTAMATIC 44: 1969-73, Knob wind, uses flash cubes.

R2* A–

INSTAMATIC 100: 1963-66, Lever wind, uses AG1 flashbulbs, first Instamatic, the most collectable.

R2* D+

R1* A

Kodak Instamatic 50, 154 and 100

INSTAMATIC 104: 1965-68, Lever wind, uses flash cubes.

R1*   **A–**

INSTAMATIC 124: 1968-71, Lever wind, uses flash cubes.

R1*   **A–**

INSTAMATIC 134: 1968-71, Spring motor drive, with light meter, uses flash cubes.

R3*   **B–**

INSTAMATIC 150: 1964-66, Spring motor drive, uses AG1 bulbs.

R2*   **A**

INSTAMATIC 154: 1965-69, Spring motor drive, uses flash cubes.

R2*   **A**

INSTAMATIC 174: 1968-71, Spring motor drive, uses flash cubes.

R2*   **A**

INSTAMATIC 250: 1965-67, Lever wind, uses AG1 bulbs, coated f2.8 lens focusing from 2.5' to infinity, shutter speeds 1/30-1/250s, made in Germany.

R2*   **B+**

INSTAMATIC 300: 1963-66, Lever wind, light meter, uses AG1 bulbs.

R2*   **A**

INSTAMATIC 300: 1965-69, Lever wind, light meter, uses AG1 bulbs.

R2*   **A–**

INSTAMATIC 304: 1965-69, Lever wind, light meter, uses Flash cubes.

R2*   **A–**

INSTAMATIC 314: 1968-71, Lever wind, light meter, uses Flash cubes.

R2*   **A–**

INSTAMATIC 324: 1966-68, Lever wind, light meter, uses Flash cubes, made in Germany.

R2*   **A–**

INSTAMATIC 400: 1963-66, Spring motor drive, light meter, uses AG1 bulbs.

R2*   **B+**

INSTAMATIC 404: 1965-69, Spring motor drive, light meter, uses Flash cubes.

R2*   **B+**

INSTAMATIC 414 : 1968-71, Spring motor drive, light meter, uses Flash cubes.

R2*   **B+**

INSTAMATIC 500: 1963-66, Lever wind, PC connection and hot shoe, light meter, f2.8 lens, speeds 1/30-1/500s, made in Germany.

R3*   **C–**

INSTAMATIC 700: 1963-66, Spring motor drive, uses AG1 bulbs, light meter, f2.8 lens, shutter speeds 1/60-1/250s.

R3*   **C–**

INSTAMATIC 704: 1965-69, Spring motor drive, uses Flash cubes, light meter, f2.8 lens, shutter speeds 1/60-1/250s.

R2*   **C–**

INSTAMATIC 714: 1968-70, Spring motor drive, uses Flash cubes, light meter, f2.8 lens, shutter speeds 1/60-1/250s.

R2*   **C–**

INSTAMATIC 800: 1964-66, Spring motor drive, AG1 bulbs, rangefinder, light meter, f2.8 lens, shutter speeds ⅟₆₀-½₅₀s.
R2*   **C**

INSTAMATIC 804: 1965-70, Spring motor drive, uses Flash cubes, built-in rangefinder, light meter, f2.8 lens, shutter speeds ⅟₆₀-½₅₀s.
R1*   **C**

INSTAMATIC 814: 1968-70, Spring motor drive, uses Flash cubes, built-in rangefinder, light meter, f2.8 lens, shutter speeds ⅟₆₀-½₅₀s.
R2*   **C**

INSTAMATIC X-15: 1970-76, Lever wind, uses "X" cubes which require no battery to be fired.
R1*   **A–**

INSTAMATIC X-15F: 1976-1986, Lever wind, uses Flip flash.
R1*   **A–**

INSTAMATIC X25: 1970-74, Spring motor drive, uses "X" cubes.
R2*   **A**

INSTAMATIC X30: 1970-74, Lever wind, light meter, uses "X" cubes.
R2*   **A**

INSTAMATIC X35: 1970-76, Lever wind, light meter, uses "X" cubes.
R2*   **A**

INSTAMATIC X35F: 1976-86, Lever wind, light meter, uses "Flip flash".
R2*   **A**

INSTAMATIC X45: 1970-74, Spring motor drive, light meter, uses "X" cubes.
R2*   **A**

INSTAMATIC X90: 1970-73, Spring motor drive, light meter, uses "X" cubes, f2.8 lens, coupled rangefinder, shutter speeds ⅟₆₀-½₅₀s.
R2*   **F**

INSTAMATIC S-10: 1967-70, Knob wind on the end of the camera body, pop out lens, uses Flash cubes.
R2*   **A–**

INSTAMATIC S-20: 1967-71, Knob wind on the end of the camera body, pop out lens, light meter, uses Flash cubes.
R2*   **A–**

INSTAMATIC 50: Lever wind, made in Rochester for the export market.
R2*   **A–**

MICKEYMATIC: 1988. Version of the Pocket Instamatic for 110 film with Mickey Mouse label. Found in blue and pink.
R2*   **A+**

HAWKEYE II: 1969. Knob wind, uses flash cubes, grey and black, used as a give-away premium.
R2*   **A–**

HAWKEYE: 1963. Lever wind, uses seperate flash gun, Chrome and olive.
R1*   **A–**

HAWKEYE-F: 1964. Lever wind, uses Flip flash.
R2*   **A–**

HAWKEYE-R4: 1965. Lever wind, uses Flash cubes.
R2*   **A–**

HAWKEYE-A1: 1969. Spring motor drive, with light meter, uses Flash cubes.
R2*   **B**

HAWKEYE-X: 1971. Lever wind, uses "X" cubes, much like the Instamatic X15.
R2*   **A–**

SIX-20 BROWNIE MODEL F: 1954. One of the more attractive Brownie box cameras, finished in buff leather cloth with brown metal front plate and polished brass trim. 8 exp on 620. Fixed focus lens for 10ft to infinity, supplementary lens built in for 5-10ft. I & B shutter. Two tripod bushes for vertical or horizontal use.

R2*   **A**

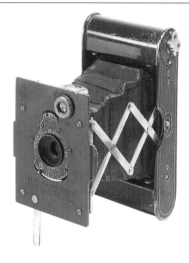

VEST POCKET KODAK: c1912. 127 roll film. Kodak Ball Bearing Shutter. A large variety of lenses were offered for the Kodak VP during it's very long life from a simple meniscus to a Zeiss Kodak Anastigmat. Later models fitted with an Autographic back.

R2*   **B**

JIFFY KODAK 127: 1935. This is an advanced version of the popular VP (vest-pocket) series of cameras. A molded bakelite body was fitted with a fixed focus doublet lens. The camera and packaging were designed by Walter Dorwin Teague. An original box greatly increases the value of the camera.

R2*   **B**

KODAK BANTAM: 1935. First model of Bantam Camera introduced by Eastman Kodak to use new film format. Unsprocketed 35mm paperbacked film for images 28x40mm. Anastigmat f6.3 lens. First model fitted with rigid viewfinder. Camera and packaging designed by Walter Dorwin Teague.

R2*   **B**

KODAK PINHOLE CAMERA: 1930. This was given as a kit to schools as part of

science projects. All the material needed for assembly (cardboard, sticky tape, a pin, and careful instructions, were included. A piece of 3¹/₄ x 4¹/₄" sheet film was used. On occasion they turn up in the original unassembled package at twice the price

R3* **D**

Kodak A.G.
Stuttgart, Germany

MINI INSTAMATIC S-40: c1977. Very compact pocket Instamatic 110 camera for 13 x 17mm images. Kodak Reomar fixed-focus f5.6, 25mm lens. Two shutter speeds automatically selected 1/40 and 1/80s. Automatic exposure control.

R2* **B**

Kogaku Seiki, Japan.

NIPPON: 1942 cfps, 1/20- 1/500s, no RFR, vfr only, screw mount K.O.L. Xebec F2.0/5cm lens. This camera was also known as the "Nippon Standard".

R5* **H–**

NIPPON: 1943 cfps, 1- 1/500s, seperate RFR/vfr windows, screw mount Sun Xebec F2.0/5cm lens. A copy of the Leica III, without diopter adjustment, this camera was also known as the "Nippon III".

R5* **H–**

Kinrad Kohnlein
Nurnberg, Germany

WIKO: 1939. Unusual for having a focal plane shutter in a Bakelite body. Models can be found with fixed focus and variable focus lenses, f4.5 and f2.8. Image size 14x18mm on paper-backed 16mm rollfilm. Shutter 1/20-1/200s.

R3* **D+**

Kolar, Prague, Czechoslovakia

Set of masks greatly increases value

KOLA: c1936, VFR camera for 4x4cm and 3x4cm images on 127 film or 24x36cm images on 35mm film. A variety of lens shutter combinations were available. Zeiss Tessar f/2.8 60mm most common. Early models have a folding VFR, later versions a tubular finder (reverse Galilean telescope). Camera sold with a complete set of three internal masks for different formats and fittings for 35mm film. Presence of all of these items greatly increases the value of the camera.

R4* **E+**

Konishiroku Photo Co., Ltd.
Tokyo, Japan

Konica C35 AF

KONICA C35AF: 1977; 35mm eye-level auto-focus camera. First auto focus production camera in the world based on a design by Honeywell Corp. in the U.S. Hexanon lens, f2.8, 38mm. Built-in electronic flash.

R2*   **B**

Konishiroku, *Japan*

SAKURA POCKET CAMERA: 1907. Folding plate camera for 8.2cm x 10.8cm glass plates. Rapid Rectiliniar f8 lens T,I,B shutter. Quite rare.

R4*   **F–**

IDEA: 1909 Folding 4 x 5 camera for glass plates or sheet film, front shifts and revolving back. Tessar f6.3/165mm lens, Compur shutter, both imported from Germany. Quite rare.

R4*   **F–**

IDEA "A": 1909-24 Folding 8cm x 10cm camera for glass plates. Many versions were made during its production, early cameras used imported lenses and shutters, either from the USA or Germany. All are quite rare.

R3*   **D**

IDEA HAND CAMERA: 1930-35 Folding, 8cm X 10.5cm or 6.5cm X 9cm camera for glass plates. Many versions were made during its production, most cameras used imported lenses and shutters, either from the USA or Germany. Less rare than the Idea "A" camera. An exception is the Idea Hand Camera of 1935, with one of the first Nikkor lenses, which is about 20 times more valuable.

R3*   **C+**

THE PEARL II: 1909 Folding roll film camera, 8cm x 10.5cm on 118 roll film. The first Japanese roll film camera. Models III, and IV could also use glass plates. All are rare.

R3*   **D+**

SPECIAL PEARL: 1913 Folding roll film camera, 8cm x 10.5cm on glass plates, or 8cm x 13.7cm on 101 roll film. Quite rare.

R3*   **D+**

PEARL NO. 2: 1923-31 Folding roll film camera, 6cm x 9cm or 6cm x 4.5cm on 120 roll film. Several versions with various shutters, Wooden body. This is the first Japanese camera to use 120 roll film.

R3*   **C+**

BABY PEARL: c1935; Folding camera; 3 x 4cm exp on 127 roll film; front cell focusing; 50mm f4.5 Hexor lens in Rox shutter B,$\frac{1}{25}$ – $\frac{1}{100s}$.

R2*   **D+**

THE LILY CAMERA: 1909-38 Folding plate cameras of various sizes, most with German lenses and shutters. Early cameras are quite rare. A tropical Lily was said to have been made in the 1930's, and was the only tropical camera to come from Japan. Either the tropical model, or a camera equipped with an Anytar lens, made by Nippon Kogaku

Semi-Pearl

Baby Pearl

(Nikon), are valued at about 20 times the value of any other Lily camera.

R3*   **C+**

PEARLETTE: 1928-40 Folding roll film camera using lazy tong struts, and 127 film. Simple fixed focus lenses or various types. Some cameras had provision for 4cm x 6.5cm and 3cm x 4cm negative sizes on 127 film. Similar in looks to the Vest Pocket Kodak. The earliest camera lacked the unusual close-up lens attached to the wire frame finder. This line was started again after the Second World War, and the Pearl name found its way to quite a number of roll film cameras, both 127 and 120.

R3*   **C+**

SEMI-PEARL: c1938. Folding rollfilm camera for 16 exposures on 120 film Hexar 7.5cm/f4.5 lens, Durex shutter, 1-¹⁄₁₀₀s.

R3*   **C–**

PEARL I: 1949 Folding roll film camera, uncoupled RFR, leaf shutter,1 – ¹⁄₅₀₀ sec, Hexar F4.5/75mm lens. 6cm x 4.5cm on 120 film. The Pearl RS used a Konirapid shutter.

R2*   **C+**

KONICA 35: 1965. 35mm camera with CRF btl shutter, speeds 1-¹⁄₅₀₀s, Hexar

50mm/f3.5 lens. marked "Made in Occupied Japan".

R3*   **D**

KONICA AUTOREFLEX: 1968. The first automatic 35mm SLR. Shutter priority, TTL metering. 52mm f1.8 standard lens. Shutter 1-1/000s.

R2*   **D**

KONICA FS-1: 1978. The first 35mm SLR to feature a built-in electric motordrive, used also for auto film load. Totally electronic shutter using twin micro solenoids to activate the first and second curtains. Copal shutter that travels vertically. Shutter priority automation, TTL metering.

R2*   **D**

E. B. Koopman, *New York*

THE PRESTO CAMERA: C 1899 meniscus lens with rotating stops; single speed shutter; 4 exp, 18 x 18cm on special roll film. Invented by H. Casler.

R4*   **F+**

Korsten, *Paris, France*

LA LITOTE: c1902. 45 x 107mm stereo; Aplanatic lenses; 3 speed guillotine shutter. Leather covered box camera.

R4*   **D**

The Presto Camera

Kowa Co., Ltd., *Nagoya, Japan*

KOMAFLEX-S: 1960. 127 roll film SLR camera; Prominar 65mm f2.8 coated lens; Seikosha-SLV shutter 1 -⅟₅₀₀s, MX synch.

R3*   **D**

RAMERA: 1959, combination portable AM radio and detective camera; Prominar 65mm f2.8 coated lens; 3 speed synch shutter; 20 exp, 10 x 14mm on 16mm film (Minolta 16 cassettes).

R3*   **D+**

KOWA 35 N: 1960: Leaf shutter, ½s – ⅟₅₀₀s, vfr only, fixed Prominar F.C. F3.5/45mm lens. interesting trigger wind mechanism.

R2*   **C–**

KOWA SW: 1964: Leaf shutter, 1 – ⅟₅₀₀s, vfr only, using a strange system, available in black or chrome. Fixed wide angle f3.2/28mm lens. Perhaps more valuable as a user camera than a collector's item.

R2*   **D+**

KOMAFLEX: 1960-64: Leaf shutter, 1 – ⅟₅₀₀s, fixed Kowa F2.0/50mm, or f1.9/50mm lens. Inexpensive 35mm SLR, with wide angle and telephoto conversion lenses available. Several models, some with built-in light meters including SE, SER, SET, SETR. Only the Kowa UW 190, sporting a fixed f4/19mm lens seems to be highly prized, bringing about 8 times the price of an ordinary Komaflex.

R2*   **C–**

Kozy Camera Company
Boston, Massachusetts

POCKET KOZY CAMERA: C1892. Meniscus lens; single speed shutter; 9 x 9cm exp on roll film

R4*   **E–**

Krasnogorsk Mechanical Works *Krasnogorsk, USSR.* (*Same as KMZ*)

FT-2 PANORAMIC CAMERA: 1958-1965. Rotating Industar 50mm f5 lens; shutter ⅟₁₀₀, ⅟₂₀₀, ⅟₄₀₀s.; 12 exp. 24x110mm on 35 mm film in special cassettes. Early models had shutter adjustment on bottom in addition to the two levers on top. Later models had a two-winged tensioning lever.

R4*   **E+**

HAPYUCC: c.1960. English corruption of the Cyrillic letters that make up the Russian name on the front of the camera. 16mm SLR. It was exported under the name Narciss (see below).

R3*   **A**

HORIZONT: 1968. Panoramic swing lens camera for 24x58mm images on 35mm giving 120° angle of view. 28mm f2.8 lens. Shutter 1/25-1/125s. Clip-on viewfinder (often missing) incorporates spirit level.

R3*   **A**

NARCISS 1961-1965; 16mm subminiature camera SLR fitted with Industar f2.8/35mm lens. Originally designed as a specialized instrument for medical photography it was eventually offered to the general public. This was the first ever miniature SLR.

R3*   **B+**

ZENIT PHOTOSNIPER: c1960, 35mm camera; Tair 300mm f4.5 coated lens, inter-changeable screw mount; cfps ⅟₃₀-⅟₅₀₀s. Zenit camera mounted on gunstock with tele-photo lens. Outfit including normal lens, filters for 300mm lens, screwdrivers, and empty film cassettes.

R2*   **E–**

ZENIT PHOTOSNIPER 12: c1970- today (written "Photosn*a*iper on the shoulder stock but referred in English translation Soviet literature without the "a".) Intro-duction of a modified Zenit 12 black camera body, which includes a built-in light meter, and integral connections to the gunstock and 300mm lens. The modified body is designated "12S". At least one Euro-pean sale for £200 in 1990, but many others at less than half that price!

R2*   **E**

ZENIT PHOTOSNIPER: Latest version of (KM100) now sporting a Zenit Automat 35mm SLR with aperture priority, a Telezenitar-K f4.5/300mm lens in "K" type bayonet mount, and a redesigned shoulder stock. Available *new*, but not found yet in great numbers in the "West".

R3*   **E**

ZENIT: c1953, 35mm SLR, interchangeable (39mm screw mount) 50mm normal lens, CFPS ⅟₃₀ – ⅟₅₀₀s, non-instant return mirror.

R2*   **C+**

ZENIT S (C): c1956, with flash synch.

R2*   **C**

ZENITH C: c.1962. 35mm SLR. Screw-thread interchangeable lenses. 50mm f3.5 Industar-50 lens. FP shutter 1/25-1/500s + B & T. Adjustable flash synch 0-12 milliseconds.

R2*   **C**

ZORKI-1: 1948-56, Cfps, ½₀ – ⅟₅₀₀s, no slow speeds, no synch, CRF. Interchangeable Leica-type screw mount, f3.5/50mm Industar-22 lens in collapsible mount, though some rigid mount lenses were made. Lens serial numbers usually indicate year of production as the first two digits. The null series camera with both FED and Zorki markings and 5cm F2 collapsible lens is worth $500. Prices are 20% higher in the United States for ordinary Zorki-1 cameras. Australian and Japanese collectors are starting to buy at higher prices too.

R2*   **D–**

FED Zorki-1 produced 1948-1949.

R4*   **F**

ZORKI-2: 1955, Cfps, 1/20 to ⅟₅₀₀s, no slow speeds, no synch, CRF. Interchangeable Leica-type screw mount, f3.5/50mm Industar-22 lens in collapsible mount, though some rigid mount lenses were made.Lens serial numbers usually indicate year of production as the first two digits. This camera differs from the Zorki-1 by the addition of a self timer. Though very few Zorki-2 cameras were made, their current price does not reflect their rarity.

R4*   **E–**

ZORKI-S (C): 1956-58, Cfps, ⅟₂₀ to ⅟₅₀₀s, no slow speeds, synch, CRF. Interchangeable Leica-type screw mount, f3.5/50mm Industar-22 lens in collapsible mount, or rigid mount f3.5/50mm Industar 50 lens. Camera serial numbers indicate year of production as the first two digits. Though not an exact copy of the Leica II(D); this camera keeps many of the features of the previous Zorki cameras. The rigid mount lens adds 15% to the value of the camera. Models in green and grey were made and add 100% or more to the price.

R2*   **D–**

ZORKI-2S (C): 1956-58 Cfps, ⅟₂₀ to ⅟₅₀₀s, no slow speeds, synch, CRF. Interchangeable Leica-type screw mount, rigid mount f3.5/50mm Industar-50 lens or F2.0/52mm Jupiter-8. Camera serial numbers indicate year of production as the first two digits. This camera differs from the Zorki-C by the addition of a self timer.

R2*   **D–**

ZORKI-3: 1954-55 Cfps, 1 to ⅟₁₀₀₀s, slow speeds, no synch, CRF. Interchangeable Leica-type screw mount, rigid mount F2.0/50mm Jupiter-8 lens. Camera serial numbers indicate year of production as the first two digits. Very few Zorki-3 cameras were made, but the collectors' market price does not reflect this.

R3*   **E–**

ZORKI-3M: 1955 Same as the Zorki-3, slow speeds moved to the top dial. Cfps, 1 to ⅟₁₀₀₀ s, slow speeds, no synch, CRF. Interchangeable Leica-type screw mount, rigid mount f2.0 Jupiter-8. Camera serial numbers indicate year of production as the first two digits. More common than the Zorki-3, but almost the same market value.

R2*   **D+**

ZORKI-3S (C): 1956. This camera adds flash synch and a redesigned top cover to the features of the Zorki-3M. Cfps, 1-⅟₁₀₀₀s, slow speeds, synch, CRF. Interchangeable Leica-type screw mount, rigid mount f2.0/50mm Jupiter-8 lens. Camera serial numbers indicate year of production as the first two digits.

R2*   **D**

ZORKI-4: 1956-73 Cfps, 1 to 1/1000 s, slow speeds, synch, CRF. Interchangeable Leica-type screw mount, rigid mount f3.5/50mm Industar-50 lens or f2.0/52mm Jupiter-8 lens. Camera serial numbers indicate year of production as the first two digits. This camera differs from the Zorki-C by the addition of a self timer. Some cameras were marked celebrating the 50th anniversary of the Communist Party in Russia. These models more than double the price of the camera. Cameras marked "50th Anniversary" **£150.**

R2*   **C+**

ZORKI-4K: 1973-77 Cfps, 1 to ⅟₁₀₀₀s, slow speeds, synch, CRF. Interchangeable Leica-type screw mount, rigid mount F2.0 52mm

Jupiter-8. Camera serial numbers indicate year of production as the first two digits. This camera is the same as the Zorki-4, with the addition of a rapid wind lever, and a fixed take-up spool. The Zorki-4K was made in large numbers, and was widely exported. Quite popular in Europe where it is commonly found, this camera fetches about 30% more in the United States.

R2*   **C+**

ZORKI-5: c1958-59 Cfps, 1 to ¹/₁₀₀₀s, slow speeds, synch, CRF. Interchangeable Leica-type screw mount, rigid mount f3.5/50mm Industar-50 lens or F2.0/52mm Jupiter-8 lens. Camera serial numbers indicate year of production as the first two digits. Incorporates a longer base rangefinder (67mm) than previous Zorki cameras, uses a combined RFR/vfr window.

R2*   **D–**

ZORKI-6: 1960-66 Cfps, 1 to 1/1000s, slow speeds, synch, CRF. Interchangeable Leica-type screw mount, rigid mount f3.5/50mm Industar-50 lens or f2.0/52mm Jupiter-8 lens. Camera serial numbers indicate year of production as the first two digits. This camera is the same as the Zorki-5, with the addition of a hinged back and a self timer. Less common in the US than in Europe.

R2*   **D–**

ZORKI-10: 1964-78. Not a Leica copy, but based on Ricoh cameras of the 1960's. Fixed lens, automatic shutter, CRF.

R3*   **C**

ZORKI-11: 1964-66. Fixed lens, automatic shutter, the same as the Zorki-10, but without a coupled rangefinder.

R3*   **C**

ZORKI-12: (ZR114); 1967-1968. Fixed lens, automatic shutter, 1/2 frame format.

R4*   **E–**

RUSSIAN ACCESSORY LENSES AFTER 1945.

20mm, f5.6, MR-2, w/o finder	**E–**
(w/finder	**F**
28mm, f6.0, Orion-15	**D**
35mm, f2.8, Jupiter-12	**D**
50mm, f1.5 Jupiter-3	**D**
85mm, f2.0, Jupiter-9	**D–**
135mm, f4.0, Jupiter-11	**D–**

Russian post-war lenses and the 2cm viewfinder

Russian pre-war lenses

RUSSIAN ACCESSORY FINDERS.

2cm optical finder	**E+**
Universal finder for 28, 35, 50, 80, and 135mm views	**B+**

RUSSIAN ACCESSORY LENSES BEFORE 1945

FED F4.5/28mm	**D**
FED F2.0/50mm	**D+**
FED F3.5/50mm, Macro	**D**
FED F3.5/50mm – close focusing	**E+**
FED F6.3/100mm	**D**
FED F6.3/100mm	**G**
FED f4.5/28mm	**D**

E. Krauss, Paris, France.

EKA: C1924. Krauss Tessar 50mm f3.5 lens; Compur shutter 1-⅓₀₀s; 100 exp, 30 x 42mm on non-perforated 35mm film. c1924.

R4*   **F+**

EKA

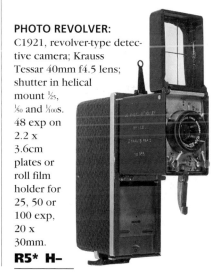

PHOTO REVOLVER:
C1921, revolver-type detective camera; Krauss Tessar 40mm f4.5 lens; shutter in helical mount ½₅, ⅙₀ and ¹⁄₁₀₀s. 48 exp on 2.2 x 3.6cm plates or roll film holder for 25, 50 or 100 exp, 20 x 30mm.

R5* H–

TAKYR: C1906. Zeiss Krauss 136mm f6.3 lens; fps. 3¼" x 4¼" exp on plates.

R4*   **E+**

G. A. Krauss
Stuttgart, Germany.

KRAUSS PEGGY I: C1935. 35mm camera; often found with Zeiss Tessar 50mm f3.5 lens, though many lens options were available; Compur shutter 1-⅓₀₀s.

R4*   **F–**

KRAUSS PEGGY II: C1935. 35mm RFR camera; often found with Schneider Xenon 45mm f2 lens, though many lens options were available; Compur shutter 1-⅓₀₀s, CRF. c1935.

R4*   **F**

ROLLETTE: c1922. Folding Rollfilm camera, 4 x 6.5cm format, front struts, Compur shutter, various lenses, simple models had Pronto shutter.

R2*   **C**

STEREO POLYSKOP: c1906. Stereo camera making images on glass plates held in changing magazine. Twin 63mm f6.3 Tessar lenses.

R3*   **E+**

STEREOPLAST: c1921. Stereo camera for 45x107mm held in push-pull changing magazine. Fitted with twin Schneider 55mm f4.5 Xenar lenses

R2*   **D+**

Stereoplast

Dr. Rudolph Krugener
Bockheim, Germany

DELTA CAMERA: C1895, folding plate camera; meniscus lens; 3 speed rotary shutter; 9 x 12cm exp on plates.

R4*   **D+**

DELTA KLAPP: c1904, Rapid Aplanatic lens; pneumatic shutter $\frac{1}{5}$-$\frac{1}{100}$s; 3¼ x 4¼" exp on plates. Double ext bellows.

R4*   **D**

DELTA MAGAZINE CAMERA: C1892, Aplanat 145mm f13 lens; string cocked guillotine shutter; 12 exp, 9 x 12cm on dry plates.

R4*   **F+**

DELTA PATRONEN FLACH KAMERA: c1903, Rapid Rectilinear lens; central shutter 1-$\frac{1}{100}$s; 3¼" x 4¼" exp on plates or roll film.

R4*   **D**

DELTA PERISKOP: c1903, Periskop 150mm f12 lens; central shutter $\frac{1}{25}$-$\frac{1}{100}$s; 3 ¼" x 4¼" exp on plates.

R4*   **D–**

DR. KRUGENER'S BOOK CAMERA: C1889, book-type detective camera; Rectilinear 60mm f12 lens; guillotine shutter; 24 exp on 40 x 40mm plate.

R5*   **H+**

DR. KRUGENER'S MILLION CAMERA: c1903, 9 x 18cm stereo camera; Rapid Periskop lenses; guillotine shutter. 9 x 18cm exp on roll film.

R4*   **D+**

MINI DETECTIVE: c1900, miniature box detective camera. Leather changing bag for 12 plates; polished mahogany wood; size: 4" x 3¼" x 7".

R4*   **F+**

NORMAL SIMPLEX: c1900, 9 x 12cm reflex camera; three diaphragm stops on sliding brass bar. Vf fitted to concealed bellows; mahogany finish.

R4*   **G+**

SIMPLEX MAGAZINE CAMERA: c1889, TLR detective camera; Achromatized Periscopic 100mm f10 lens; sector self-capping shutter; 24 exp, 6 x 8cm on dry plates.

R4*   **G**

DELTA STEREO: c1900-1909, folding stereo camera for 9cm x 18cm plates, Aplanat lenses and simple two speed shutter, some models allowed the use of roll film.

R4*   **E–**

VESTPOCKET KRONOS: c1920, strut folding VFR camera for 4.5cm x 6cm plates, Anticomar f4.2/75mm lens, Compur shutter.

R3*   **D+**

STEREO KRONOS: c1920, strut folding stereo camera for 4.5cm x 10.7cm plates, Anticomar f3.5/75mm lenses, Compur Stereo shutter.

R4*   **E+**

QUER KRONOS: c1920, metal bodied horizontal folding camera for 9cm x 12cm glass plates, Anticomar f6.3/10.5cm lens, Compur shutter.

R3*   **C–**

NESTOR: c1920, horizontal folding VFR camera for 6cm x 6cm frames on roll film, Anticomar f5.4/75mm lens, Compur shutter.

R3*   **B+**

PASTOSCOPE: c1900, strut folding stereo camera 4.5cm x 10.7cm plates, Simplex f7.7/60mm lenses, simple four speed shutter.

R4*   **E–**

Kromskop Manufactory
Philadelphia, Pa.

IVES KROMSKOP TRIPLE CAMERA: c1897 single exposure tri-colour camera using internal prisms as beam-splitters. Mahogany and brass fittings. The wooden bodies were made for Ives in England. They were shipped to Philadelphia where the prisms, filters and other items were added.

R4*   **E+**

Kunick, Walter KG
Frankfurt, Germany

LIGHTER PETIE: cigarette lighter-type detective camera; built along lines of Petie Compact, camera separable; meniscus 24mm f11 lens; single speed shutter; 16 exp, 16 x 16mm on 16mm roll film. c1957. Red, green, blue, deco or leather and chrome finish.

R3*   **F–**

PETIE: c1958, subminiature camera; meniscus 25mm f9 lens; single speed shutter; 16 exp, 14 x 14mm on 16mm.

R3*   **C+**

PETIE VANITY-CASE: c1958, ladies compact-type subminiature detective camera; 35mm f9 lens; single speed shutter. 16 exp, 14 x 14mm on 16mm roll film. Red, green, blue, deco or leather with

chrome/gold finished case contains lipstick, compact and camera.

R4*   **F**

Kürbi & Niggeloh, Bilora
Radevormwald, Germany

RADIX 56: c1950, metal 35mm VFR camera for 24 x 24mm frames on 35mm film, Biloxar f5.6/40mm lens, simple shutter, lever advance.

R2*   **B–**

RADIX 35B c1950, with Biloxar f3.5 lens.

R2*   **B–**

RADIX 35S: c1950, with Schneider Radionar f3.5/38mm lens.

R2*   **B–**

RADIX 35BH: c1951, with improved shutter, 1/2 – 1/200s.

R3*   **B**

RADIX 35SH: c1951, with improved shutter, 1/2 – 1/200s.

R3*   **B**

BOY: c1950, bakelite box camera for 6 x 4.5 frames on 127 film, simple lens and shutter.

R2*   **A**

LUXUS BOY: c1954, *red* bakelite box camera for 6 x 4.5cm frames on 127 film, f11 lens, simple shutter.

R2*   **C**

BILORA STAHL-BOX: c1950, metal box camera for 6 x 9cm frames on roll film, reflex VFRs, simple lens and shutter.

R2*   **A–**

BILORA BLITZ BOX: V1950, with synchro contacts.

R2*   **A–**

BILORA BLITZ BOX D: metal box camera for 6 x 9cm frames on roll film, simple lens and shutter, *optical* VFR allowing for better positioning of the flash.

R2*   **A–**

BILORA STANDARD BOX: c1950, metal box camera for 6 x 9cm frames on roll film, f11 lens and simple shutter.

R2*   **A–**

BILORA SPECIAL BOX: c1950, with built-in close-up lens.

R2*   **A–**

BILORA MIKRO BOX: c1953, special purpose metal box camera, *no VFR.* (one offered for £50 in April, 1991).

R3*   **C–**

BILORA BONITA 66: c1953, TLR type box camera for 6 x 6cm frames on roll film, simple lens and shutter.

R2*   **A**

BILORA BELLA: c1950, metal VFR camera for 6 x 4.5cm frames on 127 film, all black with chrome trim, simple f9 lens and shutter.

R3*   **A**

BILORA BELLA 55: c1955. With chrome top plate and simple f8 lens.

R3*   **A**

BILORA BELLA D: c1957. In "Swiss-Air Blue" and "Fashion-Grey".

R2* **A**

BILORA BELLA 44: c1959, metal VFR camera for 4 x 4cm frames on 127 film, simple f8 lens and shutter.

R2* **A–**

BILORA DC 4: c1959-60, with Trinar f5.6/55mm lens in vario shutter, or Trinar f3.5/55mm lens in Prontor shutter.

R2* **A–**

BILORA BELLA 46: c1957, metal VFR camera for 4 x 6cm frames on 120 roll film, simple lens and shutter, available in "Swiss-Air Blue" and "Fashion-Grey".

R2* **A**

BILORA BELLA 66: c1957, metal VFR camera for 6x 6cm frames on 120 roll film, simple lens and shutter, available in "Swiss-Air Blue" and "Fashion-Grey".

R2* **A**

Kyoto Seiki, *Japan*

LOVELY: c.1948. Subminiature for 17.5mm rollfilm. One of the first horizontal style subminiature cameras that led the way for Minolta and Mamiya. 14x14mm images, despite box claiming 18x18mm. Shutter 1/25-1/100s. Very rare.

R5* **H**

Reference Notes

Lamperti & Garbagnati
Italy

LAMPERTI: c1890. 9 x 18cm stereo detective camera; 13cm lens; 3 speed guillotine shutter. Leather covered wooden body; rack focusing; 9 x 18cm exp on plates.

R4*   **E+**

Lancart, *Paris, France.*

XYZ: c1935. Subminiature camera; nickel plated finish.

R4*   **F+**

J. Lancaster & Son
Birmingham, England

CAMREX DELUXE: c1900. 3¼" x 4¼"folding hand camera; RR lens; pneumatic shutter. Red leather bellows. Mahogany finish with brass fittings.

R3*   **E−**

GEM APPARATUS: c1880. 12-lens tintype camera. 12 Petzval-type 2" f4.5 lenses. Shutter: horizontally sliding panel on front of camera is operated manually. 12 exp, 1⅛"x1⅜" on ¼"x 4¼" ferrotype plates.

R5*   **H+**

INSTANTOGRAPH B: c1883. Quarter plate view camera. Brass barrel Lancaster f8 or f10 lens with iris diaphragm; rotary shutter; tapered red bellows; wood body.

R3*   **E+**

Gem Apparatus

Instantograph II

THE 1888 PATENT INSTANTOGRAPH: c1888. 4" x 5" view camera. Lancaster & Son brass lens with adjustable diaphragm. Reversible back; red Russian leather bellows. Lancaster & Son made several models of this camera.

R4*   **E+**

LADIES'CAMERA: c1897. Pocketbook-type detective camera. Achromatic lens; iris diaphragm; Lancaster see-saw single speed shutter. Quarter, half- or whole-plate pictures.

R5*   **H−**

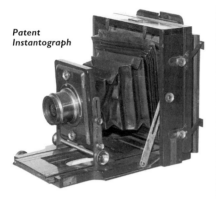

Patent Instantograph

LANCASTER'S PATENT WATCH CAMERA: c1886. Collapsible watch-type detective camera. Grubb-type achromatic 45mm f22 lens; variable speed rotary shutter. Single exp, 1" x ½"on dry plates. NSR.

R5*   **K–**

LE MERITORE: c1880-1905. Wood and brass view camera. Blue or brown double extension bellows. A range of Lancaster lenses. Quarter plate to 10" x 12".

R2*   **E**

LE MERVEILLEUX: c1888. 3¼" x 4¼" view camera. Aplanatic lens. 3¼" x 4¼" exp on plates.

R4*   **E–**

OMNIGRAPH DETECTIVE CAMERA: (LN106). c1891-1907. Box-type detective camera.

R4*   **D+**

THE ROVER DETECTIVE CAMERA: c1892. 3¼" x 4¼" box-type detective camera. Magazine load; mahogany finish.

R4*   **F–**

E. Ludwig Lausa
Dresden, Germany

LEADER: c1950. 35mm stereo camera. Leader Anastigmat 45mm f4.5 lenses; shutter TMBK ½₅-¼₀₀s. Mfd in Japan.

R3*   **C+**

R. Lechner, Vienna, Austria

JUWEL: c1909. Folding stereo camera. Achromat lens; T and I shutter; central finder; side-flaps covered retracted lens panel; leather covered metal body. 45 x 107mm exp on plates.

R4*   **E+**

LECHNER'S SCHUTZEN-CAMERA (MARKS-MAN'S CAMERA): c1892. Rifle-type detective camera. 30 exp, 3cm diameter, on roll film. A camera that attached beneath the barrel of any gun.

R5*   **NSR**

NANNA IA: c1909. Folding bellows stereo camera. Nanna Aplanat 80mm f8 lens with sliding stops; guillotine shutter. Central frame finder; 6 x 13cm exp on plates. Size: 2.5 x 19 x 10.5cm.

R4*   **E+**

Lecoultre & Cie, Le Sentier
Switzerland

COMPASS: c1938. 24 x 36mm miniature RFR camera; Kern CCL 3B Anastigmat 35mm f3.5 lens with variable stops to f16; rotary sector shutter – 22 speeds from 4½" to ½₀₀s. Pivoting mirror for right-angle viewing, CRF. Machined Duralumin body, stereoscopic head, panoramic head, built-in yellow, orange and green filters, ground glass back with focusing magnifier,

collapsible lens shade, spirit level on top of camera, built-in extinction meter visible through VFR window, hinged lens cap with depth of field scale, collapsible lens mount. Single exp on 24 x 6mm dry plates (sold ready loaded in small heavy paper "Compass envelopes" complete with dark slide). A wide range of accessories was available for the Compass. A roll film back held six exp on special 1½" film, a pocket tripod the size of a fountain pen, and an enlarger-projector that fit into a 4" x 4" x 16" box and could be powered by a 12 volt car battery. Mfg. by LeCoultre & Cie, Le Sentier, Switzerland for Compass Cameras, Ltd, London, England.

R3* **G+**

COMPASS ACCESSORIES

Tripod	**F**
Roll film back	**F**

Armand Le Docte, *Brussels.*

PHOTO DETECTIVE: c1889. Rectilinear 18cm f8 lens; flap shutter. Reflex viewer for either vertical or horizontal format. Changing mechanism for 18 plates, 8.3 x 10.8 cm.

R5* **G–**

PLASTRON: c1886. Concealed vest-type detective camera. Rectilinear 45mm lens. Size: 2cm from front to rear; 14.9cm diameter. Similar to Gray, Stirn and Photo Eclair.

R5* **NSR**

A. Lehmann
Berlin, Germany

BEN AKIBA: c1903. Cane-type detective camera. Front meniscus 35mm f9 lens; oscillating sector, self-cocking shutter. 20 exp, 16 x 20mm on special daylight loading

Ben Akiba

roll film. Handle contained extra rolls of film. Invented by Emil Kronke.

NOTE; Extreme caution required as many replicas made.

R5*   **K–**

Leidolf Kamerawerkes
Wetzlar, Germany

LEIDOX: c1950, metal VFR camera for 4 x 4cm frames on 127 roll film; Triplon f3.8, 50mm lens; Vario shutter.

R3*   **B+**

LEIDOX IIS: c1952, metal VFR camera for 4 x 4cm frames on 127 film. Triplon f2.8, 50mm lens; Prontor-S shutter.

R3*   **B+**

LORDOX: c1952, 35mm VFR camera. Lordon f2.8, 50mm lens; Prontor-SV shutter, body release, knob wind.

R3*   **B+**

LORDOMAT: c1955, 35mm RFR camera. Interchangeable Lordon f1.9 or Lordonar f2.8, 50mm lens; Prontor-SV or SVS shutter; double stroke lever advance operating from front to back; CRF; marked "Lordomat" on top.

R2*   **C–**

LORDOMAT C35: c1956, 35mm RFR camera with built-in light meter. Lordon f1.9 or Lordonar f2.8, 50mm lens; Prontor-SVS shutter; CRF; VFR with fields of view for 35mm, 90mm, and 135mm.

R3*   **C+**

LORDOMAT SLE: 1959. Modified version of the Lordomat C35. CRF camera, top plate redesigned for a neater

appearance with one window of the rangefinder incorporated into the meter window, the other in the viewfinder. Made for interchangeable lenses with frames for 35mm-135mm in viewfinder. Lenses fit into the Prontor SVS shutter speeded 1-1/300s + B. Two stroke lever wind.

R3*   **C–**

LORDOMAT SE: c1960, 35mm RFR camera. Lordon f1.9 or Lordonar f2.8, 50mm lens; Prontor SVS shutter; new body and RFR style; CRF; interchangeable lens mounting system; marked Lordomat on the front.

R3*   **C–**

LORDOX II: c1955, 35mm VFR camera. Fixed Triplon f2.8, 50mm lens; Prontor-SV shutter; same body style and double stroke lever advance.

R3*   **B+**

LORDOX 57: 1957. VFR 35mm camera. 5cm f2.8 Leidof Tripon. Prontor SVS shutter 1-1/300s. Double wind through 180° for film advance.

R2*   **B+**

LORDOX JUNIOR: c1960, 35mm VFR camera. Fixed Triplon f2.8, 50mm lens; Prontor-SVS shutter; same body style as (LY105).

R2*   **A**

LORDOX JUNIOR B: c1950, 35mm VFR camera with built-in light meter.

R2*   **A**

LORDOX BLITZ: c1960, 35mm VFR camera with built-in AG1 flash lamp holder.

R2*   **A**

LORDOMATIC: c1960, 35mm VFR camera, fixed Lordonar f2.8, 50mm lens; Prontor-SLK shutter; coupled light meter.

R2*   **A**

ACCESSORY LENSES FOR LORDOMAT CAMERAS

Lordonar f3.5/35mm lens	**B+**
Travenar f3.5/35mm lens	**B+**
Telordon f5.6/90mm lens	**B+**
Travenar f4.0/90mm lens	**B+**
Travenar f4.0/135mm lens	**C**

Ernst Leitz G.M.B.H.
Wetzlar, Germany

For further information see Leica Collectors Guide by Dennis Laney, Hove Collectors Books, 1992, also other Leica books from Hove Collectors Books listed in the advertisement at the back of this book.

N.B. Leica prices are for items in original condition, one grade higher than other makes.

O-Series Leica

LEICA I (A) ANASTIGMAT: c1925. Leitz Anastigmat f3.5, 50mm lens; CFPS ½5-½00S. Snr 126-300. Qty 175.The original Anastigmat design used five elements. A four element lens would indicate a later Leitz conversion or a counterfeit camera. When considering buying such a camera, it is suggested that a complete examination of the camera and lens be undertaken by an expert with the specialized tools and knowledge to determine the camera's authenticity. Any attempt by an inexperienced person to take apart Leitz Anastigmat lens to find out the number of elements used could drastically lower the cameras worth!

R5*   **K–**

UR Leica

UR LEICA REPLICA: c1970. Non-operational display replica.

R4*   **G**

O-SERIES LEICA: c1923. Leitz Anastigmat f3.5, 50mm lens; non-self-capping CFPS 1/20-1/500s.

R5*   **L+**

LEICA I (A) ELMAX: c1926-1930. Leitz Elmax f3.5, 50mm lens; CFPS ½0-½00 s. Snr 300-1,300. Qty 1000. The original Elmax design used five elements. A four element lens would indicate either a later Leitz conversion or a counterfeit camera.

R5*   **J**

LEICA I (A) ELMAR: c1926-1930. Leitz Elmar f3.5, 50mm lens; CFPS ⅟₂₀-⅟₅₀₀s. Snr 1,300-71,250. Qty 53,000(?). Four digit serial numbered Leica I (A):

R3*   **G+**

Five digit serial numbered Leica I (A):

R3*   **G−**

Close focus (18") model Leica I (A):

R3*   **G**

LEICA I (A) LUXUS: c1928-1931. Leitz Elmar f3.5, 50mm lens; CFPS ⅟₂₀ – ⅟₅₀₀ s. Snr 28,692-48,441. Qty 95. Gold plated Leica I(A) with red, blue, green or brown lizard skin.

R5*   **K−**

LEICA I (A) LUXUS REPLICA: Collectors and others have remanufactured replica Luxus cameras from Leica I (A) cameras.

R4*   **G+**

LEICA MIFILMCA: c1927, for use on microscope with fixed focus MIKAS attachment – using microscope optics. (one sold

at auction in April, 1991 for more than £5000).

R4*   **I+**

LEICA I (A) HEKTOR: c1930. Hektor f2.5, 50mm lens; CFPS ⅟₂₀-⅟₅₀₀s. Snr 38,662-71,230. Qty 1330. Counterfeit Hektor cameras have been offered on the market for $4000. To verify a Hektor camera, check the serial number against the factory list and inspect the rear lens bezel for alterations.

R4*   **I−**

LEICA I (B) COMPUR, DIAL-SET: c1926-1929. Leitz Elmar f3.5, 50mm lens; Compur shutter 1-1/300s. Snr 5,700-13,200(?). Qty 638.

R4*   **J−**

LEICA I (B) COMPUR, RIM-SET: c1929-1930. Leitz Elmar f3.5, 50mm lens; Compur shutter 1-⅟₃₀₀s. Snr 13150-50710. Qty 969.

R4*   **I+**

LEICA I (C) WITH NON-STANDARDIZED LENS MOUNT:
c1930-1931. Leitz Elmar f3.5, 50mm lens; CFPS ½₀-⅟₅₀₀s. Snr 37,280. When the swing-in vf mask is intact and matched 135mm and 35mm lenses are included, add $1000-$1500. First Leica with interchangeable lens mount (shown above). It is difficult to find this model in historically accurate condition (the lens flange must not have a "0" engraved at the 12 o'clock position. The rear lens bezel must be marked with the last three digits of the body serial no.) because in most cases they were standardized by E. Leitz when returned for service. **WITH HEKTOR ADD 20%.** With matched 50mm lens **G+**; with mask **H–**; with Hektor **H–**; with three lenses **I+**.

R4*   H–

LEICA I (C) WITH STANDARDIZED LENS MOUNT:
c1931. Leitz Elmar f3.5, 50mm lens; CFPS ½₀-⅟₅₀₀s. Snr 55404-99755. Qty 7231. First Leica to permit interchangeability of standardized lenses with any stan-

dardized camera body. The lens flange has a "0" engraved at the 12 o'clock position.

R3*   F

LEICA II (D):
c1932-1948. Leitz Elmar f3.5, 50mm lens; CFPS ½₀-⅟₅₀₀ s. Snr 71,200-358,650. Qty 52509.

R3*   Chrome: F–
Black: F

LEICA E (STANDARD):
c1932-1946. CFPS ½₀-⅟₅₀₀s. Snr 101,101-355,670. Qty 27,255.

R3*   F–

Postwar 1946 model with Wollensak Velostigmat 50mm f3.5 lens. Snr 355,001-355,650. Qty 650.

R4*   H

LEICA III (F):
c1933-1939. CFPS 1-⅟₅₀₀s. Snr 107,601-343,100. Qty 69,300..

R3*   Chrome: F–
Black: F

LEICA 250 (FF) REPORTER:
c1933. CFPS 1-⅟₅₀₀s. Snr 114,051-150,124. Qty 126(?).

R4*   J+

Leitz

Camera Directory

Leica III(F)

Leica 250(FF) Reporter

LEICA 250 (GG) REPORTER: c1942. CFPS 1-¹⁄₁₀₀₀s. Snr 150,125-353,800. Qty 824(?).

R4*   **J–**

LEICA IIIA (G): c1935-1950. CFPS 1-¹⁄₁₀₀₀s. Snr 156,201-357,200. Qty 92,687(?). Black

body appears on factory list, but no genuine example has been verified.

R2*   **Chrome: F+**

LEICA IIIB (G) – 1938: c1935-1950. CFPS 1-¹⁄₁₀₀₀s. Snr 240,001-368,563. Qty 32, 105.

R2*   **F–**

LEICA IIIC (1939-1945): CFPS, 1 – ¹⁄₁₀₀s, Snr 360,175-367,600, Qty, 33,750. After 1945, Snr 4,000,01-525,000, Qty 100,876.

CIVILIAN CAMERAS:

In chrome below Nr.400,000:   **F**

Above Nr.400,000:   **F–**

In blue-grey, with blue/grey body covering: **H–**

With "K" after the body SNR, standing for "Kugellager", meaning ballbearing. This special shutter was designed to operate in

Leica 250GG with Motor, c1942
Courtesy to 1996 Auction Team Breker, Köln

extremes of climatic conditions. In chrome, Qty 400: **H+**

in blue/grey: **H**

MILITARY CAMERAS:

With "Luftwaffen Eigentum" and "FL No.38079" blue-grey body only: **H**

complete with Summitar f2.0, 5cm lens, also engraved "Luftwaffen Eigentum" and "FLNo.38079" and "K" for Kugellager, in chrome and blue/grey: **H+**

Marked "HEER" (meaning "Army" with f3.5/5cm Elmar also marked "HEER": **H+**

(at auction these cameras can bring higher prices. It seems they get some collectors' blood boiling and the bidding goes sky high! One auction in autumn 1990 saw almost $4000 for this camera and lens combination, and again in April of 1991 the same price!)

LEICA IIID: c1940-1942. CFPS 1-⅟₁₀₀₀ s. Snr 360,002-360,134; 367,000-367,325. Qty 427. Similar to the Leica IIIc (1940-1946) with self-timer. An internal inspection is necessary to confirm a genuine Leica IIId camera.

R4* **I+**

LEICA IIC: c1948-1951. CFPS ⅟₃₀-⅟₅₀₀ s. Snr 440,000-451,000. Qty 11,000.

R3* **F–**

LEICA IC: c1949-1952. CFPS ⅟₃₀-⅟₅₀₀s. Snr 455,001-563,100. Qty 12,000.

R3* **F–**

LEICA IIIA "MONTE EN SARRE": c1950. Mfd in France on a Leica IIIa body. Late models had IIIf flash synch. Snr 359,xxx.

R4* **H+**

LEICA IIIF: c1950-1952. CFPS 1-⅟₁₀₀₀s. Black dial version: Snr 525,001-611,000. Qty 71,000.

R3* E+ Black **J**

RED DIAL VERSION: c1952-1954. Snr 615,000-685,000. Qty 54,000.

R3* **F–**

IIIF CANADA VERSION. Engr. Midland, Ontario

R4* **H–**

IIIF BLACK VERSION with black Elmar 50mm f3.5 lens.

R4* **J**

LEICA IIF: c1951-1952. Black dial version: CFPS ⅟₃₀-⅟₅₀₀s. Snr 451,000-574,000. Qty 8400(?).

R4* **F–**

RED DIAL VERSION: c1952-1957. CFPS ⅟₂₅-⅟₁₀₀₀s. Snr 574,000-851,000. Qty 15,240.

R4* **E+**

LEICA IF: c1952. Black dial version: CFPS ⅟₃₀-⅟₅₀₀s. Snr 562,293-564,200.

R4* **G**

RED DIAL VERSION: c1956. CFPS 1/25-1/500s. Snr 564,201-851,000.

R4* **F**

Leica IF

LEICA 72: c1954. CFPS 1-⅟₁₀₀₀s. Snr 357,301-357,500. Midland, Ontario version: qty 149.

The Leica 72 was the only screw half-frame 35mm camera marketed by Ernst Leitz. c1954.

R5*   **J**

Wetzlar, Germany version: Qty 33.

R5*   **J+**

LEICA IIIG: c1957-1960. CFPS 1-⅟₁₀₀₀ s. Snr 825,001-988,280. Qty, chrome version 41,589

R3*   **G**

LEICA IIIG SWEDISH MILITARY VERSION: black body with chrome Elmar 50mm f2.9 lens-both marked with Swedish three-crown emblem. Qty 125.

R5*   **J**

LEICA IG: c1958-1960. CFPS 1-⅟₁₀₀₀s. Qty 5,986. Snr 887,001-987,600.

R4*   **G**

LEICA M3: Intro-1954. CFPS 1-⅟₁₀₀₀s. Null series Snr 00xx, Snr 700,000-700,500. First 500:   **H–**

Double stroke: **F**

Serial numbers over 1,000,000:   **G**

Black: **H+**

Olive supplied to German army. c1954-1966.   **I+**

LEICA MP: CFPS 1-⅟₁₀₀₀s. With Leicavit black enamel version. Snr 12-150. Qty 139:

R4*   **J+**

Leica MP

Chrome version: Snr 1-11, and 151-450, qty 310, c1956-1957.

R4*   **J**

LEICA MP COUNTERFEIT: CFPS 1-⅟₁₀₀₀s. 5 counterfeit MP cameras were sold in the USA for $500-$1000 each (1972); one was resold for $2000 in Japan (it was later returned).

R4*   **G+**

LEICA M2: c1957-1967. CFPS 1-⅟₁₀₀₀ s. Snr 926,001-970,261. Button rewind release (early version). Chrome, qty 24,800.

R3*   **F+**

Leica M2 cut-away display model

Lever rewind release (late version) with self-timer. Snr 970,261-1,165,000. Chrome, qty 59,000(?).

R3*   **F+**

Black enamel, qty 1350(?).

R3*   **H**

Cut-away display model, qty $1000?

LEICA M2-M: c1956. CFPS 1-⅟₁₀₀₀s. Snr 1,163,771-1,164,046. Qty 275. Complete with motor:

R4*   **I+**

LEICA M1: CFPS 1-⅟₁₀₀₀s. Button rewind release (early version), Snr 950,001-966,729. Chrome, qty 1515(?)

R3*   **G**

Lever rewind release (late version), Snr966,730-1,102,900. Chrome, qty 7925(?):

R3*   **G**

Olive enamel, qty 325. c1959-1964.

R3*   **I**

LEICA MD: c1964-1966. CFPS 1-⅟₁₀₀₀s. Snr 1,102,501-1,160,820. Qty 3200 plus.

R3*   **G**

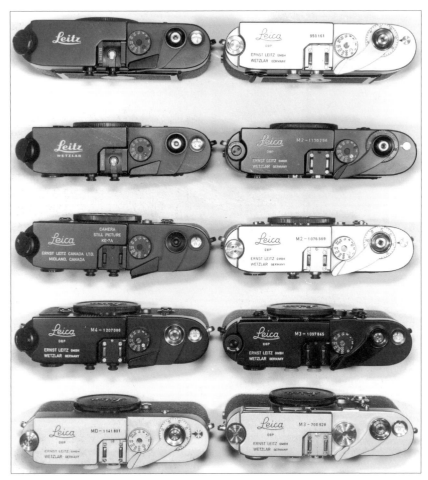

Ten different Leica 'M' cameras viewed from above: Left, top to bottom: MD-2, M4-2 (red dot), KE-7, M4 enamel, MD, Right, top to bottom: M1, M2, M2 chrome, M3, M3 chrome

LEICA M4 (1967):   CFPS 1-$\frac{1}{1000}$s. Snr 1,175,001-1,286,700. Qty chrome 47,260 plus.

R3*   **G**

Black enamel 4,590 plus.

R3*   **H+**

Military olive, qty 30 plus. c1967-1972.

R3*   **I–**

Leica M4

LEICA M4-M (MOTORDRIVE): Snr 1,206,xxx-(?). Complete with motor:

R4*   **I+**

LEICA M4 (1974): c1974-1975. CFPS 1-⅟₁₀₀₀s. Snr 1,380,000-(?). Qty black chrome, 5000 plus.

R3*   **G+**

FIFTIETH ANNIVERSARY LEICA M4, c1975. Wetzlar, Germany. Qty black chrome 1400.

R3*   **H**

FIFTIETH ANNIVERSARY LEICA M4, Midland, Canada. c1975. Qty black chrome, 350.

R3*   **H+**

LEICA M4-2: c1978. CFPS 1-⅟₁₀₀₀s. "Red-dot" version: **$2**.25k. £1.5k DM3.6k Midland, Canada version and Wetzlar, Germany version.

R3*   **G−**

LEICA MDA: c1966-1975. CFPS 1-⅟₁₀₀₀s. Snr 1,159,001-(?).

R3*   **G−**

LEICA MD-2: c1980. CFPS 1-⅟₁₀₀₀s. Body only:

R4*   **G**

Hologon lens, finder, and filter:

R4*   **I+**

LEICA M2-R: c1969-1970. CFPS 1-⅟₁₀₀₀s. Snr 1,248,201-1,250,200. Qty 2000.

R3*   **G+**

LEICA M5: c1971-1975. Leitz Summicron f2, 50mm lens; CFPS ½-⅟₁₀₀₀s. Snr 1,287,001-(?).

R3*   **G**

FIFTIETH ANNIVERSARY LEICA M5: c1975. Qty 1750. Black chrome version:

R3*   **H**

Chrome version:

R3*   **H**

LEICA KE-7A, U.S. ARMY, CAMERA-STILL PICTURE: c1972. Leitz Elcan f2, 50mm lens; CFPS 1-⅟₁₀₀₀s. Snr 1,294,xxx-(?). Qty released for the civilian market, 50(?) bodies; 70(?) Elcan lenses. Civilian version, with lens:

R4*   **I**

KE-7A with 50mm F2 lens; military version, with lens:

R4*   **I+**

The following six Leicas are not true classics in so far as they were manufactured during the past six years. But each was manufactured as a special edition to celebrate an event or anniversary and, as such, immediately became collectors' items. They are all based on the Leica M6, first made in 1984,

LEICA M6J: 1994. Body, shutter and meter as M6, but with a top plate copied from original M3, made in 1954. Made to mark 40 years of Leica cameras. Limited edition of 1,640.

R3*   **I**

RPS M6: 1994. Made to mark the centenary of the Royal Photographic Society. Top and base plates finished in satin chrome with matt black controls and top plate engraved with the RPS coat of arms. Limited edition of 100.

R3*   **I**

DANISH ROYAL WEDDING M6: 1995. Engraved with the Danish Royal Crest and the wedding date, 18th November 1995. Limited edition of 200.

R3*   **I**

ANTON BRUCKNER M6: 1996. Made to commemorate the 100th anniversary of the death of the Austrian composer, the camera is covered in grey-blue embossed iguana leather. Limited edition of 200, representing 20 cameras for each of Bruckner's 10 symphonies.

R3*   **I**

EIN STUCK M6: 1996. Made to mark the listing of Leica AG on the stock exchange. Covered in calf skin embossed with the Leica logo. Limited edition of 996.

R4*   **I**

JAGUAR M6: 1998. Commissioned by Jaguar to mark the 50th anniversary of the Jaguar XK120 sports car in 1948. Limited edition of 50 cameras, numbered XK1 to XK50.

R4*   **J**

LEICA CL: c1973-1975. Leitz Summicron f2, 40mm lens; CFPS ½-¹⁄₁₀₀₀s. Snr 1,300,001-(?).

R2*   **F+**

Fiftieth Anniversary Leica CL: qty black chrome, 1750. c1975. with lens;

R3*   **G+**

LEICAFLEX STANDARD: c1964-1968. Interchangeable bayonet mount; CFPS

1-½₀₀₀s. Snr 1,173,001-1,174,700. First SLR by Leitz. Chrome version:

R3* **F–**

black enamel version:

R3* **H–**

Leica R3 Electronic

LEICAFLEX SL: (EL152). c1968-1974. CFPS 1-½₀₀₀s. Snr 1,173,001-(?). Chrome:

R3* **F+**

Black:

R4* **G+**

LEICAFLEX SL2: (EL153). Leitz Summicron f2, 50mm lens; CFPS 1-1/2000 s.

Black:

R3* **G**

Chrome:

R3* **G+**

FIFTIETH ANNIVERSARY LEICAFLEX SL2. c1975. Qty black chrome, 1750.

Chrome H **Black H–**

LEICA R3 ELECTRONIC: c1977. Mfps 4-½₀₀₀ s. Body:

R3* **F–**

LEICA SCREW-MOUNT LENSES

21mm f4 Super Angulon lens:
Qty 1400(?). c1958-1963 **G+**
28mm f6.3 Hektor lens:
Qty 10,000(?). c1935-1953 **F–**
28mm f5.6 Summaron lens:
Qty 6200(?). c1955-1963 **F+**

33mm f3.5 Stemar lens: Complete outfit c1954-1957 **I+**
35mm f3.5 Elmar lens:
Qty 42,500(?). c1930-1950 **E–**
Nickel **E+**
35mm f3.5 Summaron lens:
Qty 80,000(?). c1949-1958 **E+**
35mm f2.8 Summaron lens:
Qty 52,000(?). c1958 **F+**
35mm f2 Summicron lens:
Qty 500(?). c1958 **G+**
50mm f3.5 Elmar lens:
Qty 360,000(?). c1926-1959 **D+**
Red scale **E+**
50mm f2.5 Hektor lens:
Qty 10,300(?). c1930-1939 **F**
50mm f2 Summar lens:
Qty 123,000(?). c1933-1939 **C+**
50mm f2 Rigid Summar lens:c1933-1939
G+ Nickel; **H–** Chrome.
50mm f1.5 Xenon lens:
Qty 6000(?). c1936-1949 **F–**
50mm f2 Summitar lens:
Qty 170,000(?). c1939-1953 **E–**
50mm f1.5 Summarit lens:
Qty 39,000(?). c1949-1960 **E+**
50mm f3.5 Wollensak Velostigmat lens:
c1947-1949 **G+**
50mm f2 Collapsible Summicron
lens:Qty61,000c1953-1961 **F–**
50mm f2 Rigid Summicron lens:
Qty 100(?). c1958-1962 **G+**
50mm f2 Compur Summicron lens and
shutter with lever **I**
50mm f2.8 Elmar lens: c1957-1962 **E–**

50mm f1.4 Summilux lens:
Qty 550(?). c1960-1963 **H+**

65mm f3.5 Elmar lens: c1960-1969.

Black **G–**

Chrome **F+**

73mm f1.9 Hektor lens:
Qty 7000(?). c1932-1940 **G–**

85mm f1.5 Summarex lens:
Qty 4000(?). c1949-1962.

Black **H+**

Chrome complete with lens hood and
caps **G+**

90mm f2 Summicron lens:
Qty 600(?). c1957-1962 **H–**

First version with removable shade **G+**

Second version with built-in lens shade.
(Original screw mount doesn't have red
dot at the base of the lens mount.) **G+**

90mm f4.5 Wollensak Velostigmat made
in USA: 1945-1950 **E–**

90mm f4 Elmar lens: Qty 114,000(?).
c1931-1964 **D+**

90mm f2.8 Elmarit lens:
Qty 2000(?). c1959-1962 **H**

90mm f2.2 Thambar lens: Qty 3000(?).
Disk shade and caps. c1935-1939. **I–**

without filter **H**

105mm f6.3 Mountain Elmar lens:
Qty 4000(?). **G+**

With shade and caps. c1932-1937. **G**

125mm f2.5 Hektor lens: Qty 3300(?).
c1954-1963. With shade and caps **G**

127mm f4.5 Wollensak Velostigmat lens;
made in USA **E+**

c1944-1951.

135mm f4.5 Elmar lens: Qty 5200(?).
c1930-1936. **F–**

135mm f4.5 Hektor lens: Qty 70,000(?).
c1933-1960 **E–**

135mm f4 Elmar lens: Qty 5000(?).
c1960. **F+**

180mm f2.8 Tele-Elmarit lens (bayonet

mount for Visoflex II, IIa and III):
c1965 **F+**

200mm f4.5 Telyt lens: Qty 11,500(?).
c1935-1960 **E+**

280mm f4.8 Telyt lens: c1961-1970 **E+**

400mm f5 Telyt lens: Qty 4000(?).
c1937-1967. **F**
With removable shade, **G+**
with built-in shade **G**

LEICA M-MOUNT LENSES

Hologon 15mm f8.0 lens with finder **I+**
Super Angulon 21mm f4.0 lens **G–**
Super Angulon 21mm f3.4 lens **G+**
Elmarit 21mm f2.8 lens **G+**
Elmarit (old style) 28mm f2.8 lens **F+**
Elmarit (new style) 28mm f2.8 lens **G+**
RF-Summicron 35mm f2.0 lens:
Chrome **F+**
400mm f5 Telyt lens: Qty 4000(?).
c1937-1967. black laquer **G+**
RF-Summaron 35mm f2.8 **G**
Summicron Chrome 35mm f2.0 lens **F+**
Summicron Black laquer 35mm f2.0
lens **H–**
Summaron 35mm f2.8 lens **F–**
Summaron 35mm f3.5 lens **E+**
Summilux 35mm f1.4 lens: **G–**
Summicron C 40mm f2.0 lens **E+**
Elmar 50mm f2.8 lens **E+**
Elmar 50mm f3.5 lens **E+**
Summarit 50mm f1.5 lens **F–**
Summicron Chrome Wetzlar 50mm f2.0
lens: Rigid **F–**
Summicron Chrome Collapsible 50mm
f2.0 lens **F–**
Summicron Black laquer Wetzlar 50mm
f2.0 lens **H–**
Dual Range Summicron 50mm f2.0 lens
with finder **F**
Summilux Black 50mm f1.4 lens **G–**
Summilux Chrome 50mm f1.4 lens **G–**
Noctilux 50mm f1.2 lens **H+**
Noctilux 50mm f1.0 lens **G+**
Summilux 75mm f1.4 lens: Chrome **G+**
Elmarit 90mm f2.8 lens **G–**

Elmar C 90mm f4.0 lens	**F–**
Tele Elmarit 90mm f2.8 lens	**G**
Elmar Rigid 90mm f4.0 lens	**E–**
Elmar Collapsible 90mm f4.0 lens	**F**
Summicron Black or Chrome 90mm f2.0 lens	**G–**
Summicron Black (new style) 90mm f2.0 lens	**G–**
Hektor 135mm f4.5 lens: Elmarit 135mm f2.8 lens	**E**
Tele Elmar 135mm f4.0 lens	**F+**
Summicron 50mm f2 lens, cutaway display model	**G**

LEICA REFLEX LENSES

Leica 15mm f3.8 R lens	**H+**
Leica 16mm f2.8 R lens	**G+**
Leica 19mm f2.8 R lens	**G**
Leica 21mm f4.0 R lens	**G+**
Leica 24mm f2.8 R lens	**G+**
Leica 28mm f2.8 R lens	**G–**
Leica 35mm f2.0 R lens	**F+**
Leica 35mm f2.8 R lens	**E+**
Leica PA-Curtigon 35mm f4 R lens	**J**
Leica 50mm f2 R lens (Canadian)	**E+**
Leica 50mm f1.4 R lens	**F+**
Leica 60mm f2.8 R lens	**G**
Leica 80mm f1.4 R lens	**G+**
Leica 90mm f2.8 R lens	**F+**
Leica 90mm f2 R lens	**F+**
Leica 100mm f4 R with mount	**F+**
Leica 135mm f2.8 R lens	**F**
Leica 180mm f3.4 APO lens	**G+**
Leica 250mm f4 R lens	**F**
Leica 180mm f2.8 R lens (Compact)	**G+**
Leica 180mm f2.8 R lens (Original)	**F+**
Leica 250mm f4 R lens lightweight	**G+**
Leica 350mm f4.8 R lens	**H**
Leica 400mm f6.8 R lens	**G**
Leica 500mm f8 Mirror-R lens	**G**
Leica 560mm f6.8 R lens	**G+**
Leica Angenieux P 45-90mm f2.8 lens	**G–**
Leica 35-70mm f3.5 R lens	**G–**
Leica 75-200mm f4.5 R lens	**G–**

Leica 2X Extender R lens	**F+**

LEICA REFLEX ACCESSORIES

Leica R4 Motor	**E–**
Leica R4 Winder	**D+**
Leica R4 Data Back	**D+**
Leica R4 Bellows	**F–**
Leicaflex Motor	**G–**
Megoflex Viewer (non-Leitz manufacture)	**F–**

Megoflex Viewer

GENERAL ACCESSORIES
Viewfinders:

Torpedo type: VISOR	**E+**
VISAX, VIUNA,VIZWO,VITRE	**E**
VIFUR	**E**
Other Universal Viewfinders:	
VIDOM, Black	**D+**
early	**E–**
Chrome	**D**
VIOOH, round body	**E–**
Earliest, unthreaded nose piece	**E–**
Later, pinched or sloped body	**D**
TUVOO, (28mm adaptor)	**E+**
Waist level viewfinders:	
AUFSU	**E+**
without shoe	**F–**
AYOOC, with swing lens 35mm	**F**
AHOOT, with swing lens 28mm	**F+**

Right angle viewfinders:

WINKO	**D+**
WINTU (in chrome or black)	**D+**

Optical viewfinders:

EARLY:

WEISU, 35mm, chrome	**E+** black **E+**
SUWOO, 50mm	**F**

LATER:

SBLOO, 35mm	**E**
SBOOI, 50mm	**D+**
SGOOD, 85mm	**F–**
SGVOO, 90mm	**D+**
SHOOC, 135mm	**D+**
SBKOO, 21mm	**E+**
SLOOZ, 28mm	**E+**
OIDYO, for Stereo Stemar	**F+**

Optical sportsfinder:

FOLDING

SUOOQ, 28mm	**F–**
SAIOO, 73mm, black or chrome	**F**
SEROO, 90mm, – black	**G**
SYEOO, 135mm, black or chrome	**E+**

NON-FOLDING.

SOODL, 50mm	**G–**
SOOAW, 73mm	**G**
SOOUT, SEVUE, 90mm	**E+**
SOOYV, 135mm	**E+**

Frame finders:

FOLDING

RASUK, 50mm & 90mm	**D**
RASUK, 35mm & 73mm	**D**
RASAL, 35mm, 73mm, 90mm, &135mm	**D+**
ROSOL, 50mm, 90mm, & 135mm	**D**

NON-FOLDING

SFTOO, 200mm	**D+**
TZOON/TZFOO, tube for 200mm	**C+**
SQTOO, 400mm	**E+**

Rangefinders:

FODIS, FOFER, long, only in black	**E–**
FOKOS, in black or chrome	**E**
HFOOK, same as FOKOS with mounting foot	**E+**

Reflex housing, complete units:

PLOOT	**D+**
VISOFLEX I	**D**
VISIFLEX II	**E–**
VISOFLEX III	**F–**

SMALL ACCESSORIES

Single exposure camera:

OLIGO/OLEYO with IBSOR shutter, H	
Self-timer: APDOO	**C–**
Slow-speed device: HEBOO	**E–**
Close-up device: NOOKY, NOOKY-HESUM	**C+**
Close-up device, 9cm: OMIFO	**F–**
Three filter turret	**E+**
Panorama head, 5cm (early) FIAMA	**D+**
Panorama head, interchangeable rings: FARUX	**D+**
De Mornay Budd Viewfinder (non-Leitz manufacture)	**E**

MOTORS AND WINDERS

MOOLY motor, one-speed	**G**
MOOLY motor, two speed	**D+**
MOOLY motor IIIc:	
black or chrome	**H+**
grey	**I–**
Rapid winder: SCNOO, chrome	**F+**
Rapid winder: SCNOO, black/nickel	**G–**
Rapid winder: SCNOO, IIIc, chrome	**G–**
Leicavit: SYOOM	**F**
Leicavit, M: SMYOM	**H–**
Leicavit, MP (black enamel)	**H+**
Remote winder: OOFRC	**H–**

Lennor Engineering Company
Chicago, Illinois, USA

DELTA STEREO: c1955. 35mm Stereo camera with optical VFR, fixed focus La Croix 50mm, f6.3 lenses, shutter speeds of ½₅-¹⁄₁₀₀s. plus B. Shutter marked for "shade" "normal" and "very bright". Blue or black plastic body with satin finished metal cover.

R2*   **D**

Leotax Camera Company
Japan. (see SHOWA)

LEADER: c1950. 35mm stereo camera. Leader Anastigmat 45mm f4.5 lenses; shutter TMBK ½₅-¹⁄₁₀₀ s. Mfd in Japan.

R3*   **C+**

Lucien Leroy, *Paris, France*

STEREO PANORAMIQUE LEROY: 1906, Metal stereo camera. Krauss 82mm, f9 Protar or similar lenses 6 x 13cm exp. Stereoscopic or panoramic pictures by rotating lens in centre of camera.

R3*   **F–**

L. Leullier, *Paris, France.*

STEREOCHROME: c1939. 35mm stereo camera. Boyer Saphir 40mm f3.5 fixed focus lens; guillotine shutter 1-¹⁄₃₀₀s.

R3*   **D**

SUMMUM: c1925. 6 x 13cm stereo camera. Boyer Saphir 85mm f4.5 lenses; Stereo Compur shutter 1-¹⁄₁₅₀s. Rising lens panel.

R3*   **E–**

SUMMUM-STERECHROME: c1950. 35mm stereo camera. Berthiot Flor f3.5 lens.

R4*   **F–**

S. J. Levi, *London, England*

THE PULLMAN DETECTIVE CAMERA: c1896. Stereo detective camera in shape of carved leather carrying case. Roller blind shutter; bellows focusing; 5" x 7" exp on plates.

R4*   **F+**

Levy-Roth, *Berlin, Germany*

MINIGRAPH: c1915. 35mm camera. Minigraph Anastigmat 54mm f3.5 or Trioplan f3 lens; flap shutter ¹⁄₅₀ s and T. 50 half-frame exp, 18 x 24mm on 35mm perforated film in special cassettes. First German 35mm camera; also used as contact printer or projector.

R4*   **G–**

W. & W.H. Lewis, *New York*

DAGUERREOTYPE CAMERA: c1855; Harrison lens (Petzval design). Most common type although it is still very rare is for ¹⁄₄ plate pictures. One of the first American cameras to use a bellows.

DAGUERREOTYPE CAMERA: c1855; Harrison or Holmes, Booth & Hayden Lenses. Overall physical appearance except for size is identical to the ¼ plate model.

R5*   **G+**

LEWIS WET PLATE CAMERA: c1862. Wet plate studio portrait camera. Exp up to 12" x 12" on wet plates.

R5*   **G+**

Lexa Manufacturing Co.
Melbourne, Australia

LEXA 20: Announced October, 1948, metal box camera for 6 x 9cm frames on 120 roll film, simple lens and shutter, a number of these cameras appeared in the mid 1980's, none, however, was complete with internal metal film carrier, leading to the assumption that production or other problems may have prevented the Lexa 20 from ever having been sold!

R3*   **B+**

L.F.O. & Co. *Paris, France*

LE FRANCEVILLE: c1908. Cardboard plate camera Meniscus lens; drop shutter; 4 x 4cm glass plates.

R3*   **D+**

V. LIEBE, *Paris, France*

MONOBLOC: c1920. 6 x 13cm stereo camera. Berthiot Flor 85mm f5.7 lenses; 6 speed shutter. Panoramic setting, rising front panel.

R3*   **E–**

Linex Corp., Division of Lionel Corp.
New York

LINEX: c1950. Subminiature 35mm stereo camera, f6 fixed focus lenses; shutter ⅛s. 8 pairs of stereo exp on 16mm film in special cassette. In the USA, prices are 50% lower. Outfit included camera, viewer and case.

R3*   **D**

Linhof Prazasions-Kamera-Werke GmbH
Munich, Germany.

LINHOF TECHNIKA IV: c1953. 4" x 5" folding press camera. Schneider Xenar f4.5 lens; Synchro Compur shutter 1 -⅟₅₀₀s, CRF.
R3* **G−**

LINHOF TECHNIKA III: 1946, black. 4" x 5" technical/press camera. Likely to be found with f4.5 Kenar lens.
R3* **F**

SPECIAL WIDEANGLE 65: 1961. Equipped with 65mm f8 Super Angulon. Two models: with Super Rolex back for 10 exp on 120, or Cine Rolex back for 50 exp on 70mm perforated film. First camera in 2¼x3¾-inch format to have this huge film capacity.
R3* **F**

Lippische Kamerafabrik Barntrup
Germany

FLEXORA: 1952. TLR with two lenses mounted on common lens board for focus link. Both are 75mm f3.5 Ennars. Prontor-S shutter. Parallax correction marks in viewfinder. Pull up wire frame finder for eye-level use.
R3* **C+**

ROLLOP: c1955. Rollei-type TLR; 6 x 6cm exp on 120 roll film; 75mm Ennagon f3.5 lens; SVS shutter;
R3* **D**

LITHOSCOPE: c1904. 8 x 17cm stereo camera. Aplanat lens; 4-speed shutter; 8 x 17cm exp.
R4* **F**

J. Lizars, *Glasgow, Scotland*

CHALLENGE DAYSPOOL TROPICAL CAMERA: c1905. Beck Symlens lens; Bausch & Lomb shutter. Teak and brass, red leather bellows.
R4* **F+**

CHALLENGE DELUXE: c1910. 4" x 5" tropical camera. Dagor 150mm lens; 4" x 5" exp on plates. Polished mahogany, brass fittings.

R4*   **G–**

CHALLENGE VIEW CAMERA: c1898. Compact folding ½ plate view camera; Lizars Kram Triple Convertible lens and shutter; front and rear tilt and swing; built-in brass tripod base; plumb bob; double ext bellows to 17"; Spanish mahogany construction. C 1898.

R4*   **E+**

CHALLENGE HAND CAMERA, MODEL C: c1902. Goerz Double Anastigmat Dagor Series III 150mm f6.8 lens; Bausch & Lomb shutter, up to ¹⁄₁₀₀s.

R4*   **E–**

CHALLENGE STEREO CAMERA, MODEL B: c1900. Aldis Anastigmat lenses; Bausch & Lomb Stereo shutter; 3¼" x 6¾" exp on plates.

R4*   **F**

CHALLENGE STEREO DAYSPOOL: Mahogany stereo camera. Aldis Anastigmat lenses; Bausch & Lomb shutter; pair of 3¼" x 3¼" exp on roll film or plates. Mahogany finish, brass hardware. c1905.

R4*   **G–**

Lollier, *Paris, France*

STEREOGRAPH (STEREO MARINE): c1903-1923. Binocular-type detective camera; revolving diaphragm 60mm f8 lens; guillotine shutter, T, I. 45 x 107mm exp. on plates.

R5*   **H**

London Stereoscopic Company
London, England

ARTIST HAND CAMERA: c1889. Black-band 4¼" x 3¼" lens. Mahogany finish.

R4*   **H–**

BINOCULAR: c1890's; Jumelle-style stereo camera. 12 exp 1½ x 2½ in plate magazine; Krauss-Zeiss f6.3 lenses;

R4*   **E+**

CARLTON: c1895. Ross Goerz Double Anastigmat 6" f7.7 lens; variable speed guillotine shutter 1-¹⁄₈₀s. 4" x 5" exp on plates – changed by gravity feed.

R4*   **F**

THE DISPATCH DETECTIVE CAMERA: c1888. Wooden box-type detective camera. Shutter to ¹⁄₁₀₀s. 8 x 10.5cm or 10.5 x 12.5cm exp on plates.

R4*   **NSR**

IMPROVED ARTIST REFLEX: c1910. Voigtlander 15cm f4.5 Heliar lens; CFPS. Rising front panel; tropical mahogany finish; green leather bellows.

R5*   **H–**

JUMELLE CAPSA DE MARIA: c1910. Zeiss Protar 85mm f8 lenses.

R3*   **E–**

THE KING'S OWN TROPICAL CAMERA: c1907. Dagor lens; Volute shutter. Roll film or plates. Teak construction, brass fittings.

R5*   **G+**

Lumiere & Cie, *Lyons, France*

ELJY: c1937. 35mm miniature camera. Folding VFR Lumiere Lypar 40mm f3.5 lens; Lumiere shutter ¹⁄₁₀-¹⁄₂₀₀s. 8 exp, 24 x 36mm on unperforated 35mm film in special cassettes; pull-out lens mount; scale focusing.

R2*   **D–**

ELJY-CLUB: c1951. 35mm miniature camera. Optical VFR mounted in top housing, early models with built-in extinction meter, while later models sport an accessory shoe. Lumiere Lypar 40mm f3.5 lens; Lumiere shutter 1-¹⁄₆₀s. 8 exp, 24 x 36mm on unperforated 35mm film in special cassettes; pull-out lens mount; scale focusing. available in Grey, yellow, red, green, white and Blue. (worth 100% more) in addition to a "Luxus" model covered in crocodile skin! (worth 200% more).

R3*   **D**

LUMICLUB: c1950. Som Berthiot Flor 75mm f3.5 lens. Built-in extinction meter; telescoping lens mount; eye-level and waist-level finders; rapid wind lever. 6 x 6cm or 4.5 x 6cm format. Made from dies prepared by the Pontiac company before going bankrupt, this camera was *originally* intended to use perforated 70mm film, less than 1000 cameras are said to have been made.

R4*   **E**

LUMIERE 6 X 6: c1952. Folding camera for 6 x 6cm or 4.5 x 6cm format on roll film. 80mm f4.5 Spector lens. Built-in extinction meter; telescoping lens mount; eye-level and waist-level finders; rapid wind lever. Sharing some of the features of the more expensive Lumiclub, this camera also shared the same short life. About 1000 cameras are thought to have been made.

R4*   **D+**

LE PERIPHOT c1910; panoramic camera of unusual design powered by a clockworks motor. The film is placed on the inside of a cylinder remaining stationary whilst the lens rotates around the cylinder. Pictures

covering a full 360 degrees are possible. Very rare, really in the unavailable category.

U   **I+**

STERELUX LUMIERE: c1947, folding stereo camera. Nacor Boyer Anastigmat 80mm f6.3 lenses; shutter ½₅-½₀₀s; 6 x 13cm exp on 116 roll film. c1920.

R3*   **E+**

LUMIX: c1947. Post WWII folding roll film camera for 8 negatives 6 x 9 on 120 film, simple lens, and one speed shutter.

R2*   **B–**

LUDAX: c1950. Folding roll film camera for 8 negatives 6 x 9 on 620 film, 105mm, f6.3 Fidor lens, shutter speeds ½₀-½₀₀s, folding optical finder, body release. Made in large numbers.

R2*   **A–**

LUMIREX: c1950. Folding roll film camera for 8 negatives 6 x 9 on 620 film. 105mm, f6.3 Fidor lens, or 105mm/f4.5 Spector lens; shutter speeds ½₀-½₀₀s; self-timer folding optical finder; body release. Along with the Ludax, made in large numbers.

R2*   **B**

LUMIREX III: c1949. Folding roll film camera for 8 negatives 6 x 9 on 620 film. 100mm, f3.5 Angenieux type 11 lens; Prontor S shutter 1-½₀₀s; optical finder built-into the top housing along with an extinc-

tion meter; body release. (At the end of production, a cheaper version having 105mm, f4.5 Spector lens and Sido shutter ½₀ – ½₀₀s was offered for the budget minded.)

R3*   **C–**

LUMIERE 6.5 X 11: c1950. Folding camera for 6.5 x 11 negs on 616 film. Folding optical finder; 125mm/f4.5 Berthiot or Topaz lens; shutter speeds 1-½₀₀s. Thought to be the last camera made for 616 film, and probably one of the few made for that film with a coated lens and flash synch.

R4*   **C+**

OPTAX: October 1948- Spring 1949. 35mm black plastic camera with folding optical VFR. 50mm, f3.5 Lypar lens in collapsible mount; shutter speeds ½₀-½₀₀s. Marking Lumiére's entry into the standard 35mm market, this first model Optax lasted only a few months in production.

R4*   **D+**

OPTAX 2ND MODEL: c1948. 35mm black plastic camera with tubular optical VFR. 40mm, f3.5 Altar lens in fixed mount, shutter speeds ½₀-½₀₀s. A continuation of the Optax line, made in large quantities and much less rare than the original Optax.

R2*   **C+**

STARTER: c1955. 35mm black plastic camera with grey plastic top housing. 45mm, f3.5 Lypar lens; shutter speeds ½₅-½₅₀s; made to capture a share of the "low" end of the camera market.

R2*   **B+**

ELAX: c1938. Pre WWII high quality precision folding camera for 3 x 4cm negatives on 127 film. 50mm, f3.5 Flor lens, lever wind mfps speeds 4 – ½₀₀₀s, Optical finder said to have been made by Leitz.

R4*   **F**

ELAX II: c1948. Post WWII version of the Elax (LM108). Thought to have been made from stocks of pre-war parts. 50mm, f3.5 Flor lens, lever wind mfps 4-¼₀₀₀S. Has a satin chrome top plate. The high price of this camera on the French market killed it.

R4*   **F**

LUMIFLEX: c1951. Black plastic twin lens reflex camera for 6 x 6 format. The 80mm, f4.5 Spector lens is not coupled to the viewing lens; shutter speeds 1-¼₀₀S; built-in extinction meter.

R2*   **B+**

LUMIREFLEX: c1950. Black plastic twin lens reflex. 80mm, f3.4 Spector taking lens coupled to the 80mm, f3.5 viewing lens; Atos shutter, speeds 1-¼₀₀S. Did not sell well and was quickly taken off the market.

R4*   **C+**

LUTAC: c1949. Simple black plastic roll film camera, very similar to the Ultra-Fex.

R2*   **A**

Reference Notes

_____

_____

_____

_____

_____

_____

_____

_____

_____

_____

_____

_____

_____

_____

_____

_____

_____

_____

_____

_____

_____

H. Mackenstein Fabricant
Paris, France.

LA FRANCIE: c1906. 45 x 107mm Press-type stereo camera. Max Balbreck Aplanatic lenses; variable speed guillotine shutter; Red leather bellows.

R3*   **E–**

Photo Livre

MACKENSTEIN TAILBOARD CAMERA: c1890. 13cm x 18cm Compact view camera. Grande Angle Gibauet brass lens; Mahogany finish; brass fittings.

R4*   **F**

PHOTO LIVRE: c1890. Book-type detective camera. Rectilinear 60mm f12 lens; guillotine shutter; 24 exp, 40 x 40mm on plates.

R5*   **H–**

STEREO JUMELLE: c1895. 6.5 x 9cm stereo camera. Goerz Dagor 110mm f6.3 lens; variable speed guillotine shutter; Magazine for 12 plates.

R3*   **E–**

Macris-Boucher *Paris, France*

NIL MELIOR STEREO: c1920. 6 x 13cm Stereo camera. Boyer Saphir or E. Krauss Tessar f4.5 lens; 7 speed spring shutter; Magazine holds 12 plates, 6 x 13cm.

R*   **D+**

HACOFLEX: c1950. 6 x 6cm TLR cmera. Japanese Copy of Rolleicord. 80mm f3.5 Tri-Lansar lens in 1-¹⁄₃₀₀ shutter.

R3*   **D**

H. Mader, *Isny, Germany.*

THE INVICIBEL: c1898. Aplanat 180mm f6 lens; double action rotary shutter; 13 x 18cm plates.
R4*   **G**

Magic Introduction Co. *New York.*

PHOTORET CAMERA: c1893. Watch-type detective camera. Meniscus lens; front-of-lens shutter; 6 exp, ½"x½" on 1¾"diameter plates. Outfit, with box and film tin. Camera only.
R4*   **F+**

Mamiya Camera Co. Ltd. *Tokyo, Japan*

MAMIYAFLEX: 1957. TLR camera. Mamiya-Sekor 105mm f3.5 coated lens, interchangeable lens mount; Seikosha-S 1-⅕₀₀s. 12 exp, 6 x 6cm on 120 roll film.
R2*   **E–**

MAMIYAFLEX JUNIOR: 1948. 6 x 6cm TLR camera; Neocon 75mm f3.5 lens in Stamina shutter. B. 1-⅕₀₀s.
R4   **C+**

Mamiyaflex

Mamiyaflex Junior

MAMIYA PISTOL CAMERA: c1954, pistol-type detective camera. 50mm lens; 6 square diaphragm stops; single speed shutter. 65 exp, 18 x 24mm on 35mm film. Made for Japanese police training.

R5*   **H+**

MAMIYA SIX: c1958. 2¼" x 2¼" RFR camera. T.S.M. Anastigmat 75mm f3.5 lens; Copal shutter 1-½₀₀s. 12 exp, 6 x 6cm on 120 roll film. Rfr coupled to movable film plane; lens remains stationary. Many variations of lens/shutter combinations found. All are worth about the same.

R2*   **D–**

MAMIYA 16: 1949. The first of several 16mm cameras made by this company. 25mm f3.5 Cute fixed focus lens. Guillotine shutter 1/25-1/100s. 10x14mm images.

R2*   **C**

MAMIYA 16 POLICE CAMERA: 1949. Made for Japanese Police Intelligence Division. As original model, but in black with detachable waist-level viewfinder. Rarest of all Mamiya 16 cameras.

R4*   **D**

MAMIYA 16 SUPER (MODEL III): c1953. 25mm f3.5 lens; shutter ½-½₀₀s. 32 x 14mm exp on 16mm film in special cassettes. Slide-in yellow filter.

R2*   **C**

MAMIYA 16 AUTOMATIC: 1959. Subminiature for 10x14mm images on 16mm film. 25mm f2.8 Sekor lens, focused by slide on body. Shutter 1/5-1/200s. Built-in yellow filter. Build-in meter with match needle automation.

R2*   **C**

MAMIYA FAMILY: c1962. 35mm SLR with leaf shutter. The first leaf-shutter SLR with instant-return mirror and instant re-opening shutter. 48mm f2.8 Sekor lens; shutter speeds ⅛ – ½₅₀s.

R3*   **C+**

MAMIYA AUTO-LUX 35: c1963. 35mm SLR camera. Co-operative design with the Canon company, derived from Mamiya Family. Practically identical externaly to the Canon Canonex, but with important

internal differences. 48mm f2.8 Mamiya sekor lens; leaf shutter.

R3*   **C+**

MAMIYA/SEKOR 1000 TL: c1960. 35mm SLR camera. FPS. B. 1-$\frac{1}{1000}$s. Interchangeable 55mm f1.4 Auto Mamiya Sekor. First Mamiya with TTL metering.

R2*   **C+**

MAMMY: c1953. Black plastic body for a 35mm camera using unsprocketed paper-backed film. Anastigmat f3.5 44mm lens. Three zone focusing with zones indicated in the viewfinder, a first for this innovation. The least expensive camera made by the Mamiya Camera Company.

R3*   **D**

MAMIYA MAGAZINE 35: c1957. 35mm camera with coupled rangefinder, Mamiya-Sekor f/2.8, 50mm. Shutter Seikosha 1-1/500s. Unusual feature was fully interchangeable magazine backs. Several different films could be used. Very few production cameras have used this feature,

the only earlier one being the Kodak Ektra of 1941.

R3*   **C+**

ARGUS 260 AUTOMATIC: c1964. Camera for 126 Instamatic film (first of Japanese manufacture) for the Argus Camera Co. in the U.S. where it was exported. Cintar lens, fixed shutter speed 1/1000s. Exposure set automatically by coupled selenium cell. Built-in miniature flashbulb and pop-up reflector.

R2*   **B+**

MAMIYAFLEX C: 1956. Mamiya's move into professional TLRs. 12 exp on 120. One of the few TLRs with interchangeable lenses. Standard lens was 105mm f3.5 Sekor. Seikosha-MX shutter 1-1/400s + B. Shutter interchangeable with the lens. Also available: 85mm and 135mm lenses.

R2*   **D**

MAMIYAFLEX C2: 1957. TLR for 12 exp on 120. Interchangeable 10.5cm f3.5 Sekor with Seikosha-S shutter 1-1/500s +B.

R2*   **D**

MAMIYAFLEX C3: 1962. TLR for 12 exp on 120. Interchangeable 80mm f2.8 Sekor with Seikosha-S shutter 1-1/500s + B.

R2*   **C+**

This is just a small selection of the earlier Mamiyaflex range of interchangeable lens TLRs. The company went on to offer various upgrades during the 1960s that included the C33 (1965), C22 (1966), C220 (1968) and C330 (1969).

Mamiyaflex C3

MFAP, Pontiac
(Manufacture Française d'Appareils Photographique)
Paris, France & Casablanca, Morocco

PONTIAC: c1938; 6 x 9cm folding roll film camera with thermaplastic bodies offered in two models. With simple lens and single speed shutter, or front focusing 105mm, f4.5 Berthiot, in MFAP shutter with speeds of ½₅ -¹⁄₁₀₀s, plus B. Closely resembles earlier Gallus and Ebner cameras of the same design.

R3*   **C–**

PONTIAC: c1938, 6 x 9cm folding roll film camera offered in brown bakelite as a "Luxus" model. Front focusing 105mm, f4.5 Berthiot, in MFAP shutter with speeds of ½₅ – ¹⁄₁₀₀s, plus B. Brown bellows.

R4*   **C+**

PONTIAC: 16 exposures on 127 roll film. Polished aluminIum body, CFPS with speeds ½₅-¹⁄₅₀₀s. SOM Berthiot Flor 50mm, f3.5 lens in collapsible mount. At first glance the lens and mount look very much like Leica. Don't be fooled into trying to unscrew the lens. You will only end up hurting your hand, and possibly damaging the lens!

R3*   **E–**

PONTIAC BLOC METAL 41: c1941-1946. 6 x 9 folding roll film camera of cast aluminium. Produced during the second World War in quite large numbers. Various 105mm, f4.5 lens and shutter combinations. The lack of quality construction material made necessary the rethinking of some design ideas, such as the use of textures body castings painted black instead of the more traditional leather covered bodies. These cameras often suffer from poor bellows and rusting nickel plated parts. The "41" indicates the year of introduction.

R2*   **C**

BLOC METAL 45: c1946. 6 x 9cm folding roll film camera with cast aluminium body. Early cameras have 105mm, f4.5 Flor Berthiot or Trylor Roussel lens in Prontor II shutter, speeds of 1-½₀₀s, textured bodies painted black while later cameras have "leather" covering, and a Gitzo shutter labelled "Zotic-l".

R3*   **C**

BLOC METAL 145: c1946. 6 x 9cm folding roll film camera with cast aluminium body. 105mm, f4.5 Flor Berthiot lens in a Compur Rapid shutter marked "licence française", speeds of 1-¹⁄₄₀₀s. Said to have been assembled in France from earlier Compur parts shipped from Germany.

R4*   **D**

LYNX-1: c1943, 3 x 4cm exp. on 127 film; between the lens shutter with speeds of ½₅-¹⁄₂₀₀s; front focusing 50mm, f3.5 Flor

COMPUR LYNX: c1946. 3 x 4cm on 127 film, fixed mount front focusing 50mm, f3.5Flor Berthiot lens; rim set Compur shutter speeds of 1-⅟₃₀₀s; cast aluminium body with textured finish. Very few made.

R4*   **E+**

STANDARD LYNX: c1948. 3 x 4cm on 127 film, CFPS ⅟₂₅-⅟₃₀₀s; fixed mount 40mm, f3.5 Flor Berthiot or Roussel lens; cast aluminium body with textured finish.

R4*   **E+**

Berthiot lens; cast aluminium body, with textured finish, often painted black. Perhaps less than 100 made.

R4*   **D**

LYNX-II: c1946. 3 x 4cm on 127 film, CFPS ⅟₂₅-⅟₃₀₀s; some cameras have self-timer; front focusing 50mm, f2.8 or f3.5 Flor Berthiot, or f2.9 Angénieux lens in collapsible mount; cast aluminium body with textured finish; often painted black. Perhaps more than 100,000 made.

R3*   **D**

LYNX DE NUIT (NIGHT LYNX): c1946. 3 x 4cm on 127 film, CFPS ⅟₂₅-⅟₃₀₀s, coated 50mm, f1.5 Flor Berthiot lens; cast aluminium body with textured finish. Very few made.

R4*   **E+**

SUPER LYNX-I: c1948. 35mm VFR camera. With cast aluminium body; CFPS ⅟₂₅-⅟₃₀₀s coupled to film advance; 50mm, f3.5 or f2.8 Flor Berthiot lens in collapsible mount; polished or painted textured body. Unlike earlier 127 roll film Lynx's, these 35mm cameras were clearly marked on the camera body above the lens.

R4*   **D+**

SUPER LYNX "STANDARD": c1950. 35mm VFR camera. With cast aluminium

body; CFPS ½s-⅕₀₀s coupled to film advance; 35mm, f3.5 Flor Berthiot wide angle lens in fixed mount; painted textured body.

R4*   **E+**

SUPER LYNX-ll: C.1953. 35mm VFR camera. With cast aluminium body; CFPS ½s-⅕₀₀s coupled to film advance; self-timer; 50mm, f3.5 or f2.8 Flor Berthiot lens in collapsible interchangeable bayonet mount; painted textured body; 28mm, f3.3 Angulor , 35mm, f3.5 Flor, 75mm, f2.8 Flor, and 90mm, f3.5 Flor accessory lenses were made for this camera. Marked "made in French Morocco" or "made in Morocco". Along with a few Super Lynx-l and Super Lynx cameras, perhaps the only camera made in Africa. A complete outfit increases the price 200%.

R4*   **F–**

SUPER LYNX: c1953. 35mm VFR camera. With cast aluminium body; CFPS ½s-⅕₀₀s coupled to film advance, 50mm, f3.5 Flor Berthiot lens in fixed collapsible mount; painted textured body. Made at the same time as the Super Lynx-ll, and post-dating the Super Lynx-l. This camera was a simplified version, without the self timer available on the Super Lynx-ll.

R4*   **E+**

BABY LYNX: c1951. 35mm VFR camera. With between the lens shutter, speeds of 1- ⅕₀₀s; front focusing 50mm, f3.5 or 2.8 Flor Berthiot lens in collapsible mount; cast aluminium body with black covering. Made in Paris and then in Morocco, early

cameras were not marked with the name. Brown body covering adds 100%.

R3*   **E–**

BABY STANDARD: c1953. 35mm camera. With between the lens shutter, speeds of ½s-½₀₀s; front focusing 50mm, f3.9 Trylor Roussel lens in collapsible mount; cast aluminium body with black covering. Sold by Central-Photo in France, a cheaper version of the Baby Lynx with a simpler Pronto shutter.

R4*   **D**

MIOM *(Manufacture d'Isolents et d'Objects Moulés)*
France

PHOTAX: c1938. Bakelite VFR camera. For 6 x 9cm or 6 x 4.5cm on roll film; simple lens and shutter; metal focusing ring with handle; similar to the Rex camera made in Argentina.

R3*   **B+**

JACKY: c1950, as PF100) but for the name.

R3*   **B+**

PHOTAX BLINDE: c1950. Bakelite VFR camera. For 6 x 9cm frames on roll film; curved film plane; simple lens and shutter; redesigned body now without metal focusing ring. Called Blindé (armoured) because of the bakelite lens/shutter cover delivered with the camera. Also made in Spain under the Fotex name.

R2*   **B+**

C. Marelli
Rosario, Argentina

MECABOX: c1950. "Rustic" metal box camera. For 6 x 9cm on roll film; simple lens and shutter.

R4*   **C–**

Mecabox

Marion & Co., Ltd.
London, England

MARION'S METAL MINIATURE CAMERA: c1888. Petzval-type 55mm f5.6 lens; rack and pinion focusing; guillotine drop shutter; 30 x 30mm dry plates.

R4*   **H**

MARION'S RADIAL DETECTIVE CAMERA: c1890. Quarter plate mahogany box camera. Plate changing mechanism.

R4*   **F+**

NO. 1 ACADEMY CAMERA: c1885. TLR camera. Petzval-type 2" f5 lens; rotary shutter in front of lens; eye-level finder. 12 plates in magazine. One of the earliest TLR cameras.

R5*   **H+**

CURLEW I: c1948. Self erecting Folding Camera. 9 X 6cm exp on 120 roll film.

R1*   **C–**

CURLEW II: c1948. As Curlew I above.

R1*   **C**

CURLEW III: c1948. As Curlew II above.

R1*   **C+**

KING PENGUIN: c1953. Self erecting roll film camera. Eight exp on 120 roll film; B.& I. Shutter.

R1*   **B–**

PENGUIN: c1953. Self erecting roll film camera.

R1*   **A**

PEREGRINE I: (mid 1950's),6 X 6cm exp on 120 roll film. F3.5, 80mm lens; shutter 1-$\frac{1}{400}$S.B.

R1*   **D–**

PEREGRINE II: (Mid 1950's). As Peregrine I above with Taylor-Hobson f2.8 lens.

R2*   **D+**

PEREGINE III: (Mid 1950's). As Peregrine II above with Taylor-Hobson Adotal f2.8 lens and coupled rangefinder.

R3*   **E+**

RAVEN: (Mid 1950's). Folding Bakelite roll-film camera. Leather effect finish on body; folding finder; f4.5, 100mm Kershaw lens.

R2*   **C+**

LE PARCEL DETECTIVE CAMERA: c1885. Wrapped-package type detective camera. Fixed focus double lens; simple shutter. 8 x 10.5cm plates in simple holder.

R4*   **I**

Soho
Tropical Reflex

RAJAR NO.6: c1929-? One of the earliest Bakelite folding body cameras.

R1*   **B+**

SOHO REFLEX: c1905. All models were made by A. Kershaw and Sons, of Leeds, for Marion, incorporating Kershaw's mirror patent of 1904.

R2*   **E+**

SOHO TROPICAL REFLEX: c1928-39. 3¼" x 4¼" tropical SLR. Dallmeyer 6½", f4.5 lens; CFPS ¹⁄₁₆-¹⁄₈₀₀s. Teak wood, brass fittings; red leather bellows. C.1928-39.

R4*   **H+**

Marshall Optical Works
Tokyo, Japan

MARSHALL PRESS CAMERA: 1966. 120/220 roll film for 6x9cm images. Nikkor f3.5, 105mm lens coupled to rangefinder. Accessory lenses were available. Shutter 1-

1/500s. A very sturdy camera which was designed by Mr Seiichi Mamiya, who founded the Mamiya Optical Company.

R3*   **G**

G. Mason & Co.
Glasgow, Scotland

G. MASON & CO. TAILBOARD CAMERA: Brass-bound mahogany field camera. Ross lens; rotating disc stops; 4¾" x 6½" tilting ground glass back; vertical and horizontal adjustment on lens board.

R3*   **F–**

Mast Development Co.
Iowa.

LUCK STRIKE: c1949-1950. Cigarette package type detective camera. 17.5mm, f2.7 lens; shutter ¹⁄₁₅, ¹⁄₁₂₅, ¹⁄₅₀₀s and B.

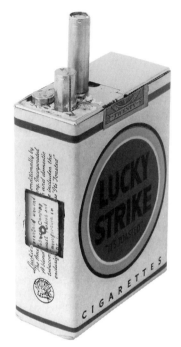

Designed to fit inside a Lucky Strike cigarette package. Three false cigarettes controlled the diaphragm, focus and shutter trip. Mfd for the U.S. Signal Corps.
R5* **NSR**

Mattioli

LA BELLE GAMINE: c1920. 45 x 107mm stereo camera. Balbreck Rapid Rectilinear lenses; 3-speed guillotine shutter. 45 x 107mm exp.
R4* **E–**

Mawson *Newcastle, England*

MAWSON: c1865. Stereo wet plate camera. Achromat lens; cylindrical diaphragm; rectangular bellows; archimedian screw focus adjustment; 3¼" x 6¾" exp on wet plates.
R5* **H+**

Mazo *Paris, France.*

LE GRAPHOSTEREOCHROME: c1910. Colour stereo folding camera. Special slide-in filters for Autochrome and Tri-colour processes. Sliding plateholder for three plates. 10 x 15cm exp and 6 x 13cm stereo exp. Designed by Abbe Tauleigne.
R5* **H–**

JUMELLE MAZO: c1900. Double Triplet 135mm, f6.5 lens; 5 speed shutter; 12 quarter plates.
R3* **D**

MEAGHER *London, England*

MEAGHER SLIDING BOX WET PLATE CAMERA: c1858. Lens with brass barrel; rack and pinion focusing; 7" x 7" ground glass. Mahogany finish.
R5* **H–**

MEAGHER STEREO CAMERA: c1860. Collapsible box-type stereo camera. Ross landscape lens.
R5* **I–**

MEAGHER WET PLATE: c1860. Dallmeyer Rectilinear lens with waterhouse stops. Ground glass focusing. Mahogany finish, maroon leather bellows.
R5* **G**

Laboratorias MC. *Argentina*

JOYA: c1950. Bakelite TLR box camera. For 6 x 6cm frames on 120 or 620 film, simple lens and shutter.
R4* **B+**

MEIKAI: 35mm TLR camera. M.K. Anastigmat 50mm, f3.8 lens. Mfd in Japan.
R3* **D–**

Joya

Meguro Kogaku Kogyo Co., Ltd.
Japan.

Melcon original with non original Canon lens

MELCON ORIGINAL: c1955. 35mm RFR csmera. CFPS, 1-⅟₅₀₀s; interchangeable Leica-type screw mount f3.5, 50mm Hexar (Konika) lens or f2.0, 50mm Nikkor-H lens. Hinged back. Less than 2000 cameras were produced, with the first two digits of the serial number giving the year of production. Quite rare.

R4*   **G–**

MELCON-II: c1957. 35mm RFR camera. CFPS, 1 – ⅟₅₀₀ sec; interchangeable Leica-type screw mount f2.0, 50mm Nikkor-H lens. Hinged back. Very few cameras were produced. This camera looks more like a Contax or Nikon than the previous model. Extremely rare.

R5*   **G+**

Mejori Optical Works
Japan

HONOR S1 (first version). c1956. 35mm camera. CFPS, 1 – ⅟₅₀₀S; seperate RFR/VFR windows; diopter adjustment. Screw mount Hexar f3.5, 50mm lens. This camera is quite similar to the Ichicon 35 camera from the Dai-ichi Optical Works.

R2*   **G**

HONOR S1 (second version). c1957. 35mm camera. CFPS, 1 – ⅟₁₀₀₀S; seperate RFR/VFR windows; diopter adjustment. Screw mount Honor f1.9, 50mm lens. Quite rare, this camera is an improved version of the Honor S1, with the addition of ⅟₁₀₀₀ sec to the shutter speeds.

R4*   **G**

Mentor Werke
Dresden, Germany

MENTOR: c1914-1931. Press-type stereo camera. Tessar 90mm, f4.5 lenses with coupled diaphragms and coupled helicoid focusing. Rising front; panoramic exp. 6 x 13cm exp.

R3*   **E+**

Meopta *Prerov,*
Czechoslovakia

(There are now two countries, the Czech Republic & the Republic of Slovakia - Instruments made prior to

the breakup of the country will continue to be to considered as having been "Made in Czechoslovakia."

MEOPTA was founded in 1946 as a united enterprise for the production of optics and precision mechanics. With the communist takeover in 1948, the firm was seized by the government becoming a state organization. Meopta had been created by the unification of a number of Czech optical manufacturers including Optikotechna, Eta, Sonet, Srb & Sty, Loschner, Bradac Brothers Co., and J. Suchanek. It was a very large operation making products for both the military and civilian markets with factories in Prague, Brno, Prerov, Hynicice, and Bratislava. In the 1970's camera production ceased when the military equipment area was expanded. As expert glassmakers, the Czechs always had a good supply of optical glasses and were considered the main source of precision optics within the old Eastern bloc.

A long awaited master list of Meopta cameras with dates of manufacture will reportedly be produced in the near future. Hopefully this will end some ongoing disagreements about production dates. The most common Meopta

cameras found in the West, are probably the Flexaret with the sub-miniature Mikroma running a close second. It is a possibility that the rarity rating on some cameras will drop with the complete opening of the country.

MIKROMA: c1946. Subminiature camera. For 11mm x 14mm size negatives on single perforated 16mm film. Four-speed shutter ½s-¹⁄₂₀₀s. Designed before WWII, but only produced from 1946.

R3*   **D**

MIKROMA II: c1964. Subminiature camera. Mirar 20mm, f3.5 lens; shutter ⅛-¹⁄₄₀₀s; with brown or green body covering. C.1964.

R2*   **D**

STEREO MIKROMA: c1965. Subminiature stereo camera. Mirar 25mm, f3.5

lenses; shutter ⅕-¹⁄₁₀₀s. 12 to 14 stereo exp on single perforation 16mm film. Viewers are still available in Czechoslovakia.

R2*   **E–**

STEREO MIKROMA II: c1970. Subminiature stereo camera. Mirar 25mm, f3.5 lenses; shutter ⅕-¹⁄₁₀₀s. 12 to 14 stereo exp on single perforation 16mm film. As first model but with improved film transport and shutter cocking systems.

R2*   **E–**

MIKRONETTE: c1945 Subminiature camera. For 240 exposures 11mmx14mm size on single perforated 16mm film. Four speed shutter ¹⁄₂₅-¹⁄₂₀₀s. Designed before WWII, and made by Optikotechna in limited numbers for the military.

R5*   **H–**

STEREO 35: c1970. Cream coloured stereo camera for 35mm film, but yielding about 80 Viewmaster size stereo pairs from a 36 exposure roll of film. Fixed focus Mirar f3.5, 25mm lenses in a simple shutter. These cameras were hard to sell,

and eventually went to state owned discount shops where they were sold out. Rare.

R4*   **D+**

OPEMA (II): c1955-60. 35mm CRF camera. CFPS, ¹⁄₂₅ – ¹⁄₅₀₀; combined RFR/VFR window; screw mount f3.5, f2.8, or f2.0, 45mm lenses. Removable back; cassette to cassette film transport. Considered by some to be a Leica copy, the Opema uses a smaller diameter screw thread than Leica. Do not try to force your Leitz lenses, you are only asking for trouble!

R3*   **E–**

OPEMA (I): c1954-59. 35mm CRF camera. CFPS, ¹⁄₂₅-¹⁄₅₀₀; as Opema II, but without RFR. Screw mount f3.5, f2.8, or f2.0, 45mm lenses. Removable back; cassette to cassette film transport.

R4*   **E–**

MILONA: c1946-50. Well made folding camera for 6 x 6 or 6 x 4.5 negatives on 120 roll film. Mirar f4.5, 80mm lens in Prontor II or Prontor S shutter. Scale

Opema (I)

focusing from 1M. Built-in slide for tilting lens to straighten converging lines when photographing buildings from a low angle. Quite rare.

R4*   **D+**

MILONA II: c1951-56. Folding camera for 6 x 6 or 6 x 4.5 negatives on 120 roll film. Mirar f3.5, 80mm lens in Prontor S shutter. Same lens tilting feature as Milona. Quite rare.

R4*   **D+**

ISKRA: c1951-56. Folding camera for 6 x 6 or 6 x 4.5 negatives on 120 roll film. Mirar f3.5, 80mm lens in Prontor S shutter. **WITHOUT** lens tilting feature. (Not to be confused with the Soviet "Iskra" which is a copy of Agfa.) Quite rare.

R4*   **C+**

MAGNOLA: c1947-53. Ground glass focusing folding metal bodied view camera. For 13 x 18cm negatives; Compound type shutter with Belar f4.5, 210 lens, three built-in levels; lens tilts and shifts. According to a factory source, this camera was exported.

R4*   **F**

FLEXARET: (ORIGINAL) c1945. Twin lens reflex camera. For 6 x 6 negatives on 120 roll film. Uncoated Mirar f4.5, 80mm taking lens in Prontor II shutter Optikotechna Anastigmat f3, 80mm viewing lens. Knob advance not coupled to shutter cocking; no provisions for double exposure prevention. Made by Opitkotechna before merging with Meopta in 1946. Quite rare.

R4*   **D**

FLEXARET II: c1946-47. TLR. camera for 6 x 6 negatives on 120 roll film. Mirar f4.5, 80mm taking lens in Prontor II shutter. Anastigmat f3, 80mm viewing lens. Knob advance not coupled to shutter cocking; no provisions for double exposure prevention. Made after merger into Meopta. Tran-

sition models still have Optikotechna marked on the lenses, but not on the camera body.

R3*   **C+**

FLEXARET III: c1948-50.TLR camera for 6 x 6 negatives on 120 roll film. Coated Mirar f3.5, 80mm taking lens in Prontor S or Metax shutter. Anastigmat f3, 80mm viewing lens; crank advance coupled to shutter cocking; automatic frame counting double exposure prevention. The only crank advance model.

R3*   **C+**

FLEXARET IV: c1950-57. TLR camera for 6 x 6 negatives on 120 roll film. Coated Belar f3.5, 80mm taking lens in Prontor SVS or Metax shutter. Anastigmat f3, 80mm viewing lens. Knob advance coupled to shutter cocking; automatic frame counting double exposure prevention. First model with depth of field scale built-into the focusing handle. Easily recognised by its strange body mounted shutter release. Quite common.

R2* C+

Flexaret VI

FLEXARET V: c1958-59 TLR camera for 6 x 6 negatives on 120 roll film. Coated Belar f3.5/80mm taking lens in Prontor SVS shutter. Anastigmat f3, 80mm viewing lens. Knob advance coupled to shutter cocking; automatic frame counting double exposure prevention. Redesigned front; focusing lever and shutter release.

R2* C+

FLEXARET VA: c1959-61. TLR Camera for 6 x 6 negatives on 120 roll film. Coated Belar f3.5, 80mm taking lens in Prontor SVS shutter. Anastigmat f3, 80mm viewing lens. Knob advance coupled to shutter cocking; automatic frame counting; double exposure prevention. Provision for using 35mm film with the appropriate adaptor. This is the first model with this

feature. (Price given is for the camera complete with 35mm adaptor set.)

R2* C+

FLEXARET VI: c1961-67. Grey covered body twin lens reflex camera for 6 x 6 negatives on 120 roll film. Coated Belar f3.5, 80mm taking lens in Prontor SVS shutter. Belar f3.5, 80mm viewing lens. Knob advance coupled to shutter cocking; automatic frame counting double exposure prevention; provision for using 35mm film with the appropriate adaptor. (Price given is for the camera complete with 35mm adaptor set -30% without adaptor).

R3* D–

FLEXARET VII: c1966-71. Grey covered body twin lens reflex camera for 6 x 6 negatives on 120 roll film. Coated Belar f3.5, 80mm taking lens in Prontor SVS shutter. Belar f3.8, 80mm viewing lens. Knob advance coupled to shutter cocking; automatic frame counting double exposure prevention; provision for using 35mm film with the appropriate adaptor. The last of the Flexarets. (Price given is for the camera complete with 35mm adaptor set (-30% without adaptor).

R3* D

OPTINETA: c1959. 35mm VFR camera. Front element focusing, coated f3, 45mm Belar lens in Metax shutter.

R3* B+

ETARETA: 1947-48. 35mm VFR camera front-cell focusing coated f3.5, 5cm Etar II lens in collapsible mount; Etaxa shutter ¹⁄₁₀ – ¹⁄₂₀₀s; marked "Eta Praha" on the lens, and "made in Czechoslovakia" on the front of the camera body.

R3* C–

SPEKTARETA: c1939. "The smallest three-colour camera in the world" (according to the National Technical Museum in Prague). Three exposures made at the same time through red, green, and blue filters to

Etareta

produce three colour seperation negatives. 12 sets of negatives 24mm x 24mm per 36 exposure roll. f2.9, 70mm Spektar lens in Compur shutter, 1 - ½₅₀s CRF; parallax correcting VFR. Made by Optikotechna, very rare.

R5*   **NSR**

COLOURETA: c1939. Three-colour camera, without CRF. Helical focusing Spektar f2.9, 70mm lens in Compur shutter, 1 - ½₅₀s. 12 sets of negatives 24mm x 24mm per 36 exposure roll. Made by Optikotechna, very rare.

R5*   **NSR**

META: c1956? Simple 35mm VFR camera. F3.5, 63mm Belar lens in focusing mount; Metax shutter, 1 - ¼₀₀s; marked "Meta" on the front of the top plate. Not produced in large numbers, quite rare.

R4*   **D**

META II: c1957? With added coupled RFR. F3.5, 63mm Belar lens; Metax shutter, 1 - ¼₀₀s. Marked "Meta" on the top plate, quite rare.

R4*   **E–**

META III; 1959? 35mm camera. With coupled RFR and interchangeable lenses; f3.5, 35mm Meopta S.O. lens in breech mount; Metax behind-the-lens shutter, 1 - ¼₀₀s; very Voightländer Prominant in appearance; was never made in large scale production and may exist only in proto-type form. No information is available concerning accessory lenses.

R5*   **G**

KAMERAD: c1936. Metal TLR for 6 x 6 exposures on 120 roll film. f3.9, 7.5cm Bellar from Ernst Ludwig Optical works, Dresden, are used for both lenses. Prontor II shutter, 1 - ¹⁄₇₅s; knob film transport with automatic frame counting. Made by the Bradéc Brothers, Hovorcovice (near Prague).

R5*   **D+**

KAMERAD MII: c1936. Metal TLR for 6 x 6 exposures on 120 roll film. f2.9, 7.5cm Trioplan lenses are used for both viewing and taking lenses. Compur shutter 1 - ½₅₀s; knob film transport with automatic frame counting. Made by the Bradéc Brothers, Hovorcovice (near Prague).

R5*   **E–**

AUTOFLEX: c1938. Metal TLR for 6 x 6 negatives on 120 roll film. f2.9, 7.5cm Trioplan lenses are used for both viewing and taking lenses. Compur shutter 1 - ½₅₀s; knob film transport with automatic frame counting. Made by Optikotechna. Rare.

R4*   **D–**

Autoflex

OPTIFLEX: c1938. Metal TLR for 6 x 6 negatives on 120 roll film. F2.9, 7.5cm Mirar lenses are used for both viewing and taking lenses. Compur shutter 1 – ½₂₅₀s; knob film transport with automatic frame counting. Made by Optikotechna. Rare.

R5*   **D–**

VEGA: c1950's. Simple 35mm VFR camera with cassette to cassette film transport. Collapsible f3.5 or f4.5 50mm lens (Druoptar or Etar) in Etaxa, Chrontax, Metax, or "no-name" shutters; with or without accessory shoe. Made by Druopta, Prague.

R3*   **C+**

DRUOFLEX I: c1950's. Bakelite TLR in the style of Lubitel, which is itself a loose copy of Voightländer Brilliant, for 6 x 6 exposures on 120 roll film. Body by Atak. Nonfocusing VFR; front cell focusing taking lens; f6.3, 75mm Druoptar in Chrontax shutter, ⅒ – ½₀₀s. Made by Druopta, Prague.

R3*   **B+**

FOKAFLEX: c1950's. Bakelite TLR for 6 x 6 exposures on 120 roll film. Boxier than the Druoflex, with unusual two piece back. Fixed focus "special" lens; Fokar 2 shutter, ½₅ – ½₀₀s. Made by Foka.

R4*   **C–**

RIX: c1950's. Bakelite TLR camera. Smoother body than the Druoflex; grey painted metal front and focusing hood; for 6 x 6 exposures on 120 roll film. Nonfocusing VFR, fixed focus fll taking lens in Fokar shutter, ½₅ – ½₅s. Made by Foka. Rare.

R4*   **C–**

PIONYR I: c1950's. Bakelite VFR camera. For 6 x 6cm or 6 x 4.5cm frames on roll film, simple lens and shutter. Made by Dufa, near Prague.

R3*   **C**

PIONYR II: c1950's. With focusing. Copied by the Chinese as the "Great Leap" camera.

R3*   **C**

MEPHISTO CAMERA: c1900. Meniscus lens, exp controlled by lens cap. 5 exp on plates. Mfd in Germany.

R5*   **G–**

STEREO MIKROMA II: c1970. Subminiature 16mm stereo camera. Mirar lenses, 25mm f3.5; shutter 1/5-1/400s. Available in several colours, green being the most common. The stereo images were usually mounted in a disc very similar to a system still used in the U.S. called "Viewmaster."

R2*   **E**

Below: Stereo Mikroma II.

Metropolitan Supply
Chicago, Illinois

THE KING CAMERA: Miniature cardboard camera. 2" x 2" x 3½" exp on glass plates.
R3* **D+**

Micro Precision Products
Surrey, England

MICROCORD: c1952. TLR camrea. 6 x 6cm, 12 exp on 120 roll film; Ross Xpres f3.5, 75mm lens; Prontor SVS 1-300s, shutter.
R1* **D–**

MICROFLEX: c1959; 6 x 6cm TLR camera. F3.5, 77mm lens in Prontor SVS shutter.
R2* **E**

MPP PRESS CAMERA: c.1950. Introduced as a technical camera and improved to make a press camera. Front panel with a 2¼-inch diameter aperture to accommodate range of lenses. Wray self-capping FP shutter with 3 tensions and 6 slit widths, 1-1/1000s + B & T.

Microcord

Double extension Rise and cross movements. Ranegfinder coupled.
R3* **D**

D. Millard & Co.
Cincinnati, Ohio

ROBINSON'S PATENT PHOTOGRAPH ALBUM: c1865. Carte-de-visite photos

Robinson's Album and Photographicon

Mimosa

MIMOSA II: c1948. Meritar 50mm f2.9 lens; Velax shutter ⅒-¹⁄₂₀₀s.

R3*   **D**

mounted on a fabric belt; displayed by turning knobs.

R4*   **E**

ROBINSON'S PHOTOGRAPHICON: c1865. Carte-de-visite photograph viewer. Early hand-coloured stencil design. Patent April 11th. 1865.

R4*   **E+**

T. Miller
Manchester, England

ADELPHI DETECTIVE CAMERA: c1899. Box-type detective camera.

R3*   **E–**

Mimosa Cameras, Germany.

MIMOSA I: c1947. 35mm box-type camera. Meyer Trioplan 50mm f2.9 lens; Compur-Rapid 1-¹⁄₅₀₀s.

R4*   **D**

Minolta – Chiyoda Kogaku Seiko Co., Ltd.
Osaka, Japan

KONAN 16 AUTOMAT: c1952. Rokkor 25mm f3.5 lens.

R3*   **D+**

BEST MODEL 1: 1934. Unusual folding camera that used three telescopic boxes in place of bellows. 75mm f8 fixed focus Coronar Anastigmat. Marble shutter 1/25-1/100s + B & T. Also known as the Minolta Vest. (Camera sometimes gets incorrectly referred to as the Marble because of the prominence of the shutter name.) Early use of plastic in body. Dual format for 8 & 16 exp on 127.

R3*   **D**

BEST MODEL II: Similar to Model I with 75mm f5.6 front focusing lens.

R3*   **D**

BEST MODEL III: Similar to Model II with 75mm f4.5 lens.

R3*   **D**

Minolta 16PS

MINOLTA 16 MG: 1966. 20mm f2.8 Rokkor. Shutter 1/30-1/250s. Match-needle metering.

R2*   **B**

MINOLTA 16 MG-S: 1969. Image size changed to 12x17mm. 23mm f2.8 Rokkor. Shutter 1/30-1/500s. Match needle metering.

R2*   **B**

MINOLTA 16 QT: 1972. Similar to MG-S, but shutter 1/30-1/250s. Auto metering.

R2*   **B+**

Best Model II

MINOLTA 16 MODEL I: 1957. Subminiature for 10x14mm images on 16mm. 25mm f3.5 Rokkor Shutter 1/25-1/200s. Push-pull Minox-style film advance. Common in chrome, rarer in gold, black, blue, red & green.

R2*   **B**

MINOLTA 16 MODEL II: 1960. Similar to first model, but with 22mm f2.8 lens and shutter 1/30-1/500s + B. Fixed focus, but with supplementary lenses for close-ups to 30 in.

R2*   **B**

MINOLTA 16 MODEL P: 1960. Simpler version with only 1/100s shutter. Symbols for aperture setting.

R2*   **B**

MINOLTA 16EE: 1962. Similar to Model II plus auto exposure via Selenium cell.

R2*   **B**

MINOLTA 16PS: 1964. Similar to Model P, but with added shutter speed 1/30s for flash.

R2*   **B+**

MINOLTA AUTO PRESS: c1935. 6 x 9cm Press camera. Promar Anastigmat Nippon 100mm f3.5 lens; Crown Rapid shutter 1-1/400s; CRF; 6 x 9cm exp on cut film and film pack.

R3*   **F–**

MINOLTA 35 I: c1947. 35mm camera. CFPS, 1 – 1/500 sec; combined Rfr/Vfr window; self-timer; unusual 24mm x 32mm frame size known as "Nippon" size, and also used by Nikon, is found on both the "Original" and type "B" cameras. Screw mount Super Rokkor F2.8, 45mm lens. 24 x 33mm frame size was used on the type "C" camera, and a 24 x 34mm frame on the type "D" and "E" cameras. Types "C", "D", and "E" though rare, bring roughly 50% of the price of the original and type "B" cameras.

R4* F   **ORIGINAL F+**

MINOLTA 35 MODEL II: c1953. 35mm camera. CFPS, 1 – ⅟₅₀₀s; combined Rfr/Vfr window; self-timer; 24mm x 34mm frame size. Screw mount Super Rokkor f2.8, 45mm or Super Rokkor f2.0, 5cm lens. This is the most common of the Minolta Leica copies.

R2*   **E+**

MINOLTA 35 MODEL IIB: c1958. CFPS, 1 – ⅟₅₀₀s; combined RfR/VfR window; self-timer; 24mm x 36mm frame size. Screw mount Super Rokkor f1.8, 5cm lens. This was the first Minolta to use the standard 24mm x 36mm frame size, and the last Minolta Leica copy. Though not particularly rare this camera is still valuable as a Leica copy.

R3*   **F–**

MINOLTA A: 1955. First Minolta to be exported. 35mm RFR camera. 45mm f3.5 Chiyoko Rokkor. Unusual shutter speed control is wheel protruding from top plate. Speeds 1-1/300s + B. 45mm f3.5 Chiyoko Rokkor

R3*   **F**

MINOLTA A5: 1961. 35mm CRF camera, more conventionally styled than the original Minolta A. 45mm f2.8 Rokkor. Optiper shutter 1-1/1000s + B. X & M synch.

R3*   **B**

MINOLTA AL: 1961. CRF 35mm camera. Unusual focusing system moves both lens and between-lens shutter together in a helical focusing mount. 45mm f2 Rokkor. Optiper Citizen MLT shutter 1-1/1000s. Shutter and aperture controls linked for match needle metering.

R3*   **B**

MINOLTA UNIOMAT: 1961. Fully auto 35mm CRF camera. 45mm f2.8 Rokkor. Optiper 'Brain' shutter, 1/8-1/100s. Shutter speeds and apertures connected to built in meter for match needle metering. Manual override if needed.

R3*   **B**

MINOLTAFLEX: c1936. TLR Camera. For 6 x 6cm exp on roll film; the first Japanese TLR; marked only "Minolta" on the front, Promar f3.5, 75mm taking lens among others; Minolta viewing lens; shutter 1 – ⅟₃₀₀s.

R3*   **E**

MINOLTAFLEX II: c1950. First post-war Minoltaflex; similar to Rokkor 75mm f3.5 lens in S-Konan shutter B.1-⅟₅₀₀s. See page 326.

R3*   **E**

Minoltaflex

Minoltaflex II

MINOLTA CLE: 1980. Cfps, 1 - ¹⁄₁₀₀₀s, electronically controlled; combined Rfr/Vfr window; "M" type bayonet mount Minolta Rokkor f2.0, 40mm lens. The limited edition model available in gold, increases the price by a factor of three.

R2*   **F**
               GOLD MODEL G

Minolta CLE

Accessory lenses for Minolta CLE

28mm/f2.8 lens:	**F**
90mm/f4.0 lens:	**E**

MINOLTA XM: (**XK** in USA)-(**X-I** in Japan). C.1973. System 35mm SLR camera. Electronic MFPS 1-¹⁄₂₀₀₀, titanium blades. Interchangeable view-finders; shutter coupled to SPD-TTL meter; Auto shutter speeds 16s ¹⁄₂₀₀₀s.

R2*   **E+**

MINOLTA AC101 COURREGES: 1983. "Designer" version of Minolta Disc Camera. f2.8, 12.5mm fixed focus lens. Strobe and exposure completely automatic. Shutter speed range 1/100-1/200s.

R3*   **C**

MINOLTA AUTOPAK 500: 1966. 126 camera with fixed 38mm Minolta Rokkor f2.8 lens. Zone-focusing. Fully programmed

Minolta AC101 Courreges

Minolta Zoom SLR MkII

shutter coupled to selenium exposure meter. Shutter operates at 1/90s.

R1*   **A**

MINOLTA HI-MATIC F: 1972. 35mm rf camera, Rokkor f2.7, 38mm lens. Seikosha shutter programmed to operate 4s to 1/720s. Available in chrome or black.

R2   **B+**

MINOLTA 110 ZOOM: 1976. First SLR 110 format. Auto exposure via CdS meter. Rokkor Macro lens 25-50mm f4.5. Shutter 10 seconds to 1/1000s.

R2*   **C**

MINOLTA ZOOM SLR MKII: 1979. Complete restyle of the Model I to look more like a miniature 35mm SLR. 25-67mm f3.5 Zoom Rokkor incorporating macro focusing. Aperture priority automation with apertures set by dial on top plate.

R2*   **D**

MINOLTA DISC 7: 1983. Fitted with a f2.8, 12.5mm fixed focus lens. Strobe and exposure control completely automatic. An unusual feature was the small mirror in front of the camera. An individual could take their own picture by framing themselves in the mirror and using the camera's self timer.

R1*   **A+**

MINOLTA SR-1: 1959. Manual control 35mm SLR. Optional Selenium meter. FP shutter 1-/500s. Synch speed 1/50s.

R2*   **C**

MINOLTA SR-2: 1958. Similar to SR-1 with 1-1/1000s and higher synch speed of 1/100s.

R2*   **D**

MINOLTA SR3: 1961. Similar to SR-2 with detachable Selenium meter and split image rangefinder.

R2*   **D**

MINOLTA SR-7: Similar to SR-3 but with built-in CdS meter for manual non TTL metering. Synch speed reduced to 1/60s.

R2* **D**

MINOLTA SRT-100: 1971. Minolta's first 35mm SLR with TTL metering. Incorporated Minolta's contrast light metering system.

R2* **C**

MINOLTA: XD-7: 1977. Come to be known as the world's first multi-mode 35mm SLR, offering shutter priority, aperture priority and manual modes, although the Savoyflex Automatique offered similar in the late 1950s. Viewfinder information via LEDs. Shutter 1-1/1000s. Synch at 1/100s. Multi-exposure capabilities.

R2* Chrome **E**

MINOLTA 7000: 1985. First 35mm SLR with body-integral autofocus. Exposure modes include shutter priority, aperture priority, manual, standard programme, wide programme and tele programme. Auto program selection takes data from autofocus lenses and translates date for most appropriate exposure mode.

R2* **D**

Note: Minolta made many more SLRs in the 1970s and 1980s, some with only minor variations in specification. They included models such as the SRM, SRT101, SRT303, SRT100b, SRT101b, SRT303b, SR-T MC-II, SRT SC-II, X-7A, X-

Minolta 7000

9, X-370, X-300, X-370s, X-500, X-700, XD-5, XE-5, XE-1, XG-1, XG-2, XG-S, XG-A, XG-M, XM and XK Motor. It is also worth noting that many of these names were subtly changed for American and Japanese markets. Full details and specifications of all these models can be found in the book Japanese 35mm SLR Cameras by Bill Hansen and Michael Dierdorff, published by Hove Books.

Minox *Geissen, West Germany*

For further information see Spy Camera, The Minox Story by Morris Moses, Hove Collectors Books, 1990.

MINOX I: c1938. Subminiature detective camera; Minostigmat 15mm f3.5 fixed aperture, 3 element lens; guillotine, front-of-lens shutter ½ -¹⁄₁₀₀₀s. 8 x 11mm exp on 9.5mm film in special cassettes. Snr 1-20,000. The original Minox was made from stainless steel; later models were made from aluminium. Valsts Electro-Techniska Fabrika, Riga, Latvia.

R3*   **F+**

MINOX I "RIGA": c1940-1941 and again 1944-1945. The two periods during which Riga was occupied by Russia during WWII. These "Russian Rigas" are engraved "Made in USSR" on the back of the camera.

R4*   **G–**

MINOX B: c1958-1972; Subminiature detective camera; 15mm f3.5 lens; shutter ½-¹⁄₁₀₀₀s; coupled light meter; two filters. Chrome version:

R2*   **D+**

Black version: Very few in Gold, at the following price guide.

R3*   **H+**

MINOX BL: c1976, subminiature camera; 15mm f3.5 lens; shutter ½-¹⁄₁₀₀₀s. Coupled CdS exp meter. Chrome.

R2*   **E**

MINOX C: c1976, subminiature detective camera; 15mm f3.5 lens; electronic shutter 10s-¹⁄₁₀₀₀s; coupled to CdS exp meter for auto exp control with manual override.

R3* Chrome model   **E**
R3* Black model   **E+**

MINOX IIIS: subminiature camera; 15mm f3.5 lens; shutter ½-¹⁄₁₀₀₀ s. Chrome model;

R3*   **E+**

Black model;   **F**

Gold model;   **H–**

MINOX LX: c1978; subminiature camera; new curved to fit the finger shutter release next to focusing dial; Three LED's next to shutter dial; both dials have milled edges; shutter to ¹⁄₂₀₀₀s.; Black or chrome finish;

R1*   **F–**

MINOX EC: c1981; Subminiature camera; f5.6 fixed focus lens; shutter release button coloured plastic; no parallax markings on Vfr.; plastic body normaly black, very few white bodies;

R1*   **D**

All prices are for cameras with chain and case or with Riga case.

Minox Accessories;

Tripod	**C**
tripod clamp	**B**
Bulb flash	**B**
Binocular attachment	**B+**

MIRANDA CAMERA COMPANY
Tokyo, Japan.

In 1946, the Orion Camera Company, predecessor of the Miranda Camera Company, Ltd., was established in

Tokyo. Although the company did manufacture a limited line of photographic related products, its main function was as a service centre for professional photographic equipment.

Among the products made by Orion were a special adaptor which allowed the use of Contax or Nikon mount lenses on Leica type screw mount bodies, and the "Focabell" close-up bellows.

In 1956, the Orion Company adopted the well known "Miranda" name.

In all, a total of 36 different basic camera models were produced before financial difficulties forced the company to close its doors in 1977. Though much maligned in the past as poor cousins to their more popular competitors, Miranda has seen recent growth in collector interest, to the point of the establishment of a Miranda Collectors Club.

Adam Geschwind, from Sydney, Australia, has put together the information which appears here, along with the photographs. He welcomes correspondence concerning all models of Miranda cameras, especially serial number information on both cameras and lenses for use in compiling a computer data base.

He may be reached at: Adam Geschwind, PO Box 28, Waverly Post Office, Waverly, Sydney, Australia, 2024

MIRAX: 1950 marked "Orion Camera Company" later version marked "Miranda Camera Company", mirror box with interchangeable reflex finder (after 1953), which allowed upright TTL viewing on Nikon, Contax, Leica, Canon, or similar 35mm camera bodies.

R4*   **E**

ORION T: c1954, 35mm SLR with interchangeable Zunow f1.9, 5cm lens in 44mm screw mount. CPFS 1 - ½₀₀s; removable pentaprism; knob wind; non-instant return

mirror; top and front mounted shutter release; chrome body; serial numbers 554xxx to 556xxx. (black body adds at least 100%) **Miranda Identification hint:** Many models contain the model designation before the serial number, on the back of the camera.

R4*   **G+**

MIRANDA T: c1956. 35mm SLR with interchangeable Zunow f1.9, 5cm, Arco f2.4, 5cm, Soligar-Miranda f1.9, 5cm or Miranda f1.9, 5cm lens in 44mm screw mount. CPFS 1 – ⅟₅₀₀s; removable pentaprism; knob wind; non-instant return mirror; top and front mounted shutter release; chrome body; serial number 558xxx. (camera illustrated shows rare black trim on advance, rewind, shutter speed, and film counter dials.)

R3*   **F**

MIRANDA S: c1959. 35mm SLR with interchangeable Soligar-Miranda f2.8/5cm lens in 44mm screw mount, ⅟₃₀-⅟₅₀₀s. Removable WL finder, pentaprism sold as accessory; knob wind; non-instant return mirror; **ONLY FRONT MOUNTED SHUTTER RELEASE,** chrome body, serial number 59xxxx.

R3*   **E–**

MIRANDA ST: c1959. 35mm SLR with interchangeable Soligar-Miranda f2.8, 5cm

lens in 44mm screw mount. 1 -⅟₅₀₀s; removable WL finder; pentaprism accessory; knob wind; non-instant return mirror; top and front mounted shutter release; chrome body; serial number 55xxxx to 56xxxx.

R3*   **E+**

MIRANDA A: c1957; 35mm SLR with interchangeable preset Soligar-Miranda f1.9, 5cm lens in either 44mm screw mount or external semi-automatic (similar to Exakta) bayonet mount. 1 -⅟₁₀₀₀s; removable finder; **LEVER WIND**; non-instant return mirror; top and front mounted shutter release; chrome body; serial number 57xxxx.

R2*   **D+**

MIRANDA AII: c1957. Small frame counter dial, and red triangles marked at 20 and 36 exposures.

R3*   **G+**

MIRANDA B: c1957. 35mm SLR with interchangeable, black finished Prominar-Miranda f1.9, 5cm external semi-automatic lens in bayonet mount . CFPS 1 -⅟₁₀₀₀s; removable finder; lever wind; instant return mirror; top and front mounted shutter release; chrome body; serial number 58xxxx.

R2*   **D+**

MIRANDA C: c1959. 35mm SLR with interchangeable black finished Prominar-Miranda f1.9, 5cm external semi-automatic lens in bayonet mount . CFPS 1 -⅟₁₀₀₀s;

removable finder; lever wind; instant return mirror; self-timer; top and front mounted shutter release; chrome body; serial number 60xxxx.

R2*   **D+**

MIRANDA D: c1960. 35mm SLR with interchangeable preset Soligor-Miranda f2.8, 5cm lens in 44mm screw mount, or bayonet mount Soligor-Miranda or Prominar-Miranda f1.9, 5cm external semi-automatic lens. CFPS 1-⅟₅₀₀s; lever wind; instant return mirror; new rounded body shape; **FRONT SHUTTER RELEASE ONLY**; serial number 63xxxx (sequence shared by Automex III (MI3xx)

R1*   **D**

MIRANDA DR: c1962. 35mm SLR with interchangeable preset Soligor-Miranda f2.8, 5cm lens in 44mm screw mount, or bayonet mount Soligor-Miranda f1.9, 5cm external semi-automatic lens. CFPS 1-⅟₅₀₀s; lever wind; instant return mirror; new rounded body shape; **FRONT SHUTTER RELEASE ONLY**; split image focusing screen standard; both "Miranda" and "MIRANDA" logos are found; no model designation on the camera back; red leatherette covering on the frame counter dial; serial number 65xxxx to 66xxxx.

R2*   **D**

MIRANDA F: c1963. 35mm SLR with interchangeable Auto Miranda f1.9, 5cm len., CFPS 1 - ⅟₁₀₀₀s, (a few cameras in this series had 1/500s top speed); depth of field

preview button on the camera body; no model designation on the camera back; serial number 67xxxx to 70xxxx. (Black body add 100%).

R1*   **D**

MIRANDA FM: (MI312): c1963. As model "F" (MI311), but for **NON-TTL** CDS pentaprism. Any "F" body could be updated simply by adding this metered pentaprism. (Black body add 100%).

R2*   **D**

MIRANDA FT: c1967. As model "F", but for **UNCOUPLED TTL** CDS pentaprism. Any "F" body could be updated simply by adding this metered pentaprism. (Black body add 100%).

R2*   **D**

MIRANDA FV: c1966. As model "F" (MI311), but for no depth of field preview, and removable shutterspeed dial, for use when using clip on meter. Model designation on the camera front; serial number 72xxxx. (Black body add 100%).

R2*   **D**

MIRANDA FvM: c1966. As model "Fv", but for **NON-TTL** CDS meter prism. Model designation "Fv" on the camera front; any "Fv" camera body could be up-dated simply by adding this metered prism(Black body add 100%).

R2*   **D**

MIRANDA FvT: c1967. As model "Fv" (MI314), but for uncoupled **TTL** CDS meter prism. Model designation "Fv" on the camera front; "T" on the prism; any "Fv" camera body could be updated simply by adding this metered prism (Black body add 100%).

R2*   **D**

MIRANDA G: c1965. 35mm SLR with interchangeable Auto Miranda f1.9, 5cm lens. CFPS 1 – ¹⁄₁₀₀₀s; removable finder; inter-

Miranda G with clip on meter

changeable **FOCUSING SCREENS; MIRROR LOCK-UP**; self-timer; top and front shutter release; removable shutter-speed dial for use when using clip-on meter; model designation on the camera front. (Black Body adds 100%).

R2*   **D**

MIRANDA GM: c1965-66. For non-TTL CDS prism finder. Any "G" camera body could be updated simply by adding this metered prism. (Black body adds 100%).

R2*   **D**

MIRANDA GT: c1967. For uncoupled TTL CDS prism finder. Model designation "G" on the camera front; "T" on the prism. Any "G" camera body could be updated simply by adding this metered prism. (Black body adds 100%)

R2*   **D**

MIRANDA SENSOMAT: c1969. 35mm SLR with interchangeable Auto Miranda f1.8, 5cm lens. CFPS 1 – ¹⁄₁₀₀₀s; coupled TTL CDS meter for stopped down metering

with two button operation; all metal lever advance; serial number 81xxxx to 83xxxx.
R2*   **D**

MIRANDA SENSOMAT RE: c1970. As previous model but for single button meter operation, and black plastic tipped lever advance. Tops of lever advance, shutter speed dial, and rewind knob are chrome, not black, serial numbers 68xxxxx.
R2*   **D**

MIRANDA SENSOMAT RS: c1970. Without meter, serial number 37xxxxx.
R2*   **D**

MIRANDA SENSOMAT RE II: c1975. 35mm SLR with interchangeable Auto Miranda EC f1.4 or f1.8, 5cm lens. CFPS 1 – ⅟₁₀₀₀s; single top mounted shutter release; "Q.I.S". "Quadrascopic Image System" circular multi image rangefinder focusing system; serial number 58xxxxx to 59xxxxx. (Black body adds 100%).
R2*   **D**

MIRANDA TM: c1975. 35mm SLR with interchangeable Auto Miranda TM f1.8, 5cm lens in 42mm (Praktica/Pentax size), CFPS 1 – ⅟₁₀₀₀s. Single top mounted shutter release; stopped down metering; serial number 46xxxxx (type I); slight variations seen over the production life serial number 56xxxxx (type II). (Also sold as the "Soligor TM".
R2*   **D**

SOLIGOR TM: c1975. Has Auto Soligor f1.8, 50mm lens.
R2*   **D**

MIRANDA AUTOMEX: c1959. 35mm SLR camera with interchangeable Soligor-Miranda f1.9, 5cm lens. CFPS 1 – ⅟₁₀₀₀s; coupled selinium light meter to 400 ASA; provision for motor wind on some cameras though no winder has yet been found; serial number 61xxxx.
R2*   **D**

MIRANDA AUTOMEX II: c1963. Redesigned flash synch and 1600 ASA sensibility; serial number 61xxxx
R2*   **D**

MIRANDA AUTOMEX III: c1964. Side mounted flash synch and CDS light meter to 1600 ASA; serial number 63xxxx.
R2*   **D**

Miranda
Automex III

Miranda Sensorex II in chrome and black

MIRANDA SENSOREX: c1967. 35mm SLR with interchangeable Auto Miranda f1.4 or f1.9, 5cm lens. CFPS 1 – ⅟₁₀₀₀s; first Miranda with open aperture metering; maximum aperture of lens in use must be set on a special dial under the front of the camera, under the rewind knob marked -1.4, 1.9, 2.8, 3.5, 4, 5.6, and 8, serial numbers 7xxxxx.

R2*   **D**

MIRANDA SENSOREX 1.8: c1968. For use with f1.8 lens instead of f1.9; serial number 9xxxxx. (Black body adds 100%).

R2*   **D**

MIRANDA SENSOREX II: c1971. 35mm SLR with interchangeable Auto Miranda f1.4 or f1.8, 5cm lens. CFPS 1 – ⅟₁₀₀₀s; first Miranda with hot shoe; lens aperture selection dial moved to under rewind knob;

serial number 83xxxxx. (Black body adds 100%).

R2*   **D**

MIRANDA SENSOREX EE: c1971. 35mm SLR with interchangeable Auto Miranda E

Miranda Sensorex EE. AIC on the camera body means Allied Impex Corporation, the American owners of Miranda Company, and official importers and distributors.

f1.4 or f1.8, 5cm lens. CFPS 1 - ⅟₁₀₀₀s; shutter speed preferred automatic TTL exposure control; top shutter release only; serial number 91xxxxx. (Black body adds 50%)

R2*   **D**

MIRANDA SENSOREX EE-2: c1974. 35mm SLR with interchangeable Auto Miranda EC f1.4 or f1.8, 5cm lens. CFPS 1 - ⅟₁₀₀₀s; shutter speed preferred automatic TTL exposure control; top shutter release only; shutter speeds visible in finder; Q.I.S. focusing system, serial number 93xxxxx. (Black body adds 100%).

R1*   **D**

*Miranda
DX-3 in black*

MIRANDA DX-3: c1975. 35mm SLR with interchangeable Auto Miranda EC f1.4 or f1.8, 5cm lens. Electronically controlled CFPS 4 - ⅟₁₀₀₀s; the only Miranda SLR with a fixed prism; motor drive capable; the last Model produced by MIranda; often found

not working; serial number 39xxxxx. (Black body **LESS** 50%).

R1*   **D+**

MIRANDA SENSORET: c1972. 35mm RFR camera with fixed Miranda Soligor f2.8, 38mm lens. Seiko ESF shutter; the only non-SLR Miranda; serial number 24xxxxx.

R3*   **C**

MIRAX LABOREC II: c1970. 35mm SLR for laboratory use. Suitable for mounting on a microscope or telescope; CFPS 1 - ⅟₁₂₅s; two bayonet mounts and one screw mount; oversized knob advance; **CABLE RELEASE ONLY TOP AND FRONT**; removable VF-5 vertical VFR; type A has button VFR lock; type B uses a locking ring located under the rewind knob; X synch only; serial number type A 113xxx - 115xxx; serial number type B 116xxx to 119xxx; it is not known if a Laborec I was ever made.

R3*   **E+**

MIRAX LADOREC ELECTRO-D: c1972. 35mm SLR for laboratory use. Black body and built-in motor winder capable of two frames/sec. 12V DC required to power the motor either from rectified/reduced AC, or from rechargeable battery unit, serial number 114xxx Mx.

R4*   **F–**

MIRANDA LABOREC: c1975. 35mm SLR for laboratory use. Miranda bayonet and 44mm screw mount, serial number 12xxxx.

R3*   **E+**

MIRANDA LABOREC III: c1975. 35mm SLR for laboratory use. Additional ½₅₀ and ½₀₀s shutter speeds; **THE ONLY LABOREC WITH MODEL DESIGNATION INDICATED ON THE CAMERA FRONT**; serial number 21xxxxx.

R3*   **E+**

ACCESSORIES AND LENSES FOR MIRANDA SLRS:

extension tube set, 8mm, 16mm, 32mm	**A**
universal helicoid	**A–**
lens adaptors, (39mm screw, 42mm screw, Exakta, etc.)	**A–**
VF-1 WL VFR	**A**
VF-3 critical focusing VFR	**B–**

VF-3 critical focusing VFR opened and closed

VF-4 critical focusing VFR	**B–**
"M" pentaprism w/CDS meter	**B–**
"T" pentaprism w/ TTL CDS meter	**B+**
Focabell twin rail bellows (Miranda "T")	**B+**
Focabell AII twin rail bellows (Sensomat)	**B+**
Focabell AIII twin rail bellows (Sensomat RE)	**B+**
Bellox JR single rail bellows (DR)	**A**
Focabell S single rail bellows (F)	**A**
pistol grip with release	**B**
microscope adaptor	**B+**
double cable release	**A–**
clip-on CDS light meter	**B–**
flash bracket	**A–**
slide copier	**A–**
focusing screens for "G" and Laborec	**A–**
Miranda Panorama head	**B+**
motor drive for Automex	**D**
motor drive for dx-3	**D**
bulk film back for dx-3	**D**
radio remote release for dx-3	**D**
scope meter for microscope use	**C**

SOLIGOR MIRANDA LENSES, PRESET OR EXTERNAL AUTOMATIC

28mm f2.8 automatic	**C+**
35mm f2.8 preset	**C**
35mm f3.5 preset	**C**
35mm f2.8 automatic	**C**
105mm f2.8 automatic	**C+**
135mm f2.8 preset	**C**
135mm f2.8 automatic	**C**
135mm f3.5 preset	**C**
135mm f3.5 automatic	**C**
135mm f3.5 bellows mount	**D**
180mm f4.5 preset	**D+**
250mm f4.5 preset	**D+**
400mm f5.5 preset	**E**

SOLIGOR MIRANDA LENSES FOR AUTOMEX CAMERAS:

28mm f2.8	**C+**
35mm f2.8	**C+**
105mm f2.8	**C+**
135mm f2.8	**C**
135mm f3.5	**C**

AUTO MIRANDA LENSES FOR AUTOMEX CAMERAS:

25mm f2.8	**D+**
28mm f2.8	**C+**
35mm f2.8	**C+**
105mm f2.8	**C+**
135mm f2.8	**C+**
135mm f3.5	**C+**
200mm f3.5	**D+**

AUTO MIRANDA LENSES FOR SENSOREX CAMERAS:

25mm f2.8	**D**
28mm f2.8	**D**
35mm f2.8	**C+**
105mm f2.8	**C+**
135mm f2.8	**C+**

135mm f3.5	**C+**
180mm f3.5	**D+**
200mm f3.5	**D+**
52mm f3.5 Macron	**D+**

AUTO MIRANDA E LENSES:

25mm f2.8	**D**
28mm f2.8	**C+**
35mm f2.8	**C+**
105mm f2.8	**D**
135mm f2.8	**C**
135mm f3.5	**C**
180mm f3.5	**D+**
200mm f3.5	**D+**
52mm f3.5 Macron	**D+**

AUTO MIRANDA EC LENSES:

28mm f2.8	**D**
35mm f2.8	**D**
105mm f2.8	**D+**
135mm f2.8	**D**
200mm f3.5	**E–**
80-200mm f3.5 zoom	**E–**
52mm f3.5 Macron	**D+**

Misuzu Kogaku Kogyo & Co. Ltd.
Japan

ALTA: 1957-59. CFPS, 1-⅕₀₀s; seperate RFR/VFR windows; diopter adjustment. Screw mount Altanon f2.0, 50mm or Altanon f3.5/50mm lens. Similar to the Leica IIIA. Maybe only 600 made.

R4*	**G+**

J.D. Moller
Hamburg, Germany

CAMBINOX-N: c1956. Binocular with subminiature camera built-in. Inter-

changeable Idemar 90mm f3.5 lens, bayonet mount (for 35mm, 135mm and 180mm lenses). 6 speed rotary FPS ⅟₅₀-⅟₈₀₀S; 10 x 14mm exp on 16mm film; after focusing the binoculars, the distance reading is transfered to the camera lens.

R4*   **G**

CAMBINOX-S: c1960. Monocular form, originally available on special order.

R4*   **NSR EST G+**

ACCESSORIES FOR CAMBINOX

Jedmar f3.5/35mm lens   **F**

Jedmar f3.5/135mm lens   **F**

Jedmar f3.5/180mm lens   **F**

Mollier *Paris, France*

LE "CENT VUES": c1924. Metal 35mm VFR camera for 100 exp, 18 x 24mm on perforated 35mm film in special cassettes. Hermagis f3.5, 40mm lens; single speed guillotine shutter or Compur shutter; also used as a projector; horizontal and vertical styles exist. Invented by Etienne N. Mollier.

R4*   **H–**

MOLTENI DETECTIVE CAMERA: Molteni Aplanat lens. Body unfolds to form vf; brass fittings. 9 x 12cm exp on plates. Mfg. in Paris, France. C 1885.

R5*   **G+**

Le "Cent Vues"

MOM *Budapest, Hungary*

MOMETTA: c1953. 35mm RFR camera. Fixed mount Ymmar f3.5, 50mm lens; CFPS ½₅ – ⅟₅₀₀S; CRF.

R3*   **E–**

MOMETTA II: c1955. With interchangeable mount (42mm screw), interesting in that the lens flange to focal plane distance is the same as that used on SLR cameras having a "Universal" screw mount. This would allow the SLR lens to be used on the Mometta camera.

R3* **E–**

MOMETTA III: c1958. With flash synch.
R3* **E–**

Monroe Camera Co.
Rochester, New York

The Monroe Camera Co. was established in 1897 in Rochester, New York. In 1899 they merged with several other companies – the Rochester Optical Co., the Rochester Camera & Supply Co., the Ray Camera Co., and the Western Camera Mfg. Co.-to form the Rochester Optical & Camera C0.

MONROE NO. 7 FOLDING PLATE CAMERA: c1898. 4" x 5" folding plate camera; Rapid Rectilinear lens; Unicum shutter. Double extension red bellows; reversible and shifting back; polished mahogany body, brass fittings; ivory label; leather covered case.

R3 * **D+**

POCKET MONROE: c1898. Folding plate camera; 3½" x 3½" exp on dry plates.

R3* **D+**

VEST POCKET MONROE: c1898, miniature camera; collapsible bellows; single exp, 3½" x 3½" on dry plates.
R3* **E–**

Montanus-Camerabau
Solingen, Germany

PLASCAFLEX V45: c1950. TLR for 6 x 6cm on 120 roll film, f4.5, 75mm lens, Vario shutter.

R3* **C+**

PLASCAFLEX PS35: c1950. TLR for 6 x 6cm on 120 roll film, f3, 75mm lens, Prontor-S shutter,.

R3* **C+**

ROCCA AUTOMATIC: c1953. TLR for 6 x 6cm on 120 roll film, Trinar f2.9 or Cassar f2.8, 80mm lens, Prontor-SVS shutter, interchangeable focusing hood.

R3* **C+**

DELMONTA: c1955. TLR for 6 x 6cm frames on 120 roll film, Pluscanar f3.5, 75mm lens, Vario shutter.

R3* **C**

MONTIFLEX: c1955. TLR for 6 x 6cm frames on 120 roll film, Pluscanar f3.5, 75mm lens, Prontor-SVS shutter.

R3* **C**

MONTANA: c1956. 35mm VFR camera, Deltamon f3.5, 45mm lens, Vario shutter.
R2* **C**

Charles Monti, *Paris*

LUMIERE MAGAZINE CAMERA: c1892. Box-type magazine camera; Rapid Rectilinear 135mm f11 lens; 2 leaf scissors behind-the-lens shutter. Waist-level finder; 12 exp, 9 x 12cm on dry plates. Invented by L. Lumiere, Lyons, France.
R4* **F**

Moore & Co.,
Liverpool, England

APTUS FERROTYPE CAMERA: c1913-1956. Black leather covered wooden ferrotype camera; meniscus lens. Suction disk takes unexposed plate and swings it into position to be exposed; after exposure, the suction disk dropped the plate into the developing tank attached to the camera. Very popular among "while you wait" beach photographers. 4.5 x 6.3cm exp on plates.

R3*   **E+**

Morita Trading Company
Japan

KIKU 16: c.1960. Subminiature made for 16mm rollfilm. 25mm f8 lens. I & B shutter set by tiny knob on front of body, giving it the appearance of a miniature Leica. Originally sold as part of a kit that contained lens hood and filter. Also known as the Gem 16 Model II.

R3*   **D**

H. Morse, *London, England*

SINGLE LENS STEREOSCOPIC CAMERA: c1865. Ross Landscape lens. Stereo exp on 3½" x 7" wet plates; camera slides laterally on rails for second exp.

R5*   **H+**

William Muller
Vienna, Austria

DELTA-STEREO FLAT CARTRIDGE: c1900. Stereo folding camera;ExtraRapid Aplanat 120mm f6.5 lens (also Anastigmat 260mm f9, Triple Anastigmat 280mm f12, or Collinear III M 300). Reflecting finder; scale focusing. 9 x 18cm exp on roll or sheet film.

R4*   **E+**

NEUE REFLEX STEREOSKOP CAMERA: c1901, box-type reflex stereo camera; Suter Anastigmat 340K lens, (also Goerz Series III 120mm 510K, Voigtlander Collinear Series III 120mm 570K); FPS. 9 x 18cm exp on stereo plates.

R4*   **F–**

MULTICOLOURE: c1905, tri-colour magazine box camera. Tri-colour filters were sequentially moved into position (behind the lens) by using external controls. Mfd in Paris, France.

R4*   **F**

LE MULTI PHOTO: c1924, all metal camera; two Boyer Saphir 40mm f4.5 lenses; FPS ½₀-⅕₀₀s. 9 exp, 27 x 27mm. Also takes stereo pictures using 10 x 15cm plate holder. Mfg. in Lyon, France.

R4*   **G+**

Multiscope & Film Co.
Burlington, Wisconsin

All Al-Vista panoramic cameras shared a common method of controlling the transit speed of the lens. A set of vanes ranging in size from about 1/2 to 1 inch were fitted to a small rotating post either on top or bottom of the cameras. The larger the vane, the greater the wind resistance and the slower the lens movement. They were usually stored inside the camera. If they all are missing, deduct at least 40% from the value of the camera and adjust the value for the number of wind vanes present.

AL-VISTA PANORAMIC CAMERA (MODEL 4B): c1900. 4" x 12" exp on roll film.

R4*   **E+**

AL-VISTA PANORAMIC CAMERA (MODEL 5B): c1900. 5" x 12" exp on roll film.

R4*   **E+**

BABY AL-VISTA: c1900, panoramic camera; 2¼"x 6¾" exp on roll film.

R4*   **F–**

Multi-Speed Shutter Co.
Morris Park, Long Island, New York; later became Simplex Photo Products Company

SIMPLEX CAMERA: c1914. 35mm camera; Bausch & Lomb Tessar 50mm f3.5 lens; built-in shutter 1-¹⁄₃₀₀s. 800-35mm half-frame exp or 400-35mm full-frame exp. The Simplex was the first commercially produced camera designed to take full-frame photographs on 35mm film. See picture opposite.

R5*   **I**

MUNDUS COLOUR: c1955. Tessar 20mm f2.7 lens; Prontor shutter 1 – ¹⁄₃₀₀s. 8 x 14mm exp on 16mm movie film. c1955.

R4*   **E+**

Murer & Duroni
Milan, Italy

MURER: c1920. 6 x 9cm camera; Murer Anastigmat 102mm f6.3 lens with heli-

The Simplex Camera – the first commercially produced camera designed to take full-frame photographs on 35mm film.

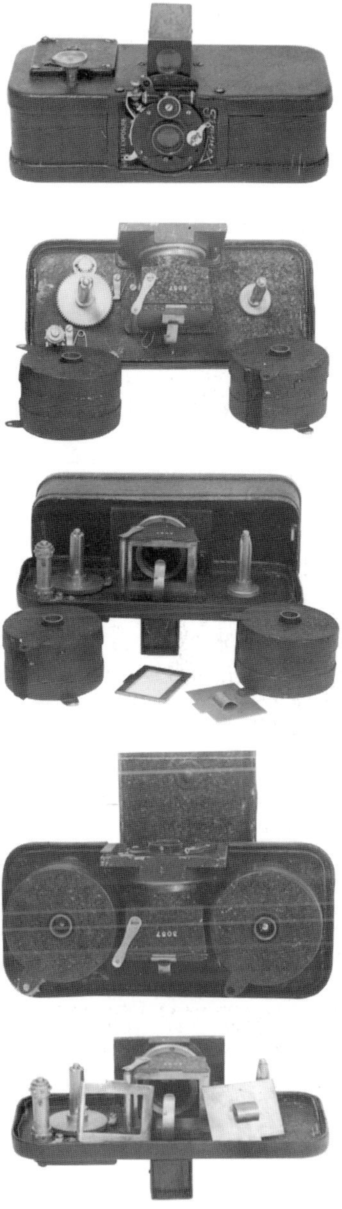

coidal focusing; FPS. Sliding lens cap with built-in viewer.

R3* **D–**

MURER EXPRESS: c1905, mirror reflex camera; Anastigmat 9cm f7 lens; FPS ¹⁄₃₀-¹⁄₁₀₀₀s. Leather covered wood body. 6 x 13cm exp on plates.

R3* **D**

MURER EXPRESS STEREO: c1896-1897. Mirror reflex stereo camera; anastigmat f6.3 lens. Aluminium body. 45 x 107mm and 6 x 13cm exp on plates. C 1896-1897.

R3* **F–**

MURER FOLDING EXPRESS: c1920. 45 x 107mm folding stereo camera; Anastigmatic 60mm f4.5 lens; FPS ¹⁄₁₅-¹⁄₁₀₀₀ s.

R4* **E–**

MURER SPRITE: c1919. 4.5 x 6cm folding camera; Rapid Aplanat 70mm f8 lens; shutter ¹⁄₂₅-¹⁄₁₀₀s. Roll film version, **$175.** Plate:

R3* **C+**

Murray & Heath
London, England

STEREOSCOPIC CAMERA: c1865. Ross lenses, sliding box focusing. Stereo exp on 9 x 17cm wet plates. Rising front; Mahogany construction.

R5* **H+**

Muse Optical Co.
Japan

MUSEFLEX: 1948. Small format TLR-style camera for Bolta size film (similar to Kodak's 828 but with different spool configurations). Early models with fixed focus meniscus lenses and single-speed shutters. Later models synch for flash and with 2 apertures. Some models with focusing lens, though not coupled to viewfinder.

R4* **D**

MUSEFLEX IIA: 1951. Similar to original Museflex, but with shutter 1/25-1/150s and coupled focusing to make it a true TLR.

R4* **D**

Mutschler, Robertson & Co.
Rochester, New York

Mutschler, Robertson & Co. was founded in 1895 by Albert Mutschler and John A. Robertson. The company name was changed to the Ray Camera Co. in 1898; located at 204 Commercial Street in Rochester, New York. In 1899 they merged with several other companies the Rochester Optical Co., the Rochester Camera & Supply Co., the Monroe Camera Co. and the Western Camera Mfg. Co. – to form the Rochester Optical & Camera Co.

RAY FOLDING PLATE MODEL A: c1898. 4" x 5" folding plate camera; Rapid Rectilinear lens; Victor shutter. Red bellows; shifting, rising and falling front; side loading.

R3* **D–**

RAY NO. 2: c1895. 5" x 7" folding plate camera; Rapid Rectilinear lens; Unicum

RAY NO. 4: c1895. 4" x 5" folding plate camera; Rapid Rectilinear lens; Unicum shutter. Leather covered exterior; mahogany interior, brass fittings; red bellows. Mutschler, Robertson & Co. brass label above lens board.

R3* **D–**

shutter. Shifting, rising and falling front. Leather covered exterior; mahogany interior, brass fittings; red bellows.

R3* **D–**

THE RAY JUNIOR: c1898, small box-type dry plate camera; 2½" x 2½" exp on dry plates.

R3* **C–**

Reference Notes

_____

_____

_____

_____

_____

_____

_____

_____

_____

_____

_____

_____

_____

_____

_____

_____

_____

_____

_____

_____

_____

Dr. August Nagel Camerawerk
Stuttgart, Germany

Pupille
with Leitz
rangefinder

PUPILLE: c1930. Metal VFR camera for 16 exp, 3 x 4cm on roll film, Schneider Xenon 50mm, f2.0 or Xenar f2.9 or f3.5 lens; Compur shutter 1-⅓₀₀s. Leitz Elmar 50mm f3.5 lens doubles the price.

R4*   **E+**

RANCA: c1931. Nagel Anastigmat 50mm f4.5 lens; Ibsor shutter 1-¹⁄₁₅₀s.

R3*   **F–**

RECOMAR: C.1928-1932. Folding plate camera; 6 x 9cm & 9 x 12cm; Leitz Elmar 10.5cm f4.5 lens in Compur shutter.

R3*   **D**

VOLLENDA 3X4, N048: c1930. Elmar 50mm f3.5 lens; Compur shutter 1-¹⁄₃₀₀s.

R4*   **F–**

Vollenda
3x4

NATIONAL COLOR CAMERA: c1938; 3¼ x 4¼ inch format; Tessar 135mm f4.5 lens; Dial set Compur shutter. The Goertz Dagor & Dogmar lenses were also very popular and found frequently on National Cameras. It is rare to find the pellicle mirrors intact. They are made of a very thin mirrored collodion membrane and were very fragile.

R4*   **F+**

VOLLENDA B: C.1930. Folding roll film camera; 5 x 7.5cm exp; 9cm f6.3 Nagal Anastigmat lens; 3 speed shutter B.T. ½₅-⅟₁₀₀s.

R4*   **C+**

National Photocolour Corp., New York

One shot or single exposure colour cameras used two internal pellicle mirrors to divide the light into three portions which made simultaneous exposures through red, green, and blue filters on high-speed black & white film or plates. These "separation negatives" were then used to make a natural colour print by the dye transfer process. The National Photocolor Corp. made a number of sizes ranging from 3¼ x 4½ inch to 5 x 7 inches.

Neidig, Germany

PERLUX: 1952. 35mm VFR camera. Die-cast light alloy body, matt chrome with black leatherette. 45mm f2.8 Kataplast with front cell focusing. Prontor-S shutter 1-1/300s + B. Depth of field indicator.

R3*   **C**

PERLUX II: 1953. Similar to first model with slightly changed body design to incorporate uncoupled rangefinder.

R3*   **C+**

PERLUX IIA: 1953. Similar to Perlux II with coupled rangefinder.

R3*   **C+**

Nettel Kamerawerk
Sontheim a/M., Germany

ARGUS CAMERA: c1911. monocular-type detective camera; Tessar 50mm f4.5 lens; single speed cylindrical shutter. 4.5 x 6cm exp on plates.

R4*   **G**

New Ideas Mfg. Co.
New York
Sold by Herbert & Huesgen Company, New York

TOURIST MULTIPLE: c1914. 35mm camera. Bausch & Lomb Zeiss Tessar 50mm f3.5 lens; 7 speed guillotine MFPS $\frac{1}{40}$ – $\frac{1}{200}$s; 750 exp, 18 x 24mm on 50' rolls of perforated 35mm cine film. Qty less than 1000. The camera originally sold for $175; the complete outfit (camera and matching projector) sold for $250. The Tourist Multiple was the first 35mm still camera produced commercially and sold in substantial quantity.

R4*   **H–**

Newman & Guardia
London, England

BABY SIBYL: c1914. Tessar 75mm f4.5 lens; Newman & Guardia shutter $\frac{1}{2}$-$\frac{1}{200}$s. c1910. Roll film version, and plate version.

R3*   **F+** RANGEFINDER VERS. **H**

Baby Sibyl
Plate Version

NEW IDEAL SIBYL: c1914. Ross Xpres f4.5 lens; Newman & Guardia shutter. 3¼" x 4¼" exp.

R3*   **E+**

NEW SPECIAL SIBYL: c1914. 6 x 9cm; Ross Xpres 112mm f4.5 lens; special Newman & Guardia shutter. Rising and sliding front; vf adjusted for use of rise and cross facility and had two sets of adjustment marks depending on which axis the vf was turned. Two spirit levels, to check for correct horizon. 6 x 9cm exp.

R3*   **E**

PATTERN B DETECTIVE CAMERA: c1895. 3¼" x 4¼" exp on plates.

R3*   **E**

NEWMAN & GUARDIA REFLEX CAMERA: c1906. Beck-Steinheil Unifocal f4.5 lens.

R3*   **E**

NYDIA: c1890. Wray Rectilinear lens; double guillotine shutter; 12 exp, magazine changed by manipulation of plates through soft leather pouch.

R3*   **F**

NYDIA: c1901-1913. Quarter-plate pocket camera; weighng one pound; Wray – Ross or Aldis lens; Pneumatic shutter; reversable finder; DD. slide; focusing screen;Newman magazine changing bag for 12 cut films in sheaths; detachable tapered bellows & struts for folding.

R3*   **G–**

SPECIAL: Magazine box camera; lens board moves vertically and horizontally; pneumatic shutter. Extended bellows for closeups and copying. 3¼" x 4¼" exp, 12 plate magazine.

R3*   **E–**

STEREO DETECTIVE CAMERA: c1895. Rectilinear 120mm f8 lens; guillotine shutter ½-⅟₁₀₀s. Leather bag changing mechanism for plates. 10 x 16cm.

R4*   **G–**

SIBYL DE LUXE: c1910-1917. Quarter-plate double ext.; folding reflector finder; fold away tripod screw; model 1 later known as model 83 with Zeiss VIIa f6.3-5" lens; model 1a with roll-film holder; model 83 had Ross F6.3 lens.

R2*   **E+**

SIBYL TRELLIS: c1910-1938. Quarter-plate Hand and stand camera; N&G focal plane shutter on reversing back; Anastigmat f4.5 lens and other lens; rising & cross front.

R3*   **F**

SIBYL "ORDINARY" POCKET CAMERA: c1906-1913. 12 models, 3¼" X 2¼" to Quarter-plate;Optical DV. Vfr.;Shutter ½s, to ⅟₁₀₀s,; lenses include Ross, Ziess, Cook.

R2*   **D+**

Nicca Camera Works
Japan

NICCA III (TYPE 3): 1949. Cfps, 1-⅟₅₀₀s; seperate RFR/VFR windows; diopter adjustment; screw mount Nikkor HC f2.0/5cm lens. Now called the Nicca Camera Works Ltd. This camera is a copy of the Leica III.

R3*   **F–**

NICCA IIIA: 1951. Cfps, 1- 1/500s; seperate RFR/VFR windows; diopter adjustment; screw mount Nikkor HC f2.0/5cm or Nikkor SC f1.5/cm lens. The company name changed once again in November 1951 to the "Nicca Camera Company Ltd." IIIA cameras can be found with both company markings. It was also distributed by Sears Roebuck and Co. as the Tower Type-3, which is valued about 10% less than cameras marked "Nicca".

R2*   **F–**

NICCA IIIB: 1951. Cfps, 1-⅟₅₀₀s; FP flash synch; seperate RFR/VFR windows; diopter adjustment; screw mount Nikkor HC f2.0, 5cm or Nikkor SC f1.5, 5cm lens. The same as the Nicca IIIA, with flash synch added It was also distributed by Sears Roebuck and Co. as the Tower Type-3B, which is valued about 10% less than cameras marked "Nicca".

R3*   **F–**

NICCA IIIS: 1952. Cfps, 1 – ⅟₅₀₀s; FP and X flash synch; seperate RFR/VFR windows; diopter djustment; screw mount Nikkor

QC f3.5, 5cm lens. It was also distributed by Sears Roebuck and Co. as the Tower Type-3S, which is valued about 10% less than cameras marked "Nicca".

R2*   **F–**

Tower camera with a Culminar 8cm/f2.8 lens – similar to Nicca 3F

NICCA 4: 1953. Cfps, 1-⅟₁₀₀₀s; FP and X flash synch; seperate RFR/VFR windows; diopter adjustment; screw mount Nikkor SC f1.5, 5cm lens.

R3*   **F**

NICCA 3S: 1954. Cfps, 1-⅟₅₀₀s; FP and X flash synch; seperate RFR/VFR windows; diopter adjustment; screw mount Nikkor QC f3.5, 5cm lens. The same as the Nicca IIIs, with new shutter speed progression, and synch at ⅟₂₅ instead of ⅟₂₀. It was also distributed by Sears Roebuck and Co. as the Tower Camera valued about 10% less than cameras marked "Nicca".

R2*   **F–**

NICCA 3F: 1956. Cfps, 1-⅟₅₀₀s; FP and X flash synch; seperate RFR/VFR windows; diopter adjustment; screw mount Nikkor H f2.0, 5cm or Nikkor S f1.4, 5cm lens. One piece top plate, hinged back. It was also distributed by Sears Roebuck and Co. as the Tower Camera valued about 10% less than cameras marked "Nicca". A 3F version with a quick wind lever was made, and is valued at about 15% less than the wind knob version.

R3*   **F–**

NICCA 5: 1955. Cfps, 1-¹⁄₁₀₀₀s; FP and X flash synch; seperate RFR/VFR windows; diopter adjustment; screw mount Nikkor S f1.4, 5cm or Nikkor S f2.0, 5cm lens. One piece top plate, hinged back. Leica IIIF copy, with synch contact under the accessory shoe. Also sold by Sears Roebuck and Co. with the f2/50mm lens as the Tower 45, and with the f1.4, 50mm lens as the Tower 46.

R2*   **F–**

NICCA 33: 1957. Cfps, ½-¹⁄₅₀₀s; FP and X flash synch; seperate RFR/VFR windows; diopter adjustment; screw mount Nicca F2.8, 50mm lens. Continued after Nicca Camera Company Ltd. was taken over by Yashica, and then known as the Yashica YE.

R3*   **F–**

NICCA IIIL: 1958. Cfps, 1-¹⁄₁₀₀₀s; FP and X flash synch; seperate RFR/VFR windows; diopter adjustment; screw mount Nikkor H f2.0, 5cm lens. Completely redesigned top plate. Continued as the Yashica YF, after the company was taken over by Yashica.

R3*   **F+**

NICNON TF BINOCULAR CAMERA: c1968. half-frame 35mm binocular camera; Nicnon 165mm f3.5 lens; Copal square MFPS ¹⁄₆₀, ¹⁄₁₂₅ and ¹⁄₂₅₀ s. The SLR camera uses right-hand optics of the binocular as an objective; springwound motor allows up to 20 exp per wind.

R4*   **F+**

NICNON S BINOCULAR CAMERA: c1970; 7x50 monocular telescope, fitted to a half frame 35mm camera. The Nicnon was one of the highest quality binocular cameras. They were frequently used by law enforcement agencies.

R4*   **F+**

Nichiryo Trading Co.
Tokyo, Japan

TEFLEX BINOCULAR CAMERA: c1968. Binoculars with a half-frame 35mm camera attached. Tefnon lens f3.5, 165mm effective focal length. Focus through right half of binocular. Camera spring driven. Nearly identical cameras were the Ricoh Teleca and The Nicnon

R4*   **F**

Niell and Simons
Brussels

LOPA: c1900, meniscus 120mm f11 lens; single speed guillotine shutter. 6.5 x 9cm exp.

R4*   **F–**

Nikon Inc., Nippon Kogaku K.K.
Tokyo, Japan

For further information see Nikon Rangefinder Cameras by Robert Rotoloni, Hove Collectors Books, 1983, and Nikon Compendium, Handbook of the Nikon System by Rudolf Hillebrand and Hans-Joachim Hauschild, Hove

Collectors Books, 1993, for SLR and underwater cameras.

NIKON I: c1948-49. 35mm RFR camera. Nikkor 50mm f2 coated lens, interchangeable bayonet mount; CFPS 1 -¹⁄₅₀₀s; CFR. 40 exp, 24 x 32mm. Qty 758. No factory installed synch; removable take-up spool. One offered in 1989 for **K** Worth at least **H** if damaged, non-working, or modified in any way.

R5* RARE   K

NIKON M: c1949-52. 35mm RFR camera. Nikkor 50mm f2 coated lens, interchangeable bayonet mount; CFPS 1 -¹⁄₅₀₀s; CFR. 36 exp, 24 x 34mm. Qty 1643. No factory installed flash synch; M prefix on serial number.With synch, (about 1700 cameras made).

R4*   G+

Without synch, (1643 cameras made).

R4*   H

NIKON S: c1950-54. 35mm RFR camera. Nikkor 50mm f2 coated lens, interchangeable bayonet mount; CFPS 1 -¹⁄₅₀₀s; CFR; flash synch. 36 exp, 24 x 36mm. Qty

36,746. Double spring synchro socket. "Made in Occupied Japan"

R4*   F+

Eight digit serial number:

R3*   F–

Others:

R2*   F–

NIKON S2: c1954-55. 35mm RFR camera. Nikkor 50mm f2 coated lens, interchangeable bayonet mount; CFPS 1 -¹⁄₁₀₀₀s; CFR; flash synch. 36 exp, 24 x 36mm. Qty 56,715. Single stroke rapid wind lever, enlarged vf.

BLACK BODY:

R4*   I–

CHROME BODY, CHROME DIAL:

R3*   F

CHROME BODY, BLACK DIAL:

R3*   F+

NIKON S3: c1958. 35mm RFR camera. Nikkor 50mm f2 coated lens, interchangeable bayonet mount; CFPS 1 -¹⁄₁₀₀₀s; CFR; flash synch. Combined range-vf for 3

lens fields. 36 exp, 24 x 36mm. Qty 14,310. Chrome body:

R3*   **G**

BLACK BODY:

R4*   **I–**

BLACK OLYMPIC:

R4*   **I**

Nikon SP with stereo Nikkor lenses

NIKON S4: c1959. 35mm RFR camera. Nikkor 50mm f2 lens, interchangeable bayonet mount; CFPS 1-¹⁄₁₀₀₀s; CFR; flash synch. 36 exp, 24 x 36mm. Qty 5698. No self-timer, manual reset frame counter.

Chrome body.

R3*   **H–**

NIKON SP: c1957. 35mm RFR camera. Nikkor 50mm f2 coated lens, interchangeable bayonet mount; CFPS 1 -¹⁄₁₀₀₀s; flash synch. Combined range-vf for 6 lens fields; 1:1 viewing, parallax correction for

normal and telephoto lenses, adjacent eye-level optical finder for 28mm and 35mm lenses. Self-timer. Qty 21,534. Electric motor drive available automatically advances film and fires shutter at maximum rate of 3 exp per second. The motor is powered by 6 pen-light or 6 C size batteries. Chrome body with normal lens:

R3*   **G+**

Black body:

R4*   **I–**

NIKON S3M: c1960. Half-frame 35mm RFR camera. Nikkor 35mm f2 coated lens, interchangeable bayonet mount; CFPS 1-¹⁄₁₀₀₀s; CFR; flash sync. 72 exp, 18 x 24mm, half-frame format. Qty 195. One offered in 1989 with matching S72 motor for $15,000. This same matched set today could easily command $20,000!Chrome: With motor;

R5*   **K**

Black:

R5*   **K**

NIKON F: Introduced in 1959. 35mm SLR with interchangeable lenses, backs, viewing screens, prisms etc. CFPS speeds 1-¹⁄₁₀₀₀s. This camera, considered by some to be the first 35mm SLR system camera has finally reached the ranks of the collectables! With Nikon RFR equipment becoming harder and harder to find, many Nikon enthusiasts have begun the search for early Nikon SLRs, particularly Nikon F Photomics. We expect to see a greater interest in the coming years in collecting these cameras. For now at least, the early Nikon "F" Photomic cameras with serial numbers from 640000 to 641000 are actively being looked for. Because of their popularity as "working" cameras, pristine examples are particularly hard to find. Competition from users is great. (price is for low numbered camera bodies only 640000-641000, black model is about 50% more, other serial numbers are about 70% cheaper)

R4*   **G+**

NIKON F CUTAWAY MODEL: non working Nikon F camera sliced in half for use as a display piece, showing some of the internal workings. Includes half a lens.

R4*   **G+**

NIKON F MADE FOR THE UNITED STATES SPACE PROGRAM: with special markings, this camera is one of the rarest

Nikon SLRs (for the moment at least!) including lens.

R5*   **H**

NIKON F MADE FOR THE UNITED STATES NAVY: with special markings, hard to find in clean condition. Price includes motor drive and lens.

R4*   **G+**

NIKKOR F: Nikon F made for the European market. Harder to find in the USA than in Germany.

R4*   **F+**

NIKON F PHOTOMIC: C.1962 – 1966. 35mm SLR camera. MFPS; 1-¹⁄₁₀₀₀s.T.B.; Cds meter; needle display; ¹⁄₆₀s. X,M. Flash exp.

R2*   **F–**

NIKON F PHOTOMIC T: c1965-1966. 35mm SLR camera. MFPS; 1-¹⁄₁₀₀₀s.T.B.;Cds meter; Needle display; ¹⁄₆₀s.X,M flash exp.

R2*   **F–**

NIKON F PHOTOMIC TN; c1967-1968. 35mm SLR cmaera. MFPS;1-¹⁄₁₀₀₀s. T.B.;Cds meter; needle display; ¹⁄₆₀s.X,M flash exp.

R2*   **F–**

NIKON F PHOTOMIC FTN; c1968-1972. 35mm SLR cmera. MFPS; 1-1/000s. T.B.; Cds meter; needle display; ¹⁄₆₀s.X.M. flash exp.

R2*   **F–**

NIKON F2; c1971-1980. 35mm SLR camera. MFPS; 10s-¹⁄₂₀₀₀s.T.B.; Cds meter; ¹⁄₈₀s.X.M.flash exp.

R2*   **E–**

NIKON F2 PHOTOMIC; c1971-1977. 35mm SLR camera. MFPS 10s.-¹⁄₂₀₀₀s.T.B.; Cds.meter; needle display;1/80s X.M. flash exp.

R2*   **E**

NIKON F2S PHOTOMIC; c1973-1976. 35mm SLR Cmaera. MFPS 10s.-¹⁄₂₀₀₀s. T.B.; Cds meter; LED display; ¹⁄₈₀s. X,M flash exp.

R2*   **E+**

NIKON F2SB PHOTOMIC: c1976-1977. 35mm SLR Camera. MFPS 10-¹⁄₂₀₀₀s. T.B.; SPD Meter; LED display;1/80s. X,M flash exp.

R2*   **F−**

NIKON F2A PHOTOMIC: c1977-1980. 35mm SLR Camera. MFPS 10-¹⁄₂₀₀₀s T.B.; Cds Meter; Needle display; 1/80s. X,M flash exp.

R2*   **F**

NIKON F2AS PHOTOMIC: (NK143) c.1977-1980. 35mm SLR cmera. MFPS 10-¹⁄₂₀₀₀s.T.B.; SPD meter; LED display; ¹⁄₈₀. X,M flah exp.

R2*   **F+**

NIKON F2T; c1978-1980. 35mm SLR camera. Titanium version of the F2 camera. First series marked with gold coloured logo "Titan" on the front later versions only had "T" to the left of the serial number; The F2T is 5 grams lighter than the F2; recognised by the textured metal surface.

R3*   **H−**

NIKON F3: 1980. The third generation of Nikon professional SLRs. Aperture priority and manual. Titanium electronic shutter 8s-1/2000s + T & B. Inter-change-able finders.

R2*   **E+**

NIKON F3T; c1982. 35mm SLR cmaera. Titanium version of the F3 camera; First series have textured silver finish of the metal. later versions are black; Both models have HP-type finder only.

R3*   **H−**

NIKON F3AF: 1983. First Nikon with autofocus capabilities. Similar to F3 but with relay contacts to link with special Nikon AF lenses. Forerunner of, but different to, the current Nikon autofocus system.

R3*   **F**

NIKON FA: 1983. Introduced Automatic Multi-Pattern Metering to measure and compare five segment areas for the most accurate reading. Aperture priority, shutter priority and manual modes. Electronic shutter 1-1/4000s.

R3*   **F**

NIKON EM: 1979. Nikon's first SLR aimed at amateur use. Aperture priority auto without manual option. Electronic shutter with 1/90s mechanical setting for flash. Audible signal when speed drops below 1/30s. Accepts Nikkor AI lenses, but launched with its own cheaper 'E' range of lenses.

R2*   **E**

NIKKORMAT FT: c1965-196. 35mm SLR camera. MFPS 1-¹⁄₁₀₀₀s. B.; ¹⁄₁₂₅s. X.flash exp; TTL Cds exp meter with needle display;

Acceptes all Nikon Lenses; single stroke winder sets shutter, switches on meter, transports film.

R2* **D**

NIKKOMAT FS: c1965-1971. 35mm SLR camera. Same as FT except No mirror lock-up; No Exp meter; (Rare model).

R3* **F+**

NIKKORMAT FTN: c1967-1975. 35mm SLR camera. MFPS 1-$\frac{1}{1000}$S.B.; $\frac{1}{125}$S X. Flash exp; Cds Meter Needle display.

R2* **D+**

NIKKORMAT EL: c1972-1977. 35mm SLR camera. Auto exp mode; MFPS 4s.-$\frac{1}{1000}$S.; $\frac{1}{125}$S. X,M flash exp.; Cds meter;exp lock;single stroke winder sets shutter, meter and film.

R2* **D+**

NIKKORMAT FT2; c1975-1978. 35mm SLR camera. MFPS 1-$\frac{1}{1000}$S. B.; $\frac{1}{125}$S. X.M. flash exp;plus & minus symbols in Vfr.

R2* **D+**

NIKKORMAT ELW; c1967-1968. 35mm SLR camera. As the EL model modified to take winder.

R2* **E**

NIKKORMAT FT3: c1977-1979. 35mm SLR camera. As the FT2 with AI auto apature coupling;Assesory shoe.

R2* **E**

NIKON FM; c1977-1984. 35mm SLR camera. Bayonet mount for all Nikon lenses; FP Copal shutter 1-$\frac{1}{1000}$S B.;$\frac{1}{125}$S. x flash exp; 2Cds/SPD/Gas meter; LED display;Accepts AW1 motor.

R2* **E**

NIKON FE: c1978-1984. 35mm SLR camera. Auto/manual version of the FM model; Interchangable screens; MFP Electronic shutter 8s.-$\frac{1}{1000}$S. B.; $\frac{1}{90}$S. M; $\frac{1}{125}$S. x.flash exp.

R2* **E**

NIKON FM2; c1982-1988. 35mm SLR camera. As FM with titanium shutter to $\frac{1}{4000}$S. and $\frac{1}{200}$ X flash exp; Cds/SPD/Gas meter; LED display.

R1* **F–**

NIKON FG: c1982-1987. 35mm SLR camera. MFPS 1-$\frac{1}{1000}$S. B.; M $\frac{1}{90}$, X $\frac{1}{125}$ flash exp.; SPD meter; LCD display; Manual & progamme exp; TTL flash metering.

R1* **D**

NIKON FE2: c1983-1989. 35mm SLR camera. As FE with shutter speeds to $\frac{1}{4000}$S.; TTL- flash control $\frac{1}{200}$S. exp.

R1* **F–**

NIKON FM2N: c1983. 35mm SLR camera. As the FM2 with flash shutter speed of $\frac{1}{250}$S.

R1* **F–**

NIKON F3/T: 1983-86. Full system 35mm SLR with titanium finish; fps 1-¹⁄₁₀₀₀s.

R3* **G+**

Note: Nikon continued to make professional SLRs throughout the 1980s that included the F3HP, F3T and F3P before introducing the F4 in 1988, which was followed by its own variations up to the F5 and on into the N series of cameras. Full details and specifications of all these models can be found in the book Japanese 35mm SLR Cameras by Bill Hansen and Michael Dierdorff, published by Hove Books.

NIKONOS I: 35mm underwater camera; Nikkor 35mm f2.8 lens.

R3* **E– CALYPSO F**

NIKON SUPER ZOOM 8: Super 8mm movie camera. Cine Nikkor Zoom 8.8mm-45mm f1.8 lens; Electric motor drive-12, 18 or 24 frames per sec.

R3* **C+**

NIKKOREX ZOOM 35: c1963. SLR fitted with non-interchangeable 43-86mm zoom lens, f3.5, 1-500s, auto-exposure. First camera with a non- inter-changeable zoom lens.

R2* **D**

NIKON ACCESSORIES

NIKON RANGEFINDER MOTOR DRIVES

Motordrive S36 for Nikon SP: chrome	**H+**
Motordrive S36 for Nikon SP: black	**H+**
Motordrive S72 for Nikon S3M	**I+**

NIKON RANGEFINDER LENSES

21mm/f4 lens w/finder	**H**
25mm/f4 lens chrome	**F+**
25mm/f4 lens black	**G–**
28mm/f3.5 lens chrome	**F**
28mm/f3.5 lens black	**F**
35mm/f3.5 lens "MIOJ"	**F**
35mm/f3.5 lens chrome	**E**
35mm/f3.5 lens black	**E+**
35mm/f2.5 lens chrome	**E+**
35mm.f2.5 lens black	**F–**
35mm/f2.5 lens black: type II	**F+**
35mm/f1.8 lens black	**F**
35mm/f1.8 lens, type II	**F**
50mm/f3.5 micro lens	**G+**
50mm/f3.5 collapsible lens	**G+**
50mm/f2 collapsible lens marked "Tokyo"	**G–**
50mm/f2 lens chrome	**D+**
50mm/f2 lens black with chrome	**E–**
50mm/f2 lens all black	**G**
50mm/f1.5 lens	**G+**
50mm/f1.4 lens marked "Tokyo"	**E**
50mm/f1.4 lens chrome	**E–**
50mm/f1.4 lens black and chrome	**E–**
50mm/f1.4 lens all black	**G+**
50mm/f1.4 lens aluminium	**H–**
50mm/f1.4 lens "Olympic"	**G+**
50mm/f1.1 lens internal mount	**G+**
50mm/f1.1 lens external mount	**H–**
85mm/f2 lens chrome	**E+**
85mm/f2 lens black	**F–**
85mm/f2 lens "MIOJ"	**F+**
85mm/f1.5 lens	**H–**
105mm/f4 lens	**G+**
105mm/f2.5 lens	**F**
135mm/f4 lens: short mount	**F**
135mm/f4 lens	**G–**
135mm/f3.5 lens chrome	**D+**
135mm/f3.5 lens black	**E–**
180mm/f2.5 lens	**G**
250mm/f4 lens manual aperture	**G–**
250mm/f4 lens pre-set aperture	**F+**
350mm/f4.5 lens	**H**
500mm/f5 lens	**I+**
1000mm/f6.3 lens black	**K–**

1000mm/f6.3 lens grey	**J**
Stereo outfit	**K–**

Nikon produced innumerable accessories for their rangefinder system. They produced chrome optical finders in 35, 85, 105, and 135mm lengths. Very early 35, 85 and 135mm finders are marked Nippon Kogaku Tokyo and cover 24 x 34. Later finders are marked Nippon Kogaku Japan and cover 24 x 36. Types marked with an L on the base were designed for Leica type cameras and covered 24 x 36. Those marked with a C were made for Contaxes and have a longer foot. The 21 and 25mm finders were produced in black finish. Nikon also produced a series of brightine finders. The 35, 85, 105 and 135 brightline finders are not uncommon. The 50mm brightline is quite rare. The stereo brightline finder is extremely desirable.

21mm finder black	**F+**
25mm finder black	**E+**
28mm finder chrome	**E–**
35mm finder chrome	**D**
35mm finder black	**E**
35mm "mini" finder	**G**
50mm finder black	**G**
85mm finder chrome	**D**
85mm finder black	**E+**
105mm finder chrome	**D**
105mm finder black	**E+**
135mm finder chrome	**D**
135mm finder black	**E**
Stereo Finder	**H**
Sportsfinder	**G–**

Nikon produced a variable finder called the Variframe similar to the Leitz Vidom. The original model is finished in dull chrome and marked 24 x 32 for use with the Model I. The black screw-in 28mm adaptor for the variframe is extremely desirable. Nikon also made a very common zoom finder covering focal lengths 35 to 135mm. Some of these have markings for the Leica type lenses as well. These are quite common. The 28mm adaptor for this finder is uncommon. Two types of sportsfinder exist with yellow and silver backs.

Variframe 24x32 dull	**I–**
Variframe 24x32 bright	**H+**
Variframe M "MIOJ"	**F**
Variframe chrome	**E**
Variframe black with shoe	**F+**
Variframe black without shoe	**F+**
28mm adaptor for variframe	**F+**
Varifocal Zoom "MIOJ"	**G**
Varifocal Zoom type I	**E**
Varifocal Zoom type II	**E**
28mm adaptor for	
Varifocal Zoom: **E+**	
RF Illuminator: **F**	
Reflex housing type I: **I–**	
Reflex housing	
type II 45 degree	**H**
90 degree prism only	**I–**
Bellows model I	**H–**
Exposure meter, grey top	**F**
Exposure meter, black top	**E**
Microflex type I	**H–**
Microflex type II	**H–**
"S" copy stand	**G+**
"SA" copy stand	**G**
"P" copy stand	**H–**
"PA" copy stand	**G**
21mm lens shade	**F–**
25mm lens shade	**E–**
50mm lens shade for f1.1lens	**E+**
Micro Collar	**F+**

LENSES FOR NIKON F:

2.1cm/f4.0 lens with finder	**F–**
2.8cm/f3.5 lens	**H–**

3.5cm/f2.8 lens	**E–**
5.0cm/f2.0 lens	**C+**
5.8cm/f1.4 lens	**E–**
5.5cm/f3.5 preset macro lens	**G**
10.5cm/f2.5 lens	**E+**
10.5cm/f4.0 lens	**F–**
13.5cm/f3.5 lens	**E–**
20.0cm/f4.0 lens	**E–**
8.5 to 25cm zoom, two touch	**F–**
8.5 to 25cm zoom, one touch	**F–**
50cm mirror lens, with case and filters	**G**
100cm mirror lens	**I–**

METERS FOR NIKON F

Model 1 meter, round type	**E+**
Model 2 meter, long window	**D+**
Nikkorex type	**D**
Model 3 meter, square type	**D+**
Booster module for the above	**C+**

MOTORS FOR NIKON F

Type one, number on the base plate	**F+**
Type two, Nippon Kogaku logo on the front	**F–**
Type three, marked Nikon, and numbered on the back	**E+**
Grey pack	**E–**
Brown battery pack	**D**
Black battery pack	**C+**
250 exposure back	**F–**

MISC. ACCESSORIES FOR NIKON F

Waist level finder, type one, with Nippon Kogaku logo	**D**
Waist level finder type two, with Nikon F markings	**C+**
Copy stand for Nikon F	**E–**
Electronic flash, S.B. 1	**D+**
Flash BC 7, for flash bulbs	**B**

NIMSLO, America

NIMSLO: 1980. First seen at photokina, then again at the next photokina in 1982 before finally reaching the market in 1983. Four-lens stereo camera invented by Jerry Nims and Allen Lo. Processing by Nimslo labs cut the four images into strips and overlaid them with screen made up of minute prisms to give 3-D effect without the need for viewer. Fixed focus, fixed aperture lens. Auto shutter. Film speeds adjustable for 100 & 400 ASA.

R2*   **C**

Nitto Shashin Yohin KK, Japan

ELEGA: c1951, 35mm VFR camera, Leica copy, Elega or Eleger f3.5/45mm lens in a fixed mount, guillotine shutter 1 -1/200s, built-in film cutter.

R4*   **F+**

With "Olympic" name: **G**

Normura Optical Co. Japan

TANZER: c.1950. Bakelite TLR-style box camera for Bolta film. 4.2cm fixed focus lens. I & B shutter.

R3*   **C**

FLASH TANZER: c.1950. Similar to first model but with flash synch.

R3*   **C**

Odeon Photo *Paris, France*

ISOGRAPHE: 6 x 13cm stereo camera, Boyer Saphir f4.5 or Berthiot Flor f5.7 lens; shutter 1-½₀₀s. Two models: 6 x 13cm exp on plates, fixed focus, or 6 x 13cm exp on 620 roll film, micrometer focusing.

R4*   **F**

Officiene Galileo
Milan, Italy

GAMI 16: 1953. Superior CRF subminiature for 12x17mm images on 16mm film. Opening lens cover winds clockwork motor drive and advances film. 25mm f1.9 Esamitar lens behind metal shutter, 1/2-1/1000s. Built in extinction meter and yellow filter. Focusing my moving film plane. Accessories included close-up lenses, developing tank, underwater housing and auxiliary telephoto lenses.

R3*   **C+**

Office General de La Photographie
Paris, France

THE EXPRESS DETECTIVE NADAR: c1888. Mahogany (reinforced with brass) box-type detective camera; Anastigmat Zeiss 86mm f18 wide angle lens; for 13 x 18cm plates or roll film with Eastman Walker back. Distributed by Nadar. Nadar was George Eastman's French representative. He added exposure counter.

R4*   **G+**

OKAM: *See Section K Odon KEYSLAR.*

R3*   **E+**

O.I.P. *(Society Belge d'Optique et d'Instruments de Precision*
Paris, France

CINESCOPIE: c. 1929. Miniature made for 24x24mm images on paper-backed 35mm film. f3.5 O.I.P. Labor lens. Lens and shutter assembly removable for use with an enlarger. Approx 300 made.

R4*   **E**

Okada Optical Co. Ltd.
Japan

GEMMY: c1950. Pistol-type detective camera; 35mm f4.5 lens; 3 speed shutter. 11 x 18mm exp on 16mm film; film advanced by trigger action.

R4*   **I**

Olympus Optical Co. Ltd.
Tokyo, Japan

SEMI OLYMPUS: 1936. The first Olympus camera. Vertical folding bellows type for 16 exp on 120. 75mm f4.5 Coroner lens. Shutter was imported rimset Compur on early models, Japanese Crown copy on later models 1/5-1/200s + T & B. Folding viewfinder

R3*   **E**

SEMI OLYMPUS II: 1938. Style changed to horizontal type. 16 exp on 120. Rigid viewfinder. 75mm f4.5 Zuiko lens, Koho shutter.

R3*   **E**

OLYMPUS SIX: 1939. Bellows camera similar to Semi Olympus Model II, but format increased for 12 exp 6x6cm on 120. 75mm f3.5 Zuiko. Koho shutter. Postwar models used improved lens and, late models used Copal shutters.

R3*   **E**

OLYMPUS CHROME SIX: 1948. Original model based on Semi Olympus II with chrome top plate. 75mm f3.5 Zuiko. Copal shutter 1-1/200s + B.

R2*   **D**

OLYMPUS CHROME SIX II: 1948. Similar to first model with f2.8 lens.

R2*   **D**

OLYMPUS CHROME SIX II: 1950. Similar to Model II plus flash synch. Found with f2.8 and f3.5 lenses

R2*   **D**

OLYMPUS PEN F: 1960. The first 35mm half-frame SLR camera made for production. Use of a porro prism does away with the familiar pentaprism hump on most other 35mm SLR cameras. FPS, to ⅟₅₀₀s; no metering system, but an accessory meter was available. With Zuiko 38mm, f1.8 lens. This camera, along with the Pen FT and Pen FV, is less rare in the USA, where prices for all Pen F cameras tend to be about 30% less than in Europe. Black version; double the prices.

R3* BLACK   **E**

CHROME   **D+**

PEN S2.8: c1960; Zuiko 30mm f2.8 lens; Copal X shutter.

R2*   **C+**

PEN EE: c1961; Fixed focus 28mm f3.5 lens large electric eye surrounds the lens.

R2*   **C+**

PEN EES: c1962. As the EE model, but with zone focusing 30mm f2.8 lens.

R2*   **C+**

PEN D: c1962. Zuiko f1.9 32mm lens; Copal X shutter; meter read out on top of camera.

R2*   **C+**

Pen EES

PEN D2: c1964. As model D, but with Cds meter.

R2*   **C+**

PEN W: c1964. As Pen S, but with 25mm f2.8 wide-angle lens; all black body.

R2*   **D+**

PEN RAPID EE.S: c1965. As the EES model, but designed to take the Agfa-rapid cassette.

R2*   **C–**

PEN RAPID EE.D: c1965. As the EED model, but with Agfa-rapid easy loading system.

R2*   **C–**

OLYMPUS PEN FT: Updated version of the Pen F, using a semi-silvered mirror to permit through-the-lens metering at full aperture; self-timer. Black version less common, and brings 50% more. With Zuiko 38mm, f1.8 lens.

R3*   **E+**

OLYMPUS PEN FV: Simplified version of the Pen FT, using a fully silvered mirror in order to brighten the finder image. This results in the loss of through-the-lens metering. The last model made. With 38mm, f1.8 Zuiko lens.

R4*   **E**

OLYMPUS PEN F MICROSCOPE CAMERA: in Chrome only.

R3*   **E**

OLYMPUS PEN FT MICROSCOPE CAMERA: in Black only.

R4*   **E**

LENSES FOR OLYMPUS PEN F SLR CAMERAS

20mm/f3.5 G Zuiko Auto W lens	**E**
25mm/f2.8 G Zuiko Auto W lens	**E**
25mm/f4.0 E Zuiko Auto W lens	**E–**
38mm/f1.8 F Zuiko Auto S lens	**C+**
38mm/f2.8 D Zuiko Auto S lens: Made for Europe during a six month period, without the diaphragm ring used for the Pen FT metering system, quite rare	**E**
38mm/f2.8 Compact E Zuilo Auto S lens	**D+**
38mm/f3.5 E Zuiko Macro lens	**E**
40mm/f1.4 G Zuiko Auto S lens	**F–**
42mm/f1.2 M Zuiko Auto S lens	**E+**
60mm/f1.5 G Zuiko Auto T lens	**F–**
70mm/f2.0 F Zuiko Auto T lens	**F–**
100mm/f3.5 E Zuiko Auto T lens	**D+**
150mm/f4.0 E Zuiko Auto T lens	**D–**
250mm/f5.0 E Zuiko Auto T lens	**F**
400mm/f6.3 E Zuiko Auto T lens	**G**
800mm/f8.0 Zuiko Mirror T lens	**G+**
50-90mm/f3.5 Zuiko Auto Zoom lens	**E**
100-200mm/f5.0 Zuiko Auto Zoom lens	**E+**
100-200mm/f5.0 Zuiko Zoom lens	**E+**

ACCESSORIES FOR PEN F SLR CAMERAS

Bellows Pen F	**D–**
Slide copier Pen F	**C**
Bellows Pen F II	**D**
Slide copier Pen F II	**C+**
Accessory light meter for Pen F and FV	**C+**
Microscope adaptor Pen F	**C+**

OLYMPUS ACE: 1958-60, The first Olympus 35mm RFR camera to be sold with interchangeable lenses. Four lenses including the E Zuiko 4.5cm, f2.8 normal lens were available for this camera, not three as is widely believed. with 4.5mm, f2.8 lens.

R3*   **D+**

OLYMPUS ACE E: 1959-61. Same as the Olympus Ace (OY105), but with the addition of match needle metering. With normal 4.5cm, f2.8 lens.

R3*   **E–**

ACCESSORY LENSES FOR OLYMPUS ACE CAMERAS

3.5cm/f2.8 E Zuiko W ACE lens   **D+**

8cm/f4.0 E Zuiko T ACE lens   **E–**

8cm/f5.6 E Zuiko T ACE lens   **E–**

OLYMPUS 35 I : 1948-49, 24 x 32mm format on 35mm film, coated 4cm, f3.5 Zuiko lens in Seikosha Rapid shutter.

R3*   **D+**

AUTO EYE: 1961. Shutter priority 35mm VFR camera. Set aperture indicated in viewfinder. Click stop focusing with feet and symbols markings. 45mm f2.8 D-Zuiko lens. Copal SV shutter to 1/500s + B.

R2*   **C–**

OLYMPUS 35 III : 1949-50. 24 x 36mm format on 35mm film, the first from Olympus in this format. coated 4cm, f3.5 Zuiko lens in Seikosha Rapid shutter. Made for only three months.

R4*   **D+**

OLYMPUS TRIP 35: 35mm VFR camera with built-in light meter, made in very large numbers.

R1*   **C**

OLYMPUS PEN W: 1964-65. Black version of the Pen S but with fixed 25mm, f2.8 lens.

R4*   **E–**

OLYMPUS M-1: C.1972. 35mm SLR camera; FPS 1-¹⁄₁₀₀₀s; full range of lenses; later to be called OM-1.

R3*   **F**

OLYMPUS: OM-1: 1972. Commercial version of the MI, made after Leica objected to the name. 35mm manual SLR. TTL metering. FP shutter 1-1/1000s.

R1*   **D**

OLYMPUS OM-1N: 1979. Similar to OM-1 with redesigned film lever and rewind, plus flash ready signal in viewfinder.

R1*   **D**

OLYMPUS OM-2: 1976. Manual metering 35mm SLR. First with Off The Film metering for flash and long speeds above 1/15s. FP shutter 60s-1/1000s.

R1*   **D**

OLYMPUS OM-10: 1978. Aperture priority auto 35mm SLR. FP shutter 2s-1/1000s. Needed manual adapter for use as manual camera.

R1*   **D+**

OLYMPUS OM-2N: 1979. Similar to OM-2 plus aperture priority automation. FP shutter 120s-1/1000s.

R1*   **D**

OLYMPUS OM-3: 1983. Similar to OM-2 with metering for centre weighting, average and 2% spot. FP shutter 1-1/2000s

R2*   **D**

OLYMPUS OM-30: 1983. 35mm SLR, made to offer autofocus capability when used with its Zuiko 35-70mm zoom AF lens with focusing mechanism built in. Otherwise used as manual focus camera. Follow focus with motor drive was claimed to be possible.

R2*   **D**

Note: This is only a selection of Olympus 35mm SLRs made during the 1970s and 1980s. Other models, with slight variations in specification, included the OM-25P, OM-3Ti, OM-4, OM4-T, OM10FC, OM10 Quartz, OM 77AF, OM101, OM20 and OM40. Some of these had name variants in the US. Full details and specifications of all these models can be found in the book Japanese 35mm SLR Cameras by Bill Hansen and Michael Dierdorff, published by Hove Books.

XA: 1979. Unusually styled 35mm CRF camera. Aperture priority automation. Manual focus with rangefinder. 35mm f2.8 Zuiko lens with sliding cover. Electronic shutter 10s-1/500s. Backlight control.

R1*   **C**

XA1: Similar to XA with Selenium meter cell around lens. Fixed focus f4 Zuiko. Programmed automation 1/30-1/250s.

R1*   **C**

XA2: Similar to XA but with focusing lens at three symbol settings. f3.5 Zuiko.

R1*   **C**

XA3: Similar to XA2 with DX film coding option.

R?   **C**

XA4: Similar style to other XA cameras, but with 28mm wideangle lens. Programmed automation. Easy film load system. Focuses down to 0.3 metres.

R1*   **C**

Optik Primar Kamera Werke VEB,
Görlitz, East Germany.

Post-War successor to the Bentzin Factory

PRIMARFLEX II: c1950, SLR for 6cm x 6cm frames on 120 roll film, interchangeable Trioplan f2.8/10cm lens, interchangeable VFR, same shutter problems as pre-war Primarflex.

R3* **E–**

STUDIO PRIMAR: c1950, SLR camera for 9cm x 12cm plates, specially reinforced lens standard and focusing rails in order to maintain "even the heaviest lenses" parallel to the film plane! CFPS 1-⅕₀₀s.

R4* **E–**

O.P.L. (Optique de Précision– Levallois)
France.

FOCA PF1 (*) ONE STAR: 1946-53. CFPS, ½₀-⅕₀₀s; viewfinder only. Non-interchangeable f3.5, 35mm model made only in 1946

Foca PF I
(*) one star

(5300 cameras made). From 1947 to 1953 the lens was interchangeable (11,900 cameras made). Vfr shows fields of view for the 35mm lens. With minor modifications this camera became the Foca Standard of 1953. (see ID and dating section in the front of the Blue Book for Foca serial number information).

R3* **E**

FOCA "POST": 1952-?. CFPS ½₅s only; 24mm x 30mm frame size; VFR not modified; 50mm, f3.5 Oplar lens; focusing between 30 and 35cm; diaphragm blocked between f5.6 and f8. Easily recognized by four ball shaped protrusions located on the front of the camera. Used to photograph telephone registers, just as the Leica "Post" cameras.

R4* **E+**

FOCA STANDARD: 1953. Cfps, ½₀-⅕₀₀s; Viewfinder only with field of view for 35mm lens; interchangeable screw mount f3.5, 35mm or f2.8, 50mm lens. Early cameras are easily distinguished from later ones by their lack of rewind lever on the front of the top plate. At least six models were made, each with slight physical variations. Not the most common of Focas, as some might think!

R3*   **E–**

FOCA PF2 (**) TWO STAR: 1946. Cfps, ½₀-⅕₀₀s; combined RFR/VFR; 36mm interchangeable screw mount f3.5, 5cm or f2.8, 5cm Oplar lens. Only the 50mm lenses couple accurately with the rangefinder. Early cameras had brown body covering, worth about 75% more.

R3*   **E–**

FOCA PF2B: The PF2b (the "b" meaning "bis", continued in French) has ⅕ – ⅟₁₀₀₀s shutter and factory installed X and M synch, otherwise the same as PF2. Same price for either camera. Military examples exist and are worth about 200% more.

R3*   **E–**

FOCA PF3 (***) THREE STAR: 1952. Cfps, 1 – ⅟₁₀₀₀s; combined RFR/VFR; 36mm interchangeable screw mount f3.5, 5cm or f2.8, 5cm Oplar lens or with faster f1.9, 5cm Oplarex lens. Only the 50mm lenses couple accurately with the rangefinder. With and without synch. Military examples do exist and are worth about 200% more.

R3*   **E**

FOCA PF3 L (***) THREE STAR: 1956. Cfps, 1 – ⅟₁₀₀₀s; combined RFR/VFR; 36mm interchangeable screw mount f3.5, 5cm or f2.8, 5cm Oplar lens or with faster f1.9, 5cm Oplarex lens. Only the 50mm lenses couple accurately with the rangefinder. Military examples do exist and are worth about 200% more.

R3*   **E**

FOCA UNIVERSEL: 1946. Cfps, 1-⅟₁₀₀₀s; combined RFR/VFR; bayonet mount f1.9 or f2.8 50mm coated lenses coupled to the RFR; X and M synch indicated by letters.

R3*   **F+**

FOCA UNIVERSEL "R": 1955. Cfps, 1-⅟₁₀₀₀s; combined RFR/VFR; bayonet mount f1.9 or f2.8 50mm coated lenses coupled to the RFR; X and M synch. An improved version of the Universel with lever wind, and a quieter shutter. Graphic symbols indicate flash synch sockets.

R3*   **F–**

FOCA UNIVERSEL "RC": 1959. Cfps 1-⅟₁₀₀₀s; combined RFR/VFR; bayonet mount

f1.9, or 2.8 lens, coupled to RFR; bright line projected frame in VFR. An improved version of the Universel "R". Less than 2000 cameras are thought to have been made. Thought by some to be the best made French 35mm camera. Some outfits were made for the French Navy, and bear the markings "Marine Nationale" on the front, along with a contract number. These cameras are worth about 300% more than normal Universel "RC".

R3*   **F**

FOCAFLEX: 1960 - 68. SLR; BTL leaf shutter, 1-¼₅₀s; fixed mount f2.8, 5cm Neoplex lens. Since no pentaprism was used, the camera body is quite slim.

R3*   **E+**

FOCAFLEX II: 1962 - 68. SLR; BTL leaf shutter, 1-¼₅₀s; interchangeable bayonet mount lenses. Retroplex f4.0, 3.5cm wide-angle lens, f2.8, 5cm Neoplex normal lens, f4.0, 9cm Teleoplex telephoto lens and

very rare f4.0, 15cm Super Teleoplex lenses were available.

R3*   **E**

FOCAFLEX AUTOMATIC: 1961 - 68. SLR; BTL leaf shutter, 1 - ¼₅₀s; fixed mount f2.8, 5cm Neoplex lens. Since no pentaprism was used, the camera body is quite slim. This camera is the same as the Focaflex, with the addition of a built-in light meter.

R3*   **D+**

FOCA SPORT : 1954. BTL leaf shutter, 1-⅟₃₀₀s; fixed f3.5, 4.5cm Neoplar lens with scale focusing, knob advance and removable back.

R2*   **D–**

FOCA SPORT I: 1956. BTL leaf shutter, 1-⅟₃₀₀s; fixed f3.5, 4.5cm Neoplar lens with scale focusing; removable back. Differs from Foca Sport by addition of lever advance.

R2*   **D–**

FOCA SPORT C: 1957. BTL leaf shutter, 1-¹⁄₃₀₀s; fixed f3.5, 4.5cm Neoplar lens with scale focusing; lever advance and removable back. Differs from Foca Sport I by the addition of a built-in light meter.

R2* **D–**

FOCA SPORT IB: 1958. BTL leaf shutter, 1-¹⁄₃₀₀s; fixed f2.8, 4.5cm Oplar-Colour lens with scale focusing; lever advance and removable back, differs from Focasport I by addition of faster lens, and projected frame in the VFR.

R2* **D–**

FOCA SPORT ID: 1958. BTL leaf shutter, 1-¹⁄₃₀₀s; fixed f2.8, 4.5cm Oplar-Colour lens with scale focusing; lever advance and removable back. Combines the projected frame and faster lens of the Foca Sport Ib with the light meter of the Foca Sport C.

R2* **D–**

FOCA SPORT II: 1963. BTL leaf shutter, 1-¹⁄₃₀₀s; fixed f2.8, 4.5cm Oplar-Colour lens coupled to RFR; lever advance and removable back.

R2* **D–**

LENSES AND ACCESSORIES FOR FOCA AND FOCAFLEX

SCREW MOUNT

28mm f4.5 Oplex	**D**
35mm f3.5 Oplex	**C+**
90mm f3.5 Oplex or Teleoplar	**D**
135mm f4.5 Teleoplar	**D**
200mm f6.3 Teleoplar, for use with "Micro Foca" mirror box	**E–**

BAYONET MOUNT

28mm f4.5 Oplex	**E**
35mm f3.5 Oplex	**D+**
90mm f3.5 Oplex or Teleoplar	**E–**
135mm f4.5 Teleoplar	**E–**
200mm f6.3 Teleoplar, for use with "Micro Foca" mirror box	**E+**

Screw mount lenses for Foca cameras. Left to right, they are the 135mm f4.5 Teleoplar, 90mm f3.5 Oplex and 28mm f4.5 Oplex.

ACCESSORIES FOR RANGEFINDER FOCAS

Foca Universel finder, fields of view for 28mm, 35mm, 50mm, 90mm, 135mm	**D**
35mm optical finder	**C+**
Sports finder	**D–**
Focanox, brightline finder for 50mm lenses	**D**
Micro Foca mirror box	**RARE F**
Focascaph underwater housing	**E+**

LENSES FOR FOCAFLEX IIF

3.5cm f4 Retroplex	**D–**
9cm f4 Teleoplex	**D**
15cm f4 Super-Teleoplex	**RARE F**

*Foca screwmount lenses are NOT the same thread size as Leica screw.

Oshira Optical Works
Japan

EMI K: 1956. Lens shutter, ¹⁄₂₅-¹⁄₃₀₀s; VFR only; fixed Eminent Colour, or Fujiyama F2.8, 50mm lens. Not often seen, but not very valuable.

R3* **C–**

EMI 35 A: 1956. Lens shutter, 1-¼₀₀s; VFR only; fixed Tri-Lausar Anistigmat f3.5, 45mm lens. Not often seen.

R3*   **C+**

Osterreichishe Telephon A.G.
Vienna, Austria

AMOURETTE: c1925. 35mm camer. Double microscope 35mm f6.3 lens; shutter ⅕ - ¼₀₀s. 50 exp on 35mm film in special double cassette. First camera to have form of interchangeable back.

R4*   **F**

Thomas Ottewill, England

OTTEWILL 8 X 10 WET PLATE CAMERA: c1856, sliding box and wet plate camera; Andrew Ross lens.

FR5*   **H**

Ottico Meccanica Italiana, OMI, Rome, Italy

SUNSHINE: c1947. Three-lens 35mm VFR camera for three colour seperation negatives, each 9 x 12mm on standard 35mm film. f3.5, 35mm lenses; simple shutter. The negatives were contact printed into positives, and then the camera was used as a projector for viewing the resulting full colour pictures! Rare and interesting, this camera has a very volatile price. (price indicated includes all parts for using as projector.)

R5*   **H–**

Owla, Japan

OWLA STEREO: c1958. 35mm VFR stereo camera. Focusing Owla Anistigmat 35mm, f3.5 lenses; shutter speeds ¼₀-¼₀₀s; top mounted accessory shoe. Two versions seem to exist with different focusing knobs.

R3*   **E**

Reference Notes

Panon Camera Co.
Tokyo, Japan

PANON CAMERA: 1952. Wide-angle panoramic VFR camera for 6 exp on 120 roll film. Panon 50mm, f2.8 coated lens; 140 degree coverage angle.

R3*   **H–**

WIDELUX: 1959. Panoramic camera for 24x59mm images on 35mm film. 26mm

f2.8 Lux lens rotates during exposure to give 140° angle of view. Speed of rotation determines shutter speeds 1/5s, 1/50s & 1/200. Apertures to f11.

R3*   **H**

Note: New models of the Widelux have been produced since this original version, right up until the present day. They include the Widelux FV, F6, F6B and F7. Later models tend to be bought for use rather than collecting.

Papigny

JUMELLE PAPIGNY: c1902. 8 x 16cm Box-type stereo camera. Chevalier 10cm, f6.5 lens; speed guillotine shutter. Bellows; rack focusing; central finder. 8 x 8cm exp on plates.

R3*   **E+**

Parker Pen Company
Janesville, Wisconsin

THE PARKER CAMERA: c1948-50. Subminiature camera. Black & white or colour daylight loading cartridge; film exposed on inner rim of cartridge through mirror.

R4*   **G+**

H.V. Parsells et Fils
France.

PARSELL'S DETECTIVE CAMERA: c1885. Wooden box-type detective camera. Rapid rectilinear lens; pneumatic front-of-lens shutter; 6 double holders, 6.5 x 6.5cm exp. Tripod in form of cane. With tripod.

R5*   **D–**

PAX GOLDEN VIEW: c1954. 35mm RFR camera. Luminor Anastigmat 45mm, f3.5 lens; ⅒-⅟₃₀₀s. Mfd in Japan.
R3* **D+**

Samuel Peck & Co.
New Haven, Connecticut

PECK FOUR-TUBE FERROTYPE CAMERA: c1868. Takes four ninth-plate tintypes.
R5* **G–**

VEB Pentacon
see Guthe & Thorsch

Perken Son & Raymewnt
London, England

OPTIMUS DETECTIVE CAMERA: c1890. Leather money-pouch type detective camera; rapid rectilinear lens; Thornton Pickard FPS. 8 x 10.5cm plates.
R5* **F+**

PERKEN, SON & RAYMENT DETECTIVE CAMERA: c1896. Thornton Pickard roller blind shutter.
R5* **F**

PERKEN, SON & CO. LTD. 4" X 5" FOLDING PLATE CAMERA: c1900's. 4" x 5" Folding plate camera; brass lens and shutter, rotating diaphragm stops. Remov-

able ground glass back; reversible back. Front standard adjustable; leather covered, brass fittings.
R3* **E**

PERKEN, SON & RAYMENT TAILBOARD CAMERA: c1910. P.S. & R. brass barrel Rapid Euryscope lens slotted for waterhouse stops. Mahogany finish, brass fittings; maroon leather bellows and lens cap.
R3* **E+**

Le Perreaux *France*

STEREO SIMDA: c1950. Roussel Microcolor 25mm, f3.5 lenses; shutter 1-⅟₂₅₀s, flash synch. 300 exp on 16mm movie film.
R4* **F**

Perry Mason & Co.
Boston, Massachusetts

THE ARGUS: c1890. Leather handbag type detective camera. 12 exp, 8cm diameter; plate changed by turning lens mount.

R5*   **G**

HARVARD CAMERA: c1880. Simple tin box camera finished in black with gold striping; meniscus lens; 2 1/2 x 4 inch pictures on individual glass plates. No shutter, exposure made by removing lens cap. A complete outfit with plates, tripod, and all developing and printing accessories cost $1.75. It was offered at a reduced price (50 cents) to subscribers of the magazine "The Youth's Companion." A variety of different models were produced over a period of about 10 years, all of them very simple. A complete intact outfit is rare indeed and worth easily 2 to 3 times the price of a stand-alone camera.

R4*   **D+**

LE PETIT POUCET: French magazine camera; 4 x 4cm plates. Mfd in France.

R3*   **C+**

Petri Camera Co.
Tokyo, Japan

FOTOCHROME: 1965. Made by Petrie for the American importer Fotochrome Inc and used for promotional purposes.

Special purpose film pre-loaded in its own cassette gave direct positive colour prints when processed by the Fotochrome company. 5.3x8cm. Film runs at right angles to lens. Auto exposure via Selenium cell surrounding lens. Focusing by distance settings and symbols. Built-in flashgun.

R2*   **C+**

W. Phillips
Birmingham, England

DEMON DETECTIVE CAMERA NO. 1: c1889. Small metal detective camera. Achromatic doublet 30mm, f10 lens; rubber band activated flap type, front-of-lens shutter; single exp, 2¼" diameter on

2¼" square dry plates. Invented by Walter O'Reilly; mfd. for American Camera Co., London, England.

R5* G

PHOENIX: H. Roussel Stylor 13.5cm, f4.5 lens; Compur shutter 1-½₀₀s. 6" x 9" exp on plates.

R3* E

Photavit-Werk
Nurnberg, Germany

PHOTAVIT I: c1930. Miniature camera for 14 exp, 24 x 24mm on 35mm film in special cassette. Schneider-Kreuznach Radionar f7, 40mm lens among others, Photavit or Prontor II shutter.

R3* D

PHOTAVIT I LUXUS: c1930. Same as (PW100) but in "Luxus" edition.

R4* E

PHOTAVIT II: c1935. Miniature camera for 14 exp, 24 x 24mm on 35mm film in special cassette. Primotar f2.9, 40mm lens among others; Compur shutter.

R2* D

BOLTAVIT: c1935. Same camera as (PW102) but for name. Much motre rare.

R4* D+

PHOTAVIT III: c1949. Miniature camera for 25 exp, 24 x 24mm on 35mm film in special cassette. Radionar f3.5, 37.5mm lens; Compur shutter.

R3* D

PHOTAVIT IV: c1950. Miniature camera for 25 exp, 24 x 24mm on 35mm film in special cassette. Xenar f2.8, 40mm lens; Compur shutter.

R3* D

PHOTAVIT V: c1950. As (PW105) but with Luxar f2.9 lens.

R3* D

PHOTINA I: c1950. TLR for 6 x 6cm frames on 120 roll film. f4.5, 75mm lens; Vario shutter.

R2* C+

PHOTINA II: c1950. TLR for 6 x 6cm frames on 120 roll film. f3.5, 75mm lens; Prontor shutter.

R2* C+

PHOTINA REFLEX: c1955. TLR for 6 x 6cm frames on 120 roll film. f3.7, 75mm lens geared to viewing lens for focusing much like the Ricohflex; Prontor shutter.

R2* C+

PHOTAVIT 36: c1956. 35mm RFR camera. The first 24 x 36mm "full frame" camera from Photavit. Interchangeable Ennit f2.8, 45mm lens; Prontor-SVS shutter; CRF.

R3*   **C+**

PHOTAVIT 36B: c1956. Built-in light meter.

R2*   **C+**

PHOTAVIT 36 AUTOMATIC: c1958. 35mm RFR camera. Interchangeable Ennalyt f1.9, 50mm lens; Prontor-SLK shutter; **COUPLED** built-in light meter.

R3*   **C+**

PHOTO CYCLE: c1895. Berthiot Eurigraphe 135mm, f8 lens; Thornton Pickard shutter, ⅕-⅒s; 10 x 12cm exp on roll film. Mfd in France.

R4*   **D+**

PHOTO-ETUI-JUMELLE: c1892. Binocular case detective camera. Rapid rectilinear 120mm, f12 lens; central guillotine shutter; 9 x 12cm plates. Patented by Frank-Valery.

R5*   **G+**

PHOTOLET: c1935. Meniscus 31mm, f8 lens; single speed rotary shutter; 20 x 20mm exp. Mfd in France. c1935.

R3*   **D**

Photo Developments Ltd.
Birmingham, England

ENVOY WIDEANGLE: 1950. Wideangle camera for 8 exp 5.5x8cm on 120. 64mm Envoy fixed focus lens gives 82° angle of view and has apertures marked to f11, but opens wider, probably to f6.5. Shutter 1/25-1/150s + T & B. Could also be used with cut film back.

R3*   **E**

Envoy Wideangle

Photogrammetry Inc., *America*

UNDERWATER PANORAMIC CAMERA: c.1950s. Drum-shaped camera, takes 70mm film in cassettes to produce 6x19cm images. Convex glass side becomes part of the optical system under water. Exposure made by rotating lens. Very rare.

R5*   **E+**

The Photo Materials Co.
Rochester, New York

THE TROKONET CAMERA: c1895. 4" x 5"Magazine camera. 30 exp, 4" x 5" or 12 glass plates.
R4*   **F–**

Photo-See Corp. New York

PHOTO-SEE: c1939. Simple camera for direct positive paper photography. After exposing the paper, it was developed and fixed in a single solution tank fitted to the camera. Really a primitive form of a street photographers camera. Not exactly an "instant" camera but results were possible in several minutes. A number of these turned up in New York in their original boxes several years ago keeping the price down.
R3*   **B+**

John Piggott London, England

ENGLISH SLIDING BOX WET-PLATE CAMERA: c1858. Petzval type lens.
R5*   **G+**

Pignons S.A.
Ballaigues, Switzerland

BOLCA I: c1942-1946. 35mm SLR camera. S.O.M. Berthiot 50mm, f2.9 lens; interchangeable bayonet mount; CFPS 1-¹⁄₁₀₀₀s. Waist level reflex finder; split image RFR. Some late models were marked "Bolsey Model A", rare.
R4*   **F+**

BOLCA (STANDARD): c1942-1946. 35mm SLR camera. S.O.M. Berthiot 50mm, f2.9 lens, interchangeable bayonet mount; CFPS 1-¹⁄₁₀₀₀s. Split image RFR.
R4*   **G+**

English Sliding Box Wet Plate Camera

ALPA (I STANDARD): c1947-1952. 35mm SLR camera. Angenieux 50mm, f2.9 lens; interchangeable bayonet mount; CFPS 1-¹⁄₁₀₀₀s, some without slow speeds, only ½₅-¹⁄₁₀₀₀s. Split image RFR. Snr begins at 11,000. Without slow speeds, prices 25% more.
R4*   **G**

ALPA (II) REFLEX: 35mm SLR camera. Angenieux 50mm, f2.9 lens, interchangeable bayonet mount; CFPS 1-⅟₁₀₀₀s. Split image RFR; waist level reflex finder with flip-up magnifier. Also sold as Bolsey Reflex; called Alpax or Bolsey Reflex G with Angenieux 50mm f2.9 lens; Alitax or Bolsey Reflex H with Angenieux 50mm, f1.8 lens. With f2.9 lens, or with f1.8.

R3*   **F+**

ALPA (III) PRISMA REFLEX: c1949-1952. 35mm SLR camera. Angenieux 50mm, f2.9 lens, interchangeable bayonet mount; CFPS 1-⅟₁₀₀₀s. Split image RFR; 45 degree Kern prism finder. Called Primitax with f1.8 lens. With either lens, also with Xenon 50mm f2.0 lens.

R3*   **F+**

ALPA 4: c1952-1960. 35mm SLR camera. Spektros Alovar f3.5 lens, interchangeable bayonet mount; CFPS 1-⅟₁₀₀₀s. on a single dial. Enclosed (fixed housing and magnifier) 90 degree reflex vf; redesigned body configuration.

R3*   **F+**

ALPA 5: c1952-1960. 35mm SLR camera. Old Delft Alfinon f2.8 or Kern Switar f1.8 lens, interchangeable bayonet mount; CFPS 1-⅟₁₀₀₀s. on single dial. 45 degree Kern eye level prism finder.

R3*   **F+**

ALPA 6: c1955-1959. 35mm SLR camera. Old Delft Alfinon f2.8 or Kern Switar f1.8 lens, interchangeable bayonet mount; CFPS 1-⅟₁₀₀₀s on single dial. Self- timer; prism RFR on ground glass.

R3*   **F**

ALPA 7: c1952-1959. 35mm SLR camera. Kern Switar f1.8 lens, interchangeable bayonet mount; CFPS 1-⅟₁₀₀₀s on single dial. Coupled RFR (vertical base) and multi-focal (50-90-135) combined vf.

R3*   **F**

ALPA 8: c1958-1959. 35mm SLR camera. Kern Switar f1.8 lens, interchangeable bayonet mount; CFPS 1-⅟₁₀₀₀s on single dial. Added coupled RFR (vertical base) and multi-focal (50-90-135) combined vf; with prism RFR.

R3*   **G**

ALPA 7S: c1958-1959. Half-frame 35mm SLR camera. Kern Switar f1.8 lens, interchangeable bayonet mount; CFPS 1-⅟₁₀₀₀s on single dial. Added coupled RFR (vertical base) and multi-focal (50-90-135) combined vf; single frame (18 x 24mm).

R4*   **G+**

ALPA 4B: c1959-1965. 35mm SLR camera. Spektros Alovar f3.5 lens, interchangeable bayonet mount; CFPS 1-⅟₁₀₀₀s on single dial. Enclosed (fixed housing and magnifier) 90 degree reflex vf; rapid return mirror; lever wind.

R3*   **F+**

ALPA 5B: c1959-1965. 35mm SLR camera. Kern Macro Switar f1.8 lens; focus to 8", interchangeable bayonet mount; CFPS 1-⅟₁₀₀₀s on single dial. 45 degree Kern eye level prism finder; rapid return mirror; lever wind.

R3*   **F+**

ALPA 6B: c1959-74. 35mm SLR camera. Macro Switar f1.8 lens, interchangeable bayonet mount; CFPS 1-¹⁄₁₀₀₀s on single dial. Self-timer, prism RFR on ground glass; rapid return mirror; lever wind.

R3*   **F**

ALPA 7B: c1959-1970. 35mm SLR camera. Macro Switar f1.8 lens, interchangeable bayonet mount; CFPS 1-¹⁄₁₀₀₀s on single dial. Coupled RFR (vertical base) and multi-focal (50-90-135) combined vf; rapid return mirror; lever wind.

R3*   **G**

ALPA 8B: c1956-1969. 35mm SLR camera. Macro Switar f1.8 lens, interchangeable bayonet mount; CFPS 1-¹⁄₁₀₀₀s on single dial. Prism RFR on ground glass; rapid return mirror; lever wind.

R3*   **F+**

ALPA 6C: c1960-1969. 35mm SLR camera. Macro Switar f1.8 lens, interchangeable bayonet mount; CFPS 1-¹⁄₁₀₀₀s on single dial. Redesigned prism, straight through viewing, and uncoupled selenium exp meter; rapid return mirror; lever wind.

R3*   **F**

ALPA 9D: c1964-1969. 35mm SLR camera. Macro Switar f1.8 lens, interchangeable bayonet mount; CFPS 1-¹⁄₁₀₀₀s on single dial. Through-the-lens match needle Cds meter, uncoupled. Some models gold or black finish with red or green covering.

R4*   **F+**

ALPA 9F: c1965-1967. 35mm SLR camera. Macro Switar f1.8 lens, interchangeable bayonet mount; CFPS 1-¹⁄₁₀₀₀s on single dial.

R3*   **G+**

ALPA 10D: c1968-1972. 35mm SLR camera. Reformulated Macro Switar f1.9 lens, interchangeable bayonet mount. Redesigned body configuration; through-the-lens match needle Cds meter; cross coupled zero centre meter. Some models gold or black finish with red or green covering.

R3*   **F+**

Coloured models   **F+**

ALPA 11E: c1970-1972. 35mm SLR camera. Reformulated Micro Switar f1.9 lens, interchangeable bayonet mount; CFPS 1-¹⁄₁₀₀₀s on single dial. Cross coupled zero centre meter with illuminated over-under exp arrows in finder. Some models gold or black finish with red or green covering.

R3*   **G**

Coloured models   **F+**

ALPA 10S: c1972. Half-frame 35mm SLR camera. Reformulated Macro Switar f1.9 lens, interchangeable bayonet mount; CFPS 1-¹⁄₁₀₀₀s on single dial. Redesigned body configuration; cross coupled zero centre meter; single frame (18 x 24mm).

R3*   **G+**

ALPA 10F: c1968-1972. 35mm SLR camera. Reformulated Micro Switar f1.9 lens, interchangeable bayonet mount; CFPS 1-¹⁄₁₀₀₀s on single dial. No meter.

R3*   **F+**

ALPA 11EL: c1972-1974. 35mm SLR camera. Reformulated Micro Switar f1.9 lens, interchangeable bayonet mount; CFPS 1-¹⁄₁₀₀₀s on single dial. Cross coupled zero centre meter with illuminated over-under exp arrows in finder.

R3*   **G**

ALPA 11SI: 35mm SLR camera. Reformulated Microc1976-1978. Switar f1.9 lens, interchangeable bayonet mount; CFPS 1-¹⁄₁₀₀₀s on single dial. Cross coupled zero centre meter (red, green, yellow L.E.D.'s). Most have black finish.

R3*   **G+**

Gold models   **H**

ALPA 11Z: c1977. Half-frame 35mm SLR camera. Reformulated Micro Switar f1.9 lens, interchangeable bayonet mount; CFPS ¹⁄₆₀s. No meter; single frame (18 x 24mm). Very rare.

R3*   **H–**

ALPA 11FS: c1977. Half-frame 35mm SLR camera. Reformulated Micro Switar f1.9 lens, interchangeable bayonet mount; CFPS 1-¹⁄₁₀₀₀ s on single dial. Cross coupled zero centre meter; single frame (18 x 24mm).

R3*   **G+**

Pinnock Rty. Ltd.
Sydney, Australia

GYMEA MINOR: c1948. Metal box camera for 6 x 6cm frames on roll film. Simple lens and shutter. Perhaps fifty prototype cameras were made for Pinnock which itself made photographic darkroom equipment and sewing machines. The Gymea was never sold to the public.

R5*   **NSR**

PINNOCK 35: Announced January, 1947. 35mm camera. Copy of the Leica Standard, at least one prototype camera was made, and was seen by Australian lens designer and manufacturer Eric Waterhouse. No camera is known to exist today.

R5*   **NSR**

Plaubel & Co.
Frankfurt, Germany

PLAUBEL MAKINA I: c1924. 6.5 x 9cm Press camera. Anticomar 100mm, f2.9 lens, front elements removable; can be replaced with wide-angle and telephoto components; Compur dial-set shutter 1-¹⁄₂₀₀s. The

Makina I was introduced in 1920 and discontinued in 1932. It came with non-removable 100mm, f4.5 Anticomar lens until 1924; after this it came with 100mm, f2.9 Anticomar lens with removable front elements. 6.5 x 9cm exp on sheet film.

R3*   **E**

PLAUBEL MAKINA II (1938): c1938. 6.5 x 9cm Press camera. Anticomar 100mm, f2.9 lens; Compur shutter 1-½₀₀s. 6.5 x 9cm exp on sheet film.

R3*   **E**

PLAUBEL MAKINA III: c1949. 6.5 x 9cm press camera; Anticomar 100mm f2.9 lens; Compur shutter 1-½₀₀s.

R3*   **F**

PLAUBEL MAKINETTE: c1935. Miniature roll film camera. Supercomar 45mm, f2 lens; Compur shutter 1-⅓₀₀s. 1¼" x 1⅝" exp on 127 roll film.

R4*   **F+**

PLAUBEL ROLLOP: c1935. Folding roll film camera. Anticomar 75mm, f2.8 lens; Compur Rapid shutter 1-¼₀₀s; CRF; 16 exp on 120 roll film.

R3*   **E**

VERIWIDE: 1960. Wideangle camera giving a 100° angle of view on 120 film. 47mm f8 Super Angulon lens. Similar in style to Contarex Hologon, but made for rollfilm rather than 35mm.

R4*   **A**

PLUCKER'S POCKET STEREOGRAPH: c1871. Darlot 21cm, f8 Planigraph lens; built-in circular shutter; 13 x 18cm exp on plates. Mfg. by various opticians, including Dubroni.

R5*   **G+**

Polaroid Inc.
Cambridge, Massachusetts

MODEL 95: 1948. The first instant picture camera. Folding design. Apertures f11-f45, speeds 1/8-1/60s, linked and controlled by single dial, numbered 1-8. Took Polaroid's first instant rollfilm to make sepia pictures in around a minute. Early models had rigid viewfinder mast, later models had folding mast.

R3*   **F**

POLAROID 95A:
R2*   **B+**

POLAROID 95B:
R2*   **B+**

POLAROID 80:
R2*   **A**

POLAROID 80A:
R2*   **A**

POLAROID 80B:
R2*   **A**

POLAROID J33: 1961. Programmed automation 1/15s at f19 to 1/1000s at f64. Built in flashgun for AG1 bulbs.

R2*   **A**

POLAROID J66:
R2*   **A**

AUTOMATIC 100: 1963. World's first camera with fully automated electronic shutter. First Polaroid camera for flat pack film in place of previous rollfilm.

R2*   **A**

POLAROID 101:
R2*   **A**

POLAROID 110:
R2*   **B**

POLAROID 110A:
R2*   **C**

POLAROID 110B:
R2*   **C**

POLAROID 150:
R2*   **A**

POLAROID 160:
R2*   **B+**

POLAROID 180:
R3*   **E+**

POLAROID 195:
R3*   **F–**

POLAROID 210:
R2*   **B–**

POLAROID 420:
R1*   **B–**

POLAROID 450:
R1*   **B–**

POLAROID 800:
R1*   **B–**

POLAROID 900:
R1*   **B–**

HIGHLANDER: 1954. First Model 80 uses similar exposure system to Model 95. Model 80S changes numbers to exposure values. Model 80B with parallax correction marks in viewfinder.
R2*   **B**

ELECTRIC EYE: 1960. First Polaroid camera to offer auto exposure with

Polaroid

programmed automation from 1/2s at f8.8 to 1/600s at f82. Lighten darken control for manual adjustment.

R2*   **B**

POLAROID SX70:

R2*   **D–**

POLAROID SX70, MODEL II:

R2*   **D**

POLAROID SX70 SONAR:

R2*   **C+**

BIG SHOT: 1971. Made specifically for portraiture. Lens fixed focus at 1 metre with built-in rangefinder set for same

distance. Flashcube slots behind diffuser panel on top.

R2*   **B+**

POLAROID COOL-CAM: c1980. Simple to use inexpensive point and shoot auto focus, auto exposure, instant imaging camera for images 3x3½". Originally sold with sunglasses. Pink for the ladies.

R2*   **B+**

Popular Photograph Co.
New York

NODARK FERROTYPE CAMERA: c1899. Wooden box camera. Magazine loading; 26 exp, 2½" x 3½" on ferrotype plates.

R4*   **F+**

Xavier Portafax *France*

PHOTO VOLUME: c1894. Book-type detective camera. Rapid rectilinear or Zeiss lens; direct vf. 9 x 12cm plates.

R5*   **G**

Premier Instrument Corp.
New York, USA

KARDON: 1945. Leica copy. Cfps, 1-$\frac{1}{1000}$s; diopter adjustment; screw mount f2, 47mm

Kodak Ektar. (The exact year of manufacture can be determined using the code described in the ID section of this book.) The military model has enlarged shutter winding and release controls, allowing use of the camera while wearing gloves. The military model now sells for about 20% less than the civilian model. Price given is for a civilian model with lens.

R3* **F**

Kardon (military version)

Left: Kardon (Leica facsimile)

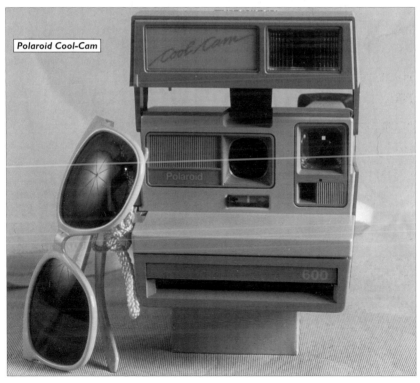

Polaroid Cool-Cam

Ray Camera Co.
refer to Mutschler, Roberson & Co.

THE RECORD CAMERA: TLR box camera. All wooden body; single exp, 3¼" x 4". Mfr unknown – English construction.

R5*   **G**

Rectaflex Starea *Rome, Italy*

RECTAFLEX 1000: c1949. 35mm SLR with interchangeable Xenon f2, 50mm lens among others. CFPS 1-¹⁄₁₀₀₀s. Historically important, along with the Contax S, as being the first 35mm SLR with fixed pentaprism sold on the marketplace.

R3*   **F**

RECTAFLEX 1300: c1950. 35mm SLR camera with interchangeable Angenieux f1.8, 50mm lens, among others. CFPS 1-¹⁄₁₃₀₀s.

R3*   **F**

RECTAFLEX ROTOR WITH GUNSTOCK: c1950. With special rotating mount for

three different lenses, including Angenieux f1.8, 90mm, f1.8, 50mm and f2.8, 35mm.

R4*   **H**

RECTAFLEX JUNIOR: c1950. 35mm SLR with interchangeable Xenon f2.8, 50mm lens among others. CFPS ¹⁄₂₅-¹⁄₅₀₀s. The cheaper version of the Rectaflex.

R3*   **E+**

RECTA: c1953. 35mm RFR camera with interchangeable Westar f3.5, 50mm lens. CFPS 1-¹⁄₁₀₀₀s. Made in only small numbers, (some say 6!) this camera never made it to the market place.

R5*   **NSR**

DIRECTOR 35: c1954. 35mm VFR camera. 39mm screw mount; FPS; made only in prototype units, never delivered to the public.

R5*   **NSR**

Reflex Camera Co.
Newark, New Jersey

FOCAL PLANE POSTCARD CAMERA: c1912. Postcard size camera; FPS. Ground glass focusing back; 3¼" x 4¼" exp.

R4*   **E–**

JUNIOR REFLEX CAMERA: c1903..3¼" x 4¼" box-type SLR; fixed focus lens; 4-speed shutter.

R3*   **D**

REFLEX CAMERA: c1898. Anastigmat 210mm f16 lens; variable speed FPS; 5" x 7" plates, space for 3 double holders.

R3*   **E+**

Reid & Sigrist Ltd.
Leicester, England

Reid II

REID III: 1951-55. Cfps, 1 – ¹⁄₁₀₀₀s. Type I had no flash synch, while type II used synch contacts marked "E" for electronic flash, and "B" for bulbs. Screw mount Taylor-Hobson f2, 2 inch lens. This camera is a high quality copy of the Leica III B. In 1958 Reid announced Models II and IA. Type II cameras are valued 25% less than type I cameras. Price given is for type I camera with normal lens.

R3*   **F+**

REID II: 1953. Similar to the original Reid III but with flash synch added. Flash is connected via two sockets beside the slow speed dial. Sockets marked 'E' for electronic flash or F class bulbs, or 'B' for normal expendable bulbs.

R4*   **H**

REID I: 1958-62. Cfps, 1/20 – ¹⁄₁₀₀₀s; no Rfr; Vfr only. Screw mount Taylor-Hobson f2, 2 inch lens. Originally offered at £20 less than the Reid III camera, the Reid I is found mostly in the ex-military version. This military version can easily be identified by the code impressed into the leather on the back of the camera body, consisting of the letters A.P., A.P.F., or F. followed by the numbers 8810, or marked entirely in numbers, such as 0553/8810. These markings are known, though others may exist. It is thought about 1500 of these cameras were made.

R3*   **R**

Revere Camera Co.
Chicago, Illinois

REVERE STEREO 33: c1952. 35mm stereo camera. Wollensak Revere Amaton 35mm f3.5 lenses; Synchromatic or Rapax shutter ½-¹⁄₂₀₀₀ s; MFX synch; crf..

R3*   **E–**

Revere Stereo 33

Rex Magazine Camera Co.
Chicago, Illinois

REX MAGAZINE CAMERA: c1899, meniscus lens; single speed shutter. Magazine load: 4" x 5" dry plates changed by wooden sheath.

R3*   **E–**

REX PHOTOGRAPHIC OUTFIT: cardboard box camera, covered with black paper; 2" x 2" exp on dry plates.

R3*   **C–**

Jules Richard *Paris, France*

LE GLYPHOSCOPE STEREO CAMERA: meniscus lenses; guillotine shutter. c1905.

R2*   **D**

HOMEOS: c1914-1920. 35mm stereo camera. Zeiss Tessar 30mm, f4.5 lens; horizontal guillotine shutter ⅙-¼2s; 2 finders,

one on top for horizontal exp, one on left side for vertical exp. 27 stereo exp, 2.5 x 1.9cm or 54 single exp on 35mm film. Qty 1500(?). The Homeos was the first 35mm stereo camera.

R5*   **H–**

HOMEOSCOPE 1897; Early Richard stereo available for two formats. Fitted with Anastigmat Zeiss Krauss lenses, f/6.3 124mm focal length. Guillotine shutter.

R3*   **E**

VERASCOPE: c1905. Goerz Double Anastigmatic 85mm f6.8 lens; 6 speed guillotine shutter. Plate and roll film magazine.

R3*   **D**

VERASCOPE F40: c1938. 35mm stereo camera. Optis f4.5 or Berthiot 40mm, f3.5 lens; shutter 1-½₅₀s; 40 stereo pairs on 35mm film, also single-frame.

R4*   **F**

Ricoh Co. Ltd. *Tokyo, Japan*

GOLDEN RICOH "16" Subminiature camera. Ricoh 25mm, f3.5 lens; sector shutter ⅕₀-½₀₀s; 20 exp on 16mm film on special cassettes. c1956.

R2*   **E–**

RICOH "16" c1956. Subminiature camera. Ricoh 25mm, f2.8 interchangeable lens; shutter ⅕₀-½₀₀s; 24 exp, 10 x 14mm on 16mm film in special cassettes.

R2*   **E**

Ricoh 16

RICOLET: c1950. 35mm Camera. Ricoh Anastigmat 45mm, f3.5 coated lens; Riken ½₂₅-½₅₀ s.

R2*   **B+**

RICOH 35: 1955. Similar in shape to the Richolet, but with crf. Riken shutter, speeds 1-½₂₀₀s; 4.5cm, f3.5 Riken Ricomat lens.

R3*   **D**

RICOHFLEX MODEL III: c1950. Twin lens reflex, fitted with Ricoh anastigmat f3.5 80mm lens. Riken shutter 1/25-100s. 120 rollfilm yielded 12 6x6cm images. There were a total of 20 Ricohflex models through about 1959.

R3   **C**

SUPER 44: 1959. TLR for 12 exp on 127. 6cm f3.5 Riken lens. Shutter 1-1/400s. Depth of field sale linked to focusing knob.

R3*   **D**

RICOH XRS: c.1980s. 35mm SLR that used solar panels to charge internal

---

battery. Otherwise conventional aperture priority SLR.

R3*   D

Note: From the mid-1960s, through to the 1990s, Ricoh produced a significant range of quality SLRs, of which the XRS is probably the only one worth collecting due to its solar panels. Like the company's contemporaries (Chinon, Cosina), early models adopted the M42 Universal screw lens mount made popular by Pentax, then switched to the K-mount bayonet when Pentax introduced that in the 1970s. In this way, Ricoh cameras could be used with the vast variety of independent lenses made for these two popular mounts. Few of these cameras are of real interest to the collector, but full details of Ricoh SLRs can be found in the book Japanese 35mm SLR Cameras by Bill Hansen and Michael Dierdorff, published by Hove Books.

Rietzschel GmbH Optische Fabrik, Munich, Germany

HELI-KLACK: c1920. Folding stereo camera. 3 Interchangeable lenses; Compound shutter; rising front; rack focusing; double extension bellows. 9 x 18cm exp.

R4*   F+

KOSMO KLACK: c1914-1925. 45 x 107mm Stereo camera. Combinable Rietzschel 65mm, f4.5 lens; Stereo Compur 1-½₅₀s. Panoramic setting; rising lens panel.

R4*   E+

Riken Optical Industry
Tokyo, Japan

STEKY II: 1950; 16mm subminiature camera. Stekinar Anastigmat 25mm f3.5

Kosmo Klack

coated lens; 1/25-1/100s; 24 exp, 10x14mm on 16mm film in cassettes.

R4*   E+

Marked "Made in TOKYO"

R4*   E+

Riley Research
Santa Monica, California.

RILEX: 1946-47. 2¼" x 3¼" View camera. Kodak Anastigmat Spec. 127mm lens.

R4*   D–

John Roberts
Boston, Massachusetts

JOHN ROBERTS DAGUERREOTYPE CAMERA (1850): c1850. 8" x 10" daguerreotype camera; Jamin Darlot Sr. Landscape 350mm, f11 lens, sliding box focusing. 8" x 10" or 6½" x 8½" plates. Largest known American daguerreotype camera.

R5*   **J–**

JOHN ROBERTS DAGUERREOTYPE CAMERA (1854): c1854. Holmes, Booth & Hayden, New York lens with reversing prism; ¼ plate daguerreotypes. Boston Box style daguerreotype camera.

R5*   **I**

C. N. Robinson
Philadelphia, Pennsylvania

CAMERA OBSCURA: c1820-1830. 32.5 x 18.5 x 19.5cm; mahogany with dovetail construction; sliding box focusing; 15 x 16cm image.

R5*   **H+**

J. Robinson & Sons
England

LUZO DETECTIVE CAMERA: c1890, first British-made box camera; Aplanat 2½", f11 lens; variable speed sector shutter. Used Eastman-type roll film, 100 exp, 6 cm diameter.

R4*   **G**

Robot-Berning & Co.
Dusseldorf, Germany

ROBOT I: c1934-1938. 35mm Motor drive camera. Zeiss Tessar 32.5mm, f2.8 lens; interchangeable screw mount; rotary metal shutter 1-⅕₀₀s; 24 x 24mm exp on 35mm film in special cassettes. "Detective-type" swivelling vf. Spring motor: 24 exp on one winding.

R3*   **D+**

ROBOT II: c1938-1950. 35mm Motor drive camera. Zeiss Biotar 40mm, f2 lens, interchangeable screw mount; rotary metal shutter 1-⅕₀₀s; 24 x 24mm exp on 35mm film in special daylight loading cassettes. Spring motor: 24 exp on one winding; optional motor was available for 48 exp on one winding.

R3* **D+**

LUFTWAFFE ROBOT: c1940. 35mm Motor drive camera. Schneider Tele-Zenar 75mm, f3.5 lens, interchangeable screw mount; rotary metal shutter ½-⅕₀₀s; 24 x 24mm exp on 35mm film in special cassettes. Manufactured for the German Air Force during WWII. One variation has the double spring for 48 exp on a single wind. The finish is black enamel; internal film channel is made from black plastic material. "Luftwaffen Eigentum" always marked on rear of top cover; the Tele-Zenar 75mm f35 is marked "Luftwaffen Eigentum" on rear of lens mount or on side of barrel. Shutter speeds

Luftwaffe Robot

below ⅟₁₀₀s. have been ground off the shutter speed dial in some examples.

R3* **F**

ROBOT IIA: c1951-1953. 35mm Motor drive camera. Schneider Xenon 40mm, f1.9 lens, interchangeable screw mount; rotary metal shutter ½ - ⅕₀₀s; 24 x 24mm exp on 35mm film in special cassettes. Spring motor for 24 exp on one winding; optional motor was available for 48 exp on one winding.

R3* **D+**

ROBOT JUNIOR: c1951-1953. Similar to Robot IIa except does not have adjustment for right angle viewing.

R2* **D+**

ROBOT ROYAL 24: c1956-1959. 35mm Motor drive camera. Schneider Xenar

45mm, f2.8 coated lens; rotary metal shutter ½-⅟₅₀₀s; crf. 24 x 24mm exp. **Has auto "burst" operation.**

R2*   **F**

ROBOT ROYAL 36: c1956-1959. 35mm Motor drive camera. Schneider Xenar 45mm, f2.8 coated lens, interchangeable bayonet mount; rotary shutter ½ – ⅟₅₀₀s, crf. 24 x 36mm exp. No auto "burst" operation.

R3*   **F+**

ROBOT STAR I: c1952-1959. 35mm Motor drive camera. Schneider Xenon 40mm, f1.9 coated lens, interchangeable screw mount; rotary metal shutter 1/2 -⅟₅₀₀ s. 24 x 24mm exp on 35mm film in standard cartridge. Spring motor for 24 exp on one winding; optional motor was available for 48 exp on one winding.

R3*   **E–**

ROBOT STAR II: c1958-63. 35mm Motor drive camera. Schneider Xenar f2.8, 38mm or Xenon f1.9, 40mm coated lens, inter-

changeable screw mount; rotary metal shutter ½-⅟₅₀₀s. 24 x 24mm exp on 35mm film in standard cartridge. Spring motor for 18 exp on one winding; optional motor was available for 50 exp on one winding, electromagnetic shutter release, field of view for 40mm and 75mm in VFR.

R3*   **E+**

ROBOT STAR 25: c1960. 35mm Motor drive camera for 25-24 x 24mm frames on standard 35mm film with one winding of the built-in spring motor, Xenar f2.8, 38mm lens, burst operation up to 6 frames per second, all metal rotary shutter, ¼-⅟₅₀₀s, electromagnetic release.

R3*   **E–**

ROBOT STAR 50: c1960. With 50 shot spring motor.

R3*   **H**

ROBOT 400: c1955. Royal Robot 24 with built-in long film holder for 400 frames 24 x 24 on standard 35mm film, electric motor drive was available in addition to built-in spring motor.

R3*   **F+**

ROBOT ROYAL II: c1955. As Royal Robot 24 but **without RFR,** and **without burst operation.**

R3*   **F–**

ROBOT RECORDER 24: c1958. As Robot Royal 24, but **without any finder at all, or burst operation.**

R3*   **F**

ROBOT RECORDER 36: c1958. As Robot Royal 36 , but **without any finder at all.**

R3*   **F**

ACCESSORIES FOR ROBOT CAMERAS

Ennalyt f4/24mm lens	**E–**
Primotar f3.5/30mm lens	**D**
Xenogon f2.8/35mm lens	**E–**
Tele-Xenar f3.8/75mm lens	**E–**

Tele-Arton f4/90mm lens	**E–**
Sonnar f2/90mm lens	**F–**
Tele-Xenar f4/135mm lens	**E**
Tele-Xenar f4/150mm lens	**E**
Tele-Xenar f5.5/200mm lens	**E+**
universal finder 30mm-150mm	**D**
30mm optical finder	**D**
folding finder for 40mm and 75mm	**C+**
90mm optical finder	**D**
135mm optical finder	**D**
200 optical finder	**E–**
accessory coupled RFR for Robot II	**E–**
under-water housing	**F**
beam-splitter microscope adaptor	**E**
series flash lamp holder (4 lamps)	**D+**

Rochester Optical and Camera Company
Rochester, New York

The Rochester Optical Company was producing "Premo" cameras in 1893; it merged with several other companies in 1900 to form the Rochester Optical and Camera Company. In 1907 the firm was acquired by the Eastman Kodak Company. From 1907 to 1917 the designation was Rochester Optical Division, Eastman Kodak Company; from 1918 to 1922 – Rochester Optical Department, Eastman Kodak Company.

THE CARLTON TWIN LENS CAMERA: c1895. 4" x 5" plate TLR camera.

R5*   **NSR**

CARLTON VIEW CAMERA: c1890's. $6^1/2$" x $8^1/2$" View camera. Brass tripod base built into lens bed; reversible double swing

back; polished wood body with brass fittings. 8 sizes from 4" x 5" to 11" x 14".

R4*   **4 X 5 SIZE E+**
            11 X 14 SIZE F–

THE EMPIRE STATE CAMERA: c1895. View camera.

R3* 5 X 7 SIZE   **E**
8 X 10 SIZE   **E+**
11 X 14 SIZE   **F–**

FOLDING GEM POCO: c1890's. $3^1/4$" x $4^1/4$" Folding plate camera. Built-in shutter. Polished wood finish, red bellows. Folded size 6" x $5^1/4$" x $1^1/2$" ; weight 1 lb.

R3*   **D+**

THE FOLDING PREMIER: c1895. Folding plate camera. Bausch & Lomb pneumatic shutter with built-in rotating waterhouse stops.

R2*   **D**

Folding Gem Poco

THE HANDY: c1895. Box-type camera. 4" x 5" exp on plates.

R2*   **C**

THE IDEAL CAMERA: c1895. View camera. Made in 4" x 5" 5" x 7" 8" x 10" **SIZES.**

R3*   **D+**

THE KENWOOD CAMERA: c1895. Compact view camera. Wide front for stereo lenses. 5" x 7", 8" x 10".

R3*   **E–**

KING POCO: c1890's. 6½" x 8½" Folding plate camera. Rochester Symmetrical Convertible lens; Unicum shutter. Double extension red leather bellows; horizontal or vertical format swing back; mahogany. Sizes: 4" x 5" to 8" x 10".

R3*   **D+**

KING VIEW CAMERA: c1890's. 8" x 10" View camera. Rising and falling front; front and rear swings; double extension red leather bellows; polished mahogany, lacquered brass fittings. Sizes: 5" x 7" to 11" x 14". Top of the line view camera, original price $36.

R3*   **E**

THE LONG FOCUS PREMO: c1895. 5" x 7" Folding plate camera.

R3*   **D+**

MIDGET POCKET CAMERA: c1895. Compact view camera. c1895. 4" x 5" exp on plates.

R2*   **D**

THE MONITOR CAMERA: c1895. Compact view camera. 4" x 5", 8" x 10".

R3*   **E**

NEW MODEL CAMERA: c1895. View camera. 4" x 5"; 5" x 7"; 8" x 10".

R3*   **E–**

NEW MODEL IMPROVED CAMERA: c1895. View camera. Polished wood finish, nickel plated fittings. 4" x 5"; 5" x 7"; 10" x 8".

R3*   **E**

NEW MODEL STEREO CAMERA: c1895. Stereo view camera.

R4*   **F**

THE PREMO: c1895. 4" x 5" folding plate camera.

R2*   **C+**

POCO, SERIES A: c1890's, 4" x 5" Folding plate camera. Symmetrical brass lens. Shifting, rising and falling front; wood interior, red bellows.

R3*   **D**

POCO, SERIES B: c1890's. 4" x 5" Folding plate camera. Rapid Rectilinear Symmetrical lens; Unicum shutter. Single swing back; rising front; Poco reversible finder; red bellows.

R3*   **D–**

POCO, SERIES E: c1890's. 4" x 5" Folding plate camera; built-in lens and shutter. Polished wood finish, red bellows and leather covered bed; reversible finder. Original price $8. Also in 5" x 7" size.

R3*   **D**

PONY PREMO NO. 6: c1890's. 4" x 5" Folding plate camera. Goerz Double Anastigmat 5" lens; Eastman Kodak Bausch & Lomb shutter. Reversible back with swings; shifting, rising and falling front; double extension red bellows.

R3*   **D**

THE PREMARET: c1895. Box-type camera. 4" x 5" exp on plates.

R3*   **C+**

THE PREMIER: c1895. Box-type detective camera. Brass lens; built-in shutter in front swing down face; 4" x 5" exp on plates. Leather exterior, cherrywood interior.

R3*   **D–**

THE PREMO B: c1895. Folding plate camera. 4" x 5" exp on plates.

R2*   **C+**

THE PREMO C: c1895. 4" x 5" Folding plate camera.

R2*   **C+**

THE PREMO D: c1895. 4" x 5" Folding plate camera.

R2*   **C+**

THE PREMO SR: c1895. 4" x 5" Folding plate camera.

R2*   **C+**

REVERSIBLE BACK PREMO: c1900. Folding plate camera. Goerz Double Anastigmat 10⅜", f11 lens; Bausch & Lomb "Iris Diaphragm" shutter. Whole plate size, 6½" x 8½"

R3*   **D**

ROCHESTER OPTICAL CO. 8" X 10" VIEW CAMERA: c1900's. 8" x 10" view camera; rear Folmer & Schwing FPS; rising and falling front. Polished wood finish, brass fittings; red leather bellows.

R3*   **E**

STANDARD VIEW CAMERA: c1890's. 8" x 10" view camera; rear focus; reversible back; mahogany finish, brass fittings. 7 sizes: 3¼" x 4¼" to 8" x 10" (single or double swing back).

R3*   **D+**

THE STEREOSCOPIC PREMO: c1895. 5" x 7" Folding plate camera.

R4*   **F−**

TELEPHOTO POCO A: c1902. Rapid Rectilinear lens; Bausch & Lomb shutter. 5" x 7" exp on plates. Polished wood interior, red leather bellows.

R3*   **D+**

TELEPHOTO CYCLE B: c1900. 5" x 7" Folding. Telephoto Triple Convertible lens or Zeiss, Goerz, Wide Angle or Voigtlander; double extension; reversible back; rising and falling front; back swings horizontally or vertically; mahogany, brass fittings;

covered in Moroccan leather. 4 sizes: 4"x 5" to 8"x10".

R3*   **E**

UNIVERSAL CAMERA: c1890's. Compact folding 5" x 7v view camera. Wide-angle brass lens; rack and pinion focusing; swinging, rising and falling front; polished wood finish with brass fittings. 11 sizes from 3¼" x 4¼" to 17" x 20" in single and double swing models.

R3*   **E+**

NEW MODEL VIEW CAMERA: c1895. Wood bellows view camera with a modest number of tilts and swings. The instrument pictured is for 5x8" glass plates but they were available in many sizes ranging from 4x5 to 8x10". They are occasionally found with a simple front mounted shutter, just a slide of wood pulled by gravity past the lens.

R3*   **D**

Dr. Rodehuser Kamera Mechanik
Heessen, Germany

PANTA: c1948. Metal VFR camera for 6 x 4.5cm frames on 120 roll film. Ennar f4.5, 74mm lens in collapsible tube mount among others, Vario or other shutter.

R2*   **B+**

Panta

Rokuwa *Tokyo, Japan*

STEREO ROCCA: c1955. Stereo camera. Single meniscus 42mm lens; shutter ⅟₃₀s, B, flash. Direct vision optical finder; 24 pairs, 24 x 3mm on 120 roll film.

R3* **D+**

ROLAND: c1931. 15/8" x 21/4" RFR camera. Kleinbild Plasmat 70mm, f2.7 lens; Compur Rapid shutter 1-⅟₄₀₀ s, crf. 16 exp, 15/8" x 2¼" on 120 roll film. Probably the

first combined range-viewfinder in a commercially produced camera. See picture overleaf.

R4* **G**

Andrew Ross *London, England*

ANDREW ROSS STEREO WET PLATE: Sliding box stereo camera. Dovetailed mahogany; brass lenses; rack and pinion focusing.

R5* **H–**

Thomas Ross & Co. *London, England*

PHOTOSCOPE: c1889. Binocular-type detective camera. Special cassette from roll film allowing 3.5x4cm exp. Patented by William Sanders.

R5* **NSR**

ROSS DIVIDED: c1895. 3¼" x 4¼" TLR camera. Goerz Doppel Anastigmat f7.7 lenses.

R4* **F**

ROSS 13" X 18" TAILBOARD CAMERA: c1880's. 13" x 18" tailboard camera. Voigtlander & Son, Brauschweig lens; shifting front for stereo; rear tilts and swings; double extension.

R3* **F–**

ROSS TWIN LENS REFLEX: c1891. Ross Homocentric 7" f6.3 lens; Bausch & Lomb pneumatic shutter 1-⅟₁₀₀₀s. 4" x 5" plates; rotating back.
R4* **F+**

Rouch *London, England*

EUREKA DETECTIVE CAMERA: c1888. Mahogany box-form camera. 150mm f6 Doublet lens; behind-the-lens roller blind shutter; flexible leather plate changing bag.
R4* **F**

ROUCH EXCELSIOR HAND CAMERA: c1890. Two mahogany boxes joined by leather bellows; rack and pinion focusing.
R4* **F**

Roussel *Paris, France*

STELLA JUMELLE: c1900. 9 x 12cm Stereo camera; Anti Spectroscopique 130mm f7.7 lens; 7 speed guillotine shutter.
R3* **E**

RUBIX: c1950. Subminiature camera. Hope 5mm f3.5 lens; shutter ⅟₂₅-⅟₁₀₀s; 50 exp, 10 x 14mm on 16mm film. Mfg. in Japan.
R4* **E–**

Royer, *France*

SAVOYFLEX AUTOMATIQUE: c.1958. 35mm SLR with Selenium cell to offer automation. Shutter and aperture priorities. 50mm f2.8 Som Berthiot lens. Prontor Reflex shutter 1-1/300s + B.
R4* **D**

TELEROY: 1951. Folding camera for 8 or 16 exp on 120 or 620. Coupled split image rangefinder. 100mm f3.5 Angenieux lens. Shutter 1-1/300s + B. Synch at 1/25s.
R3* **D+**

Reference Notes

Saint-Etienne, France

UNIVERSAL: c. 1908. Folding plate camera that could be adapted for rollfilm with the addition of a special back. f6.8 Beckers lens stopping down to f64. Unicum shutter 1/2-1/100s.

R4*   **F**

Sakura *Japan*

PETAL: c1950. Watch-type detective camera. 6 Circular exp, on 25mm diameter disc of film. C 1950. Round style, Hexagonal style, Petal Outfit: film cutter, developing holder and two tins of film discs, in wooden boxes with directions.

R3*   **F**

Hexagonal style.   **F**
Round style.   **E**

Samei Sangyo *Japan*

SAMOCA 35II: c1957. 35mm Camera. C. Ezumar 50mm, 3.5 lens; shutter ½s-¹⁄₁₀₀s.

R2*   **B+**

SAMOCA 35III: c1958. 35mm Camera. Ezumar Anastigmat 50mm, 3.5 lens; very similar to the Samoca II, except for the name and faster shutter!

R2*   **B+**

SAMOCA SUPER: c1956. 35mm Camera. C. Ezumar 50mm, 2.8 lens; CRF and (sometimes) built-in lightmeter; btl shutter speeds 1-½₀₀s. Its value lies in its strange looks!

R3*   **C**

SAMOCAFLEX: 1955. 35mm TLR. Waist-level finder with split image rangefinder,

plus direct vision viewfinder. First model with Seikosha Rapid shutter, following year with Seikosha MX shutter. 50mm f2.8 lenses. 1-1/500s + B.

R4*   **E+**

VIEW-MASTER PERSONAL STEREO CAMERA: c1952-1960. 35mm Stereo camera. Anastigmat 25mm, f3.5 coated lenses; guillotine shutter ⅒-¹⁄₁₀₀₀s; flash. Double run 5mm film produces 37 pairs on 20 exp film, or 69 pairs on 36 exp film. View master format.

R3*   **E**

VIEW-MASTER ACCESSORIES

Close-up attachment – 24" with case	**D**
Close-up attachment – 36" with case	**D**
Viewmaster film cutter	**D+**

San Georgio, *Italy*

PARVA: 1947. Very rare 16mm subminiature. 2cm f3.5 San Giorgio Essegi interchangeable lens (though no evidence of other lenses). FP shutter 1/40s, 1/100s & 1/150s. Eye-level finder.

R5*   **J**

Sawyers Inc. *Portland, Oregon*

MARK IV: c1959. 127 Roll film TLR camera. Topcor 6cm, f2.8 coated lens; shutter 1-¹⁄₅₀₀s; 12 exp on 127 roll film.

R2*   **C+**

VIEW-MASTER STEREO COLOUR CAMERA: c1950. German made for the European market. 35mm stereo vfr camera for viewmaster format stereo pairs. Rodenstock Trinar 20mm, f2.8 fixed focus lenses shutter coupled to lens opening using EV scale; slanting film travel allows all the frames to be made without rewinding the film, as on the Viewmaster Personal Stereo Camera. More often seen in Europe than the USA, where the price is often 25% lower.

R3*   **E–**

VIEW-MASTER STEREO EUROPE: Manufactured in Germany.

R   **E–**

A. Schaeffner *Paris, France*

PHOTO ALBUM: c1890. Book detective camera. Achromat 120mm, f12 lens; guillotine shutter. 9 x 12cm plates in metal double plate holders. Also available with rapid rectilinear lens and central guillotine shutter. Invented by Cadot.

R5*   **H**

Schlesicky & Strohlein of Leipzig

THE COMFORT: c1890. Leather covered detective camera. Achromatic 80mm, f7.5 lens; vertical guillotine shutter; 6 x 7.3cm exp on 8 dry plates. A turn of a spool brings the new plate into position. Invented by C. F. Schlesicky.

R4*   **F–**

FIELD CAMERA: c1880's. 24 x 30mm Field camera. Brass convertible lens. Blue bellows; mahogany finish; brass fittings; black striped edges.

R3*   **E–**

Schmitz & Theinemann
Dresden, Germany

UNIFLEX: c1933. Unar 75mm, f4.5 lens; self-cocking Pronto shutter coupled to the mirror

R3*   **D–**

UNIFLEX REFLEX METEOR: c1931. Trioplan 105mm, f4.5 lens; Pronto shutter; front element focusing. Box camera for 6 x 9cm exp.

R3*   **D**

Scovill Mfg. Co.
proprietors of American Optical Co., New York.

AMERICAN OPTICAL REVOLVING BACK CAMERA: c1888. 5" x 8" Revolving back camera. Front focus; revolving back (Flaming's patent); Daisy dry plate holder. Sizes: 4" x 5" to 8" x 10".

R3*   **E–**

AMERICAN OPTICAL VIEW CAMERA: c1883. Brass fittings and lens; lens slotted for waterhouse stops; 5½" x 8½" exp on plates.

R3*   **D+**

ANTIQUE OAK DETECTIVE CAMERA: c1892. Wooden box-type detective camera. 4" x 5" exp on plates.

R4*   **F**

KLONDIKE: c1898. Meniscus lens; rotary shutter, T and I. 4" x 5" dry plates.

R3* **C+**

KNACK DETECTIVE CAMERA: c1891. Box-type detective camera. 4" x 5" exp on plates.

R4* **E**

BOOK CAMERA: c1892. Book-type detective camera. Achromatized periscopic 75mm, f12 lens; variable speed horizontal guillotine shutter. Single exp on 4" x 5" dry plates.

R5* **I+**

SCOVILL 4" X 5" VERTICAL VIEW CAMERA: c1881. R. Morrison N.Y. lens, rotating stops. No rising front. With holder and case.

R3* **D+**

CENTENNIAL STEREO OUTFIT: c1876. 5" x 8" Stereo outfit. Matched pair of stereo lenses, single achromatic Scovill lens; swing back; polished mahogany, brass fittings. Nickel plated label: American Optical Co., New York. Scovill Mfg. Co. proprietors.

R4* **F+**

SCOVILL 5" X 8" VIEW CAMERA: c1888. Waterbury lens; rotating stops; original box in brass and light mahogany.

R3* **D+**

THE TRIAD CAMERA: c1892. Leather covered box-type detective camera. 4" x 5" Exp on plates or roll film – using an Eastman Walker roll holder.

R4* **E**

WATERBURY 5" X 8" FIELD CAMERA: c1885. Rubber-band shutter. Original price, $17.

R4*   **F–**

SCOVILL DETECTIVE CAMERA: c1886. Leather covered box-type detective camera. 4 x 5 Size; Instantaneous lens; variable speed rotary shutter. 4" x 5" exp on plates. 4 sizes: 8 x 10.5cm; 10.5 x 12.5cm; 11.5 x 16.5cm; 13 x 18cm. In 1888 a pivoting vf was adapted to the camera.

R4*   **F+**

WATERBURY DETECTIVE CAMERA (ORIGINAL MODEL): c1888. Black painted box type detective camera. String cocking shutter; 4" x 5" exp on plates. Storage for extra plate holder in recessed base of camera; "T" bar extends through base of camera for focusing.

R4*   **E+**

WATERBURY DETECTIVE CAMERA (SECOND MODEL): c1890. Leather covered box-type detective camera. 4" x 5" Exp on plates. "T" bar extend through base of camera for focusing.

R4*   **E+**

IMPROVED WATERBURY DETECTIVE CAMERA: c1892. Leather covered box-type detective camera. 4" x 5" Exp on dry plates. The focusing knob has been positioned on the top front of the camera body.

R4*   **E+**

Sears, Roebuck & Co.
Chicago, Illinois

KEWPIE KAMERA: c1921. Leatherette covered box roll film camer.; 2¼" x 3¼" Exp on 120 roll film.

R1*   **A**

SEROCO 8" X 10" VIEW CAMERA: c1920. 8" x 10" View camera. Conley lens; Auto shutter. Front and rear focusing; rising and falling front; mahogan; nickel-plated.

R3*   **E–**

SEROCO STEREO CAMERA: c1920. Seroco 4" x 5" Rapid Symmetrical lenses; Wollensak shutter; 5" x 7" exp on plates. Brown leather covered wood, red bellows.

R4*   **E+**

TOWER TYPE 3: c1950, 35mm RFR camera, Nikkor 50mm f2 coated lens, interchangeable screw mount; CFPS 1-¹⁄₅₀₀ s, Copy of Leica IIIa, made in Japan by Nicca Camera Company, (Nicca III or IIIA) sold by Sears, Roebuck & Co.

R3*   **F–**

TOWER TYPE 3S: c1951. Added flash synch, (Nicca IIIB).

R3* **F−**

TOWER 35: c1956. 35mm RFR camera with interchangeable Nikkor f2.8, 50mm lens; CFPS 1 − ⅟₁₀₀₀s, (Nicca 3F) with

lever or knob wind.

R3* **F−**

TOWER 45: c1957. 35mm RFR camera with interchangeable f2, 50mm Nikkor screw mount len; CFPS 1-⅟₁₀₀₀s; flash calculator on the hinged back, (Nicca 5L).

R3* **F−**

TOWER 46: c1957. Delivered with Nikkor f1.4, 50mm lens.

R3* **F**

TOWER STEREO: c1954. 35mm Stereo camera. Vfr; Isconar 35mm, f3.5 lenses; Prontor S shutter 1-⅟₃₀₀s. Made by Wilhelm Witt of Hamburg, West Germany for Sears. similar to the Iloca Stereo II.

R3* **D+**

Secam, *Paris, France*

STEREOPHOT: c1955. Stereo version of pen camera. Consists of two Stylophot cameras mounted on a bracket, with tripod attachment. Leather carrying case.

R4* **E−**

STYLOPHOT STANDARD: 1955. Pen-type detective camera. f6.3 Coated lens; fixed shutter speed of 1/50s. 10 x 10mm on 16mm film in a special cassette. Camera is in shape of large pen. Auto film transport advances film and cocks shutter.

R4* **E−**

STYLOPHOT DELUXE: c1956. Pen-type detective camera. Roussel Anastigmat 27mm, f3.5 lens; fixed shutter speed of ⅟₅₀s.

18 exp, 10 x 10mm on 16mm film in a special cassette.

R4* **E**

H. SEEMANN STEREO CAMERA: c1910. Wooden stereo camera. Pair of Goerz Dagor 120mm lenses, original cap; sliding front focus; ground glass screen; black ebonized wood, nickel plated fittings.

R4* **F−**

Stylophot
Standard

Some of the different styles of Sida camera.

SIDA GMBh, Germany

SIDA: c.1936. Simple Bakelite camera for 25x25mm images on special rollfilm. 35mm f8 fixed focus lens. Single speed shutter. Found in black, red, green and brown.

R2*   **C**

SIDA STANDARD: 1938. Similar to original Sida, but made in cast metal.

R2*   **C**

Note: Although manufacture of Sida camera began in Germany, production moved around Europe post-war and cameras with the name Sida were also manufactured in France, England and even Poland.

Seitz Phototechnic
Switzerland

ROUNDSHOT: Subminiature panoramic camera for 10 images on Minox 9.5mm

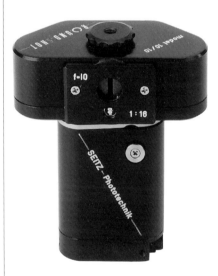

Roundshot

film. 10mm f16 fixed focus lens. Camera rotates on its handle to give pictures from 100° to full 360°.

R4*   **NSR**

SEM, Sociéte des Etablissements Modernes
SA Aurec, France.

Established after the second world war, by Paul Royet, the company produced cameras affordable to every household in France. From the first Sem Kim in 1946 , to the last Semflex of 1978, these cameras left their mark with the camera enthusiasts of France. Though they didn't find their way out of France in any great numbers, they are still seen at fairs and fleamarkets in France, and sometimes hanging around the necks of provincial visitors to Paris! A total of more than 350,000 Semflex cameras are estimated to have been made.

SEMFLEX I: 1948-49, TLR for 6cm x 6cm frames on roll film. Angénieux or Berthoit f4.5, 75mm taking lens; f3.3 viewing lens; knob advance; shutter 1-¹⁄₄₀₀s; framing counting by ruby window

R2* **C**

SEMFLEX T950: 1950-54. TLR for 6cm x 6cm frames on roll film. Angénieux or Berthoit f4.5, 75mm taking lens; f3.3 viewing lens; knob advance; shutter ¹⁄₁₀ – ¹⁄₂₅₀s; grey body

R2* **C**

SEMFLEX STANDARD 4.5: 1955. TLR for 6cm x 6cm frames on roll film. Angénieux or Berthoit f4.5, 75mm taking lens; f3.3 viewing lens; knob advance; shutter ¹⁄₁₀ – ¹⁄₂₅₀s; grey body; sports finder.

R2* **C**

SEMFLEX STANDARD 4.5: 1956-60, as previous model but for cast "Semflex" logo inside a raised frame.

R2* **C**

SEMFLEX STANDARD 61: 1961-67. Cast "Semflex" logo inside a raised frame with grey relief

R2* **C**

SEMFLEX SI: 1950-54. TLR for 6cm x 6cm frames on roll film. Angénieux or Berthoit f3.8,75mm taking lens ; f3.3 viewing lens; knob advance; shutter ¹⁄₁₀-¹⁄₂₅₀s; grey body; sports finder. (Angénieux lens adds 25%)

R2* **C**

SEMFLEX STANDARD 3.5: 1953-55. TLR for 6cm x 6cm frames on roll film. Angénieux or Berthoit f3.5, 75mm taking lens; f3.3 viewing lens; knob advance; Synchro Sem shutter 1-1/400s; grey body; sports finder; large lens bezels. (Angeenieux lens adds 25%).

R2* **C**

SEMFLEX STANDARD 3.5: 1956-63. Cast "Semflex" logo inside a raised frame.

R2* **C**

SEMFLEX II: 1948-49. TLR for 6cm x 6cm frames on roll film. Angénieux or Berthoit f3.5, 75mm taking lens; f3.3 viewing lens; knob advance; black body.

(Angénieux lens adds 25%).

R2* **C**

SEMFLEX S II: 1950-53. Sports finder.

R2* **C**

SEMFLEX STANDARD 3.5: 1954. Sports finder; larger focusing knob which incorporates a film reminder; second ruby window for 28mmx 40mm framing.

R2* **C+**

SEMFLEX STANDARD 3.5 B: 1960-64. As previous model but for lack of film reminder; totally grey; possibility of 24mm x 36mm or 4cm x 4cm on 120 film; cast "Semflex" logo inside raised frame with grey relief

R2*   **C+**

SEMFLEX STANDARD 3.5 B: 1965-69. As previous model but for bayonet filter mount.

R2*   **D–**

SEMFLEX STUDIO REFLEX: 1954. TLR for 12 exp on 120 film. Longer than usual 150mm short tele lens made it ideal for portraiture. Taking lens at f5.4, finder lens at f3.9. Two move together for focusing. Shutter 1-1/400s + B. Flash synch. Film wind by two strokes of lever.

R?   **A**

SEMFLEX OTOMATIC I: 1949. TLR for 6cm x 6cm frames on roll film. Angénieux or Berthoit f4.5, 75mm taking lens; f3.3 viewing lens; double throw crank advance; 1 – ⅓₀₀S.

R2*   **C**

SEMFLEX OTO SI: 1950-52. TLR for 6cm x 6cm frames on roll film. Angénieux or Berthoit f3.8, 75mm taking lens; f3.3 viewing lens; double throw crank advance; 1 – ⅓₀₀S; sports finder; grey body

R2*   **C+**

SEMFLEX SEMI OTOMATIC 3.5 B: 1956-64. TLR for 6cm x 6cm frames on roll film. Angénieux or Berthoit f3.5, 75mm taking lens; f2.8 viewing lens; crank advance with double exposure protection; 1 – ¼₀₀s; sports finder; film reminder; bayonet filter mount; leather body covering.

R2*   **D–**

SEMFLEX III: 1948. TLR for 6cm x 6cm frames on roll film. Angénieux or Berthoit f3.5, 75mm taking lens; f3.3 viewing lens;

shutter speed and aperture visible from above.

R5*   **NSR**

SEMFLEX OTO II: 1949. TLR for 6cm x 6cm frames on roll film. Angénieux or Berthoit f3.5, 75mm taking lens; f3.3 viewing lens; crank advance; shutter 1 – ¼₀₀s; condensing lens on VFR ground glass.

(Angénieux lens adds 25%).

R2*   **C+**

SEMFLEX OTO S II: 1950-53. as (SX218) but for addition of sportfinder and large magnifyer in the VFR.

(Angénieux lens adds 25%).

R2*   **C+**

SEMFLEX OTO 154: 1954. Decorative lens bezels; film reminder; side mounted shutter release and second ruby window for 28mm x 40mm.

(Angénieux lens adds 25%).

R2*   **C+**

SEMFLEX OTO 3.5 B: 1955-62. Berthoit f3.5, 75mm taking lens. Angénieux or Berthoit f3.3 viewing lens; shutter cocking coupled to crank film advance; black body

R2*   **C**

SEMFLEX OTO 3.5 B: 1959-71. As previous model, but grey body, possible 24mm x 36mm or 4cm x 4cm on 120 film; Compur shutter available on special order. (Compur shutter lens adds 100%)

R2*   **D–**

SEMFLEX 72: 1972-74. TLR for 6cm x 6cm frames on 120 roll film. Berthiot or Tourret-Narrat f3.5, 75mm lens (four elements); Orec or Compur shutter; reinforced advance mechanism; film loading possible while mounted on a tripod; 36mm or 4cm x 4cm on 120 film; black body; about 1000 cameras made. (Compur shutter lens adds 100%).

R4*   **E–**

NB: Semflex Studio cameras are usually found in well used condition, as they were the workhorse studio camera for many French portrait photographers.

SEMFLEX STUDIO OTO: 1953-54. TLR for 6cm x 6cm frames on 120 roll film. Shutter 1 – $\frac{1}{400}$s; ground glass with condensing lens; sport finder; crank advance; lens panel black enamel.

R3* **E–**

SEMFLEX STUDIO OTO: 1955-58. Lens panel black crinkle finish.

R3* **E–**

SEMFLEX STUDIO STANDARD: 1955-59. Knob advance.

R3* **E–**

SEMFLEX STUDIO OTO MODEL 2: 1959-71. Logo cast in relief; black or grey available.

R3* **E–**

SEMFLEX STUDIO STANDARD 2: 1959-71. Logo cast in relief; black or grey available.

R3* **E–**

SEMFLEX STUDIO 72: 1972-78. Compur shutter.

R3* **E–**

SEMFLEX STUDIO: "ATELIER" C1976. New film loading permitting changing rolls while attached to a tripod; a protective heavy wire frame around taking and viewing lenses served as a prudent precaution while doing this manoeuvre.

R4* **E+**

SEMFLEX "JOIE DE VIVRE" 3.5: 1956-64. TLR for 6cm x 6cm frames on roll film. Berthiot f3.5, 75mm taking lens (four elements); f2.8 viewing lens; simple shutter 1/50s; side mounted release. (Complete outfit comprising hard case, flash, eveready case, and camera adds 50%)

R3* **D+**

SEMFLEX "JOIE DE VIVRE" 4.5: 1959-64. TLR for 6cm x 6cm frames on roll film. Berthiot f4.5, 75mm taking lens (three elements); f2.8 viewing lens; simple shutter 1/50s, front mounted shutter release; decorative front plate; large "S" on the VFR hood, possible 24 frames on 120 roll film.

R3* **D+**

SEMFLASH STANDARD: 1951-56. TLR for 6cm x 6cm frames on roll film. Berthiot f4.5/75mm taking lens (three elements); simple shutter 1/50s; focusing scale has seven numbers which allow distance/diaphragm flash control; delivered in a hard carrying case.

R4* **E–**

SEMFLASH COUPLE: 1951-59. With diaphragm coupled directly to the focusing mechanism. Sometimes marked "Semflash Location".

R4* **D+**

SEMFLASH COUPLE: 1960. With fixed "chimney" type VFR.

R4* **E–**

GRENAFLEX: 1955-57. sold under the "Grenaflex" name.

R3* **C+**

PHOTOHALL: 1955-57. Sold under the "Photo Hall" name.

R3* **C+**

NO NAME SEMFLEX: 1955-57. Sold without name brand by Manufrance.

R4* **D–**

A. Semmendinger
Fort Lee, New Jersey

EXCELSIOR WET PLATE CAMERA:
c1872. Wet plate camera. 5" x 5" ground glass.

R5*   **G–**

Seneca Camera Co.
Rochester, New York

BUSY BEE: c1903. 4" x 5" Box-type detective camera. 4" x 5" exp on plates.

R3*   **C+**

CHAUTAUQUA: c1912. 3½" x 4½". Folding plate camera.

R3*   **C**

NEW IMPROVED SENECA VIEW CAMERA: c1900's. 5" x 7" View camera. Seneca Triple convertible lens and shutter. Horizontal and vertical swings; double extension reversible back; double tongued bed; plumb bob; black ebonite wood. 7 sizes from 5" x 7" to 17" x 20".

R3*   **5 x 7 size E**
              17 x 20 size F–

SENECA FOLDING ROLL CAMERA: c1915. Ground glass focusing on special Vidax film.

R3*   **C+**

SENECA NO. 8: Folding plate camera. Seneca Sym-Convertible lens; Seneca Auto

Seneca Folding Roll Camera

shutter. Reversible back; black double extension bellows.

R3*   **C+**

SENECA STEREO VIEW CAMERA: c1910. Wollensak Optical Co. stereo shutter. 5" x 7" exp on plates.

R3*   **E**

SEPTON CAMERA: c1953. Pen-type detective camera. 20mm, f2.8 lens; 14 x 14mm exp on 16mm roll film. Mfd in Japan.

R4*   **F**

SFOMAX: c1950. fomax 30mm, f3.5 lens; shutter ⅓₀-¼₀₀s, CRF; 20 exp on 16mm film in special cassettes; slide-in yellow filter.

R4*   **F–**

Shanghai Camera Factory
Shanghai, China

SHANGHAI 58-I: 1958. Cfps, 1-¹⁄₁₀₀₀ sec; seperate Rfr/Vfr windows; diopter adjustment. Screw mount Shanghai f3.5, 50mm lens. A copy of the Leica IIIB, this camera was in production for less than one year. Fewer than 2000 cameras were made, and few survived the violence of China in the 60's. Serial numbers always begin 58XXXXX. Quite rare.

R5*   **H–**

Shanghai 58-I

SHANGHAI 58-II: 1958-63. Cfps, 1 - ¹⁄₁₀₀₀ sec; combined Rfr/Vfr windows; flash synch. Screw mount Shanghai f3.5, 50mm lens. A continuation of the camera line started by the Shanghai 58-I. Several types exist, the earliest ones having strap lugs, five screws in the accessory shoe, and diopter adjustment, while later cameras have no strap lugs, no diopter adjustment, and only three screws in the accessory shoe. Serial numbers always begin 58XXX.

R3* **F–**

SHANGHAI 203: 1963. Folding 120 roll film camera with between the lens leaf shutter, 1 - ¹⁄₃₀₀s. Coupled RFR; flash synch; self-timer; built-in mask for 6x6 or 6x4.5 frame size. Coated f3.5, 75mm lens. This camera was produced in small numbers just before the brand name changed to "Seagull". Rare even in China.

R3* **D+**

SEAGULL 203: 1964-1986. Folding 120 roll film camera with between the lens leaf shutter, 1 - ¹⁄₃₀₀s. Coupled RFR; flash synch; self-timer; built-in mask for 6 x 6 or 6 x 4.5

frame size. Coated f3.5, 75mm lens. Somewhat Zeiss Ikon like in its styling, the Seagull 203 exists in several models, the earliest having no accessory shoe, and the latest having a black plastic top plate, and hot shoe. Common in China, though not often seen in the West.

R3* **C+**

SHANGHAI TLR: 1958-63. TLR camera with between the lens leaf shutter, 1 - ¹⁄₃₀₀s. Flash synch; self-timer; automatic frame counting; knob advance; manual shutter cocking. Coated F3.5, 75mm lens. This well made TLR survived after 1963 as the Seagull 4 TLR. Serial numbers always begin 63XXX.

R3* **D–**

SEAGULL 4: 1964. TLR camera with between the lens leaf shutter, 1 - ¹⁄₃₀₀s. Flash synch; self-timer; automatic frame counting; knob advance; manual shutter cocking. Coated f3.5, 75mm lens. A continuation of the Shanghai TLR. The serial numbers always begin 4-63XXX. Not to be confused with the Seagull 4A, exported in the 1970's, the Seagull 4 has Knob film advance, while the 4A uses a crank, not unlike Rollei TLRs.

R3* **D+**

SEAGULL 4A: 1970's. TLR camera with between the lens leaf shutter, 1 - ¹⁄₃₀₀ s. Flash synch, self-timer; automatic frame counting; crank advance; manual shutter cocking. Coated f3.5, 75mm lens. A continuation of the Shanghai TLR. The serial numbers always begin 4A-XXX. the Seagull 4A has automatic frame counting, and no provision for 6 x 4.5 framing.

R3* **C**

SEAGULL 4B: 1965. TLR camera with between the lens leaf shutter, 1 - ¹⁄₃₀₀s. Flash synch; self-timer; ruby window frame counting; removable metal mask for 6 x 4.5 frame size.

R3* **C**

SEAGULL 4C: 1968. TLR camera with manually set between the lens leaf shutter, 1 - ⅟₃₀₀s. Flash synch; self-timer; ruby window frame counting; removable metal mask for 6 x 4.5 frame size. Special adapter for using 35mm film, with built-in exposure counter. Not often seen in China.

R3*   **D**

Seagull DFAB with f1.4/50mm lens

SEAGULL DFAB: 1970's. Cfps, 1 - ⅟₆₀s, no viewing system. Sometimes equipped with f2, 58mm lens or f1.4, 50mm lens (the same as used on the Red Flag 20 camera) in 42mm screw mount for use as a CRT camera. Available without a lens for use on microscopes. Made at the same time as the Red Flag 20 camera, and using some of the same parts. Not very popular, and quickly replaced on the marketplace by specialty Japanese cameras. Rare, even in China.

R4*   **E+**

EAST WIND: 1970[clq]s. Lens shutter, 1-⅟₁₀₀₀s on the normal lens, 1-⅟₅₀₀ on all others, waist level Vrf, interchangeable magazine backs. Bayonet mount F2.8/80mm normal lens, with f4/50mm wide angle and f4/150mm telephoto lenses available. This Hasselblad copy was made in very small numbers at the order of Jiang Ching, the wife of Chairman Mao. Very rare even in China, usually seen in quite used condition. A complete set including filters, backs, and all three lenses adds 100% to the price. Prices are higher in Japan.

R4*   **I–**

RED FLAG 20: 1971-77. Cfps, 1 - ⅟₁₀₀₀ sec, combined Rfr/Vfr windows, field of view for 35mm, 50mm, and 90mm lens automatically selected upon mounting lens. "M" type bayonet Red Flag f1.4, 50mm lens, with f1.4, 35mm and f2, 90mm lenses available. A copy of the Leica M4 camera, the Red Flag 20 was made in very small numbers, surely less than 200. The first two digits of the serial number indicate the year of manufacture. Prices have gone down from a high of £6,000 for a complete set in the early 1980's. Camera and all three lenses add 100% to the price. Prices are higher in Japan. Quite rare.

R4* H+   **Lenses G** each

Sharp & Hitchmough
Liverpool, England

APTUS PIC-NIC-BASKET: c1889. Picnic basket-type detective camera. 8 x 10.5cm or 10 x 12.5cm plates.

R5*   **H**

LE SHERLOCK HOLMES: c1912. Valise-type detective camera. Fixed focus meniscus lens; close-up lens swings into position; single speed shutter; 6.5 x 9cm plates.

R5*   **G–**

J. F. Shew & Co.
London, England

ALUMINIUM XIT: c1905. Goerz Dagor Series III f6.8 lens; mahogany and aluminium construction.

R2*   **E–**

ECLIPSE: c1888. Denlot rapid rectilinear lens; Rotary shutter.

R3*   **E–**

FOCAL PLANE ECLIPSE: c1895. Same as Eclipse with FPS;

R3*   **F–**

STEREOSCOPIC ECLIPSE: c1891-1900. 6 ¾ x 3¼ plates; with two lenses; removable partition for non-stereoscopic use;

R3*   **G**

SHEW TAILBOARD 4" X 5" CAMERA: c1870's. Shew lens; Waterhouse stops; rubberband powered shutter. Glass plates; finder; book-type holders; original box. C 1870s.

R3*   **F**

Showa Optical Works
Japan

GEMFLEX: c1954. Subminiature TLR camera. Gem 25mm, f3.5 lens; Swallow ½₅-¹⁄₁₀₀s; 10 exp, 14 x 14mm on 16mm roll film.

R3*   **F**

Showa Optical Co. Japan

(Marked Showa Kogaku, this section also contains cameras marked Leotax Camera Co. Ltd.)

LEOTAX (ORIGINAL): 1940. Cfps, ¹⁄₂₀ – ¹⁄₅₀₀; un-coupled RFR; screw mount Letana Anastigmat f3.5, 50mm lens. Viewed from the front, the vfr window is to the left of both the RFR windows, unlike most other Leica copies, and just the opposite of the later Leotax Special A and Special B cameras. Reportedly about 50 cameras made.

R5*   **G+**

LEOTAX SPECIAL A: 1942. Cfps, ½₀ -½₀₀; coupled RFR; seperate RFR/vfr windows; screw mount Letana Anastigmat f3.5, 50mm lens. Viewed from the front, the vfr window is to the right of both the RFR windows, unlike most other Leica copies, and just the opposite of the earlier Leotax (original).

R4*   **G+**

LEOTAX SPECIAL B: 1942. Cfps, 1-½₀₀; coupled RFR; seperate RFR/vfr windows; screw mount Letana Anastigmat f3.5, 50mm lens. The same as the Leotax Special A, except with slow speeds.

R4*   **G+**

LEOTAX SPECIAL: 1946. Cfps, ½₀-½₀₀; coupled RFR; seperate RFR/vfr windows; screw mount Letana Anastigmat f3.5, 50mm or State f3.5, 50mm lens. The same as the Leotax Special A, but produced after the end of the Second World War.

R4*   **G**

LEOTAX SPECIAL DII: 1947. Cfps, ½₀-½₀₀; coupled RFR; seperate RFR/vfr windows; screw mount C. Similar f3.5, 50mm lens. This camera is the first Leotax to have the front vfr window between the two RFR windows.

R4*   **G**

LEOTAX SPECIAL DIII: 1947. Cfps, 1-½₀₀; coupled RFR; seperate RFR/vfr windows; screw mount C. Similar f3.5, 50mm lens. The same as the Leotax Special DII, except

Leotax Special DIII NR III variation for the US Army

with slow speeds. (Also produced as the NR III, and marked "made in occupied Japan". Only about 50 such examples were made.)

R4*   **G**

LEOTAX DIV: 1950. Cfps, 1-½₀₀, coupled RFR; seperate RFR/VFR windows; screw mount Similar f1.5, 50mm lens. Body strap lugs. Not so rare as earlier Leotax's.

R3*   **F**

LEOTAX S: 1952. Cfps, 1-½₀₀; coupled RFR; F and FP synch; seperate RFR/VFR windows; screw mount Similar f1.5, 50mm lens. Body strap lugs. The same as Leotax DIV, with addition of synch.

R3*   **F+**

LEOTAX F: 1954. Cfps, 1-½₀₀₀; coupled RFR; F and FP synch; seperate RFR/vfr windows; screw mount Topcor f1.5, 50mm lens. Single piece top plate, body strap lugs. The first Leotax camera with ½₀₀₀ s shutter. In 1956, the company name changed to Leotax Camera Company, and Leotax F cameras made after that time were so marked, and are considered second version F cameras.

R2*   **F–**

LEOTAX K: 1955. Cfps, ⅒₅ – ⅟₅₀₀; coupled RFR; flash synch; seperate RFR/vfr windows; screw mount Topcor f3.5, 50mm lens. Single piece top plate, body strap lugs.

R2*   **F–**

LEOTAX T: 1955. Cfps, 1-⅟₅₀₀; coupled RFR; flash synch; seperate RFR/vfr windows; screw mount Topcor f3.5, 50mm lens. Single piece top plate, body strap lugs. Similar to Leotax F, but lacking 1/1000 s shutter speed.

R2*   **F–**

The following cameras are marked Leotax Camera Co. Ltd, not Showa.

Leotax TV with Topcor f3.5/ 50mm lens

LEOTAX TV: 1957. CFPS, 1-⅟₅₀₀; coupled RFR; self-timer; seperate RFR/VFR windows; screw mount Topcor f2.0, 50mm lens. Single piece top plate, body strap lugs.

R2*   **F**

LEOTAX FV: 1958. CFPS, 1-⅟₁₀₀₀; coupled RFR; self-timer; seperate RFR/VFR windows; screw mount Topcor f2.0, 5cm or Leonon f2.0, 50mm lens. Single piece top plate, body strap lugs. First Leotax using lever instead of knob advance.

R3*   **F**

LEOTAX K3: 1958. CFPS, ⅛ – ⅟₅₀₀; coupled RFR; seperate RFR/VFR windows; screw mount Fujinon f2.8, 5cm lens. Single piece top plate, body strap lugs.

R3*   **F**

LEOTAX T2: 1958. CFPS, 1 – ⅟₅₀₀; coupled RFR; seperate RFR/VFR windows; screw mount Fujinon f2.0, 50mm lens. Single piece top plate, body strap lugs.

R2*   **F**

Leotax TV2 (Merit) with f2/50mm Topcor

LEOTAX TV2 (MERIT): 1958. CFPS, 1-⅟₅₀₀; coupled RFR; self-timer; separate RFR/VFR windows; screw mount Topcor f2.0, 5cm or Leonon f2.0, 5cm lens. Single piece top plate, body strap lugs. Lever advance.

R2*   **F**

LEOTAX T2L (ELITE): 1959. CFPS, 1-⅟₅₀₀; coupled RFR; seperate RFR/VFR windows; screw mount Topcor f2.0, 5cm or Leonon f2.0, 5cm lens. Single piece top plate, body strap lugs. Lever advance.

R2*   **F**

LEOTAX G: 1961. CFPS, 1-⅟₁₀₀₀; coupled RFR; self-timer; seperate RFR/VFR windows; screw mount Topcor f1.8, 5cm or Leonon f2.0, 5cm lens. Single piece top plate, body strap lugs. Lever advance. More a Leica M copy in body style, the last Leotax.

R4*   **G+**

Shock & Co. KG
Feinmechanik-Optik-Geratebau
Bergkamen, Germany

PANTA: C1954. Metal VFR camera for 6 x 4.5cm frames on 120 roll film. Steiner f3.5, 75mm lens; Vario shutter. A continuation of the Panta camera made by Dr. Rodehuser.

R2*   **B+**

J. Guido Sigrist
Paris, France

JUMELLE SIGRIST STEREO: c1900. Tessar 100mm, f3.5 and tele-Quatryl 150mm, f4.5 lenses; special FPS ⅟₆₀-⅟₄₀₀₀s. 6 x 13cm plates.

R4*   **J–**

SIGRIST: c1898. Krauss-Zeiss Planar 110mm, f3.6-f32 lens; iris diaphragm; variable speed MFPS ⅟₄₀-⅟₄₀₀₀s. 18 exp, 6.5 x 9cm on dry plates. Shutter cocked automatically when plate changed. First camera with ⅟₄₀₀₀ s shutter speed.

R4*   **I**

Simmon Bros. Inc. *New York*

OMEGA 120: c1954-55. 2¼" x 2¾" RFR camera. Omicron 90mm, f3.5 lens; Wollensak-Rapax 1-⅟₄₀₀ s. 9 exp, 2¼" x 2³/₄" on 120 roll film. Eye level optical vf with parallax compensation – coupled RFR. Push-pull film advance coupled to shutter cocking; large focusing heel with depth of field scale. Omega flash attachment automatically coupled to film advance permitting 6 flash bulb exp in rapid sequence. The Omega 120 was the prototype for the Koni-Omega Rapid cameras.

R3*   **E**

Omega 120

James Sinclair & Co. Ltd.
London, England

SINCLAIR TRAVELLER UNA: c1930. Ross Combinable lens; "NS" Perfect shutter. Duralumin construction. 2½" x 3½" exp on plates.

R4*   **I**

SINCLAIR TROPICAL UNA: c1907-1929. Ross Con-vertible lens; Optimo shutter. Teak, brass fittings.

R4*   **G+**

SINCLAIR UNA: c1920. ½ plate camera. N & S Perfect shutter ½-¹⁄₁₀₀s. Double extension bellows; rising front; revolving back; double spirit levels.

R3*   **F+**

UNA CAMEO: c1925. 9 x 12cm folding plate camera. Aldis Uno Anastigmat f7.7 lens.

R3*   **D+**

Thomas Skaife
London, England.

PISTOLGRAPH: c1859. Dallmeyer Petzval-type 50mm, f2.2 lens; double flap shutter. 28mm circular exp on 30 x 40mm wet collodion plates.

U*   **NSR**

SMART STEREO: c1910. Meniscus 110mm f11 lenses; guillotine shutter ¹⁄₁₀-¹⁄₁₀₀s. Stereo exp on 8 x 10cm dry plates.

R4*   **E+**

F. W. Smith & Co. New York

MONOCULAR DUPLEX: c1884. F.W. Smith & Co. Rapid Rectilinear 180mm f5.6 lens; guillotine shutter (operates in conjunction with mirror); variable speed by tension adjustment. 4" x 5" exp on plates.

R5*   **H–**

Jas J. Smith Chicago, Illinois

THE SUNFLOWER MULTIPLYING CAMERA: c1885. Portrait lens; pneumatic flap shutter. Multiple exp: 2 to 32 exp on a 4¾" x 6½" plate. Mahogany finish.

R4*   **G–**

Sanders & Crowhurst
Brighton, England

BIRDLAND REFLEX: c1908. ¼ plate SLR camera. Aldis Anastigmat f8 lens. Ebonized pear wood finish.

R4*   **F–**

SNAPPY: c1950. Meniscus lens; shutter ½₅-¹⁄₁₀₀₀s; 14 x 14mm exp on 16mm roll film. Mfd in Japan.

R3*   **D**

SOLA: c1939. Schneider Xenar 25mm, f2 lens; rotary shutter 1-¹⁄₅₀₀ s; reflex and frame vf; 13 x 18mm exp on 16mm roll film.

R5*   **G+**

Sirius

ACTION TRACKER: c.1980. Unusual 35mm compact camera for four images from four lenses on standard 35mm frame. Images are exposed sequentially to capture sporting sequences. Fixed aperture, speed and focus. Fold up frame viewfinder. Black and red versions. Made in China.

R1*   **C**

Societa Construzioni Articoli Technici
Rome, Italy

SCAT: c1950. Subminiature camera. 7x9mm exp on Minox cassettes. Mfd in Italy.

R4*   **E–**

Soligor *Japan*

SOLIGOR SEMI-AUTO: c1950. 2¼" x 2¼" TLR camera. Soligor 80mm, f3.5 lens; Rektor shutter 1-⅟₃₀₀s; 12 exp, 2¼" x 2¼" on 120 roll film.

R2*   **B+**

Sony, *Japan*

MAVICA: 1982. Announced as the first digital camera to record images on

magnetic disc, rather than film. The name was a corruption of Magnetic Video Camera. SLR with interchangeable lens. 50 exp to a disc. Prototypes exist, but the camera never went into commercial production.

R4*   **NSR**

Spartacus Corp. *Chicago*

SPARTUS 35: 35mm Camera. Brown and gray plastic.

R1*   **A**

Star-Kist Food Inc. *USA*

CHARLIE TUNA: 1971, toy plastic camera in shape of a tuna fish. 8 exp, 126 cartridge. C 1967.

R3*   **C**

Star Mfg. Co.
Brooklyn, New York

STAR 8" X 10" VIEW CAMERA: c1930's. Century Planograph Convertible lens. Roller blind shutter, lens board moves hori-

zontally and vertically. Double ext bellows; polished wood finish, brass fittings.

R4*   **E**

STAR WATCH CAMERA: c1912. Watch-style detective camera, resembles Lancaster. Mfd in Japan.

R5* NSR   **J+**

Steineck Kamerawerk
Germany

STEINECK A.B.C: c1948. Subminiature watch-style detective camera. Steinheil 12.5mm, f2.5 lens; rotary MFPS ½₂₅s; 8 exp, 6mm diameter on 25mm diameter film in metal cassette.

R3*   **F+**

G. A. Steinheil Sons
Munich, Germany

STEINHEIL CASCA I: c1948. Culminar 50mm f2.8 lens; FPS ½₂₅-¹⁄₁₀₀₀ s.

R3*   **E–**

Range-finder version.   **E+**

DETECTIVE CAMERA: c1888. Magazine loading box-type wooden detective

Steinheil Detective Camera

finished in tan leather. Designed by Seton Rochwhite. Only 150 mfd.

R4*   **G+**

camera. Achromatic lens; 9 x 12cm on plates.

R4*   **F+**

Stereo Corporation
Milwaukee, Wisconsin

CONTURA 35MM STEREO CAMERA: c1950. 35mm stereo camera. Volar f2.7 lens; flash. Combined range-vf window at base of camera. Double exp prevention device with override. Aluminium body

Stereo Crafters Inc.
Milwaukee, Wisconsin, U.S.A

VIDEON: c1953. Black plastic and aluminium bodied 35mm stereo vfr camera. Front focusing Ilex Stereon Anistigmat 35mm, f3.5 lenses; shutter speeds ¹⁄₁₀-¹⁄₁₀₀s. Also sold as the "Videon Challenger".

R3*   **C+**

VIDEON II: c1954. Black plastic and aluminium bodied 35mm stereo vfr camera. Front focusing Ilex Stereon Anistigmat 35mm, f3.5 lenses; shutter speeds ¹⁄₁₀-¹⁄₁₀₀s. Quite similar to the Videon, with only a few minor changes.

R3*   **C+**

H. Steward *England.*

J. H. STEWARD MAGAZINE CAMERA: c1890. Detective drop plate magazine camera. Rising, falling and sliding front.

R4*   **D+**

C. P. Stirn, Stirn & Lyon
New York

STIRN'S AMERICA DETECTIVE CAMERA: c1887. Wooden box-type detective camera. Periscopic 105mm, f17 lens; 25 exp, 7.5 x 10cm on Eastman 85mm film. Probably the first camera especially made for flexible film. Invented by R. Gray, New York; mfd by Rudolph Stirn, Germany. C 1887.

R5*   **NSR H+**

STIRN'S CONCEALED VEST CAMERA, NO. 1: c1886. 6" Diameter detective camera. 6 circular 1¾" exp on glass plate. Nickel, or brass. With wooden case.

R5*   **G+**

STIRN'S CONCEALED VEST CAMERA, NO. 2: c1886. 7" Diameter detective camera; 4 circular 2½" exp on glass plate.

R5*   **H−**

STIRN'S DETECTIVE CAMERA: c1891. Mahogany magazine camera. Aplanatic lens; variable speed rotating shutter; 2 vf. 12 exp on 6 x 8cm plates; leather changing bag back. It's rare to find these cameras with the wooden case intact. Without wooden box, R4 and value reduced.

R5*   **G**

STIRN'S STEREO DETECTIVE CAMERA: c1893. Aplanatic 90mm f11 lens; variable speed rotating shutter; 9 x 18cm plates – changing mechanism with leather bag.

R5*   **NSR G+**

Suffize & Molitor
Paris, France

SUMO STEREO CAMERA: c1912. 6x13cm stereo pairs were made on glass plates carried in changing magazines. Compur shutters, Krauss Tessar f4.5 lenses. These cameras were most commonly used for making Lumiere Autochromes and are frequently found with changing magazines for use with Autochrome plates. They could, however, be used with any standard glass plates.

R2*   **E**

Sugaya Optical Co. Ltd.
Japan.

MINIMAX 110EE: 1978. Resembles a small-scale 35mm camera, but made for 110 film. Detachable flashgun out of proportion to camera. 32mm f2 Minimax lens, auto shutter, CdS meter.

R3*   **C+**

MINIMAX-LITE: Combination camera and lighter, made for 8x11mm images on Minox film. Fixed focus f8 lens.

R3*   **C+**

MYCRO III A: c1950. Mycro 20mm, f4.5 lens; shutter ½s-¹⁄₁₀₀s; 10 exp, 10 x 14mm on 16mm roll film.

R3*   **C+**

MYRACLE: c1949. Subminiature camera. 10 x 14mm exp on roll film.

R3*   **D**

Sunart Photo Co.
Rochester, New York

SUNART VIDI NO. 2: c1898. Leather covered folding plate camera. Red bellows, mahogany interior.

R4*   **D–**

Sunpak Corporation
Tokyo, Japan

NIMSLO-3D: c1982. Stereo using the lenticular principle. The camera has four lenses about 2cms apart. The four images require special processing and result in an image with significant apparent depth. No special glasses are required for viewing. The first version of the Nimslo-3D was manufactured in Scotland c1978-9 before production was moved to Japan. Depending on location R2 for first model, R1 for second

R2* or R1*   **D**

E. Suter*Basle, Switzerland*

SUTER'S DETECTIVE MAGAZINE CAMERA: c1890. Suter Detective lens; rotating shutter. Leather covered mahogany box camera, brass fittings.

R4*   **E+**

SUTER'S STEREO DETECTIVE CAMERA: c1897. Rectilinear lenses; rotating shutter. Changing mechanism for 9 x 18cm plates.

R3*   **F+**

Suzuiki Optical Co. *Japan*

ECHO 8: c1951. Cigarette lighter-type detective camera. Echor 15mm, f3.5 lens; shutter 1/50 s. 8 exp, 6 x 6mm on 8mm film.

R4*   **F+**

Echo 8

Swank Mfg. Co. *USA*

SCHNAPPS-O-FLEX: c1965. Liquor container in shape of a camera. Flash reflector uncorks from flashgun revealing clay container with one pint capacity.

R2*   **C**

T

Takahashi Kogaku *Japan*

ARSEN: c.1938. Small camera for 12 exp on 127. Similar style to the Gelto D III.

R3*   **C+**

Romain Talbot Berlin
Germany

ERRTEE BUTTON TINTYPE CAMERA: c1910. Cannon shaped street camera. Laak 50mm, f4.5 lens; single speed shutter; 100 exp, 1" diameter tintype plates.

R5*   **NSR**

Walter Talbot *Berlin, Germany*

TALBOT INVISIBLE CAMERA: c1914-1930. Belt-type detective camera; Anastigmat f5.5 lens; shutter ⅟₂₅s; 15 to 30 exp on 35mm film. Rapid trigger release to cock shutter and advance film. Long, thin rectangular (7 x 34cm) shape. Camera was worn on a belt under coat, with lens protruding through button hole.

R5*   **NSR**

Tanaka Optical Co. Ltd.
Japan

TANACK II C: 1953. Cfps, ⅟₂₀-⅟₅₀₀; FP flash synch; hinged back seperate Rfr/Vfr windows. First produced with a screw mount Tanar f3.5, 50mm lens. Later cameras used screw mount Tanar f2.8/50mm lens. Similar to the Leica IIIB, but without slow speeds.

R4*   **F–**

TANACK IIIF: 1954. Cfps, 1 -⅟₅₀₀; FP flash synch; seperate Rfr/Vfr windows. First produced with a screw mount Tanar f3.5, 50mm lens or Tanar F2.8, 50mm lens. Same as the Tanak IIC, but with slow speeds.

R4*   **F–**

TANACK IIIS: 1954-55. Cfps, 1-⅟₅₀₀; FP and X flash synch; seperate Rfr/Vfr windows. With screw mount Tanar f3.5, 50mm lens or Tanar f2.8, 50mm lens. Similar to the Tanak IIIF but with additional X synch contact, and one piece top plate.

R3*   **F–**

TANACK IV-S: 1955-58. Cfps, 1-⅟₅₀₀; FP and X flash synch; seperate Rfr/Vfr windows. With screw mount Tanar f3.5, 50mm lens ,Tanar f2.8, 50mm lens or Tanar f2.0,

50mm lens. Late cameras had a film type reminder dial added to the wind knob.

R3* F–

TANACK SD: 1957. Cfps, 1-¹⁄₁₀₀₀ sec; flash synch; self-timer; combined Rfr/Vfr windows; bright line parallax corrected finder. Screw mount Tanar f2.0, 50mm or Tanar f1.5, 50mm lens. Very few of these cameras were made. More like the Contax II or Nikon S2, but using screw mount lenses.

R4* F

TANACK V3: 1958. Cfps, 1-¹⁄₅₀₀sec; flash synch on the right side next to the rewind crank; combined Rfr/Vfr window; film type reminder in the back of the camera; no self-timer. Bayonet mount Tanar f2.8, 50mm or Tanar f1.9, 50mm or Tanar F1.5, 50mm lens. Though similar to the Leica M type bayonet mount, the Tanack V3 camera used three lugs instead of four. Screw mount lenses could be used by means of a bayonet to screw mount adaptor.

R3* F

TANACK VP: 1959. Cfps, 1-¹⁄₅₀₀sec; flash synch; combined Rfr/Vfr window; film type reminder in back of camera; no self-timer. Screw mount Tanar F1.8, 50mm lens. Development of the V3 camera, the VP used only screw mount lenses.

R4* F

TASCO BINOCULAR CAMERA: c1978. Subminiature 4 x 20mm binocular camera.

Tele-Tasco 112mm, f5.6 coated lens; 12 exp on 110 cartridge. Mfd in Japan.

R3* E+

A. & G. Taylor
London, England.

A & G TAYLOR TAILBOARD CAMERA: c1890's. 13" x 18" Tailboard camera. Brass Clement Gilmer lens. Mahogany finish, brass fittings; leather bellows.

R4* E

Tek Serra & Co.
Torino, Italy

TELECA: c1950. Subminiature binocular-type detective camera. Telesigmar 35mm, f4.5 coated lens; shutter ¹⁄₂₅,¹⁄₅₀,¹⁄₁₀₀s; binoculars function as vf. 10 x 14mm exp on 16mm film in special cassette. Mfd in Japan.

R4*   **G**

A. Themsteyr

PHOTO SPORT: c1926. Laako Dyalitar 45mm, f4.5 lens; Compur shutter 1-¼₀₀s. 24 x 30mm exp on 35mm film.

R4*   **E+**

THOMAS OF PALL MALL WET PLATE: c1860. Mahogany sliding box camera. Ross portrait lens, Waterhouse stops. Multiplying back takes 2 exp on horizontal plate.

R5*   **H–**

W. J. Thompson Co. Inc.
New York

THOMPSON TINTYPE CAMERA: c1910. Suitcase-type street camera.

R4*   **E–**

Thornton Pickard Mfg. Co.
Altrincham, England

AERIAL CAMERA TYPE A: c1915-?. Mahogany and brass camera. 4 x 5" plates in special magazines; FPS; Type C as A except Long body accomodates Ross Xpres f4.5-10" lens.

R4*   **I–**

AMBER: c1899-1906. Compact folding field camera. Quarter to whole-plate sizes; tripod turntable; lens and shutter protude through base when closed; cheaper version of the Ruby.

R3*   **F–**

COLLEGE: c1912-1926. Compact double extension folding field camera. Mahogany with brass fittings; 9 x 12 to 18 x 24cm; TP roller-blind shutter; Rectoplant lens.

R3*   **F–**

DUPLEX RUBY REFLEX TROPICAL: c1920. Teak and brass reflex camera, for the overseas market; 6.5 x 9cm or quarterplate; double extension orange bellows; FPS ¼₀₀₀; Cook Anastigmat f6.3 lens.

R4*   **H+**

HYTHE GUN CAMERA: c1915. Lewis gun style camera for training British RAF machine gunners during WWI. Copied by Japanese in WWII. 300mm, f8 lens; central shutter; 16 exp, 4.5 x 6cm or 11 exp, 6 x 6cm on 120 roll film.

R4*   **G**

IMPERIAL TRIPLE EXTENSION; (TP108) c1904-1926. Field camera. Triple ext. tapered bellows; mahogany with brass fittings; Beck Symmetrical or TP Rectoplant lenses.

R3*   **F**

Hythe Gun Camera

RUBY: c1899-1905. Compact folding field camera. Ruby RR lens; TP roller blind shutter.

R3*   **F**

ROYAL RUBY: c1904-1930. Triple extension version of the Ruby.

R3*   **F+**

RUBY DUPLEX TROPICAL REFLEX: c1916. Tropical SLR camera. Cooke Series IIa 6½" f3.5 lens; CFPS 1-¹⁄₁₀₀₀s; 2¼" x 3¼" exp on film pack.

R4*   **H+**

RUBYETTE: c.1934. One of the smaller SLRs from this company, made for 6x9cm plates and cut film, or 120 rollfilm if used with a rollfilm back. 4-inch f4.5 Dallmeyer Anastigmat. FP shutter 1-1/100s. Shutter release linked to mirror movement to give return after exposure.

R3*   **D+**

STEREO PUCK: c1926. Roll film stereo box camera.

R2*   **D**

THORNTON PICKARD STEREO CAMERA: Roll blind shutter. Mahogany finish, brass fittings.

R4*   **F+**

Thornton Pickard Stereo Camera

J. Thorpe
New York

THORPE FOUR-TUBE CAMERA: c1862. Four lens camera for Carte-de-visite or wet plate. 5" x 7" exp.

R5*   **G+**

THURY & AMEY STEREO FOLDING CAMERA: c1890. Zeiss Protar 120mm, f9 lenses; Thury & Amey 4-speed guillotine shutter. Mfd in Geneva, Switzerland.

R4*   **E–**

Tiranti
Rome, Italy

SUMMA REPORT: c.1950s. Unusual and rare camera for 6x9 plates, cut film or rollfilm. Four lenses mounted on revolving turret, two for taking and two or viewing. Standard pair 105mm f4 Xenar coupled with f4 Galileo Reflar, wideangle pair 65mm f6.8 Schneider Angulon coupled with f3.5 Galileo Reflar. As well as optical finder, extra frame finder on top of body.

R5*   **NSR**

Summa Report

Ph. Tiranty
Paris, France

SIMDA: c1957. 16mm Camera for either single exposure or stereo pairs using either single or double perforated cine film. Fixed focus Angénieux 25mm, f3.5 of Roussel Special 25mm, f3.5 lenses, shutter speeds 1-¹⁄₂₅₀s, holds enough film for 100 shots. Available in either black or grey. Also known as the "Panoramascope 3D".

R4*   **F+**

A. Tischlere Heinemann & Dressler
Munich, Germany

MONACHIA: c1889. Meniscus lens; front of lens rotary shutter. 35 x 40mm exp.

R4*   **F–**

Tisdell & Whittelsey
New York

TISDELL & WHITTELSEY DETECTIVE CAMERA: c1887. Box-type detective camera. Achromatic meniscus lens; variable speed shutter; 3¼" x 4¼" exp on dry plates.

Leather covered model

R4*   **G–**
Wooden model   **H–**

Tisdell Camera and Mfg. Co.
Scranton, Pennsylvania

TISDELL HAND CAMERA: c1893. Leather covered box-type detective camera. 4" x 5" exp on dry plates.

R4*   **F–**

Tisdell Hand Camera

Tizer Company *Tokyo, Japan*

COCA COLA CAMERA: c.1978. The original can camera later copied by Taiwan. Fixed focus, aperture and shutter speed. Takes 110 film. Some models have hot shoes synch for flash.

R1*   **A**

SNOOPY CAN CAMERA: 1979. 110 camera in the form of a soft drink can decorated with cartoon character Snoopy. Fixed-focus meniscus lens, shutter works at about 1/75s. Also made as a Coca-Cola can.

R3*   **D+**

TKC, *Japan.*

KALIMAR A: c1956. 35mm Camera. Teri-onon 45mm, f3.5 coated lens; shutter ½s-¹⁄₂₀₀ s.

R3*   **B–**

Toakoki Seisakusho
Japan

GELTO D III (PRE-WAR MODEL): 1938. Small, neatly designed camera for 16 ex on 127. 5cm f4.5 Grimmel lens extends on collapsible tube. Shutter 1/5-1/250s. Eye-level viewfinder. Black body.

R2*   **C+**

GELTO D III (POST-WAR MODEL): 1950. Similar to pre-war version, but with f3.5 lens and made in silver or gold. Very attractive camera.

R3*   **D**

Tokiwa Seiki Co.
Tokyo, Japan

PENTAFLEX: 1955. SLR for eye-level viewing, the first Japanese camera with this feature. A penta mirror worked like a pentaprism. Tokinon Anastigmat f3.4, 50mm lens which was interchangeable. Behind the lens shutter 1-1/400s.

R3*   **F–**

Tokyo Optical Co.
Tokyo, Japan

TOPCON RE SUPER: 1963. SLR fitted with Auto-Topcor f1.8, 5.8cm interchangeable lens. Focal plane shutter 1-1000s. First SLR to be fitted with a TTL exposure meter.

R2*   **D**

Tokyo Koki *Japan*

RUBINA 16 MODEL II: c.1950. Better than average quality 16mm subminiature for 10x14 mm images. Styled like a small 35mm camera. 25mm f3.5 Ruby Anastigmat lens, focusing down to 1 metre. Shutter 1/25-1/100s. Miniature accessory shoe on top plate, though no evidence of accessories. Model I unknown.

R3*   **E**

Tokyo Shashin *Japan*

MIGHTY: 1947. Japanese subminiature. Meniscus lens; single speed shutter; 13 x 13mm exp on 16mm roll film; Double vf; adjustable diaphragm. A 2x telephoto was an available accessory. Unusual for a very simple sub-miniature.

R3*   **D**

TONE: 1949. Subminiature camera. Tone Anastigmat 25mm, f3.5 lens. Direct optical vf and waist level reflex finders. Mfd in Japan.

R3*   **C+**

Topper Toy Division
De Luxe Reading Corporation
New Jersey

SECRET SAM ATTACHE CASE CAMERA: c1965. Toy spy attache case, pistol assembly and camera. Takes 127 roll film. Includes a toy pistol, plastic bullets.

R4*   **E–**

SECRET SAM'S SPY DICTIONARY: c1965. Plastic book-type detective camera; 16 exp on 127 film

R4*   **D+**

Tougo-Do Mfg. Co.
Tokyo, Japan

HIT: c1948. Sub-miniature camera for 14x14mm images on paper-backed roll-film. Lens meniscus f11, 30mm. Single speed shutter works at about 1/30s. It was made in very large quantities under a variety of names.

R2*   **B**

Hit

STEREO HIT: Roll film stereo camera. S-Owla 4.5cm coated lenses; guillotine shutter, I, B. 8 stereo exp on 127 film (single frame capacity). Mfd in Japan.

R3*   **D+**

Triad Corporation
Encino, California

FOTRON III: c1960. Automatic camera. 10 exp, 1" x 1" on cartridge film, 35mm wide. Built-in electronic flash with rechargeable batteries; electric film advance.

R3*   **B+**

TURF FOLDING CAMERA: c1935. Folding camera with thermoplastic body for 16 exp 6x4.5cm on 120 film. Front cell focusing Turf Extra Anistigmat 7cm, f3.8 lens; btl shutter, speeds ½₅-¹⁄₁₀₀s. Made in Germany C. 1935

R4*   **F–**

W. Tylar *Birmingham, England*

GNU STEREOSCOPIC MAGAZINE HAND CAMERA: c1904. Box form magazine camera. Single achromat lens; rotating Waterhouse stops; shutter, T, I. Single exp option; reflecting finder. 2 sets of 12 plates, 4¾" x 3¼".

R4*   **F**

TYLAR DETECTIVE CAMERA: c1890. Guillotine shutter; ¼ plate exp on dry plates.

R4*   **E**

Tynar Corporation
Los Angeles, California.

TYNAR: c1950. Subminiature camera. 45mm, f6.3 lens; single speed guillotine shutter. 10 x 14mm exp on 16mm cassettes.

R3*   **C**

Reference Notes

Ulca Camera Corp.
Pennsylvania, USA

ULCA: c.1930s. Subminiature for 20x20mm images on special rollfilm. Although generally known as an American camera, models were also made in Germany (where it was designed and patented) and Britain. Fixed focus, aperture and speed. Varying models include the Ulca TSL, STI, STM and TMS.

R3* **C**

Four of the several different styles of Ulca.

United Feature Syndicate Inc.

SNOOPY-MATIC CAMERA: c1966. Meniscus lens; sector shutter. 12 exp on 126 roll film.

R3* **D–**

United Optical Instruments
Essex, England

MERLIN: 1936. Simple subminiature for 20x20mm images on special rollfilm. Fixed focus, aperture and speed. Fold-up viewfinder. No markings on body. Uncommon in black, rare in red and green. (This camera was later incorporated into a Bakelite shell shaped vaguely liked a pistol and called the Erac.)

R4* **D**

Unitek Mfg. Co.
Monrova, California

UNITEK PRECISION INTRA-ORAL DENTAL CAMERA: c1965. Geared belt-driven moving prism with internal light source is used for oral photographs on 3¼" x 4¼" Polaroid film. A separate power unit charges the camera's nicad batteries and warms the optical assembly.

R4* **E–**

Universal Camera Corporation
New York

BUCCANEER: c1945. 35mm Camera with CRF. Built-in extinction meter; Bakelite construction; collapsible Tricor 50mm f3.5 lens; Chrono-matic shutter ⅒-⅟₃₀₀s, flash synch.

R2* **B+**

CORSAIR I: c1938. 35mm VFR camera with built-in extinction meter for special perforated film. Bakelite construction, similar to Vitar. Collapsible Univex Anastigmat f4.5, 50mm lens; shutter ⅟₂₅-⅟₂₀₀s.

R2* **B+**

CORSAIR II: c1946. 35mm VFR camera. With built-in extinction meter. As previous model except uses standard 35mm film. Bakelite construction. Similar to Vitar. Collapsible Univex Anastigmat f4.5, 50mm lens, shutter ⅟₂₅-⅟₂₀₀s.

R2* **B+**

IRIS: c1939. Dark painted metal bodied VFR camera. Collapsible Ilex Vitar 50mm, f7.9 lens. T. B. I. shutter, 8 exp 1x1.5" on 00 universal roll film.

R2* **B+**

IRIS DELUX: c1939. Metal bodied VFR camera. Collapsible Ilex Vitar 50mm, f7.9 lens; T. B. I. Shutter. 8 exp 1 x 1.5" on 00 universal roll film, polished metalwork synchronised version add 50% .

R2* **B+**

MERCURY I: c1947. Metal bodied half-frame 35mm VFR camera. Interchangeable Tricor 35mm, f3.5 lens, rotary sector MFPS ⅟₂₀-⅟₁₀₀₀s. Using 35mm film in special rolls.

R2* **C+**

MERCURY I, MODEL CC1500. c1947. Metal bodied half-frame 35mm VFR. Interchangeable Tricor f3.5 or f2.7, 35mm lens; rotary sector MFPS ⅟₂₀-⅟₁₅₀₀s. Using 35mm film in special rolls; as (UC103) but for ⅟₁₅₀₀s shutter speed.

R4* **D**

MERCURY II: c1948. Metal bodied half-frame 35mm VFR camera. Interchangeable Universal Tricor 35mm, f2.8 lens; rotary sector MFPS ½₀ -¹⁄₁₀₀₀s. Using standard 35mm film.

R2*   **C+**

METEOR: c1949. metal bodied VFR camera. For 6cm x 6cm frames on 620 roll film; fll lens in collapsible tube; simple shutter; built-in extinction meter.

R2*   **A**

MINICAM: c1938. Brown metal bodied strut folding camera for 00 film. Ilex-Achromar 50mm lens; simple shutter.

R3*   **B+**

MINUTE 16: c1950. Subminiature camera. Meniscus lens; guillotine shutter. 10 x

14mm exp on 16mm film in special cartridge.

R3*   **C+**

NORTON: c1935-1936. Black plastic camera. 6 Exp, 1⅛" x 1½" on No. 00 universal roll film.

R2*   **B+**

ROAMER I: c1949. Metal bodied folding VFR camera. For 6cm x 9cm frames on either 120 or 620 film. Universal Anastigmat f6.3, 100mm lens; synchromatic shutter; as (UC122) but for lens.

R2*   **B−**

ROAMER II: c1949. Metal bodied folding VFR camera. For 6cm x 9cm frames on either 120 or 620 film. Universal Anastigmat f4.5, 100mm lens; synchromatic shutter.

R2*   **B−**

ROAMER 63: c1949. Metal bodied folding VFR camera For 6cm x 9cm frames on either 120 or 620 film. Universal Anastigmat Synchromatic 100mm, f6.3 lens; 6cm x 9cm frames on 120 roll film.

R2*   **B−**

STER-ALL: c1957. 35mm stereo VFR camera. Tricor f3.5 fixed focus lens; shutter ⅕₀s.

R3*   **D**

STEREO UNIVEX MODEL A: c1938. Paired Univex cameras attached by bracket.

R4*   **E**

Stereo Univex Model A

TWINFLEX: c1938. Meniscus lens; sector shutter; reflex viewing. 6 exp on No. 00 roll film.

R3* **B+**

UNIVEX AF: c1937. Compact metal bodied strut folding camera for 00 roll film.

R2* **B+**

UNIVEX AF-2: c1938. Compact metal bodied strut folding camera for 00 roll film.

R2* **B+**

UNIVEX AF-3: c1938. Compact metal bodied strut folding camera for 00 roll film.

R2* **B+**

UNIVEX MODEL A CAMERA: c1940. VFR camera. For 6 exp on Univex 00 roll film. Bakelite construction.

R2* **B–**

UNIFLASH: c1940. Simple VFR camera. For 00 film. Bakelite construction. Vitar 60mm lens. Sold with flash.

R2* **A**

VITAR: c1950. 35mm VFR camera. Bakelite construction. Universal Tricor Anastigmat 50mm f3.5 lens; Flash Chronomatic shutter ½₅-¼₀₀s; built-in extinction meter. (prices higher in Europe).

R2*   **B+**

UNIVEX ZENITH: 1939. Similar style to Univex Iris Delux, but with f4.5 lens, shutter 1/25-1/200s + T & B. Rigid lens mount. Flashgun hot shoe and body release via add-on accessory screwed to top plate. Rare.

R4*   **D+**

UNIVEX: c1950?. Bakelite VFR camera. For 6x4.5 frames on roll film; simple lens and shutter; marked "Univex", but the shutter is marked "P and I" like a French camera would be.

R4*   **C–**

Usines Gallus
Courbevoie, France

GALLUS 00: c1924. 6 x 13cm plate magazine camera. Detachable shutter unit.

R4*   **D+**

GALLUS 0: c1924. 6 x 13cm plate magazine camera. For use as a stereoscope.

R4*   **E**

GALLUS 100: c1924. 6 x 13cm plate magazine camera. Fixed focus Gallus 75mm,

f6.3 lens; guillotine shutter ⅛-½₀₀s.T.B. Rising front.

R4*   **D+**

GALLUS 110: c1924. 6 x 13cm plate magazine camera. Leather covered Gallus 100.

R4*   **D+**

GALLUS 120: c1924. 6 x 13cm plate magazine camera. Fixed focus Gallus 75mm, f6.3 lens; Ibsor shutter 1-¼₀₀s. Ring front; leather covered..

R4*   **D+**

GALLUS 130: c1924. 6 x 13cm plate magazine camera. Helicoidal focusing; Compur shutter.

R4*   **D+**

GALLUS 140: c1924. 6 x 13cm plate magazine camera. Helicoidal focusing; shutter 2-⅓₀₀s.

R4*   **D+**

GALLUS 150: c1924. 6 x 13cm plate magazine camera. optical finder.

R4*   **D+**

GALLUS: c1938. 6 x 9cm Bakelite roll film camera. With various lens and shutter combinations. Looks the same as the Pontiac and Ebner cameras of that era. Though not as often seen.

R4*   **C+**

CADY-LUX: c1940. Metal bodied folding camera. Making 6 x 9cm or 6 x 6cm negatives on roll film through the use of two ruby windows and internal masks. Fixed optical finder and adjustable depth of field gauge on the camera top plate. Front focusing 105mm, f4.5 Berthiot Special lens in a Gallus shutter, speeds of ½₅-¼₀₀s.

R3*   **C**

DERBY-GALLUS: c1939. 3 x 4cm on roll film camera. CFPS speeds of ½₅ -¼₀₀s. Optical VFR; front focusing 50mm, f3.5 Saphir lens. This camera is the continuation of the famous "Foth" Derby, originally made in Berlin, Germany. Because of the beginning of WWII, not many cameras were made.

R3*   **D**

DERLUX: c1947, 3 x 4cm on roll film camera. CFPS speeds of ½₅-¹⁄₅₀₀s. Optical VFR, front focusing 50mm, f3.5 or f2.8 Saphir lens or the more often found 50mm, f3.5 Gallix lens. Early cameras use the old style "Foth" body, with a new polished aluminium lens board, later cameras were entirely polished aluminium.

R3*   **D+**

LENSES FOR GALLUS 1924 MODELS: Hermagis Aplanastigmatic 75mm, f6.8; Dogmar 75mm, f6.3; Stylor 75mm, f4.5 or f6.3; Berthiot Perigraphe 75mm, f6.8; Olor 75mm, f6.8 or f5.7; Tessar 75mm, f6.3.

Utility Mfg. Co. *Chicago, USA*

NB, to make life simple, cameras made by the "Falcon Camera Company" (Chicago and New York) and the "Spartus Camera Company" are also included in this listing. Someday, it may be made clear when and how these three companies went their seperate ways, here is a sample from each. Most of these cameras are much less expensive in the USA.

SPARTUS FULL-VUE: c1950. Bakelite TLR box camera. For 6 x 6cm on roll film, simple lens and shutter.

R2*   **A**

SPARTUS PRESS FLASH: c1946. Bakelite box camera for roll film. Built-in flash reflector.

R2*   **B–**

SPARTUS 35: c1950, Bakelite 35mm VFR. Simple lens and shutter.

R2*   **B+**

SPARTUS 35F: c1950. With flash synch. (price includes flash).

R2*   **B+**

SPARTUS: c1939. Bakelite strut folding camera. For 3 x 4cm on 127 roll film; simple lens and shutter.

R3*   **B+**

FALCON JUNIOR MODEL: c1947. Made by Falcon.

R2*   **B+**

FALCON MINIATURE: c1947. Bakelite VFR camera. For 3 x 4cm on 127 roll film; simple lens and shutter. Several variations.

R2*   **B+**

FALCON MINIATURE DELUXE: c1947. In brown.

R3*   **B+**

FALCON ROCKET: c1947. Streamlined Bakelite VFR camera. For 3 x 4cm on 127 roll film; simple lens and shutter.

R3*   **B+**

FALCON G: c1937. Bakelite VFR camera. For 3 x 4cm on 127 roll film; f3.5 lens in collapsible tube focusing mount in Deltax shutter ½₅-¹⁄₁₀₀s.

R3*   **B+**

FALCON F: c1937. With f4.5 lens.

R3*   **B+**

FALCON SPECIAL: Built-in extinction meter.

R3*   **B+**

FALCON PRESS FLASH: C.1939.

R3*   **B+**

D.F. Vasconcellos
Sao Paulo, Brazil

Kapsa

BIEKA: c1950. Metal box camera. For 6 x 9cm frames on roll film; simple lens and shutter.

R3* **B–**

KAPSA: c1950. Well made Bakelite box camera. For 6 x 9cm or 6 x 4.5 cm on roll film; simple lens and shutter.

R3* **C**

Vega Co. *Geneva, Switzerland*

TELEPHOTE VEGA: c1901. 13 x 18cm; Achromatic 120mm, f20 lens; FPS up to ½₀₀s. Compact structure – long focal length achieved by reflecting light beam with two mirrors.

R5* **H+**

VEGA: c1900. Book-style detective camera. Aplanatic 180mm f7.8 lens; guillotine shutter ½-⅟₁₀₀s; closing and opening this book-style camera operates the plate changing mechanism.

R5* **G–**

LE VEROGRAPHE: c1920. Krauss Tessar 90mm, f6.3 lenses;5-speed guillotine shutter; 2 plate magazine. Mfd in Paris, France.

R3* **D+**

VESTKAM: c1947, subminiature camera. TKK shutter. Mfd in Japan.

R3* **D**

Vidmar Camera Co. *U.S.A.*

VIDAX: c1951. Press camera. Using 120 roll film and 2¼" x 3¼" sheet film; Schneider Xenotar 80mm, f2.8 coated lens in interchangeable mount; Synchro-Compur 1-⅟₅₀₀s, X, M flash synch. Variable crf; interchangeable backs; 8, 12 or 16 exp on 120 roll film. Rare.

R5* **G**

VISCAWIDE 16: c1961, subminiature panoramic camera. Ross 25mm f3.5 coated lens; shutter ⅟₆₀-⅟₅₀₀s. 10 x 52mm exp on 16mm film in special cassette. Mfd in Japan. Only 16mm panoramic camera ever made.

R3* **E+**

Vive Camera Co.
Chicago, Illinois

VIVE SOUVENIR CAMERA: c1897. Premium box camera.

R3* **D**

VIVE NO. 1: c1898. Simple lens; single speed shutter; 12 exp, 11 x 11cm on dry plates, manipulated through light tight sleeve. First American camera to use the dark sleeve to change plates.

R3* **D–**

VIVE NO. 2, IMPROVED MODEL: c1897. Box magazine camera. Self-capping shutter; 12 exp, 4¼" x 4¼" on dry plates.

R3* **C+**

VIVE NO. 4: c1895. 4" x 5" plate camera.

R3* **C+**

VIVE STEREO CAMERA: c1899. Stereo box camera. 6" x 3½" exp on dry plates in magazine.

R4* **F–**

Josef Vojta *Prague, Bohemia*
(Austro-Hungarian Empire)

STEREO DRY PLATE CAMERA: c1910. 9x18cm images on glass plates in holders. Matched anastigmat lenses f7. Many of Vojta's cameras were fitted with a front mounted curtain shutter of his design.

R5* **E**

Voigtlander A.G.
Braunschweig, Germany

VOIGTLANDER DAGUERREOTYPE CAMERA (REPLICA): c1956. Replica of the first portrait camera produced in 1841. Brass construction. Petzval 159mm, f3.7 lens was 20 times faster than lens used by Daguerre in 1859. Exposure time was reduced to 1½ minutes or less on sunny days, 80mm diameter sensitized daguerreotype plate was contained in circular brass holder. Those made by others, 20% less.

R4* **H+**

Stereo Dry Plate Camera

Bergher

ALPIN: c1912. Folding plate camera. Voigtlander Collinear 120mm, f6.8 lens; Kolios shutter 1-⅓₀₀s; 9 x 12cm plates.

R3*   **E**
Stereo version   **F+**

AVUS: c1920. 9 x 12cm Folding camera. Skopar 105mm, f4.5 lens; Compur shutter 1-¼₅₀s. 9 x 12cm exp on sheet film.

R2*   **B+**

BERGHEIL: c1930. Folding plate camera. Heliar 12cm f4.5 lens; Compur shutter 1-½₀₀s. 6.5 x 9cm exp on plates..

R2*   **C**

BERGHEIL DE LUXE: c1930. Folding plate camera. Heliar 105mm, f4.5 lens; Compur shutter 1-½₀₀s; rising and cross front; 6.5 x 9cm exp on plates. Covered with green leather.

R3*   **F**

BESSA 6 X 6 (BABY BESSA): c1930. Folding roll film camera. Heliar 75mm, f3.5 lens; Compur-Rapid shutter 1 -⅓₀₀s; 6 x 6cm exp on roll film.

R3*   **C**

BESSA I: 1952. Folding camera for 8 or 16 exp on 120. Fitting the accessory mask for the smaller format automatically removes cover from second red window. Four masks in viewfinder give views at

close distances and infinity for the two formats. 105mm f4.5 Vaskar, Prontor-S shutter 1-1/250s. Flash synch.

R3*   **C+**

BESSA II: c1960. Roll film folding camera. Colour-Heliar 105mm, f3.5 coated lens; Synchro-Compur shutter 1-⅟₅₀₀s. crf; 8 exp, 6 x 9cm on 120 roll film.

R3*   **F**

With Skopar lens   **F+**

APO Lanthar lens   **H**

BRILLIANT: c1932. Roll film TLR camera. Voigtar 75mm, f7.7 lens. Not a true TLR, effectively a box camera with a large reflecting vfr., much like the Kodak Duoflex. In 1938, a focusing Brilliant appeared, bakelite body and a very different appearance. It had gears to couple the focusing mounts of the two lenses, a system used by the Kodak Reflex. Until recently, a Russian-made copy of the focusing Brilliant was sold in Britain as the Lubitel.

R2*   **B+**

PERKEO I: c1960. 6 x 6cm roll film camera. Colour Skopar 75mm, f3.5 lens.

R2*   **C**

Perkeo I

PERKEO II: c1960. 6 x 6cm roll film camera. Colour Skopar 75mm, f3.5 lens; Synchro-Compur shutter.

R2*   **C+**

PROMINENT (1932): c1932. Roll film folding camera. Voigtlander Heliar 10.5cm, f4.5 lens; Compur shutter 1-½₅₀s; crf.; 8 exp, 2¼" x 3¼" on 120 roll film. Built-in extinction meter; cast metal body.

R4*   **G**

Stereoflektoscop

PROMINENT: c1958. 35mm RFR camera. Ultron 50mm, f2 coated lens, interchangeable mount; Synchro-Compur shutter 1-¹⁄₅₀₀S, crf. Version 1, C.1953-1954. detachable accessory shoe; knob-wind film advance. Version 2, integral accessory shoe, knob-wind film advance. Version 3, rapid wind film advance lever (two stroke). Prices for version 3, versions 1 and 2 25% less.

R3*   **E**

PROMINENT II: c1959. With bright frame lines for 35mm, 50mm and 100mm lenses in a redesigned VFR.

R3*   **F+**

ACCESSORIES FOR PROMINENT

Scoparon f3.5, 35mm lens   **D**

Dynaron f4.5, 100mm lens   **D+**

Super-Dynaron f4.5, 150mm lens   **E+**

Reflex viewer with

Telomar f5.5, 100mm lens   **F–**

STEREFLEKTOSCOP: c1914. Stereo plate camera. Heliar 65mm, f4.5 lenses; Compur shutter 1-¹⁄₂₅₀S; 45 x 107mm exp on plates.

R4*   **E+**

SUPERB: c1938. 6 x 6cm TLR camera. Heliar 75cm, f3.5 lens; Compur shutter 1-¹⁄₂₅₀S; 12 exp. 6 x 6cm on 120 roll film.

R4*   **E+**

Superb

VAG: c1930. Folding plate camera. Voigtar f6.3 or Skopar f4.5 lens; Compur shutter 1-¹⁄₂₀₀S.

R2*   **B+**

VIRTUS: c1935. Folding roll film camera. Heliar 75mm, f3.5 lens; Compur shutter 1-$\frac{1}{250}$s; 16 exp on 120 roll film.

R4*   **F–**

VITESSA: c1956. 35mm RFR camera. Fixed mount Colour Skopar f3.5 or f2.8 or Ultron f2, 50mm coated lens. Synchro-Compur shutter, LVS 1-$\frac{1}{500}$s; CRF. Camera has unique rapid film advance plunger that advances the film and cocks the shutter. With and without built-in light meter.

R3*   **F–**

VITESSA T: c1956. 35mm RFR camera. As previous model but now with rigid

interchangeable mount lenses; built-in light meter.

R3*   **E–**

ACCESSORIES FOR VITESSA T:

Skoparet f3.4, 35mm lens   **D**

Dynaret f4.8, 100mm lens   **D**

Turnit VFR for 35mm, 50mm, and 100mm   **D**

VITO: c1950. Folding 35mm VFR camera. Skopar f3.5, 5cm coated lens; Prontor II shutter.

R2*   **B+**

VITO II: c1951. With redesigned top plate and Colour Skopar lens.

R2*   **C–**

VITO IIA: c1953. With lever advance.

R2*   **C**

VITO III: c1951. Folding 35mm RFR camera. Untron f2, 50mm lens; Compur shutter; CRF.

R4*   **E**

VITO B: c1954. 35mm VFR camera. Solid mount Skopar f3.5 or f2.8, 50mm lens; Pronto or Prontor shutter.

R2*   **B+**

VITO BL: c1956. With built-in light meter.

R2*   **C–**

VITO CLR: c1961. 35mm camera. With CRF Colour-Skopar 50mm, f2.8 lens; Prontor 500 LK shutter speeds $\frac{1}{15}$ -$\frac{1}{500}$s.; coupled light meter, needle visible in finder and also on the top plate. One of the last photographic products in a 120 year history of continuous camera manufacturing.

R3*   **C+**

BESSAMATIC: c1959. 35mm SLR camera. With interchangeable Skopar f2.8, 50mm lens in Synchro Compur shutter. Coupled built-in light meter.

R2*   **D**

BESSAMATIC M: c1962. No light meter.

R3*   **E–**

BESSAMATIC CS: c1965. With TTL metering.

R2*   **E–**

ULTRAMATIC: c1961. 35mm SLR camera. With interchangeable Septon f2 or Skopar f2.8, 50mm lens; Synchro Compur shutter. Built-in light meter, shutter priority full automatic exposure.

R2*   **E**

ULTRAMATIC CS: c1965. With TTL metering.

R3*   **E**

ACCESSORY LENSES FOR BESSAMATIC AND ULTRAMATIC CAMERAS

Skoparex f3.4, 35mm lens	**D**
Skopagon f2, 40mm lens	**E+**
Dynarex f3.4, 90mm lens	**E+**
Super-Dynarex f4, 135mm lens	**D**
Super-Dynarex f4, 200mm lens	**E+**
Super-Dynarex F4, 350mm lens	**F+**
Zoomar f2.8, 36-82 zoom lens	**F**

Vokar Corporation, USA

VOKAR I: c1946. 35mm RFR camera. Vokar Anastigmat 50mm, f2.8 lens; leaf shutter ½₀₀s.

R2*   **C–**

VOOMP, Experimental Factory
Leningrad, USSR. (now St. Petersburg, Russia).

PIONEER: c1934. 35mm RFR camera. Leica copy. Screw mount VOOMP f3.5, 50mm lens; CFPS ½₀-⅕₀₀s. No accessory shoe. 200-300 made.

R4*   **H–**

Vredeborch G.m.b.H.
Nordenham, West Germany

NORDETTA 3-D: c1950. Strut type folding stereo camera for 127 roll film. Fixed focus 8cm, f11 lenses; single speed shutter; PC flash synch; and top mounted accessory shoe.

R3*   **C+**

NORDINA I: 1953. 12 exp on 620. Lens on telescopic extension. 75mm f4.5 lens. Vario shutter.

R2*   **B**

NORDINA II: 1953. Similar to Model I but with f/3.5 Steinar.

R2*   **B**

NORDINA III: c. 1956. New redesigned top plate. Retractable lens in square housing. 75mm f2.9 Steinar. Prontor SVS shutter 1-1/300s + B.

R2*   **B+**

Bernard Wachtl.

STOCK APPARAT: c1893. Cane handle detective camera. Round exp, 42mm diameter.

R5*   **NSR I+**

Walker Mfg. Co.
Palmyra, New York

THE TAKIV CAMERA: c1892. Cardboard and leatherette multiple exp camera. Rotary shutter. 4 exp, 2½" x 2½" on dry plates.

R5*   **F+**

Warzawskie Zaklady Foto-Optyczne, (WZFO)
Warsaw, Poland

ALFA-2: c1950. Grey and white vertically styled metal 35mm VFR camera. Emitar f4.5, 45mm lens.

R4*   **D**

DRUH: c1950's. Bakelite VFR camera. For 6 x 6cm on roll film. Simple lens and shutter.

R3*   **B–**

WATLZ, Japan

AUTOMAT: 1960. TLR for 12 exp on 127. 60mm f2.8 Zunow lenses. Copal shutter 1-1/500s + B

R3*   **C**

ENVOY 35: c.1959. 35mm CRF camera. 48mm f1.9 Kominar. Copal SLV shutter 1-1/500s.

R3*   **C**

W. Watson & Sons
London, England

VANNECK: c1890. Taylor and Hobson Cooke lens; shutter mechanism works by means of the mirror's upward and downward action ½s-¹⁄₁₀₀s. Changing mechanism for 12 plates 3¼" x 4¼".

R4*   **F–**

WATSON'S DETECTIVE CAMERA: c1886. Wooden box-type detective camera. Rectilinear lens; front-of-lens guillotine shutter. 8 x 11.5cm exp on plates (adapter for roll film).

R4*   **F+**

WATSON TAILBOARD CAMERA: c1880's. Rising and falling front. Red Russian leather bellows.

R3*   **E+**

WATSON TWIN LENS REFLEX: c1890. Wray Anastigmat f8 lenses.

R4*   **F–**

WATSON VIEW CAMERA: c1890's. 13" x 18" View camera. Bush Rapid Symmetrical lens; Thornton Pickard behind-lens shutter. Reversible and tilting back. Mahogany finish with brass fittings.

R3*   **E+**

Watson View Camera

Webster Industries Inc.
Webster, New York

WINPRO 35: c1948. Simple sturdy fixed focus 35mm camera, fitted with a Crystar 40mm lens. The camera was made with Tenite, a tough Kodak plastic. The Winpro enjoyed a brief period of popularity at the end of WWII.

R4*   **F–**

Welta Kamera Werke
Waurich & Weber, Freital, Germany. (after 1946, VEB Welta)

WELTI (PRE-WAR): c1936. Folding 35mm VFR camera. Xenar f3.5 or f2.8 or Tessar

f2.8, 50mm lens in Compur shutter 1-⅓₀₀s or Compur Rapid.shutter to 1/500s.

R2*   **C–**

WELTIX: c1938. Folding 35mm VFR camera. Xenar f3.5 or Cassar f2.9, 50mm f2.9 lens in Compur shutter 1-1/300s.

R2*   **C–**

WELTI (POST-WAR): c1946. Folding 35mm VFR camera. Meritar f3.5, 50mm lens in Compur shutter.

R2*   **B+**

WELTI I: c1954. Folding 35mm VFR camera. Tessar f3.5, 50mm lens in Cludor or Ovus shutter.

R2*   **B+**

WELTI IC: c1955. Folding 35mm VFR camera. Tessar f2.8, 50mm lens; Vebur shutter. New designed top plate.

R2*   **B+**

WELTINI: c1935. Folding 35mm camera. With coupled RFR; Xenar f2.8, Xenon f2, Elmar f3.5, or Tessar f2.8, 50mm lens; Compur-Rapid shutter. (add 200% or more for Elmar lens!).

R2*   **D**

WELTUR: c1934. 6 x 6 or 6 x 9 folding roll film camera. (6 x 4.5 possible with adapter) coupled RFR, Tessar f2.8 or f4.5, Xenar f2.8 or 3.8, or Trinar f3.8 lens. Compur or Compur Rapid shutter.

R3*   **B+**

WELTAX (PRE-WAR): c1937. Folding VFR camera. For 6 x 9cm frames on roll film(6 x 4.5 with adapter). Trioplan f4.5, Xenar f2.8, Tessar f2.8 or Cassar f2.9, 105mm lens. Prontor II, Compur or Compur Rapid shutter.

R3*   **B+**

WELTAX (POST-WAR): c1946. Folding VFR camera. For 6 x 9cm frames on roll film (6 x 4.5 with adapter). Meritar f3.5, 75mm lens, Junior shutter.

R2*   **B+**

TRIO: c1935-1937. Folding VFR camera. For 6 x 9cm frames on roll film (6 x 4.5 with adapter). Trioplan f4.5, Tessar f4.5 or Trinar f3.8, 105mm lens. Prontor II,Compur or Compur Rapid shutter.

R2*   **B+**

SYMBOL: c1935-1937. Folding VFR camera. For 6 x 9cm frames on roll film (6 x 4.5 with adapter); Weltar f6.3, 105mm lens, Prontor II or Vario shutter.

R2*   **B**

SOLIDA: c1935. Folding camera. For 6 x 9 frames on roll film; coupled RFR; Xenar f3.9. Radionar f4.5 or Tessar f4.5 lens. Compur shutter.

R3*   **B+**

WELTA: c1930. Horizontal folding plate camera. For either 9 x 12cm or 10 x 15cm exp. FPS ⅒-¹⁄₁₀₀₀s. Trinar, Eurynar or Xenar lenses in 135mm or 150mm were available, with or without Compur shutter.

R3*   **C+**

DUBLA: c1933. Horizontal folding plate camera. As previous model, but only in 10 x 15cm, FPS ⅒-¹⁄₁₀₀₀s. Trinar, Eurynar or Xenar 165mm lens, with or without Compur shutter.

R3*   **C+**

WELTA: c1932. Folding VFR camera. For 6 x 9 frames on roll film, Weltar f9, 105mm lens, single speed shutter.

R2*   **B+**

WELTA: c1931. Folding VFR camera. For 6 x 4.5mm frames on roll film, Weltar f6.3, 90mm lens, Prontor shutter.

R2*   **B+**

PERLE: c1936. Folding VFR camera. For 6 x 4.5mm frames on roll film, Weltar f4.5, Xenar f4.5, Trioplan f2.9 or Xenar f2.9, 75mm lens, Prontor or Compur shutter.

R3*   **C+**

PERLE: c1937. Folding VFR camera. For 6 x 6 frames on roll film, Cassar f2.9, 50mm lens in Compur shutter; parallax correcting VFR.

R3*   **C+**

GARANT: c1938. 6 x 9cm folding rollfilm camera. Trioplan f4.5 or Trinar f3.8, 105mm lens; Compur shutter.

R2*   **B+**

GUCKI: c1937, strut type folding VFR roll film camera for 3 x 4cm on 127 roll film. Trinar 5cm, f2.9 lens; Compur shutter.

R3*   **C–**

GUCKI: c1935. Bed type folding VFR roll film camera. For 4 x 6.5cm frames, Xenar f2.9, 50mm lens; Compur shutter.

R3*   **C**

WELTA PERFEKTA: c1934. Folding TLR camera. Meyer f3.5, 75mm lens; Compur

shutter 1-⅓₀₀s. 12 exp, 6 x 6cm on 120 roll film.

R4*   **E+**

REFLEKTA (PRE-WAR): c1938. TLR camera. Pololyt f3.5 or f4.5, 75mm lens; Blitz shutter. 6 x 6cm exp on 120 roll film.

R3*   **B+**

REFLEKTA II (POST-WAR): c1952. TLR camera. Pololyt f3.5, 75mm lens; Prontor shutter. 6 x 6cm exp on 120 roll film. Often marked "Made in USSR Occupied Germany" Quite common in the USA.

R2*   **B+**

WELTAFLEX: c1954. TLR camera. Trioplan f3.5 or Rectan f3.5, 75mm lens; Vebur or Prontor SVS shutter.

R3*   **D**

WELTA SUPERFEKTA: c1934. 6 x 9cm TLR camera. Trioplan 10cm f3.8 lens; Compur shutter 1 – ½₅₀s. Horizontal and

vertical format; 6 x 9cm exp on 120 roll film.

R4* G   **Perfekta F**

SICA: c1950. Plastic 6 x 6 box camera. Wefo-Sicar lens.

R3*   **A**

ORIX: c1958. Metal half-frame (18 x 24mm) VFR camera. Film transport and shutter arming by rod extending from the side of the camera. Gold coloured front and back with Blue, Red, Green or Brown coloured body. Trioplan f3.5, 30mm lens. Three speed shutter.

R3*   **C+**

PENTI: c1959. Metal half-frame (18 x 24mm) VFR camera. Film transport and shutter arming by rod extending from the side of the camera. Gold coloured front and back with Blue, Red, Green or Brown coloured body. Trioplan f3.5, 30mm lens, three speed shutter. Some people feel that this camera was made by VEB Pentacon. Probably VEB Welta assumed some manufacturing role in the grander VEB Pentacon complex, since both factories were located relatively close in Freital and nearby Dresden, respectively. Now with the unification of Germany, in the near future a clearer picture may come to light concerning the relationships of East German camera manufacturers, and the relationship of VEB Pentacon with its "socialist" partners.

R2*   **C**

PENTI I: c1959. Metal half-frame (18 x 24mm) VFR camera. Film transport and shutter arming by rod extending from the side of the camera. Gold coloured front and back with Blue, Red, Green or Brown coloured body. Dimoplan f3.5, 30mm lens; three speed shutter.

R2*   **C**

PENTI II: c1959. Metal half-frame (18 x 24mm) VFR camera. Film transport and shutter arming by rod extending from the side of the camera. Gold coloured body, Dimoplan f3.5, 30mm lens, three speed shutter. Almost the same body as (WL128).

R2*   **C**

Weiner Kamera Werkstatte
Vienna, Austria

WICA: c1948-50. 35mm camera with coupled RFR. Leica copy. CFPS 1 - ⅟₁₀₀₀S; flash synch; interchangeable Angénieux f2.9 or f1.8, Berthiot f2.8 or Heligon f2, 50mm lens; focusing mount to lenses of different focal lengths. Early model has wide seperation between the RFR/VFR eyepieces, two synch contacts and strap lugs, while later ones use close together eyepieces, one flash synch and no strap lugs. Quite rare.

R4*   **G+**

Gebr. Wenke
Nurnberg, Germany

WENKA: c1955 35mm camera. With CRF 24 x 30mm frame size, interchangeable Xenar f2.8, 50mm lens in 40mm screw mount; odd "FPS" located just behind the lens ⅟₂₅ - ⅟₈₀₀S; CRF. Early models marked "24 x 30" on the top plate. Considered by

some to be a Leica copy. About 1000 camera produced

R4*   **F+**

WENKA I: c1951-52. Top shutter speed shutter marked ⅟₅₀₀S.

R4*   **F+**

WENKA II: c1951-52. Green flash selector indicator.

R4*   **F+**

Wescon Camera Company
Milwaukee, WI, USA

WESCON: c1955. 35mm RFR camera. Collapsible f3.5, 50mm Wollensak lens, Alphax shutter ⅟₁₀ - ⅟₂₀₀S, CRF.

R4*   **NSR**

Western Electric Co.
New York

Gray's Vest Camera: 1886; Thin round detective camera worn under a man's vest. The upper "button" was the lens and the middle changed the plate and cocked the shutter. Six exposures each 1⅝" diameter were made on a 5½ inch round plate. Its possible that Gray the inventor made the first cameras himself. In less than a year Western Electric a prominent maker of

telegraph equipment briefly became the manufacturer. CP Stirn purchased the rights and began to make the camera in the US, Great Britain, France, and Germany.

R5* **H–**

Western Mfg. Co.
Chicago, Illinois

MAGAZINE CYCLONE NO. 2: c1897. Drop plate box camera. 12-Plate magazine; after each exposure a key releases one plate to the storage chamber, a spring slides the next plate into film plane.

R3* **C+**

MAGAZINE CYCLONE NO. 3:

R3* **B+**

MAGAZINE CYCLONE NO. 4:
R3* **B+**

MAGAZINE CYCLONE NO. 5:.
R3* **B+**

David White Co. USA

REALIST 45: c1956. 35mm stereo camera. VFR; Steinheil Munchen Cassar S 35mm, f3.5 lenses; Vero shutter ½s-¹⁄₂₀₀s. Made by Wilhelm Witt Iloca, Hamburg, West Germany for Realist Inc.

R2* **E–**

REALIST MACRO STEREO (MODEL 1060): c1971. 35mm macro stereo camera. Realist Stereo Anastigmat 35mm, f3.5 coated lens, permanently set at f25. Self-cocking, behind-lens shutter 1-¹⁄₁₂₅s. Close up focus from 3½" to 4½".

R4* **G+**

Realist 45

STEREO REALIST (MODEL 1041): c1951. 35mm stereo camera. David White Co. Anastigmat 35mm, f3.5 coated lenses. Shutter 1-¹⁄₁₅₀s; CRF. Focus adjustment moves film plane.

R2*   **E**

STEREO REALIST (MODEL 1042): c1951. 35mm stereo camera. Kodak Ektar 35mm, f2.8 coated lenses or David White Anastigmat 35mm, f2.8 coated lenses. Shutter 1 – ¹⁄₂₀₀s. CRF.

R4*   **F**

STEREO REALIST CUSTOM (MODEL 1050): c1960. 35mm stereo camera. Realist 35mm, f2.8 coated lenses; made in Germany; Shutter 1 – ¹⁄₂₀₀s; CRF. Larger wind and rewind knobs and different frame counter than the Realist 2.8.

R4*   **F+**

Whitehouse Products Inc.
Brooklyn, USA

BEACON: c1954-55. Metal and plastic VFR camera. For 3 x 4cm frames on 127 film. Simple lens and shutter. available in black, white, red, brown, green and blue. (Euro-

pean prices higher, colour other than black add 50% or more).

R2*   **A**

BEACON 225: c1954-55. Metal and plastic VFR camera. For 6 x 6cm frames on roll film. Doublet 70mm coated lens and simple shutter mounted in a collapsible square tube. (European prices higher).

R2*   **A**

BEACON REFLEX: 1947. TLR-style camera with non coupled lenses. Two-

Stereo Realist

tone grey plastic. Fixed focus and shutter. Apertures marked for B&W and col.

R2*   **B**

Wilca Kamerabau
Germany

WILCA AUTOMATIC: c.1960. Subminiature for 24 exp on 16mm film in special cassettes. Built-in meter with film speed set by coding on film cartridge. 16mm f2 fixed focus Wilcalux lens. Shutter 1/25-1/250s. Auto programmed exposure.

R4*   **F**

Wm. R. Whittaker Co. Ltd.
Los Angeles, California

MICRO 16: c1950. 16mm Subminiature camera. Doublet lens with three Waterhouse stops marked "bright", "dull" and "colour". Sector shutter with fixed speed

of ⅟₆₀s. 20 exp on 16mm film in special cassettes.

R3*   **C+**

PIXIE: c1950. Microtar f6.3 lens; sector shutter; 16mm film in special cassettes.

R3*   **C+**

FLASH PIXIE: c.1950. Version of the Pixie with detachable flashgun, twice the size of the camera! Otherwise as original model.

R4*   **D**

Windsor Camera Co., USA

WINDSOR: c1957. 35mm stereo camera. Windsor f3.5 lens; shutter ⅟₂₅-⅟₆₀s. Focusing scale; direct vision optical finder.

R4*   **D+**

Simon Wing Charleston
Massachusetts

NEW GEM CAMERA: c1901. Multiple exposure camera. Darlot achromatized periscopic 120mm, f6 lens; 2 blade scissor-type shutter. 15 separate exp, 1" x1¼" on a single 5" x 7" ferrotype plate, dry plate or sheet film.

R5*   **G**

SIMON WING/A.S. SOUTHWORTH MULTIPLYING CAMERA: Patent April

10th 1858. Wet plate camera for multiple images on 4" x 5" wet collodion plates.

R5*   **I–**

SIMON WING NINE LENS MULTIPLYING VIEW CAMERA: c1895.

R5*   **H+**

WING 4" X 5" MULTIPLYING VIEW CAMERA: c1900. Lens standard has vertical and horizontal adjustments, to photograph multiple images on a single plate.

R4*   **F+**

Wirgin Brothers
Wiesbaden, Germany

GEWIRETTE: c1936. Metal VFR camera. For 3 x 4cm on 127 roll film; Collapsible Trioplan f2.9, 50mm lens; Compur shutter; tubular optical finder.

R3*   **B+**

KLEIN EDINEX: c1937. Metal VFR camera. For 3 x 4cm exp on 127 roll film, collapsible Cassar f2.8, 50mm lens. Prontor shutter; accessory shoe; tubular optical finder.

R2*   **B+**

EDINEX (24 X 36): c1927. Metal 35mm VFR camera. Radionar f3.5,50mm lens; Compur Rapid shutter; tubular optical finder; accessory shoe for "Fokas" RFR. Black body indicates early cameras, chrome bodies are mostly post-war. (deduct 50% for chrome body).

R3*   **C+**

EDINEX I (PRE-WAR) : c1938. Metal 35mm VFR camera. Collapsible Cassar f2.8, 50mm lens; Prontor-S shutter; accessory shoe and optical finder in one piece top plate.

R2*   **B+**

EDINEX I (POST-WAR): c1949. Metal 35mm VFR camera. Collapsible Radionar f2.9 or Xenon f2,50mm lens; Prontor-S or Compur Rapid shutter. Accessory shoe and optical finder in one piece top plate.

R2*   **B+**

EDINEX III (PRE-WAR): c1939. Metal 35mm camera. Coupled RFR; Heligon f2, 50mm lens; Compur Rapid shutter.

R4*   **C+**

EDINEX III (POST-WAR): c1949. Metal 35mm camera. Coupled RFR; Radionar f2.9 or Xenon f2 50mm lens; Prontor-S or Compur Rapid shutter.

R4*   **C+**

WIRGIN: c1938. TLR camera for 6 x 6 on roll film. Trioplan f3.5, 73mm lens; Compur shutter. Identical to Welta Reflecta but for the name plate. The same style camera was exported to the USA and sold by Peerless camera of New York as the Peerflekta.

R3*   **C−**

EDINA: c1952-54. Metal 35mm camera with CRF. Cassar f3.5 or Isconar f2.8, 43mm lens; Pronto or Prontor-S shutter. Lever wind.

R3*   **B+**

EDIXA: c1954. Metal 35mm camera with CRF. Cassar f3.5 or Isconar f2.8, 43mm lens; Prontor-SVS shutter; Lever wind.

R2*   **B+**

EDIXA I: c1954. Metal 35mm camera. Cassar f3.5 lens; Vario shutter; lever wind.

R2*   **B+**

EDIXA IIL: c1955. Metal 35mm camera with CRF. Cassar f3.5 or Isconar f2.8, 43mm lens; Pronto or Prontor-SVS shutter. EV system on shutter.

R2*   **C−**

EDIXA REFLEX: c1953. 35mm SLR camera. Interchangeable Cassar f2.8, 50mm lens (among others, some with automatic aperture); CFPS ½s-¹⁄₁₀₀₀s; interchangeable finder. Originally advertised as the "Komet", this camera model never made it big in the USA. Australia seems to be the one place where a collector has no problem finding a good example.

R3*   **C+**

EDIXA REFLEX II-B: c1957. 35mm SLR camera. Interchangeable Travenar f2.8, 50mm lens (among others); CFPS 1-¹⁄₁₀₀₀s; interchangeable finder.

R3*   **C+**

EDIXA REFLEX II-C: c1957. 35mm SLR camera. Interchangeable Travenar f2.8, 50mm lens (among others); CFPS 1-¹⁄₁₀₀₀s; interchangeable finder; built-in uncoupled light meter.

R3*   **C+**

EDIXA REFLEX II-D: c1957. 35mm SLR camera. Interchangeable Westromat f1.9, 50mm lens (among others); CFPS ¹⁄₁₀₀₀s; interchangeable finder; self-timer.

R3*   **C+**

EDIXAMAT REFLEX-B: c1960. 35mm SLR camera. Interchangeable Xenon f1.9, 50mm lens (among others); CFPS; 1-¹⁄₁₀₀₀s; interchangeable finder, also model BL.

R3*   **C+**

EDIXAMAT REFLEX-C: c1960. 35mm SLR camera. Interchangeable Iscolar f2.8, 50mm lens (among others); CFPS 1-¹⁄₁₀₀₀s; built-in uncoupled light meter.

R3*   **D−**

EDIXAMAT REFLEX-D: c1960. 35mm SLR camera. Interchangeable Westromat f1.9, 50mm lens (among others); CFPS 1-¹⁄₁₀₀₀s; interchangeable finder; self-timer; slow speed and self-timer, also model DL.

R3*   **D**

Edixamat Reflex C

EDIXA STANDARD: c1961. 35mm SLR camera. Interchangeable Xenon f1.9, 50mm lens (among others); CFPS ½-⅟₅₀₀s; interchangeable finder. A cheap version of the then current Edixamat Reflex-B.

R3* **C+**

EDIXA KADETT: c1961. 35mm SLR camera. Interchangeable Auto-Casseron f2.8, 50mm lens (among others). CFPS ⅟₃₀-⅟₅₀₀s; interchangeable finder. A cheap version of the then current Edixa Standard with simplified shutter.

R3* **C+**

EDIXA PRISMAFLEX: c1967. 35mm SLR camera. Interchangeable Iscotar f2.8, 50mm lens (among others). CFPS ¼-⅟₁₀₀₀s. Stopped down TTL metering, finder.

R3* **C+**

EDIXA PRISMAT: c1970. 35mm SLR camera. Interchangeable Xenon f1.9, 50mm lens (among others). CFPS 1-⅟₁₀₀₀s. Open TTL metering.

R3* **C+**

EDIXA STEREO IA: c1950. 35mm stereo camera. Steinheil Cassar f3.5, 35mm lenses; Vario or Prontor shutter ½₅-⅟₂₀₀s.

R3* **D**

EDIXA STEREO IB: c1954. 35mm stereo camera. Edinar f3.5, 35mm lenses; Velio shutter, speeds ⅟₁₀-⅟₂₀₀s.

R3* **D**

EDIXA STEREO IIA: c1958 35mm stereo camera. Coupled RFR; Steinheil Cassar f3.5, 35mm lenses; Pronto SVS shutter 1-⅟₃₀₀s.

R3* **D+**

EDIXA STEREO IIIA: c19585. 35mm stereo camera. Coupled RFR; Steinheil Cassar f3.5, 35mm lenses; Prontor SVS shutter 1-⅟₃₀₀s. Built-in meter.

R3* **D+**

EDIXA 16: c1960. Subminiature VFR camera. Travear or Trinar f2.8, 25mm lens. 12 x 16mm exp on 16mm film. Coupled meter available as accessory.

R3* **C+**

Edixa Stereo IA

EDIXA 16MB: c1969. Subminiature VFR camera. Travear or Trinar f2.8, 25mm lens. 12 x 16mm exp on 16mm film. Coupled meter available as accessory. Redesigned camera back, and film transport.

R3* **C+**

Witt Iloca
Hamburg, Germany

CITASCOPE: c1951. Reflex stereo camera. Tessar lens; 45 x 107mm exp. Lenticular viewing screen.

R4* **E+**

ILOCA: c1950. 35mm VFR camera. Iling Hamburg f3.5, 45mm lens; Pronto II shutter 1-1/250s.

R3* **B+**

ILOCA I: c1950. Metal 35mm VFR camera. Ilitar f3.5, 45mm lens; Vario or Prontor-S shutter; knob wind.

R2* **B+**

ILOCA IA: c1951. Metal 35mm VFR camera. Ilitar f2.9, 45mm lens; Prontor-S shutter; knob wind; body mounted shutter release.

R2* **B+**

ILOCA II: c1950. Metal 35mm camera. Coupled RFR; Ilitar f3.5, 45mm lens; Prontor-S shutter; knob wind; no accessory shoe.

R3* **C**

ILOCA IIA: c1952. Metal 35mm camera. Coupled RFR; Ilitar f3.5, 45mm lens; Prontor-S shutter; knob wind; no accessory shoe. Body mounted shutter release, and redesigned top.

R3* **C**

ILOCA QUICK A: c1954. Metal 35mm VFR camera. Ilitar f3.5, 45mm lens; Vero shutter; no accessory shoe; knob wind.

R2* **B–**

ILOCA QUICK B: c1954. Metal 35mm camera. Coupled RFR, Ilitar f2.9 or Ilitar f3.5, 45mm lens; Prontor-S shutter; accessory shoe; knob wind; body mounted shutter release.

R2* **B+**

ILOCA QUICK S: c1954. Metal 35mm VFR camera. Ilitar f3.5, 45mm lens; Prontor-S shutter; accessory shoe; knob wind; body mounted shutter release.

R3* **B**

ILOCA QUICK R: c1956. Metal 35mm VFR camera. Cassar f2.8, 45mm lens, Vero shutter, lever advance, accessory shoe.

R3* **B+**

ILOCA RAPID: c1956. Metal 35mm VFR camera. Ilitar f2.8 or Cassar f2.8/45mm lens, Prontor SV shutter, folding lever advance, accessory shoe.

R2* **B+**

ILOCA RAPID B: c1956. Metal 35mm camera. Coupled RFR, Ilitar-Super f2.8, Cassar-S or Cassarit f2.8, 45mm lens; Prontor SV shutter; folding lever advance; accessory shoe.

R2* **C**

ILOCA RAPID I: c1956. Metal 35mm VFR camera. Cassarit f2.8, 45mm lens; Compur shutter; lever advance; accessory shoe.

R3* **B+**

ILOCA RAPID IL: c1956. Metal 35mm VFR camera. Ilitar or Cassar f2.8, 45mm lens; Prontor SV shutter; lever advance; accessory shoe. Built-in light meter.

R3* **B+**

ILOCA RAPID IIL: c1956. Metal 35mm camera. With coupled RFR; Cassar-S or Cassarit f2.8 or Heligon f2, 50mm lens; lever advance; accessory shoe; Gauthier shutter or Compur Rapid shutter with EV settings.

R3*   **C**

REPORTER: c1953. Metal 35mm VFR camera. Reporter 3.5, 45mm lens; Prontor-S shutter; accessory shoe; knob wind; body mounted shutter release. Made by Iloca for sale by other retailers.

R3*   **B+**

ILOCA STEREO: c1951. 35mm VFR stereo camera. Ilitar f3.5, 45mm individually focused lenses. Prontor S shutter 1-⅟₃₀₀s.

R2*   **E−**

ILOCA STEREO II: c1954. 35mm VFR stereo camera. Ilitar f3.5, 35mm lenses; Prontor S shutter 1-⅟₃₀₀s.

R3*   **E−**

ILOCA STEREO RAPID: c1955. 35mm stereo camera. CRF; lever wind; Steinheil Cassarit f2.8, 35mm lenses; Prontor S shutter 1-⅟₃₀₀s. Also available as the Iloca Stereo Rapid 3.8, a modified version of which was made for Realist Inc, and sold in the USA as the Realist 45.

R3*   **E−**

Wohler, *Saaland*

FAVOR II: c.1950. 35mm VFR camera in satin chrome and black plastic imitation leather. 45mm f2.8 Docar lens, Prontor Shutter 1-1/300s.

R3*   **D**

Wolfgang Simons & Co.
Bern, Switzerland.

SICO: c1923. 35mm miniature camera. Rudersdorf Anastigmat 60mm, f3.5 lens; Dial-set Compur shutter 1-⅟₃₀₀s. 25 exp, 30 x 40mm on unperforated 35mm paper-backed roll film. Dark brown wooden body with brass trim. Only pre-Leica 35mm with wooden body.

R5*   **I−**

Wollensak Optical Co.
Rochester, New York

WOLLENSAK STEREO: c1950. 35mm stereo camera. Wollensak Amaton f2.7 lens; Rapax shutter ½-⅟₃₀₀s,CRF. Similar to Revere design.

R3*   **E**

Wratten & Wainwright
London, England

WRATTEN AND WAINWRIGHT TAIL-BOARD CAMERA: c1890. 13" x 18" Tailboard camera. Excelsior 3 Rochester Optical Company brass lens. Shifting stereo lens panel. Dark red Russian leather bellows.

R4* **E+**

Wray Optical Works
London, England.

PECKHAM-WRAY: 1955. 5x4 SLR designed by Cyril Peckham, Chief Photographer at Hawker Siddeley. Originally designed for air-to-air photography. Designed to be hand-held. 135mm f4.5 Wray Lustrar. FP shutter 1/15-1/800s + B & T. Folding frame finder.

R3* **E**

WRAYFLEX I: 1950. Originally known simply as the Wrayflex. The 'I' was added when subsequent models were launched. Early eye-level 35mm SLR that uses mirrors in place of a pentaprism. Satin chrome and black grained leather. 50mm f2 Unilite lens. FP shutter 1/2-1/500s + B. Film wind by key on base. Takes 40 exp 24x32mm. Around 700 made.

R3* **E**

WRAYFLEX IA: 1954. 35mm SLR. Not a replacement for the first model, but made to sell as an alternative. Similar specification, but film format changed to standard 36 exp 24x36mm and flash synch socket changed to 3mm co-ax type. 50mm f2.8 Unilux launched with this model. This model was originally referred to by Wray as the Wrayflex Mark III. Around 1,700 made.

R3* **E**

WRAYFLEX II: 1959. 35mm SLR. Basically the same spec as the first two models, but with a taller top plate to incorporate a pentaprism in place of the mirror system previously used. Only around 300 made.

R4* **E+**

WRAY STEREO GRAPHIC: c1950's. Simple ⅕₀ sec shutter; coated Wray F4.0, 35mm lenses. Made under license from Graflex Corp. Basically the same camera as the Stereo Graphic.

R2* **D**

Wrayflex II

Emil Wunsche, Reick
Dresden, Germany

EMIL WUNSCHE'S POSTAGE STAMP
CAMERA:c1900. 12 exp, 25 x 30mm on
a 13 x 18cm plate.

R5* **H–**

MARS DETECTIVE CAMERA: c1893.
Mahogany box form camera. Aplanat
130mm, f8 lens; rotary shutter. 9 x 12cm
exp.

R5* **F–**

MARS BOX CAMERA: c1900. Leather
covered box camera. For 8 x 10cm plates,
internal plate changing mechanism for 12
plates, external shutter.

R4* **NSR est E+**

MARS 99: c1900. Leather covered box
camera. For 9 x 12cm plates; external
shutter.

R4* NSR est **E+**

BOSCO: c1900. Leather covered box
camera. Exp. 9 x 9cm on roll film; external
shutter.

R4* **D+**

ELITE STEREO: c1900. Leather covered
box camera. Exp. 9 x 18cm stereo frames
on glass plates; internal plate changing
mechanism for 12 plates. Two speed
shutter.

R4* **F–**

SPORT STEREO: c1908. Leather covered
box camera. Taking 8.5 x 17cm stereo
frames on glass plates. Two speed shutter.

R4* **F**

VICTRIX STEREO: c1908. Leather covered
folding camera. Taking 6 x 13cm stereo
frames on glass plates. CFPS $\frac{1}{25}$ – $\frac{1}{200}$. Rapid-
Aplanate lenses.

R4* **NSR est F**

VICTRIX: c1908. Strut type folding camera.
For 9 x 12cm plates. Tessar f6.3, 135mm
lens; CFPS, $\frac{1}{25}$ – $\frac{1}{200}$S.

R3* **D+**

KOBOLD:c1904. Leather covered box
camera. Taking 9 x 12cm plates; internal
changing mechanism for 6 glass plates.
Two speed shutter; meniscus lens.

R3* **C+**

NOVA: c1908. Leather covered box
camera. Taking 9 x 12cm plates; internal
changing mechanism for 12 glass plates.
Dagor lens. Internal pneumatic shutter.
Automatic frame counting.

R4* NSR est **D**

LEGION: Leather covered box camera. With nickel plated fittings. Taking 9 x 12cm plates. Offered as a "tropical" model in catalogues of the day.

R4* NSR est   D

NIXE (ROLL FILM): c1900. Leather covered folding camera. For roll film only, 8.3 x 10.8cm and 6 x 9cm sizes. Many different lens shutter combinations, typically Mars-Anastigmat f6.8 lens, Univers shutter. 50% Less for simpler less decorative models.

R3*   C

NIXE (ROLL FILM & PLATES): c1900. Leather covered folding camera. Taking roll film or glass plates, 8.3 x 10.8cm on roll film. 9 x 12cm on glass plates. Many different lens shutter combinations, typically Dynar lens, Compound shutter. 50% Less for simpler less decorative models.

R3*   C+

APFI 6 X 9: c1900. Leather covered folding camera. Taking 9 x 12cm plates. Many lens and shutter combinations; typically Extra-Rapid-Aplanat f8 lens; Automat shutter.

Camera interior polished Mahogany or Walnut.

R3*   G–

AFPI "QUERFORMAT": c1904. Leather covered folding camera. Two models: 9 x 12cm or 13 x 18. Square design allows the making of horizontal and vertical photos by simply turning the removable camera back 90 degrees. Many lens and shutter combinations, typically Imagonal f6 lens; S.V Automat shutter. Double extension bellows. Camera interior polished Mahogany or Walnut.

R3*   C+

MINIMUM: Leather covered folding camera for 9 x 12cm glass plates or film packs. Double extension bellows. Many lens and shutter combinations; typically Rapid Aplanat f8 lens; Compound shutter.

R3*   C+

NYMPHE: c1904. Leather covered scissors type folding camera. Taking 9 x 9cm Exp. on roll film. Anastigmat lens. Two speed shutter.

R4*   D

Reference Notes

_____

_____

_____

_____

_____

_____

_____

_____

_____

_____

Yashica Co. Ltd.
Tokyo, Japan.

Yashica 44LM

YASHICA ATORON ELECTRO:c1970. Subminiature detective camera. Yashinon 18mm, f2.8 coated lens. Camera flash and right-angle finder.

R2*   **C+**

YASHICA 44: c1956. TLR camera for 4 x 4cm exp on 127 roll film. Yashicor f3.5, 60mm lens. Copal SV shutter 1-1/500s. Crank advance. Usually found in grey.

R2*   **D–**

YASHICA 44A: c1959. TLR camera for 4 x 4cm exp on 127 roll film. Yashicor F3.5, 60mm lens. Copal shutter 1/25 – 1/300s. Knob advance. Usually found in grey.

R3*   **D–**

YASHICA 44LM:c1962. TLR camera for 4 x 4cm exp on 127 Roll film.Yashinon f3.5, 60mm lens. Copal SV shutter 1 – 1/500s. Knob advance, built-in light meter. Usually found in grey.

R2*   **D–**

YASHICA YF: C.1959. RFR camera. CFPS, 1 – 1/1000s. FP and X flash synch. Seperate Rfr/Vfr windows. Diopter adjustment. Screw mount Nikkor H. f2.0, 5cm lens. Completely redesigned top plate. The same as the Nicca IIIL.

Yashica YF

Produced by the Nicca Camera Company LTD.

R3*   **F**

YASHICA YE: c1959. RFR Camera. CFPS. 1/2 – 1/500s. PF And X flash synch.

Separate Rfr/Vfr windows. Diopter adjustment. Screw mount Niccor f2.8, 50mm lens. The same as the Nicca 33. Produced by the Nicca Camera Company Ltd.

R2*   **E+**

YASHICAMAT: c1959. TLR camera. Taking 6 x 6cm exp on 120 roll film; Yashicor f3.5, 80mm lens. Copal shutter 1 – 1500s.

R2*   **C+**

Yashicamat 635

YASHICAMAT 635: c1959. TLR Camera. For 6 x 6cm exp on 120 roll film or 24 x 36mm on 35mm film with adaptor. Yashicor f3.5, 80mm lens. Copal shutter 1 -1⁄500s. (Price includes 35mm adaptor)

R2*   **C+**

YASHICA A: c1959 TLR Camera. Taking 6 x 6cm exp on 120 roll film. Yashikor f3.5, 80mm lens. Copal shutter ¼₅ – ¹⁄₅₀₀s. Knob advance not coupled to shutter. Screw mount filters.

R2*   **C+**

YASHICA C: c1960. TLR Camera. For 6 x 6cm exp on 120 roll film.Yashikor f3.5, 80mm lens. Copal shutter 1 - ¹⁄₅₀₀s.Knob advance, coupled to shutter. Bayonet mount filters.

R2*   **C**

YASHICA D: c1960. TLR Camera. Taking 6 x 6cm exp on 120 roll film. Yashikor f3.5, 80mm lens. Copal shutter 1 - ¹⁄₅₀₀s. Knob advance coupled to shutter. Bayonet mount filters.Users pay more than collectors.

R2*   **C+**

YASHICA LM: c1960. TLR Camera. For 12 exp. 6 x 6cm on 120 roll film. Yashikor f3.5, 80mm lens. Copal shutter 1 - ¹⁄₅₀₀s. Built-in light meter. Knob advance coupled to shutter. Bayonet mount filters.

R2*   **C+**

PENTAMATIC: 1961. 35mm SLR. Probably one of the first cameras to utilise the rewind knob for opening the back. Interchangeable, bayonet-fit 55mm f1.8 Auto-Yashinon lens. FP shutter 1-1/1000s.

R2*   **C**

RAPIDE: c1962. Vertically styled 35mm half-frame (18 x 24mm) camera. Yashion f2.8, 28mm lens. Copal shutter 1 – ¹⁄₅₀₀s. Built-in light meter.

R3*   **C+**

SEQUELLE: c1962. 35mm Half-frame (18 X 24mm) camera. Yashinon f2.8, 28mm lens. Seikosha shutter, ¹⁄₃₀ - ¹⁄₂₅₀s. Built-in light meter.

R3*   **C+**

Rapide

Yamato Optical Co.
Tokyo, Japan

PAX I: 1952. According to the Collector's Guide to Japanese Cameras this is the smallest of the Leica type of 35mm camera. Fitted with a Luminor Anastigmat f3.5, 45mm lens and coupled to a rangefinder. Shutter 1/25-1/150s. It was just slightly over 4¼" (11cms) wide.

R4* **C+**

PAL 4: 1960. Pocket size 35mm CRF camera. 45mm f2.8 Luminor lens. Shutter 1/10-1/300s

R* **C**

Reference Notes

Z

Paul Zeh Kamerawerk
Dresden, Germany

ZECAFLEX: c1938. Folding TLR camera. For 12 exp. 2¼" x 2¼" on roll film. Xenar or Tessar f3.5. or f4.5, 75mm lens in Compur Rapid shutter 1-¼₀₀s.

R4*   **G+**

GOLDI: c1938. Folding camera for 3 x 4cm frames on roll film. Zecanar f2.9, 50mm lens in Compur shutter.

R3*   **C+**

BELTAX: c1938. Folding camera for 6 x 9cm or 6 x 4.5cm on roll film. Trinar f4.5, 105mm lens. Pronto or Compur shutter.

R3*   **C–**

Zeiss Ikon A.G.
Dresden, Germany

For further information see Zeiss Compendium and Zeiss Ikon Cameras 1926-39, reissued 1993. Hove Collectors Books.

Zeiss Ikon A.G. was founded at Dresden, Germany in 1926 by the merger of a number of leading German camera manufacturers, among them: Contessa-Nettel A.G., Stuttgart; Ernemann Werke A.G., Dresden; Optisch-Anstalt C.P. Goerz, Berlin; and Ica A.G., Dresden. Camera production ceased in 1971, although

Two views of the Zecaflex folding twin lens camera

assembly continued into 1972 at Stuttgart.

In a single year (1927) Zeiss offered 104 different models with an average of three formats each with more than three lens and shutter combinations – 936 choices of "stock" models in one catalogue! The camera model with the most variations was the Deckrullo later called "Nettel" press camera.

It could be ordered in five formats (4.5 x 6cm, 6.5 x 9cm, 9 x 12cm, 10 x 15cm and 13 x 18cm). All except the smallest size were available in Tropical models with varnished teak wood construction and brown leather bellows. A selection of 30 different lenses was available for the nine models – 39 possible variations for this single model. This was in the 1927 catalogue, before any of the really famous Zeiss Ikon cameras such as the Contax, Contarex, Kolibri, and Super Ikonta cameras had been introduced.

From the above you can get some idea of the complexity of identifying and pricing all Zeiss Ikon cameras, so please regard this list as covering only the more usual types and those of special interest. Where the Zeiss Ikon model number is likely to be found on the camera it is included in the description. The number is usually expressed as a fraction – 250/7 for a 9 x 2cm Ideal and 250/3 for a 6.5 x 9cm Ideal. The second part of the fraction gives the film size according to the following table. (1) These film size numbers were used from 1927-1960; decimal numbers were used after 1960. The focal length of the most usual lens for the format is also shown.

NUMBER	SIZE	USUAL LENS
none	4.5 x 6cm	75mm
none	22 x 31mm	45 or 50mm
1	4.5 x 10.7cm	twin 65mm
2	6 x 9cm	105mm
3	6.5 x 9cm	105mm
4	6 x 13cm	twin 75mm
5	8.5 x 11.5cm	135mm
6	8 x 14cm	150mm
7	9 x 12cm	135mm
8	9 x 14cm (ICA)	Stereo
9	10 x 15cm	165mm
10	9 x 18cm (ICA)	Stereo
11	13 x 18cm (5" x 7")	210mm
12	4 x 6.5cm	75mm
13	13 x 18cm (ICA)	210mm
14	5 x 7.5cm	90mm
15	6.5 x 11cm	120mm
16	6 x 6cm	80mm
17	8 x 10.5cm	120mm
18	3 x 4cm	50mm
19		
24	24 x 36mm	50mm
27	24 x 24mm	40mm

BABY BOX TENGOR: c1931. Small box camera marked "Baby Box" on front or rear. 3 x 4cm. Frontar f11 lens. Plain leather front.

R **C**

BABY BOX TENGOR: c1931-1934. 3 x 4cm. Novar f6.3 focusing lens. Black metal front plate.

R3* **D**

BABY DECKRULLO: c1929. 4.5 x 6cm
Plate camera. 80mm, f4.5 or f2.7 lens; FPS.
Chrome struts, door closes. Focus knob on
top.

R4*   **F**

BABY IKONTA: c1931. 3 x 4cm roll film
camera. C.1936. Novar 50mm, f3.5 lens.
price 20% less. Tessar 50mm, f3.5 lens.
Novar f6.3 and Tessar f4.5 lens.

R2*   **C– to D–**

BALDUR BOX: c1938. Metal box camera.
Taking 6 x 4.5cm. frames on roll film.
Named for the leader of the Hitler Youth,
and sold to its members!.

R3*   **C+**

BALDUR BOX: c1938. 6 x 9cm. frames.

R3*   **D–**

BALDUR BOX: c1938. Metal box camera
for 6 x 4.5cm. frames on roll film. Named
after the Facist Youth organization in Italy
the "Balilla" for children 11 to 13 years old.
Only one camera has been recently discov-
ered, where one might expect there to
have been many thousands produced. The
story of its production still waits to be told.

R5*   **E**

BEBE: c1928. 4.5 x 6cm camera. With
struts and unpleated bellows. Tessar
75mm, f4.5 or Triotar f3.5 lens (front cell
focus). Dial-set Compur. C.1930. Rim-set
Compur (Z342/3), 6.5 x 9cm; Tessar
105mm, f4.5 lens, Tessar 105mm, f3.5 lens,
Rim-set shutter, adds 20% to the price.

R3*   **E**

BOB: c1931-1941. 4.5 x 6cm or 6 x 9cm
Folding camera. Nettar lenses. Inexpensive black camera.

R2*   **B+**

BOB IV AND V: c1927. Clean up of Ernemann 4 x 6.5cm, 6 x 6cm, 6 x 9cm, 6.5 x
11cm and 7.25 x 12.5cm cameras. 33
different lens/shutter combinations.

Smaller sizes.

R2* **C–**

Larger sizes. **C+**

BOBETTE I: c1929. Folding roll film camera. With struts 2.2 x 3.1cm format. Frontar 50mm, f9 lens. Ernoplast 50mm f4.5 or Erid f8 lens add 50% to the price.

R3* **D**

BOBETTE II: c1929. Folding roll film camera taking 2.2 x 3.1cm format. Ernon 40mm,f3.5 or Ernostar 42mm,f2 lens. Earliest f2 lens on a miniature roll film camera. Used the so-called "N" size film for 5 x 7.5cm film size

R4* **F+**

BOX TENGOR (127 ROLL FILM SIZE – 5 X 7.5CM.). c1928-1934. Two models, both with Frontar f11 lens. First model had plain leather covered front with the two finder lenses located vertically – upper left. Winding knob on left side at bottom. Second model C.1928-1934. Similar, except the two finder lenses are located horizontally across top of front, priced 25% less.

R3* **D–**

BOX TENGOR (HALF OF 120 ROLL FILM SIZE – 4.5 X 6CM.). c1934-1939. All models had the Frontar f11 lens. Rotating Waterhouse stops and close-up lens (controlled from front of camera). Diamond shaped winding knob. 2 ruby windows.

R3* **D–**

BOX TENGOR (FULL 120 ROLL FILM SIZE – 6 X 9CM.). Six models. c1926-1928. Frontar f11 lens. Plain leatherette front. Vfr. objectives located vertically – one above the other – on the upper left of front. Winding knob on left side at bottom.

R3* **B+**

c1928-1934. Similar to above, except Vfr. objectives located horizontally across top of front. Winding knob on left side at top. Frontar f11 lens with waterhouse stops and close-up lens. Varieties include the following:

C–

c1934-1938. Frontar f11 lens with Waterhouse stops and close-up lens in centre of hexagonal shaped front plate. Black enamel trim around front edge of camera. Diamond shaped winding knob located on left side at top.

C–

c1938. Similar to above, except release button moved to top left of camera.

C+

c1939. Similar to above, except serrated round winding knob with leatherette centre. Black enamel front trim. Double exp interlock coupled to winding knob.

C+

c1948-1956. Chrome trim. Lever-type shutter release on lower front. Frontar f9 lens.

C–

Box Tengor Cameras

BOX TENGOR (116 ROLL FILM SIZE – 6.5 X 11CM.). c1926-1928. Three models. Vfr. windows of ground glass the objectives located one above the other on the left front. Winding knob on left side at bottom. Variations include the following:

C+

c1928-1933. Mirror on front of shutter. Vfr. objectives located horizontally across top of front. Winding knob on left side at top. Controls for diaphragm and close-up lens located on top of camera.

C–

c1933-1939. Similar to above, except has elongated hexagonal design on front around lens. Brilliant vfr with rectangular lenses. Control for diaphragm and close-up lens located on front metal plate. This size was discontinued after 1938-1939.

R3* **C**

COCARETTE: 1926-1932. Roll film folding camera. Frontar, Periskop, Novar, Dominar or Tessar lenses. Derval, Klio or Compur shutters – 64 possible combinations. To load film, the finder and film track are removed from the side of the camera, the back does not open. (similar to loading film in a Leica camera). All models were finished in black. Five sizes, single extension. Variations include the following:

Three sizes, single extension no vertical lens adjustment, lever focus.

Two sizes, single extension, vertical lens adjustment, lever focus.

Two sizes, same as above. A plate model also exists. C.1928. All variations.

R2*	**C+**

COCARETTE LUXUS: Covered in brown leather with polished metal fittings. Dial-set Compur shutter. Double ext bellows. Two sizes. 6 x 9cm. with Dominar 105mm, f4.5 lens or Tessar 105mm, f4.5 lens. 8 x 10.5cm. Dominar f4.5 or Tessar f4.5 lens.

with Tessar lens.

R3*	**E+**
with Dominar lens	**E–**

COCARETTE (1930): Black models were manufactured with Compur rim-set shutters. They are worth £5 to £10 more than models with dial-set shutters. No Cocarettes were offered after 1930.

R3*	**C+**

COLOURA: c1963-1965. Inexpensive 35mm camera. Novicar 50mm, f2.8 lens in Prontar 125 shutter, X synch. Camera is marked "Coloura" on right side of top. The Novicar is an unusual lens.

R3*	**B+**

COLOURA "F": Similar to above, except accessory shoe (on top) tips back to become reflector for AG-1 flash bulbs, the flash socket is uncovered as the shoe tips back. Flash calculator built into rewind knob. C.1963-1965.

R3*	**B+**

Contaflex TLR 1935; This was one of the most advanced cameras of its time. Seven interchangeable lenses were available ranging from 35 to 135mm. (see following

listing) The 80mm viewing lens was fixed and provided an usually bright focusing surface. An albada type eye-level viewfinder was used for most of the lenses. It was the first camera to be fitted with a built-in but non-coupled electric exposure meter. Even cameras in mint cosmetic condition rarely have a fully functional shutter and exposure meter, unless it has been serviced recently. Since the camera is rarely actually used by collectors, overall cosmetisc condition is of extreme importance when determining price.

R3*	**G+**

CONTAFLEX TLR LENSES

Biogon 35mm lens, with viewfinder	**G**
Sonnar 50mm f/2 lens	**F**
Sonnar 50mm f/1.5 lens	**F+**
Sonnar 50mm f2.8 lens	**F+**
Sonnar 80mm f/2 lens	**F+**
Triotar 85mm f/4 lens	**F+**
Sonnar 135mm f/4 lens	**F+**

All interchangeable lenses are rare and difficult to find.

CONTAFLEX I: c1953-1958. 35mm SLR camera. Tessar 45mm, f2.8 lens. Synchro-Compur shutter. No exp meter.

R2*　　　　　　　　　　　　**C+**

CONTAFLEX II: c1954-58. Similar to above except, has built-in exp meter.

R2*　　　　　　　　　　　　**C+**

CONTAFLEX III: c1956-1958. 35mm SLR camera. Tessar 50mm lens, interchangeable front element. Last model with knob wind for film advance. No built-in meter. Stereo attachment £200. "O" stereo viewer, £180 "OO" stereo viewer, £100 C.1957-1959. Camera alone.

R3*　　　　　　　　　　　　**C+**

CONTAFLEX IV: c1957-1959. Similar to above, except has LVS settings on shutter. Built-in exp meter with hinged door.

R2*　　　　　　　　　　　　**C+**

CONTAFLEX "ALPHA": c1958-1959. Inexpensive version of Contaflex III. Pantar 45mm, f2.8 lens, interchangeable front element for Pantar series lenses.

R2*　　　　　　　　　　　　**C+**

CONTAFLEX "BETA": (Z10.1251). c1957-58. Similar to "Alpha" model, except has exp meter.

R2*　　　　　　　　　　　　**D–**

CONTAFLEX "RAPID": 1958-60. Tessar 50mm, f2.8 lens, interchangeable front element. Three special features first appeared on this camera and succeeding models: rapid film advance lever, accessory shoe on prism housing, interchangeable magazine backs.

R2*　　　　　　　　　　　　**D**

CONTAFLEX "PRIMA": c1959-1965. Similar to "Rapid" except has Pantar 45mm, f2.8 lens. Uncovered match needle exp meter (right side).

R2*　　　　　　　　　　　　**D**

CONTAFLEX "SUPER": c1959-1962. Similar to "Rapid" except has coupled exp meter. The uncovered meter window is in the front of the prism housing. Meter adjustment wheel, is on the right front of the camera (the only Contaflex with external wheel).

R1*　　　　　　　　　　　　**D+**

CONTAFLEX "SUPER" (NEW STYLE): c1962-1967. Tessar 50mm, f2.8 lens. Shutter marked "Synchro-Compur Z". Larger exp meter window marked "Zeiss Ikon". Top mount exp meter window shows two red arrows – no numbers. Internal RFR images shows small "2x" (visible at top of exp meter slot – right side). No auto exp control.

R1* **E–**

CONTAFLEX "SUPER B": c1963-1968. Similar to above, except shows numbers in top mounted exp meter and in vfr. Shutter marked "Synchro-Compur" under lens. Auto exp control.

R1* **E–**

CONTAFLEX "SUPER BC": c1967-1970. Similar to above, except has no external exp meter window. Has through-the-lens CdS photo-electric meter. Marked "Zeiss Ikon" in rectangle above lens. Battery compartment with door located at 9 o'clock from lens. Was produced in chrome or black finish.

Black model.

R3* **E+**
Chrome model. **E–**

CONTAFLEX "S" AUTOMATIC: c1970-72. Similar to above, except has no external exp meter window. Has through-the-lens CdS photo-electric meter. Marked "Zeiss Ikon" in rectangle above lens. Battery compartment with door located at 9 o'clock from lens. Produced in chrome or black finish.

Black model.

R3* **D–**

Chrome model. **E–**

LENSES FOR CONTAFLEX SLR (35MM: 24 X 36MM)

Teleskop 1.7x (fits models I and II only).Complete with bracket **D+**

Steritar A (stereo prism for Teleskop 1.7x) **E+**

Pro-Tessar 35mm f4-takes filters with 49mm external thread **D+**

Pro-Tessar 35mm, f3.2-takes filters with 60mm external thread **D+**

Pro-Tessar 85mm, f4-takes filters with 60mm external thread **D+**

Pro-Tessar 85mm, f3.2-takes filters with 60mm external thread **D+**

Pro-Tessar 115mm, f4-takes filters with 67mm external thread **E–**

Pro-Tessar M-1:1 Macro lens **D+**

LENSES FOR CONTAFLEX ALPHA, BETA, PRIMAR AND CONTINA III

Pantar 30mm f4 lens **C+**

Pantar 75mm f4 lens **D–**

Steritar "D" **E–**

LENSES FOR CONTAFLEX III TO "S"

Steritar "B" **E+**

CONTAFLEX 126: 1966-71. Tessar 45mm, f2.8 or Colour Pantar 45mm, f2.8 lens. FPS. Automatic exp control. Marked Contaflex "126" on front of camera.

28 x 28mm exp on 26 Instamatic cartridge. Seven interchangeable lenses were available, 25 to 200mm.

R3*   **E–**

LENSES FOR CONTAFLEX 126

(28 X 28MM)

Distagon 25mm, f4. Rare   **E**

Distagon 32mm, f2.8   **D**

Colour Pantar 45mm, f2.8   **C**

Tessar 45mm, f2.8   **C**

Sonnar 85mm, f2.8   **D+**

Tele-Tessar, 135mm f4   **D+**

Tele-Tessar, 200mm f4   **E+**

Contarex cameras are marked "Contarex"; the microscope version is not marked.

CONTAREX "BULLSEYE": 1959-66. Planar 50mm, f2 (chrome) lens, interchangeable mount. Coupled exp meter has large round window on front of pentaprism. Early models lacked data strip slot at rear of camera

R2*   **F**

CONTAREX "SPECIAL": c1960-66. Script style logo "Contarex". Interchangeable vfr – reflex or prism. No meter.

R4*   **G**

CONTAREX "PROFESSIONAL": 1966-67. Fixed prism finder. No meter. Logo "Professional" on front at 11 o'clock position from lens.

R4*   **G+**

CONTAREX "SUPER": Logo "Super" marked on front. C.19668-75. First model had through-the-lens exp meter on front at 2 o'clock. (Black add 30%). Second model had switch under winding lever.

R3*   **G**

CONTAREX "ELECTRONIC": c1968-75. Marked "Electronic" at 11 o'clock from lens. Chrome or black (rare) finish. Seldom offered.

R3*   **G+**

CONTAREX "HOLOGON": (outfit). c1969-75. Hologon 15mm, f8 fixed focus (fixed opening) lens. (linear type, not a fisheye). Outfit: camera, grip, cable release, special neutral density graduated filter and combination case.

R4* **H+**

CONTAREX MICROSCOPE CAMERA: marked "Zeiss Ikon" on top. No lens, vfr. or exp meter. Takes interchangeable backs.

R4* **F+**

CONTAREX LENSES: manufactured between 1959 and 1973 by Carl Zeiss, Oberkochen. These lenses have seldom been equalled and never surpassed, even with modern technology. Prior to 1965, lenses with focal length of 135mm and shorter were finished in chrome; those of 180mm focal length and longer were finished in black; after 1965 all lenses were finished in black. Distagon Fisheye 16mm, f2.8. C 1973. Rare **G**

Distagon 18mm, f4, with adapter ring for B96 filters. C 1967-1973 **G+**

Biogon 21mm, f4.5, won't work on Contarexes after Bullseye model. C 1960-1963 **G**

Distagon 25mm, f2.8. C 1963-1973. Chrome **G–**

Black **G**

Distagon 35mm, f4. C 1960-1963 **E+**

Blitz Distagon 35mm, f4, built-in flash automation. C 1966-1973 **F–**

Distagon 35mm, f2. C 1965-1973 **G–**

Tessar 50mm, f2.8. Chrome or black **E+**

Planar 50mm, f2. C 1960-1973. Chrome **E+**

Blitz-Planar 50mm, f2. C 1966-1973. Chrome **F–**

S-Planar 50mm, f4, for critical closeups to 3". C 1963-1968 **G+**

Planar 55mm, f1.4 C 1965-1973.

Chrome, **F–** Black, **F+**

Sonnar 85mm, f2. C 1960-1973.

Chrome, **F–** Black, **F+**

Planar 85mm, f1.4. C 1974. Rare **H**

Tessar 115mm, f3.5, for use with bellows. C 1960-1973 **G**

Sonnar 135mm, f4. C 1960-1973.

Chrome **E**

Black **F–**

Olympia-Sonnar 135mm, f2.8. C 1965-1973 **F+**

Olympia-Sonnar 180mm, f2.8. C1967-1973 **H**

Sonnar 250mm, f4, manual preset ring focus. C 1960-1963 **G–**

Olympia-Sonnar 250mm, f4, knob focus auto stop down. C 1963-1973 **G**

Mirotar 500mm, f4.5, Catadioptric. C 1963-1973 **I**

Mirotar 1000mm, f5.6, Catadioptric. C 1964-1970. Rare, only four known to have been offered in last fourteen years, negotiated price, around **J**

Tele-Tessar 400mm, f5.6. C 1970-1973. Rare **H+**

Vario-Sonnar 40-120mm, f2.8. C 1970-1973. Rare **H**

Vario-Sonnar 85-250mm, f4. C 1970-1973. Rare **H**

Monocular 8 x 30B c1969. With 27mm thread at eyepiece to fit Contaflex SLR or Contarex with an adapter. First model had eyepiece focus and line for 140 feet. C.1960. Second model had front end focusing and a distance scale. This was the most common type. **E** C.1963. Third model had a porroprism and front end focus. The shape is straight, it looks like a small refracting telescope **F–**

Curtagon 35PA f4, c1973. Automatic stop-down with perspective control by lateral movement of up to 7mm in any of four directions. Mfd by Schneider, mounted and sold by Zeiss Ikon. Stuttgart. Rare.

R5* **H–**

CONTAX SERIES.

Introduced in 1932, the Contax I was the most advanced 35mm system camera of its time. Early Zeiss literature stresses many competitive advantages: the long base RFR with pivoting gold-plated prism; the MFPS with 1/1000s top speed; the interchangeable bayonet lens mount; availability of a wide range of lenses and accessories; and the removable back for convenient film loading and cleaning. Production of subsequent models continued (except for the period from 1944 to 1952) until 1961.

Many design changes occurred during the production span of the Contax I (1932-1936). These variations have been grouped into six models, designated: I(a); I(b); I(c); I(d); I(e) and I(f). Dissimilar and yet similar, they shared many features: the rectangular body with removable back finished in black enamel; the logo "CONTAX" was marked on the front, above the lens mount in white letters; the bayonet lens mount; and the combination film wind knob and shutter setting dial located on the front of the body, to the left of the lens mount.

Price codes shown below include the value of the correct (period) lens.

CONTAX I(A): 1932-36. No slow (below ½₅s) shutter speeds. No "foot" on tripod socket. Some models had one or more raised "dimples" on the front of the camera (covering ends of shafts). The Vfr. window eyepiece is to the right of the RFR window

(looking at the rear). The distance scale around the base of the lens mount is finished in black enamel with white numerals. Serial numbers start with "AU" or "AV".

R4*   **G**

CONTAX I(B): Similar to I(a) except front bezel extends across front of camera to Vfr and RFR window.

R4*   **F+**

CONTAX I(C): Slow shutter speeds added. Pivoting "foot" added to tripod socket. Lens bezel has guard attached which surrounds slow speed setting ring.

R4*   **F+**

Note: the preceding models did not have a button to unlock the infinity stop when lenses with an external bayonet were in use.

CONTAX I(D): Similar to I(c), except has button to release infinity lock located at 1 o'clock from lens. Distance scale around base of lens mount finished in chrome with black numerals.

R3*   **F+**

CONTAX I(E): Similar to I(d), except the Vfr window (viewing body from rear). A shallow vertical groove in the front bezel separates the area containing the logo "CONTAX" and the focus wheel.

R3*   **F+**

CONTAX I(F): Similar to I(e), except accessory shoe has four screws. The marker for setting the shutter speeds was changed from a slotted screw head to a small pointer.

R3*   **F+**

CONTAX II: c1936-1942. Sonnar 50mm, f2 lens. MFPS to ¹⁄₁₂₅₀s. No synch. Combined range and Vfr. Narrow frame around left

RFR window. Chrome finish. Winding knob with shutter speed dial on top left.

R3*   **E+**

CONTAX III:c1936-1942. Similar to Contax II. Except had uncoupled selenium photo-electric exp meter on top, and higher rewind knob.

R3*   **E+**

"NO NAME" CONTAX, CONTAX S, D AND CONTAX F: Several variations of the Contax were produced in East Germany after WWII. The Contax S was the first 35mm camera to use a pentaprism.

R2*   **F**

CONTAX IIA: 1950-61. A superb 35mm camera produced at Stuttgart. Chrome finish; "CONTAX" logo marked on front. Wide frame around left RFR window. Film speed and type indicator on rewind knob. C.1950-1961. First model had black numerals on shutter speed dial. The synch connection looks like a flat plunger in socket – a special attachment is required to convert mechanical motion to electrical contact. £200. Second model similar, except the numbers on the shutter speed dial were in colour – 1 -⅕s. Black. ⅕₀s. Yellow. ⅟₁₀₀-⅟₁₂₅₀s. Red. Regular P.C. flash connector on rear.

R3*   **F**

CONTAX IIIA: similar to Contax IIa, except has uncoupled selenium photo-electric exp meter on top. First model: Black dial. Second model: Coloured dial.

Black dial.

R3*   **F+**

Coloured dial.   **F+**

CONTAX LENSES (PREWAR) Collectors prefer the early Contax lenses with black enamel finish and chrome trim (to the later chrome finished versions); early lenses, therefore, usually bring a higher price. The snr range is approximately 1,350,000 to 2,700,000.

Tessar 28mm, f8 non-coupled lens   **E**

Biogon 35mm, f2.8 lens, will not fit post-war Contaxes **E–**

Orthometer 35mm, f4.5 lens, rare **F**

Biotar 40mm and 42.5mm, f2 lenses, chrome **H**

Black **H**

Tessar 50mm, f3.5 lens **D**

Tessar 50mm, f2.8 lens **D**

Sonnar 50mm, f2 lens **D+**

Sonnar 50mm, f1.5 lens **D+**

Triotar 85mm, f4 lens **D+**

Sonnar 85mm, f2 lens **E–**

Sonnar 135mm, f4 lens **D+**

Tele-Tessar K 180mm, f6.3 lens, direct mount **G+**

Sonnar 180mm, f2.8 lens, direct mount **H–**

Sonnar 180mm, f2.8 lens, in Flektoskop (inverted image) with case **G+**

Tele-Tessar K 300mm, f8 lens, direct or Flektoskop mount **I–**

Fern 500mm, f8 lens (distance), in direct or Flektoskop mount. Rare **I**

POSTWAR CONTAX LENSES. Chrome finish, except the Fern 180mm and 500mm, f2 lenses, and the Tessar 115mm, f3.5 lens, were offered in black.

Biogon 21mm, f4 lens with finder **G**

Topogon 25mm, f4 lens. Rare. NSI. Estimate **G+**

Biometer 35mm, f2.8 lens **F–**

Planar 35mm, f3.5 lens **F–**

(Z563/09), Biogon 35mm, f2.8 lens **F–**

Tessar 50mm, f3.5 lens **E–**

Sonnar 50mm, f2 lens **E–**

Sonnar 50mm, f1.5 lens **E–**

Biotar 75mm, f1.5 lens, rare. Estimate: **G+**

Sonnar 85mm, f2 lens **F–**

Triotar 85mm, f4 lens **E–**

Panflex Tessar 115mm, f3.5 lens, for bellows, rare **G+**

Sonnar 135mm, f4 lens **E–**

Sonnar 180mm, f2.8 lens, direct or Flektoskop mount, rare **H–**

Sonnar 300mm, f4 lens, Flektoskop mount, rare **H+**

Direct mount, rare **I–**

Tele-lens 500mm, f8 lens, with Flektoskop or Panflex mount, and case. This lens sold for $835 in October 1952. Rare, Est **I–**

Stereotar "C" outfit, stereo lens outfit: prism, special vf, closeup lenses and leather case. Rare, estimate **H+**

CONTESSA 35: Tessar 45mm, f2.8 lens. Compur-Rapid shutter, X synch only. Dual-range uncoupled selenium photo-electric exp meter. Logo "Contessa" marked in gold-leaf letters on leather covered lens bed. Round RFR window above lens. Film advance coupled to shutter cocking.

First version. C.1950-1953. Second version. C.1953-1955. Similar except had Synchro-Compur shutter, MX synch.

Third version. C.1960-1961. Redesigned body with built-in exp meter. Tessar 50mm, f2.8 lens in rigid mount. Pronto

1/30-1/250s. shutter. Logo "Contessa" on top cover.

All three versions have lately been selling around the same price.

R3* **D+**

CONTESSA LK: c1963-1965. Tessar 50mm, f2.8 lens. Prontor 500 LK shutter. coupled match needle exp meter. No RFR. Marked "Contessa LK" on top cover.

R2* **C+**

CONTESSA LKE: c1963-1965. Similar to LK except had coupled RFR. Marked with logo "Contessa LKE" on top cover.

R2* **C+**

CONTESSA S-310: c1971. Tessar 40mm, f2.8 lens, rigid mount. Pronto S500 Electronic shutter coupled to photo-electric exp meter (max exp-8s). Logo "S-310" marked on front.

R3* **C+**

CONTESSA S-312: Similar to S-310. Except has coupled RFR and marked with logo "S-312" on front.

R3* **D+**

CONTESSAMATIC "E": c1960-1963. Tessar 50mm, f2.8 lens. Prontor SLK "Special" 1-$\frac{1}{500}$ s, MX synch. Coupled RFR. Coupled photo-electric exp meter. Marked

with logo "Contessa" on front above lens mount. top cover is not marked.

R2* **B+**

CONTESSAMATIC: c1960-1961. Similar to "E" except has Prontor SLK shutter. No RFR.

R1* **C**

CONTESSAMAT: c1964-1965. Colour Pantar 45mm, f2.8 lens. Prontormatic $\frac{1}{30}$-$\frac{1}{125}$s. shutter. Coupled photo-electric exp meter. No RFR. Logo "Contessamat" on top cover.

R2* **C+**

CONTESSAMAT "SE": c1964-1965. Similar to Contessamat (above), except has Prontormatic 1-$\frac{1}{500}$s. shutter. CRF. Logo "Contessamat SE" marked on top cover.

R2* **C+**

CONTESSAMAT "STE": c1965. Similar to SE except has Tessar 50mm, f2.8 lens. Prontormatic 500 SL 1-$\frac{1}{500}$s. shutter. Logo "Contessamat STE" marked on top cover.

R2* **D–**

CONTESSAMAT "SBE": c1963-1967. Similar to STE, except top cover has a cover over the flash contacts. Marked "flashmatic" in red letters and "Contessamat SBE" in black letters. Linkage between distance and diaphragm setting provided auto flash exp control.

R2* **C+**

CONTINA I: c1956-1957. 35mm folding camera. Novar 45mm, f3.5 lens. Prontor SV shutter, X synch. Also came with Tessar 45mm, f2.8 lens in Synchro-Compur shutter X synch. Model number impressed in leather on rear of body near latch.

R2* **B+**

CONTINA I: c1956-1957. Novicar 45mm, f2.8 lens, rigid mount. Prontor SVS 1-$\frac{1}{300}$s. MX synch. Came with Pantar 45mm, f2.8 lens in 1958. Marked "Contina" under lens

and on bezel at 1 o'clock from lens. Model number impressed in leather on rear of body near latch.

R2*   **B+**

CONTINA II: c1952-1953. Opton-Tessar 45mm, f2.8 lens. Synchro-Compur 1-⅟₅₀₀s. MX synch. Also with Novar 45mm, f3.5 lens and Prontor SV shutter. Uncoupled RFR. Marked "Contina" on leather of lens bed. Model number impressed in leather on rear of body near latch.

R2*   **C+**

CONTINA IIA: c1956-1958. Novar 45mm, f35 lens, rigid mount or Novicar 45mm, f2.8 lens. Prontor 1-⅟₃₀₀s. MX synch. Rapid wind film advance. Top mounted uncoupled match-needle exp meter. Marked "Contina" on front under lens. Model number on back.

R2*   **C−**

CONTINA III: c1956-1958. Similar to IIa, except has Pantar 45mm, f2.8 convertible lens – uses all lenses of Contaflex "Alpha" series. Marked "Contina" on front bezel at upper left (not under the lens as in IIa); model number on back.

R2*   **D−**

CONTINA III LENSES AND FINDERS

Pantar 30mm, f4 lens   **D−**

Pantar 75mm, f4 lens   **D**

Steritar "D", for 3D pictures   **E+**

Wide-angle (30mm) finder   **C+**

Telephoto finder   **C+**

Telephoto rangefinder,(correct field of view for 75mm Pantar)   **D−**

Universal finder for all above items **E−**

CONTINA II MICROSCOPE CAMERA: Modified III body used with standard Zeiss Microscope Connecting funnel. No lens. Has Ibsor B self-cocking 1-⅟₁₂₅s. X synch. No exp meter. No RFR. No vfr. Marked "Zeiss Ikon" in middle of rear. No other markings. Usual shutter release button does not release shutter but must be depressed to advance film.

R4*   **E**

CONTINA: c1962-1965. 35mm camera. Colour Pantar 45mm, f2.8 lens, rigid mount. Pronto 1-⅟₂₅₀s. X synch. Self-timer. Marked "Contina" on top cover.

R2*   **C−**

CONTINA "L": c1964-1965. Similar to Contina. Except has built-in uncoupled exp meter. Prontor ⅟₃₀-⅟₂₅₀s. Marked "Contina L" on top cover.

R1*   **C−**

CONTINA "LK": c1963-1965. Similar to "L" except has coupled exp meter. Marked "Contina LK" on top cover.

R1*   **C−**

CONTINETTE: c1960-1961. Lucinar 45mm, f2.8 lens, rigid mount. Pronto ⅟₃₀-⅟₂₅₀s. Self-timer. The Continette was the only camera by Zeiss Ikon to use the Lucinar lens. Marked "Continette" on front next to vfr.

R1*   **C−**

CITOSKOP: c1929. 45 x 107mm stereo camera. Tessar 65mm, f4.5 lenses. Dial-set Stereo Compur shutter. Reflex vfr.

R4*   **E+**

DONATA: c1927-1931. Inexpensive folding plate camera. Tessar f4.5 or

Dominar f4.5 lens. Compur shutter.
Marked "Donata" on or under handle. 6.5
x 9cm or 9 x 12cm exp on cut film.

R3* **C+**

ELEGANTE: c1927-1934. Field camera
with square bellows and rigid front.
Polished wood finish. Brass fittings.

R4* **F–**

ERA-BOX: c1934-1938. Inexpensive
version of Box Tengor. Marked "ERA-BOX"
around lens. Two formats: 16 exp, 4.5 x
6cm or 8 exp, 6 x 9cm exp on 120 film.

R2* **C–**

ERGO: c1927-1931. Monocular-style detective camera. Tessar 55mm f4.5 lens. Self-
cocking shutter. Rare.

R4* **G+**

ERMANOX: c1927-1931. 4.5 x 6cm plate
camera. Ernostar 85mm, f1.8 lens, rigid
mount with helical focus. FPS ½₀-½₀₀s.
Shutter speed to $^1/_{1000}$s

R4* **G+**

ERMANOX: C.1927. Ernostar f1.8 lens.
FPS to ½₀₀₀s. Bellows with struts. 6.5 x 9cm
on plates.

Rare. **G+**

ERNOSTAR 165MM, F1.8 LENS, 9 x
12cm exp on plates. Two other sizes – 10
x 15cm and 5" x 7" are listed in period catalogues.

R5* **NSR**

ERMANOX-REFLEX: c1927-1929. 4.5 x
6cm SLR camera. Ernostar 105mm, f1.8
lens, rigid mount with helical focus. FPS
1/20-1/1200s.

R4* **H+**

ERNI: c1927-1930. Box camera with celluloid "ground glass". Rare.

R3* **E**

FAVORIT: c1927-1935. Plate camera.
Tessar f4.5 or Dominar f3.5 lens. Usually
marked with number or "Favorit" on
handle. Number usually marked on rear
door near hinge. 9 x 12cm or 10 x 15cm
(rotating back). £120. 5" x 7". Rare.

R4* **NSR**

FAVORIT: c1917-1931. Tropical plate
camera. Tessar or Dominar f4.5 lens in
Compur shutter. Polished teak construction. Brown leather handle marked with
name "Favorit" and model number.

R4* **F+**

HOCHTOURIST, **KOSMOPOLIT,**
PERFEKT: c1930. View cameras of
polished wood with brass fittings; square
bellows. Sizes: 5" x 7", 8" x 10", and 10" x
12" exp on plates. Although these cameras
are not marked with a model name, they
usually have a round metal plate with logo

"Zeiss Ikon". These are rare and are seldom offered on the market. Estimate

R4* **E+**

HOLOGON: refer to Contarex.

ICARETTE: c1927-1936. Sizes. 4 x 6.5cm, 6 x 6cm, 6 x 9cm, 6.5 x 11cm, 8 x 10.5cm and a combination model which used 6 x 9cm roll film or 6.5 x 9cm plates. There were more than 60 different lens and shutter combinations and four different bodies. Usually marked "Icarette" on handle or impressed in leather of body.

R2* **C–**

ICAREX 35 (BM): c1967-1973. Colour Pantar 50mm, f2.8 lens in interchangeable bayonet mount. CFPS ½-¹⁄₁₀₀₀s. x synch. Interchangeable viewing screens and vfr. With Colour Pantar 50mm, f2.8 lens £80. With Tessar 50mm, f2.8 lens.

R2* **D+**

ICAREX 35 (TM): c1967-1973. Marked TM at 1 o'clock position from lens. With Tessar

50mm, f2.8 lens or Ultron 50mm, f1.8 lens.

R2* **E–**

Either of the above cameras became an "Icarex CS" with the addition of a pentaprism D. Vfr containing a through-the-lens CdS meter the finder is marked "Icarex 35-CS". With the vfr.

R2* **C+**

ICAREX 35S: Available in both "TM" and "BM" models, the "35S" differed from the previous two models Due to the vfr and viewing screens were not interchangeable. The CdS meter is built-in and coupled to the diaphragm by stop-down metering. Four Zeiss lenses were available for the "TM" model. With nine lenses for the "BM" model. Some of the early black models were marked "PRO". ("TM" designates 42mm thread mount, "BM" designates bayonet mount).

35S (TM) or 35S (BM), with Pantar **D+**

35S (TM) or 35S (BM) with Tessar f2.8 lens **E–**

Icarex 35S with Super Dynarex 200mm f/4

35S (TM) or 35S (BM) with Ultron f1.8 lens **D+**

Black models are worth additional **C+**

R2*

ICAREX SL-706: c1972-1973. Front of body marked "SL-706" at 11 o'clock from lens mount. Open aperture metering with Zeiss lenses. With Ultron 50m f1.8 lens:

R3* **E**

ICAREX LENSES – all accept 50mm bayonet or 56mm threaded filters and sunshades.

Skoparex 35mm, f3.4 lens	**C**
Colour Pantar 50mm, f2.8 lens	**C**
Tessar 50mm, f2.8 lens	**C+**
Dynarex 90mm, f3.4 lens	**E–**
Super Dynarex 135mm, f4 lens	**E–**
Super Dynarex 200mm, f4 lens	**E+**
Telomar 400mm, f5 lens, rare	**F–**
Zooman 36-82mm, f2.8 lens	**F–**
Ultron 50mm, f1.8 lens	**D–**
Distagon 25mm, f2.8 lens, rare	**E+**
Skoparex 35mm, f3.4 lens	**D+**
Tessar 50mm, f2.8 lens	**C**
Ultron 50mm, f1.8 lens	**D**
Super Dynarex 135mm, f4 lens	**D+**

IDEAL: c1927-1938. Folding plate camera. Dominar, Tessar or Double Protar lenses. Usually marked with name "Ideal" and model number on leather under the handle. Double ext bellows. Removable "pop-off" holders.

6.5x9cm; 9 x 12cm	**B+**
10 x 15cm	**C+**
13 x 18cm	**D**

Ideal

IKOFLEX (ORIGINAL): c1935-1960. Novar 80mm, f6.3 or Novar f4.5 lens in Derval, Klio or Compur-Rapid shutter. Marked "Ikoflex" on shutter above lens. Called the "coffee can" model by collectors. All black enamel finish on body. Has 2 film counters; one for 120 film, and one for 620 film. Lever focus beside lens.

R3*   **E–**

folding shutter release. Focusing hood opens and closes with simple action. Magnifiers over diaphragm and shutter speed dials. No exp meter. Price for Novar lens. Tessar lens 20% more.

R2*   **C+**

Ikoflex I

IKOFLEX I: c1936-1950. Tessar 70mm, f3.5 or Novar 75mm, f3.5 lens in Compur shutter to ⅟₃₀₀s. until 1939. Klio shutter to ⅟₂₅0s. after 1939. Chrome plate inscribed with "Ikoflex" at top front of camera. Models from first production year had lever focus on right side; later models had a knob.

R3*   **C+**

IKOFLEX I(A): c1952-1956. Novar 75mm, f3.5 or Tessar 75mm, f3.5 lens in Prontor SV shutter to ⅟₃₀₀s. No folding shutter release. Marked "Ikoflex" in chrome on black background on front of Vfr.

R2*   **C+**

IKOFLEX I(B): c1956-1958. Similar to I(a). But improved model. Tessar or Novar 75mm, f3.5 lens. Only Novar was available in 1957-1958. Prontor SVS shutter with

IKOFLEX I(C): c1956-1958. Similar to I(b). Except has built-in exp meter needle visible on ground glass inside hood.

R2*   **D–**

IKOFLEX II: c1937-1939. Tessar 75mm, f3.5 lens in Compur Rapid shutter to ⅟₃₀₀s. Auto film counter; double exp prevention. Viewing lens in extended chrome tube (as compared to other models). Marked "Ikoflex" on chrome plate on front. 1937 models had focus lever, 1938 and later had focusing knob.

R2*   **D–**

IKOFLEX II(A): c1950-1952. Similar to II. Except has flash synch. Magnifiers on peep windows over shutter speed and aperture setting dials (these are set by levers below the shutter housing).

R2*   **D**

IKOFLEX II(A): c1953-1956. Similar to previous model, except the viewing lens bezel is black. The peep windows are directly over the lens. Shutter and aperture settings are adjusted with wheels. Does not have LVS settings as does the Favorit.

R3*   **D**

Ikoflex Favorit

IKOFLEX III: c1939-1940. Tessar 80mm, f2.8 lens. Only Ikoflex with huge Albada finder on front of viewing hood (similar to Albada finder on Contaflex TLR). Crank-type film advance coupled to shutter cocking mechanism.

R3*   **E+**

IKOFLEX FAVORIT: c1956-1960. Last model of the Ikoflex line. Tessar 75mm, f3.5 lens in Synchro-Compur shutter. Built-in LVS cross-coupled exp meter. Shutter and aperture adjustment set by wheels.

R3*   **E+**

IKOMATIC "A": c1964-1965. Inexpensive instamatic camera for 126 cartridge film. Colour Citar 45mm, f6.3 lens in two speed shutter ⅙₀s. for daylight ⅓₀s. for flash. Built-

in photo-electric exp control. Hot shoe. Marked "Ikomatic A" on lower right front of camera.

R2*   **B+**

IKOMATIC "F": c1964-1965. Similar to above except Frontar fixedfocus lens. No exp control. Built-in pop-up reflector for AG-1 flash bulb (top right of camera). Marked "Ikomatic F" on lower right front of camera.

R2*   **B+**

IKONETTE: c1929-1931. Small 127 roll film camera. Frontar 80mm, f9 lens in self-cocking shutter. Removable back for film loading. There were at least two variations of the body latch mechanism.

R3*   **C–**

IKONETTE 35: c1958-1960. 35mm camera of gray plastic. Novar 45mm, f3.5 lens in Pronto shutter, X synch. Unusual combination film advance lever and shutter release. Close fitting blue plastic case. Red

Ikonette 35

signal appears in Vfr. when film advance lever is not cocked.

R2*   **C–**

IKONTA SERIES. c1929-1956. Early model was called "Ikomat". All had lenses with front cell focus.

IKONTA: c1931. 5 x 7.5cm folding roll film camera. Novar 80mm, f6.3 lens and Derval shutter. 40% less.

Price with Tessar 80mm, f4.5 lens and Compur shutter.

R2*   **C–**

IKONTA A: c1933-1940. Half 120 film size. Compur shutter. Novar 80mm, f4.5 lens. 40% less than price with Tessar 80mm, f3.5 lens.

R2*   **C+**

IKONTA A: Postwar version. Tessar 75mm, f3.5 lens and Synchro-Compur shutter. Novar 75mm, f4.5 or f3.5 and Prontar shutter. 40% less.

R2*   **C+**

Ikonta A

IKONTA C:6 x 9cm folding roll film camera. C.1930-1940. Tessar 105mm, f4.5 lens £25. Novar 105mm, f8.3 lens £20. C.1936-1937 Tessar 105mm F3.8 lens £30. After 1937 Tessar 105mm, f3.5 lens.

R2* **C**

IKONTA II: c1950-1956. 6 x 9cm folding roll film camera. Heavy chrome trim on top cover. Novar 105mm, f3.5 or f4.5, or Tessar 105mm, f3.5 lens.

R2* **D+**

IKONTA D: c1931-1939. Early version used 126 film; later version used 616 film. Most Ikomats are of this size. Novar 120mm, f6.3 lens and Derval shutter. Tessar 120mm, f4.5 lens and Compur shutter.

R2* **C–**

IKONTA B: c1937-1939. 12 exp. 6 x 6cm on 120 film. Novar 75mm, f3.5 or f4.5 in Compur or Klio shutter. Tessar 75mm, f3.5 lens and Compur-Rapid shutter.

R2* **C+**

IKONTA B: c1948-1953. Similar to above, except had more chrome trim and chrome lens mount. with Tessar lens.

R2* **C**

IKONTA B: c1954-1956. Similar to above, except had chrome top plate. Prontor SV or Synchro-Compur shutter.

R2* **C+**

IKONTA B: c1954-1956. 6 x 6cm roll film camera. With built-in uncoupled RFR. Novar 105mm, f3.5 or f4.5 lens and Prontor SV shutter. Tessar 105mm, f3.5 lens and Synchro-Compur shutter.

R2* **D+**

IKONTA 35: c1949-1953. 35mm folding camera. Novar 45mm, f3.5 or Tessar 45mm, f2.8 lens. The Xenar 45mm, f2.8 lens was supplied during the first two years. Rigid front lens bed – centre of camera. Marked "Ikonta" on leather on rear of camera.

R2* **C+**

JUWEL: c1927-1938. 9 x 12cm leather covered metal case, plate camera. Revolving back; rising, falling, shifting and tilting front. Removable backs. Triple ext bellows. Double rack and pinion knobs on folding bed, one moves back and front, other moves lens stand. Bayonet mount interchangeable lenses. Marked "Juwel" or "Universal Juwel" on or under handle.

Price depends on condition and lens.

R4* **F**

JUWEL: c1927-1938. 13 x 18cm plate camera. Lens interchanges with aluminium board. Otherwise similar to above. Tessar or Triple convertible Protar. This was the most expensive camera mfg by Zeiss throughout the pre-war years. Camera used extensively by Ansel Adams. Rare and still usable. With Tessar 210mm f4.5 lens or Protar lens.

R3* **F**

KOLIBRI: c1930-1935. Compact 127 roll film camera. Lens extends for picture taking on brightly polished chrome tube. Unique shaped brown or black case. "Kolibri" in leather below lens. Hinge on

Kolibri, Dial-Set Compur

Kolibri f/3.5 Tessar, Rim-set Compur

reversing back, rising and sliding front, (no swing). Wood finish with brass fittings.

R4* **E**

LILLIPUT: c1927-1928. 4.5 x 6cm. 6.5 x 9cm. Tiny strut-type folding plate camera. f12.5 lens. Celluloid "ground glass". Struts inside bellows.

R2* **D+**

LLOYD: c1928-1931. Black leather covered folding roll film camera. Tessar 120mm, f4.5 lens in Compur shutter. Ability to use cut film with ground glass focusing by sliding out back cover plate. Marked "Lloyd" in leather on front of camera.

R2* **B+**

MAXIMAR A: c1927-1939. 6.5 x 9cm. Folding plate camera. Tessar 105mm, f4.5 lens in Compur shutter. Slide in holders. Marked "Maximar" in leather on rear of camera.

R2* **C+**

MAXIMAR B: c1927-1939. 9 x 12cm. Folding plate camera. Similar to above. Tessar 135mm, f4.5 lens in Compur shutter..

R2* **C+**

MAXIMAR: c1927-1937. 10 x 15cm. Folding plate camera. Similar to above. Tessar 165mm, f4.5 lens in Compur shutter. Rare.

R* **D**

MIROFLEX A: c1927-1936. 6.5 x 9cm. Folding SLR plate camera. FPS ⅓ -¹⁄₂₀₀s. Reflex viewing and sportsfinder. Marked "Miroflex" in leather on front of camera.. Tessar 120mm, f4.5 lens. With Tessar 135mm, f3.5 or Bio Tessar 135mm, f2.8 lens.

R4* **F–**

Miroflex A

rotating RFR window attached to interchangeable lens. FPS to ⅟₁₀₀₀s.

Tessar 50mm, f2.8 lens, rare	**F+**
Tessar 50mm, f3.5 lens, rare	**G–**
Extra for telephoto (rare),	
Triotar 105mm, f5.6 lens	**F–**
R4*	**Code**

MIROFLEX B: c1934-1938. Takes 9 x 12cm film or plates. Similar to above. Tessar 165mm, f4.5 lens. £175. Tessar 165mm, f3.5 or Bio Tessar 165mm, f2.8 lens, more common.

R4*	**E+**

NETTAR: c1934-1941. 4.5 x 6cm., 6 x 9cm. The Bob camera. Was known as Nettar 510 in England. Inexpensive folding roll film camera with Nettar or Novar lens. "Nettar" impressed on leather. Postwar version. C.1949-1957. Fancier style with body release and chrome top. Sixteen possible lens/shutter combinations. Novar models. Tessar models.

R2*	**B+**

NETTAR II: c.1950. Self erecting folding VFR camera for 12 exp on 120. 3in f4.5 Novar, Pronto shutter 1/25-1/200s + B.

R2*	**A**

NETTAX: c1936-1938. 35mm camera looks somewhat like Contax II, except has

NETTAX: c1955-1957. 6 x 6cm. Folding roll film camera. Novar 75mm, f4.5 lens. Pronto shutter. Built-in uncoupled exp meter. Chrome top cover. Rare.

R4*	**C+**

NETTEL: c1929-1937. 4.5 x 6cm. 6.5 x 9cm., 9 x 12cm. Most common. 10 x 15cm., 5" x 7". "Nettel" marked on right side of camera below FPS winding and setting knob. Black leather covered. 12 lens/shutter/format combinations.

R2*	**C+**

NETTEL, TROPEN: c1930-37. Tropical model. Made in four larger sizes shown above. Focal plane press camera. Polished teak, brown leather bellows.

R3*	**F**

STEREO NETTEL, TROPICAL MODEL: c1927. Makes 6x13cm images on glass dry plates. Focal plane shutter and matched Tessar lenses f4.5. The tropical model made from teakwood is at least twice the

value of the regular leather covered instrument.

R3*   **F**

NIXE: c1927-1934. Folding camera. Dominar, Tessar or Double Protar lens. Double ext bellows. 8 x 10.5cm. Roll film or 9 x 12cm cut film. Marked "Nixe" on handle or impressed in leather of body.

R2*   **B+**

NIXE: Similar to above, except 8 x 14cm roll film or 9 x 14cm cut film.

R2*   **C–**

ONITO: c1927-1929. 6.5 x 9cm. 9 x 12cm. Inexpensive folding plate camera. Novar f6.3 lens. Single ext bellows. Lever focus.

R2*   **B+**

ORIX: c1928-1934. 10 x 15cm. Folding plate camera. Tessar 150mm, f4.5 lens. Double ext bellows. Rack and pinion focusing. Was used as press camera. Special model with spring back was available.

R2*   **C**

PALMOS-O: c1927-1928. 4.5 x 6cm. Plate camera. Tessar 80mm, f2.7 (high-speed) lens. FPS 1/50-1/1000s. Struts. Folding door. Sold in Europe (1927) as Minimum Palmos.

R3*   **F–**

PICCOLETTE: c1927-1930. Inexpensive all metal strut-type camera; Achromat 75mm, f11, Novar 75mm, f6.3 or Tessar 75mm, f4.5 lens. Marked "Piccolette" below lens; "Zeiss Ikon" at 11 o'clock from lens; 3 x 4cm exp on 127 roll film. In Germany; available until 1932 in U.S.

R3*   **C+**

PICCOLETTE-LUXUS: c1927-1930. 4 x 6.5cm. Top-of-the-line model, with folding bed. Dominar 50mm, f4.5 or Tessar 75mm, f4.5 lens. Dial-set Compur shutter. Lazy tong struts. Brown leather covering. Brown bellows.

R3*   **E+**

PLASKOP: c1927-1930. Inexpensive Stereo box camera. Marked "Plaskop" on front under left lens. 4.5 x 10.5cm exp.

R3*   **D+**

PLASKOP: c1927-1930. Stereo box camera. Novar 60mm, f6.8 lenses. Marked

"Plaskop" on oval label – left front. 4.5 x 10.5cm exp.

R3*   **D+**

PLASKOP: c1927-1930. Stereo box camera. Similar to above, except has brilliant finder – top centre. 6 x 13cm. exp.

R3*   **E**

POLYSKOP: c1927-1930. Precision Stereo box camera. Tessar 65mm, f4.5 lenses. Compur Dial-set stereo shutter. Brilliant finder – top centre. Covered with black leather. 12 exp, 4.5 x 10.5cm. on plates in septum magazine.

R3*   **E**

POLYSKOP: c1927-1930. Similar to above except it has Tessar 75mm, f4.5 lenses. 6 x 13cm. exp on plates.

R3*   **E**

SIMPLEX: c1928-1930. Inexpensive folding plate camera. For 9 x 12cm plates. Frontar 140mm, f9 lens or Novar 135mm, f6.3 lens. Marked "Simplex" on leather under handle. "Zeiss Ikon" under lens on front of lens standard.

R2*   **B+**

SIMPLEX: Brown plastic bodied 6 x 9cm. roll film camera. Nettar 105mm, f6.5 lens. Telma or Derval shutter. Marked "Simplex". The hardware and struts vary on this model.

R3*   **C–**

SIMPLEX-ERNOFLEX: c1929-30. 4.5 x 6cm. 6.5 x 9cm. 9 x 12cm. SLR focal plane camera. Ernoplast f4.5 or f3.5. Ernon f3.5 or Tessar f4.5 lens. CFPS On/20-¹⁄₁₀₀₀s. The early model was marked "Ernemann" On right side and back. "Zeiss Ikon" on round metal plate. In 1930 it was marked

"Simplex Ernoflex" over lens. "Zeiss Ikon." On right side and door of focusing hood.

4.5cm X 6cm, Size.

R3*   **NSR G+**
6.5 X 9cm and 9 X 12cm Sizes.   **F–**

SIRENE: c1927. Inexpensive folding plate camera (9 x 12cm or 6.5 x 9cm). Marked "Sirene" under handle. The same model number used later on Volta cameras.

R2*   **B+**

SIRENE: c1930-1931. Similar to above, 3¼" x 4¼" size for American market. Dominar 135mm, f4.5 lens. Compur shutter. Rare.

R4*   **C**

SONNET: c1927-1930. 4.5 x 6cm. Tropical folding plate camera. Novar 80mm or 75mm, f6.3. Dominar or Tessar 75mm, f4.5 lens. Teak wood construction. Brown leather door covering and brown bellows.

R3*   **G**

SONNET: c1927-1930. Tropical 6.5 x 9cm folding plate camera. Similar to above, except 6.5 x 9cm size. Novar 105mm, f6.3 or Dominar or Tessar 120mm f4.5 lens.

R4*   **F+**

STEREOLETTE-CUPIDO: c1927-1928. 4.5 x 10.7cm. Folding Stereo plate camera. Black leather covered. Marked "Stereolette-Cupido" on handle. "Stereolette" on outside of door.

R3*   **E**

STEREOCO: c1927-1930. 4.5 x 10.7cm. Leather covered Stereo box plate camera. Tapered shape. Tessar 55mm, f6.3 lenses. Derval or Dial-set Compur shutters. Marked "Stereoco" on upper front between lenses. "Zeiss Ikon" below lenses.

R3*   **E**

STEREO-ERNOFLEX: c1927-1929. Folding stereo camera. Ernotar 75mm, f4.5. Ernon 75mm, f3.5 or Tessar 75mm, f3.5 lenses.

CFPS ½₀-¹⁄₁₀₀₀s. Full length viewing hood cover.

R4*   **H–**

STEREO-SIMPLEX-ERNOFLEX: c1927-1930. Non-folding Stereo box camera. Ernon 75mm, f3.5 or Tessar 75mm or 80mm, f4.5 lenses. CFPS. Marked "Ernemann" on front between lenses. Viewing hood cover is on ½ of camera top. Pop-up frame finder on other half.

R3*   **F+**

STEREO IDEAL: c1927-1928. 6 x 13cm. Folding stereo camera. Tessar 90mm, f4.5 lenses. Dial-set Compur shutter on 1927 version. Compound shutter on 1928 versions. Marked "Stereo-Ideal-651" on handle. "Zeiss Ikon" inside door. Covered with black leather.

R4*   **E**

STEREO NETTEL: c1927-1930. 6 x 13cm. Scissors strut Stereo camera. Tessar 90mm, f4 lenses. FPS. Wire finder. Focusing knob on right side (over shutter winding knob). Internal roller blind separates two images (removable for full frame use).

Black leather,   **E+**

Tropical model.Teak wood. Brown bellows.

R4*   **G–**

STEREO NETTEL: c1927-1930. Similar to above, except 10 x 15cm model. Tessar 120mm, f4.5 lenses.

Black leather.   **E+**

Tropical model. Teak wood. Bbrown bellows.

R4*   **G–**

SUPER IKONTA SERIES

Folding roll film camera: lenses had front cell focusing, coupled to a coincidence type built-in RFR. Postwar

models had factory installed flash synch.

SUPER IKONTA "A": (Z530). 1934-1937.

R2*   **E**

SUPER IKONTA "A": 1937-1950.

R2*   **E+**

SUPER IKONTA "A": 1950-1956.

R2*   **E+**
Synchro Compur   **G**

SUPER IKONTA "B": 1935-1937.

R2*   **E+**

SUPER IKONTA "B":1937-1951.
R2*   **E+**

SUPER IKONTA "B": 1951-1956.
R2*   **F–**

SUPER IKONTA "BX": 1937-1952.
R2*   **E+**

*Super
Ikonda BX*

SUPER IKONTA "BX": 1952-1957.
R2*   **F–**

SUPER IKONTA III: 1954-1958.
R2*   **F–**

SUPER IKONTA IV: 1956-1960.
R2*   **F**

SUPER IKONTA "C": 1934-1936.
R2*   **E**

SUPER IKONTA "C": 1936-1950.
R2*   **E+**

SUPER IKONTA "C": 1950-1955.
R2*   **F–**

SUPER IKONTA "D": 1934-1936,.
R3*   **E**

*Super
Ikonda C*

*Super
Ikonta "C"*

SUPER IKONTA "D": 1936-1939.

R4*   **E+**

SUPER NETTEL: c1934-1937. 35mm folding bellows camera.

Tessar 50mm, f3.5 or f2.8 lens. 1935 – Triotar 50mm, f3.5 lens offered. The Tessar lens was discontinued in 1936. FPS 1/5-¹⁄₁₀₀₀s. Black enamel finish with leather covering. Marked "Super Nettel" in leather on door.

R3*   **F+**

SUPER NETTEL II: c1936-1938. Similar to above, except had polished chrome door. Top cover was finished with matte chrome. Tessar 50mm, f2.8 lens.

R4*   **G**

SYMBOLICA: c1959-1962. 35mm camera. Tessar 50mm, f2.8 lens. Coupled match-needle exp meter. No RFR; Lens had front cell focus. Marked "Symbolica" on top.

R2*   **B**

TAXO: c1927-1931. 6.5 x 9cm., 9 x 12cm. Inexpensive folding plate camera. Periskop 105mm, f11. Novar 105mm or 135mm, f6.3 lens (Frontar or Dominar lens later). Derval shutter. Single ext bellows. Marked "Taxo" on body under handle. Lens had slide on track for focusing.

R2*   **B**

TAXO: 6.5 x 9cm., 9 x 12cm. Similar to above, except had radial focusing lever. C.1927-1930.

R2*   **B**

TAXONA: Post WWII 35mm camera. 24 x 24mm. Made from captured Tenax I parts. Tessar 37.5mm, f3.5 lens. Marked "TAXONA" around lens. See Tenax below. 24 x 24mm exp on 35mm film.

R2*   **C**

TENAX: c1927. Popular strut folding plate camera. 16 different lenses offered. Compound shutter. 4.5 x 6cm. 6.5 x 9cm. 4.5 x 10.7cm. (stereo). Clean-up items which were never actually mfd by or marked "Zeiss Ikon". Marked "TENAX" or "Taschen Tenax" on front or top.

R3*   **D**

TENAX I: c1930-1941. Novar 35mm, f3.5 lens. Compur shutter. Lever on right side advanced film and cocked shutter. No RFR. 35mm film. 50 exp. 24 x 24mm on 36 exp roll. Marked "TENAX" under lens.

R2*   **D**

TENAX I: c1948. Similar to above, except Tessar 37.5mm, f3.5 coated lens. Flash synch contact on top of shutter. Marked "Zeiss Ikon"above lens. "TENAX" below lens. Possibly East German.

R2*   **D+**

TENAX II: c1938-1941. 24 x 24mm format. Interchangeable lenses. Coupled rangefinder. Shoe for Vfr. and Contameter. A rare microscope (or X-ray) version exists with dark slide and without lens. C.1938-1941.

Tessar 40mm f2.4 lens	**F–**
Sonnar 40mm f2 lens	**F–**

R4*

ACCESSORY LENSES FOR TENAX II:

Sonnar 75mm, f4 (telephoto) lens with vf	**F**
Orthometer 27mm, f4.5 W/A lens with vf	**F**

TENAX AUTOMATIC: c1960-1963. Full frame 35mm camera. Tessar 50mm, f2.8 lens. Prontormat shutter. No RFR. Front cell focus. Auto Exp control with selsnium photo-electric cell. Marked "Tenax" at 11 O'Clock from lens on Exp meter window.

R2*   **B–**

TENGOFLEX; c1941-1942. Box camera. 6 X 6cm. exp on 120 roll film. Large brilliant finder on top gives appearance of TLR. Marked "Tengoflex" on front. Rare.

R4*   **F–**

TESSCO; c1927-1928. 9 X 12cm. Folding plate camera. 5 different lenses range from, Periskop f11 to Tessar f4.5. Double ext bellows. Marked "Tessco" on leather handle.

R4*   **C**

TRONA: c1929-1938. 6.5 x 9cm., 9 x 12cm. Tessar f3.5 lens. Compur shutter (Rim-set after 1930). The original ground glass back was of aluminium and it is rare today. The camera is usually found with standard back. "TRONA" and model number marked under handle.

R2*   **C–**

TROPEN ADORO: c1927-1936. Tropical folding plate camera. Tessar 105mm or 120mm, 135mm or 150mm. 9 x 12cm. Tessar 165mm or 180mm, f4.5 lens 10 x 15cm. Compur shutter in all models.

Trona Cameras

Double ext bellows. Brown leather covering on door and back. Brown bellows. "TROPEN ADORO" and model number marked on leather of door.

R4* **F+**

TROPICA: c1927-1931(1935 in foreign catalogues). 9 x 12cm., 10 x 15cm., 5" x 7". Folding plate camera. Polished teak wood construction (even the door to the ground glass back is of teak wood) with hardware of German silver. Rotating back. Marked "Zeiss Ikon" between knobs on front standard. 14 different lenses, all in Compur shutters. All sizes are rare today, especially the 5" x 7" size. NSR. Estimate.

R5* **G+**
5" X 7" size. **H–**

UNETTE: c1927-1930. Leatherette covered wooden box camera. 40mm, f12.5 lens. Metal frame finder on top (rear). 22 x 31mm exp on roll film. Marked "UNETTE" on front over lens in the leatherette. "Zeiss Ikon" over lens. "Ernemann" on right side. Rare, only one sale known.

R5* **est E**

VICTRIX: c1927-1931. Small folding plate camera. Novar 75mm, f6.3. Dominar 75mm, f4.5 and Tessar lens. Compur shutter. 4.5 x 6cm exp. Marked "Victrix 101" in leather on top of camera. "Zeiss Ikon" marked on lens, between knobs and on door. Rare.

R4* **D–**

VOLTA: c1927-1931. Inexpensive folding plate camera. Novar, Dominar or Tessar lenses. Compur or Klio shutters. Single ext bellows. Radial arm focusing.

R4* **B+**

VOLTA: Similar to above but without radial arm focusing. C.1926-1927.

R4* **B+**

Zorki see Kraznogorsk Mechanical Works

Zuiho Precision Optical Company *Japan*

HONOR SL: c1959. 35mm RFR camera. CFPS. 1 – ¹⁄₁₀₀₀s. Combined RFR/VFR window. Lever advance and folding crank rewind. Honor 50mm f1.9 lens. This camera has a redesigned top plate and has lost some of its "Leica copy" looks. Now, more like a Canon VT or Tanack V3. Quite rare.

R4* **G**

Honor

HONOR : c1956. 35mm RFR camera. CFPS. 1-⅟₅₀₀s; seperate RFR/VFR windows. Honor or Hexanon 50mm, f1.9 or Hexar 50mm, f3.5 lens. Quite "Leica" like!

R4* **F+**

Reference Notes

_____

_____

_____

_____

_____

_____

_____

_____

_____

_____

_____

_____

_____

_____

_____

_____

_____

_____

_____

_____

_____

I nevitably with the passage of time, manufacturers information may be lost or destroyed. We have included these cameras in this section. If any of our readers can supply us with more data, it will be incorporated in subsequent editions.

Probably Czechoslovakia

NOVA: c1938-39. Unusual simple camera. Two boxes extend the lens from a cast metal body. Shutter operated between 1/25-1/100s. Paper-backed rollfilm made images 30x40cm. These unusual cameras are difficult to locate in really good condition.

R3 **C**

Made in France

WET PLATE STEREO CAMERA: c1865. This is typical of a camera type much in use during the wet-plate era. Focus by sliding

a box-in-box. This particular camera is fitted with American made lenses by Harrison & Harrison but many other makes both European and American were used.

R3* **D**

LE REVE: c1908. 3¼" x 4¼" camera; Anastigmatic Roussel 135mm f6.3 or Beck 135mm f6.3 lens; Unicum or pneumatic shutter. 3¼" x 4¼" plates or roll film with special roll film back. Mfd in Paris, France.

R3* **D**

PHOTO OMNIA: c1925; 45 x 107mm stereo camera. Anastigmat 60mm f/6 lenses. Variable speed shutter.

R3* **D**

Europe & USA

Wet Plate Camera Outfit: c1865; Wet Plate Camera Outfits were made by a number of makers in Europe and the United States. They came in a variety of sizes from what we now call "medium format" to very large indeed, up to 16x20 inches and larger. A complete outfit would have consisted of a camera, tripod, plate holders, sensitizing and developing tanks, and the paraphernalia used to manipulate the glass plates. If you are uncertain whether a camera was designed for wet plate or early dry-plate photography, check the holders and camera body. Wet plate cameras invariably have black stains from the silver halide salts.

R5* **G+**

WONDER TRICK CAMERA: c1970. toy "camera" with squeaking mouse. Toy mouse squeaks and jumps out of the camera when shutter is tripped. Mfd in Japan.

R3* **B+**

Wonder Trick Camera

Hong Kong

MICRO 110 KEY CHAIN CAMERA: c1988. The camera itself consists of a very simple shutter and lens, a 110 film cassette actually makes the back of the camera. When not in use, a coin holder takes the place of a film cartridge.

R1*   **D**

DONKEY BOOK CAMERA: c1980. 110 camera in the form of a small book. Back of book rotates revealing meniscus lens. Shutter works at about ¹⁄₅s.

R3*   **D**

Japan

BABY FLEX c1950. Sanko 20mm f3.5 lens; Peace Model 2 shutter ¹⁄₅₀-¹⁄₂₅₀; 10 exp, 13x14mm on special roll film. The Japanese maker of this simple camera is unknown. It is considered very rare in Japan.

R4*   **G**

JAPANESE PHOTOGRAPHIC RIFLE: c1930, anti-aircraft training rifle; copy of Thornton Pickard rifle. Mfd in Japan.

R4*   **H-**

England

WEMBLEY SPORTS: c.1950. Ugly Bakelite camera made in England for 8 exp. on 120. Lens extends on large diameter helical screw and click-stops at five positions for focusing. 8.5cm f11 London Sportar lens. Shutter 1/25-1/100s.

R2*   **E-**

Above: Micro 110 Key Chain Camera

Reference Notes

Manufacturers and Camera Index

A-Z

Manufacturers Index

Hanau; 231
Hare, George; 231
Hasselblad, Victor; 231
Hensold, Dr. Hans - see ISO
Herco, Herbert George Co.;
  232
Hermagis, J. Fleury; 232
Herzog, A; 232
Hesekiel, Dr. Adolf & Co.;
  232
Hess-Ives Corp; 233
Hetherington & Hibben; 233
Hofert Emil, Eho Kamera
  Fabrik; 233
Horne & Thornthwaite; 233
Horsman, E.I. & Co.; 234
Houghton & Son Ltd,
  George; 234
Houghton Sanderson; 240
Hunter Ltd., R.F.; 242
Hurlbut Manufacturing Co.;
  242
Huttig A.G.; 242

Ica A.G.; 243
Ideal Toy Corp.; 248
Ihagee Kamerawerk; 248
Ikkosha Co. Ltd.; 254
Ilford Ltd; 254
Ingersoll & Bros; 256
International Metal &
  Ferrotype Co.; 256
I.O.R.; 256
ISO, Industria Scientifica
  Ottica S.R.L.; 256
Ising Eugen; 257
Ives Corp.; 257

J

Japy & Cie; 258
Jeanneret and Co.; 258
Johnson and Harrison; 258
Jonte, F; 258
Joseph Peter; 258
Joux, L; 258
Jumeau & Jannin; 259
Jurnick, Max; 259

Kalart Co.; 260
kalso Kamerabau; 260
Kamera Werkstütten, see
  Guthe & Thorsch;
Kashiwa Seiko; 260
Keio department Store; 261
Kemper, Alfred C; 260
Kennedy Instruments; 261
Kern; 261
Kerr, Thomas; 262
Keys Stereo products; 262
Keyzlar, Odon; 262
KGB; 262
Kilburn, Benjamin; 264
Kilfit; 264
Kin-Dar Corporation; 264
Kinn; 265
Kinrad Kohnlein; 297
Kochmann, Franz; 265
Kodak Co, Eastman; 266
Kodak AG; 297
Kolar; 297
Kogaku Seiki; 297
Konishiroku Photo Co. Ltd.;
  298
Konishiroku; 298
Koopman, E.B.; 300
Korsten; 300
Kowa Co. Ltd.; 300
Kozy Camera Company; 301
Krasnogorsk Mechanical
  Works (same as KMZ);
  301
Krauss, E.; 305
Krauss, G.A.; 306
Krugener, Dr. Rudolph; 307
Kromskop Manufactory; 308
Kunick, Walter KG; 308
Kürbi & Niggeloh, Bilora;
  309
Kyoto Seiki; 310

Lamperti & Garbagnati; 311
Lancart; 311
Lancaster, J. & Son; 311
Lausa, E. Ludwig; 312
Lechner, R; 312

Lecoultre & Cie; 313
Le Docte, Armand; 313
Lehmann, A; 313
Leidolf Kamerawerkes; 314
Leitz GmbH, Ernst; 315
Lennor Engineering
  Company; 329
Leotax Camera Company,
  see SHOWA; 329
Leroy, Lucien; 329
Leullier, L; 329
Levi, S.J.; 329
Levy-Roth; 329
Lewis, W. & W.H.; 329
Lexa Manufacturing Co.; 330
L.F.O. & Co.; 330
Liebe, V; 330
Linex Corp. Division of
  Lionel Corp; 330
Linhof Prazasions-Kamera-
  Werke GmbH; 331
Lippische Kamerafabrik; 331
Lizars, J; 331
Lollier; 332
London Stereoscopic
  Company; 332
Lumiere & Cie; 333

Mackenstein Fabricant, H;
  336
Macris-Boucher; 336
Mader, H; 337
Magic Introduction Co.; 337
Mamiya Camera Co. Ltd.;
  337
MFAP, (Manufacture
  Francaise d'Appareils
  Photographique); 340
MIOM (Manufacture
  d'Isolents et d'Objects
  Moulés); 342
Marelli C.; 342
Marion & Co. Ltd.; 343
Marshall Optical Works; 344
Mason G. & Co.; 344
Mast Development Co.; 344
Mattioli; 345
Mawson; 345
Mazo; 345
Meagher; 345

Camera Index

Super Frankanette E; 194
Super Frankanette EL; 194
Super Frankanette L; 194
Super Frankanette SLK; 194
Super Frankanette; 194
Super Ikonta "A"; 518
Super Ikonta "B"; 518
Super Ikonta "BX"; 519
Super Ikonta "C"; 519
Super Ikonta "D"; 519
Super Ikonta III; 519
Super Ikonta IV; 519
Super Lynx; 342
Super Lynx "standard"; 341
Super Lynx-I; 341
Super Lynx-II; 342
Super Nettel II; 520
Super Nettel; 520
Super Paxette I; 124
Super Paxette Ib; 124
Super Paxette II; 125
Super Paxette IIB; 125
Super Paxette IIBL; 125
Super Paxette IIL; 125
Super Paxette IL; 124
Super Speed Graphic; 222
Super Sport Dolly Model A; 149
Super Sport Dolly Model C; 149
Super Sporti; 256
Super Stereo; 261
Super-Fex; 189
Superb; 470
Super-Pontura; 111
Suter's Detective Magazine Camera; 450
Suter's Stereo Detective Camera; 450
Swiftshot; 190
Symbol; 475
Symbolica; 520

T

Takiv Camera, The; 473
Takyr; 306
Talbot Invisible Camera; 452
Tanack IIC; 452
Tanack IIIF; 452
Tanack IIIS; 452
Tanack IV-S; 452

Tanack SD; 453
Tanack V3; 453
Tanack VP; 453
Tanzer; 389
Tasco Binocular Camera; 453
Taxo; 158
Taxo; 520
Taxona; 520
Taylor Tailboard Camera, A.G; 453
Teflex Binocular Camera; 381
Tele-Rolleiflex; 201
Teleca; 453
Telephoto Cycle B; 425
Telephoto Poco A; 425
Telephoto Vega; 466
Teleroy; 427
Telescopic Graphic Camera; 216
Telescopic Stereo Graphic; 216
Telka-I; 171
Telka-II; 171, 521
Telka-III "Professional"; 170
Telka-III (Dehel Super); 170
Telka-IIIA; 170
Telka-IIIB; 170
Telka-Sport; 171
Telka-X; 170
Telka-XX; 170
Tenax Automatic; 484
Tenax I; 520
Tenax II acccessory lenses; 521
Tenax II; 521
Tenax; 210
Tenax; 520
Tengoflex; 521
Tessco; 158, 521
Tessina; 155
Tessina Accessories; 155
Thomas of Pall Mall Wet Plate; 454
Thompson Tintype Camera; 454
Thornton Pickard Stereo Camera; 455
Thorpe Four-Tube Camera; 455
Thread Mount Lenses; 418

Thury & Amey Stereo Folding Camera; 455
Ticka; 239
Tisdell & Whittelsey Detective Camera; 456
Tisdell Hand Camera; 456
Tom Thumb Camera Radio; 259
Tom Thumb Camera; 259
Tone; 458
Topcon RE Super; 458
Tourist Buckeye, No.1; 77
Tourist d'Enjalbert, Le; 178
Tourist Graflex; 216
Tourist Hawkeye Special Camera; 120
Tourist Hawkeye; 120
Tourist Multiple; 378
Tower 35; 433
Tower 45; 433
Tower 46; 433
Tower Stereo; 433
Tower Type 3; 432
Tower Type 3S; 433
Triad Camera, The; 431
Trilby Nr.11; 247
Trilby Nr.12; 247
Trilby Nr.13; 247
Trilby Nr.14; 247
Trilby Nr.17; 247
Trilby Nr.18; 247
Trilby Nr.20; 247
Trilby Nr.29; 247
Trilby Nr.31; 247
Trilby Nr.33; 248
Trilby Nr.5; 247
Trio; 475
Triple Lens Stereo Graphic; 216
Trivision Camera; 262
Trixette I; 207
Trixette; 207
Trokonet Camera, The; 405
Trolita; 81
Trona Nr.210; 248
Trona; 521
Tropen Adoro; 521
Tropica; 248, 522
Tropical Heag XI; 181
Tropical Klapp; 182
Tropical Watch Pocket Carbine No.4; 240

Technical Photographic Publishers 2000

HASSELBLAD®

HASSELBLAD
SYSTEM COMPENDIUM

Richard Nordin

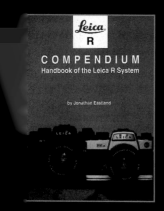
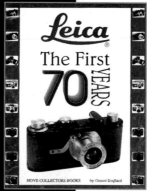
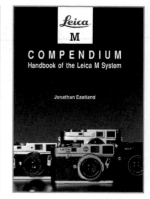
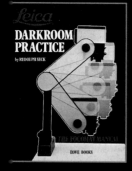

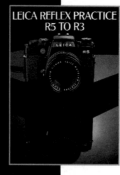

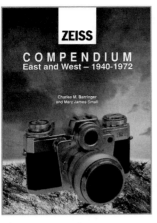

ZEISS
COMPENDIUM
East and West – 1940-1972

Charles M. Barringer
and Marc James Small

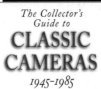

The Collector's Guide to
CLASSIC CAMERAS
1945-1985

John Wade

Leica
Pocket
Books

LEICA®

International Price Guide

Seventh Edition

Preisführer
Guide De Prix
Guida Ai Prezzi

Cameras, lenses and accessories

HOVE COLLECTORS BOOKS

Walther Benser

MY LIFE WITH THE
Leica

Kodak Cameras
THE FIRST HUNDRED YEARS

Leica
Accessory Guide

2ND EDITION

HOVE COLLECTORS BOOKS

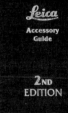

HASSELBLAD®

HASSELBLAD
SYSTEM COMPENDIUM

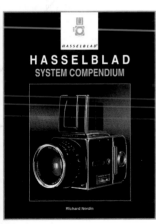

Richard Nordin

Canon

COMPENDIUM
Handbook of the Canon System

Leica
Pocket Book

6TH EDITION

HOVE COLLECTORS BOOKS

Technical Photographic Publishers 2000

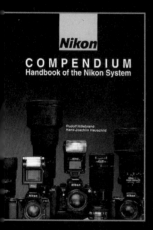

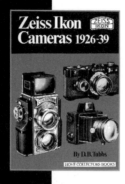

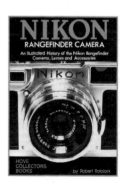

Leica

GENERAL CATALOGUE
FOR 1936

ERNST LEITZ, WETZLAR AND LONDON

Leica

INSTRUCTIONS
for use of Reproduction Devices
including Visoflexes and Bellows etc.

ERNST LEITZ, WETZLAR AND LONDON

Leica

INSTRUCTIONS
for the use of the Leica Camera
Models c, f & g

ERNST LEITZ, WETZLAR AND LONDON

Leica

INSTRUCTIONS
for Models—Standard, IIIa & 250
and Accessories

ERNST LEITZ, WETZLAR AND LONDON

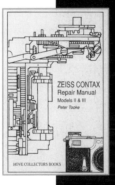

Leitz

Leica
c a m e r a

CATALOGUE FOR 1931

ZEISS CONTAX
Repair Manual
Models II & III
Peter Tooke

HOVE COLLECTORS BOOKS

Leitz WETZLAR

1961
General Catalogue
for Leica Dealers

Models M1, M2, M3
and their accessories

Leica

INSTRUCTIONS
for the use of the Leica Camera
Models M5, CL, Leicaflex,
Leicaflex SL & SL2, including
SL MOT Motor Drive,
Focusing Bellows – R, Elpro Lenses
and Extension Tubes

ERNST LEITZ, WETZLAR

Leica

GENERAL
CATALOGUE
FOR 1933

ERNST LEITZ WETZLAR AND LONDON

Leica

GENERAL CATALOGUE
FOR 1955/56

Models If, IIf and IIIf
Ig, IIIg and "72"

ERNST LEITZ, WETZLAR AND LONDON

Leitz WETZLAR

1961
General Catalogue
for Leica Dealers

Models M1, M2, M3
and their accessories

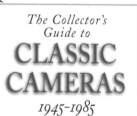

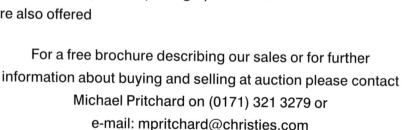